SETTLE ANY ARGUMENT
WITH THE DEFINITIVE
REFERENCE GUIDE
TO OUR WORLD OF WONDERS

MOST EFFICIENT MOTHER: A woman in Russia gave birth to 69 children—including 16 pairs of twins, 7 sets of triplets, and 4 sets of quadruplets—from about 1725 to 1765. [p. 357]

WHAT A HATRACK: The largest antler spread from any living species is a 6-foot 6$\frac{1}{2}$-inch rack from a moose killed in the Yukon Territory in 1897. [p. 343]

THE CASSEROLE OF ETERNAL LEFTOVERS: The world's largest delicacy is roasted whole camel, a Bedouin wedding dish that is stuffed with eggs, fish, cooked chickens, and a roasted sheep's carcass. [p. 32]

THE 15-FOOT 5-INCH PIGGY BANK! [p. 8]
THE 26-HOUR SQUARE DANCE! [p. 422]
THE 830-POUND ICE-CREAM SANDWICH!
[p. 33]
THE 56-FOOT 3-INCH KALEIDOSCOPE! [p. 142]

OR [p. 374]
T [p. 375]
RSICKNESS BAG
COLLECTION [p. 44]
THE MOST EXPENSIVE WEDDING [p. 29].

THE
GUINNESS
BOOK
OF
WORLD
RECORDS
1998

GUINNESS MEDIA, INC.

BANTAM BOOKS
NEW YORK • TORONTO • LONDON • SYDNEY • AUCKLAND

This edition contains the complete text of the original hardcover edition.
NOT ONE WORD HAS BEEN OMITTED.

THE GUINNESS BOOK OF WORLD RECORDS 1998
*A Bantam Book / Published by arrangement with
Guinness Publishing, Ltd.*

Bantam edition / March 1998

*"Guinness International" is a registered trademark
of Guinness Publishing Ltd.*

INTRODUCTION

WELCOME TO THE 1998 EDITION OF *THE GUINNESS BOOK OF WORLD RECORDS*.

The Guinness Book of World Records was the brainchild of Sir Hugh Beaver, the managing director of Guinness Brewing. In 1951, after a day of game shooting in Ireland, Beaver and his shooting party were involved in an argument as to whether the golden plover was Europe's fastest game bird. Beaver could not find the answer in any of the reference books in his host's house, Castlebridge House. Three years later, the dispute flared again.

UNABLE TO FIND the answer a second time, Beaver thought that there must be numerous such arguments going on nightly in pubs and inns throughout the British Isles, while patrons partook of his employer's brew. He decided to produce a book that would settle these disagreements. Beaver commissioned Norris and Ross McWhirter, editors and statisticians in London, to compile a book of records. The first copy was bound by the printers in 1955. The book shot to the top of the British best-seller list, and each successive annual edition has done the same.

OVER THE YEARS the book has become a worldwide success. The first United States edition was published in 1956. Editions in France (1962) and Germany (1963) followed. The 1998 edition will be published in 77 different countries in 38 different languages. Total sales of all editions passed 50 million in 1984, 75 million in 1994 and will pass the 100 million mark early in the next millennium.

THE GUINNESS BOOK OF WORLD RECORDS

CEO/PUBLISHER
Mark C. Young

MANAGING EDITOR
Christine Heilman

RESEARCH MANAGER
John W. Hansen

SENIOR WRITER
Glenn M. Speer

WRITERS
Tobey Grumet, Herbert Hadad, Stacy Kamisar,
David J. Stiewe, Karen Romano Young

ACKNOWLEDGMENTS

The creation of a new edition of *The Guinness Book of World Records* is very much a team effort. Space prevents me from mentioning all of the talented and dedicated people who put together the 1998 edition. There are, however, certain individuals whose contributions have been especially valuable. They are as follows:

Pat Collins and Jennifer Harrak of Penguin Putnam, Inc.; Rick Thompson, Picture Network International; Peter Orlowsky and Jackie Jèske, Allsport Photography, USA; Don Bowden, Associated Press/Wide World Photos; Pat McLaughlin, Animals Animals; Marco DePaul, National Geographic Society; Kathy Strawn, NASA; Jocelyn Clapp, Corbis Bettmann; Valerie Zars and Konstantine Mol, Gamma Liaison; Vince Casey, National Football League; Evan Silverman, National Basketball Association; Rick Campbell, Gary Johnson and Jim Wright, NCAA; Adam Schwartz and Tamir Lipton, National Hockey League; Farah Yale, Nathan Brookwood and Martin Reynolds, Dataquest; Jennifer Genco and Beth Ashfield, New York Stock Exchange; Jennifer McCarter, NASA Office of Space Flight; Angela Corio, Recording Industry Association of America; Gail Perkins, Maritime Administration, United States Department of Transportation; Jim Lockhart, American Petroleum Institute; Scott McDonald, Advertising Age; Richard Cerrone, New York Yankees; Jay Horwitz and Chris Leible, New York Mets; Andy Shearer, Boneau/Bryan-Brown; Brad Topper, New York Knicks; Linda Woods and Angela Lee, University of North Carolina Men's Basketball Program; Deputy Assistant Secretary of State for Public Affairs Lula Rodriguez, Kitty Bartels and Deb Godfrey, State Department; Vicki Rivas-Vazquez, office of United Nations Ambassador Bill Richardson; Michael Borowski; Estee Portnoy, Falk Associates Management Enterprises (FAME); Betsy Fischer, NBC News; Debbie Zealley, Advantage International; Carolyn Grunwalder, IMG; Geoff Baker; Bill Coyle, New York Shakespeare Festival; Jude Clark and Kate Hunter, Royal Shakespeare Festival; Colleen Hughes; MaryLee McNulty, National Theatre; Tamar Thomas; David Parfitt; Cleone Clark; Mike Murray, Detroit Lions; Ray Flynn; Chris Gilbert; Gigi Ravera and Nadia Guerriero, Gold Medal Management; Springer/Chicoine Public Relations; Jeff Bradley, New York/New Jersey MetroStars; Arthur Greene; Marsha DeFilippo; Monique Reilly; Jonathan Kamisar; and our colleagues at Guinness Publishing Ltd., with special thanks to Clive Carpenter, Amanda Brooks, Elaine Prenzlau and Mary Hill.

I would also like to thank the individuals and organizations who took time to help us with our research, and the record-breakers, whose enthusiasm and hard work inspire us to make the book better every year.

Mark C. Young, CEO/Publisher

TABLE OF CONTENTS

FANTASTIC FEATS

Big Deals 2
Fantastic Feats 10
Food 30

HOBBIES AND PASTIMES

Fruits & Vegetable
  Growing 40
Collections 44
Models 48
Buildings for
  Leisure 51
Games 60

TRANSPORTATION

Cars 71
Driving 73
Bicycles &
  Motorcycles 82
Specialized
  Vehicles 86
Trains &
  Subways 91
Bridges &
  Tunnels 96
Aircraft 101
Airlines &
  Airports 105
Flying 109
Ballooning 113
Ships 117

SCIENCE AND TECHNOLOGY

Chemistry &
  Physics 128
Biotechnology . . . 133
Archaeology 135
Machines &
  Instruments 140
Measures &
  Calculations . . . 145
Energy 148
Communications . . 152
Computers 157

EARTH AND SPACE

The Universe 162
The Solar System . 165
Space Exploration . 170
Telescopes 174
The Earth 178
The Oceans 186
Rivers & Lakes . . . 190
Dams & Canals . . . 194
Weather 198
Natural Disasters . . 203

HUMAN WORLD

Geography 208
Population 212
Accidents &
  Disasters 217
Housing 221

Government **227**
U.S. Government . . **232**
Military & Defense . **237**
Education &
  Awards **242**
Religion **248**
Monuments **252**
Language **256**
Law **262**
Crime **267**

COMMERCE
Economics **274**
Business **278**
Advertising **283**
Commercial
  Buildings **286**
Money & Wealth . . **291**
Gems & Precious
  Metals **296**
Agriculture **300**

LIVING WORLD
Plants & Trees . . . **306**
Prehistoric Life . . . **310**
Microbes &
  Fungi **315**
Invertebrates **319**
Insects **323**
Spiders &
  Scorpions **327**
Fish **329**
Reptiles &
  Amphibians **333**
Birds **336**
Mammals **342**

Pets & Domestic
  Animals **351**

HUMAN BEING
Birth & Life **357**
The Body **361**
Height & Weight . . **366**
Disease &
  Medicine **371**

ARTS AND
ENTERTAINMENT
Visual Arts **377**
Antiques &
  Collectibles **381**
Literature **388**
Newspapers &
  Magazines **394**
Music &
  Instruments **399**
Composers &
  Performers **402**
Television &
  Radio **407**
Recorded Music . . . **416**
Dancing **420**
The Circus **423**
Theater **427**
Movies **440**

SPORTS
Baseball **450**
Basketball **467**
Football **493**
Hockey **513**
Soccer **523**

Other Team Sports . **529**
Bowling **536**
Golf **541**
Tennis **552**
Other Racket Sports **562**
Horse Racing **567**
Other Equestrian
  Sports **572**
Automotive Sports . **578**
Cycling **589**
Extreme Sports . . . **595**
Swimming **609**
Sailing **620**
Other Aquatic
  Sports **625**

Skiing **635**
Other Winter Sports **640**
Gymnastics **646**
Track & Field **651**
Multievent Sports . . **675**
Target Sports **679**
Martial Arts **686**
Combat Sports . . . **690**
Weightlifting **695**
Olympics **701**

*Rules and advice for
record attempts* . . . **707**

Index **717**

Photo credits **745**

On Your Mark: Get Set,
  Grow!
  April Lavender: Tree
  planting 24

Stuck On Magnets
  Louise J. Greenfarb:
  Magnet Collection . . . 46

A Penchant for Parks
  Allan K. Hogenauer:
  Visiting the National
  Parks 58

It's a Gas!
  Jay Lowe and Ted
  Jacobs: Fuel economy
  drive 76

Rising to the Challenge
  Steve Fossett: Longest
  balloon flight 114

Everything But Waterskiing
  Joe Farcus: Largest
  cruise ship 124

Working In Extremes
  Dr. Charles P. Covino:
  Lowest friction. 130

Cheddar Man
  Adrian Targett: Most
  distant ancestor 136

Senior Spaceman
  Dr. Story Musgrave:
  Oldest astronaut. . . . 172

The Middle of Nowhere
  Brendan Dalley:
  Remotest inhabited
  island. 214

America's House
  John Zweifel: Largest
  dollhouse 223

At the Helm of the Ship of
  State
  Madeleine Albright:
  Highest-ranking
  woman in U.S.
  government 234

Now That's a Senior!
  Jean Bowman:
  Oldest high school
  graduate 244

Footsteps from the Past
  Dr. Martin G. Lockley:
  Longest dinosaur
  trackway 312

Dynamic Duo
  John and Greg Rice:
  Shortest living twins . 368

No Stranger to the Best-
Seller List
Stephen King:
Most books on the
best-seller list 390

Lots of Plots!
Paul S. Newman:
Most prolific
comic book writer . . 397

Th 51st State
Tim Russert: Longest-
running TV show . . . 408

Hey, Man, Homer's
Number One
Matt Groening:
Longest-running
prime-time cartoon . . 410

Yada, Yada, Yada
Jerry Seinfeld: Most
expensive TV series
renewal 412

And the Winner Is . . .
Alfred Uhry: Multiple
award winner 432

Catching the Record
Todd Hundley:
Most home runs in
a season (catcher). . . 452

The Stuff of Dreams
Michael Jordan:
Most wins in
a season 476

The Dean of Coaching
Dean Smith: Most
wins in a career 482

Moore Catches
Herman Moore:
Most pass receptions
in a season. 498

Maracana Magic
Brazil: Most World
Cup Wins 524

Mr. 900
Jeremy Sonnenfeld:
Highest individual
bowling score 538

Wunderkind
Martina Hingis:
Youngest champion
(singles) 554

A Man in a Hurry
Jeff Gordon:
Youngest Daytona 500
winner 580

Fastest Man Alive
Donovan Bailey:
100-meter world
record 658

Double Champion
Michael Johnson:
Fastest 200-meter
sprint. 702

Largest onion	41
Motorcycle ramp jumping	85
Largest edible fungus	317
Basketball dribbling	478
Golf ball balancing	550
Cycling	592
Most push-ups	650
Fastest marathon tossing a pancake	663
Million and one up	683

FANTASTIC FEATS

BIG DEALS

Ax A steel ax 60 feet long, 23 feet wide and weighing 7.7 tons was designed and built by BID Ltd. of Woodstock, New Brunswick, Canada. The ax was presented to the town of Nackawic, also in New Brunswick, on May 11, 1991 to commemorate the town's selection as Forestry Capital of Canada for 1991.

Balloon sculpture The largest balloon sculpture consisted of 41,241 colored balloons forming the Rabelo Boat, for an exhibition in Vila Nova de Gaia, Portugal on October 30, 1996.

Banner On November 15, 1995, a banner measuring 4 mi. 1,698 yd. long was made by Nestlé's Milo. It was part of an effort by the Ministry of Education, the Thailand Amateur Sports Associations Club and Nestlé to promote the Thai team in the South East Asian Games.

Basket A hand-woven maple basket measuring 48 by 23 by 19 feet was made by the Longaberger Company of Dresden, OH in 1990.

Blanket A hand-knitted, machine-knitted and crocheted blanket measuring a record 186,107.8 square feet was made by members of the Knitting and Crochet Guild worldwide, coordinated by Gloria Buckley of Bradford, England, and assembled at Dishforth Airfield, Thirsk, England on May 30, 1993.

Blown glass vessel A bottle standing 7 ft. 8 in. tall with a capacity of about 188 gallons was blown at Wheaton Village, Millville, NJ on September 26–27, 1992 by a team led by glass artist Steve Tobin. The attempt was made during the "South Jersey Glass Blast," part of a celebration of the local glassmaking heritage.

Bottle A soda bottle 10 ft. 2 in. tall and 11 ft. 6 in. in circumference was filled with Schweppes Lemonade in Melbourne, Australia on March 17, 1994 to celebrate 200 years of Schweppes.

Bottle cap pyramid "Interstrong," a team of 570 people led by Oleg and Vadim Goryunov, constructed a pyramid of 400,995 bottle caps at the Moscow Polytechnical Museum, Moscow, Russia between December 27, 1995 and February 19, 1996.

Can construction A 1:4 scale model of the Basilica di Sant'Antonio di Padova was built from 3,245,000 empty beverage cans in Padova (Padua), Italy by the charities AMNIUP, AIDO, AVIS and GPDS. The model, measuring 96 by 75 by 56 feet, was completed on December 20, 1992 after 20,000 hours of work.

Can pyramid In the same competition, two 10-person teams built pyramids consisting of 6,201 empty cans each in 30 minutes, at Tamokutekihiroba Ouike Park, Tokai, Japan on September 1, 1996.

Bryan Berg proves that no adhesives were used in the construction of his 105-story house of cards.

House of cards The greatest number of stories achieved in building a free-standing house of standard playing cards is 105, to a height of 20 ft. 1¾ in., built by Bryan Berg of Spirit Lake, IA in Des Moines, IA and completed on June 27, 1997. No adhesives were used to hold together the construction, which required over 60 hours of work and almost 700 decks of cards to complete.

Carpets A 52,225-square-foot, 31.4-ton red carpet was laid on February 13, 1982, by the Allied Corporation, from Radio City Music Hall to the New York Hilton along the Avenue of the Americas, in New York City.

The world's longest clothesline, covered with freshly laundered clothes, stretched to 17,298 feet.

Most finely woven The most finely woven carpet known is a silk hand-knotted example with 4,224 knots per square inch, measuring 14 by 22 inches. It was made over a period of 22 months by the Kapoor Rug Corporation of Jaipur, India and completed in May 1993.

Chainsaw A working chainsaw 22 ft. 11 in. long and six feet high was made by Moran Iron Works, Inc. of Onaway, MI in 1996. Named "Big Gus," it was put on display at Da Yoopers Tourist Trap, Ishpeming, MI.

Chair The largest is the Washington Chair, a 53-ft.-4-in.-high replica of the chair George Washington sat in when he presided over the Constitutional Convention in Philadelphia in 1787. Built by NSA and first displayed in Los Angeles, CA on December 9, 1988, the chair was designed to withstand earthquakes and 70-mph winds.

Chandelier The world's largest chandelier was created by the Kookje Lighting Co. Ltd. of Seoul, South Korea. It is 39 feet high, weighs 11.8 tons and has 700 bulbs. Completed in 1988, the chandelier occupies three floors of the Lotte Chamshil Department Store in Seoul.

Christmas cracker The largest functional Christmas cracker was 150 feet long and 10 feet in diameter. It was made by Ray Price for Markson

Sparks! of New South Wales, Australia and pulled at Westfield Shopping Town, Chatswood, Sydney, Australia on November 9, 1991.

Christmas tree   A 221-foot Douglas fir (*Pseudotsuga menziesii*) was erected at Northgate Shopping Center, Seattle, WA in December 1950.

Clothesline   The longest continuous clothesline measured 17,298 feet and was erected in Bavel, Netherlands on June 2, 1996. Freshly washed laundry was hung along the entire length of the line.

Crochet chain   On July 14, 1986, Ria van der Honing (Netherlands) completed a crochet chain that measured 38 mi. 1,471 yd. long.

Daisy chain   The longest daisy chain measured 6,980 ft. 7 in. and was made in seven hours by villagers of Good Easter, England on May 27, 1985. The team in this competition is limited to 16.

Doll   The largest rag doll is 41 ft. 11 in. in total length, and was created by Apryl Scott at Autoworld in Flint, MI on November 20, 1990.

Dress train   The world's longest wedding dress train measured 670 feet and was made by Hege Solli for the wedding of Hege Lorence and Rolf Rotset in Norway on June 1, 1996. The train needed 186 bridesmaids and pageboys to carry it.

Egg   The largest and most elaborate jeweled egg stands two feet tall and was fashioned from 37 pounds of gold, studded with 20,000 pink diamonds. Designed by British jeweler Paul Kutchinsky, the Argyle Library Egg took six British craftsmen 7,000 hours to create and has a price tag of £7 million ($12 million). It was unveiled on April 30, 1990 before going on display at the Victoria and Albert Museum, London, England.

Embroidery   An 8-inch-deep, 1,338-foot-long embroidery of scenes from C. S. Lewis's Narnia children's stories was worked by Margaret S. Pollard (Great Britain) to the order of Michael Maine. Its total area is about 937 square feet.

Fan   A handpainted fan made of chintz and wood, measuring 26 ft. 3 in. when unfolded and 14 ft. 8 in. high, was made by Victor Troyas Oses of Peralta, Spain in October 1994.

Fireworks   The largest firework ever made was Universe I Part II, exploded for the Lake Toya Festival, Hokkaido, Japan on July 15, 1988. The 1,543-pound shell was 54.7 inches in diameter and burst to a diameter of 3,937 feet.

Catherine wheel   A self-propelled horizontal firework wheel measuring 47 ft. 4 in. in diameter, built by Florida Pyrotechnic Arts Guild, was displayed at the Pyrotechnics Guild International Convention in Idaho Falls, ID on August 14, 1992. It functioned for 3 min. 45 sec.

Flag   The largest flag in the world, measuring 505 by 255 feet and weighing 1.36 tons, is the American "Superflag," owned by Ski Demski of Long

Beach, CA. On May 1, 1996, "Superflag" was unfurled and suspended from cables strung across Hoover Dam.

The largest flag flown from a flagpole was a Brazilian national flag measuring 65 ft. 6 in. by 46 ft. 9 in.

Float The largest float was 184 ft. 8 in. long. It was produced by the World of Dreams Foundation for the St. Patrick's Day parade, Montreal, Quebec, Canada in 1993.

Bouquet of flowers On April 11, 1997, members of the Sri Chinmoy Marathon Team constructed a bouquet of 27,713 carnations in Jamaica, NY. The finished bouquet was 56 ft. 11 in. long and was wrapped with a bow made from 18-inch-wide satin.

The largest bouquet of flowers contained 27,713 carnations.

Garbage can The largest garbage can was made by Natsales of Durban, South Africa for "Keep Durban Beautiful Association Week," September 16–22, 1991. The 19-ft.-9-in.-tall fiberglass can is a replica of Natsales' standard model and has a capacity of 11,493 gallons.

Globe The revolving "Globe of Peace," built between 1982 and 1987 by Orfeo Bartolucci of Apecchi, Pesaro, Italy, is 33 feet in diameter and weighs 33 tons.

Gum wrapper chain The longest gum wrapper chain on record measured 18,721 feet long, and was made by Gary Duschl of Waterdown, Ontario, Canada between 1965 and 1996.

Hanging basket A hanging basket measuring 26 ft. 5 in. in diameter and containing about 2,000 fuchsias was created by Fuchsiavrienden de Kempen VZW of Neerpelt, Belgium in 1996. The basket was 13 ft. 11 in. deep and weighed an estimated 22 tons after it was filled.

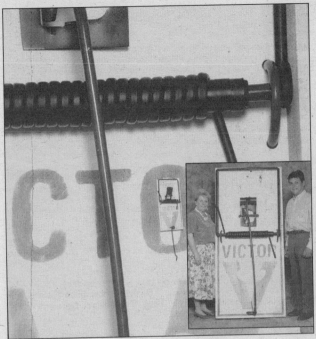

A normal mousetrap is dwarfed by its Texas-size cousin, the world's largest working mousetrap.

Jack-o'-lantern The largest jack-o'-lantern in the world was carved from an 827-pound pumpkin by Michael Green, Regina Johnson and Daniel Salcedo at Nut Tree, CA on October 30, 1992.

The record for most lit jack-o'-lanterns in one place at one time is 13,044, on October 26, 1996, at the Pumpkin Festival in Keene, NH.

Jigsaw puzzle The world's largest jigsaw puzzle measures 51,484 square feet and consists of 43,924 pieces. Assembled on July 8, 1992, it was devised by Centre Socio-Culturel d'Endoume in Marseilles, France and was designed on the theme of the environment.

Jukebox A jukebox 41 ft. 4 in. high and 63 feet wide was built by Namco Ltd. and unveiled in Tokyo, Japan in July 1996. Various features of the jukebox come to life when the music starts.

Knife The penknife with the greatest number of blades is the Year Knife, made by cutlers Joseph Rodgers & Sons, of Sheffield, England, whose trademark was granted in 1682. The knife was made in 1822 with 1,822 blades, and a blade was added every year until 1973, when there was no more space. It was acquired by British hand tool manufacturers Stanley Works (Great Britain) Ltd. in 1970.

Matchstick model   Joseph Sciberras (Malta) built an exact replica, including the interior, of St. Publius Parish Church, Floriana, Malta, consisting of over 3 million matchsticks. The model, made to scale, is 6½ by 6½ by 5 ft.

Mousetrap   Mel McDaniel and Joseph Melancon unveiled a 6-ft.-4-in. long mouse trap in Cleburne, TX in February 1997. The mouse trap is fully functional and is intended to spark children's interest in science and physics.

Origami   It took residents of the district of Gunma, Maebashi, Japan six hours to fold a paper crane measuring 52 ft. 6 in. tall, with a wingspan of 117 ft. 2 in., on October 28, 1995.

Paper chain   A paper chain 40.6 miles long was made by 60 students from the University of Missouri–Rolla on behalf of Rolla Area Big Brothers/ Big Sisters on March 1–2, 1997. The chain consisted of over 450,000 links and was made within a 24-hour period.

Pencil   A pencil measuring 8.9 feet long and weighing 53 pounds was constructed by students at Huddersfield Technical College, Huddersfield, England in 1995.

Piggy bank   The world's largest piggy bank is 15 ft. 5 in. long, 8 ft. 8 in. tall and 21 ft. 4½ in. in circumference. Named "Maximillion," it was constructed by the Canadian Imperial Bank of Commerce in Canada in November 1995.

Piñata   The world's biggest piñata measured 27 feet high, with a diameter of 30 feet, a circumference of 100 feet and a weight of 10,000 pounds. It was built in March 1990 during the celebrations for Carnaval Miami in Miami, FL.

Pinhole camera   A pinhole camera was created from a Portakabin unit measuring 34 by 9½ by 9 feet by John Kippen and Chris Wainwright at the National Museum of Photography, Film and Television in Bradford, England on March 25, 1990. The unit produced a direct positive measuring 33 feet by 4 ft. 2 in.

Pottery   The largest thrown vase on record is one measuring 18 ft. 7 in. high. It was completed on February 10, 1996 by Ray Sparks of The Creative Clay Company, Esk, Queensland, Australia.

Quilt   The world's largest quilt was made by the Saskatchewan Seniors' Association of Saskatchewan, Canada. It measured 155 ft. 4½ in. by 82 ft. 8 in., and was completed on June 13, 1994.

Rope   A rope measuring 610 feet long was made for the annual festival in Naha City, Japan in October 1996. It is the largest rope made from natural materials and weighs 1,345 pounds.

Rube Goldberg machine   The Rube Goldberg Society of Monache High School, Porterville, CA successfully ran the world's largest Rube Goldberg machine on July 31, 1997. The machine incorporates 113 steps, including a flushing toilet, a turning riverboat wheel, a rotating turntable and an empty Guinness Stout bottle. Designed and built by a team of students led by Kinsey G. Blomgren, the machine serves as a coin changer. Two quarters are placed in the machine, and after all 133 steps connect, 50 pennies are dispensed.

Santa Claus   The world's largest Santa Claus was 51 feet high and 36 feet wide, and weighed 2.76 tons. Constructed from polyfoam and metal, it stood at the entrance to the Tanglin Mall, Singapore from November 10, 1996 to January 3, 1997.

Scarf   The longest scarf ever knitted measured 20 miles long. It was knitted by residents of Abbeyfield Houses for the Abbeyfield Society in Potters Bar, England and was completed on May 29, 1988.

Silver   The largest single pieces of silver are a pair of water jugs of 10,408 troy ounces (4.77 cwt) made in 1902 for the Maharaja of Jaipur (1861–1922). They are 5 ft. 3 in. tall, with a circumference of 8 ft. 1½ in., and have a capacity of 2,160 gallons. They are now in the City Palace, Jaipur, India.

Snowman   The tallest snowman was built by a team of local residents at Ohkura Village, Yamagata, Japan. They spent 10 days and nights building the 96-ft.-7-in.-tall snowman, which was completed on March 10, 1995.

Sofa   In May 1995, a red leather sofa 24 feet long was made by Art Forma (Furniture) Ltd. of Castle Donington, England for the Swiss company Spühl AG.

String ball   The largest ball of string on record is one 13 ft. 2½ in. in diameter, 41 ft. 6 in. in circumference, amassed by J. C. Payne of Valley View, TX between 1989 and 1991.

Stuffed toy   Students at Veien School, Honefoss, Norway created a stuffed snake 1,377 feet long in June 1994.

Table   The longest table was set up in Pesaro, Italy on June 20, 1988 by the U.S. Libertas Scavolini basketball team. It was 10,072 feet long and seated 12,000 people.

Tablecloth   The world's largest tablecloth is 1,502 feet long and 4½ feet wide, and was made by the Sportex division of Artex International in Highland, IL on October 17, 1990.

Tapestry   The largest tapestry ever woven is the History of Iraq, with an area of 13,370.7 square feet. It was designed by the Yugoslavian artist Frane Delale and produced by the Zivtex Regeneracija Workshop in Zabok, Yugoslavia. The tapestry was completed in 1986, and it now adorns the wall of an amphitheater in Baghdad, Iraq.

Toy brick tower A pyramid measuring 82 ft. 2 in. tall was built by a team of 800 to commemorate the inauguration of Taiwanese president Lee Teng-hui. It was completed in Taipei on May 18, 1996.

Yo-yo A yo-yo measuring 10 ft. 4 in. in diameter and weighing 897 pounds was devised by J. N. Nichols (Vimto) Ltd. and made by engineering students at Stockport College, Stockport, England. It was suspended from a 187-foot crane in Wythenshawe, England on August 1, 1993, and "yo-yoed" about four times.

Zipper The world's longest zipper was laid around the center of Sneek, Netherlands on September 5, 1989. The brass zipper, made by Yoshida (Netherlands) Ltd., is 9,353.56 feet long and has 2,565,900 teeth.

FANTASTIC FEATS

Apple peeling The longest single unbroken apple peel on record measures 172 ft. 4 in. It was peeled by Kathy Wafler of Wolcott, NY in 11 hr. 30 min. at Long Ridge Mall, Rochester, NY on October 16, 1976. The apple weighed 20 ounces.

Apple picking The greatest recorded performance is 15,830 pounds picked in eight hours by George Adrian of Indianapolis, IN on September 23, 1980.

Balancing on one foot Amresh Kumar Jha balanced on one foot for 71 hr. 40 min. in Bihar, India from September 13 to September 16, 1995. In this activity, the free foot may not be rested on the standing foot, nor may any object be used for support or balance.

Balloon release A mass release of 1,592,744 balloons was staged by Disney Home Video at Longleat House, England on August 27, 1994.

Barrel rolling The record for rolling a full 36-gallon metal beer barrel over a measured mile is 8 min. 7.2 sec., by Phillip Randle, Steve Hewitt, John Round, Trevor Bradley, Colin Barnes and Ray Glover of Haunchwood Collieries Institute and Social Club, Nuneaton, England on August 15, 1982.

A team of 10 people from Tecza Sports Club, Lodz, Poland rolled a 140-pound barrel 124 mi. 560 yd. in 24 hours, September 1–2, 1995.

Barrow pushing A one-wheeled barrow loaded with bricks weighing a gross 8,275 pounds was pushed a distance of 243 feet by John Sarich in London, Ontario, Canada on February 19, 1987.

Barrow racing The fastest time attained in a one-mile wheelbarrow race is 4 min. 48.51 sec., by Piet Pitzer and Jaco Erasmus at Transvalia High School, Vanderbijlpark, South Africa on October 3, 1987.

Members of the Tecza Sports Club of Lodz, Poland rolled a 140-pound barrel over 124 miles in a day.

Bathtub racing The record for a 36-mile bathtub race (with the bathtub used as a boat on water) is 1 hr. 22 min. 27 sec., by Greg Mutton at the Grafton Jacaranda Festival, New South Wales, Australia on November 8, 1987. Tubs are limited to 75 inches and 6-hp motors.

The greatest distance for paddling a hand-propelled bathtub in still water in 24 hours is 90½ miles, by 13 members of Aldington Prison Officers Social Club, near Ashford, Kent, England, May 28–29, 1983.

Bed making The pairs record for making a bed with one blanket, two sheets, an undersheet, an uncased pillow, one bedspread and "hospital" corners is 14.0 seconds, by Sister Sharon Stringer and Nurse Michelle Benkel of the Royal Masonic Hospital, London, England on November 26, 1993.

The record time for one person to make a bed is 28.2 seconds, by Wendy Wall, 34, of Sydney, Australia on November 30, 1978.

Bed pushing A wheeled hospital bed was pushed 3,233 miles by a team of nine employees of Bruntsfield Bedding Center, Edinburgh, Scotland, June 21–July 26, 1979.

Bed race The course record for a 10-mile bed race is 50 minutes, by the Westbury Harriers' 3-man bed team at Chew Valley, Avon, England.

Beer coaster flipping Terry Cole (Great Britain) caught 1,309 beer coasters in one hand, out of 1,310 stacked on his forearm and released in a downward movement, on the British television program *The Big Breakfast* on October 3, 1996.

Beer keg lifting George Olesen raised a keg of beer weighing 138 lb. 11 oz. above his head 737 times in six hours in Horsens, Denmark on May 1, 1994.

Beer stein carrying   Duane Osborn covered a distance of 49 ft. 2½ in. in 3.65 seconds with five full steins in each hand in Cadillac, MI on July 10, 1992.

Brick balancing   John Evans balanced 100 bricks weighing a total of 407 pounds on his head for 14 seconds at London Zoo, London, England on November 18, 1996.

Brick carrying   The greatest distance achieved for carrying a 10-pound brick in one ungloved hand using an uncradled downward pincer grip is 73.4 miles, by Jamie Borges (U.S.) in Jupiter, FL in May 13–14, 1996.

The women's record for carrying a 9-lb.-12-oz. brick is 22.5 miles, by Wendy Morris of Walsall, England on April 28, 1986.

Bricklaying   Travis McGee of Monroe, NC laid 1,494 bricks in 60 minutes on May 17, 1996. The record was set under the normal working conditions of an average bricklayer in a charity event for Habitat for Humanity in Dallas, TX.

Brick lifting   Russell Bradley of Worcester, England lifted 31 bricks laid side by side off a table, raising them to chest height and holding them there for two seconds, on June 14, 1992.

The greatest weight of bricks lifted was by Fred Burton of Cheadle, Staffordshire, England, who lifted 20 bricks weighing 202 lb. 5 oz. on March 21, 1997, holding them for two seconds.

Bubble blowing   Alan McKay of Wellington, New Zealand created a bubble 105 feet long on August 9, 1996. He made it using a bubble wand, dish-washing liquid, glycerine and water.

Bubble-gum blowing   The greatest reported diameter for a bubble-gum bubble under the strict rules of this highly competitive activity is 23 inches, by Susan Montgomery Williams of Fresno, CA on July 19, 1994.

Camping out   The silent Indian fakir Mastram Bapu ("contented father") remained on the same spot by the roadside in the village of Chitra for 22 years, from 1960 to 1982.

Carriage pushing   The greatest distance covered in 24 hours while pushing a baby carriage is 350.22 miles, by 60 members of the Oost-Vlanderen branch of Amnesty International in Lede, Belgium on October 15, 1988.

A 10-man team from the Royal Marines School of Music, Deal, England, with an adult "baby," covered 271.7 miles in 24 hours, November 22–23, 1990.

The fastest time to complete 10 kilometers (6.2 miles) is 38 min. 38 sec., by Craig McGarry, pushing his son James, in Melbourne, Australia on November 17, 1996.

Car washing   Students from Carroll High School, Yakima, WA washed 3,844 cars in eight hours on May 7, 1983.

Cherry stem tying   Al Gliniecki (U.S.) tied 833 cherry stems into knots with his tongue in one hour on April 21, 1995.

Cigar box balancing Terry Cole of London, England balanced 220 unmodified cigar boxes on his chin for nine seconds on April 24, 1992.

Coal shoveling The record for filling a 1,120-pound hopper with coal is 26.59 seconds, by Wayne Miller in Wonthaggi, Victoria, Australia on April 17, 1995. The record by a team of two is 15.01 seconds, by Brian McArdle and Rodney Spark at the Fingal Valley Festival in Fingal, Tasmania, Australia on March 5, 1994.

CPR training session On May 19, 1997, the American Heart Association, Dutchess Region trained 1,320 people in CPR and Early Defibrillation Awareness at the Casperkill Conference Center, Dutchess County, NY.

Crawling The longest continuous voluntary crawl (progression with one knee or the other in unbroken contact with the ground) on record is 31.5 miles, by Peter McKinlay and John Murrie, who covered 115 laps of an athletic track at Falkirk, Scotland, March 28–29, 1992.
 Over a 15-month period ending on March 9, 1985, Jagdish Chander crawled 870 miles from Aligarh to Jamma, India to propitiate his revered Hindu goddess, Mata.

Cucumber slicing Norman Johnson (Great Britain) set a record of 13.4 seconds for slicing a 12-inch cucumber, 1½ inches in diameter, at 22 slices

The world's largest plastic duck race, with 100,000 competitors, took place on the River Avon in Bath, England.

to the inch (total 264 slices) at Westdeutsche Rundfunk in Cologne, Germany on April 3, 1983.

Diving   The record depth for the dangerous (and ill-advised) activity of breath-held diving is 428 feet, by Francisco "Pipín" Ferreras (Cuba) off Cabo San Lucas, Mexico on March 10, 1996. He was underwater for 2 min. 11 sec.

The record dive with scuba gear is 925 feet, by Jim Bowden (U.S.) in a cave in Zacaton, Mexico in April 1994.

Duck racing   A hundred thousand yellow plastic ducks raced down the River Avon, Bath, England on May 26, 1997 in the world's largest duck race. It took 2 hr. 15 min. for duck number 24359, owned by Chris Green (Great Britain) to finish the half-mile race.

Egg and spoon racing   Dale Lyons of Meriden, England ran 26 mi. 385 yd. (the classic marathon distance) while carrying a dessert spoon with a fresh egg on it in 3 hr. 47 min. on April 23, 1990.

Egg balancing   Kenneth Epperson of Monroe, GA balanced 210 eggs simultaneously on September 30, 1990.

A class from Bayfield School, Bayfield, CO simultaneously balanced 467 eggs on March 20, 1986.

Egg hunt   The greatest egg hunt in the United States involved 120,000 plastic and candy eggs at an Easter egg hunt at Coquina Beach in Manatee, FL on March 23, 1991. The event, hosted by Meals on Wheels PLUS of Manatee, Inc., entertained 1,870 children.

Longest incarceration in an elevator   Graham Coates (Great Britain) was trapped in an elevator in Brighton, England for 62 hours, May 24–27, 1986.

Escalator riding   The record distance traveled on a pair of up and down escalators is 133.18 miles, by David Beattie and Adrian Simons at Top Shop in London, England, July 17–21, 1989. They each completed 7,032 circuits.

Fire bucket brigade   The longest fire company bucket brigade stretched over 11,471 feet, with 2,271 people passing 50 buckets along the complete course, at the Centennial Parade and Muster, Hudson, NY on July 11, 1992.

Garbage collecting   The greatest number of volunteers involved in collecting garbage in one location in one day is 50,405, along the coastline of California on October 2, 1993, in conjunction with the International Coast Cleanup.

Glass balancing   Ashrita Furman of Jamaica, NY balanced 57 pint glasses on his chin for 11.89 seconds on May 18, 1996.

Gold panning   The fastest time for panning eight planted gold nuggets in a 10-inch-diameter pan is 7.55 seconds, by Don Roberts of Diamond Bar, CA in the 27th World Gold Panning Championship on April 16, 1989 in Dahlonega, GA. The women's record is 8.30 seconds, by Desiree Fauscett of Crandall, GA at the 32nd World Ladies Gold Panning Contest on April 16, 1994 in Dahlonega, GA.

Grape catching The greatest distance at which a grape thrown from level ground has been caught in the mouth is 327 ft. 6 in., by Paul J. Tavilla in East Boston, MA on May 27, 1991. The grape was thrown by James Deady.

Hair cutting The greatest number of haircuts given in an hour is 18, by Trevor Mitchell in London, England on October 27, 1996. During this attempt, he also completed one haircut in a record 2 min. 20 sec. The haircuts met guidelines set down by the Organisation Artistique Internationale de la Coiffure.

Fifty-seven glasses, one chin, Ashrita Furman sets the glass-balancing record.

Hair splitting　Alfred West (Great Britain) split a human hair 17 times into 18 parts on eight occasions.

Handshaking　Yogesh Sharma shook hands with 31,118 different people in eight hours at the Gwalior Trade Fair, Gwalior, Madhya Pradesh, India on January 14, 1996.

Hopscotch　The greatest number of games of hopscotch successfully completed in 24 hours is 390, by Ashrita Furman of Jamaica, NY, April 2–3, 1995.

Human centipede　The largest "human centipede" to move 98 ft. 5 in. (30 meters), with ankles firmly tied together, consisted of 1,665 students from the University of Guelph in Canada on September 2, 1996. Nobody fell over in the course of the walk.

Human fly　The longest climb on the vertical face of a building occurred on May 25, 1981, when Daniel Goodwin climbed a record 1,454 feet up the outside of the Sears Tower in Chicago, using suction cups and metal clips for support.

Joke telling　Working on the premise that a joke must have a beginning, a middle and an end, Felipe Carbonell (Peru) told 345 jokes in one hour on July 29, 1993.

Mike Hessman of Columbus, OH told 12,682 jokes in 24 hours on November 16–17, 1992.

Juggling　*"Juggled" means that the number of catches made equals the number of objects multiplied by the number of hands. "Flashed" means the number of catches made is equal to at least the number of objects, but less than a "juggle."*
*　　* These records are reported to have been achieved, but indisputable evidence is not available.*

Most objects aloft　826 jugglers kept 2,478 objects in the air simultaneously, each person juggling at least three objects, in Glastonbury, England on June 26, 1994.

11 rings (juggled)　Albert Petrovski* (USSR), 1963; Eugene Belaur* (USSR), 1968; Sergei Ignatov* (USSR), 1973.

12 rings (flashed)　Albert Lucas (U.S.), 1995 (1984*); Anthony Gatto (U.S.), 1993.

7 clubs (juggled)　Albert Petrovski* (USSR), 1963; Sorin Munteanu* (Romania), 1975; Jack Bremlov* (Czechoslovakia), 1985; Albert Lucas (U.S.), 1996 (1985*); Anthony Gatto (U.S.), 1988; Bruce Tiemann (U.S.), 1995.

8 clubs (flashed)　Anthony Gatto (U.S.), 1989; Scott Sorensen (U.S.), 1995.

10 balls (juggled)　Enrico Rastelli* (Italy), 1920s; Bruce Sarafian (U.S.), 1996.

10 balls (bounce juggled)   Tim Nolan* (U.S.), 1988.

12 balls (flashed)   Bruce Sarafian (U.S.), 1995.

8 plates (juggled)   Enrico Rastelli* (Italy), 1920s; Albert Lucas, 1997.

8 plates (flashed)   Albert Lucas (U.S.), 1993.

7 flaming torches (juggled)   Anthony Gatto (U.S.), 1989.

Passing 11 clubs (juggled)   Owen Morse and John Wee (U.S.), 1995.

Passing 15 balls (flashed)   Peter Kaseman and Rob Vancko (U.S.), 1995.

5 balls inverted   Bobby May (U.S.), 1953.

Ball spinning (on one hand)   François Chotard (France), 9 balls, 1990.

Basketball spinning   Bruce Crevier (U.S.), 18 basketballs (whole body), 1994.

Duration: 5 clubs without a drop   45 min. 2 sec., Anthony Gatto (U.S.), 1989.

Duration: 3 objects without a drop   11 hr. 4 min. 22 sec., Terry Cole (Great Britain), 1995.

Kissing   Alfred A. E. Wolfram of New Brighton, MN kissed 10,504 people in eight hours at the Minnesota Renaissance Festival on August 19, 1995.
The most couples kissing simultaneously in one place was 1,420, at the University of Maine, Orono, ME on February 14, 1996.

Kite flying   The following records are all recognized by *Kite Lines Magazine*:

Highest   A record height of 31,955 feet was reached by a train of eight kites over Lindenberg, Germany on August 1, 1919.
The altitude record for a single kite is 12,471 feet, in the case of a kite flown by Henry Helm Clayton and A. E. Sweetland at the Blue Hill Weather Station, Milton, MA on February 28, 1898.

Longest   The longest kite flown was 3,394 feet long. It was made and flown by Michel Trouillet and a team of helpers in Nimes, France on November 18, 1990.

Largest   The largest kite flown was 5,952 square feet. It was first flown by a Dutch team on the beach at Scheveningen, Netherlands on August 8, 1991.

Fastest   The fastest speed attained by a kite was 120 mph for a kite flown by Pete DiGiacomo in Ocean City, MD on September 22, 1989.

Most figure eights   The greatest number of figure eights achieved with a kite in an hour is 2,911, by Stu Cohen in Ocean City, MD on September 25, 1988.

Most on a single line   The greatest number of kites flown on a single line is 11,284, by Sadao Harada and a team of helpers in Sakurajima, Kagoshima, Japan on October 18, 1990.

Longest duration   The longest recorded flight is one of 180 hr. 17 min., by the Edmonds Community College team at Long Beach, WA, August 21–29, 1982. Managing the flight of this J-25 parafoil was Harry N. Osborne.

Knitting   The world's fastest hand-knitter was Gwen Matthewman of Featherstone, England. She attained a speed of 111 stitches per minute in a test at Phildar's Wool Shop, Leeds, England on September 29, 1980.

The Exeter Spinners—Audrey Felton, Christine Heap, Eileen Lancaster, Marjorie Mellis, Ann Sandercock and Maria Scott—produced a sweater by hand from raw fleece in 1 hr. 55 min. 50.2 sec. on September 25, 1983 at British Broadcasting Corporation Television Centre, London, England.

Knot tying   The fastest recorded time for tying the six Boy Scout Handbook knots (square knot, sheet bend, sheepshank, clove hitch, round turn and two half hitches, and bowline) on individual ropes is 8.1 seconds, by Clinton R. Bailey Sr. of Pacific City, OR on April 13, 1977.

Ladder climbing   A team of 10 firefighters from the Pietermaritzburg Msunduzi Fire Services climbed a vertical height of 56.23 miles up a standard fire department ladder in 24 hours in Pietermaritzburg, South Africa, April 28–29, 1995.

Leapfrogging   The greatest distance leapfrogged is 996.2 miles, by 14 students from Trancos dormitory at Stanford University, Stanford, CA. They started leapfrogging on May 16, 1991 and stopped 244 hr. 43 min. later on May 26.

Log rolling   The record number of International Championships won is 10, by Jubiel Wickheim of Shawnigan Lake, British Columbia, Canada, between 1956 and 1969.

Mantle of bees   Jed Shaner was covered by a mantle of an estimated 343,000 bees weighing an aggregate of 80 pounds in Staunton, VA on June 29, 1991.

Mathematical computation   Shakuntala Devi multiplied two randomly selected 13-digit numbers (7,686,369,774,870 × 2,465,099,745,779) at Imperial College, London, England on June 18, 1980, in 28 seconds. Her answer, which was correct, was 18,947,668,177,995,426,462,773,730.

Memorization   Bhandanta Vicittabi Vumsa (1911–93) recited 16,000 pages of Buddhist canonical texts in Yangon, Myanmar in May 1974.

Gon Yangling, 26, memorized more than 15,000 telephone numbers in Harbin, China, according to the Xinhua News Agency.

Memorizing cards Dave Farrow (U.S.) memorized on a single sighting a random sequence of 52 separate decks of cards (2,704 cards in all) that had been shuffled together, with six mistakes, at the Guinness World of Records Museum, Niagara Falls, Canada on June 24, 1996.

The fastest time to memorize a single deck of shuffled cards is 38.29 seconds, by Dominic O'Brien (Great Britain) at London Zoo, London, England in June 1996.

Memorizing pi Hiroyuki Goto of Tokyo, Japan recited pi to 42,195 places at the NHK Broadcasting Center, Tokyo on February 18, 1995.

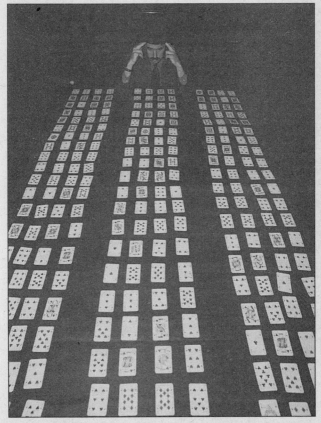

Dominic O'Brien memorized a deck of cards in 38.29 seconds.

Milk bottle balancing   The greatest distance walked by a person continuously balancing a milk bottle on the head is 72 miles, by Terry Cole (Great Britain) around the City of London, England on June 4–5, 1996. It took him 25 hours to complete the walk.

Milk crate balancing   Terry Cole of Walthamstow, England balanced 29 crates on his chin for the minimum time of 10 seconds on May 16, 1994.

John Evans of Marlpool, England balanced 94 crates (each weighing three pounds) on his head for 16 seconds on the British television show *The Big Breakfast*, filmed in Birmingham, England, on October 2, 1996.

Motionlessness   Radhey Shyam Prajapati (India) stood motionless for 18 hr. 5 min. 50 sec. at Ghandi Bhawan, Bhopal, India on January 25–26, 1996.

Needle threading   On February 21, 1996, Dean Gould (Great Britain) threaded a piece of thread through a number 13 needle 3,471 times in two hours.

Oyster opening   The record for opening oysters is 100 in 2 min. 20.07 sec., by Mike Racz in Invercargill, New Zealand on July 16, 1990.

Paper clip chain   A 9.33-mile-long chain of paper clips was made by 40 members of Boon Lay Community Centre Youth Group, Singapore, July 13–14, 1996.

Pass the parcel   The largest game of pass the parcel involved 3,464 people who removed 2,000 wrappers in two hours from a parcel measuring 5 by 3 by 3 feet at Alton Towers, Alton, England on November 8, 1992. The event was organized by Parcelforce International.

Pedal-boating   Kenichi Horie of Kobe, Japan set a pedal-boating distance record of 4,660 miles, leaving Honolulu, HI on October 30, 1992 and arriving in Naha, Okinawa, Japan on February 17, 1993.

Pogo stick jumping   The greatest number of jumps achieved is 177,737, by Gary Stewart at Huntington Beach, Los Angeles, CA, May 25–26, 1990. Ashrita Furman (U.S.) set a distance record of 23.11 miles in 12 hr. 27 min. on June 22, 1997 in Bayside, New York.

Pole sitting   Modern records do not come close to that of St. Simeon the Younger (*c.* A.D. 521–97), called Stylites, a monk who spent his last 45 years on top of a stone pillar on the Hill of Wonders, near Antioch, Syria. His achievement is the longest-standing record in *The Guinness Book of World Records*.

Mellissa Sanders lived in a shack measuring six feet by seven feet at the top of a pole in Indianapolis, IN, from October 26, 1986 to March 24, 1988, a total of 516 days.

Glen Boyden stayed in a 180-gallon barrel at the top of a pole in Sherwood Park, Alberta, Canada, for 54 days from June 8 to August 1, 1996.

Potato peeling   On September 19, 1992, Marj Killian, Terry Anderson, Barbara Pearson, Marilyn Small and Janene Utkin peeled 1,064 lb. 6 oz. (net) of potatoes to an institutional cookery standard with standard kitchen knives in 45 minutes at the 64th Annual Idaho Spud Day celebration, held in Shelley, ID.

Rappeling A team of four Royal Marines set an overall distance record of 3,627 feet, by each rappeling down the Boulby Potash Mine, Cleveland, England from 25 feet below ground level to the shaft bottom on November 2, 1993.

The longest descent down the side of a building is one of 1,465 feet by two teams of twelve people representing the British Royal Marines and the Canadian School of Rescue Training. All 24 people rappeled to the ground from the Space Deck of the CN Tower in Toronto, Ontario, Canada on July 1, 1992. Two ropes were used, and the first member of each team reached the ground at exactly the same time.

The greatest distance rappeled by 10 people in an 8-hour period is 67.68 miles, by a team from the British 10th (Volunteer) Battalion, Parachute Regiment. They rappeled 1,427 times down the side of Barclays Bank on Fenchurch Street, London, England on May 6, 1995.

Rope slide The greatest distance recorded in a rope slide is 5,730 feet, by Lance Corporal Peter Baldwin of the British Royal Marines and Stu Leggett of the Canadian School of Rescue Training, from the top of Mt. Gibraltar, near Calgary, Canada down to level ground on August 31, 1994. Some of the descent was done at speeds in excess of 100 mph.

Portraying Santa Claus Dayton C. Fouts has played Santa Claus every year since 1937. He appeared as Santa for 55 years in Harvey, IL and now continues the tradition in Tucson, AZ.

Shaving Denny Rowe shaved 1,994 men in 60 minutes with a retractor safety razor in Herne Bay, England on June 19, 1988, taking an average of 1.8 seconds per volunteer and drawing blood four times.

Dayton C. Fouts has played Santa Claus every year since 1937. It's hard to find reindeer in Tucson, AZ, but Guinness record-holders know how to improvise.

Tom Rodden of Chatham, England shaved 278 volunteers in 60 minutes with a straight razor on November 10, 1993, averaging 12.9 seconds per face. He drew blood seven times.

Shoe shining   The greatest number of shoes shined "on the hoof" by four people in eight hours is 14,975. This was achieved by four members of the London Church of Christ, London, England on June 15, 1996.

Spitting   The greatest recorded distance for spitting a cherry stone is 95 ft. 1 in., by Horst Ortmann in Langenthal, Germany on August 27, 1994.

The record for projecting a watermelon seed is 75 ft. 2 in., by Jason Schayot in De Leon, TX on August 12, 1995.

David O'Dell of Apple Valley, CA spat a tobacco wad 49 ft. 5½ in. at the 19th World Tobacco Spitting Championships, Calico Ghost Town, CA on March 26, 1994.

Stair climbing   The 100-story record for stair climbing was set by Dennis W. Martz in the Detroit Plaza Hotel, Detroit, MI on June 26, 1978, at 11 min. 23.8 sec.

Brian McCauliff ran a vertical mile (ascending and descending eight times) on the stairs of the Westin Hotel, Detroit, MI in 1 hr. 38 min. 5 sec. on February 2, 1992.

The record for the 1,760 steps (vertical height 1,122 feet) in the world's tallest freestanding structure, the CN Tower, Toronto, Canada, is 7 min. 52 sec., by Brendan Keenoy on October 29, 1989.

Geoff Case raced up the 1,575 steps of the Empire State Building, New York City in 10 min. 18 sec. on February 16, 1993.

Russell Gill climbed the 835 steps of the Rhodes State Office Tower, Columbus, OH 53 times (for a total vertical height of 26,712 feet) in 9 hr. 16 min. 24 sec. in February 1994. He descended by elevator each time.

Standing   The longest period on record that anyone has continuously stood is more than 17 years in the case of Swami Maujgiri Maharaj when performing the Tapasya or penance from 1955 to November 1973 in Shahjahanpur, Uttar Pradesh, India. When sleeping he would lean against a plank. He died at age 85 in September 1980.

Step-ups   Terry Cole of Walthamstow, England completed 2,970 step-ups in one hour on May 24, 1996, using a 15-inch-high exercise bench.

Stone skipping   The video-verified stone skipping record is 38 skips, achieved by Jerdone in Wimberley, TX on October 20, 1991.

Stretcher bearing   The record for carrying a stretcher case with a 140-pound "body" is 186 mi. 1,160 yd. in 59 hr. 19 min., May 27–30, 1996, by two 4-man teams from 1 Field Ambulance, Canadian Forces Base Calgary. They started in Edmonton, Alberta and finished in Calgary.

Tailoring   The shortest time for production of a 3-piece suit from sheep to finished article was 1 hr. 34 min. 33.42 sec., by 65 members of the Melbourne College of Textiles, Pascoe Vale, Victoria, Australia on June 24, 1982. Catching and fleecing took 2 min. 21 sec., and carding, spinning, weaving and tailoring occupied the remaining time.

Lifting with teeth   Walter Arfeuille (Belgium) lifted weights totaling 621 pounds a distance of 6¾ inches off the ground with his teeth in Paris, France on March 31, 1990.

Pulling with teeth   Robert Galstyan of Masis, Armenia pulled two railroad cars coupled together, weighing a total of 483,197 pounds, a distance of 23 feet along a railroad track with his teeth at Shcherbinka, Greater Moscow, Russia on July 21, 1992.

Tightrope walking   The oldest tightrope walker was "Professor" William Ivy Baldwin, who crossed the South Boulder Canyon in Colorado on a 320-foot wire with a 125-foot drop on his 82nd birthday on July 31, 1948.

The tightrope endurance record is 205 days, by Jorge Ojeda-Guzman of Orlando, FL, on a wire 36 feet long and 35 feet above the ground. He was there from January 1 to July 25, 1993 and entertained onlookers by walking, balancing on a chair and dancing. His main luxury was a wooden cabin measuring 3 by 3 feet at one end of the tightrope.

Ashley Brophy of Neilborough, Victoria, Australia walked 7.19 miles on a wire 147.64 feet long and 32.81 feet above the ground in Adelaide, Australia on November 1, 1985 in 3½ hours.

The greatest drop over which anyone has walked on a tightrope is 10,335 feet above the French countryside, by Michel Menin (France) on August 4, 1989.

Toast   The greatest number of people simultaneously participating in a toast was 50,304. The Great Guinness Toast was staged on February 28, 1997 at 11:00 P.M. EST, in pubs, restaurants and bars in 31 United States metropolitan areas.

Top spinning   A team of 25 from the Mizushima Plant of Kawasaki Steel Works in Okayama, Japan spun a giant top 6 ft. 6¾ in. tall and 8 ft. 6¼ in. in diameter, weighing 793.6 pounds, for 1 hr. 21 min. 35 sec. on November 3, 1986.

Train pulling   Juraj Barbaric single-handedly pulled a train weighing 396.8 tons a distance of 25 ft. 3 in. along a train track in Kosice, Slovakia on May 25, 1996.

Traveling   John D. Clouse of Evansville, IN had visited all 192 sovereign countries and all but six of the nonsovereign or other territories that existed in early 1996.

Couple   Dr. Robert and Carmen Becker of Pompano Beach, FL have visited all of the sovereign countries and all but seven of the nonsovereign or other territories.

U.S. counties   Allen F. Zondlak of St. Clair Shores, MI visited all 3,142 counties and county equivalents in the United States, completing his travels in 1991.

Tree climbing   On July 3, 1988, Guy German of Sitka, AK climbed up a 100-foot tree trunk and back down to the ground in 24.82 seconds at the World Championship Timber Carnival in Albany, OR.

ON YOUR MARK, GET SET, GROW!

*A*nd you thought planting your flower garden was back-breaking work. Imagine planting 14,000 trees in just under three hours. That's what 158 volunteers from the Georgia Forestry Association accomplished this year, reforesting 16 acres of reclaimed farmland and breaking the world record all in less than half a day.

"I'm sure there were lots of blisters and sore backs, but it was worth it," says April Lavender, the communications director of the forestry association, a lobby group representing the interests of Georgia's landowners, saw mills, pulp mills, loggers and paper manufacturers.

When the forestry association brainstormed on a public relations campaign to show their commitment to reforestation, an attempt to break the world tree-planting record seemed a natural. The group quickly recruited 158 volunteers who gathered on February 21, Georgia's Arbor Day, to make history.

The volunteers were divided into groups of two, with one member of each pair responsible for digging and the other for planting the seedling in the ground. The teams worked so quickly that they completed the project before their scheduled lunch break. After just three hours and 45 minutes, they had added 14,000 Loblolly Pines to the Charlie Elliott Wildlife Center, a state park.

"Everyone came together for a common goal and when the goal was reached they were elated," says Lavender, adding that the volunteers "hooted and hollered" when they learned that a world record had been broken.

According to Lavender, the day was overcast and the crew of volunteers worked under the threat of storms. The weather held during the planting and subsequent ceremony, but the skies opened up as soon as the last of the equipment was packed.

"We like to think that God was watching over us," Lavender quips, "because those trees really needed that water."

TREE PLANTING

On February 21, 1997, 158 volunteers organized by the Georgia Forestry Association, Inc. planted 14,000 native tree seedlings in 3 hr. 45 min. at the Charlie Elliott Wildlife Center, Jasper County, GA.

Tree planting   On February 21, 1997, 158 volunteers organized by the Georgia Forestry Association, Inc. planted 14,000 native tree seedlings in 3 hr. 45 min. at the Charlie Elliott Wildlife Center, Jasper County, GA.

The one-week record for an unlimited number of volunteers is 101,165. The trees were planted in Vanderbijlpark, South Africa on November 1–2, 1996.

Tree sitting   The duration record for staying in a tree is more than 25 years, by Bungkas, who went up a palm tree in the Indonesian village of Bengkes in 1970 and has been there ever since. He lives in a nest made from branches and leaves. Repeated efforts have been made to persuade him to come down, but without success.

Typewriting   The highest recorded speeds attained with a 10-word penalty per error on a manual machine are as follows: Five minutes: 176 wpm by Carole Forristall Waldschlager Bechen in Dixon, IL on April 2, 1959; one hour: 147 wpm by Albert Tangora (U.S.) on an Underwood Standard, October 22, 1923. The official 1-hour record on an electric typewriter is 9,316 words (40 errors) on an IBM machine, giving a net rate of 149 wpm, by Margaret Hamma (later Dilmore) in Brooklyn, NY on June 20, 1941.

In an official test in 1946, Stella Pajunas (later Garnand) typed 216 words in one minute on an IBM machine in Chicago, IL.

Gregory Arakelian of Herndon, VA set a speed record of 158 wpm, with two errors, on a personal computer in the Key Tronic World Invitational Type-off, which attracted some 10,000 entrants worldwide. Arakelian recorded this speed in a 3-minute test in the semifinal on September 24, 1991.

Mikhail Shestov of Fredriksberg, Denmark set a numerical record for a PC on April 2, 1996, by typing spaced numbers from 1 to 801 in five minutes at Baruch College, New York City. He did not make any errors and was not aided by a correction device.

Les Stewart of Mudjimba Beach, Queensland, Australia had typed the numbers 1 to 894,000 in words on 17,770 quarto sheets as of April 11, 1996. His target is to become a "millionaire."

Unsupported circle   An unsupported circle of 10,323 employees of the Nissan Motor Co. was formed at Komazawa Stadium, Tokyo, Japan on October 23, 1982.

Walking   Arthur Blessitt of North Fort Myers, FL has walked 32,002 miles in more than 26 years since December 25, 1969. He has been to 367 countries on all seven continents, carrying a 12-foot cross and preaching while he walked.

Rick Hansen (Canada), who was paralyzed from the waist down in 1973 as a result of a car accident, wheeled his wheelchair 24,901.55 miles through four continents and 34 countries. He started his journey from Vancouver, British Columbia on March 21, 1985 and arrived back there on May 22, 1987.

Trans-Americas   George Meegan (Great Britain) walked 19,019 miles from Ushuaia, in the southern tip of South America, to Prudhoe Bay in northern Alaska, taking 2,426 days from January 26, 1977 to September 18, 1983.

Trans-America Sean McGuire (U.S.) walked 7,327 miles from the Yukon River, north of Livengood, AK to Key West, FL in 307 days, from June 6, 1978 to April 9, 1979.

John Lees (Great Britain) walked 2,876 miles across the United States from City Hall, Los Angeles to City Hall, New York City in 53 days 12 hr. 15 min. (averaging 53.75 miles a day) between April 11 and June 3, 1972.

Trans-Canada Clyde McRae walked 3,764 miles from Halifax to Vancouver in 96 days, from May 1 to August 4, 1973.

Whip cracking The longest whip ever cracked (i.e., the end made to travel faster than the speed of sound) is one of 184 ft. 6 in., excluding the handle, wielded by Krist King of Pettisville, OH on September 17, 1991.

Wine glass stacking Alain Fournier (Canada) put in position and held 45 wine glasses in one hand on "Live! With Regis and Kathie Lee" on July 20, 1994.

Writing During the mid 1950s, Horace Dall of Luton, England built a pantograph—which reduces movement—fitted with a diamond stylus, with which he engraved writing small enough to fit 140 Bibles to one square inch.

In the 1990s, the movement of small atoms under an electron microscope now allows engraving of letters five atoms tall. At this size, several Bibles could be printed on a single bacterium.

Yodeling The most rapid recorded yodel is 22 tones (15 falsetto) in one second, by Thomas Scholl of Munich, Germany on February 9, 1992.

Yo-yo Fast Eddy McDonald of Toronto, Canada completed 21,663 loops in three hours on October 14, 1990 in Boston, MA. McDonald also set a one-hour speed record of 8,437 loops in Cavendish, Prince Edward Island, Canada on July 14, 1990.

The fastest time to complete 100 meters (328 feet) is 13.9 seconds, by Taro Yamashita at the 1996 Yolympics in Portsmouth, NH, April 22, 1994.

MARRIAGES

Longest engagement The longest engagement was between Octavio Guillén and Adriana Martínez. They took the plunge after 67 years in Mexico City in June 1969, when they were 82 years old.

Most marriages The greatest number of marriages contracted by one person in the monogamous world is 28, by former Baptist minister Glynn "Scotty" Wolfe (1908–97) of Blythe, CA, who first married in 1927.

The most monogamous marriages by a woman is 22, by Linda Lou Essex of Anderson, IN, who has been married to 15 different men since 1957. Her most recent marriage was in October 1991, but that ended in divorce, like the others.

The record for bigamous marriages is 104, by a man using the name Giovanni Vigliotto, from 1949 to 1981 in 27 states and 14 countries. On March 28, 1983 in Phoenix, AZ, Vigliotto received a sentence of 28 years for fraud and six for bigamy, and was fined $336,000.

Oldest bride and bridegroom   The oldest recorded bridegroom was Harry Stevens, age 103, who married Thelma Lucas, 84, in Beloit, WI on December 3, 1984.

The oldest bride was Minnie Munro, age 102, who married Dudley Reid, 83, in Point Clare, New South Wales, Australia on May 31, 1991.

It's never too late to find Mr. Right. Minnie Munro was 102 years old when she married Dudley Reid.

Youngest married couple   In 1986 an 11-month-old boy was married to a 3-month-old girl in Bangladesh to end a 20-year feud over a disputed farm.

Longest marriages   The longest marriages were both of 86 years. Sir Temulji Bhicaji Nariman and Lady Nariman were married from 1853 until 1940, when Sir Temulji died in Bombay, India. Lazarus Rowe of Greenland, NH and Molly Webber married in 1743. She died in 1829, also after 86 years of marriage.

Golden weddings   The most golden weddings in a family is 10. The six sons and four daughters of Joseph and Sophia Gresl of Manitowoc, WI celebrated golden weddings between 1962 and 1988; the six sons and four daughters of George and Eleonora Hopkins of Patrick County, VA celebrated golden weddings between 1961 and 1988; and the five sons and five daughters of Alonzo and Willie Alpharetta Cagle of McLennan County, TX celebrated golden weddings between 1971 and 1993.

Oldest to divorce   A divorce was granted to Simon Stern, 97, and his wife Ida, 91, in Milwaukee, WI on February 2, 1984.

Wedding ceremonies   The largest mass wedding was one of 35,000 couples officiated over by Sun Myung Moon of the Holy Spirit Association for the

Unification of World Christianity in Seoul, South Korea on August 25, 1995. Another 325,000 couples around the world took part through a satellite link.

Most ceremonies   Richard and Carole Roble of South Hempstead, NY have renewed their vows 56 times, starting in 1969.

Most expensive   The wedding of Mohammed, son of Shaik Rashid Bin Saeed Al Maktoum, to Princess Salama in Dubai in May 1981 lasted seven days and cost $44 million.

Best man   Ting Ming Siong (Malaysia) served as best man at 1,089 weddings between September 1975 and March 1997.

PROJECTILE THROWING

Longest throw   The longest independently authenticated throw of any inert object heavier than air is 1,265 ft. 9 in., for a lead weight with a long string tail attached, thrown by David Engvall in El Mirage, CA on October 17, 1993. The record for an object without any velocity-aiding feature is 1,257 feet by Scott Zimmerman, with a flying ring on July 8, 1986 in Fort Funston, CA.

Boomerang juggling   The greatest number of consecutive catches with two boomerangs, keeping at least one boomerang aloft at all times, is 555, by Yannick Charles (France) in Strasbourg, France on September 4, 1995.

Boomerang throwing   The greatest number of consecutive 2-handed catches is 817, by Michael Girvin (U.S.) on July 17, 1994 in Oakland, CA.

Longest out-and-return distance   489 ft. 3 in., by Michel Dufayard (France) on July 5, 1992 in Shrewsbury, England.

Longest flight duration (with self-catch)   2 min. 59.94 sec. by Dennis Joyce (U.S.) in Bethlehem, PA, June 25, 1987.

Brick   146 ft. 1 in. (standard 5-pound building brick), Geoff Capes (Great Britain) at Braybrook School, Orton Goldhay, England on July 19, 1978.

Cow chip   The greatest distance under the "non-sphericalization and 100 percent organic" rule is 266 feet, by Steve Urner at the Mountain Festival, Tehachapi, CA on August 14, 1981.

Egg (fresh hen's)   323 ft. 2½ in. (without breaking it), Johnny Dell Foley to Keith Thomas in Jewett, TX on November 12, 1978.

Rolling pin   175 ft. 5 in. (two pounds), Lori La Deane Adams at Iowa State Fair, IA on August 21, 1979.

Slingshot   1,565 ft. 4 in. (50-inch-long sling and a 2¼-ounce dart), David P. Engvall in Baldwin Lake, CA on September 13, 1992.

Spear throwing   848 ft. 6½ in. (using an atlatl or hand-held device that fits onto a short spear), David Engvall in Aurora, CO on July 15, 1995.

Flying disc throwing (formerly Frisbee)   The World Flying Disc Federation distance records are: *(men)* 656 ft. 2 in., by Scott Stokely (U.S.) on May 14, 1995 in Fort Collins, CO; *(women)* 447 ft. 3 in., by Anni Kreml (U.S.) on August 21, 1994, also in Fort Collins, CO.

The throw, run and catch records are: *(men)* 303 ft. 11 in., by Hiroshi Oshima (Japan) on July 20, 1988 in San Francisco, CA; *(women)* 196 ft. 11 in., by Judy Horowitz (U.S.) on June 29, 1985 in La Mirada, CA.

The 24-hour distance records for a pair are: *(men)* 367.94 miles, by Conrad Damon and Pete Fust (U.S.) on April 24–25, 1993 in San Marino, CA; *(women)* 115.65 miles, by Jo Cahow and Amy Berard (U.S.), December 30–31, 1979 in Pasadena, CA.

The records for maximum time aloft are: *(men)* 16.72 seconds, by Don Cain (U.S.) on May 26, 1984 in Philadelphia, PA; *(women)* 11.81 seconds, by Amy Bekken (U.S.) on August 1, 1991.

FOOD

Bagel   On July 24, 1996 Kraft Foods and Lender's Bagels in Mattoon, IL made a bagel weighing 563 pounds and measuring 59³/₁₆ inches in diameter and 12½ inches high.

Banana split   The longest banana split ever created measured 4.55 miles long, and was made by residents of Selinsgrove, PA on April 30, 1988.

Burrito   A burrito weighing 4,456.3 pounds and measuring 3,578.8 feet long was created by La Costeña and Burrito Real Restaurants at Rengstorff Park, Mountain View, CA on May 3, 1997.

Cake Largest   The largest cake ever created weighed 128,238 lb. 8 oz., including 16,209 pounds of icing. It was made to celebrate the 100th birthday of Fort Payne, AL, and was in the shape of Alabama. The cake was prepared by a local bakery, EarthGrains, and the first cut was made by 100-year-old resident Ed Henderson on October 18, 1989.

Tallest   The tallest cake was 101 ft. 2½ in. high. It was created by Beth Cornell Trevorrow and her team of helpers at the Shiawassee County Fairgrounds, MI. The cake consisted of 100 tiers, and work was completed on August 5, 1990.

Oldest   The Alimentarium Food Museum in Vevey, Switzerland has on display the world's oldest cake, which was sealed and "vacuum-packed" in the grave of Pepionkh, who lived in ancient Egypt around 2200 B.C. The

This bumper burrito, made by La Costeña and Burrito Real Restaurants, weighed 4,456.3 pounds.

4.3-inch-wide cake has sesame on it and honey inside, and was possibly made with milk.

Candy The largest candy was a marzipan chocolate weighing 4,078 lb. 8 oz., made at the Ven International Fresh Market, Diemen, Netherlands, May 11–13, 1990.

Cereal treat The Wood Company created a 1,413-pound Kellogg's Rice Krispies treat in Bethlehem, PA on March 15, 1997.

Cheese The largest cheese ever created was a cheddar weighing 57,508 lb. 8 oz., made on September 7, 1995 by Loblaws Supermarkets Limited and Agropur Dairies in Granby, Quebec, Canada. It was taken on tour in a refrigerated truck that had been specially designed for the purpose.

Chocolate model The largest chocolate model weighed 4.4 tons, and was in the shape of a traditional Spanish sailing ship. It was made by Gremi Provincial de Pastisseria, Confiteria i Bolleria school, Barcelona in February 1991 and measured 42 ft. 8 in. by 27 ft. 10½ in. by 8 ft. 2½ in.

Cookie On April 2, 1996, a chocolate chip cookie with an area of 5,241.5 square feet and a diameter of 81 ft. 8 in. was made by Cookie Time, in Christchurch, New Zealand. It contained 2.8 tons of chocolate.

Crepe The largest crepe was 49 ft. 3 in. in diameter and one inch deep, and weighed 6,614 pounds. It was made and flipped in Rochdale, England on August 13, 1994.

Crepe tossing The greatest number of times a crepe has been tossed in two minutes is 349, by Dean Gould in Felixstowe, England on January 14, 1995.

Dish The largest item on any menu in the world is roasted camel, prepared occasionally for Bedouin wedding feasts. Cooked eggs are stuffed into fish, the fish stuffed into cooked chickens, the chickens stuffed into a roasted sheep's carcass and the sheep stuffed into a whole camel.

Doughnut The largest doughnut ever made weighed 3,739 pounds. It was 16 feet in diameter and 16 inches high in the center. The jelly doughnut was made by representatives from Hemstrought's Bakeries, Donato's Bakery and radio station WKLL-FM in Utica, NY on January 21, 1993.

Easter egg The heaviest chocolate Easter egg on record, and also the tallest, weighed 10,482 lb. 14 oz., and was 23 ft. 3 in. high. It was made by the staff of Cadbury Red Tulip at their factory at Ringwood, Victoria, Australia, and completed on April 9, 1992.

Float On May 18, 1996, the Thomas Kemper Soda Company of Seattle, WA concocted a 2,166.5-gallon root beer float. Some 500 people enjoyed the finished product.

Garlic string A string of garlic 149 ft. 11¼ in. long was made by Francs of Chester and measured at Chester Town Hall, Chester, England on September 12, 1996.

Gingerbread house   A gingerbread house 52 feet high and 32 feet square was built by David Sunken and Roger A. Pelcher of the Bohemian Club of Des Moines, IA and 100 volunteers on December 2, 1988. The house was made of 2,000 sheets of gingerbread and 1,650 pounds of icing.

Hamburger   The largest hamburger on record weighed 5,520 pounds and was 21 feet in diameter. The burger was made at the Outagamie County Fairgrounds, Seymour, WI on August 5, 1989.

Ice-cream bar   The world's largest ice-cream bar was a vanilla, chocolate and nut one of 19,357 pounds, made by the staff of Augusto Ltd. in Kalisz, Poland, September 18–29, 1994.

Ice-cream sandwich   Interbake Dairy Ingredients made an 830-pound ice-cream sandwich, measuring 3 feet by 8 feet by 1 foot, on June 22, 1995.

Ice-cream sundae   The largest ice-cream sundae weighed 54,914 lb. 13 oz., and was made by Palm Dairies Ltd. under the supervision of Mike Rogiani in Edmonton, Alberta, Canada on July 24, 1988. It consisted of 44,689 lb. 8 oz. of ice cream, 9,688 lb. 2 oz. of syrup and 537 lb. 3 oz. of topping.

Jell-O   A 9,246-gallon watermelon-flavored pink Jell-O was made by Paul Squires and Geoff Ross at Roma Street Forum, Brisbane, Australia on February 5, 1981, in a tank supplied by Pool Fab.

Jelly bean jar   The largest jar of jelly beans was 96 inches high and contained 378,000 jelly beans weighing a total of 2,910 pounds. The Disney Channel sponsored the jar, which was unveiled in October 1992 at Westside Pavilion, Los Angeles, CA.

Lasagna   The largest lasagna weighed 8,188 lb. 8 oz. and measured 70 feet by 7 feet. It was made by the Food Bank for Monterey County in Salinas, CA on October 14, 1993.

Loaf   The longest loaf on record was a Rosca de Reyes measuring 30,184 feet long, baked in Acapulco, Mexico on January 6, 1996.
  The largest pan loaf weighed 3,163 lb. 10 oz. and measured 9 ft. 10 in. by 4 ft. 1 in. by 3 ft. 7 in. It was made by the staff of Sasko in Johannesburg, South Africa on March 18, 1988.

Lobster roll   On June 29, 1997, the Whatever Family Festival in Augusta, ME featured a 50.-ft.-11^{7}/8-in. lobster roll. The roll was baked as a single unit and then filled with 45 pounds of topping, made with the meat from 89 Maine lobsters, plus mayonnaise, celery, lettuce and other ingredients.

Lollipop   A peppermint-flavored lollipop weighing 3,011 pounds was made by the staff of BonBon in Holme Olstrup, Denmark, April 22, 1994.

Meat pie   A chicken pie weighing 22,178 pounds and measuring 12 feet in diameter was made by KFC in New York City on October 18, 1995.

Milk shake   A 4,333-gallon strawberry milk shake was made by Age Concern East Cheshire and Lancashire Dairies in Macclesfield, England on August 18, 1996.

Noodle making Simon Sang Koon Sung (Singapore) made 8,192 noodle strings from one piece of dough in 59.29 seconds during the Singapore Food Festival on July 31, 1994.

Omelet The largest omelet had an area of 1,383 square feet and contained 160,000 eggs. It was cooked by representatives of Swatch in Yokohama, Japan, March 19, 1994.

Omelet making The greatest number of 2-egg omelets made in 30 minutes is 427, by Howard Helmer in Atlanta, GA on February 2, 1990.

Pastry The longest pastry was a cream puff 3,403 feet long, made by employees of Pidy, in Ypres, Belgium, September 4–5, 1992.

Pie A pecan pie weighing 40,266 pounds and measuring 40 feet in diameter was baked on June 16, 1989 for the Pecan Festival in Okmulgee, OK.

Pizza The largest pizza was 122 ft. 8 in. in diameter with an area of 11,816 square feet. It was made at Norwood Hypermarket in Norwood, South Africa on December 8, 1990.

Pizza delivery Eagle Boys Dial-a-Pizza in Christchurch, New Zealand regularly delivers pizza to Scott Base, Antarctica for members of the U.S. and New Zealand Antarctic Program. Pizzas are freshly made, packaged for the trip and delivered to the military air base in Christchurch. After a 9-hour scheduled C-130 Hercules flight, the pizzas arrive, complete with reheating instructions.

Popcorn A container measuring 40 feet long, 28 feet wide and 6 ft. 8 in. high was filled with 7,466 cubic feet of popped corn by students from Pittsville Elementary School, Pittsville, WI, with help from local residents, March 22–26, 1996.

Popcorn ball The Boy Scouts of America Gateway Area Council created a 2,377-pound popcorn ball in La Crosse, WI, September 23–27, 1995. The finished ball was 7 ft. 7 in. tall and 23 ft. 5 in. in circumference.

Popsicle A 17,450-pound orange popsicle was made in Millinocket, ME on July 30, 1995 on behalf of the Katahdin Nursing Home.

Salami The longest salami was 68 ft. 9 in. long with a circumference of 25 inches, and weighed 1,492 lb. 5 oz. It was made by A/S Svindlands Pølsefabrikk, Flekkefjord, Norway, July 6–16, 1992.

Sausage The longest continuous sausage was one of 28.77 miles, made by M & M Meat Shops in partnership with J. M. Schneider Inc. in Kitchener, Ontario, Canada on April 28–29, 1995.

Shortcake A strawberry shortcake measuring 175 ft. 4 in. by 4 feet was made for the 3rd Annual Strawberry Dessert Festival in Watsonville, CA on May 25, 1997. The 260 sheet cakes were covered with 2,400 pounds of sliced, sweetened strawberries and 600 pounds of nondairy whipped topping.

Strawberry shortcake enthusiasts should have been in Watsonville, CA for the construction of this 2,400-pounder.

Spice Hottest   The hottest spice is believed to be Red "Savina" Habanero (1994 special), developed by GNS Spices of Walnut, CA. A single dried gram will produce detectable "heat" in 1,272 pounds of bland sauce.

Most expensive   Prices for wild ginseng from the Chan Pak Mountain area of China were reported in 1979 to be as high as $23,000 per ounce in Hong Kong.

Strawberry bowl   The largest bowl of strawberries had a net weight of 5,266 pounds. The strawberries were picked at Joe Moss Farms near Embro, Ontario, Canada and the bowl was filled at the Kitchener-Waterloo Hospital, Ontario, on June 29, 1993.

Sushi roll   The Seattle Cherry Blossom and Japanese Cultural Festival created a 101-foot sushi roll on April 26, 1997 at Seattle Center, Seattle, WA. It was made with 162 sheets of nori seaweed and more than 55 pounds of rice and other ingredients, all rolled and pressed into a single continuous unit.

The longest sushi roll was assembled and rolled into a single 101-foot-long treat.

DRINKS

Most alcoholic drink When Estonia was independent, between the two World Wars, the Estonian Liquor Monopoly marketed 98 percent alcohol (196 proof) distilled from potatoes.

Everclear, 190 proof or 95 percent alcohol by volume, is marketed by the American Distilling Co. "primarily as a base for home-made cordials."

Strongest beer Baz's Super Brew, brewed by Barrie Parish and on sale at The Parish Brewery, Somerby, England, has an alcohol volume of 23.0 percent.

Champagne cork flight The longest flight of a cork from an untreated and unheated bottle four feet from level ground is 177 ft. 9 in., reached by Prof. Emeritus Heinrich Medicus, Rensselaer Polytechnic Institute, at the Woodbury Vineyards Winery, NY on June 5, 1988.

Champagne fountain The greatest number of stories achieved in a champagne fountain, successfully filled from the top and using traditional long-stem glasses, is 47 (height 25 ft. 9 in.), by Moet et Chandon Champagne with 23,642 glasses at Caesars Palace, Las Vegas, NV, July 19–23, 1993.

Cocktail The largest cocktail on record was a 6,859.4-gallon Juicy Duce mixed at the Buderim Tavern, Buderim, Queensland, Australia on October 19, 1996.

Liquor Most expensive A bottle of 50-year-old Glenfiddich Scotch was sold for a record price of 99,999,999 lire (approximately $71,200) to an anonymous Italian businessman at a charity auction in Milan, Italy.

Wine Most expensive £105,000 ($131,250) was paid for a bottle of 1787 Château Lafite claret engraved with Thomas Jefferson's initials, sold to Christopher Forbes (U.S.) at Christie's, London, England on December 5, 1985.

The first glass of Beaujolais Nouveau 1993 (from Maison Jaffelin) was bought for Fr8,600 ($1,447) by Robert Denby at Pickwick's, a British pub in Beaune, France, on November 18, 1993.

Wine tasting At a wine tasting staged by KQED on November 22, 1986 in San Francisco, CA, 4,000 tasters consumed 9,360 bottles of wine.

FEASTS AND CELEBRATIONS

Largest banquet There were 150,000 guests at the renunciation ceremony of Atul Dalpatlal Shah, when he became a monk, in Ahmedabad, India on June 2, 1991.

Indoor The greatest number of people served indoors at a single sitting was 18,000 municipal leaders at the Palais de l'Industrie, Paris, France, August 18, 1889.

Largest barbecue The record attendance at a one-day barbecue was 44,158 at Warwick Farm Racecourse, Sydney, Australia on October 10, 1993.

The greatest meat consumption at a barbecue was at the Lancaster Sertoma Club's Chicken Bar-B-Que in Lancaster, PA, on May 21, 1994, when 44,010 pounds or 31,500 chicken halves were consumed in eight hours.

Most restaurants visited   Fred E. Magel of Chicago, IL dined out 46,000 times in 60 countries over 50 years as a restaurant grader. He claimed that the restaurant that served the largest helpings was Zehnder's Hotel, Frankenmuth, MI. Magel's favorite dishes were South African rock lobster and mousse of fresh English strawberries.

Largest party   The International Year of the Child children's party in Hyde Park, London, England, May 30–31, 1979 was attended by 160,000 children.

Birthday   The world's biggest birthday party was attended by an estimated 100,000 people in Aberdeen, Scotland on July 24, 1994. It was held to celebrate the 200th birthday of Union Street, the main street in the city.

The largest birthday party held for someone who actually went to the party was attended by an estimated 35,000 people in Louisville, KY on September 8, 1979, to celebrate the 89th birthday of Col. Harland Sanders, the founder of Kentucky Fried Chicken.

Christmas   The largest Christmas party was thrown by the Boeing Co. in the 65,000-seat Kingdome, Seattle, WA. The party was held in two parts on December 15, 1979, and a total of 103,152 people attended.

Teddy bear picnic   The largest teddy bear picnic ever staged was attended by 33,573 bears and their owners at Dublin Zoo, Dublin, Ireland on June 24, 1995.

HOBBIES AND PASTIMES

FRUIT & VEGETABLE GROWING

FLOWERS, FRUITS AND VEGETABLES

In the interest of fairness and to minimize the risk of mistakes being made, all plants should, where possible, be entered in official international, national or local garden contests. Only produce grown primarily for human consumption will be considered for publication.

Apple   3 lb. 4 oz.; Hanners family, Hood River, OR, 1994

Beet   40 lb. 8 oz.; Ian Neale, Newport, Wales, 1994

Broccoli   35 lb.; John and Mary Evans, Palmer, AK, 1997

Cabbage   124 lb.; Bernard Lavery, Llanharry, Wales, 1989

Cantaloupe   62 lb.; G. Draughtridge, Rocky Mount, NC, 1991

Carrot   15 lb. 11½ oz.; Bernard Lavery, Llanharry, Wales, 1996

Celery   48 lb. 1 oz.; Ian Neale, Newport, Wales, 1996

Chrysanthemum   14 ft. 3 in.; Bernard Lavery, Spalding, England, 1995

Collard   41¼ in. tall; B. Rackley, Rocky Mount, NC, 1989

Corn   31 ft. tall; D. Radda, Washington, IA, 1946

H. Hurley's record green bean measures 48¾ inches.

LARGEST ONION

The world's largest onion weighed 12 pounds 4 ounces. It was grown by Mel Ednie of Anstruther, Scotland in 1994.

For rules, see page 707.

TOP THIS

Corn cob   36¼ in.; Bernard Lavery, Llanharry, Wales, 1994

Cucumber   21 lb. 4½ oz.; P. Glazebrook, Newark, England, 1996

Dahlia   25 ft. 7 in.; R. Blythe, Nannup, Western Australia, 1990

Eggplant   7.324 pounds; J. Costanza, Hammond, LA, 1996

Garlic   2 lb. 10 oz.; R. Kirkpatrick, Eureka, CA, 1985

Gourd, bushel   231.5 lb.; Richard Wright, NJ, 1992

Gourd, long   110⅝ in.; Peter Waterman, NY, 1994

Grapefruit   6 lb. 12 oz.; D. Hazelton, Queensland, Australia, 1995

Grapes   20 lb. 11½ oz.; Bozzolo y Perut Ltda, Santiago, Chile, 1984

Green bean   48¾ in.; H. Hurley, Fuguay-Varina, NC, 1996

Kohlrabi   36 lb.; E. Krejci, Mt. Clemens, MI, 1979

Leek, pot   12 lb. 2 oz.; P. Harrigan, Linton, England, 1987

Lemon   8 lb. 8 oz.; C. and D. Knutzen, Whittier, CA, 1983

The 1,000-pound pumpkin barrier was broken by Nathan and Paula Zehr, who grew this 1,061-pound whopper.

Lemon, Ponderosa   13 lb. 2 oz.; J. Coody, West Palm Beach, FL; 1997

Lima bean   14 in.; N. McCoy, Hubert, NC, 1979

Okra   19 ft. 9⅝ in.; David Mikulka, FL, 1994

Onion   12 lb. 4 oz.; Mel Ednie, Anstruther, Scotland, 1994

Parsnip   171¾ in.; Bernard Lavery, Llanharry, Wales, 1990

Peanut   4 in.; E. Adkins, Enfield, NC, 1990

Pepper   13½ in.; J. Rutherford, Hatch, NM; 1975

Pepper plant   12 ft. 3 in.; F. Melton, Jacksonville, FL, 1992

Petunia   13 ft. 8 in.; B. Lawrence, Windham, NY, 1985

Philodendron   1,114 ft.; F. Francis, University of Massachusetts, 1984

Pineapple   17 lb. 12 oz.; E. Kamuk, Ais Village, WBNP, Papua New Guinea, 1994

Potato   7 lb. 13 oz.; K. Sloane, Patrick, Isle of Man, 1994

Pumpkin   1,061 lb.; Nathan and Paula Zehr, Watson, NY, 1996

Radish   37 lb. 15 oz.; Litterini family, Tanunda, South Australia, 1992

Rhubarb   5 lb. 14 oz.; E. Stone, East Woodyates, England, 1985

Runner bean   39½ in.; J. Taylor, Shifnal, England, 1986

Rutabaga   62 lb. 3 oz.; N. Craven, Stouffville, Ontario, Canada, 1993

Squash   900 lb. 8 oz.; J. & C. Lyons, Baltimore, Canada, 1994

Strawberry   8.17 oz.; G. Anderson, Folkestone, England, 1983

Sunflower   25 ft. 5½ in.; M. Heijms, Oirschot, Netherlands, 1986

Sweet potato   40¾ lb.; O. Harrison, Kite, GA, 1982

Tomato   7 lb. 12 oz.; G. Graham, Edmond, OK, 1986

Tomato plant   53 ft. 6 in.; G. Graham, Edmond, OK, 1985

Tomato plant, cherry   28 ft. 7 in.; C. H. Wilber, Crane Hill, AL, 1985

Watermelon   262 lb.; Bill Carson, Arrington, TN, 1990

Zucchini   64 lb. 8 oz.; B. Lavery, Llanharry, Wales, 1990

COLLECTIONS

Because of the infinite number of objects it is possible to collect, we can include only a small number of claims—those that in our experience reflect proven widespread interest. We are more likely to consider claims for items accumulated on a personal basis over a significant period of time.

Airsickness bags Niek Vermeulen (Netherlands) has the world's largest collection of airsickness bags. As of May 1997, he had amassed 2,112 different bags representing 470 airlines.

Bags Heinz Schmidt-Bachem (Germany) has collected 60,000 paper bags since 1975.

Barbie dolls Tony Mattia (Great Britain) had collected 900 Barbie dolls as of March 1997. He has about half of all the Barbie models produced since 1959 and many versions of Ken. He changes every doll's costume once a month.

Beer cans William B. Christiensen of Madison, NJ collected over 75,000 different cans from 125 different countries, colonies and territories.

Beer labels Jan Solberg of Oslo, Norway collected 424,868 different labels from around the world.

Books John Q. Benham of Avoca, IN has a private collection of over 1.5 million books. Benham's house is full, so he also keeps books in his 6-car garage and stacked under tarpaulins outside.

Bottle caps Starting in 1956, Paul Høegh Poulsen of Rødovre, Denmark amassed 82,169 different bottle caps from 179 countries.

Bottles George E. Terren of Southboro, MA collected 31,804 miniature liquor bottles.

The record for beer is 8,131 unduplicated full bottles from 110 countries, collected by Peter Broeker of Geesthacht, Germany.

David L. Maund (Great Britain) has a collection of 11,742 miniature Scotch whisky bottles.

Edoardo Giaccone of Gardone Rivieria, Brescia, Italy has a total of 5,502 unduplicated full-size whisky bottles in his collection, which is housed in his specially-built "whiskyteca."

Christopher Weide of Jacksonville, FL collected 6,510 different soda bottles.

Largest antique car collection Harold LeMay of Tacoma, WA has a collection of 1,900 antique and vintage vehicles.

Cigarette lighters Francis Van Herle has a collection of 58,259 different lighters.

Coasters The world's largest collection of coasters is owned by Leo Pisker of Langenzersdorf, Austria, who has collected 150,125 different coasters from 165 countries.

Credit cards The largest collection of valid credit cards to date is one of 1,397 (all different) by Walter Cavanagh of Santa Clara, CA. The cost of acquisition for "Mr. Plastic Fantastic" was zero, and he keeps the cards in the world's longest wallet—250 feet long, weighing 38 lb. 8 oz. and containing cards worth more than $1.65 million in credit.

Earrings Carol McFadden of Oil City, PA had collected 24,167 different pairs of earrings as of April 1997.

Four-leaf clovers Beginning in 1995, George Kaminski (U.S.) collected 13,382 four-leaf clovers during his recreation time at the State Correctional Institute, Somerset, PA. Because prison policy does not allow inmates to collect anything, the clovers were sent to Kaminski's sister.

Fruit stickers Antoine Secco (France) has a collection of 11,000 fruit labels (stickers), all of which are different.

Gnomes Since 1978, Anne Atkin (Great Britain) has collected 2,010 gnomes and pixies, all of which "live" in a 4-acre Gnome Reserve near Bradworthy, England.

Golf balls Ted J. Hoz of Baton Rouge, LA has a collection of 38,554 different logo golf balls. Hoz estimates that there are 100,000 logo balls in existence, and his storage cabinets have space for another 22,284 balls.

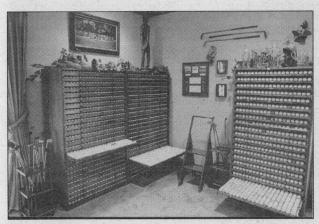

The most valuable golf tip for duffers looking for their errant drives may be Ted Hoz's phone number. He certainly knows how to find golf balls.

STUCK ON MAGNETS

Most people are always searching for more magnets to hang up notes on their refrigerators. Not Louise Greenfarb; she could use a few more refrigerators to showcase her record-breaking collection of 19,300 magnets.

Louise, a.k.a. the Magnet Lady, has spent more than 30 years amassing her collection. It all began when Louise, as a young mother, would stroll her children into downtown Brooklyn, New York. The kids would beg to put money in machines that offered prizes. The prizes, of course, were magnets, and Louise, afraid her children would choke on their toys, would put them up on her fridge.

"In the late 70s I was doing a Tupperware party in my home. A guest went in the kitchen for some cream and said, 'Oh, I love your magnet collection.' I thought, collection, why not?" says Louise.

Because her husband was in the army, Louise and her family traveled abroad. While living in Korea and Germany, she had a more difficult time tracking down local magnet manufacturers. Yet her persistence won out, and when she returned to the United States in 1989, she had more than 3,500 magnets to display.

Louise now showcases her collection in her Las Vegas home. Her refrigerator is covered top to bottom with 1,000 magnets and she arranges them in categories. Her collection runs the gamut from magnets advertising doctors and plumbers to Disney characters and telephones that ring. She

even has a full set of Monopoly magnets and some that double as finger puppets. There's not one duplicate in the bunch.

After a local news program ran a story on her hobby, other collectors began corresponding with Louise. Today, she keeps up with Mag Pals across the world, who exchange magnets from their local areas.

"The magnets are a real conversation piece," says Louise, who once covered her guest bathroom with her collectibles. "I never have to worry about people coming to my house and having nothing to talk about."

Some people carry photo books displaying their grandchildren. Louise carries one that showcases her magnets. When she shops at garage sales and shows her pictures, says Louise, people run into their homes and grab magnets off their refrigerators for her to keep. "They just want to be a part of my collection," she says. In fact, she even has her own magnet to give in return. It's a tiny refrigerator that reads:

A magmento from the Magnet Lady,
Louise, largest fridge magnet collector in the world.

REFRIGERATOR MAGNETS

Louise J. Greenfarb of Henderson, NV had collected 19,300 refrigerator magnets as of January 1997.

Greeting cards   Craig Shergold of Carshalton, England was reported to have collected a record 33 million get-well cards by May 1991, when his mother pleaded for no more.

Matchbook covers   Ed Brassard of Seattle, WA collected 3,159,119 different matchbook covers.

Matchbox labels   Teiichi Yoshizawa (Japan) has 743,512 different matchbox labels (including advertising labels) from 130 countries.
   Robert Jones of Indianapolis, IN has 280,000 matchbox labels (excluding advertising labels).

Movie cameras   Demetrios Pistiola has 305 movie cameras dating from 1901 to the present.

Passports   Guy Van Keer (Belgium) owns 3,880 used passports and travel documents. They represent 130 countries or passport-issuing authorities, many of which no longer exist, and were issued between 1616 and the present.

Pens   As of May 1997, Angelika Unverhau of Dinslaken, Germany had a collection of 108,500 different ballpoint pens.

Piggy banks   Ove Nordstrom of Spanga, Sweden has collected 3,575 different money holders in pig form over the past 40 years.

Pliers   LeRoy Baeur of Shakopee, MN had 1,834 different types of pliers in his collection as of May 1997.

Refrigerator magnets   Louise J. Greenfarb of Henderson, NV had collected 19,300 refrigerator magnets as of January 1997.

Ties   Tom Holmes (Great Britain) had collected 10,624 ties as of April 1997. His collection, which he started 50 years ago, includes yearly birthday ties from the British Prime Minister.

MODELS

MODEL AIRCRAFT

Highest model aircraft flight   Maynard L. Hill (U.S.), flying a radio-controlled model, established the world record for altitude of 26,919 feet on September 6, 1970.

Fastest model aircraft   The speed record is 245.84 mph by a model flown on control lines by Leonid Lipinski (USSR) in 1971. The record for a radio-controlled model is 242.91 mph, set by Walter Sitar (Austria) in 1977.

Longest model aircraft flight   Maynard Hill and Robert Rosenthal hold the closed-circuit distance record of 776.7 miles, achieved on June 26, 1995.

Hill and Rosenthal also hold the record for the longest flight in a straight line to a nominated landing point, with 458.5 miles, from Bealeton, VA to Ridgeland, SC in 8 hr. 43 min. on August 29, 1995.

The record duration is 33 hr. 39 min. 15 sec. by Maynard Hill, with a powered model, October 1–2, 1992.

An indoor model with a wound rubber motor, designed by Robert Randolph (U.S.), set a duration record of 55 min. 6 sec. on December 5, 1993.

Jean-Pierre Schiltknecht flew a solar-driven model aircraft for 10 hr. 43 min. 51 sec. in Wetzlar, Germany on July 10, 1991.

Largest model aircraft   The largest radio-controlled model aircraft was a glider weighing 360 pounds, with a wingspan of 25 ft. 6 in. It was made by the Melton Mowbray (England) and District Model Club.

Smallest model helicopter   A motorized helicopter $^{15}/_{16}$ths of an inch long and $^5/_{16}$ths of an inch high, with a rotor diameter of half an inch, was made by the Institut für Mikrotechnik Mainz GmbH in Mainz, Germany in 1996. The helicopter can move up a guide wire to a height of $5^1/_4$ inches.

The smallest model helicopter can climb $5^1/_4$ inches up a guide wire.

Largest paper aircraft   The largest flying paper airplane, with a wingspan of 45 ft. 10 in., was constructed by a team of students from the Faculty of Aerospace Engineering at Delft University of Technology, Netherlands and flown on May 16, 1995. It was launched indoors and flew 114 ft. 2 in.

Longest paper aircraft flight   The level flight duration record for a hand-launched paper aircraft is 20.9 seconds, by both Chris Edge and Andy Currey at Cardington Hangar, Bedford, England on July 28, 1996.

An indoor distance of 193 feet was recorded by Tony Felch at the La Crosse Center, La Crosse, WI on May 21, 1985.

MODEL BOATS

Longest model boat run Members of the Lowestoft Model Boat Club crewed a radio-controlled model boat on August 17–18, 1991 in Doncaster, England and set a 24-hour record of 111 mi. 317 yd.

24-hour run David and Peter Holland of Doncaster, England, of the Conisbrough and District Modelling Association, crewed a 28-inch-long scale model boat of the trawler *Margaret H* continuously on one battery for 24 hours, and recorded a distance of 33.45 miles, at Doncaster Leisure Park, Doncaster, England, August 15–16, 1992.

MODEL CARS

Smallest car To celebrate its 60th anniversary in 1997, Toyota created the world's smallest model car, at 0.0264 inches. It was called the Toyota Model AA.

Longest drive A Scalextric Jaguar XJ8 ran nonstop for 866 hr. 44 min. 54 sec. and covered 1,771.2 miles from May 2 to June 7, 1989. The event was organized by the Rev. Bryan G. Apps and church members of Southbourne, Bournemouth, England.

24-hour slot car race On September 4–5, 1994, H.O. Racing and Hobbies of San Diego, CA achieved a distance of 375.079 miles for a 1:64 scale car.

Under the rules of the B.S.C.R.A. (British Slot Car Racing Association), the 24-hour distance record by a 1:64 scale car is 198.987 miles, set by a team of four in Derby, England on November 11–12, 1995.

On July 5–6, 1986, the North London Society of Model Engineers team achieved a 24-hour distance record of 305.949 miles for a 1:32 scale car in Southport, England.

Longest slot car track The longest slot car track measured 1,459 ft. 4 in. and was built in Rochdale, England, May 31–June 2, 1996. One car successfully completed a full lap.

MODEL TRAINS

Smallest model railroad A miniature model railroad with a scale of 1:1,400 was made by Bob Henderson of Gravenhurst, Ontario, Canada. The engine runs on a 4½-volt battery and measures ³/₁₆ of an inch overall.

Longest run A standard Life-Like BL2 HO scale electric train pulled six 8-wheel coaches for 1,207.5 hours without stopping, from August 4 to September 23, 1990, and covered a distance of 909.5 miles. The event was organized by K&MH, Akron, OH.

24-hour run The 7¼-inch-gauge model steam locomotive "Peggy" covered 167.7 miles in 24 hours at Weston Park Railway, Weston Park, England, June 17–18, 1994.

Longest model train The world's longest model train measured 228 feet in length and consisted of 650 cars hauled by four locomotives. It was run by the Arid Australia model railroad group in Perth, Australia on June 3, 1996.

Largest model railway The Northlandz railway in Flemington, NJ occupies 52,000 square feet. Eight miles of track carry 135 model trains through cities and towns, over 40-foot bridges, and around 35-foot-high mountains.

This is just part of the Northlandz model railway, the largest in the world. Visitors have to cover more than a mile to tour the entire miniature "world."

BUILDINGS FOR LEISURE

STADIUMS

Largest stadium The Strahov Stadium in Prague, Czech Republic was completed in 1934 and could accommodate 240,000 spectators.

Largest in use The Maracanã Municipal Stadium in Rio de Janeiro, Brazil has a normal capacity of 205,000, of whom 155,000 can be seated. A crowd of 199,854 was accommodated for the World Cup soccer final between Brazil and Uruguay on July 16, 1950.

Largest covered stadium   The Aztec Stadium, Mexico City, opened in 1968, has a capacity of 107,000 for soccer, with almost all seats under cover. A record 132,274 people watched Julio César Chávez (Mexico) defend his boxing title against Greg Haugen (U.S.) on February 20, 1993.

Largest indoor stadium   The 273-foot-tall Louisiana Superdome in New Orleans, LA, covering 13 acres, has a maximum seating capacity of 97,365 for conventions or 76,791 for football.

Largest roof   The transparent acrylic "marquee" roof over the Munich Olympic Stadium, Germany measures 914,940 square feet in area, resting on a steel net supported by masts.
   The largest roofspan in the world is 787 ft. 4 in. for the major axis of the elliptical Texas Stadium, completed in 1971 in Irving, TX.

Largest retractable roof   The roof covering the SkyDome, Toronto, Ontario, Canada, completed in June 1989, covers eight acres, spans 674 feet at its widest point and rises to 282 feet.

Largest air-supported building   The 80,311-capacity octagonal Pontiac Silverdome Stadium, Detroit, MI is 600 feet wide and 770 feet long. The 10-acre translucent Fiberglas roof is 202 feet high and is supported by compressed air.

Largest dome   The Louisiana Superdome, New Orleans, LA has a diameter of 680 feet.

RESORTS

Largest amusement resort   Disney World is set in 30,000 acres of Orange and Osceola counties, 20 miles southwest of Orlando, FL. It opened on October 1, 1971.

Largest indoor waterpark   The Ocean Dome in Miyazaki, Japan is 985 feet long, 328 feet wide and 125 feet high and contains a beach 460 feet long.

Largest recreational beach   Virginia Beach, VA has 28 miles of beachfront on the Atlantic Ocean and 10 miles of estuary frontage on Chesapeake Bay. The area covers 310 square miles, with 147 hotel properties and 2,323 campsites.

Largest casino   Foxwoods Resort Casino, Ledyard, CT includes a total gaming area of 193,000 square feet. There are 3,854 slot machines, 234 table games and 3,500 bingo seats.

Largest naturist resort   Domaine de Lambeyran, near Lodève in southern France, covers 840 acres. The Centre Helio-Marin at Cap d'Agde, also in southern France, is visited by around 250,000 people per year.

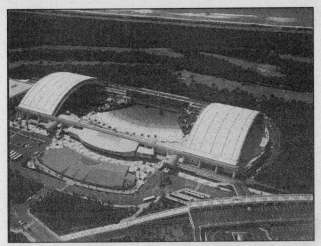

The beach inside the Ocean Dome in Miyazaki, Japan is 460 feet long.

FAIRS

Largest fair   The Louisiana Purchase Exposition in St. Louis, MO in 1904 covered 1,271.76 acres and was attended by 19,694,855 people. Events of the 1904 Olympic Games were staged in conjunction with the fair.

Largest exhibition center   The Hannover Fair Exhibition Complex in Lower Saxony, Germany has 5,154,830 square feet of covered space in 26 halls.

Largest Ferris wheel   The Cosmoclock 21 in Yokohama City, Japan is 344½ feet high and 328 feet in diameter, with illumination by laser beams and acoustic effects by synthesizers. The 60 arms holding the gondolas serve as second hands for the 42½-foot-long clock mounted at the hub.

Largest swing   A glider swing 30 feet high was constructed by Kenneth R. Mack, Langenburg, Saskatchewan, Canada for Uncle Herb's Amusements in 1986. The swing is capable of taking its four riders 25 feet off the ground.

Tallest scarecrow   "Stretch II," constructed by the Speers family of Paris, Ontario, Canada and a crew of 15 at the Paris, Ontario Fall Fair on September 2, 1989, measured 103 ft. 6¾ in. tall.

Largest bonfire   Residents and off-duty firefighters from Workington, England lit a bonfire 122 ft. 6 in. high, with an overall volume of 250,700 cubic feet, on November 5, 1993.

Largest maze The largest maze ever constructed was the Quadricycle Amazing Maize Maze in Dearborn, MI. It was cut from a cornfield and covered an area of 263,790 square feet, with a path length of 3.0113 miles. It was in existence from August to October 1996.

The largest permanent maze is the Dole Pineapple Garden Maze at the Dole Plantation, Honolulu, HI, with an area of 100,000 square feet. It also has the greatest path length, at 1.7 miles.

ROLLER COASTERS

Oldest operating roller coaster Rutschebahnen (Scenic Railway) Mk.2 was constructed at the Tivoli Gardens, Copenhagen, Denmark, in 1913. This coaster opened to the public in 1914.

Longest roller coaster *The Ultimate* at Lightwater Valley Theme Park in Ripon, England has a run of 1 mi. 740 yd.

Tallest roller coaster The tallest and fastest roller coaster in the world is *Superman the Escape* at Six Flags Magic Mountain, Valencia, CA. This lin-

Superman the Escape is the world's tallest and fastest roller coaster.

ear induction-powered dual-track reverse-point free-fall coaster was designed by Intamin AG of Switzerland and features a 415-foot steel support structure and a design speed of 100 mph.

The tallest traditional complete-circuit roller coaster is Fujiyama at the Fujikyu Highland Amusement Park, Japan. It is 259 feet tall and has a lift height of 234 ft. 7 in., a vertical drop of 230 feet and a design speed of 81 mph.

Greatest number of loops/inversions   The roller coaster with the greatest number of loops or inversions is the Dragon Khan at Port Aventura, Salou, Spain. It was designed by Bolliger and Mabillard of Mothey, Switzerland. Riders are turned upside-down eight times over the steel track, which extends for 4,166 ft. 1 in.

Most roller coasters   Cedar Point Amusement Park/Resort in Sandusky, OH has 12 roller coasters.

BARS AND RESTAURANTS

Largest bar   The world's largest beer-selling establishment is the Mathäser, Bayerstrasse 5, Munich, Germany, where daily sales can reach 84,470 pints. It was established in 1829, demolished in World War II and rebuilt by 1955. It seats 5,500 people.

Tallest bar   The bar at Humperdink's Seafood and Steakhouse in Irving, TX is 25 ft. 3 in. high with two levels of shelving containing over 1,000 bottles. The lower level has four rows of shelves approximately 40 feet across and can be reached from floor level. The upper level, with five rows of shelves, is reached by ladder.

The largest British pub is the Moon Under Water in Manchester, England. The converted movie theater has 8,845 square feet of floor space.

Longest bar   The world's longest permanent continuous bar is the 405-ft.-10-in.-long counter in the Beer Barrel Saloon at Put-in-Bay, South Bass Island, OH, opened in 1989. The bar is fitted with 56 beer taps and surrounded by 160 bar stools. Longer temporary bars have been erected, notably for beer festivals.

Oldest restaurant   The Casa Botín was opened in Madrid, Spain in 1725.

Largest restaurant   The Royal Dragon (Mang Gorn Luang) restaurant in Bangkok, Thailand, opened in October 1991, can seat 5,000 customers. In order to cover the 4-acre service area more quickly, the 541 service staff wear roller skates. Up to 3,000 dishes are served every hour.

Highest restaurant   The restaurant in the Chacaltaya ski resort, Bolivia is at an altitude of 17,519 feet.

SHOPPING CENTERS

Largest shopping center   The West Edmonton Mall in Alberta, Canada covers 5.2 million square feet on a 121-acre site and contains over 800 stores and services as well as 11 major department stores. Parking is provided for 20,000 cars, and more than 20 million shoppers visited in 1995.

Longest mall   The £40 million ($68 million) shopping center in Milton Keynes, England is 2,360 feet long.

BOOKSTORES AND LIBRARIES

Largest bookstore   The bookstore with the most titles and the longest shelving (30 miles) in the world is W. & G. Foyle Ltd. of London, England. First established in 1904 in a small store, the company now has a site of 75,825 square feet.

The most capacious individual bookstore in the world measured by square footage is the Barnes & Noble Bookstore at 105 Fifth Avenue at 18th Street, New York City. It covers 154,250 square feet and has 12.87 miles of shelving.

Largest library   The United States Library of Congress (founded on April 24, 1800) in Washington, D.C. contains 108,433,370 items—including 16,764,805 books in the classified collections, 25,934,708 other print materials, and 82,498,662 audio and visual materials. The library has 532 miles of shelving and employs 4,600 people.

Nonstatutory   The world's largest nonstatutory library—not funded or operated by the state—is the New York Public Library on Fifth Avenue, New York City. It has 525,276 square feet of floor space and 172 miles of shelving, plus an underground extension with the capacity for another 84 miles. Its collection, including 82 branch libraries, contains 4.6 million volumes and 38 million items of research material.

Most overdue book   A book in German on the Archbishop of Bremen, published in 1609, was borrowed from Sidney Sussex College, Cambridge, England by Colonel Robert Walpole, 1667–68. It was found by Prof. Sir John

Plumb in the library at Houghton Hall, Norfolk, England and returned 288 years later. No fine was charged.

MUSEUMS

Oldest museum   The world's oldest museum is the Ashmolean in Oxford, England, built between 1679 and 1683 and named after the collector Elias Ashmole (1617–92).

Largest museum   The Smithsonian Institution comprises 16 museums containing over 140 million items and has over 6,000 employees.

The American Museum of Natural History in New York City was founded in 1869 and comprises 23 interconnected buildings in an 18-acre park. The buildings of the museum and the planetarium cover 1.2 million square feet of floor space, accommodating more than 30 million artifacts and specimens. Its exhibits are viewed by more than 3 million visitors each year.

Most popular museum   The highest attendance on a single day for any museum is over 118,437 on April 14, 1984 at the Smithsonian's National Air and Space Museum, Washington, D.C., opened in July 1976. The record-setting day required the doors to be temporarily closed.

ZOOS, AQUARIUMS AND PARKS

Oldest zoo   The Zoological Society of London, England was founded in 1826. Its collection includes 3,413 different species, housed in Regent's Park, London, England and at Whipsnade Park, England.

Largest aquarium   In terms of volume, the Living Seas Aquarium, opened in 1986 at the Epcot Center near Orlando, FL, is the largest, with a capacity of almost 6.7 million gallons. It contains over 3,000 fish, representing 65 species.

The Monterey Bay Aquarium in California contains over 364,593 specimens (571 species) of fauna and flora.

Largest park   The National Park of North-Eastern Greenland covers 375,289 square miles and stretches from Liverpool Land in the south to Odaaq Ø, off Pearyland. Established in 1974, the park is largely covered by ice and is home to a variety of protected flora and fauna, including polar bears, musk-ox and birds of prey.

Most national parks visited   Alan K. Hogenauer of Oakdale, NY has visited 1,025 parts of the U.S. National Park System, including the 374 official units, since 1953.

A PENCHANT
FOR PARKS

In 1953, a young man by the name of Alan K. Hogenauer first toured the Statue of Liberty, not unlike millions of other people. What Hogenauer has accomplished since that day, however, earns him a spot in *The Guinness Book of World Records*. He personally wishes every American could follow in his footsteps. Hogenauer has journeyed to each of the U.S. Park System's 374 official units, giving him the record of most national parks visited.

"I started keeping a daily diary in '55 as a teenager," he explains, "and kept it up for 26 years." It was right about then that he realized he had a shot at the record, although the experience compelled him more than anything else. "It became a quest motivated by the goal itself, not necessarily by the record. Once I visited a few, I became aware that they were all connected, all part of the national park system."

Hogenauer continues his quest to this day, and plans to add to the 1,025 official visits he has already tallied, not for the record but for a much larger reason. "These are really first-class facilities," he points out. "People need to be made aware of that. Every time I went to one of these things, not only was I learning about that particular site, but I realized that if you visited all the sites, you've touched every facet of American history. You can link them together to see the larger picture of our whole country. It's all there."

"What has amazed me more than anything," he adds, "is how few people appreciate the diversity and dimensions of this thing we've created in our midst. These parks need to be marketed. If you go, they will treat you magnificently, but no one will ever invite you."

Though his interest in travel has propelled him all over the country and the world, Hogenauer admits to a personal favorite: the Aniakchak Crater in Alaska. "It's actually a blown-out volcano in the Aleutian Islands, and for most of the year it's shrouded in fog. Very few people have ever seen it. It's really pretty elusive." Not elusive enough to keep Hogenauer away, however. He's been there twice, and will undoubtedly return.

RECORD
ON THE

MOST NATIONAL PARKS VISITED

Alan K. Hogenauer of Oakdale, NY has visited 1,025 different parts of the U.S. National Park System, including the 374 official units, since 1953.

GAMES

CROQUET

International trophy The MacRobertson Shield (instituted in 1925 and held every three years) has been won a record nine times by Great Britain, in 1925, 1937, 1956, 1963, 1969, 1974, 1982, 1990 and 1993.

A record seven appearances have been made by John G. Prince (New Zealand), in 1963, 1969, 1975, 1979, 1982, 1986 and 1990; on his debut he was the youngest-ever international, at 17 yr. 190 days.

World Championships The first World Championships were held at the Hurlingham Club, London, England in 1989. The most wins is three, by Robert Fulford (Great Britain), 1990, 1992 and 1994.

USCA National Championships The first United States Championships were played in 1977. J. Archie Peck has won the singles title a record four times, 1977, 1979–80 and 1982. Ted Prentis has won the doubles title four times, 1978, 1980–81 and 1988. The teams of Ted Prentis and Ned Prentis (1980–81), Dana Dribben and Ray Bell (1985–86), and Reid Fleming and Debbie Cornelius (1990–91) have each won the doubles title twice. The New York Croquet Club has won a record six National Club Championships, 1980–83, 1986 and 1988.

FISHING

Largest single catch The largest officially ratified fish ever caught on a rod was a great white shark (*Carcharodon carcharias*) weighing 2,664 pounds and measuring 16 ft. 10 in. long, caught on a 130-pound test line by Alf Dean in Denial Bay, near Ceduna, South Australia on April 21, 1959.

A great white shark weighing 3,388 pounds was caught by Clive Green off Albany, Western Australia on April 26, 1976 but will remain unratified because whale meat was used as bait.

The largest fish taken underwater was an 804-pound giant black grouper by Don Pinder of the Miami Triton Club, FL in 1955.

Longest fight The longest recorded individual fight with a fish is 37 hours, by Bob Ploeger (U.S.) with a King salmon on July 12–13, 1989.

International Game Fish Association (IGFA) The heaviest freshwater category recognized by the International Game Fish Association is for the sturgeon; the record weight in this category is 468 pounds, caught by Joey Pallotta III on July 9, 1983 off Benicia, CA.

World Freshwater Championship France won the European title in 1956 and 13 world titles between 1959 and 1995. The individual title has been won a record three times by Robert Tesse (France), 1959–60 and 1965; and by Bob Nudd (England), 1990–91, 1994.

The record weight (team) is 76.52 pounds in three hours by West Germany on the Neckar in Mannheim, Germany on September 21, 1980.

The ones that didn't get away. Top left: largest wahoo, 158 lb. 8 oz., caught by Keith Winter, Baja California, Mexico, June 10, 1996; bottom: largest Pacific halibut, 459 lb., caught by Jack Tragis, Dutch Harbor, AK, June 11, 1996; top right: largest red snapper, 50 lb. 4 oz., caught by Capt. Doc Kennedy, Gulf of Mexico, LA, June 23, 1996.

The individual record is 37.45 pounds, by Wolf-Rüdiger Kremkus (West Germany) in Mannheim on September 20, 1980. The most fish caught is 652, by Jacques Isenbaert (Belgium) in Danaújváros, Hungary on August 27, 1967.

Fly fishing World fly fishing championships were inaugurated by the CIPS (Confédération Internationale de la Pêche Sportive) in 1981. The most team titles is five, by Italy, 1982–84, 1986, 1992. The most individual titles is two, by Brian Leadbetter (Great Britain), 1987 and 1991.

Casting The longest freshwater cast ratified under ICF (International Casting Federation) rules is 574 ft. 2 in., by Walter Kummerow (Germany), for the Bait Distance Double-Handed 30 g event held in Lenzerheide, Switzerland in the 1968 Championships.

At the currently contested weight of 17.7 g, known as 18 g Bait Distance, the longest Double-Handed cast is 457 ft. ½ in., by Kevin Carriero (U.S.) in Toronto, Ontario, Canada on July 24, 1984.

The longest Fly Distance Double-Handed cast is 319 ft. 1 in., by Wolfgang Feige (Germany) in Toronto, Ontario, Canada on July 23, 1984.

FOOTBAG

Open singles The record for keeping a footbag airborne is 63,326 consecutive kicks or hacks in 8 hr. 50 min. 42 sec., by Ted Martin (U.S.) at Lions Park, Mount Prospect, IL on June 14, 1997.

Women's singles The women's record is held by Constance Constable (U.S.), with 18,936 kicks in 3 hr. 14 min. 42 sec. on August 1, 1995 in Menlo Park, CA.

Open doubles The record is 123,456 hacks, by Tricia George and Gary Lautt (both U.S.) on November 12, 1995 at Lia Way Rec Center, Chico, CA. The pair kept the footbag aloft for 19 hr. 38 min. 20 sec.

Women's doubles The record is 34,543 kicks, by Constance Constable and Tricia George (both U.S.) on February 18, 1995. The pair kept the footbag aloft for 5 hr. 38 min. 22 sec.

Most kicks—five minutes Andy Linder (U.S.) achieved 1,017 kicks in five minutes on March 29, 1996 in Carol Stream, IL. The women's record is 769 by Ida Bettis-Fogle (U.S.) on April 13, 1996 in Columbia, MO.

Largest footbag circle The largest continuous circle of people playing footbag was 932. This gathering was staged at St. Patrick High School Campus, Chicago, IL on May 3, 1996.

HORSESHOE PITCHING

World Championships Most titles (men) Ted Allen (U.S.) has won 10 world titles: 1933–35, 1940, 1946, 1953, 1955–57 and 1959.

Most titles (women) Vicki Winston (née Chapelle) has won a record 10 women's titles: 1956, 1958–59, 1961, 1963, 1966–67, 1969, 1975 and 1981.

Longest perfect game At the 1968 World Championship, Elmer Hohl (Canada) threw 56 consecutive ringers.

Most perfect games In World Championship play, only three pitchers have thrown perfect games: Guy Zimmerman (U.S.), 1948; Elmer Hohl (Canada) in 1968; and Jim Walters (U.S.) in 1993.

JUMP ROPE

10-mile skip–run Vadivelu Karunakaren (India) jumped rope 10 miles in 58 minutes in Madras, India, February 1, 1990.

Most turns of the rope One hour 14,628, by Park Bong Tae (South Korea) in Pusan, South Korea, July 2, 1989.

On a single rope, team of 90 206, by students from the Minamikayabe Chyoritu-Makou Elementary School, Hokkaido, Japan on August 19, 1995.

On a tightrope 521 (consecutive), by Walfer Guerrero (Colombia) in Haarlem, Netherlands on June 1, 1995.

Most people on a rope (50-meter [164-foot] rope, minimum 12 turns obligatory) 220, by a team at the International Rope Skipping Competition, Greeley, CO on June 28, 1990.

POOL

American Straight Pool (14.1) World Championship The two most dominant 14.1 players were Ralph Greenleaf (U.S.), who won the "world" professional title six times and defended it 13 times (1919–37), and Willie Mosconi (U.S.), who dominated the game from 1941 to 1956, winning the title six times and defending it 13 times.

Most balls pocketed The greatest number of balls pocketed in 24 hours is 16,497, by Paul Sullivan in Selby, England, April 16–17, 1993.

Pool pocketing speed The record times for pocketing all 15 balls are: *(men)* 32.72 seconds, by Paul Sullivan at the Excelsior Pool and Snooker Club, Leeds, England on September 26, 1995; *(women)* 42.28 seconds, by Susan Thompson at the Ferry Inn, Holmsgarth, Shetland Isles on January 28, 1995.

TUG OF WAR

Most titles In the World Championships, England has won 16 titles in all categories, 1975–93. Sweden has won the 520 kg and the 560 kg three times at the Women's World Championships (held biennially since 1986), 1986–94.

Longest pulls Duration The longest recorded pull (prior to the introduction of AAA rules) is one of 2 hr. 41 min. when "H" Company beat "E" Company of the 2nd Battalion of the Sherwood Foresters (Derbyshire Regiment) in Jubbulpore, India on August 12, 1889.

The longest recorded pull under AAA rules (in which lying on the ground or entrenching the feet is not permitted) is one of 24 min. 45 sec. for the first pull between the Republic of Ireland and England during the world championships (640 kg class) in Malmö, Sweden on September 18, 1988.

The record time for "The Pull" (instituted 1898), across the Black River, between freshman and sophomore teams at Hope College, Holland, MI, is 3 hr. 51 min. on September 23, 1977, but the method of bracing the feet precludes this replacing the preceding records.

Distance The record distance for a tug of war contest is 3,962 yards, between Freedom Square and Independence Square, in Lodz, Poland on May 28, 1994.

TWISTER

Most participants The greatest number of participants in a game of Twister is 4,160 people, at the University of Massachusetts at Amherst on May 2, 1987. Allison Culler won the game.

BOARD GAMES

Biggest board game The world's biggest commercially available board game is Galaxion, created by Cerebe Design International of Hong Kong. The board measures 33 by 33 inches.

Most expensive board game The deluxe version of Outrage!, produced by Imperial Games of Southport, England, retails for £3,995 ($6,392). The object of the game is to steal the Crown Jewels from the Tower of London.

BACKGAMMON

Shortest backgammon game Alan Beckerson devised a game of 16 throws in 1982.

BINGO

Largest house The largest "house" in bingo sessions was 15,756, at the Canadian National Exhibition, Toronto on August 19, 1983, staged by the Variety Club of Ontario Tent Number 28. There was total prize money of $Cdn250,000 with a record one-game payout of $Cdn100,000.

Earliest and latest full house A "full house" call occurred on the 15th number by Norman A. Wilson at Guide Post Working Men's Club, Bedlington, England on June 22, 1978; by Anne Wintle of Brynrethin, Wales, on a bus trip to Bath, England on August 17, 1982; and by Shirley Lord at Kahibah Bowling Club, New South Wales, Australia on October 24, 1983.

"House" was not called until the 86th number at the Hillsborough Working Men's Club, Sheffield, England on January 11, 1982. There were 32 winners.

CARDS

Card holding Ralf Laue held 326 standard playing cards in a fan in one hand, so that the value and color of each one was visible, in Leipzig, Germany, on March 18, 1994.

Card throwing Jim Karol of Catasauqua, PA threw a standard playing card 201 feet at Mount Ida College, Newton Centre, MA on October 18, 1992.

Shortest solitaire game The shortest time to complete the game of solitaire is 10.0 seconds, by Stephen Twigge in Scissett Baths, England on August 2, 1991.

CHECKERS

World champion Walter Hellman (U.S.) won a record eight world titles during his tenure as world champion, 1948–75.

Youngest and oldest national champion Asa A. Long became the youngest U.S. national champion, at age 18 yr. 64 days, when he won in Boston, MA on October 23, 1922. He became the oldest, age 79 yr. 334 days, when he won his sixth title in Tupelo, MS on July 21, 1984.

Most opponents Charles Walker played a record 306 games simultaneously, winning 300, drawing 5 and losing 1, at Dollywood, Pigeon Force, TN on October 22, 1994.

The largest number of opponents played without a defeat or draw is 172, by Nate Cohen of Portland, ME in Portland on July 26, 1981. This was not a simultaneous attempt, but consecutive play over four hours.

Newell W. Banks played 140 games simultaneously, winning 133 and drawing seven, in Chicago, IL in 1933. His total playing time was 145 minutes, thus averaging about one move per second. In 1947, he played blindfolded for four hours per day for 45 consecutive days, winning 1,331 games, drawing 54 and losing only two, while playing six games at a time.

Longest game In competition, the prescribed rate of play is not less than 30 moves per hour, with the average game lasting about 90 minutes. In 1958, a game between Dr. Marion Tinsley (U.S.) and Derek Oldbury (Great Britain) lasted 7 hr. 30 min. (played under the 5-minutes-a-move rule).

CHESS

World Championships World champions have been officially recognized since 1886. The longest undisputed tenure was 26 yr. 337 days, by Dr. Emanuel Lasker of Germany, 1894–1921.

The women's world championship title was held by Vera Francevna Stevenson-Menchik (USSR, later Great Britain) from 1927 until her death in 1944, and was successfully defended a record seven times.

Team The USSR won the biennial men's team title (Olympiad) a record 18 times between 1952 and 1990, with Russia winning twice, in 1992 and

1994. The women's title has been won 11 times by the USSR from its introduction in 1957 to 1986, with Georgia winning in 1992 and 1995.

Youngest world champion Maya Chiburdanidze (USSR; b. January 17, 1961) won the women's title in 1978 when she was only 17. Gary Kasparov (USSR) won the title on November 9, 1985 at age 22 yr. 210 days.

Oldest world champion Wilhelm Steinitz (Austria, later U.S.) was 58 yr. 10 days when he lost his title to Emanuel Lasker on May 26, 1894.

Most active world champion Anatoliy Karpov (USSR) in his tenure as champion, 1975–85, averaged 45.2 competitive games per year, played in 32 tournaments and finished first in 26.

Youngest Grand Master On March 22, 1997 Etienne Bacrot (France) became the youngest individual to qualify as an International Grand Master, at age 14 yr. 59 days.

The youngest female Grand Master is Judit Polgar (Hungary), at age 15 yr. 150 days on December 20, 1991.

Youngest Master In January 1995, Vinay Bhat of San Jose, CA became the youngest person in the history of the United States Chess Foundation to attain a master rating, at 10 yr. 176 days.

Highest rating The highest rating ever attained on the officially adopted Elo System (devised by Arpad E. Elo) is 2,815, by Gary Kasparov (USSR) in 1993.

The women's record is held by Judit Polgar, who achieved a peak rating of 2,675 in 1996.

IBM's Deep Blue, the fastest chess computer, can look at 200 million chess positions per second. Grandmaster Gary Kasparov was bested by Deep Blue in May 1997.

Fewest games lost by a world champion   José Raúl Capablanca (Cuba) lost only 34 games (out of 571) in his adult career, 1909–39. He was unbeaten from February 10, 1916 to March 21, 1924 (63 games) and was world champion 1921–27.

U.S. Championships   The most wins since the U.S. Championships became determined by match play competition in 1888 is eight, by Bobby Fischer, 1957–66.

Most consecutive games   The record for most consecutive games played is 663, by Vlastimil Hort (Czechoslovakia, later Germany) over 32½ hours in Porz, Germany, October 5–6, 1984. He played 60–120 opponents at a time, scoring over 80 percent wins and averaging 30 moves per game.

Eric G. J. Knoppert (Netherlands) played 500 games of 10-minute chess against opponents, averaging 2,002 on the Elo scale, September 13–16, 1985. He scored 413 points (1 for win, ½ for draw), a success rate of 82.6 percent.

Most simultaneous games   Ulf Andersson (Sweden) played 310 games simultaneously (with two defeats) in Alvsjo, Sweden on January 6–7, 1996.

Most moves   The Master chess game with the most moves on record was one of 269 moves, when Ivan Nikolic drew with Goran Arsovic in Belgrade, Yugoslavia on February 17, 1989. The game took 20 hr. 15 min.

Slowest moves   In a 15-hour chess game between Louis Paulsen (Germany) and Paul Charles Morphy (U.S.) at the first American Chess Congress, NY on October 29, 1857 (before time clocks were used), a total of 56 moves were made. The game ended in a draw, Paulsen having used about 11 hours of play.

Grand Master Friedrich Sämisch (Germany) ran out of the allotted time (2 hr. 30 min. for 45 moves) after only 12 moves, in Prague, Czechoslovakia, in 1938.

The slowest move played since time clocks were introduced was in Vigo, Spain in 1980 when Francisco R. Torres Trois took 2 hr. 20 min. for his seventh move vs. Luis M. C. P. Santos.

Oldest chess pieces   The oldest chess pieces were found in Nashipur, and were dated to *c*. A.D. 900.

CONTRACT BRIDGE

Biggest tournament   The Epson World Bridge Championship, held June 20–21, 1992, was contested by 102,000 players playing the same hands, at 2,000 centers worldwide.

Most world titles   The World Championship (Bermuda Bowl) has been won a record 14 times by the U.S., 1950–51, 1953–54, 1970–71, 1976–77, 1979, 1981, 1983, 1985, 1987 and 1995. Italy's Blue Team (Squadra Azzura) won 13 world titles and an additional three team Olympiads between 1957 and 1975. Giorgio Belladonna was on all the Italian winning teams.

The U.S. has six wins in the women's world championship for the Venice Trophy, 1974, 1976, 1978, 1987, 1989 and 1991, and three women's wins in the World Team Olympiad, 1976, 1980 and 1984.

Most world championship hands   In the 1989 Bermuda Bowl in Perth, Australia, Marcel Branco and Gabriel Chagas, both of Brazil, played a record 752 out of a possible 784 boards.

CRIBBAGE

Rare hands   Five maximum 29-point hands have been achieved by Sean Daniels of Astoria, OR, 1989–92. Paul Nault of Athol, MA had two such hands in eight games in a tournament on March 19, 1977.

Most points in 24 hours   The most points scored by a team of four, playing singles in two pairs, is 139,454, by Colin Cooper, John Dunk, Peter Hyham and John Wilson at Her Majesty's Prison, Doncaster, England, September 16–17, 1995.

CROSSWORD PUZZLES

Largest crossword puzzle   In July 1982, Robert Turcot (Canada) compiled the largest crossword puzzle ever published, comprising 82,951 squares. It contained 12,489 clues across, 13,125 down, and covered 38.28 square feet.

Fast crossword puzzle solution   The fastest time for completing *The Times* (London) crossword puzzle under test conditions is 3 min. 45 sec., by Roy Dean (Great Britain) on December 19, 1970.

DOMINOES

Domino toppling   The greatest number set up single-handedly and toppled is 281,581 out of 320,236, by Klaus Friedrich, 22, in Fürth, Germany on January 27, 1984. The dominoes fell within 12 min. 57.3 sec., having taken 31 days (10 hours daily) to set up.

Thirty students at Delft, Eindhoven and Twente Technical Universities in the Netherlands set up 1,500,000 dominoes representing all the European Community countries. Of these, 1,382,101 were toppled by one push on January 2, 1988.

Domino stacking   Aleksandr Bendikov of Mogilev, Belarus stacked 522 dominoes on a single supporting domino on September 21, 1994.

MAGIC THE GATHERING

Youngest world champion   Tom Chanpheng (Australia) became world champion at age 19 in 1996.

Most championships   The United States has won the team world championship twice, in 1995 and 1996.

SCRABBLE

Highest scores   The highest competitive game score is 1,049 by Phil Appleby in June 1989. His opponent scored 253, and the margin of victory, 796 points, is also a record. His score included a single turn of 374 for the word "OXIDIZERS."

The highest competitive single-turn score recorded, however, is 392, by Dr. Saladin Karl Khoshnaw (of Kurdish origin) in Manchester, England in April 1982. He laid down "CAZIQUES," which means "native chiefs of West Indian aborigines."

Under North American rules, the record of 311 is shared by Joe Koczan, who laid down "CRAZIEST" at the Milwaukee Scrabble Club in May 1996, and Teresa A. Sanders, who laid down "BRAZIERS" in an NSA-sanctioned tournament in Tyler, TX in January 1997.

The highest score achieved on a single opening move is 124, by Sam Kantimathi in Portland, OR in July 1993. He laid down "CAZIQUE."

The highest score in a tournament game (American-style competitive) is 770 points by game inventor Mark Lansberg (Los Angeles) at the Scrabble tournament in Eagle Rock, CA on June 13, 1993. His opponent, Alan Stern, scored 338 points; their combined total of 1,108 points is also a record for American-style competitive tournament play.

Most tournaments Chuck Armstrong of Saline, MI, won the most tournaments—70 to the end of 1995.

Tom Chanpheng was the youngest Magic the Gathering champion, at 19.

TRANSPORTATION

CARS

PRODUCTION

Largest annual production   The number of vehicles constructed worldwide in 1996 was 51,513,000, of which a record 37,318,000 were cars.

Largest manufacturer   The world's largest manufacturer of motor vehicles and parts (and the largest manufacturing company) is General Motors Corporation of Detroit, MI. The company has on average 647,000 employees. In the 1996 fiscal year, the company's annual revenues were $168.4 billion and its annual net income was $4.96 billion. In 1996, General Motors produced 8.8 million cars, trucks and buses.

Largest plant   The largest single automobile plant in the world is the Volkswagenwerk in Wolfsburg, Germany, with 60,000 employees and a capacity for producing 4,000 vehicles per week (208,000 per year). The factory buildings cover an area of 371 acres and the whole plant covers 1,878 acres, with 46 miles of rail sidings.

Longest in production   A total of 21,240,657 Volkswagen "Beetles" have been produced since 1937. Two production lines continue to produce the car—Puebla, Mexico and São Paulo, Brazil.

The Morgan 4/4, built by the Morgan Motor Car Co. of Malvern, England, celebrated its 60th birthday in December 1995. There is still a waiting list of 6–8 years to buy this model.

Largest car   Of cars produced for private use, the largest was the Bugatti "Royale" type 41. First built in 1927, this machine has an 8-cylinder engine of 12.7-liter capacity, and measures over 22 feet long. The hood is over seven feet long.

Over 21 million Beetles have been produced since 1937. A new edition, seen here, is scheduled for launch before the end of the century.

Longest car   A 26-wheeled limousine measuring 100 feet long was designed by Jay Ohrberg of Burbank, CA. It has many special features, including a swimming pool and a king-sized water bed.

Largest engine   The largest engine capacity of a production car is 13.5 liters, for the U.S. Pierce-Arrow 6–66 Raceabout of 1912–18, the U.S. Peerless 6–60 of 1912–14, and the Fageol of 1918.

Most powerful car   The most powerful current production car is the McLaren F1 6.1; it develops in excess of 627 bhp.

Heaviest car   The heaviest car recently in production (up to 25 were made annually) appears to be the Soviet-built Zil–41047 limousine with a 12.72-foot wheelbase. It weighs 7,352 pounds (3.7 tons).

A "stretched" Zil was used by former USSR president Mikhail Gorbachev until December 1991. It weighed 6.6 tons and was made of 3-inch armor-plated steel. The 8-cylinder, 7-liter engine guzzled fuel at a rate of six miles per gallon.

Lightest car   Louis Borsi of London, England has built and driven a 21-pound car with a 2.5-cc engine. It is capable of 15 mph.

Smallest street-legal car   The smallest registered street-legal car in the United States has an overall length of 88¾ inches and a width of 40½ inches. It was built by Arlis Sluder and is now owned by Jeff Gibson.

Most expensive car   The most expensive car was the U.S. Presidential 1969 Lincoln Continental Executive delivered to the U.S. Secret Service on October 14, 1968. It has an overall length of 21 ft. 6¼ in. with a 13-ft.-4-in. wheelbase, and with the addition of 2.2 tons of armor plate, weighs six tons. The estimated cost of research, development and manufacture was $500,000, but it is rented at $5,000 per year.

Used   The greatest confirmed price paid is $15 million, including commission, for the 1931 Bugatti Type 41 Royale Sports Coupé by Kellner, sold to Meitec Corporation of Japan on April 12, 1990.

Most inexpensive car   The cheapest car of all time was the 1922 Red Bug Buckboard, built by the Briggs & Stratton Co. of Milwaukee, WI, listed at $125–$150. It had a 62-inch wheelbase and weighed 245 pounds. Early models of the King Midget cars were sold in kit form for as little as $100 in 1948.

Longest parade of cars   A parade of 2,223 Corvettes traveled from Springfield, IL to Athens, IL and back again on June 25, 1994.

Most expensive license plate   License plate No. 9 was sold at a Hong Kong government auction for HK$13 million (approximately $1.7 million) on March 19, 1994 to Albert Yeung Sau-Shing. "Nine" sounds like the word "dog" in Chinese, and the purchase was considered lucky because 1994 was the Year of the Dog.

Car wrecking   In a career lasting 40 years until his retirement in 1993, stuntman Dick Sheppard of Gloucester, England wrecked 2,003 cars.

SPEED RECORDS

Fastest land vehicle   The official one-mile land-speed record is 633.468 mph, set by Richard Noble on October 4, 1983 over the Black Rock Desert, NV in his 17,000-pound-thrust Rolls-Royce Avon 302 jet-powered *Thrust* 2, designed by John Ackroyd.

Fastest rocket-engined vehicle   The fastest speed attained by any wheeled land vehicle is 631.367 mph by *The Blue Flame*, a rocket-powered 4-wheeled vehicle driven by Gary Gabelich (U.S.) on the Bonneville Salt Flats, UT on October 23, 1970. Gabelich momentarily exceeded 650 mph. The car was powered by a liquid natural gas/hydrogen peroxide rocket engine developing a thrust of up to 22,000 pounds.

The fastest reputed land speed figure in one direction is 739.666 mph, or Mach 1.0106, by Stan Barrett (U.S.) in the *Budweiser Rocket*, a rocket-engined 3-wheeled car, at Edwards Air Force Base, CA on December 17, 1979. This speed is not sanctioned by the U.S.A.F.

Fastest piston-engined car   The fastest speed measured for a wheel-driven car is 432.692 mph by Al Teague in *Speed-O-Motive/Spirit of '76* at Bonneville Salt Flats, UT on August 21, 1991 over the final 132 feet of a mile run (av. 425.230 mph for the whole mile).

Fastest diesel car   The prototype 3-liter Mercedes C 111/3 attained 203.3 mph in tests on the Nardo Circuit in Italy, October 5–15, 1978, and in April 1978 averaged 195.4 mph for 12 hours, thus covering a world record 2,344.7 miles.

Fastest steam car   On August 19, 1985 Robert E. Barber broke the 79-year-old record for a steam car driving No. 744, *Steamin' Demon*, built by the Barber-Nichols Engineering Co., which reached 145.607 mph at Bonneville Salt Flats, UT.

Fastest electric car   The highest speed achieved by an electric vehicle is 183.822 mph over a 2-way flying kilometer by General Motors' *Impact*, driven by Clive Roberts (Great Britain) at Fort Stockton Test Center in Texas on March 11, 1994.

Fastest road car   The fastest speed ever attained by a standard production car is 217.1 mph for a Jaguar XJ220, driven by Martin Brundle at the Nardo Circuit, Italy on June 21, 1992.

The highest road-tested acceleration reported for a street-legal car is 0–60 mph in 3.07 seconds for a Ford RS200 Evolution, driven by Graham Hathaway at the Boreham Proving Ground, Essex, England on May 25, 1994.

DRIVING

Amphibious circumnavigation   The only circumnavigation by an amphibious vehicle was by Ben Carlin (Australia) in the amphibious jeep *Half-Safe*.

He completed the last leg of the Atlantic crossing (the English Channel) on August 24, 1951. He arrived back in Montreal, Canada on May 8, 1958, having completed a circumnavigation of 39,000 miles over land and 9,600 miles by sea and river. He was accompanied on the transatlantic stage by his ex-wife Elinore (U.S.) and on the transpacific stage by Broye Lafayette De-Mente (U.S.).

One-year drive   The greatest distance ever covered in one year is 354,257 miles, by two Opel Rekord 2-liter passenger sedans, both of which covered this distance between May 18, 1988 and the same date in 1989 without any major mechanical breakdowns. The vehicles were manufactured by the Delta Motor Corporation, Port Elizabeth, South Africa, and were driven on tar and gravel roads in the Northern Cape by a team of company drivers from Delta.

Trans-Americas drive   Garry Sowerby (Canada), with Tim Cahill (U.S.) as co-driver and navigator, drove a 1988 GMC Sierra K3500 4-wheel-drive pickup truck powered by a 6.2-liter V8 Detroit diesel engine from Ushuaia, Tierra del Fuego, Argentina to Prudhoe Bay, AK, a distance of 14,739 miles, in a total elapsed time of 23 days 22 hr. 43 min. from September 29 to October 22, 1987. The vehicle and team were surface-freighted from Cartagena, Colombia to Balboa, Panama so as to bypass the Darién Gap.

Oldest car to cross the United States   Raymond H. Carr drove across the United States in a 1902 Northern, the oldest car ever to make the trip. Traveling at 15–20 mph, Carr left San Diego, CA on May 8, 1994 and arrived at Jekyll Island, GA on May 31, 1994.

Carr also crossed the United States in a 1912 Baker Electric Runabout, the oldest electric car to make the crossing, starting in Astoria, OR on May 28, 1995 and finishing in Atlantic City, NJ on July 3, 1995.

Longest skid marks   The skid marks made by the jet-powered *Spirit of America*, driven by Craig Breedlove, after the car went out of control at Bonneville Salt Flats, UT, on October 15, 1964, were nearly six miles long.

Highest mileage   The highest recorded mileage for a car is 1,613,281 miles for a 1963 Volkswagen Beetle owned by Albert Klein of Pasadena, CA. "Old Faithful" was totaled in an accident on March 29, 1997.

The highest recorded mileage for a car with the original gasoline motor without an overhaul is 684,397 miles to August 5, 1997 for a 1979 Cadillac DeVille owned by Don Champion of Louisville, KY.

Lowest gas consumption   A vehicle specially designed by Team 1200 from Honda in Suzuka City, Japan achieved 9,426 mpg in the Pisaralla Pisimmalle mileage marathon in Nokia, Finland on September 1, 1996. The best performance by a street-legal vehicle is 568 mpg by the diesel-powered Combidrive "Mouse" at the 1996 Shell Mileage Marathon in Silverstone, England.

Longest fuel range   The greatest distance driven without refueling on a single fill-up in a standard vehicle (38.2 gallons carried in factory-optional twin fuel tanks) is 1,691.6 miles, by a 1991 Toyota LandCruiser diesel station wagon. Driven by Ewan Kennedy with Ian Lee (observer) from Nyngan, New South Wales, Australia to Winton, Queensland, Australia and back from May 18 to May 21, 1992, the car averaged 37.3 mph, giving 44.2 mpg.

The greatest distance traveled by an unmodified production car on the contents of a standard fuel tank is 1,338.1 miles, giving 75.94 mpg. Stuart Bladon and Robert Procter drove the length of Great Britain, July 26–28, 1992, from John o' Groat's to Land's End, and returned to Scotland driving an Audi 100 TD1 diesel car. The fuel in the 17.62-gallon fuel tank ran out after 35 hr. 18 min.

Fuel economy—United States drive   Jay Lowe and Ted Jacobs drove 7,229.3 miles, visiting all 48 of the contiguous states and using 163.64 gallons of gasoline, in a 1-liter, 3-cylinder, 5-speed 1992 Chevrolet Geo Metro, April 29–May 4, 1997.

Driving in reverse   Charles Creighton and James Hargis of Maplewood, MO drove their Model A Ford 1929 roadster in reverse for 3,340 miles from New York to Los Angeles, CA, from July 26 to August 13, 1930 without once stopping the engine. They arrived back in New York in reverse on September 5, having completed 7,180 miles in 42 days.

Brian "Cub" Keene and James "Wilbur" Wright drove their Chevrolet Blazer 9,031 miles in reverse in 37 days (August 1–September 6, 1984) through 15 states and Canada.

The highest average speed attained in any nonstop reverse drive exceeding 500 miles is 36.3 mph, by John Smith, who drove a 1983 Chevrolet Caprice Classic 501 miles in 13 hr. 48 min. at the I-94 Speedway, Fergus Falls, MN on August 11, 1996.

Longest battery-powered car journey   David Turner and Tim Pickhard of Turners of Boscastle Ltd., Cornwall, England traveled 875 miles from Land's End to John o' Groat's, Great Britain in a Freight Rover Leyland Sherpa, powered by a Lucas electric motor, December 21–25, 1985.

Two-side-wheel driving Car   On May 24, 1989 Bengt Norberg of Äppelbo, Sweden drove a Mitsubishi Colt GTi-16V on two side wheels nonstop for a

Goran Eliason drove a car on two wheels at over 100 mph.

IT'S A
GAS!

When Jay Lowe was a little boy, he would curl up with his father's copy of *The Guinness Book of World Records* and dream of the feats he hoped to accomplish. Little did he know that some 30 years later he would be honored for a record of his own—maintaining the lowest fuel consumption on a 48-state drive.

"I can picture exactly where I was when I read my dad's book for the first time, and when I drove across the finish line, I had flashes of that boy," says Lowe, 42, a Texas insurance agent, who along with business associate Ted Jacobs traveled 7,229.3 miles while achieving an average of 44.178 miles per gallon.

It all began when the two men joked over lunch about the time it would take to travel the 48 contiguous states. Jacobs, the planner of the duo, went home that evening and began computing the mileage involved. He called Lowe with his forecast and a plan was hatched. "It started out as a simple conversation," said Jacobs, "but then you put the challenge out and you have to just rise to it."

Originally, the pair attempted to break the world record for completing the drive in the fastest time. Although they completed the trip, Guinness had by then retired the record for safety reasons. Undaunted, the two persevered and decided to attempt the drive again—this time reaching for the record of the lowest fuel consumption. Lowe and Jacobs spent close to six months researching their route, calling truckers and State Farm agents in other states to ascertain the best roads to use in each area. Next, they devised a route that ensured they would miss rush hour in each city, cutting down on time spent idling in traffic. "Each gallon of gas meant everything to us," said Lowe, who computed tailwinds into their timing for at least 60 percent of the trip. "Not only were we trying the break the world record, we were trying to keep the next guy from breaking ours."

Finding the perfect car to achieve their goal was not easy. The two 6-foot men completed their first cross-country tour in a roomy van. This time, they had to become fuel-efficient, so they targeted a manual 5-speed Geo Metro as their dream-mobile. They arranged for a

rental from an agency, but three weeks before their scheduled start, they learned that the car had an automatic transmission.

Fate, though, smiled upon the pair. Six days before their scheduled departure, a still carless Lowe spotted a five-speed Geo Metro parked right in front of their office. He ran from store to store, yelling for the owner, and found her in the local hair salon. He told the young woman their predicament; intrigued, she agreed to lend them the car.

Lowe and Jacobs began their adventure on April 29 from Four Corners Monument, where Utah, Colorado, New Mexico and Arizona meet. They then traveled clockwise throughout the country, ending their journey in Tom, Oklahoma on May 4, 164 gallons of gas later. During the 6-day trip, the car never stopped for more than five minutes at a time. The men used the bathroom during gas breaks, grabbing whatever food they could find from the convenience marts at the stations.

"I get great personal inner satisfaction from having risen to the challenge," Jacobs said. "I could go the rest of my life and never tell anyone about it." Lowe, on the other hand, has a spot on his wall earmarked for his world record confirmation. "When I heard that we officially had broken the record, I said, 'Thanks for making a little boy's dream come true.' "

FUEL ECONOMY—UNITED STATES DRIVE

Jay Lowe and Ted Jacobs drove 7,299.3 miles, visiting all 48 of the contiguous states and using 163.64 gallons of gasoline, in a 1-liter, 3-cylinder, 5-speed 1992 Chevrolet Geo Metro, April 29–May 4, 1997.

distance of 192.873 miles in a time of 7 hr. 15 min. 50 sec. He also achieved a distance of 27.842 miles in one hour at Rattvik Horse Track, Sweden on the same day.

Goran Eliason (Sweden) achieved a speed of 111.4 mph over a 100-meter (328-foot) flying start on two wheels of a Volvo 850 Turbo on April 20, 1996.

Truck   Sven-Erik Söderman drove a Daf 2800 7.5-ton truck on two wheels for a distance of 6.73 miles at Mora Siljan Airport, Mora, Sweden on May 19, 1991.

Bus   Bobby Ore (Great Britain) drove a double-decker bus a distance of 810 feet on two wheels at North Weald Airfield, England on May 21, 1988.

Ramp jumping in a car   The longest ramp jump in a car (with the car landing on its wheels and being driven on) is 232 feet, by Jacqueline De Creed in a 1967 Ford Mustang at Santa Pod Raceway, Bedfordshire, England on April 3, 1983.

Most durable driver   Goodyear Tire and Rubber Co. test driver Weldon C. Kocich drove 3,141,946 miles from February 5, 1953 to February 28, 1986, thus averaging 95,210 miles per year.

Oldest drivers   Layne Hall (b. December 24 or 25, 1884 or March 15, 1880) of Silver Creek, NY was issued a driver's license valid until his birthday in 1993, when, based on the birthdate on the license, he would have been 113 years old. However, he died on November 20, 1990 at age 105, according to the death certificate.

Mrs. Maude Tull of Inglewood, CA, who took up driving at age 91 after her husband died, was issued a license renewal on February 5, 1976 when she was 104.

Most driving tests   Mrs. Fannie Turner of Little Rock, AR passed the written test for drivers on her 104th attempt in October 1978.

Worst driver   It was reported that a 75-year-old male driver received 10 traffic tickets, drove on the wrong side of the road 4 times, committed 4 hit-and-run offenses and caused 6 accidents, all within 20 minutes, in McKinney, TX on October 15, 1966.

Most parking tickets   Mrs. Silvia Matos of New York City set a record for unpaid parking tickets, totaling $150,000. She collected the 2,800 tickets between 1985 and 1988, but authorities were unable to collect any money; she registered her car under 19 addresses and 36 license plates and could not be found.

SERVICES

Largest filling station   There are 204 pumps—96 Tokheim Unistar and 108 Tokheim Explorer—in Jeddah, Saudi Arabia.

Highest filling station   The highest filling station in the world is at Leh, Ladakh, India, at 12,001 feet, operated by the Indian Oil Corporation.

Largest garage The largest private garage is one of two stories built outside Bombay, India for the private collection of 176 cars owned by Pranlal Bhogilal.

The KMB Overhaul Center, operated by the Kowloon Motor Bus Co. (1933) Ltd., Hong Kong, is the world's largest multistory service center. Built expressly for double-decker buses, it has four floors occupying more than 11.6 acres.

Largest parking lot The lot in the West Edmonton Mall, Edmonton, Alberta, Canada can hold 20,000 vehicles, and there are overflow facilities for 10,000 more cars.

Longest tow Great Britain's Automobile Association used a Land Rover to tow a replica Model T Ford van 4,995 miles, starting in Ascot, England on May 4, 1993 and ending up in Widmerpool, England on May 12, 1993.

ROADS

Greatest length of road The United States has more miles of road than any other country, with 3,880,151 miles of graded road.

Longest driveable road The Pan-American Highway, from northwest Alaska to Santiago, Chile, then eastward to Buenos Aires, Argentina and

The country with the greatest length of graded roads is the United States, with 3,880,151 miles.

terminating in Brasilia, Brazil, is over 15,000 miles long. There is, however, a small incomplete section in Panama and Colombia known as the Darién Gap.

Worst exit to miss   The longest distance between controlled access exits in the United States is 51.1 miles from Florida Turnpike exit 193 (Yeehaw Junction, FL) to exit 242 (Kissimmee, FL). The longest distance on any interstate highway is 37.7 miles from I-80 exit 41 (Knolls, UT) to exit 4 (Bonneville Speedway, UT).

Highest trail   The highest trail in the world is an 8-mile stretch of the Gangdise between Khaleb and Xinji-fu, Tibet, which in two places exceeds 20,000 feet.

Highest road   The highest road in the world is above the Changlung Valley in Aksai, China (administered by China but claimed by India), at an altitude of 19,320 feet. This military road is closed to foreign traffic.

Lowest road   The lowest road is along the Israeli shores of the Dead Sea at 1,290 feet below sea level.

Widest road   The Monumental Axis runs for 1^1/$_2$ miles from the Municipal Plaza to the Plaza of the Three Powers in Brasilia, the capital of Brazil. The dual 6-lane boulevard, opened in April 1960, is 820.2 feet wide.

The San Francisco–Oakland Bay Bridge Toll Plaza has 23 lanes (17 westbound) serving the bridge in Oakland, CA.

Highest traffic volume   The most heavily traveled stretch of road is Interstate 405 (San Diego Freeway), in Orange County, CA, which has a rush-hour volume of 25,500 vehicles. This volume occurs on a 0.9-mile stretch between Garden Grove Freeway and Seal Beach Boulevard.

Highest traffic density   In 1993, Gibraltar had 767 vehicles per mile of serviceable road, giving a density of 6 ft. 10^1/$_2$ in. per vehicle.

Longest traffic jam   On February 16, 1980, a traffic jam stretching 109.3 miles from Lyons to Paris, France was reported.

A record traffic jam was reported for 1.5 million cars crawling bumper-to-bumper over the East–West German border on April 12, 1990.

Longest street   The longest designated street in the world is Yonge Street, running north and west from Toronto, Ontario, Canada. The first stretch, completed on February 16, 1796, ran 34 miles. Its official length, now extended to Rainy River on the Ontario–Minnesota border, is 1,178.3 miles.

Narrowest street   The world's narrowest street is in the village of Ripatransone in the Marche region of Italy. It is called Vicolo della Virilita ("Virility Alley") and is 1 ft. 5 in. wide.

Shortest street   Elgin Street, in Bacup, England, measures just 17 feet long.

Steepest street   Baldwin Street, Dunedin, New Zealand has a maximum gradient of 1 in 1.266.

BICYCLES & MOTORCYCLES

UNICYCLES

Tallest unicycle The tallest unicycle ever mastered is 101 ft. 9 in. tall. It was ridden by Steve McPeak (with a safety wire suspended by an overhead crane) for a distance of 376 feet in Las Vegas, NV in October 1980.

Smallest unicycle Peter Rosendahl (Sweden) rode an 8-inch-high unicycle with a wheel diameter of 0.78 inches, with no attachments or extensions fitted, a distance of 7 ft. 2 in. in Hamburg, Germany on December 14, 1995.

One hundred miles Takayuki Koike of Kanagawa, Japan set a unicycle record for 100 miles of 6 hr. 44 min. 21.84 sec. on August 9, 1987 (average speed 14.83 mph).

Longest unicycle journey Akira Matsushima (Japan) unicycled 3,261 miles from Newport, OR to Washington, D.C. from July 10 to August 22, 1992.

Unicycling backwards Ashrita Furman (U.S.) rode backwards for a distance of 53 miles 300 yards at Forest Park, Queens, NY on September 16, 1994.

Fastest unicycle sprint Peter Rosendahl set a sprint record for 100 meters (328.1 feet) of 12.11 seconds (18.47 mph) in Las Vegas, NV on March 25, 1994.

BICYCLES

Longest bicycle The longest true bicycle (i.e., without a third stabilizing wheel) was designed and

The first rule of backwards unicycling is to learn how to maintain balance while looking over your shoulder. Ashrita Furman managed it for a record 53 miles 300 yards.

built by Terry Thessman of Pahiatua, New Zealand. It measures 72 ft. 11½ in. long and weighs 750 pounds. It was ridden by four riders a distance of 807 feet on February 27, 1988. Turning corners proved to be a problem.

Smallest bicycle The smallest-wheeled ridable bicycle has 0.76-inch-diameter wheels. It was ridden by its constructor, Neville Patten of Gladstone, Queensland, Australia for a distance of 13 ft. 5½ in. on March 25, 1988.

The smallest ridable bicycle in terms of length was built by Jacques Puyoou of Pau, Pyrénées-Atlantiques, France, whose tandem is 14.1 inches long. The bicycle has been ridden by him and Madame Puyoou.

Largest bicycle The largest bicycle as measured by the front-wheel diameter is "Frankencycle," built by Dave Moore of Rosemead, CA and first ridden by Steve Gordon of Moorpark, CA, on June 4, 1989. The wheel diameter is 10 feet and the bicycle itself is 11 ft. 2 in. high.

Largest tricycle The Dillon Colossal Tricycle was designed by Arthur Dillon, It has rear wheels 11 feet in diameter, constructed by David Moore, and a front wheel 5 ft. 10 in. high.

Longest wheelie Leandro Henrique Basseto set a record of 10 hr. 40 min. 8 sec. in Madaguari, Paraná, Brazil on December 2, 1990.

Underwater tricycling A team of 32 divers pedaled a distance of 116.66 miles in 75 hr. 20 min. on a standard tricycle at Diver's Den, Santa Barbara, CA on June 16–19, 1988.

At 72 feet 11½ inches, the world's longest bicycle is built for straight roads. Cornering is more difficult.

HUMAN-POWERED VEHICLES

Fastest human-powered vehicle The world speed records for human-powered vehicles (HPVs) over a 200-meter (656.2-foot) flying start (single rider) are 65.484 mph by Fred Markham at Mono Lake, CA on May 11, 1986 and 62.92 mph (multiple riders) by Dave Grylls and Leigh Barczewski at the Ontario Speedway, CA, on May 4, 1980.

The one-hour standing start (single rider) record is held by Pat Kinch, riding Kingcycle Bean, averaging a speed of 46.96 mph on September 8, 1990 at Millbrook Proving Ground, Bedford, England.

Fastest water cycle The men's 6,562-foot (single rider) record is 12.84 mph, by Steve Hegg in Flying Fish off Long Beach, CA on July 20, 1987.

MOTORCYCLES

Longest motorcycle Gregg Reid of Atlanta, GA designed and built a Yamaha 250-cc motorcycle that measures 15 ft. 6 in. long and weighs 520 pounds. It is street legal and has been insured.

Smallest motorcycle Simon Timperley and Clive Williams of Progressive Engineering Ltd., Ashton-under-Lyne, England designed and constructed a motorcycle with a 4.25-inch wheelbase, a seat height of 3.75 inches and a wheel diameter of 0.75 inches for the front and 0.95 inches for the back. It was ridden 3.2 feet.

MOTORCYCLE SPEED RECORDS

Fastest speeds Dave Campos (U.S.), riding a 23-foot-long streamliner named Easyriders, powered by two 91-cubic-inch Ruxton Harley-Davidson engines, set AMA and FIM absolute records with an overall average of 322.150 mph and completed the faster run at an average of 322.870 mph on Bonneville Salt Flats, UT on July 14, 1990.

The fastest time for a single run over 440 yards from a standing start is 6.19 seconds by Tony Lang (U.S.) riding a supercharged Suzuki at Gainesville, FL in 1994.

The highest terminal velocity at the end of a 440-yard run from a standing start is 231.24 mph, by Elmer Trett (U.S.) at Virginia Motorsports Park, Petersburg, VA, in 1994.

Fastest production road machine The 151-hp 1-liter Tu Atara Yamaha Bimota 6th edition EI has a road-tested top speed of 186.4 mph.

Dave Barr motorcycled from the Breton coast of France to Vladivostok, Russia between December 8, 1996 and March 24, 1997. He covered 9,375 miles.

RAMP JUMPING

The longest distance ever long-jumped from ramp to ramp on a motorcycle is 251 feet. Doug Danger (real name Doug Senecal), performed the feat at the New Hampshire International Speedway, Loudon, NH, on June 22, 1991. He was riding a 1991 Honda CR500.

For rules, see page 707.

TOP THIS

MOTORCYCLE RIDING

Longest motorcycle ride　Emilio Sciotto of Buenos Aires, Argentina rode over 456,729 miles across 214 countries from January 17, 1985 to April 2, 1995. He set off on his Honda Gold Wing, which he nicknamed "The Black Princess," with $300 and no previous travel experience. Along the way, Sciotto learned five languages, became a Muslim, and married his girlfriend in India.

Longest scooter ride　A Kinetic Honda DX 100 cc, ridden by Har Parkash Rishi, Amarjeet Singh and Navjot Chadha, covered a distance of 19,241 miles nonstop in 1,001 at Traffic Park, Pune, Maharashtra, India between April 22 and June 3, 1990.

Largest pyramid　The "Dare Devils" team from the Signal Corps of the Indian army established a record with a pyramid of 140 men on 11 motorcycles. The pyramid was held together by muscle and determination only, with no straps, harnesses or other aids. It traveled a distance of 218 yards in Jabalpur, India on February 14, 1996.

Ramp jumping　The longest distance ever achieved by a motorcycle long-jumping is 251 feet, by Doug Danger on a 1991 Honda CR500 in Loudon, NH on June 22, 1991.

Longest wheelie　Yasuyuki Kudo covered 205.7 miles nonstop on the rear wheel of his Honda TLM 220 R 216-cc motorcycle at the Japan Automobile Research Institute, Tsukuba, Japan on May 5, 1991.

Fastest wheelie　The highest speed attained on a rear wheel of a motorcycle is 157.87 mph, by Jacky Vranken (Belgium) on a Suzuki GSXR 1100 at St. Truiden Military Airfield, Belgium on November 8, 1992.

Wall of death　The greatest endurance feat on a "wall of death" was 7 hr. 0 min. 13 sec., by Martin Blume, Berlin, Germany on April 16, 1983. He rode over 12,000 laps on the 33-foot-diameter wall on a Yamaha XS400, averaging 30 mph for the 181½ miles.

Most on one machine　The record for the most people on a single machine is 47, established by the Army Corps of Brasília, Brazil on a 1,200-cc Harley-Davidson on December 15, 1995.

SPECIALIZED VEHICLES

LARGEST LAND VEHICLES

Largest automotive land vehicle　"Big Muskie," a 13,200 ton walking dragline (a machine that removes dirt from coal), was built by Bucyrus Erie for the Central Ohio Coal Co.'s Muskingum, OH site. It is no longer in use.

Longest land vehicle The Arctic Snow Train, owned by Steve McPeak (U.S.), has 54 wheels and is 572 feet long. It was built by R.G. Le Tourneau, Inc. of Longview, TX for the U.S. Army. Its gross train weight is 441 tons, with a top speed of 20 mph, and it was driven by a crew of six when used as an "overland train" for the military. It generates 4,680 shp and has a fuel capacity of 7,832 gallons.

Heaviest load On July 14–15, 1984, John Brown Engineers & Contractors BV moved the Conoco Kotter Field production deck with a roll-out weight of 325 tons for the Continental Netherlands Oil Co. of Leidsenhage, Netherlands.

BUSES

Longest buses The articulated DAF Super CityTrain buses of Zaire have room for a total of 350 passengers each. The buses are 105.64 feet long and weigh 32 tons empty.

Rigid The longest rigid single bus, built by Van Hool of Belgium, is 49 feet long and carries 69 passengers.

Largest bus fleet The 11,282 single-deck buses in São Paulo, Brazil make up the world's largest bus fleet.

Longest bus route Operated by Expreso Internacional Ormeño S.A., the regular scheduled 6,003-mile-long service between Caracas, Venezuela and Buenos Aires, Argentina takes 214 hours, with a 12-hour stopover in Santiago, Chile and a 24-hour stopover in Lima, Peru.

United States The longest scheduled bus route currently in use in the United States is operated by Greyhound from Los Angeles to New York City. It is 3,023 miles long and takes 70 hr. 10 min. to complete, employing nine drivers, with no change of bus.

Greatest passenger volume The city with the greatest passenger volume in the United States as of December 1996 was New York City, with unlinked passenger trips of 637.7 million for buses and 1.35 billion for trains. In 1996, the city with the highest aggregate for passenger miles traveled was also New York City, where riders logged approximately 8.1 billion miles.

CAMPERS

Largest camper In 1990, Sheik Hamad Bin Hamdan Al Nahyan of Abu Dhabi, United Arab Emirates built a 2-wheeled, 5-story vehicle measuring 66 feet long, 39 feet wide and 39 feet high. Weighing 120 tons, it has 8 bedrooms, 8 bathrooms, 4 garages and water storage for 6,340 gallons.

Longest camper journey Harry B. Coleman and Peggy Larson covered 143,716 miles in 133 countries in a Volkswagen Camper, August 20, 1976–April 20, 1978.

Fastest camper A Roadster camper towed by a 1990 Ford EA Falcon, driven by Charlie Kovacs, achieved 126.76 mph at Mangalore Airfield, Seymour, Victoria, Australia on April 18, 1991.

CRAWLERS

Largest crawler   The two Marion 8-caterpillar crawlers, used for conveying spacecraft to their launch pads at Cape Canaveral, FL, each measure 131 ft. 4 in. by 114 feet. The loaded train weight is 9,000 tons.

FIRE ENGINES

Tallest fire engine   The Bronto Skylift F72HLA has a maximum working height of 236 feet and a working outreach of 75 ft. 6 in. The 50-ton vehicle is manufactured in Finland by Bronto Skylift Oy Ab.

Shortest fire engine   "Little Squirt," a working fire engine built by Fire Chief Henry W. Preston of the City of Lebanon (TN) Fire Department, is only 118 inches long but carries scaled-down versions of all the equipment

The shortest working fire engine is 118 inches long.

found on a normal fire engine, including sirens, lights, hoses, fire extinguishers, axes, ladders and hydrant wrenches.

Greatest pumping capacity   The fire appliance with the greatest pumping capacity is the 860-hp 8-wheel Oshkosh firetruck, which weighs 66 tons and is used for aircraft and runway fires. It can discharge 50,200 gallons of expanded foam through two turrets in 2 min. 30 sec.

Fire pumping   The greatest gallonage stirrup-pumped by a team of eight in an 80-hour charity pump is 37,898 gallons, by firefighters at the Knaresborough Fire Station, Knaresborough, England, June 25–28, 1992.

Fire pump handling   The longest unaided tow of a fire appliance in excess of 1,120 pounds in 24 hours on a closed circuit is 223 miles, by a 32-man team from the Dublin Fire Brigade with a 1,144-pound fire pump, Dublin, Ireland, June 20–21, 1987.

The ultimate fireman's lift is the Bronto Skylift.

LAWN MOWERS

Widest lawn mower　The widest gang mower in the world is the 5-ton 60-foot-wide 27-unit "Big Green Machine" used by turf farmer Jay Edgar Frick of Monroe, OH. It mows an acre in 60 seconds.

Longest lawn mower drive　Ian Ireland of Harlow, England drove an Iseki SG15 power lawn mower 3,034 miles between Harlow and Southend Pier, England, August 13–September 7, 1989.

SNOW PLOWS

Largest snow-plow blade　A blade measuring 50 ft. 3 in. long and four feet high, with a clearing capacity of 1,095 cubic feet in one pass, was made by Aero Snow Removal Corporation of New York, NY in 1992 for use at JFK International Airport.

SOLAR-POWERED VEHICLES

Fastest solar-powered land vehicle　The fastest speed attained by a solely solar-powered land vehicle is 48.71 mph, by Molly Brennan, driving the General Motors Sunraycer at Mesa, AZ on June 24, 1988.
　The fastest speed of 83.88 mph using solar/battery power was achieved by Star Micronics' solar car Solar Star, driven by Manfred Hermann on January 5, 1991 at Richmond R.A.A.F. Base, Richmond, Australia.

TAXIS

Largest taxi fleet　Mexico City has a taxi fleet of 60,000 taxis, including regular taxis, communal fixed-route taxis and airport taxis.

Most durable taxi driver　Carmen Fasanella was continuously licensed as a taxicab owner and driver in the Borough of Princeton, NJ for 68 yr. 243 days, February 1, 1921–November 2, 1989.

Longest taxicab ride　The longest taxicab ride on record is one of 21,691 miles at a cost of £40,000 (approximately $68,000). Jeremy Levine, Mark Aylett and Carlos Aresse traveled from London, England to Cape Town, South Africa and back, June 3–October 17, 1994.

TRACTORS

Largest tractor　The $459,000 U.S. Department of Agriculture Wide Tractive Frame Vehicle, completed by Ag West of Sacramento, CA in June 1982, measures 33 feet between its wheels, which are designed to run on permanent paths, and weighs 24.5 tons.

Longest tractor journey　The Young Farmers Group of Devon, England left their native country on October 18, 1990 in one tractor and supporting trailer, and drove overland to Zimbabwe, a total of 14,500 miles, arriving on March 4, 1991.

TROLLEYS

Oldest trolley   Motor cars 1 and 2 of the Manx Electric Railway date from 1893. They run regularly on the 17³/₄-mile railroad between Douglas and Ramsey, Isle of Man, Great Britain.

Most extensive trolley system   St. Petersburg, Russia has the most extensive trolley system, with 2,402 cars on 64 routes and 429.13 miles of track.

Longest trolley journey   The longest trolley journey now possible is from Krefeld St. Tönis to Witten Annen Nord, Germany. With luck at the eight interconnections, the 65¹/₂-mile trip can be completed in five and a half hours.

TRUCKS

Largest truck   The Terex Titan 33-19 manufactured by General Motors Corporation and now in operation at Westar Mine, British Columbia, Canada has a loaded weight of 604.7 tons and a capacity of 350 tons. When tipped, its height is 56 feet. The 16-cylinder engine delivers 3,300 hp.

Largest tires   Bridgestone Corporation of Tokyo, Japan manufactures tires measuring 12 ft. 6³/₄ in. in diameter for giant dump trucks.

Longest wheelie   Steve Murty, driving a Pirelli High Performer, established the record for the longest wheelie in a truck, covering 1,794.9 feet in Blackpool, England on June 28, 1991.

WRECKERS

Most powerful wrecker   The Twin City Garage and Body Shop's 22.7-ton, 36-foot-long International M6-23 "Hulk" 1969 is stationed at Scott City, MO. It can lift in excess of 325 tons on its short boom.

TRAINS & SUBWAYS

TRAINS

Fastest train   The fastest speed attained by a railed vehicle is Mach 8, by an unmanned rocket sled over the 9¹/₂-mile-long rail track at White Sands Missile Range, NM on October 5, 1982.

The fastest speed recorded on any national rail system is 320.2 mph by the French SNCF high-speed train TGV Atlantique between Courtalain and Tours on May 18, 1990. The TGV Sud-Est was brought into service on September 27, 1981. TGV Atlantique and Nord services now run at up to 186 mph. The fastest point-to-point schedule is between Paris and St. Pierre des Corps, near Tours. The 144 miles are covered in 55 minutes—an average of 157 mph. The Eurostar service from London to Paris also runs at 186 mph on the French side of the Channel.

New Series 500 trains for Japan's JR West rail system are also designed to run at 186 mph in regular service.

Fastest steam locomotive   The highest speed ever ratified for a steam locomotive was 125 mph over 1,320 feet, by the LNER 4–6–2 No. 4468 Mallard (later numbered 60022), which hauled seven coaches weighing 267.9 tons down Stoke Bank, near Essendine, England on July 3, 1938. Driver Joseph Duddington was at the controls with fireman Thomas Bray. The engine suffered some damage to the middle big-end bearing.

On July 3, 1938 the Mallard reached 125 mph, the highest speed ever ratified for a steam locomotive.

Largest steam locomotive   The largest operating steam locomotive is the 207-ton South African Railways GMA Garratt type 4-8-2+2-8-4, built between 1952 and 1954.

Most powerful steam locomotive   In terms of tractive effort, the most powerful steam locomotive was No. 700, a triple-articulated or triplex 6-cylinder 2–8–8–8–4 engine built by the Baldwin Locomotive Works in 1916 for the Virginian Railway. It had a tractive force of 166,300 pounds when working compound and 199,560 pounds when working simple.

Strongest rail carrier The 36-axle "Schnabel" has a capacity of 890 tons, measures 301 ft. 10 in. long, and was built for a U.S. railroad by Krupp, Germany in March 1981.

The heaviest load ever moved on rails is the 11,971-ton Church of the Virgin Mary (built in 1548 in the village of Most, Czech Republic), which was obstructing coal operations. In October–November 1975, it was moved 2,400 feet at 0.0013 mph over four weeks, at a cost of $17 million.

Longest train On August 26–27, 1989, a 4½-mile-long train weighing 77,720 tons (excluding locomotives) made a run on the 3-ft.-6-in.-gauge Sishen–Saldanha railroad in South Africa. Carrying the largest number of cars ever recorded, the train consisted of 660 cars each loaded to 105 tons gross, a tank car, and a caboose. It was moved by nine 50 kV electric and seven diesel-electric locomotives distributed along the train. It traveled 535 miles in 22 hr. 40 min.

Longest passenger train A train belonging to the National Belgium Railway Company measured 1,895 yards long, consisted of 70 coaches, and had a total weight of over 3,071 tons. The train was powered by one electric locomotive and took 1 hr. 11 min. 5 sec. to complete the 38-mile journey from Ghent to Ostend on April 27, 1991.

Heaviest train The heaviest train was a BHP Iron Ore train weighing 79,577 tons. The 10 locomotives and 540 ore cars ran from Newman to Port Hedland, Western Australia, a distance of 253.9 miles, on May 28, 1996.

TRACKS

Longest track The world's longest run without change of train is one of 5,777 miles on the Trans-Siberian line from Moscow to Vladivostok, Russia. There are 70 stops on the fastest regular journey, which is scheduled to take 6 days 12 hr. 45 min.

Longest straight track The Commonwealth Railways Trans-Australian line over the Nullarbor Plain, from Mile 496 between Nurina and Loongana, Western Australia to Mile 793 between Ooldea and Watson, South Australia, is 297 miles dead straight, although it is not level.

Widest and narrowest gauge The widest in standard use is 5 ft. 6 in. This width is used in Spain, Portugal, India, Pakistan, Bangladesh, Sri Lanka, Argentina and Chile. The narrowest gauge on which public services are operated is 10¼ inches on the Wells Harbor (0.7 miles) and Wells–Walsingham Railways (four miles) in Norfolk, England.

Highest line At 15,806 feet above sea level, the standard gauge (4 ft. 8½ in.) track on the Morococha branch of the Peruvian State Railways at La Cima is the highest in the world.

Lowest line The Seikan Tunnel, which crosses the Tsugaro Strait between Honshu and Hokkaido, Japan, reaches a depth of 786 feet below sea level. The tunnel was opened on March 13, 1988 and is 33.46 miles long.

Steepest railway   The Katoomba Scenic Railway in the Blue Mountains of New South Wales, Australia is 1,020 feet long, with a gradient of 1 in 0.82. A 220-hp electric winding machine hauls the car by twin steel cables of $7/8$-inch diameter. The ride takes 1 min. 40 sec., and the railway carries about 420,000 passengers a year.

Greatest length of railroad   As of August 1997, the United States had 170,433 miles of road (route miles) operated for all classes of track. There were 125,072 miles of class I track (freight only) and 45,361 miles of non-class I track operated. There was a total of 180,419 miles of track owned by class I railroads, including sidings and yards.

Steepest gradient   The world's steepest gradient worked by adhesion is 1 in 11, between Chedde and Servoz on the meter-gauge SNCF Chamonix line, France.

Busiest system   The railroad that carries the largest number of passengers is the East Japan Railway Co. In 1995–96, a total of 6.067 million journeys were made.

Spike driving   In the World Championship Professional Spike Driving Competition, held at the Golden Spike National Historic Site in Utah, Dale C. Jones, 49, of Lehi, UT, drove six 7-inch railroad spikes in a time of 26.4 seconds on August 11, 1984. He incurred no penalty points under the official rules.

TRAIN TRAVEL

Most countries in 24 hours   The greatest number of countries traveled through entirely by train in 24 hours is 11, by Alison Bailey, Ian Bailey, John English and David Kellie, May 1–2, 1993. Their journey started in Hungary and continued through Slovakia, the Czech Republic, Austria, Germany, back into Austria, Liechtenstein, Switzerland, France, Luxembourg, Belgium and the Netherlands, where they arrived 22 hr. 10 min. after setting off.

Most miles traveled   Mona Tippins of Booneville, AR traveled 79,841 unduplicated rail miles in 33 countries in North America and Europe between October 7, 1994 and February 11, 1997.

H. Frank Martin of Muscatine, IA traveled 22,857 unduplicated miles within the United States on Amtrak, May 13–June 13, 1994.

Most miles in one week   Andrew Kingsmell and Sean Andrews of Bromley, England and Graham Bardouleau of Crawley, England traveled 13,105 miles on the French National Railway System in 6 days 22 hr. 38 min., November 28–December 5, 1992.

Fastest handpumped railcars   A speed of 20.58 mph for a 984-foot course was achieved by a 5-man team (one pusher, four pumpers) at Rolvenden, England, August 21, 1989, recording a time of 32.61 seconds.

STATIONS

Largest railway terminal Grand Central Terminal, Park Avenue and 42nd Street, New York City, was built 1903–13. It covers 48 acres on two levels, with 41 tracks on the upper level and 26 on the lower. On average, there are more than 550 trains and 210,000 commuters daily, in addition to the 500,000 people who walk through the terminal daily to visit the shops and restaurants or greet travelers boarding or getting off trains.

The Greater Moscow Metro is the world's busiest subway system.

Oldest station Liverpool Road Station, Manchester, England is the world's oldest station. It was first used on September 15, 1830 and was finally closed on September 30, 1975. Part of the original station is now a museum.

Highest station Condor Station in Bolivia is situated at 15,705 feet on the meter-gauge Rio Mulato-to-Potosi line.

Largest waiting rooms The four waiting rooms in Beijing Station, Chang'an Boulevard, Beijing, China, which were opened in September 1959, have a total standing capacity of 14,000.

Longest railroad platform The Kharagpur platform in West Bengal, India measures 2,733 feet long.

Largest freight yard Bailey Yard in North Platte, NE covers 2,850 acres and has 260 miles of track. It handles an average of 108 trains and some 8,500 freight cars every day.

SUBWAY SYSTEMS

Most extensive subway system   The most extensive underground or rapid transit railway system in the world is the London Underground, England, with 253 miles of route, of which 95 miles is bored tunnel and 20 miles is "cut and cover." The system is operated by a staff of 16,865; there are 267 stations, and 3,985 cars form a fleet of 547 trains. Passengers made 784 million journeys in 1995–96.

Most stations   The subway with the most stations is the Metropolitan Transportation Authority/New York City Transportation Authority subway. There are 469 stations in a network that covers 230 route miles. It serves an estimated 7.2 million passengers per day.

Busiest subway system   Greater Moscow Metro (opened 1935) in Russia had as many as 3.3 billion passenger journeys per year at its peak, but the figure has now declined to 3.2 billion. It has 4,143 railcars, 158 stations and 158.9 miles of track.

Longest subway platform   The State Street Center subway platform on "The Loop" in Chicago, IL measures 3,500 feet long.

Shortest system   Opened in 1875, the Istanbul Metro, Istanbul, Turkey is just 2,133 feet long.

Worst subway disaster   The worst subway accident in the United States occurred on November 1, 1918, in Brooklyn, NY, when a BRT Line train derailed on a curve on Malbone St. in the Brighton Beach section. There were 97 fatalities on the scene, and five more people died later from injuries sustained in the crash. The BRT line went bankrupt on December 31, 1918 as a result of the tragedy.

BRIDGES & TUNNELS

BRIDGES

Oldest bridge   The oldest datable bridge still in use is the slab stone single-arch bridge over the River Meles in Izmir, Turkey, which dates from *c.* 850 B.C.

Busiest bridge   The San Francisco–Oakland Bay Bridge was used by an average of 274,000 vehicles a day in 1996, making 100 million vehicles a year.

Fastest bridge building   A team of British soldiers from 21 Engineer Regiment, based in Nienburg, Germany, constructed a bridge across a 26-ft.-3-in. gap using a 5-bay single-story MGB (medium-girder bridge) in 8 min. 44 sec. in Hameln, Germany on November 3, 1995.

Bridge sale   The largest antique ever sold was London Bridge, in England in March 1968. Ivan F. Luckin of the Court of Common Council of the

Corporation of London sold it to the McCulloch Oil Corporation of Los Angeles, CA for £1,029,000 ($2,469,600). The 11,800 tons of stonework were reassembled in Lake Havasu City, AZ and rededicated in October 1971.

Longest bridge The Second Lake Pontchartrain Causeway, which joins Mandeville and Metairie, LA, is 126,055 feet (23.87 miles) long.

Longest bridge over sea The Confederation Bridge, which joins Prince Edward Island to New Brunswick, Canada, is 8 miles 90 ft. long including approaches.

The Confederation Bridge is over eight miles long. It was made curved to hold the attention of drivers.

Longest cable suspension bridge The 6,532-foot main span of the Akashi-Kaikyo bridge, joining the Japanese island of Awaji to the island of Honshu, was completed in 1997. It will be open to traffic in 1998.

The longest cable-stayed bridge is the Pont de Normandie in Le Havre, France.

Cable-stayed   The Pont de Normandie in Le Havre, France has a cable-stayed main span of 2,808 feet.

The Mackinac Straits Bridge between Mackinaw City and St. Ignace, MI is the longest suspension bridge between anchorages (1.58 miles), and has an overall length, including approaches, of five miles.

Suspension bridge walking   Donald H. Betty of Lancaster, PA has walked over 98 different suspension bridges, including 17 of the 20 longest suspension bridges in the world.

Longest cantilever bridge   The Quebec Bridge over the St. Lawrence River in Canada is 1,800 feet between the piers and 3,239 feet overall.

Longest covered bridge   The covered bridge in Hartland, New Brunswick, Canada measures 1,282 feet overall.

Longest drawbridge   The Erasmus Bridge in Rotterdam, Netherlands was opened in September 1996. One of its components is the world's longest bascule (drawbridge), which is 269 feet long.

Longest floating bridge   The Second Lake Washington Bridge, Seattle, WA has a total length of 12,596 feet and a floating section that measures 7,518 feet.

Longest rail and road bridge   The 40,374-foot-long Seto-Ōhashi double-deck road and rail bridge links Kojima, Honshu with Sakaide, Shikoku, Japan.

The Tsing Ma Bridge, Hong Kong, China was opened in April 1997. The road and rail suspension bridge has the world's longest single span of 974 ft. 5 in.

Fireworks and laser beams light up the night sky at the opening of the Tsing Ma Bridge in Hong Kong on April 27, 1997.

Longest concrete arch bridge   The east span of Krk-I Bridge, linking Krk Island to the mainland of Croatia, is 1,279 feet long. It opened to traffic in 1980.

Longest concrete girder bridge   The 978-foot span of the Raftsundet Bridge, linking the main islands in the Lofoten group in Norway, was completed in 1997.

Longest steel arch bridge   The New River Gorge Bridge, near Fayetteville, WV, has a span of 1,700 feet.

Longest stone arch bridge   The 3,810-foot-long Rockville Bridge, north of Harrisburg, PA, has 48 spans containing 216,050 tons of stone.

The longest stone arch span is the Wuchaohe Bridge in Fenghuang, Hunan Province, China, at 394 feet.

Widest long-span bridge   The 1,650-foot Sydney Harbor Bridge, Sydney, Australia is 160 feet wide. It carries two railroad tracks, eight road lanes, and bicycle and pedestrian lanes.

Highest road bridge   The suspension bridge in the Royal Gorge in Colorado is 1,053 feet above the Arkansas River and has a main span of 880 feet.

Highest railroad bridge   The Mala Reka viaduct of Yugoslav Railways at Kolasin on the Belgrade–Bar line is 650 feet high.

Tallest bridge towers   The towers of the Akashi-Kaikyo Bridge (*see* LONGEST CABLE SUSPENSION BRIDGE on page 97) are 974 ft. 5 in. tall.

Longest bicycle/pedestrian bridge   The Old Chain of Rocks Bridge, Madison, IL is 5,350 feet long.

Longest railway viaduct   The rock-filled Great Salt Lake Railroad Trestle, carrying the Southern Pacific Railroad 11.85 miles across the Great Salt Lake, UT, was opened as a pile and trestle bridge in 1904, but converted to rock fill in 1955–60.

Longest ancient aqueduct   The aqueduct of Carthage in Tunisia ran 87.6 miles from the springs of Zaghouan to Djebel Djougar. It was built by the Romans during the reign of Publius Aelius Hadrianus (A.D. 117–138), also known as Hadrian. In 1895, 344 arches still survived. Its original capacity was 7 million gallons per day.

Longest modern aqueduct   The California State Water Project aqueduct, completed in 1974, has a total length of 826 miles, of which 385 miles is canalized.

TUNNELS

Longest tunnel   The longest tunnel of any kind is the New York City West Delaware water-supply tunnel, begun in 1937 and completed in 1944. It has a diameter of 13½ feet and runs for 105 miles from the Rondout Reservoir into the Hillview Reservoir in Yonkers, NY.

Longest rail tunnel The 33.46-mile-long Seikan Rail Tunnel was bored to 787 feet beneath sea level and 328 feet below the seabed of the Tsugaru Strait between Tappi Saki, Honshu, and Fukushima, Hokkaido, Japan.

Undersea The Channel Tunnel runs under the English Channel between Folkestone, England and Calais, France. The length of each twin rail tunnel is 31.03 miles and the diameter 24 ft. 11 in. The undersea section is 9.1 miles longer than the undersea section of the Seikan Rail Tunnel (*see above*), although the overall length of the Channel Tunnel is less.

Longest subway tunnel The Moscow Metro Kaluzhskaya underground railroad line from Medvedkovo to Bittsevsky Park is 23½ miles long.

Longest road tunnel The 10.14-mile-long 2-lane St. Gotthard road tunnel from Göschenen to Airolo, Switzerland opened to traffic on September 5, 1980.

Largest road tunnel The largest-diameter road tunnel in the world is the one blasted through Yerba Buena Island, San Francisco, CA. It is 77 ft. 10 in. wide, 56 feet high and 540 feet long. More than 250,000 vehicles pass through on its two decks every day.

Deepest road tunnel The Hitra Tunnel in Norway, which links the mainland to the island of Hitra, reaches a depth of 866 feet below sea level. It is 3½ miles long and has three lanes.

Longest irrigation tunnel The 51½-mile-long Orange–Fish Rivers tunnel, South Africa, was bored between 1967 and 1973. The lining to a minimum thickness of nine inches gave a completed diameter of 17 ft. 6 in.

Largest sewerage tunnel The Chicago Water Reclamation District Tunnel and Reservoir Project (TARP) in Illinois, also known as the "Deep Tunnel," will have 131 miles of sewerage tunneling when it is complete. As of January 1996, 75.4 miles were in operation and 18 miles were under construction. The estimated cost of the total project, including the three 41-billion-gallon total capacity reservoirs, is $3.7 billion.

Longest bridge-tunnel The Chesapeake Bay bridge-tunnel extends 17.65 miles from the Eastern Shore region of the Virginia Peninsula to Virginia Beach, VA. It was opened to traffic on April 15, 1964. The longest bridged section is Trestle C (4.56 miles long) and the longest tunnel section is the Thimble Shoal Channel Tunnel (1.09 miles).

Longest and largest canal tunnel The Rove Tunnel on the Canal de Marseille au Rhône in the south of France was completed in 1927 and is 23,359 feet long, 72 feet wide and 37 feet high. Built to be navigated by seagoing ships, it was closed in 1963 following a collapse and has not been reopened.

Oldest navigable tunnel The Malpas tunnel on the Canal du Midi in southwest France was completed in 1681 and is 528 feet long. Its completion enabled vessels to navigate from the Atlantic Ocean to the Mediterranean Sea via the river Garonne to Toulouse and via the Canal du Midi to Sète.

Longest unsupported tunnel The longest unsupported machine-bored tunnel is the Three Rivers water tunnel, 5.82 miles long with a 10-ft.-6-in. diameter, constructed for the city of Atlanta, GA from April 1980 to February 1982.

AIRCRAFT

Largest wingspan The Hughes H4 Hercules flying boat (*Spruce Goose*) had a wingspan of 319 ft. 11 in. and measured 218 ft. 8 in. long. The 8-engined 213-ton aircraft was raised 70 feet into the air in a test run of 3,000 feet, piloted by Howard Hughes, off Long Beach Harbor, CA, on November 2, 1947, but after this it never flew again.

Among current aircraft, the Ukrainian Antonov An-124 has a span of 240 ft. 5³/₄ in. The U.S.A.F. C-5B cargo plane has a wingspan of 222 ft. 8¹/₂ in., which is the greatest for any United States military aircraft.

Heaviest aircraft The Ukrainian Antonov An-225 *Mriya* has the highest standard maximum takeoff weight, at 661 tons (1,322,750 pounds). This aircraft lifted a payload of 344,582 pounds to a height of 40,715 feet on March 22, 1989, piloted by Capt. Aleksandr Galunenko and a crew of seven.

Most capacious aircraft The Airbus Super Transporter A300-600ST *Beluga* has a main cargo compartment volume of 49,441 square feet and a maximum takeoff weight of 165 tons. Its overall length is 184 ft. 3 in. and the usable length of its cargo compartment is 123 ft. 8 in.

Heaviest commercial cargo Ukrainian aircraft designer Antonov and British charter company Air Foyle carried out the heaviest commercial air cargo movement, by taking three transformers weighing 47.4 tons each and other equipment from Barcelona, Spain to Nouméa, New Caledonia (Pacific), January 10–14, 1991. The total weight carried in the An-124 *Ruslan* was 154.3 tons.

Air Foyle and Antonov also set the record for carrying the heaviest single piece of cargo, by flying a 136.7-ton power plant generator from Düsseldorf, Germany to New Delhi, India on September 22, 1993. Again, the aircraft used was the Ukrainian An-124 *Ruslan*. Because of the huge weight, the plane had to make six refueling stops during the 5,600-mile flight.

Largest single items airlifted Beginning in February 1997, a Russian-built Antonov-124 transporter plane carried a series of RAF Nimrod fuselages one at a time from the coast of Scotland to Bournemouth, England for refurbishment. The Nimrods had their wings and tails cut off so that the 110-foot fuselages would fit into the Antonov's hold. It was more economical to transport them in this way than to rehabilitate the Nimrods to fly under their own power to Bournemouth.

Smallest aircraft The smallest biplane ever flown was the *Bumble Bee Two*, designed and built by Robert H. Starr of Arizona. It was 8 ft. 10 in. long, with a wingspan of 5 ft. 6 in., and weighed 396 pounds empty. The fastest speed it attained was 190 mph. On May 8, 1988, after flying to a height of approximately 400 feet, it crashed and was destroyed.

Fastest time to refuel The Sky Harbor Air Service line crew refueled a 1975 Cessna 310 (N29HH) with 102.7 gallons of 100 octane avgas in 3 min. 42 sec. on July 5, 1992. The plane had landed at Cheyenne (WY) Airport during an around-the-world race.

The Airbus Super Transporter A300-600ST *Beluga* is the world's most capacious aircraft.

Largest aircraft manufacturer   The world's largest aerospace company is Boeing of Seattle, WA, with 1996 sales of $22.7 billion and a workforce of 143,000 people worldwide. As of 1996, Cessna Aircraft Company of Wichita, KS has manufactured the most aircraft, with 178,637 since 1911.

BOMBERS

Heaviest bomber   The former Soviet 4-jet Tupolev Tu-160 has a maximum takeoff weight of over 600,270 pounds.

Longest bomber   The Boeing B-52G is the longest bomber in the U.S.A.F. at 160 ft. 11 in. with a wingspan of 185 feet. The B-52H has the greatest thrust of a bomber in the U.S. fleet, at 136,000 pounds, and the greatest unrefueled range of over 8,800 miles.

AIRLINERS

Oldest jet airliner   According to the British-based aviation information and consultancy service company Airclaims, the oldest jet airliner still flying is a Boeing 707-138 currently in operation with the Royal Saudi Arabian Air Force. It was completed on February 11, 1959 and delivered to Qantas; Saudi Arabia acquired the airliner in 1987.

Largest jet airliner   The highest capacity jet airliner is the Boeing 747-400, which entered service with Northwest Airlines on January 31, 1989. It has a wingspan of 213 feet, a range of 8,290 miles and can carry 566 passengers. The original Boeing 747-100 "Jumbo Jet" has a capacity of 385–560 and cruises at a speed of 640 mph. Its wingspan is 195 ft. 8 in. and its length 231 ft. 10 in. The plane entered service in January 1970.

Greatest passenger load   The greatest passenger load carried by any single commercial airliner was 1,088 during Operation Solomon, which began on May 24, 1991 when Ethiopian Jews were evacuated from Addis Ababa to Israel on a Boeing 747 belonging to El Al. This figure includes two babies born during the flight.

Most flights—propeller-driven airliner   General Dynamics (formerly Convair) reported in March 1994 that some of its CV-580 turboprop airliners had logged over 150,000 flights, typically averaging no more than 20 minutes, in short-haul operations.

Most flights by a jet airliner   A McDonnell Douglas DC-9 Series 14 had made 100,746 flights by February 1, 1996. It was originally delivered to Delta Airlines in September 1966 and is currently in service with Northwest Airlines.

The most hours recorded by a jet airliner still in service is 99,825 hours reported for a Boeing 747-200F on March 1, 1996. The aircraft was delivered to Lufthansa in March 1972 and is now in service with Korean Air.

HELICOPTERS

Fastest helicopter   Under FAI rules, the world's speed record for helicopters was set by John Trevor Eggington with co-pilot Derek J. Clews, who averaged 249.09 mph over Somerset, England on August 11, 1986 in a Westland Lynx company demonstrator helicopter.

Largest helicopter The former Soviet Mil Mi-12 was powered by four 6,500-hp turboshaft engines and had a span of 219 ft. 10 in. over its rotor tips, with a length of 121 ft. 4½ in. It weighed 114 tons. The aircraft was demonstrated at the Paris Air Show but never entered formal service.

The largest rotorcraft was the Piasecki Heli-Stat, which used four Sikorsky S-58 airframes attached to a Goodyear ZPG-2 airship. Powered by four 1,525-hp piston engines, it was 343 feet long, 111 feet high and 149 feet wide.

Smallest helicopter The single-seat Seremet WS-8 ultralight helicopter was built in Denmark in 1976. It had a a rotor diameter of 14 ft. 9 in. and an empty weight of 117 pounds.

Highest helicopter altitude Jean Boulet flew an Aérospatiale SA315B Lama at 40,820 feet over Istres, France on June 21, 1972.

Longest hover Doug Daigle, Brian Watts and Dave Meyer of Tridair Helicopters, together with Rod Anderson of Helistream, Inc. of California, maintained a continuous hovering flight in a 1947 Bell 47B model for 50 hr. 50 sec. from December 13 to December 15, 1989.

Greatest load lifted On February 3, 1982 at Podmoscovnoe in the USSR, a Mil Mi-26 heavy-lift helicopter, crewed by G. V. Alfeurov and L.A. Indeyev, lifted a mass of 62.58 tons to a height of 6,560 feet.

Longest helicopter flight Under FAI rules, the record for the longest unrefueled nonstop flight was set by Robert Ferry, flying a Hughes YOH-6A, over a distance of 2,213.1 miles from Culver City, CA to Ormond Beach, FL in April 1966.

Fastest helicopter circumnavigation Ron Bower and John Williams (both U.S.) flew around the world in a Bell helicopter in a record time of 17 days 6 hr. 14 min. 25 sec. They left Fair Oaks, London, England on August 17, 1996 and flew west, arriving back at Fair Oaks on September 3.

AIRSHIPS

Largest airship The 235-ton German *Hindenburg* (LZ 129) and its sister ship *Graf Zeppelin II* (LZ 130) each had a length of 803 ft. 10 in. and a capacity of 7,062,100 cubic feet. The *Hindenburg* first flew in 1936 and the *Graf Zeppelin II* in 1938.

Nonrigid The largest nonrigid airship ever constructed was the U.S. Navy ZPG 3-W, which had a capacity of 1.5 million cubic feet, a length of 403 feet and a diameter of 85.1 feet. It first flew in 1958 but crashed into the sea in 1960.

Longest flight The longest recorded flight by an airship (without refueling) is 264 hr. 12 min. by a U.S. Navy Goodyear-built ZPG-2 class ship (Cdr. J.R. Hunt, U.S.N.) that flew 9,448 miles, leaving from South Weymouth Naval Air Station, MA on March 4, 1957 and landing in Key West, FL, on March 15.

The FAI-accredited straight-line distance record for airships is 3,967.1 miles, set by the German *Graf Zeppelin* LZ 127, captained by Dr. Hugo Eckener, October 29–November 1, 1928.

From November 21 to November 25, 1917, the German *Zeppelin* (L 59) flew from Yambol, Bulgaria to a point south of Khartoum, Sudan and returned, covering a minimum of 4,500 miles.

Greatest passenger load The most people carried in an airship was 207, in the U.S. Navy Akron in 1931. The transatlantic record is 117, carried by the German *Hindenburg* in 1937.

AIRLINES & AIRPORTS

AIRLINES

Oldest airline Koninklijke-Luchtvaart-Maatschappij NV (KLM), the national airline of the Netherlands, was established on October 7, 1919. It opened its first scheduled service (Amsterdam–London, England) on May 17, 1920.

Chalk's International Airline has been flying amphibious planes from Miami, FL to the Bahamas since July 1919. The founder, Albert "Pappy" Chalk, flew from 1911 to 1975.

Largest airline The Russian state airline Aeroflot was instituted on February 9, 1923. In its last complete year of formal existence (1990) it employed 600,000 people (more than the top 18 U.S. airlines put together) and flew 139 million passengers, with 20,000 pilots, along 620,000 miles of domestic routes.

Since the breakup of the Soviet Union, the company that carries the greatest number of passengers is Delta Air Lines, with 93,244,865 in 1996.

Busiest airline system The country with the busiest airline system is the United States, where the total number of passengers for air carriers in scheduled domestic operations exceeded 558.2 million in 1996.

Busiest international route The city-pair with the highest international scheduled passenger traffic is London/Paris. More than 3.3 million passengers fly between the two cities annually. The busiest intercontinental route is London/New York, with more than 2.3 million passengers flying between the two cities annually.

AIRPORTS

Largest airport The King Khalid International Airport, Riyadh, Saudi Arabia covers 87 square miles (55,040 acres).

Terminal   The terminal at Hartsfield International Airport, Atlanta, GA has floor space covering 5.7 million square feet (approximately 131 acres) and 182 gates. In 1996, the terminal serviced 63,303,171 passengers, although it has a capacity for 70 million.

The Hajj Terminal at the King Abdul-Aziz Airport near Jeddah, Saudi Arabia is the world's largest roofed structure, covering 370 acres.

The $3.5 billion King Khalid International Airport outside Riyadh, Saudi Arabia is the world's largest airport.

Busiest airport   O'Hare International Airport, Chicago, IL had 69,153,528 passengers and 909,593 aircraft movements in 1996.

BAA Heathrow, London, England handles more international traffic than any other airport, with an estimated 55 million international passengers per year.

Bien Hoa Air Base, South Vietnam, handled 1,019,437 takeoffs and landings in 1970.

Largest heliport   The heliport at Morgan City, LA, owned and operated by Petroleum Helicopter Inc., is one of a string used by helicopters flying energy-related offshore operations into the Gulf of Mexico. The heliport is spread over 52 acres and has pads for 48 helicopters.

The world's largest helipad was at An Khe, South Vietnam, during the Vietnam war. It covered an area of 1¼ by 1¾ miles and could accommodate 434 helicopters.

Highest landing field   The highest is La Sa (Lhasa) Airport, Tibet, People's Republic of China, at 14,315 feet.

Highest heliport   The heliport at Sonam, on the Siachen Glacier in Kashmir, is at an altitude of 19,500 feet.

Lowest landing field   The lowest landing field is El Lisan on the east shore of the Dead Sea, 1,180 feet below sea level, but during World War II

Hanger 375 at Kelly Air Force Base in San Antonio, TX is the world's largest freestanding hangar.

The tower at Denver International Airport gives air traffic controllers a 3-mile line of sight.

BOAC Short C-class flying boats operated from the surface of the Dead Sea at 1,292 feet below sea level.

The lowest international airport is Schiphol, Amsterdam, Netherlands, at 15 feet below sea level.

Longest runway The runway at Edwards Air Force Base, Muroc, CA measures 37,676 feet (7.13 miles) long. Civil The runway at Pierre van Ryneveld Airport, Upington, South Africa is 3.04 miles long. It was constructed in five months from August 1975 to January 1976.

Largest hangar Hangar 375 ("Big Texas") at Kelly Air Force Base, San Antonio, TX has four doors each 250 feet wide, 60 feet high, and weighing 681 tons. The high bay is 2,000 by 300 by 90 feet in area and is surrounded by a 44-acre concrete apron. It is the largest freestanding hangar in the world.

Tallest control tower The tower at Denver International Airport, Denver, CO is 327 feet tall, giving air traffic controllers a 3-mile view.

Largest baggage handling unit Denver International Airport, Denver, CO has the world's largest airport conveyor system. There are 22 miles of track and six miles of conveyor belts. The system is controlled through 14 million feet of wiring.

SCHEDULED FLIGHTS

Longest scheduled flight The longest nonstop scheduled flight currently operating is the 7,968-mile flight from New York to Johannesburg on South African Airways. In terms of time taken, the longest is 15 hr. 55 min. for the flight from Chicago to Hong Kong on United Airlines.

Shortest scheduled flight Using Britten-Norman Islander twin-engined 10-seat transports, Loganair has been flying between the Orkney Islands of Westray and Papa Westray, Great Britain since September 1967. The check-in time for the 2-minute flight is 20 minutes.

Fastest circumnavigation The fastest circumnavigation on scheduled flights was made in 44 hr. 6 min., by David J. Springbett of Taplow, England, January 8–10, 1980. His route took him from Los Angeles, CA eastwards via London, Bahrain, Singapore, Bangkok, Manila, Tokyo and Honolulu, over a 23,069-mile course. A minimum distance of 22,858.8 miles (the length of the Tropic of Cancer or Capricorn) must be flown.

Antipodal points David Sole of Edinburgh, Scotland traveled around the world on scheduled flights, taking in exact antipodal points, in 64 hr. 2 min., May 2–5, 1995. Leaving from London Heathrow, he flew to Madrid, Spain, back to Heathrow, and then to Napier, New Zealand via Singapore and Auckland. From Napier he went by helicopter to Ti Tree Point, the point exactly opposite Madrid Airport on the other side of the world. Returning to London via Los Angeles, Sole traveled a total distance of 25,917 miles.

Brother Michael Bartlett of Sandy, England achieved a record time for flying around the world on scheduled flights, but just taking in the airports closest to antipodal points, when he flew via Shanghai, China and Buenos Aires, Argentina in a time of 58 hr. 44 min. He started and finished at Zürich, Switzerland and traveled a distance of 25,816 miles, February 13–16, 1995.

Most flights in 24 hours   Brother Michael Bartlett made 42 scheduled passenger flights with Heli Transport of Nice, France between Nice, Sophia Antipolis, Monaco and Cannes in 13 hr. 33 min. on June 13, 1990.

FLYING

SPEED RECORDS

Official airspeed record   Capt. Eldon W. Joersz and Major George T. Morgan, Jr. flew at 2,193.2 mph in a Lockheed SR-71A "Blackbird" near Beale Air Force Base, CA over a 15$^{1}/_{2}$-mile course on July 28, 1976.

Fastest fixed-wing aircraft   The U.S. North American Aviation X-15A-2, powered by a liquid oxygen and ammonia rocket-propulsion system, flew for the first time (after modification from the X-15A) on June 25, 1964. The landing speed was 242 mph. The fastest speed attained was Mach 6.7, by Major William J. Knight (U.S.A.F.) on October 3, 1967.

The space shuttle *Columbia*, commanded by Capt. John W. Young (U.S.N.) and piloted by Capt. Robert L. Crippen (U.S.N.), was launched from the Kennedy Space Center, Cape Canaveral, FL on April 12, 1981. *Columbia* broke all records in space by fixed-wing craft, with 16,600 mph at main engine cutoff. After reentry from 75.8 miles, experiencing temperatures of 3,920°F, it glided home weighing 107 tons, and with a landing speed of 216 mph, on Rogers Dry Lake, CA on April 14, 1981.

Fastest jet   The U.S.A.F. Lockheed SR-71, a reconnaissance aircraft, was first flown in its definitive form on December 22, 1964. It has an altitude ceiling of 85,000 feet, and its reported range at Mach 3 is 2,982 miles at 78,750 feet.

Fastest bomber   The world's fastest operational bombers include the French Dassault Mirage IV, which can fly at Mach 2.2 at 36,000 feet.

The American variable-geometry or "swing-wing" General Dynamics FB-111A has a maximum speed of Mach 2.5, and the Soviet swing-wing Tupolev Tu-22M has an estimated over-target speed of Mach 2.0 but could be as fast as Mach 2.5.

Fastest airliner   The Tupolev Tu-144, first flown on December 31, 1968, was reported to have reached Mach 2.4, but normal cruising speed was Mach 2.2. Scheduled services began on December 26, 1975, flying freight and mail.

The supersonic BAC/Aérospatiale Concorde, first flown on March 2, 1969, cruises at up to Mach 2.2 and became the first supersonic airliner used in passenger service on January 21, 1976. The New York–London, England record is 2 hr. 54 min. 30 sec., set on April 14, 1990.

Fastest biplane   The fastest is the Italian Fiat CR42B, with a 1,010-hp Daimler-Benz DB601A engine, which attained 323 mph in 1941. Only one was built.

The U.S.A.F. Lockheed SR-71, the fastest jet aircraft in the world, is refueled in flight by a KC-135 tanker.

Fastest piston-engined aircraft   On August 21, 1989, in Las Vegas, NV, *Rare Bear*, a modified Grumman Bearcat F8F piloted by Lyle Shelton, set the FAI-approved world record for a 3-km run of 528.3 mph.

Fastest propeller-driven aircraft   The fastest propeller-driven aircraft in use is the former Soviet Tu-95/142 "Bear" with four 14,795-hp engines driving 8-blade counter-rotating propellers with a maximum level speed of Mach 0.82.

Fastest coast-to-coast flight   The record aircraft time from coast to coast is 67 min. 54 sec. by Lt. Col. Ed Yeilding, pilot, and Lt. Col. J. T. Vida, reconnaissance systems officer, aboard the SR-71 Blackbird spy plane on March 6, 1990. The Blackbird refueled over the Pacific Ocean at 27,000 feet before starting a climb to 83,000 feet, heading east from the west coast near Los Angeles and crossing the east coast near Washington, D.C.

Fastest transatlantic flight   Major James V. Sullivan (U.S.) and Major Noel F. Widdifield (U.S.) flew eastward across the Atlantic in 1 hr. 54 min. 56.4 sec. in a Lockheed SR-71A Blackbird on September 1, 1974. The average speed, slowed by refueling from a KC-135 tanker aircraft, for the New York–London stage of 3,461.53 miles was 1,806.96 mph.

Solo   On March 12, 1978, Capt. John J. A. Smith flew from Gander, Newfoundland, Canada to Gatwick, London, England in 8 hr. 47 min. 32 sec., in a Rockwell Commander 685 twin-turboprop. He achieved an average speed of 265.1 mph.

Fastest London–New York flight   The record time from central London, England to downtown New York City by helicopter and Concorde is 3 hr. 59 min. 44 sec., and for the return, 3 hr. 40 min. 40 sec., both by David J. Springbett and David Boyce, February 8–9, 1982.

Fastest circumnavigational flight   The fastest flight under the FAI rules, which permit flights that exceed the length of the Tropic of Cancer or Capricorn (22,858.8 miles), was one of 31 hr. 27 min. 49 sec. by an Air France Concorde (Capt. Michel Dupont and Capt. Claude Hetru) flying east from JFK airport in New York via Toulouse, Dubai, Bangkok, Guam, Honolulu and Acapulco on August 15–16, 1995. There were 80 passengers and 18 crew on board flight AF1995.

Fastest 7-continents flight   The National Aeronautic Association's record for the fastest time to visit all seven continents is held by Bill Signs and Ruth Jacobs (both U.S.). They left Love Field, Dallas, TX on December 30, 1995 in a Cessna 210-L. During the course of their trip, they landed in many different places, including Manaus, Brazil; Base Marambio, Antarctica; Luxor, Egypt; Malaga, Spain; Chiang Mai, Thailand; and Brisbane, Australia. They returned to Dallas on February 18, 1996, having covered 39,543 miles in 50 days 1 hr. 16 min. 24 sec.

Fastest climb   Heinz Frick of British Aerospace took a Harrier GR5 powered by a Rolls-Royce Pegasus 11-61 engine from a standing start to 39,370 feet in 2 min. 6.63 sec. above the Rolls-Royce flight test center, Filton, England on August 15, 1989.

Aleksandr Fedotov (USSR) flew a Mikoyan E 266M (MiG-25) aircraft to establish the fastest time-to-height record on May 17, 1975. He reached 114,830 feet in 4 min. 11.7 sec. after takeoff from Podmoscovnoe, Russia.

DURATION RECORDS

Longest nonservice flight   The longest flight on record is 64 days 22 hr. 19 min. 5 sec., by Robert Timm and John Cook in the Cessna 172 Hacienda. They took off from McCarran Airfield, Las Vegas, NV just before 3:53 P.M.

local time on December 4, 1958 and landed at the same airfield just before 2:12 P.M. on February 7, 1959. They covered a distance equivalent to six times around the world, being refueled without any landings.

The longest nonstop flight by a commercial airliner was one of 10,008 nautical miles (11,523 miles) from Auckland, New Zealand to Le Bourget, Paris, France in 21 hr. 46 min., June 17–18, 1993 by the Airbus Industrie A340–200. It was the return leg of a flight that had started at Le Bourget the previous day.

PERSONAL AVIATION RECORDS

Oldest and youngest passengers Airborne births are reported every year. The oldest person to fly is Charlotte Hughes (Great Britain). She was given a flight on Concorde from London to New York as a 110th birthday present on August 4, 1987 and flew again when she was 115 in February 1992.

Oldest pilot Col. Clarence Cornish (b. November 10, 1898) of Indianapolis, IN flew a Cessna 172 on December 4, 1995, when he was 97 years old. His first flight was on May 6, 1918 and his first solo flight 21 days later.

Hilda Wallace (Canada) became the oldest person to qualify as a pilot when she obtained her license on March 15, 1989 at age 80 yr. 109 days.

Circumnavigation Strict circumnavigation of the globe requires the aircraft to pass through two antipodal points, covering a minimum distance of 24,859.73 miles. Fred Lasby completed a solo around-the-world flight at age 82 in his single-engined Piper Comanche. He left Fort Meyers, FL on June 30, 1994, flew 23,218 miles with 21 stops, and arrived back in Fort Meyers on August 20, 1994.

Most flying hours *Pilot* John Edward Long (U.S.) logged 62,654 hours of flight time as a pilot between May 1933 and April 1997. This adds up to more than seven years.

Evelyn Bryan Johnson, manager of Moore Murrell Airport, Morristown, TN, logged the women's record of 54,600 hours in flight as a pilot and flight instructor, 1945–95.

Passenger The record for a supersonic passenger is held by Fred Finn, who has made 709 Atlantic crossings on Concorde. He commutes regularly from New Jersey to London, England, and had flown a total distance of 11,960,000 miles by the end of May 1997.

Most planes flown Capt. Eric Brown has flown 487 different basic types of aircraft as a command pilot. A World War II fighter pilot, he became chief naval test pilot at the Royal Aircraft Establishment in Farnborough, England and is Britain's leading test pilot of carrier-based aircraft.

Most transatlantic flights Between March 1948 and his retirement on September 1, 1984, Flight Service Manager Charles M. Schimpf logged a total of 2,880 Atlantic crossings.

Longest-serving flight attendant Juanita Carmichael has been a flight attendant on American Airlines since July 10, 1944.

Most experienced passenger   Edwin A. Shackleton of Bristol, England has been a passenger in 603 different types of aircraft. His first flight was in March 1943 in a D.H. Dominie R9548; other aircraft have included helicopters, gliders, microlights, and balloons.

Plane pulling   David Huxley single-handedly pulled a Qantas Boeing 747-400 weighing 206 tons a distance of 179 ft. 6 in. across the tarmac at Sydney Airport, Australia on April 2, 1996.
    Sixty people pulled a 226-ton British Airways Boeing 747 328 feet in 61.0 seconds at Heathrow Airport, London, England, May 25, 1995.

Wing walking   Roy Castle flew on the wing of a Boeing Stearman airplane for 3 hr. 23 min. on August 2, 1990, from Gatwick, England to Le Bourget, near Paris, France.

BALLOONING

HELIUM BALLOONING

Longest balloon flight   Steve Fossett (U.S.) left St. Louis, MO on January 13, 1997 in the balloon *Free Spirit* in an attempt to fly around the world. He landed in Sultanpur, India on January 20, having traveled a record total of 10,406 miles.
    Fossett also set the FAI endurance record for a gas and hot-air balloon, at 6 days 2 hr. 50 min.

Highest balloon altitude Unmanned   The highest altitude attained by an unmanned balloon was 170,000 feet, by a Winzen balloon with a 47.8 million-cubic-foot capacity, launched at Chico, CA in October 27, 1972.

Manned   The highest altitude reached in a manned balloon is an unofficial 123,800 feet, by Nicholas Piantanida (1933–66) of Bricktown, NJ, from Sioux Falls, SD on February 1, 1966. He landed in a cornfield in Iowa but did not survive.
    The official record (closed gondola) is 113,740 feet by Cdr. Malcolm D. Ross (U.S.N.R.) and Lt. Cdr. Victor A. Prother (U.S.N.), in an ascent from the deck of the U.S.S. *Antietam* over the Gulf of Mexico on May 4, 1961 in a balloon of 12 million-cubic-foot capacity.
    Scientists Harold Froelich and Keith Lang of Minneapolis, MN made an unplanned ascent in an open gondola, without pressure suits or goggles, to an altitude of 42,126 feet on September 26, 1956.

Largest balloon   The largest balloon ever built had an inflatable volume of 70 million cubic feet and stood 1,000 feet tall. It was unmanned, and was manufactured by Winzen Research Inc. (now Winzen Engineering Inc.) of South St. Paul, Minnesota. The balloon did not get off the ground and was destroyed at launch on July 8, 1975.

RISING TO THE CHALLENGE

"There's a lot that can go wrong with the launch," reflects Steve Fossett on his attempt to circumnavigate the globe in a balloon, "so I was delighted when I climbed out of Busch Stadium. That's a big accomplishment in itself."

For Fossett, however, this was only the beginning of a record-setting journey. Though the *Solo Spirit* flight would come up short of its original goal, it would instead establish new world records for both duration and distance of flight.

Six days, two hours and 44 minutes later after taking off from St. Louis, Fossett returned to earth in Sultanpur, India, having traveled a total distance of 10,406 miles. "By the time I was in Chad, my fuel calculations revealed that I didn't have enough to make it across the Pacific. I went backwards from there and determined that India would be the best place to land."

Fossett spent the six days of his flight floating more than 24,000 feet above the earth in an unpressurized gondola that measured 6 ft. 6 in. long, 4 feet wide, and only 5 ft. 8 in. high. Temperatures ranged between 15 and 45 degrees Fahrenheit, thanks to a cabin heater that couldn't quite keep up. "The conditions are definitely tough. I have a bubble hatch that I can open so I can stand up and stretch, and I have a lot to do as far as the flight itself, but the time doesn't go by that fast. You definitely know it's six days!"

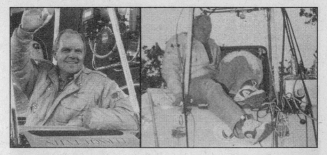

So how disappointed was he at the prospect of cutting the trip short? "Not too disappointed, really," Fossett confesses. "I did enjoy watching the changing terrain. Flying over the Sahara, for example, was spectacular. And even when I decided to set down in India, I still saw the flight as an opportunity to set a very good distance and duration record, and that became the new objective."

New objectives and challenges are always on his mind. In addition to ballooning, Fossett is an accomplished sailor, having set world records in that endeavor as well. He also completed the Ironman triathlon as part of his training for the *Solo Spirit* flight. "I've chosen to take on projects which interest me and which I consider to be major personal challenges. I'm not doing it to make a living or to be a celebrity, but for the satisfaction and sense of accomplishment."

ON THE RECORD

LONGEST BALLOON FLIGHT

Steve Fossett left St. Louis, MO on January 13, 1997 in the balloon *Solo Spirit* in an attempt to fly around the world. He landed in Sultanpur, India on January 20, having traveled a record 10,406 miles.

HOT-AIR BALLOONING

Largest hot-air balloon Richard Branson (Great Britain) and his pilot, Per Lindstrand (Great Britain), crossed the Pacific in the *Virgin Otsuka Pacific Flyer* from the southern tip of Japan to Lac la Matre, Yukon, Canada, January 15–17, 1991 in a 2.6 million-cubic-foot capacity hot-air balloon, the largest ever flown.

The greatest mass ascent of hot-air balloons was 128 balloonists, from a site in Bristol, England in 1987.

Highest hot-air balloon ascent   Per Lindstrand (Great Britain) reached 64,997 feet in a Colt 600 hot-air balloon over Laredo, TX on June 6, 1988.

Highest launch   Two balloons flew over the summit of Mt. Everest on October 21, 1991. They were *Star Flyer 1*, piloted by Chris Dehurst (Australia) with cameraman Leo Dickinson (Great Britain), and *Star Flyer 2*, piloted by Andy Elson with cameraman Eric Jones (both Great Britain). The two 240,000-cubic-foot balloons set hot-air records for the highest launch, at 15,536 feet, and the highest touchdown, at 16,200 feet.

Largest mass ascent   On August 15, 1987, 128 balloonists at the Ninth Bristol International Balloon Festival in Bristol, England made the greatest mass ascent of hot-air balloons from a single site within one hour.

Most passengers in a balloon   The balloon *Super Maine*, with a capacity of 2.6 million cubic feet, was built by Tom Handcock of Portland, ME. Tethered, the balloon rose to a height of 50 feet with 61 passengers on board on February 19, 1988.

Henk Brink (Netherlands) made an untethered flight, with 50 passengers and crew, in the 850,000-cubic-foot capacity *Nashua Number One* on August 17, 1988. The flight began at Lelystad Airport, Netherlands and lasted 25 minutes; the balloon reached an altitude of 328 feet.

Oldest hot-air balloon passenger   Florence Laine made a hot-air trip near Christchurch, New Zealand on September 26, 1996 at the age of 102 yr. 92 days.

SHIPS

SHIPS AND BOATS

Oldest vessel   A pinewood dugout found in Pesse, Netherlands was dated to *c.* 6315 B.C. ± 275 years.

Oldest boat   A 27-foot-long, 2½-foot-wide wooden canoe dated to *c.* 4490 B.C. was discovered at Tybrind Vig on the Baltic island of Fünen.

Oldest paddle wheeler   The D/S *Skibladner*, built in Minnesund, Norway by the Swedish shipyard Motala Mek. Werkstad, has continuously plied Lake Mjøsa, Norway since 1856.

Longest canoe   The "Snake Boat" *Nadubhagóm*, 135 feet long, from Kerala, India, has a crew of 109 rowers and nine "encouragers."

Heaviest wooden ship   The *Richelieu*, 333 ft. 8 in. long and weighing 9,548 tons, was launched in Toulon, France on December 3, 1873.

Longest wooden ship   The New York-built *Rochambeau* (1867–72), formerly the *Dunderberg*, measured 377 ft. 4 in. overall.

Largest human-powered ship   *Tessarakonteres*, a 3-banked catamaran galley with 4,000 rowers, built for Ptolemy IV *c.* 210 B.C. in Alexandria, Egypt, measured 420 feet, with eight men to a 57-foot oar.

Largest and most powerful tug   The *Nikolay Chiker* (SB-135) and *Fotiy Krylov* (SB-134) were commissioned in 1989 and built by Hollming Ltd. of Finland for V/O Sudoimport, in the former USSR. They have 25,000 bhp, are capable of 291 tons bollard pull at full power, and measure 325 feet long and 64 feet wide. *Fotiy Krylov* is reported to be under charter to the Tsavliris Group of Companies of Piraeus, Greece, and may for a time have been named *Tsavliris Giant*.

Most powerful icebreakers   The *Rossiya* and its sister ships *Sovetskiy Soyuz* and *Oktyabryskaya Revolutsiya* are the most powerful icebreakers in the world. The *Rossiya* weighs 28,000 tons, is 460 feet long, and is powered by 75,000 hp nuclear engines. It was built in Leningrad (now St. Petersburg), Russia and completed in 1985.

Most powerful dredger   The 468.2-foot-long *Prins der Nederlanden*, weighing 10,586 gross tons, can dredge up 22,400 tons of sand from a depth of 115 feet via two suction tubes.

Largest propeller   The largest propeller in the world has a diameter of 29 ft. 6 in. and weighs 103 tons. It was designed and manufactured by Stone Manganese Marine Ltd., Birkenhead, England for P&O containerships built at IHI Kure Shipyard in Japan.

Largest hydrofoil   The 212-foot-long *Plainview* (346 tons full-load) naval hydrofoil was launched by the Lockheed Shipbuilding and Construction Co. in Seattle, WA on June 28, 1965. It has a service speed of 57.2 mph.

Message in a bottle   A message in a bottle was released on the seabed 24 miles southwest of the island of Foula on June 12, 1914 by Capt. C. H. Brown of the Scottish Office Agriculture and Fisheries Department as part of a survey of currents. It was found on August 21, 1996 in the nets of a fishing trawler, 5 miles from the release site.

Deepest underwater escapes   The deepest underwater rescue ever achieved was of the *Pisces III*, in which Roger R. Chapman and Roger Mallinson were trapped for 76 hours when their vessel sank to 1,575 feet, 150 miles southeast of Cork, Ireland on August 29, 1973. It was hauled to the surface on September 1 by the cable ship *John Cabot* after work by *Pisces V*, *Pisces II* and the remote-control recovery vessel *Curv* (Controlled Underwater Recovery Vehicle).

The greatest depth from which an unaided escape without equipment has been made is 225 feet, by Richard A. Slater from the rammed submersible *Nekton Beta* off Catalina Island, CA on September 28, 1970.

The record for an escape with equipment was by Norman Cooke and Hamish Jones on July 22, 1987. During a naval exercise they escaped from a depth of 601 feet from the submarine HMS *Otus* off Bergen, Norway. They were wearing standard suits with a built-in life jacket.

Deepest salvage   The greatest depth at which salvage has been successfully carried out is 17,251 feet, in the case of a helicopter that crashed into the

Pacific Ocean in August 1991 with the loss of four lives. The crew of the U.S.S. *Salvor* and personnel from East Port International raised the wreckage to the surface on February 27, 1992 so that the authorities could try to determine the cause of the accident.

The deepest salvage operation ever achieved with divers was on the wreck of HM cruiser *Edinburgh*, sunk on May 2, 1942 in the Barents Sea off northern Norway, inside the Arctic Circle, in 803 feet of water. Over 32 days (September 7–October 7, 1981), 12 divers worked on the wreck in pairs, using a bell from the *Stephaniturm* (1,594 tons).

MERCHANT SHIPPING

Shipbuilding   Worldwide production completed in 1995, excluding naval auxiliaries, nonpropelled vessels, the U.S. Reserve Fleet, vessels restricted to harbor or river/canal service, and vessels of less than 100 gross registered tonnage, was 24.3 million gross registered tonnage. The figures for Russia, Ukraine, the People's Republic of China and Denmark are incomplete. Panama completed 7.9 million gross registered tonnage (32.5 percent of the world total) in 1996.

The world's leading shipbuilder in 1996 was Hyundai Heavy Industries Co. Ltd. of South Korea, which completed 42 ships of 2.68 million gross tons.

Largest ship owner   The China Ocean Shipping Group's (COSCO) fleet of owned vessels totaled 11,275,664 gross tonnage in January 1997.

Largest fleet   Panama's merchant fleet had a gross registered tonnage of 79.1 million tons at the end of 1996.

Fastest Pacific crossing   The fastest crossing from Yokohama, Japan to Long Beach, CA—4,840 nautical miles (5,567.64 miles)—took 6 days 1 hr. 27 min. (June 30 to July 6, 1973) by the containership *Sea-Land Commerce* (56,353 tons), at an average speed of 33.27 knots (38.31 mph).

Fastest shipbuilding   The fastest times in which complete ships of more than 10,000 tons were ever built were achieved at Kaiser's Yard, Portland, OR during the World War II program for building 2,742 Liberty ships. In 1942, No. 440, named *Robert E. Peary*, had its keel laid on November 8, was launched on November 12, and was operational on November 15 after 4 days 15½ hr. It was broken up in 1963.

Fastest riveting   The world record for riveting is 11,209 rivets in nine hours, by John Moir at the Workman Clark Ltd. shipyard, Belfast, Northern Ireland in June 1918. His peak hour was his seventh, with 1,409 rivets, an average of nearly 23½ per minute.

TANKERS

Largest tanker   The largest ship of any kind is *Jahre Viking*, which weighs 564,763 tons deadweight. The tanker measures 1,499 feet long overall, with a beam of 225 ft. and a draft of 80 ft. 5 in.

The world's largest ship of any kind is the oil tanker *Jabre Viking*.

Largest wreck The 354,041-ton deadweight very large crude carrier (VLCC) *Energy Determination* blew up and broke in two in the Strait of Hormuz, Persian Gulf on December 12, 1979.

Largest wreck removal In 1979, Smit Tak International removed the remains of the 120,000-ton French tanker *Betelgeuse* from Bantry Bay, Republic of Ireland. The exercise took 20 months.

Most massive collision On December 16, 1977, 22 miles off the coast of southern Africa, the tanker *Venoil* (330,954 deadweight tons) struck its sister ship *Venpet* (330,869 deadweight tons).

CARGO VESSELS

Largest cargo vessel The largest ship carrying dry cargo is the Norwegian ore carrier *Berge Stahl*, 402,082.6 tons deadweight, built in South Korea for the Norwegian owner Sig Bergesen. It has a length of 1,125 feet, a beam measuring 208 feet and was launched on November 5, 1986.

Largest containership The *Regina Maersk* was built at Odense, Denmark and completed in January 1996. Since then five sister ships have been built: *Knud Maersk*, *Katrine Maersk*, *Kate Maersk*, *Karen Maersk*, and *Kirsten Maersk*. Each vessel has a gross tonnage of 81,488 and a capacity of 6,000 TEU.

Largest barges The largest RoRo (roll-on, roll-off) vessels are four El Rey class barges, which are 580 feet long and weigh 18,400 tons. Each barge can carry 376 truck-trailers.

Largest ferry The largest car and passenger ferry is the 59,914 gross registered tonnage *Silja Europa*, which entered service in 1993 between Stockholm, Sweden and Helsinki, Finland. Operated by the Silja Line, the ferry is 662 feet long and can carry 3,000 passengers, 350 cars and 60 trucks.

Fastest ferry Built in Finland, Stena Line's HSS *Explorer* has a cruising speed of 40 knots and a top speed of 44 knots.

The ferry can carry 1,500 passengers and 375 cars. The catamaran hulls are 415 feet long and 131 feet abeam.

SUBMARINES

Largest submarines The Russian Typhoon class submarine is believed to have a dive displacement of 29,211 tons, to measure 562.7 feet overall and to be armed with 20 multiple warhead SS-NX-20 missiles with a range of 4,500 nautical miles. Six of these submarines are now in service.

United States The largest submarines in the U.S. Navy are of the Ohio class. Each of the 17 ships in active service has a displacement of 18,700 tons and a length of 560 feet.

Smallest submarine William G. Smith of Bognor Regis, England constructed a fully functional submarine 9 ft. 8 in. long, 3 ft. 9 in. wide and 4 ft. 8 in. high. It can reach depths of around 100 feet and remain underwater for four hours.

Fastest submarine The Russian Alpha class nuclear-powered submarines had a reported maximum speed of over 40 knots, and were believed to be able to dive to 2,500 feet. It is thought that only one now remains in service, used for testing purposes.

Deepest submarine dive The U.S. Navy deep submergence vessel *Sea Cliff* (DSV 4), 30 tons, commissioned in 1973, reached a depth of 20,000 feet in March 1985.

Longest submarine patrol The longest submerged and unsupported patrol made public is 111 days, by HM Submarine *Warspite* in the South Atlantic, November 25, 1982–March 15, 1983.

Fastest human-powered submarine On March 30, 1996, *SubStandard*, designed, built and crewed by William Nicoloff (U.S.), set a record for the fastest speed attained by a human-powered propeller submarine of 6.696 ±0.06 knots (11.3 feet per second).

Nonpropeller The fastest speed attained by a human-powered nonpropeller submarine is 2.9 ±0.1 knots (4.88 feet per second), by *SubDUDE* on August 21, 1992. The submarine was designed by the Scripps Institution of Oceanography, University of California, San Diego.

WARSHIPS

Largest aircraft carriers The warships with the largest full-load displacement are the Nimitz class U.S. Navy aircraft carriers U.S.S. *Nimitz, Dwight D. Eisenhower, Carl Vinson, Theodore Roosevelt, Abraham Lincoln, George Washington,* and *John C. Stennis,* the last three of which displace 114,240 tons. The ships are 1,092 feet in length overall, with 4½ acres of flight deck, and can reach speeds in excess of 30 knots. Their full complement of personnel is 5,986.

Most aircraft landings The greatest number of landings on an aircraft carrier in one day was 602, achieved by Marine Air Group 6 of the United States Pacific Fleet Air Force aboard the U.S.S. *Matanikau* on May 25, 1945 between 8 A.M. and 5 P.M.

Largest battleships The Japanese battleships *Yamato* (sunk southwest of Kyushu, Japan by U.S. planes on April 7, 1945) and *Musashi* (sunk in the Philippine Sea on October 24, 1944) were the largest battleships ever commissioned, each with a full-load displacement of 78,387 tons. With an overall length of 863 feet, a beam of 127 feet and a full-load draft of 35 ft. 5 in., they were armed with nine 18.1-inch guns that fired 3,200-pound projectiles.

United States The largest U.S. battleships were the U.S.S. *Missouri*, an Iowa class battleship, and the U.S.S. *Wisconsin*, 887 feet long with a full load displacement of 64,400 tons. Both were first commissioned in 1944 and then recommissioned in 1986 and 1988 respectively. Both ships have now been withdrawn from service.

Fastest armed vessel A U.S. Navy hovercraft, the 78-foot-long 110-ton test vehicle SES-100B, achieved a speed of 91.9 knots (105.8 mph), on January 25, 1980. (*See FASTEST HOVERCRAFT, page 123.*)

Fastest destroyers The fastest speed attained by a destroyer was 45.25 knots (51.83 mph) by the 3,120-ton French destroyer *Le Terrible* in 1935. It was built in France and was powered by four Yarrow small-tube boilers and two Rateau geared turbines, giving 100,000 shp.

United States The fastest destroyers in the U.S. Navy arsenal are the Spruance class, Kidd class ships, and *Arleigh Burke* which can reach 33 knots (38 mph).

SAILING SHIPS

Oldest active sailing ship The oldest active sailing vessel is the *Star of India* (formerly *Euterpe*), built on the Isle of Man in 1863. It is 205 feet long, with a gross tonnage of 1318. It originally carried passengers between Great Britain and New Zealand. Today it is operated by the Maritime Museum Association of San Diego, CA.

Largest sailing ship The *France II*, weighing 5,806 gross registered tons, was launched at Bordeaux, France in 1911. The ship was a steel-hulled, 5-masted barque with a hull measuring 418 feet overall. It was wrecked off New Caledonia on July 12, 1922.

Largest in service The 357-foot-long *Sedov* was built in 1921 in Kiel, Germany. It is 48 feet wide, with a displacement of 6,944 tons, a gross registered tonnage of 3,556 and a sail area of 45,123 square feet.

Largest sails The largest spars ever carried were those in HM Battleship *Temeraire*, completed at Chatham, England on August 31, 1877 and broken up in 1921. The fore and main yards measured 115 feet long. The foresail contained 5,100 feet of canvas weighing 2.24 tons, and the total sail area was 25,000 square feet.

Tallest mast   *Zeus*, an American-built sloop completed in 1994, is said to be the tallest single-masted yacht in the world. The yacht is 150 feet long and the single-piece mast, which is made of carbon fiber, is 173 feet high.

PASSENGER VESSELS

Largest passenger liner   Carnival Cruise Lines' *Carnival Destiny* is the largest passenger vessel ever built, with a displacement of 101,353 gross registered tons. It is 893 feet long and 125 feet wide.

The longest passenger liner ever built is the *Norway*, completed in 1960, measuring 1,035 ft. $7\frac{1}{2}$ in. long, of 76,049 gross registered tonnage, and with a capacity of 2,032 passengers and 900 crew. It cruises in the Caribbean for the Royal Viking Line and is based at Miami, FL.

Largest riverboat   The world's largest inland boat is the 382-foot *Mississippi Queen*, designed by James Gardner of London, England. The vessel was commissioned on July 25, 1976 in Cincinnati, OH and is now in service on the Mississippi River.

Largest yacht *Royal*   The Saudi Arabian royal yacht *Abdul Aziz*, built in Denmark and completed in 1984 at Vospers Yard, Southampton, England, is 482 feet long.

Nonroyal   The largest private yacht is the *Alexander*, a former ferry converted to a private yacht in 1986, at 400 feet overall.

Largest passenger hydrofoil   Three 185-ton Supramar PTS 150 MkIII hydrofoils can carry 250 passengers at 40 knots across the Öre Sound between Malmö, Sweden and Copenhagen, Denmark.

HOVERCRAFT

Fastest hovercraft   The 78-foot-long 110-ton U.S. Navy test hovercraft SES-100B attained a speed of 91.9 knots (105.8 mph) on January 25, 1980 on the Chesapeake Bay Test Range, MD.

Largest hovercraft   The SRN4 Mk III, a British-built civil hovercraft, weighs 341 tons and can carry 418 passengers and 60 cars. It is 185 feet long and can travel at over 65 knots.

Longest hovercraft journey   Under the leadership of David Smithers, the British Trans-African Hovercraft Expedition traveled 5,000 miles through eight West African countries in a Winchester class SRN6, between October 15, 1969 and January 3, 1970.

Highest hovercraft   The highest altitude reached by a hovercraft was on June 11, 1990 when *Neste Enterprise* and her crew of 10 reached the navigable source of the Yangzi River, China at 16,050 feet.

Everything But Waterskiing

In November 1996, the cruise ship MS *Carnival Destiny* sailed out of the Port of Miami and into *The Guinness Book of World Records*. Weighing in at 101,353 tons and running 893 feet from stem to stern, and 125 feet wide at its maximum beam, *Carnival Destiny* is the world's largest passenger ship.

Commissioned by Carnival Cruise Lines in 1993, *Carnival Destiny* left its birthplace—the Fincantieri Shipyard in Monfalcone, Italy—three years later. Among the countless numbers of people involved in the design and construction of the ship is Carnival's interior architect, Joe Farcus, who points out the challenges *Carnival Destiny* presented.

"For many people, bigness in a ship can be a negative," Farcus admits. "We took that bigness and created something only a big ship enables you to create. The result is more public rooms and larger public spaces with efficient, comfortable guest access." Among the common areas aboard this floating village are pools, restaurants, bars, and dance floors, not to mention a casino, a fitness center, a children's play area, a library, a video arcade, even a small shopping mall complete with its own portrait studio.

In addition, and much like a small town on shore, electricity, running water, fire and police protection, and medical services must also be provided. When the ship is fully manned, a small army of 1,086 crew members tends to the needs of up to 3,400 passengers. "Not only is a ship comparable to a hotel, for example, but it also has to carry all of its requirements on board. There are no extension cords running to shore," Farcus laughs.

Despite *Carnival Destiny*'s world record weigh-in, Farcus insists the intention was never to build the biggest ship in the world, but rather the best. He had no idea it would wind up in *The Guinness Book of World Records*

ON THE RECORD

LARGEST PASSENGER LINER

Carnival Cruise Lines' *Carnival Destiny* is the largest passenger vessel ever built, with a displacement of 101,353 gross registered tons. It is 893 feet long and 125 feet wide.

when he started the project, he says, "but that became apparent the longer we worked on it."

So when does Farcus think the finished product is at its most impressive? "I think on its initial viewing. When you're standing dockside and you look up and see this behemoth parked there. And then there are times when it's in port and you realize it's far and away the biggest thing on the island. "

PORTS

Largest port   The Port of New York and New Jersey has a navigable waterfront of 755 miles (295 miles in New Jersey), stretching over 92 square miles, with a total berthing capacity of 391 ships at a time. The total warehouse floor space covers 422.4 acres.

Busiest port   The busiest port and largest artificial harbor is Rotterdam, Netherlands, which covers 38 square miles, with 76 miles of quays. It handled 323 million tons of seagoing cargo in 1996.

Although the port of Hong Kong handles less tonnage than Rotterdam in total seaborne cargo, it is the world's leading container-port, and handled 13.5 million TEUs in 1996.

Largest dry dock   With a maximum shipbuilding capacity of 1.2 million deadweight tons, the Daewoo Okpo No. 1 Dry Dock, Koje Island in South Korea measures 1,740 feet long by 430 feet wide and was completed in 1979. The dock gates, 46 feet high and 33 feet thick at the base, are the world's most massive.

Longest deep-water jetty   The 5,000-foot Quai Hermann du Pasquier at Le Havre, France is part of an enclosed basin and has a constant depth of water of 32 feet on both sides.

A cargo ship is loaded at Hong Kong, the world's busiest container port.

SCIENCE AND
TECHNOLOGY

CHEMISTRY & PHYSICS

ELEMENTS

Rarest natural element   Only 0.0056 ounces of astatine (At) is present in the earth's crust; the isotope astatine 215 (At 215) accounts for only 1.6×10^{-10} ounces. The least abundant element in the atmosphere is radon (Rn), with a volume of 6×10^{-18} parts by volume.

Most common element   Hydrogen (H) accounts for over 90 percent of all known matter in the universe and 70.68 percent by mass in the solar system.

The commonest element in the earth's atmosphere is nitrogen (N), which is present at 78.08 percent by volume (75.52 percent by mass). Iron (Fe) is the commonest element in the earth itself, making up 36 percent of its mass.

Heaviest element   The newest and heaviest element is 112, which was produced in February 1996 at the Gesellschaft für Schwerionenforschung, Darmstadt, Germany. It has a mass of 277 and decays in 240 millionths of a second.

Highest and lowest density Solid   The densest solid at room temperature is osmium (Os) at 0.8161 pounds per cubic inch.

The least dense element at room temperature is the metal lithium (Li) at 0.01927 pounds per cubic inch, although the density of solid hydrogen at its melting point of $-434.546°F$ is only 0.00315 pounds per cubic inch.

Gas   The densest gas at NTP (Normal Temperature and Pressure, 0°C and one atmosphere) is radon (Rn) at 0.6274 pounds per cubic foot. The lightest gas is hydrogen (H) at 0.005612 pounds per cubic foot.

Highest melting and boiling points   Metallic tungsten or wolfram (W) melts at 6,177°F and boils at 10,550°F. The graphite form of carbon (C) sublimes directly to vapor at 6,699°F and can only be obtained as a liquid above a temperature of 8,546°F and a pressure of 100 atmospheres.

Lowest melting and boiling points   Helium (He) cannot be obtained as a solid at atmospheric pressure; the minimum pressure is 24.985 atmospheres at $-458.275°F$. Helium also has the lowest boiling point, at $-458.275°F$. Mercury (Hg) has the lowest melting and boiling points of any metallic element, at $-37.892°F$ and 673.92°F.

Hardest element   The diamond allotrope of carbon (C) has a Knoop value of 8,400.

Highest and lowest thermal expansion   The element with the highest expansion is cesium (Cs), at 94×10^{-5} per degree C, while the diamond allotrope of carbon (C) has the lowest expansion at 1.0×10^{-6} per degree C.

Most ductile element   One ounce of gold (Au) can be drawn to a length of 43 miles.

Highest tensile strength   Boron (B) has a tensile strength of 5.7 GPa 8.3 × 105 lbf/in².

Strongest pure metal   The strongest pure metal appears to be iridium (Ir) with a typical tensile strength of 550MPa (8.0×10^4 lbf/in²).

Shortest and longest liquid ranges   Based on the differences between melting and boiling points, the element with the shortest liquid range (on the Celsius scale) is neon (Ne), at only 2.542 degrees (from −248.594°C to −246.052°C [−415.469°F to −410.894°F]).
   Neptunium (Np) has the longest liquid range, at 3,453 degrees (from 637°C to 4,090°C [1,179°F to 7,394°F]).

Most toxic element   The severest restriction placed on any element in the form of a radioactive isotope is 2.4×10^{-16}g/m³ in air for thorium 228 (Th-228) or radiothorium.

Nonradioactive   Beryllium has a threshold limit value in air of 2 g/m³.

Most and fewest isotopes   There are at least 2,670 isotopes, and tin (Sn) has the most, with 38. Tin also has the greatest number of stable isotopes, with 10. Hydrogen (H) has the fewest isotopes, with just three.

Most and least stable isotopes   The most stable radioactive isotope is tellurium 128, with a half-life of 1.5×10^{24} years. The least stable is lithium 5, which decays in 4.4×10^{-22} seconds.

Strongest alloy   Carbon-manganese steel music wire measuring 0.004 inches wide has a required tensile strength in the range of 3.40–3.78 GPa (4.93×10^5 to 5.48×10^5 lbf/in²).

CHEMICAL EXTREMES

Strongest acid   The strongest super acid is an 80 percent solution of antimony pentafluoride in hydrofluoric acid (fluoroantimonic acid HF: SbF5). This solution has not been measured directly, but a 50 percent solution is 1018 times stronger than concentrated sulfuric acid.

Bitterest substance   The bitterest-tasting substances are based on the denatonium cation and are produced commercially as benzoate and saccharide. Taste detection levels are as low as one part in 500 million, and a dilution of one part in 100 million will leave a lingering taste.

Sweetest substance   Talin from katemfe (*Thaumatococcus daniellii*), discovered in West Africa, is 6,150 times as sweet as a 1 percent sucrose solution.

Least dense solids   In February 1990, a silica aerogel with a density of only five ounces per cubic foot was produced at Lawrence Livermore National Laboratory in Livermore, CA.

WORKING IN EXTREMES

"*I* put five materials together and composited them into a lubricant. And it worked the first time," declares Dr. Charles P. Covino, the inventor of Hi-T-Lube, a surface lubricant that registers the lowest coefficient of static and dynamic friction of any material.

Covino, the founder and C.E.O. of General Magnaplate Corporation, invented Hi-T-Lube for use in fighter aircraft in the late 1950s. He had been testing F105s that had been involved in a series of accidents and discovered that the speedbrake pedals were constantly jamming because of exposure to the jet flame. "The pedals were cooking hot and then freezing when the exhaust was opened and the airstream hit them. They would go immediately subzero and lots of 105s were being crashed," says Covino. The inventor realized that the solution was a new metal alloy that would take the heat, swell up, then go back and compress. Covino named the alloy Hi-T-Lube.

In the mid-1960s, Hi-T-Lube gained fame because of its critical role in the development of the space program. It is impossible to use oils or wet ma-

LOWEST FRICTION

The lowest coefficient of static and dynamic friction of any solid is 0.03, for Hi-T-Lube with an MOS2 burnished (B) exterior.

terials in a vacuum, because they will stop the engine. As machines have to work in a vacuum when flying in space, NASA was faced with a severe problem. "They tried everything, including metals like graphite and silver, but everything migrated once it got into a high vacuum. They would actually grow whiskers, which would then either jam things up or short them out," says Covino.

The problem was solved when Covino put gold on top of the Hi-T-Lube alloy he had used on the F105s. "It was the only thing that held together and could lubricate in high heat, cold zones, sunshine or a vacuum," says Covino. Hi-T-Lube was used for the first trip to the moon, and subsequently for trips to Venus and Mars. The Mars Probe had approximately 400 pieces lubricated with the alloy.

Back on earth, Covino believes that his invention can be used to help preserve fragile natural resources. "Certain metals are going to be in short supply and we're going to end up with a fast depletion of energies and materials we can extract from the earth. If lower cost metals, such as aluminum or magnesium, are coated with Hi-T-Lube, they will be less likely to corrode, bend, wear or fracture, keeping them environmentally safe and sound."

Most powerful nerve gas Ethyl S-2-diisopropylaminoethylmethylphosphonothiolate or VX, developed at the Chemical Defense Experimental Establishment, Porton Down, England in 1952, is 300 times more powerful than the phosgene ($COCl_2$) used in World War I. The lethal dosage is 10 mg-minute per cubic meter airborne or 0.3 mg orally.

Most lethal man-made chemical TCDD (2, 3, 7, 8-tetrachloro-dibenzo-p-dioxin), the most dangerous dioxin, is 150,000 times more deadly than cyanide.

Most absorbent substance "H-span" or Super Slurper, composed of one-half starch derivative and one-fourth each of acrylamide and acrylic acid, can, when treated with iron, retain water 1,300 times its own weight.

Most refractory substance The most refractory substance is tantalum carbide (TaC0.88), which melts at 7,214°F.

Most heat-resistant substance The existence of a complex material known as NFAARr or Ultra Hightech Starlite was announced in April 1993. Invented by Maurice Ward (Great Britain), it can temporarily resist plasma temperature (18,032°F).

Highest superconducting temperature In 1993, bulk superconductivity with a transition to zero resistance at –221.3°F was achieved at the Laboratorium für Festkörperphysik, Zurich, Switzerland, in a mixture of oxides of mercury, barium, calcium and copper.

PHYSICAL EXTREMES

Highest temperature The highest temperature produced in a laboratory is 918,000,000°F on February 17, 1995, in the Tokamak Fusion Test Reactor at the Princeton University Plasma Physics Laboratory, Princeton, NJ using a deuterium-tritium plasma mix (see *GREATEST FUSION POWER*, page 151).

Hottest flame The hottest-burning substance is carbon subnitride (C_4N_2), which, at one atmosphere pressure, can produce a flame calculated to reach 9,010°F.

Lowest temperature Absolute zero, 0 K on the Kelvin scale, corresponds to –459.67°F. The lowest temperature ever reached is 2.8×10^{-10}K in a nuclear demagnetization device at the Low Temperature Laboratory, Helsinki University of Technology, Finland, announced in 1993.

Highest pressure A sustained laboratory pressure of 170 GPa (11,000 tons per square inch) was achieved in the giant hydraulic diamond-faced press at the Carnegie Institution's Geophysical Laboratory, Washington, D.C. in June 1978.

Highest vacuum In January 1991, K. Odaka and S. Ueda of Japan obtained a vacuum of 7×10^{-16} atmospheres in a stainless steel chamber.

Lowest friction Solid The lowest coefficient of static and dynamic friction of any solid is 0.03, for Hi-T-Lube with an MOS2 burnished (B) exterior.

The 0.03 result was achieved by sliding Hi-T-Lube (B) against Hi-T-Lube (B). This material was developed for NASA in 1965 by General Magnaplate Corp., Linden, NJ.

Lubricant Tufoil, manufactured by Fluoramics Inc. of Mahwah, NJ, has a coefficient of friction of .029.

Highest velocity The highest velocity at which any solid visible object has been projected is 334,800 mph in the case of a plastic disc at the Naval Research Laboratory, Washington, D.C., in August 1980.

Most magnetic substance The most magnetic substance is neodymium iron boride ($Nd_2Fe_{14}B$), with a maximum energy product of up to 280 kJ per cubic meter.

Strongest magnetic field The strongest continuous field strength achieved was 38.7 ± 0.3 teslas, at the Massachusetts Institute of Technology, Cambridge, MA in 1994.

Most powerful electric current In 1996, scientists at Oak Ridge National Laboratory, Oak Ridge, TN sent a current of 2 million amperes/cm^2 down a superconducting wire.

Highest voltage The highest potential difference obtained in a laboratory was 32 ± 1.5 million volts by the National Electrostatistics Corporation, Oak Ridge, TN on May 17, 1979.

Brightest light Scientists at the University of Michigan achieved 10–20 watts/cm^2 with a pulse in an argon laser. The pressure in the laser's plasma was 1 billion atmospheres.

Longest echo There is a 15-second echo following the closing of the door of the Chapel of the Mausoleum, Hamilton, Scotland, built 1840–55.

BIOTECHNOLOGY

Most advanced cloning technique In 1996, scientists from the Roslin Institute, Edinburgh, Scotland and PPL Therapeutics used cells from the udder of a sheep to produce a clone. "Dolly" is the first mammal to be created from non-reproductive tissue taken from an adult animal. In theory, this technique would make it possible to clone adult human beings.

Oldest cryonically preserved body After his death on January 12, 1967, Dr. James H. Bedford was placed in a cryocapsule or "dewar" filled with liquid nitrogen at a temperature of –196°C (–320°F). Bedford's dewar has been replaced twice, but his body temperature has never been allowed to rise above freezing. The goal of cryonics is to preserve bodies until future technological advances permit them to be "resuscitated" and cured of illnesses that are incurable today. *Below top*, Bedford's original cryocapsule on display at Alcor Life Extension Foundation; *below bottom*, Bedford's body is placed into a new dewar in 1991.

ARCHAEOLOGY

HUMAN ORIGINS

Earliest primates Primates appeared in the Paleocene epoch, about 65 million years ago. The earliest members of the suborder Anthropoidea are known from both Africa and South America in the early Oligocene, 30–34 million years ago. Finds from the Fayum, Egypt may represent primates from the Eocene period, 37 million years ago.

Earliest hominoid A jawbone with three molars, found in the Otavi Hills, Namibia on June 4, 1991, was dated at 12–13 million years and named *Otavipithecus namibiensis*.

Earliest hominid Fossils of *Ardepithecus ramidus*, found in Aramis, Ethiopia, are 4.4 million years old.

Earliest of the genus Homo The oldest definitively dated fossil of the genus *Homo* was found in Hadar, Ethiopia in November 1994. The age of the 2.33 million-year-old jawbone was announced by a team of American, Canadian, Ethiopian and Israeli scientists in November 1996. In the absence of a complete skull, the scientists were not able to determine which species of *Homo* the fossil represents.

The earliest stone tools are abraded core-choppers dating from *c.* 2.6 million years ago. They were found in Hadar, Ethiopia in November–December 1976 by Hélène Roche (France).

Earliest Homo erectus The oldest example of *Homo erectus* ("upright man"), the direct ancestor of *Homo sapiens*, was discovered by Eugène Dubois (Netherlands) in Trinil, Java in 1891. Javan *H. erectus* was redated to 1.8 million years in 1994. Fossils of *H. erectus* from Kenya are also about 1.8 million years old.

Earliest Homo sapiens *Homo sapiens* ("wise man") appeared about 300,000 years ago as the successor to *Homo erectus*.

ANCIENT STRUCTURES

Oldest human structure In January 1960, Dr. Mary Leakey discovered what may be the footings of a windbreak built 1.75 million years ago in the Olduvai Gorge, Tanzania. The site consists of a rough circle of loosely piled lava blocks associated with artifacts and bones on a work-floor.

Oldest freestanding structure The megalithic temples of Mgarr, Skorba and Ggantija in Malta date from *c.* 3250 B.C., three and a half centuries before the first Egyptian pyramid.

Oldest wooden structure The oldest extant wooden buildings in the world are the Pagoda, Chumanar Gate and Temple of Horyu (Horyu-ji) in Nara, Japan, dating from *c.* A.D. 670.

CHEDDAR MAN

A̲N UNASSUMING 42-YEAR-OLD HISTORY TEACHER in Britain made history himself in March 1997 when he was found to be the living link to the oldest known family tree in the world. Scientists took a DNA sample from the molar of a male skeleton discovered in a cave in Cheddar Gorge, Somerset, in southwest England and found a near-perfect match in Adrian Targett, who lives less than a half mile away.

"My nickname in the newspapers was 'modern-day Fred Flintstone,'" says Targett, referring to the cartoon series that featured a family of cave-dwellers. "I used to watch it on the television when I was little. There was Fred and Wilma and Pebbles. Insert a gap of 9,000 years and then there's me." Reflecting on his entry into *The Guinness Book of World Records*, Targett says, "This is a story about roots. Most people like to know where they came from. We all have ancestors, don't we? Now I know who mine are."

Targett, who used to trace his family tree just four generations back on his mother's side, pays tribute to Dr. Bryan Sykes of Oxford University's Institute of Molecular Medicine and his team for the discovery. Sykes explains that the study, commissioned for a TV documentary, aimed to reconstruct the origins of British and European populations. "We have shown that genes present in the population now were also present 10,000 years ago," he says. "It goes against the idea that hunter-gatherers were swept aside and overwhelmed by farmers coming from the Middle East 10,000 years ago. This shows it didn't happen."

The skeleton, found in 1903, was named Cheddar Man for the region in which Cheddar cheese supposedly originated. The DNA study involved Targett and some 20 other local residents, including some of his students, but eventually will involve 10,000 people all over Britain. Cheddar Man and Targett are linked through a female line of descent. Cheddar Man is twice as old as Ice Man, found in the Italian Alps five years ago and who also yielded DNA samples.

When the story of the link first broke, reporters and TV crews swarmed into Cheddar, Targett says, making a big impression on his teenage students. But he can't discuss Cheddar Man in class indefinitely. "Our curriculum is prescribed. There's no way I can get my ancestor into 20th century world history and 19th century British history."

MOST DISTANT ANCESTOR

Adrian Targett is related to "Cheddar Man," a 9,000-year-old skeleton found in Cheddar, England, through a female line of descent of roughly 300 generations.

Oldest habitation   The remains of 21 huts containing hearths or pebble-lined pits and delimited by stake-holes, found in October 1965 at the Terra Amata site in Nice, France, are thought to belong to the Acheulian culture of approximately 400,000 years ago.

The oldest human settlement in the Americas is the Monte Verde site in Chile. Radiocarbon dating of bone and charcoal established the age of the site as approximately 12,500 years. The excavation, led by Dr. Tom Dillehay, started in 1977, and confirmation of the site's age was announced in 1997.

OTHER FINDS

Oldest mummy   A mummy at the Nevada State Museum, thought to be about 2,000 years old when it was discovered in a Nevada cave in 1940, was tested using modern dating techniques in April 1996. The Spirit Cave man was found to be more than 9,400 years old. Anthropologists hope the well-preserved body will give insights into life at the end of the ice age.

Egyptian   The oldest known Egyptian mummy is that of a high-ranking young woman who was buried *c.* 2600 B.C. near the Great Pyramid of Cheops at Giza, or Al-Gizeh, Egypt. Her remains were discovered on March 17, 1989, but only her skull was intact.

The oldest complete Egyptian mummy is of Wati, a court musician of *c.* 2400 B.C., from the tomb of Nefer in Saqqâra, Egypt, found in 1944.

Oldest weapons   The oldest complete hunting weapons are three wooden spears found in a coal mine in Schoningen, Germany. In 1997, radiocarbon dating established the age of the 6–7½-foot javelins as 380,000–400,000 years.

Oldest shipwreck   The oldest shipwreck found at sea is one off Uluburun, near Kas, Turkey, dated to 1316 B.C.

Oldest fabric   The oldest fabric, dated to 7000 B.C., was reported in July 1993 to have been discovered in southeastern Turkey. The semi-fossilized cloth is believed to be linen.

Oldest mural   In 1961, clay relief leopards were discovered by James Malaart on manmade walls at level VII at Catal Hüyük in southern Anatolia, Turkey. They date from *c.* 6200 B.C.

Oldest sculpture   An animal head carved on a woolly rhinoceros vertebra from Tolbaga, Siberia is thought to be 34,860 years old.

The oldest stone figurine is a 31,790-year-old serpentine female statuette from Galgenberg, Austria.

About 32,000 years ago, several ivory figurines of humans and animals were deposited in caves in southern Germany. These are generally more sophisticated and more animated than the sculpture of subsequent periods.

Oldest measures   The oldest known measure of weight is the beqa of the Amratian period of Egyptian civilization *c.* 3800 B.C., found at Naqada, Egypt. The cylindrical weights weigh 6.65–7.45 ounces.

The oldest freestanding structures are the megalithic temples of
Mgarr, Skorba, and Ggantija in Malta. Dated to c. 3250 B.C., these
structures predate the Egyptian pyramids by 350 years.

Oldest wine   Physical evidence of wine dating from *c.* 5000 B.C. has been found in the remains of an ancient pottery jar found in 1968 in Hajji Firuz Tepe, Iran. Residue in the jar contains two characteristic ingredients of wine.

Oldest chewing gum   A piece of 6,500-year-old birch tar with human tooth impressions was described by Elizabeth Aveling in the February 1997 issue of *British Archaeology*. The chewer of the piece of "gum," which was found in a bog in Sweden, was 30–40 years old and had a cavity in one tooth.

MACHINES & INSTRUMENTS

SCIENTIFIC INSTRUMENTS

Largest scientific instrument   The Large Electron–Positron (LEP) storage ring at CERN, Geneva, Switzerland is 12½ feet in diameter and 17 miles in circumference.

Smallest manmade object   The tips of probes for scanning tunneling microscopes are shaped to end in a single atom.

Finest balance   The Sartorius Model 4108, manufactured in Göttingen, Germany, can weigh objects of up to 0.018 ounces to an accuracy of 3.5×10^{-10} ounces, equivalent to little more than $1/60$th of the weight of the ink on this period.

Smallest thermometer   Dr. Frederich Sachs, a biophysicist at the State University of New York at Buffalo, developed an ultra-microthermometer for measuring the temperature of single living cells. The tip is one micron in diameter, about $1/50$th the diameter of a human hair.

Largest barometer   An oil-filled barometer, of overall height 42 feet, was constructed by Allan Mills and John Pritchard of the Department of Physics and Astronomy, University of Leicester, Leicester, England in 1991. It attained a standard height of 40 feet (at which pressure mercury would stand at 2½ feet).

Smallest microphone   Prof. Ibrahim Kavrak of Bogazici University, Istanbul, Turkey developed a microphone for fluid flow pressure measurement in 1967. It has a frequency response of 10 Hz–10 kHz and measures 0.06×0.03 inches.

Finest cut   The large optics diamond turning machine at the Lawrence Livermore National Laboratory, Livermore, CA was reported in June 1983 to be able to sever a human hair 3,000 times lengthwise.

Sharpest objects   The sharpest manufactured objects are glass micropipette tubes whose beveled tips have an outer diameter of 0.02 mm and a

0.01-mm inner diameter. The latter is 6,500 times thinner than a human hair. The tubes are used in intracellular work on living cells.

Most powerful microscope The scanning tunneling microscope (STM) invented at the IBM Zürich research laboratory, Switzerland, in 1981 has a magnification of 100 million times and a resolution of $1/100$th the diameter of an atom (3×10^{-10} m), making it the world's most powerful microscope.

Most powerful particle accelerator The world's highest-energy "atom-smasher" is the 1.25-mile-diameter proton synchroton "Tevatron" at the Fermi National Accelerator Laboratory (Fermilab) near Batavia, IL. On November 30, 1986 a center of mass energy of 1.8 TeV (1.8×10^{12} eV) was achieved by colliding protons and antiprotons.

Heaviest magnet The heaviest magnet is in the Joint Institute for Nuclear Research at Dubna, near Moscow, Russia, for the 10 GeV synchrophasotron measuring 196 feet in diameter and weighing 42,000 tons.

Largest electromagnet The octagonal electromagnet in the L3 detector, an experiment on LEP (Large Electron–Positron collider), consists of 7,055 tons of low carbon steel yoke and 1,213 tons of aluminum coil. Thirty thousand amperes of current flow through the aluminum coil to create a uniform magnetic field of five kilogauss.

Most powerful magnet The world's most powerful magnet was completed by the Lawrence Berkeley National Laboratory in California in 1997. The superconducting electromagnet has a coil made from 14 miles of niobium-tin wire and has a field strength of 13.5 tesla, 250,000 times stronger than the magnetic field of Earth.

The Lawrence Berkeley National Laboratory produced the world's most powerful magnet in 1997.

Largest kaleidoscope The Kaatskill Kaleidoscope at Catskill Corners, Mt. Tremper, NY measures 56 ft. 3 in. long. Viewers can step inside the kaleidoscope to experience *America: The House We Live In*, an adventure through 200 years of American history.

Most powerful laser The "Petawatt" Laser at the Lawrence Livermore National Laboratory, Livermore, CA produces laser pulses of more than 1.3 quadrillion watts (1.3 petawatts) at peak power. This is more than 1,300 times the entire electrical capacity of the United States, although each pulse lasts less than half a trillionth of a second.

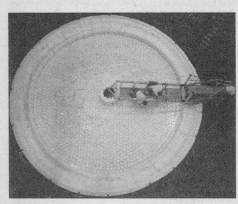

Largest one-piece glass mirror The Steward Observatory Mirror Laboratory at the University of Arizona produced a 27-ft.-9-in. borosilicate glass mirror for a telescope.

Smallest ruler In 1994 a ruler used for measuring objects under an electron microscope was developed at the Institute for Microstructural Sciences at Canada's

The world's largest one-piece mirror took 10 weeks to cast.

National Research Council. The ruler's smallest division is 18 atoms, and 10 of the rulers stacked end to end would equal the diameter of a human hair.

Thinnest glass The thinnest glass, type D263, has a minimum thickness of 0.00098 inches and a maximum thickness of 0.00137 inches. It is made by Deutsche Spezialglas AG, Grünenplan, Germany for use in electronic and medical equipment.

MACHINES

Largest blast furnace The no. 5 furnace at the Cherepovets works in Russia has a volume of 5,500 cubic meters.

Longest conveyor belt The longest single-flight conveyor belt is 18 miles long. It is in Western Australia and was installed by Cable Belt Ltd. of Camberley, England.

Most powerful gantry crane The 92.3-foot-wide Rahco gantry crane at the Grand Coulee Dam Third Powerplant in Washington State was tested to

Largest turbines The largest hydraulic turbines are 32 feet in diameter with a 449-ton runner and a 350-ton shaft. Rated at 815 MW, they were installed by Allis-Chalmers (now Voith Hydro) at the Grand Coulee Third Powerplant in Washington State.

Smallest turbine A gas turbine with compressor and turbine wheels measuring 1.6 inches and an operating speed of 100,000 rpm, was developed at the University of New South Wales, Sydney, Australia.[o]

MEASURES & CALCULATIONS

MATHEMATICS

Largest numbers The largest lexicographically accepted named number in the system of successive powers of 10 is the centillion, first recorded in 1852. It is the hundredth power of a million, or 1 followed by 600 zeros.

Highest prime number The highest known prime number was discovered by Joel Armengaud and George Woltman, who led a team of mathematicians connected over the Internet. This prime number has 420,921 digits, enough to fill over 33½ pages of *The Guinness Book of World Records*. In mathematical notation it is expressed as $2^{1,398,269}-1$, which denotes two multiplied by itself 1,398,269 times, minus one. Prime numbers expressed in this form are known as Mersenne primes, after Father Marin Mersenne, a 17th-century French monk who spent years searching for prime numbers of this type.

The largest known twin primes are $1,706,595 \times 2^{11,235}-1$ and $1,706,595 \times 2^{11,235}+1$, found on August 6, 1989 by a team in Santa Clara, CA.

Lowest composite number The lowest nonprime or composite number (excluding 1) is 4.

Lowest and highest perfect numbers A number is said to be perfect if it is equal to the sum of its divisors other than itself, e.g., $1 + 2 + 4 + 7 + 14 = 28$. The lowest perfect number is 6 ($=1 + 2 + 3$).

The highest known perfect number is $(2,859,433 -1) \times 2,859,433$. It has a total of 517,430 digits (enough to fill over 41 pages of *The Guinness Book of World Records*), and it is derived from the largest known Mersenne prime.

Smallest calculator James Gimzewski and a team of scientists at IBM Research Division's Zurich Research Laboratory, Zurich, Switzerland created a calculating device with a diameter of less than one millionth of a millimeter. The molecular abacus consists of 10 molecules of carbon 60, also called buckminsterfullerenes, that can be moved along a microscopic groove on a copper surface with the tip of a scanning tunneling microscope to carry out simple calculations.

The creators of the smallest calculating device (*left*) and a series of images (*right*) showing the tiny calculator's 10 carbon 60 atoms in each of their possible configurations.

Most difficult math problem Fermat's last theorem has precipitated more incorrect proofs than have been published for any other theorem. Pierre de Fermat inspired centuries of hopeless searching when he wrote the theorem in a notebook, adding, "I have found an admirable proof of this theorem, but the margin is too narrow to contain it." In June 1993, Andrew J. Wiles of Princeton University announced his discovery of the proof of the theorem. Subsequent study revealed flaws, but Wiles corrected them, and in 1997 he was awarded the Wolfskehl prize for his final proof.

Princeton University professor Andrew Wiles was awarded the Wolfskehl Prize in 1997 for solving the world's most difficult math problem, Fermat's last theorem.

Most-proved theorem A book published in 1940 entitled *The Pythagorean Proposition* contained 370 different proofs of Pythagoras' theorem.

Longest proof The proof of the classification of all finite simple groups is spread over more than 14,000 pages in nearly 500 papers in mathematical journals, contributed by more than 100 mathematicians over a period of more than 35 years.

Most prolific mathematician   Leonard Euler (Switzerland; 1707–83) was so prolific that his papers were still being published for the first time more than 50 years after his death. His collected works have been printed bit by bit since 1910 and will eventually occupy more than 75 large volumes.

Most accurate version of pi   Professor Yasumasa Kanada (Japan) calculated the value of pi (π) to 51,539,607,552 places in 1997, surpassing the previous record by more than 48 billion.

Most inaccurate version of pi   In 1897, the General Assembly of Indiana enacted Bill No. 246, stating that pi was de jure 4.

CLOCKS AND WATCHES

Most accurate clock   A commercially available atomic clock manufactured by Hewlett-Packard of Palo Alto, CA was unveiled in December 1991. Designated the HP 5071A primary frequency standard with cesium II technology, the device, costing $54,000 and about the size of a desktop computer, is accurate to one second in 1.6 million years.

The world's most accurate clock is the HP 5071A, manufactured by Hewlett-Packard. It is accurate to one second in 1.6 million years.

Oldest clock   The faceless clock, dating from 1386, or possibly earlier, at Salisbury Cathedral in England was restored in 1956, having struck the hours for 498 years and ticked more than 500 million times.

Largest clock   The astronomical clock in the Cathedral of St.-Pierre, Beauvais, France was constructed between 1865 and 1868. It contains 90,000 parts and is 40 feet high, 20 feet wide and nine feet deep.

Largest clock face   The clock face on the floral clock constructed at Matsubara Park, Toi, Japan on June 18, 1991 is 101 feet in diameter.

Highest clock   The highest clock is at the top of the Morton International Building, Chicago, IL. It is 580 feet above street level.

Largest sundial   Designed by Arata Isozaki of Tokyo, Japan as the center-piece of the Walt Disney World Co. headquarters in Orlando, FL, the largest sundial has a base diameter of 122 feet and is 120 feet high, with a gnomon (projecting arm) of the same length.

Longest pendulum   The longest pendulum measures 73 ft. 9¾ in. and is part of the water-mill clock installed by the Hattori Tokeiten Co. in the Shinjuku NS building in Tokyo, Japan in 1983.

Largest watch   A Swatch 531 ft. 6 in. long and 65 ft. 7½ in. in diameter was made by D. Tomas Feliu and set up on the site of the Bank of Bilbao building, Madrid, Spain, December 7–12, 1985.

Smallest watches   Jaeger le Coultre of Switzerland produces the smallest watches. Equipped with a 15-jeweled movement, they measure just over half an inch long and ³⁄₁₆ inches wide. Movement and case weigh under a quarter of an ounce.

Longest measure of time   The longest measure of time is the para in Hindu chronology. It is equivalent to the length of the complete life of Brahma, or 311,040,000,000,000 years (68,500 times the estimated age of Earth).

ENERGY

ELECTRICITY

Largest generator   A turbo generator of 1,450 MW (net) is being installed at the Ignalina atomic power station in southern Lithuania.

Largest power plant   The most powerful power station is the Itaipu power station on the Paraná River near the Brazil–Paraguay border. Opened in 1984, the station has now attained its ultimate rated capacity of 13,320 MW.

The Itaipu power station has a rated capacity of 13,320 MW.

Largest transformers   The world's largest single-phase transformers are rated at 1,500,000 kVA. Eight of these are in service with the American

Electric Power Service Corporation. Of these, five step down from 765 to 345 kV.

Longest transmission lines The longest span between pylons of any power line is 17,638 feet, across the Ameralik Fjord near Nuuk, Greenland. Erected by A.S. Betonmast of Oslo, Norway in 1991–92 as part of the 132 kV line serving the 45 MW Buksefjorden Hydro Power Station, the line weighs 42 tons.

Highest transmission lines The transmission lines across the Straits of Messina, Italy have towers of 675 feet (Sicily side) and 735 feet (Calabria side), 11,900 feet apart.

Highest-voltage transmission lines The highest voltages carried on a DC are 1,330 kV over a distance of 1,224 miles on the DC Pacific Inter-Tie in the United States, which stretches from approximately 100 miles east of Portland, OR to a location east of Los Angeles, CA.

The highest voltages carried on a 3-phase AC are 1,200 kV in Russia over a distance greater than 1,000 miles. The first section carries the current from Siberia to the province of North Kazakhstan, while the second takes the current from Siberia to Ural.

Biggest blackout The greatest power failure in history struck seven northeastern U.S. states and Ontario, Canada on November 9–10, 1965. About 30 million people in 80,000 square miles were plunged into darkness. Two people died as a result of the blackout. In New York City the power failed at 5:27 P.M. and was not fully restored for 13½ hours.

Largest battery The 10 MW lead-acid battery in Chino, CA has a design capacity of 40 MW/h. It is currently used at an electrical substation for leveling peak demand loads. This project is a cooperative effort by Southern California Edison Company Electric Power Research Institute and International Lead Zinc Research Organization, Inc.

OIL

Largest oil producer Saudi Arabia produced an estimated 8.218 million barrels per day in 1996.

Largest oil importer In 1996, the United States imported 9.478 million barrels per day of crude oil and its by-products. Venezuela was the leading supplier, providing 1.676 million barrels per day, which represented 17.7 percent of U.S. imports.

Largest oil consumer The United States used 18.23 million barrels per day in 1996, 25.4 percent of the world's total.

Largest refinery Lagovan Company's refinery at Judibana (Falcon), Venezuela has a capacity of 571,000 barrels per day.

Largest catalytic cracker The Tosco Refining Company plant in Linden, NJ had a peak fresh feed rate of 159,500 barrels (6,699,700 gallons) per day in 1995. Tosco Refining Company is a division of Tosco Corporation of Stamford, CT.

Largest oil field The largest oil field is the Ghawar Field in Saudi Arabia, developed by Aramco and measuring 150 by 22 miles, with an estimated ultimate recovery of 82 billion barrels.

Largest oil tanks The five ARAMCO 1½-million-barrel storage tanks at Ju'aymah, Saudi Arabia are 72 feet tall with a diameter of 386 feet and were completed in March 1980.

Heaviest platform The Pampo platform in the Campos Basin off Rio de Janeiro, Brazil was built and is operated by Petrobrás. It weighs 26,455 tons and processes 33,000 barrels per day. The platform operates 377 feet above the seabed.

Tallest platform In May 1997, the Ram-Powell tension-leg platform was installed in the Gulf of Mexico. Designed and engineered by Shell Oil Company, it set a new water-depth record for a production platform, extending 3,214 feet from seabed to surface.

Greatest oil gusher The greatest wildcat ever recorded blew at Alborz No. 5 well, near Qum, Iran on August 26, 1956. The oil gushed to a height of 170 feet at 120,000 barrels per day. It was closed after 90 days' work by B. Mostofi and Myron Kinley of Texas.

Worst oil spill A marine blow-out beneath the drilling rig Ixtoc I in the Gulf of Campeche, Gulf of Mexico on June 3, 1979 produced a slick that reached 400 miles by August 5, 1979. It was capped on March 24, 1980 after a loss of 505,600 tons.

On January 19, 1991, Iraqi president Saddam Hussein ordered the pumping of Kuwaiti crude oil into the Persian Gulf. Estimates put the loss at 6–8 million barrels.

The *Exxon Valdez* struck a reef in Prince William Sound, AK on March 24, 1989, spilling 10 million gallons of crude. The slick spread over 2,600 square miles.

Longest oil pipeline The Interprovincial Pipe Line Inc. installation, which spans North America from Edmonton, Alberta, Canada through Chicago to Montreal, is 2,353 miles long.

Most expensive pipeline The total cost of the Alaska oil pipeline, running 800 miles from Prudhoe Bay to Valdez, was $9 billion. The pipe's capacity is 2.1 million barrels per day.

NATURAL GAS

Largest gas producer Russia produced 22.707 trillion cubic feet of natural gas in 1996.

Largest gas deposit The gas deposit at Urengoi, Russia has an EUR (estimated ultimate recovery) of 285 trillion cubic feet.

The worst gas fire erupted at Gassi Touil in the Algerian Sahara on November 13, 1961. It was finally extinguished on April 28, 1962.

Greatest gas fire A gas fire burned at Gassi Touil in the Algerian Sahara from November 13, 1961 to April 28, 1962. The pillar of flame rose 450 feet. It was eventually extinguished by "Red" Adair of Houston, TX, using 550 pounds of dynamite.

Longest natural gas pipeline The TransCanada Pipeline transported a record 2.352 trillion cubic feet of gas through 8,671 miles of pipe in 1995.

NUCLEAR POWER

Greatest fusion power The highest level of controlled fusion power attained is 10.7 MW, in the Tokamak Fusion Test Reactor at the Princeton University Plasma Physics Laboratory, Princeton, NJ in November 1994.

A section of solar panels that form part of the Harper Lake Site, the world's largest solar electric power plant.

Largest nuclear reactor   The largest single nuclear reactor in the world is the Ignalina station, Lithuania, which came fully on line in January 1984 and has a net capacity of 1,380 MW.

Largest nuclear power station   The 6-reactor Zaporozhe power station in the Ukraine gives a gross output of 6,000 MW.

Largest solar power plant   In terms of nominal capacity, the largest solar electric power plant is the Harper Lake Site in the Mojave Desert, California, run by UC Operating Services. The two solar electric generating stations have a nominal capacity of 160 MW. The site covers 1,280 acres.

STEAM AND WATER POWER

Oldest water mill   The water mill with the oldest continuous commercial use is at Priston Mill near Bath, England, first mentioned in A.D. 931 in a charter to King Athelstan (924/5–939). It is driven by the Conygre Brook.

Oldest steam engine   The oldest working steam engine is the Smethwick Engine, dating from 1779. Designed by James Watt (1736–1819) and built by the Birmingham Canal Company, the pump originally had a 24-inch bore and a stroke of eight feet. It worked on the canal locks at Smethwick, England until 1891. The engine was presented to the Birmingham Museum of Science and Industry in 1960 and is regularly steamed for the public.

Largest steam engine   The largest single-cylinder steam engine was designed by Matthew Loam of Cornwall, England and built by the Hayle Foundry Co. in 1849 for land draining at Haarlem, Netherlands. The cylinder was 12 feet in diameter and each stroke lifted 16,140 gallons of water.

Most efficient steam engine   The most efficient steam engine recorded was Taylor's engine, built by Michael Loam for United Mines of Gwennap, England in 1840. It registered only 1.7 pounds of coal per horsepower per hour.

WIND POWER

Largest wind generators   The GEC MOD-5A installation on the north shore of Oahu, HI produces 7,300 kW with its 400-foot rotors when the wind reaches 32 MPH.

Tallest windmill   The tallest windmill in the world is St. Patrick's Distillery Mill in Dublin, Republic of Ireland. It is 150 feet tall.

COMMUNICATIONS

TELEPHONES

Most telephones   The country with the most phones is the United States, with 165 million in 1996.

Liechtenstein has the most subscribers per capita, at 1.5 for every receiver.

Most phone calls   The most calls made in any country is in the United States, with just over 550 billion in 1994.

Most mobile phones   The country with the greatest number of cellular telephone subscribers is the United States, with 35 million in early 1996. The country with the greatest penetration is Sweden, which has 229 subscribers per 1,000 people.

Largest telephone   The world's largest operational telephone was exhibited at a festival on September 16, 1988 to celebrate the 80th birthday of Centraal Beheer, an insurance company based in Apeldoorn, Netherlands. It was 8 ft. 1 in. high and 19 ft. 11 in. long, and weighed 3.8 tons. The handset, which was 23 ft. 5 in. long, had to be lifted by crane.

Smallest telephone   An operational telephone measuring 1.8 by 0.3 by 0.8 inches was created by Jan Piotr Krutewicz (U.S.) in September 1996.

Busiest telephone route   The busiest international phone route is between the United States and Canada. In 1995, there were 6.1 billion minutes of telephone traffic between the two countries.

Busiest exchange   The busiest telecommunications exchange was the Bellsouth network used at the International Broadcast Center, Atlanta, GA during the 1996 Olympic Games from July 19 to August 4. It could transmit 100 billion bits of information per second.

Largest switchboard   The switchboard in the Pentagon, Arlington, VA has 34,500 lines and handles almost a million calls per day. Its busiest day was June 6, 1994—the 50th anniversary of D day—when there were 1,502,415 calls.

Longest telephone cable   The longest submarine telephone cable is FLAG (Fiber-optic Link Around the Globe), which runs for 16,800 miles from Japan to the United Kingdom and can carry 600,000 phone calls at a time.

FAX MACHINES

Largest fax machine   Manufactured by WideCom Group Inc. of Mississauga, Ontario, Canada, the "WIDEFax 36" can process documents up to 36 inches.

Smallest fax machine   The Real Time Strategies, Inc. hand-held device Pagentry combines various functions including the transmission of fax messages. It measures 3 by 5 by ³/₄ inches.

FIBER OPTICS

Greatest fiber optics transmission   The highest rate of transmission is 1.1 terabits per second, which is equivalent to 17 million simultaneous telephone calls. This was achieved by Fujitsu Laboratories, Kawasaki, Japan in March 1996.

Longest fiber optics transmission The longest distance over which signals have been transmitted without repeaters is 156.3 miles, by British Telecom (now BT), Martlesham, England in 1985.

The longest transmission distance at a data rate of 20 gigabits per second over a path containing repeaters is 78,000 miles, achieved by using a recirculating fiber loop at BT Laboratories, Martlesham, England and reported in September 1994.

Disneyland's "Light Magic," the world's largest fiber optic display (above), uses 2,500 miles of fiber optic strands to create over a million points of light.

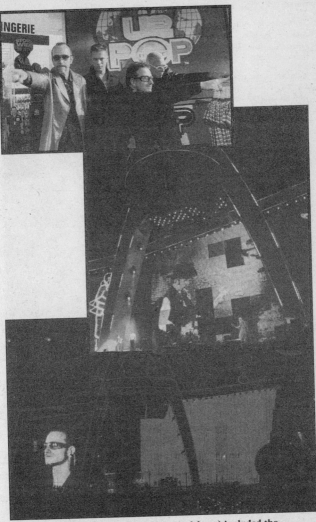

The stage set for U2's 1997 Pop Mart tour (above) included the world's largest LED screen, measuring 170 by 56 feet and containing a million light-emitting diodes. Among the images it displayed were abstract and animated pieces by artists Keith Haring and Roy Lichtenstein.

RADAR

Largest radar installation The largest of the three installations in the U.S. Ballistic Missile Early Warning System (BMEWS) is near Thule, in Greenland, 931 miles from the North Pole. It was completed in 1960 at a cost of $500 million.

Smallest radar system Electronic engineer Tom McEwan invented a radar device on a 1½-inch-square silicon chip. It can detect moving objects up to 164 feet away and is used as a virtual dipstick in industrial liquid tanks and as an electronic stethoscope.

The world's smallest radar system, invented by Tom McEwan, fits on a silicon chip.

POSTAL SERVICES

Largest mail service The country with the largest mail service is the United States. Its population mailed 182.66 billion letters and packages during the 1996 fiscal year. The U.S. Postal Service employs 760,966 people, and there are 38,212 post offices in the U.S.

Most post offices The country with the greatest number of post offices is India, with 152,792 in March 1995.

Stamp licking Dean Gould of Felixstowe, England licked and affixed 450 stamps in four minutes outside Tower Ramparts Post Office, Ipswich, England on November 24, 1995.

COMPUTERS

COMPUTING

Fastest computer   The fastest general-purpose vector-parallel computer is the CRAY Y-MP C90 supercomputer, with two gigabytes (gigabyte = one billion bytes) of central memory and with 16 CPUs (central processing units), giving a combined peak performance of 16 gigaflops (gigaflop = one billion floating point operations per second).

Several suppliers now market "massively parallel" computers which, with enough processors, have a theoretical aggregate performance exceeding that of a C90, though the performance on real-life applications can be less. This is because it may be harder to harness the power of a large number of small processors than a small number of large ones.

Fastest chip   The world's fastest microprocessor is the Alpha 21164, developed by Digital Equipment Corporation of Maynard, MA. It can run at 300 MHz.

Supercomputing speed record   The world supercomputing speed record was set in December 1994 by a team of scientists from Sandia National Laboratories and Intel Corporation. They linked together two of the largest Intel Paragon parallel-processing machines. The system achieved a performance of 281 gigaflops on the Linpack benchmark. The massively-parallel supercomputer also achieved 328 gigaflops running a program used for radar signature calculations. The 2-Paragon system used 6,768 processors working in parallel.

Highest-capacity disk drive   The disk drive with the highest capacity is a 23.4-gigabyte, 5.25-inch model, the Elite 23, produced by Seagate Technology of Scotts Valley, CA.

Largest computer network   The number of computers connected to the Internet has doubled every year since 1987, and in January 1996, there were at least 9,472,000. There may be substantially more than this, since many host or server computers are hidden behind firewalls designed to exclude unwanted visitors, including hackers.

Largest Internet service provider   The world's largest Internet service provider is America Online, based in Dulles, VA. Founded in 1985, the company had 8.04 million subscribers as of March 31, 1997.

Biggest Internet crash   On April 25, 1997 at approximately 11:30 A.M. EST, the global computer network experienced major problems and much of the system became unusable. Human error and equipment failure led a network in Florida to claim "ownership" of 30,000 of the Internet's 45,000 routes. There was widespread disruption, data packets were routed incorrectly, and connections failed across the Internet. Although some service providers took action within 15 minutes, problems persisted until 7:00 P.M. EST.

Most visited web site On July 8, 1997, the home page of NASA's web site for *Mars Pathfinder* had 46 million hits, a one-day record.

Pathfinder's landing on Mars on July 4, 1997 generated record Internet use; 46 million people visited the Pathfinder Web site on July 8.

Most wired community Montgomery County, VA claims to be the community with the most e-mail and Internet users relative to its size. According to a 1995 survey, there were approximately 30,000 users of wired data communications out of a population of 70,000. Around 20,000 users were connected through their local university, Virginia Tech.

Largest online interview The greatest number of questions asked of an individual over the Internet was 3 million, of Paul McCartney, who answered about 200 of the questions during a 90-minute session on May 17, 1997.

Largest-capacity memory chip The largest-capacity memory device is a 4-gigabit dynamic random access memory chip developed by NEC Corporation, Tokyo, Japan. The chip integrates 4.4 billion elements in one device, a memory capacity capable of storing six hours of audio data, equal to about one CD-ROM, or 64 copies of the complete works of Shakespeare.

Largest software company The largest software company is Microsoft Corporation of Redmond, WA. The company's highest annual revenues were

$8.7 billion in 1996; its highest annual net income was $2.2 billion in 1996. Microsoft had 20,561 employees worldwide in 1996.

Although software is not its primary business, International Business Machines Corporation (IBM) of Armonk, NY sold the most software in a single year, with software revenues of $13.05 billion in 1996.

America Online has more subscribers than any other Internet service provider.

Largest computer manufacturer   The world's largest manufacturer of computers is International Business Machines Corporation (IBM) of Armonk, NY. The company's highest annual revenues were $75.95 billion in 1996, and its net income in 1996 was $5.43 billion. IBM had 240,615 employees worldwide in 1996.

Largest personal computer manufacturer   The largest manufacturer of personal computers is Compaq Computer Corporation of Houston, TX. The company's highest annual revenues were $18.1 billion in 1996, and its highest annual net income was $1.3 billion in 1996. Compaq had 18,863 employees in 1996.

Compaq also sold the most personal computers in one year, with 7.13 million in 1996.

Largest computer chip manufacturer   Intel Corporation of Santa Clara, CA had its highest annual revenues, $20.85 billion, in 1996; its highest annual net income was $5.16 billion in 1996. Intel had 48,500 employees worldwide in 1996.

Fastest transistor   A transistor capable of switching 230 billion times per second was announced by the University of Illinois at Urbana–Champaign in October 1986. The devices were made of indium gallium arsenide and aluminum gallium arsenide and were developed in collaboration with General Electric Company.

Smallest modem   The smallest modem is the SRM-3A, which is 2.4 inches long, 1.2 inches wide, and 0.8 inches high, and weighs 1.1 ounces. It is currently manufactured by RAD Data Communications Ltd. of Tel Aviv, Israel.

Smallest robot   The world's smallest robot is the "Monsieur" microbot, developed by the Seiko Epson Corporation of Japan in 1992. The light-sensitive robot measures less than 0.06 cubic inches, weighs 0.05 ounces and is made of 97 separate watch parts (equivalent to two ordinary watches). Capable of speeds of 0.4 inches per second for about five minutes when charged, the "Monsieur" has earned a design award at the International Contest for Hill-Climbing Micromechanisms.

Largest CD-ROM library   MicroPatent of East Haven, CT, the commercial publisher of patent information, has a collection of 1,730 discs containing almost 20 million pages listing every U.S. utility patent from 1976 to the present day.

Biggest computer fraud   Between 1964 and 1973, 64,000 fake insurance policies were created on the computer of the Equity Funding Corporation in the United States, involving $2 billion.

Stanley Mark Rifkin was arrested in Carlsbad, CA by the FBI on November 6, 1978 and charged with defrauding a Los Angeles bank of $10.2 million by manipulation of a computer system. He was sentenced to eight years' imprisonment in June 1980.

EARTH AND SPACE

THE UNIVERSE

GALAXIES

Largest structure in the Universe   In June 1994, the discovery of a cocoon-shaped shell of galaxies about 650 million light-years across was announced by Georges Paturel (France) and his colleagues.

Remotest galaxy   The remotest galaxy is the radio galaxy 8C 1435 + 635. It has a red shift of 4.25, equivalent to a distance of 13 billion light-years. Tentative evidence was obtained during 1994 by a European Southern Observatory (ESO) team for a galaxy of red shift 4.38, equivalent to a distance of 13.1 billion light years.

Largest galaxy   The central galaxy of Abell 2029 is 1.07 billion light-years away in the Virgo cluster. The galaxy has a major diameter of 5.6 million light-years, which is 80 times the diameter of the Milky Way galaxy, and a light output 2 trillion times that of the Sun.

Most luminous galaxy   The highest luminosity reported for a galaxy is 4.7×10^{14} times that of the Sun for the hyperluminous IRAS (Infra Red Astronomy Satellite) galaxy FSC 10214 + 4724, which has a red shift of 2.282, equivalent to a distance of 11.6 billion light-years. However, this value is 10 to 100 times too large due to the lensing effect of intervening galaxies. If that is so, the brightest galaxy would then be the hyperluminous IRAS F15307 + 3252, with a luminosity 1.0×10^{13} times that of the Sun. Although it has a red shift of only 0.926, equivalent to a distance of 8.1 billion light-years, the luminosity of this galaxy may also be enhanced by lensing.

Farthest visible object   The remotest object visible to the naked eye is the Great Galaxy in Andromeda (magnitude 3.47). Known as Messier 31, it is a rotating spiral nebula at a distance of about 2.31 million light-years from Earth.

Under ideal conditions, Messier 33, the Spiral in Triangulum (magnitude 5.79), can be glimpsed by the naked eye at a distance of 2.53 million light-years.

QUASARS

Remotest object   The record red shift is 4.897 for the quasar PC 1247 + 3406. This quasar appears to be 13.2 billion light-years away.

Brightest object   The most luminous object in the sky is the quasar HS 1946 + 7658, which is 1.5×10^{15} times more luminous than the Sun. This quasar is 12.4 billion light-years away.

STARS

Largest star Betelgeuse (Alpha Orionis) is 310 light-years away. It has a diameter of 400 million miles, about 500 times greater than that of the Sun, and it is surrounded by a gas halo up to 530 billion miles in diameter.

Most massive star The variable Eta Carinae, 9,100 light-years away in the Carina Nebula, is estimated to have a mass 150–200 times greater than the mass of the Sun. The most massive stars whose masses have actually been determined are the two stars of the binary known as Plaskett's Star (discovered by K. Plaskett in 1992), which both have masses 60–100 times greater than the Sun.

Smallest star Neutron stars, which may weigh up to three times as much as the Sun, have diameters of only 6–19 miles. Although black holes are pointlike sources, their distortion of local space–time means that they appear as black stars, with a diameter of 37 miles for one weighing 10 times the mass of the Sun.

Lightest star The white dwarf companion to the millisecond pulsar PSR B1957 + 20 has a mass of only 0.02 that of the Sun (20 Jupiter masses) and is being evaporated away by the fast-spinning neutron star.

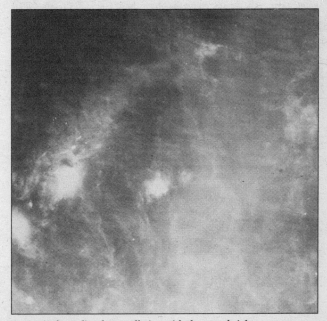

Taurus is the zodiacal constellation with the most bright stars.

The brown dwarf star Gliese 229B has a mass estimated to be between 20 and 50 Jupiter masses. Normal stars (those undergoing continuous fusion of hydrogen) cannot have a mass less than 80 times that of Jupiter.

Nearest star   The closest star other than the Sun is the very faint Proxima Centauri, which is 4.225 light-years away.

The nearest star visible to the naked eye is the Southern Hemisphere binary Alpha Centauri (4.35 light-years away), which has an apparent magnitude of –0.27.

Brightest star   If all the stars could be viewed at the same distance, Eta Carinae would be the brightest, with a total luminosity 6.5 million times that of the Sun. However, the visually brightest star viewed through a telescope is the hypergiant Cygnus OB2 No. 12, which is 5,900 light-years away. It has an absolute visual magnitude of –9.9 and is therefore visually 810,000 times brighter than the Sun.

Brightest star seen from Earth   Sirius A (Alpha Canis Majoris), 8.64 light-years away, is the brightest star in the sky, with an apparent magnitude of –1.46. It has a mass 2.14 times the mass of the Sun and is visually 24 times brighter.

Faintest star   The faintest star is the brown dwarf Gliese 229B, orbiting 4.1 billion miles from the main star Gliese 229A, which is 18.6 light-years away from Earth. The B star has a luminosity 500,000 times less than the Sun and a visual brightness 500 million times less. Its surface temperature of less than 1,300°F is the lowest observed stellar temperature.

Youngest stars   The youngest stars appear to be two protostars known collectively as IRAS–4 buried deep in dust clouds in the nebula NGC 1333, which is 1,100 light-years away. These protostars will not blaze forth as full-fledged stars for at least another 100,000 years.

Slowest pulsar   The pulsar with the slowest spin-down rate, and therefore the most accurate stellar clock, is PSR J0034 - 0534, at only 6.7×10^{-21} seconds per second.

Fastest pulsar   For pulsars whose spin rates have been accurately measured, the fastest-spinning is PSR B1937 + 214. It is in the constellation Vulpecula, 11,700 light-years away, and has a pulse period of 1.5578064949 milliseconds, which is equivalent to a spin rate of 641.9285218 revolutions per second.

Brightest supernova   The brightest supernova ever seen is believed to be SN 1006, seen near Beta Lupi in April 1006. It flared for two years and attained an estimated magnitude of –9 to –10.

Largest constellation   Hydra (the Sea Serpent) covers 1302.844 square degrees, or 3.16 percent of the whole sky, and contains at least 68 stars visible to the naked eye. The constellation Centaurus (Centaur), which ranks ninth in area, contains at least 94 such stars.

Zodiacal Virgo is the largest zodiacal constellation, with an area of 1,294.428 square degrees. Taurus has the most bright stars, with 125 down to magnitude 6.

Smallest constellation Crux Australis (Southern Cross) has an area of only 0.16 percent of the sky, or 68.477 square degrees, compared with the 41,252.96 square degrees of the whole sky.

Zodiacal The smallest zodiacal constellation is Capricornus (Capricorn), with an area of 413.947 square degrees.

THE SOLAR SYSTEM

Largest model of the solar system The biggest scale model of the solar system was developed by the Lakeview Museum of Arts and Sciences in Peoria, IL and inaugurated in April 1992. The planetary orbit of the model measures 60 miles across.

THE SUN

Largest object in the solar system The Sun is classified as a yellow dwarf type G2, but its mass of 2 octillion tons is 332,946.04 times the mass of Earth and represents over 99 percent of the total mass of the solar system. The Sun's diameter is 865,040 miles.

Greatest Earth–Sun distance Earth's orbit is elliptical, so its distance from the Sun varies. At aphelion, the outermost point, Earth is 94,509,200 miles from the Sun, compared with 91,402,600 miles at perihelion, the closest point.

Largest sunspot A sunspot recorded on April 8, 1947 had an area of about 7 billion square miles, with an extreme longitude of 187,000 miles and an extreme latitude of 90,000 miles.

Most sunspots In October 1957, a smoothed sunspot count showed 263, the highest recorded index since records started in 1755.

Longest-lasting sunspot In 1943, one sunspot persisted for 200 days, from June to December.

PLANETS

Largest planet Jupiter, with an equatorial diameter of 88,846 miles, has a mass 317.828 times, and a volume 1,323.3 times, that of Earth. It also has the shortest period of rotation; Jupiter's day is 9 hr. 50 min. 30.003 sec. long at the equator.

Smallest planet   Pluto has a diameter of 1,442 miles.

Coldest planet   Although the surface temperature of Pluto is only approximately known, its surface composition suggests that the temperature must be similar to the value of –391°F measured for Neptune's moon Triton, the lowest observed surface temperature of any natural body in the solar system.

Hottest planet   Venus has an estimated surface temperature of 864°F, based on measurements taken by the Russian *Venera* and U.S. *Pioneer* surface probes.

Outermost planet   The Pluto–Charon system orbits at a mean distance from the Sun of 3.674 billion miles.
   The remotest solar system object is the Kuiper Belt object 1995 WY2, which orbits at a mean distance of 4.420 billion miles.

Nearest planet to Earth   Venus can come to within 24 million miles of the Earth, but its average distance is 25.7 million miles inside Earth's orbit.

Fastest planet   Mercury, which orbits the Sun at an average distance of 35,983,100 miles, has an orbital period of 87.9686 days, thus giving it the highest average speed in orbit of 107,030 mph.

Highest surface feature   The highest surface feature of any planet is Olympus Mons in the Tharsis region of Mars. It has a diameter of 310–370 miles and an estimated height of 16 miles above the surrounding plain.

Brightest planet   Viewed from Earth, the brightest of the five planets normally visible to the naked eye (Jupiter, Mars, Mercury, Saturn, and Venus) is Venus, with a maximum magnitude of –4.4.

Faintest planet   Uranus, with a magnitude of 5.5, can be seen with the naked eye under certain conditions. The faintest of the nine planets as seen from Earth is Pluto (magnitude 15.0), which can only be viewed through a telescope.

Densest planet   Earth has an average density 5.515 times that of water.

Least dense planet   Saturn has an average density only about an eighth of Earth's density or 0.685 times the density of water.

Greatest conjunction   The most dramatic recorded conjunction of the seven principal members of the solar system besides Earth (Sun, Moon, Mercury, Venus, Mars, Jupiter and Saturn) occurred on February 5, 1962, when 16° covered all seven during an eclipse in the Pacific area.

ASTEROIDS

Largest asteroid   The largest asteroid is 1 Ceres, with an equatorial diameter of 596 miles.

Smallest asteroid   The smallest asteroid is 1993KA2, with a diameter of about 16 feet.

Brightest asteroid   The brightest asteroid is 4 Vesta (discovered on March 29, 1807) with an absolute magnitude of 3.16.

Faintest asteroid   The faintest asteroid is 1993KB2, whose absolute magnitude of 29 makes it the faintest object ever detected.

Nearest to the Sun   Most of the estimated 45,000 asteroids orbit between Mars and Jupiter, but the orbits of only about 7,200 have been computed. The Aten asteroid 1995 CR (discovered on February 3, 1995) is only 11,130,000 miles from the Sun at perihelion.

Farthest from the Sun   The Kuiper belt object 1994 JS is 4.933 billion miles away from the Sun at aphelion.

Closest approach to Earth   The asteroid 1994XM1, which is 33 feet in diameter, was discovered by James Scotti (U.S.) on December 9, 1994, 14 hours before it passed within 62,000 miles of Earth.

SATELLITES

Largest satellite   The largest and heaviest satellite is Ganymede (Jupiter III), which is 2.017 times as heavy as Earth's moon and has a diameter of 3,273 miles, compared with 2,159.3 miles for Earth's moon.

Smallest satellite   Of satellites whose diameters have been measured, the smallest is Deimos, the irregularly shaped outermost moon of Mars, which has an average diameter of 7.8 miles.

Most satellites   Of the 61 satellites in the solar system, 18 belong to Saturn.

Shortest planet–satellite distance   Phobos orbits Mars at a distance of 5,287 miles from the planet's center.

Longest planet–satellite distance   Jupiter's outer satellite Sinope orbits the planet at 14.7 million miles from its center.

MOON

Shortest Earth–Moon distance   In this century, the closest approach to Earth by the Moon (the smallest perigee) was 221,441 miles center-to-center on January 4, 1912.

Longest Earth–Moon distance   On March 2, 1984, the Moon was 252,718 miles from Earth, the farthest distance this century.

Largest craters   The largest impact basin on the Moon, and the largest and deepest crater in the solar system, is the far-side South Pole Aitken, which is 1,550 miles in diameter and an average 39,000 feet deep. The largest wholly visible crater is the walled plain Bailly, which is 183 miles across, with walls rising to 14,000 feet.

Highest mountains   In the absence of a sea level, lunar altitudes are measured relative to an adopted reference sphere with a radius of 1,080 miles.

On this basis, the highest elevation is 26,000 feet for the highlands north of the Korolev Basin, on the far side of the Moon.

Highest temperature   When the Sun is overhead, the temperature on the lunar equator reaches 243°F.

Lowest temperature   Around sunset, the temperature at the lunar equator is 58°F, and after nightfall it sinks to –261°F.

METEORITES

Oldest meteorite   The Krähenberg meteorite has been dated at 4.6 billion ± 20 million years, which is just within the initial period of solar system formation.

Largest meteorite   The largest known meteorite was found in 1920 at Hoba West, near Grootfontein in Namibia. It is a block nine feet long by eight feet wide, estimated to weigh 65 tons.

The largest meteorite exhibited in a museum is the "Cape York" meteorite, which weighs 68,000 pounds. It is on display in the Hayden Planetarium in New York City.

Largest meteor shower   On the night of November 16–17, 1966, the Leonid meteors were visible between western North America and eastern Russia. Meteors passed over Arizona at a rate of 2,300 per minute for a period of 20 minutes starting at 5 A.M. on November 17, 1966.

Largest crater   In 1962, a crater 150 miles in diameter and half a mile deep in Wilkes Land, Antarctica was attributed to a meteorite. The crater could have been created by a 14.33 billion-ton meteorite striking at 44,000 mph.

There is a craterlike formation or astrobleme 275 miles in diameter on the eastern shore of Hudson Bay, Canada.

The largest and best-preserved crater that was definitely formed by an asteroid is the Coon Butte or Barringer Crater, near Canyon Diablo, Winslow, AZ. It is 4,150 feet in diameter and now about 575 feet deep, with a parapet rising 130–155 feet above the surrounding plain. It has been estimated that an iron–nickel mass of some 2.2 million tons and with a diameter of 200–260 feet gouged out this crater *c.* 25,000 B.C.

ECLIPSES

Longest eclipse   The maximum possible duration of a solar eclipse is 7 min. 31 sec. The longest recent eclipse was on June 20, 1955 (7 min. 8 sec.), west of the Philippines, although it was clouded out along most of its track.

Most eclipses in one place   The only recent example of three total solar eclipses occurring in one location was at a point 44° N, 67° E in Kazakhstan, in September 1941, July 1945, and February 1952.

COMETS

Brightest periodical comet   Appearances of Halley's Comet, which has a period of 76 years, have been traced back to 467 B.C. The comet was first depicted in the Nuremburg Chronicle of A.D. 684.

Largest comet   The object 2060 Chiron has a diameter of 113 miles. The coma of the comet of 1811 was 1.2 million miles in diameter. The tail of the Great Comet of 1843 trailed for 205 million miles.

Longest period   The longest period computed for a comet is 1,550 years, for Comet McNaught-Russell, equivalent to a mean distance from the Sun of 12 billion miles.

Shortest period   The periodic comet that returns most frequently is the increasingly faint Encke's Comet, first identified in 1786. It has an orbital period of 1,198 days (3.28 years) and has the closest approach to the Sun (30.8 million miles at perihelion, when its speed is 158,000 mph).

Closest approach to Earth   On July 1, 1770, Lexell's Comet came within 745,000 miles of Earth.

Earth is believed to have passed through the tail of Halley's Comet on May 19, 1910.

It has been estimated that more people observed Hale-Bopp than any other comet to pass within Earth's orbit.

SPACE EXPLORATION

SPACE FLIGHT

Highest rocket velocity   The fastest escape velocity from Earth was 34,134 mph, achieved by the ESA *Ulysses* spacecraft, powered by an IUS–PAM upper stage after deployment from the space shuttle *Discovery* on October 7, 1990, en route to an orbit around the Sun via a flyby of Jupiter.

Most powerful rocket   The NI booster of the former USSR, first launched on February 21, 1969, had a thrust of 5,200 tons, but it exploded at takeoff + 70 seconds. Its current booster, *Energya*, first launched on May 15, 1987, has a thrust of 3,900 tons. It is capable of placing 116 tons into low Earth orbit. Four strap-on boosters powered by single RD-170 engines were used.

Most powerful rocket engine   The most powerful rocket engine was built in the former USSR by Scientific Industrial Corporation of Energetic Engineering in 1980. The engine has a thrust of 900 tons in open space and 830 tons at Earth's surface. The RD-170 burns liquid oxygen and kerosene.

Largest objects orbited   The 440-pound U.S. RAE (Radio Astronomy Explorer) B, or *Explorer 49*, launched on June 10, 1973, was the largest object orbited, with antennae 1,500 feet from tip to tip.

The heaviest object orbited was the combined Russian *Mir 1* space station and U.S. space shuttle *Atlantis*, which docked on June 29, 1995 and together weighed 245.8 tons.

The longest object ever placed in space was the Italian Tethered Satellite, deployed from *Columbia STS 75*, which extended 12.3 miles before the tether snapped on February 26, 1996. The satellite and the length of tether continued to orbit until March 19, 1996.

Closest approach to the Sun   The research spacecraft *Helios B* approached within 27 million miles of the Sun, carrying both U.S. and German instrumentation, on April 16, 1976.

Fastest spacecraft   The fastest solar system speed of approximately 158,000 mph is reached by the NASA–German *Helios B* solar probe when it reaches the perihelion of its solar orbit.

Remotest manmade object   *Pioneer 10*, launched from Cape Canaveral, FL on March 2, 1972, was 6.39 billion miles from Earth by July 8, 1997. The *Pioneer* mission formally ended on March 31, 1997, but the spacecraft will continue to travel indefinitely toward the constellation Taurus.

Most distant remote-controlled land vehicle   The most distant remote-controlled land vehicle is *Sojourner*, deployed from *Mars Pathfinder* shortly after its landing on Mars on July 4, 1997. Controllers on Earth communicated with *Sojourner* using radio waves, which took 10 min. 39 sec. to travel approximately 119 million miles from Earth to Mars.

(See also MOST VISITED WEB SITE, page 158.)

Longest manned spaceflight   Dr. Valeriy Polyakov (Russia) was launched to *Mir* aboard *Soyuz TM-18* on January 8, 1994. He landed in *Soyuz TM-20* on March 22, 1995, after a spaceflight lasting 438 days 18 hr.

The longest space flight by a woman was 188 days 4 hr. 0 min. 14 sec. by Dr. Shannon Lucid (U.S.), who was launched to *Mir* on *STS 76* on March 22, 1996 and landed on *STS 79* on September 26, 1996.

Under the FAI Category P for aerospacecraft, the longest spaceflight is by *Columbia STS 78*, which lasted 16 days 21 hr. 48 min., June 20–July 7, 1996.

Shortest manned spaceflight   Cdr. Alan B. Shepard, Jr. (U.S.N.) made a spaceflight aboard *Mercury 3* on May 5, 1961. His suborbital mission lasted 15 min. 28 sec.

Fastest spaceflight   The fastest speed at which humans have traveled is 24,791 mph, when the command module of *Apollo 10*, carrying Col. (now Brig. Gen.) Thomas Patten Stafford (U.S.A.F.), Cdr. Eugene Andrew Cernan (U.S.N.) and Cdr. (now Capt.) John Watts Young (U.S.N.), reached this maximum value at the 75.7-mile altitude interface on its trans-Earth round-trip flight on May 26, 1969.

Most space journeys   Two astronauts have completed six space flights. Capt. John Watts Young (U.S.N. ret.) flew *Gemini 3*, *Gemini 10*, *Apollo 10*, *Apollo 16*, *STS 1* and *STS 9*. Dr. Story Musgrave (U.S.) flew on *STS 6*, *STS 5F/Spacelab 2*, *STS 33*, *STS 44*, *STS 61* and *STS 80*.

The women's record is five, by Shannon Lucid (*STS 51G*, *STS 34*, *STS 43*, *STS 58* and *STS 76/STS 79*).

Most time in space   Valeriy Polyakov, a physician and research cosmonaut, has the most accumulated time in space, with 16,312 hr. 36 min. (nearly 680 days) in two missions.

The most experienced female space traveler is Shannon Lucid (U.S.), who has spent 223 days 2 hr. 54 min. 40 sec. in space on five missions. (*See also* LONGEST MANNED SPACEFLIGHT, *above*.)

Oldest astronaut   The oldest astronaut was Dr. Story Musgrave (U.S.; b. August 19, 1935), who flew on *Columbia STS-80* (November 19–December 7, 1996) at age 61 yr. 3 mo. 2 days.

Youngest astronaut   Major (later Lt.-Gen.) Gherman Stepanovich Titov (b. September 11, 1935) was 25 yr. 329 days old when launched in *Vostok 2* on August 6, 1961. The youngest woman in space was Valentina Tereshkova, age 26.

Largest crew   The largest crew on a single space mission was eight, launched on October 30, 1985 on *Challenger STS 61A*, the 22nd shuttle mission, which carried the German *Spacelab D1* laboratory. The mission, commanded by Hank Hartsfield, lasted 7 days 44 min. 51 sec.

The largest crew on a single spacecraft was 10, when the crew of the *Soyuz TM 21* mission (two Russians and one American) joined the crew of the *Atlantis STS 71* mission (five Americans and two Russians) aboard the Russian *Mir 1* space station on June 29, 1995.

SENIOR SPACEMAN

As a boy, Story Musgrave would slip out of his western Massachusetts farmhouse at night, lie on his back and gaze at the stars, never imagining their importance in his future. For when the space shuttle began its 17-day journey on November 8, 1996, the 61-year-old civilian became the world's oldest astronaut.

Musgrave, a medical doctor, totaled 1,281 hours, 59 minutes and 22 seconds in space over six flights. "Being the oldest is a source of pride," he says. "I've done it for 30 years and if you keep doing it you end up being the oldest. I'm the only person who flew on every shuttle. That record will probably stand forever because most people stay in the program for only eight or nine years."

But his pride is reflective, not boastful. "Space is my calling. It is a spiritual quest. My interest in space preceded medicine. My deep-rooted love for nature began on my family farm, and space is just a different point of view of nature," he says.

As it turned out, the 1,000-acre farm, now the site in Stockbridge, MA of the Norman Rockwell Museum, was not a happy place. Musgrave's family was torn by conflict. He had trouble completing high school and joined the Marines. Determined to acquire an education, he also began a pursuit that never ceased. Besides his

OLDEST ASTRONAUT

Dr. Story Musgrave (U.S.: b. August 19, 1935) flew on *Columbia STS-80* at age 61 yr. 3 mo. 2 days.

medical diploma, he has received a half-dozen degrees in everything from literature and mathematics to physiology and biophysics. Recently he was working on new master's degrees in psychology and history.

Musgrave joined the National Aeronautics and Space Administration (NASA) in 1967. "It just seemed like I had been preparing all my life for it," he says. "When the space program came along, bang, the epiphany struck and there was no going back." In space, he has cared for his fellow astronauts. "It's not like I did heart surgery," he says, "it was stuffy noses and headaches, nausea, ear blocks, like a family practitioner." As for his thirst for knowledge, "I didn't do homework in space. I worked very hard and every spare moment was used to catch the experience of space—what was in my heart and in my head."

Musgrave is grateful to the U.S. for his astronaut's career. "But space tends to transcend nationalism and national boundaries. You tend to see the entire planet. One reason we're in space is to elevate the human spirit."

Most people in space   The greatest number of people in space at one time was 13, by the crews of the 7-person American mission *STS-67* aboard *Endeavour*, and the combined Russian teams *Soyuz TM-20* and *Soyuz TM-21*, each of which consisted of three crew members (one American). From March 14 to March 18, 1995, all parties were in space conducting joint scientific experiments.

Farthest person from Earth   The greatest distance from Earth attained by humans was when the crew of *Apollo 13* were at apocynthion (i.e., their farthest point), 158 miles above the Moon and 248,655 miles from Earth, at 1:21 A.M. EST on April 14, 1970. The crew consisted of Capt. James Arthur Lovell Jr. (U.S.N.), Fred Wallace Haise Jr. and John L. Swigert.

Most isolated human being   The farthest a human has been removed from the nearest living fellow human is 2,235 miles, by the command module pilot Alfred M. Worden on the U.S. *Apollo 15* lunar mission of July 30–August 1, 1971, while David Scott and James Irwin explored the moon's surface.

Longest spacewalk   The longest spacewalk ever made was 8 hr. 29 min., by Pierre Thuot, Rick Hieb and Tom Akers on *Endeavour STS 49* on May 13, 1992. The longest spacewalk by a woman was 7 hr. 49 min., by Kathryn Thornton (U.S.) on *Endeavour STS 49* on May 14, 1992.

Untethered   Capt. Bruce McCandless II (U.S.N.), from the space shuttle *Challenger*, engaged in untethered EVA (extravehicular activity), at an altitude of 164 miles above Hawaii, on February 7, 1984.

Most spacewalks   Russian cosmonaut Aleksandr Serebrov completed a record ninth spacewalk on October 22, 1993.

Most flights by a shuttle   As of August 14, 1997, *Columbia* and *Discovery* had each flown 23 missions.

Greatest spaceflight disaster   The greatest published number to perish in a spaceflight is seven, aboard *Challenger 51L* on January 28, 1986, when an explosion occurred 73 seconds after liftoff, at a height of 47,000 feet.

TELESCOPES

Largest telescope   The world's largest telescopes are Keck I and Keck II on Mauna Kea, HI. Each one has a 10-meter primary mirror made up of 36 segments. Keck I and Keck II work together as an interferometer. Theoretically, they would be able to see a car's headlights separately from a distance of 15,500 miles.

Largest reflector   The largest single-mirror telescope in use is the 19-ft.-8-in. reflector on Mount Semirodriki, near Zelenchukskaya, Russia.

Largest infrared reflector The UKIRT (United Kingdom Infrared Telescope) on Mauna Kea, HI has a 147-inch mirror. It is so good that it can be used for visual work as well as infrared.

Largest metal-mirror reflector A 72-inch reflector was set up at Birr Castle, County Offaly, Ireland in 1845 by the third Earl of Rosse. The reflector was last used in 1909, but it is being restored and should be operational again in the near future.

Largest multiple-mirror telescope The MMT (Multiple-Mirror Telescope) at the Whipple Observatory at Mount Hopkins, AZ uses six 72-inch mirrors together, giving a light-grasp equal to a single 176-inch mirror.

Largest solar telescope The McMath solar telescope at Kitt Peak, AZ has a 6-ft.-11-in. primary mirror; the light is sent to it via a 32° inclined tunnel from a coelostat (rotatable mirror) at the top end.

The Keck telescopes are theoretically capable of seeing a car's headlights separately from a distance of 15,500 miles.

Largest submillimeter telescope The James Clerk Maxwell telescope on Mauna Kea, HI has a 49-ft.-3-in. paraboloid primary, and is used for studies of the submillimeter part of the electromagnetic spectrum.

Largest refractor A 62-foot-long refractor completed in 1897 is situated at the Yerkes Observatory, Williams Bay, WI and belongs to the University of Chicago, IL. The 40-inch refractor is still in full use on clear nights.

Largest radio telescope The largest radio telescope is the partially-steerable ionospheric assembly built over the natural bowl at Arecibo, Puerto Rico. The dish is 1,000 feet in diameter and covers 18½ acres suspended under a 600-ton platform.

Largest radio installation The Australia Telescope includes dishes at Parkes, Siding Spring and Culgoora. There are also links with tracking stations at Usuada and Kashima, Japan, and with the TDRS (Tracking and

Data Relay Satellite). This is equivalent to a radio telescope with an effective diameter of 17,102 miles.

The VLA (Very Large Array) of the U.S. National Science Foundation is Y-shaped, with a total of 27 mobile antennae, each with a diameter of 82 feet. Each arm of the "Y" is 13 miles long. The installation is 50 miles west of Socorro, NM.

Largest Schmidt telescope The largest Schmidt telescope is the 6-ft.-6³/₄-in. instrument at the Karl Schwarzschild Observatory in Tautenberg, Germany. It has a clear aperture of 52³/₄ inches with a 78³/₄-inch mirror, focal length 13 feet.

Largest space telescope The Edwin P. Hubble Space Telescope weighs 12 tons and is 43 feet in overall length, with a 94¹/₂-inch reflector. It was placed in orbit at 381 miles altitude by a U.S. space shuttle on April 24, 1990.

Oldest observatory The oldest observatory building is the "Tower of the Winds" used by Andronichus of Cyrrhus in Athens, Greece *c.* 100 B.C.

Highest observatory The observatory on Chacaltaya, Bolivia is at 17,060 feet. It is equipped with gamma ray sensors rather than telescopes.

Lowest observatory The lowest "observatory" is at Homestake Mine, SD, where the "telescope" is a tank of cleaning fluid (perchloroethylene), which contains chlorine, and can trap neutrinos from the sun. The installation is 1.1 miles below ground level so that experiments are not confused by cosmic rays.

Oldest planetarium The Adler Planetarium in Chicago, IL, which opened on May 12, 1930, is the oldest planetarium in the United States. Its dome is 68 feet in diameter, and it seats 433 people.

Largest planetarium The planetarium at the Ehime Prefectural Science Museum, Niihama City, Japan has a dome with a diameter of 98 ft. 5 in. Up to 25,000 stars can be displayed, and viewers can observe space as it would look from other planets.

Longest extraterrestrial search The longest-running SETI (search for extraterrestrial intelligence) project is the Ohio SETI Program at Ohio State University, Columbus, OH, which has searched the universe for extraterrestrial radio signals for 23 years, beginning in 1973.

Largest extraterrestrial search The most comprehensive search for extraterrestrial life is Project Phoenix (originally NASA SETI), which is conducted by the SETI Institute of Mountain View, CA. The project will be stationed in Green Bank, WV from the fall of 1996, using a 140-foot-diameter telescope to listen for radio signals from the neighborhoods of approximately 1,000 nearby sunlike stars by the year 2000.

Most powerful extraterrestrial search A system for analyzing signals from space was installed at the Arecibo Observatory (*see LARGEST RADIO TELESCOPE,* page 175) in 1997. Called Serendip IV (Search for Extraterrestrial Radio Emissions from Nearby Developed Intelligent Populations), the equipment can scan 168 million frequency channels every 1.7 seconds.

The Hubble Space Telescope has opened new horizons to
astronomers. The spectacular images on this page are a tiny sample
of its work.

THE EARTH

Deepest penetration into the earth A geological exploratory drilling near Zapolarny in the Kola Peninsula of Arctic Russia, begun on May 24, 1970, was reported in April 1992 to have surpassed a depth of 40,230 feet.

The deepest penetration made into the ground by human beings is in the Western Deep Levels Mine at Carletonville, Transvaal, South Africa, where a record depth of 11,749 feet was attained on July 12, 1977. The virgin rock temperature at this depth is 131°F.

CONTINENTS

Largest continent Of the earth's surface, only about 57,151,000 square miles (29.02 percent) is land above water, with a mean height of 2,480 feet above sea level. The Eurasian landmass is the largest, with an area (including islands) of 20,700,000 square miles.

The Afro-Eurasian landmass, separated artificially by the Suez Canal, covers an area of 32,700,000 square miles.

There is strong evidence that about 300 million years ago, the earth's land surface comprised a single primeval continent of 60 million square miles, now termed Pangaea.

Smallest continent The Australian mainland has an area of 2,941,526 square miles.

Land farthest from the sea The point of land remotest from the sea is at Lat. 46° 16.8′ N, Long. 86° 40.2′ E in the Dzungarian Basin, which is in the Xinjiang Uygur autonomous region of China. It is at a straight-line distance of 1,645 miles from the nearest open sea—Baydaratskaya Guba to the north (Arctic Ocean), Feni Point to the south (Indian Ocean) and Bohai Wan to the east (Yellow Sea).

Largest peninsula The world's largest peninsula is Arabia, with an area of about 1.25 million square miles.

United States The Alaskan peninsula is the longest in the United States, with a length of 471 miles. The longest in the conterminous 48 states is the Florida peninsula, at 383 miles.

ROCKS

Oldest rock The greatest reported age for any scientifically dated rock is 3.962 billion years in the case of the Acasta Gneisses, found 200 miles north of Yellowknife, Northwest Territories, Canada.

Older minerals that are not rocks have also been identified. Zircon crystals discovered in the Jack Hills, 430 miles north of Perth, Western Australia, were found to be 4.276 billion years old. These are the oldest fragments of the earth's crust discovered so far.

United States   The oldest rocks in the United States are the 3.6 billion-year-old Morton Gneisses, scattered over an area of 50 miles from New Ulm to Renville Co., MN.

Largest rock   The largest exposed monolith in the world is Ayers Rock, known to Aborigines as Uluru, which rises 1,143 feet above the surrounding desert plain in Northern Territory, Australia. It is 1.5 miles long and a mile wide.

Called Uluru by aboriginal Australians, Ayers Rock is the world's largest exposed monolith.

Longest natural arch   Kolob Arch in Zion National Park, Utah, has a span of 90–310 feet, a width of 41 feet and its height to the top surface is 330 feet. While Kolob Arch is set 50 feet from the wall of a cliff, Landscape Arch, in Arches National Park, Utah is a stand-alone arch with a span of 291–306 feet and the height to the top surface is 106 feet. In one place erosion has narrowed it to six feet wide.

Landscape Arch, one of the two longest natural arches, is just six feet wide at its narrowest point.

CAVES

Deepest cave   The Reseau Jean Bernard in the French Alps has been explored to a depth of 5,256 feet.

Longest cave   The most extensive cave system in the world is in Mammoth Cave National Park, KY. Explorations by many groups of cavers have revealed that interconnected cave passages beneath the Flint, Mammoth Cave, Toohey and Joppa ridges make up a system with a total mapped length that is now 350 miles.

Largest cave   The world's largest cave chamber is the Sarawak Chamber, Lubang Nasib Bagus, in the Gunung Mulu National Park, Sarawak, Malaysia. Its length is 2,300 feet, its average width is 980 feet, and it is not less than 230 feet high at any point.

Longest underwater cave   The Sistema Ejido Jacinto Pat in Quintana Roo, Mexico has over 35 miles of mapped passages.

Longest dive into a cave   The longest dive into a single flooded cave passage is 13,300 feet into the Doux de Coly, Dordogne, France by Olivier Issler (Switzerland) on April 4, 1991.

The longest underwater traverse in a cave is 10,000 feet from King Pot to Keld Head, North Yorkshire, England by Geoff Yeadon and Geoff Crossley on August 3, 1991.

The deepest cave dive was to 925 feet in Zacaton, Mexico by Jim Bowden (U.S.) in April 1994.

Deepest descent into a cave   The world depth record was set by the Groupe Vulcain in the Gouffre Jean Bernard, France at 5,256 feet in 1989. However, this cave has never been entirely descended, so the "sporting" record for the greatest descent into a cave is recognized as 4,947 feet in the Shakta Pantyukhina in the Caucasus Mountains of Georgia by a team of Ukrainian cavers in 1988.

Longest stalactite   The longest freehanging stalactite in the world is believed to be one measuring 92 feet long in Gruta do Janelão, Minas Gerais, Brazil.

Tallest stalagmite   The tallest known stalagmite in the world is one measuring 200 feet high in the cave of Tham Nam Klong Ngu, at Kanchanaburi, Thailand. It is difficult to see whether or not it is joined to the cave roof; if it is, it should correctly be termed a cave column. The tallest stalagmite may in that case be one measuring 105 feet tall in the Krasnohorska cave, near Roznava in Slovakia.

The tallest known cave column is considered to be the Flying Dragon Pillar, 128 feet high, in Daji Dong, Guizhou, China.

Deepest cave   The deepest cave in the United States is Lechuguilla Cave in Carlsbad Caverns National Park, Carlsbad, NM, which currently measures 1,567 feet deep and has a mapped length of 89.35 miles.

Highest rock pinnacle   The highest rock pinnacle is Ball's Pyramid, near Lord Howe Island in the Pacific, which is 1,843 feet high but has a base axis of only 660 feet.

GLACIERS

Longest glacier   The Lambert Glacier, which drains about a fifth of the East Antarctic ice sheet, is up to 40 miles wide and, with its seaward extension, the Amery Ice Shelf, it measures at least 440 miles long.

Fastest glacier   The fastest-moving major glacier is the Columbia Glacier, between Valdez and Anchorage, AK, which travels an average of 82 feet per day.

DESERTS

Largest desert   The Sahara in North Africa stretches 3,200 miles from east to west at its widest point. From north to south it is 800–1,400 miles long, and it covers 3,579,000 square miles.

Largest sand dunes   The world's highest measured sand dunes are those in the Saharan sand sea of Isaouane-N-Tifernine of east-central Algeria. They have a wavelength of three miles and are as high as 1,526 feet.

POLAR EXPLORATION

Longest sled journey   The longest polar sled journey was undertaken by the International Trans-Antarctica Expedition (six members), who traveled about 3,750 miles by sled in 220 days, from July 27, 1989 (Seal Nunataks) to March 3, 1990 (Mirnyy). The expedition was supported by aircraft.

The longest self-supporting polar sled journey was one of 1,350 miles from Gould Bay to the Ross Ice Shelf by Sir Ranulph Fiennes and Dr. Michael Stroud, November 9, 1992–February 11, 1993.

Oldest to reach both poles   Major Will Lacy (Great Britain) went to the North Pole on April 9, 1990 at age 82 and the South Pole on December 20, 1991 at age 84. He traveled by aircraft on both trips.

Youngest to reach both poles   Robert Schumann (Great Britain) went to the North Pole on April 6, 1992 at age 10 and the South Pole on December 29, 1993 at age 11. He reached the North Pole by air and the South Pole by mountain bike (having flown to within a short distance of the pole).

Fastest Antarctic crossing   The 2,600-mile trans-Antarctic leg from Sanae to Scott Base of the 1980–82 British Trans-Globe Expedition was achieved in 67 days and eight rest days, from October 28, 1980 to January 11, 1981, the expedition having reached the South Pole on December 15, 1980. The 3-man snowmobile team comprised Sir Ranulph Fiennes, Oliver Shepard and Charles Burton.

MOUNTAINS

Highest mountain   Recent satellite measurements indicate that Mt. Everest, a peak in the eastern Himalayas on the Tibet–Nepal border, is 29,029 feet high.

The mountain whose summit is farthest from the earth's center is the Andean peak of Chimborazo (20,561 feet), 98 miles south of the equator in Ecuador. Its summit is 7,054 feet farther from the earth's center than the summit of Mt. Everest.

The highest island mountain in the world is Puncak Jaya in Irian Jaya, Indonesia, at 16,023 feet.

Tallest mountain   Measured from its submarine base in the Hawaiian Trough to its peak, Mauna Kea (White Mountain), on the island of Hawaii, has a total height of 33,480 feet, of which 13,796 feet are above sea level.

From its submarine base in the Hawaiian Trough to its summit on the island of Hawaii, Mauna Kea measures 33,480 feet.

Longest mountain range   The submarine Mid-Ocean Ridge extends 40,000 miles from the Arctic Ocean, around Africa, Asia and Australia, to North America. Its highest point is 13,800 feet above the base ocean depth.

Land   The longest land mountain range is the Andes of South America, which is 4,700 miles long.

Highest mountain range   The Himalaya-Karakoram range contains 96 of the world's 109 peaks of over 24,000 feet.

Longest line of sight   Vatnajökull (6,952 feet), Iceland has been seen by refracted light from the Faeroe Islands 340 miles away. In Alaska, Mt. McKinley (20,320 feet) has been sighted from Mt. Sanford (16,237 feet), a direct distance of 230 miles.

Greatest plateau   The most extensive high plateau in the world is the Tibetan Plateau in Central Asia. Its average altitude is 16,000 feet and its area is 715,000 square miles.

Highest sea cliffs   The cliffs on the north coast of Moloka'i, HI near Umilehi Point descend 3,300 feet to the sea at an average inclination of more than 55°.

VALLEYS

Deepest valley   The Yarlung Zangbo valley in the Himalayas is 16,650 feet deep. The peaks of Namche Barwa (25,436 feet) and Jala Peri (23,891 feet) are 13 miles apart, with the Yarlung Zangbo River in between.

Largest gorge   The Grand Canyon on the Colorado River in north-central Arizona extends from Marble Gorge to the Grand Wash Cliffs, a distance of 277 miles. It averages 10 miles in width and is one mile deep.
   The submarine Labrador Basin, between Greenland and Labrador, Canada, is 2,150 miles long.

Deepest canyon   A canyon or gorge is generally defined as a valley with steep rock walls and a considerable depth in relation to its width.
   The Grand Canyon (*see LARGEST GORGE, above*) has the characteristic vertical sections of wall, but is much wider than its depth.
   The Vicos Gorge in the Pindus mountains of northwest Greece is 2,950 feet deep and 3,600 feet between its rims.

Deepest submarine canyon   The submarine canyon 25 miles south of Esperance, Western Australia is 6,000 feet deep and 20 miles wide.

ISLANDS

Largest island   Discounting Australia, which is usually regarded as a continental landmass, the largest island in the world is Greenland, with an area of about 840,000 square miles.

Sand   The largest sand island in the world is Fraser Island, Queensland, Australia, with a sand dune 75 miles long.

Freshwater The largest island surrounded mostly by fresh water (18,500 square miles) is the Ilha de Marajó in the mouth of the Amazon River, Brazil.

Remotest island Bouvet Island (Bouvetøya), an uninhabited Norwegian dependency in the South Atlantic, is 1,050 miles north of the nearest land, Queen Maud Land in Antarctica.

(*See also* REMOTEST INHABITED ISLAND, *page 214.*)

Greenland is the largest island on Earth.

Northernmost land The islet of Odaaq Ø, 100 feet across and 0.8 miles north of Kaffeklubben Ø off Pearyland, Greenland, is 438.9 miles from the North Pole.

Southernmost land The South Pole, unlike the North Pole, is on land. At the South Pole the ice sheet is drifting at a rate of 33 feet per year away from the geographic pole along the 40th meridian west of Greenwich.

Newest island An island in Tonga's Ha'apai group, covering an area of 12 acres and with a maximum height of 131 feet, is the world's newest island. The unnamed island is located halfway between the islands of Kao and Late and was formed as a result of submarine volcanic activities. The earliest date that the island can be said to have existed is June 6, 1995, when volcanic activity was first observed.

Greatest archipelago The world's greatest archipelago is the crescent of more than 17,000 islands, 3,500 miles long, that forms the Republic of Indonesia.

Largest atoll The largest atoll in the world is Kwajale in the Marshall Islands, in the central Pacific Ocean. Its coral reef, 176 miles long, encloses a lagoon of 1,100 square miles.

The atoll with the largest land area is Christmas Atoll, in the Line Islands in the central Pacific Ocean. It has an area of 251 square miles, of which 124 square miles is land.

Longest reef　The Great Barrier Reef off Queensland, northeastern Australia is 1,260 miles long. It actually consists of thousands of separate reefs. Large areas of the central section have been devastated by the crown-of-thorns starfish (*Acanthaster planci*).

MOUNTAINEERING

Climbing Mount Everest Most conquests　Ang Rita Sherpa has scaled Mount Everest (29,029 feet) eight times, with ascents in 1983, 1984, 1985, 1987, 1988, 1990, 1992, and 1993, all without the use of bottled oxygen.

Most climbers　The Mount Everest International Peace Climb, a team of American, Russian and Chinese climbers, led by James W. Whittaker (U.S.), succeeded in putting the greatest number of people on the summit, 20, on May 7–10, 1990.

Most in a day　Nine separate expeditions (32 men and 8 women from the United States, Canada, Australia, Great Britain, Russia, New Zealand, Finland, Lithuania, India and Nepal) reached the summit on May 12, 1992.

Sea level to summit　Timothy John Macartney-Snape (Australia) traversed Mt. Everest's entire altitude from sea level to summit. He set off on foot from the Bay of Bengal near Calcutta, India on February 5, 1990 and reached the summit on May 11, having walked approximately 745 miles.

Oldest　Ramon Blanco (Spain) was 60 years old when he reached the summit on October 7, 1993.

Most summits　Reinhold Messner scaled all 14 of the world's mountains of over 26,250 feet, all without oxygen.

Oldest mountain climber　Ichijirou Araya (Japan) climbed Mt. Fuji (12,388 feet) at the age of 100 yr. 258 days on August 5, 1994.

Greatest walls　The highest final stage in any wall climb is the one on the south face of Annapurna I (26,545 feet). It was climbed by the British expedition led by Christian John Storey Bonington, when, from April 2 to May 27, 1970, using 18,000 feet of rope, Donald Whillans and Dougal Haston scaled to the summit.

The longest wall climb is on the Rupal-Flank from the base camp, at 11,680 feet, to the South Point, at 26,384 feet, of Nanga Parbat—a vertical ascent of 14,704 feet. This was scaled by the Austro-German-Italian expedition led by Dr. Karl Maria Herrligkoffer in April 1970.

Highest bivouac　Four Nepalese summiters bivouacked at more than 28,870 feet in their descent from the summit of Everest on the night of April 23, 1990. They were Ang Rita Sherpa, on his record-breaking sixth ascent of Everest; Ang Kami Sherpa; Pasang Norbu Sherpa; and Top Bahadur Khatri.

Highest unclimbed mountain   The highest unclimbed mountain is Kankar Punsum (24,741 feet), on the Bhutan–Tibet border. It is the 67th highest mountain in the world.

The highest unclimbed summit is Lhotse Middle (27,605 feet), one of the peaks of Lhotse, in the Khumbu district of the Nepal Himalaya. It is the tenth highest individually recognized peak in the world, Lhotse being the fourth highest mountain.

THE OCEANS

Largest ocean   The Pacific Ocean represents 45.9 percent of the world's oceans and covers 64,186,300 square miles. Its average depth is 12,925 feet.

The saltiest water in a marine environment is found in a basin off the southwest coast of Crete. The water, a solution of magnesium chloride, is a third more dense than normal seawater.

Deepest ocean   The deepest point of the world's oceans is in the Marianas Trench in the Pacific Ocean. It was pinpointed in 1951 by the British Survey Ship *Challenger*, and on January 23, 1960, the manned U.S.N. bathyscaphe *Trieste* descended to the bottom. On March 24, 1995, the unmanned Japanese probe *Kaiko* also reached the bottom and recorded a depth of 35,797 feet.

Deepest ocean drilling   In 1993, the Ocean Drilling Program's vessel *JOIDES Resolution* drilled 6,926 feet into the seabed in the eastern equatorial Pacific. The deepest site at which drilling has been conducted is 23,077 feet below the surface on the western wall of the Marianas Trench, Pacific Ocean, by the Deep Sea Drilling Project's vessel *Glomar Challenger*.

Smallest ocean   The Arctic Ocean covers 5,105,700 square miles. Its average depth is 3,407 feet.

Largest sea   The South China Sea has an area of 1,148,500 square miles.

Remotest spot from land   The world's most distant point from land is a spot in the South Pacific, 47° 30′ S, 120° W, which is 1,600 miles from Pitcairn Island, Ducie Island and Cape Dart, Antarctica. Surrounding this spot is a circle of water with an area of 8,041,200 square miles—about a million square miles larger than Russia, the world's largest country.

Largest bay   The largest bay measured by shoreline length is Hudson Bay, Canada, which has a shoreline of 7,623 miles and an area of 476,000 square miles.

Measured by area, the Bay of Bengal, in the Indian Ocean, is larger, at 839,000 square miles.

A trio of Hudson Bay sights. The shoreline of the bay is a record 7,623 miles long.

Largest gulf   The Gulf of Mexico covers 596,000 square miles and has a shoreline extending 3,100 miles, from Cape Sable, FL to Cabo Catoche, Mexico.

Longest fjord   The Nordvest Fjord arm of the Scoresby Sound in eastern Greenland extends 195 miles inland from the sea.

Most southerly ocean   The most southerly part of the oceans is located at 87° S, 151° W, at the snout of the Scott Glacier, 200 miles from the South Pole.

Lowest sea temperature   The temperature of water at the surface of the White Sea can be as low as 28°F.

Highest sea temperature   In the shallow areas of the Persian Gulf, the surface temperature can reach 96°F in summer.

The highest temperature recorded in the ocean is 759°F in a hot spring 300 miles off the west coast of the United States, measured in 1985 by an American research submarine.

Clearest sea   The Weddell Sea, 71° S, 15° W off Antarctica, has the clearest water of any sea. A Secchi Disk one foot in diameter was visible to a depth of 262 feet on October 13, 1986, as measured by Dutch researchers at the German Alfred Wegener Institute. Such clarity is comparable to the clarity of distilled water.

Greatest ocean descent   The record ocean descent was achieved in the Challenger Deep of the Marianas Trench, where the U.S. Navy bathyscaphe *Trieste*, manned by Dr. Jacques Piccard (Switzerland) and Lt. Donald Walsh (U.S.N.), reached a depth of 35,797 feet on January 23, 1960. The descent took 4 hr. 48 min. and the ascent 3 hr. 17 min.

Longest survival at sea   Tabwai Mikaie and Arenta Tebeitabu, two fishermen from the island of Nikunau in Kiribati, were found alive on May 12, 1992 after surviving for a record 177 days adrift at sea in their 13-foot open dinghy.

Longest on a raft   The longest survival alone on a raft is 133 days (4½ months) by Second Steward Poon Lim of Great Britain's Merchant Navy, whose ship, the SS *Ben Lomond*, was torpedoed in the Atlantic 565 miles west of St. Paul's Rocks at Lat. 00° 30′ N, Long. 38° 45′ W at 11:45 A.M. on November 23, 1942. He was picked up by a Brazilian fishing boat off Salinópolis, Brazil on April 5, 1943.

STRAITS

Longest straits   The Tatarskiy Proliv or Tartar Straits, between Sakhalin Island and Russia, run 500 miles from the Sea of Japan to Sakhalinsky Zaliv.

Broadest straits   The broadest named straits in the world are the Davis Straits between Greenland and Baffin Island, Canada, with a minimum width of 210 miles. The Drake Passage, a deep waterway between the

Diego Ramirez Islands, Chile and the South Shetland Islands, is 710 miles across.

Narrowest strait   The narrowest navigable strait is the Strait of Dofuchi, between Shodoshima Island and Mae Island, Japan. At the bridge linking the two islands, the strait is 32 ft. 7 in. wide.

WAVES

Highest waves   The highest officially recorded sea wave was calculated at 112 feet from trough to crest; it was measured during a 68-knot hurricane by Lt. Frederic Margraff (U.S.N.) from the U.S.S. *Ramapo*, traveling from Manila, Philippines to San Diego, CA on the night of February 6–7, 1933.

The highest instrumentally measured wave was 86 feet high, and was recorded by the British ship *Weather Reporter* in the North Atlantic on December 30, 1972 at Lat. 59° N, Long. 19° W.

Highest tsunamis   On July 9, 1958, a landslip on land caused a 100-mph wave to wash 1,720 feet high along the fjord-like Lituya Bay in Alaska.

The highest tsunami triggered by an underwater landslide struck the island of Lanai in Hawaii *c.* 105,000 years ago. It deposited sediment up to an altitude of 1,230 feet.

The highest tsunami caused by an offshore earthquake appeared off Ishigaki Island, Ryukyu island chain, Japan on April 24, 1771. It was possibly 279 feet high, and it tossed an 830-ton block of coral more than 1½ miles inland.

Most deadly tsunami   The worst tsunami in the United States occurred on September 8, 1900 in Galveston, TX, killing more than 5,000 people.

CURRENTS

Greatest ocean current   On the basis of measurements taken in 1982 in the Drake Passage, between Chile and Antarctica, the Antarctic Circumpolar Current or West Wind Drift was found to be flowing at a rate of 4.3 billion cubic feet per second. Results from computer modeling in 1990 estimate a higher figure of 6.9 billion cubic feet per second.

Fastest ocean current   The Somali current flows at 9 mph in the northern Indian Ocean.

Strongest currents   In Nakwakto Rapids, Slingsby Channel, British Columbia, Canada (Lat. 51° 06′ N, Long. 127° 30′ W), the flow rate may reach 16 knots.

Largest area of calm water   The Sargasso Sea in the North Atlantic covers about 2.33 million square miles of relatively still water. Its surface is largely covered with sargassum, a seaweed.

TIDES

Greatest tide   The greatest tides occur in the Bay of Fundy, which divides the peninsula of Nova Scotia, Canada from Maine and the Canadian province of New Brunswick. Burntcoat Head in the Minas Basin, Nova Scotia has the greatest mean spring range, at 52 ft. 6 in. Comparable tides have been reported in Leaf Basin, in Ungava Bay, Quebec.

Least tide   Tahiti, in the mid-Pacific Ocean, experiences virtually no tide.

ICEBERGS

Largest iceberg   A tabular iceberg 208 miles long and 60 miles wide was sighted 150 miles west of Scott Island, in the South Pacific Ocean, by the U.S.S. *Glacier* on November 12, 1956.

Tallest iceberg   In 1958, the U.S. icebreaker *East Wind* reported a 550-foot-high iceberg off western Greenland.

Most southerly arctic iceberg   An arctic iceberg was sighted in the Atlantic by a U.S.N. weather patrol at Lat. 28° 44′ N (about the same latitude as Miami, FL), Long. 48° 42′ W, in April 1935.

Most northerly antarctic iceberg   A remnant of an antarctic iceberg was seen in the Atlantic by the ship *Dochra* at Lat. 26° 30′ S (roughly the same latitude as Rio de Janeiro, Brazil), Long. 25° 40′ W, on April 30, 1894.

RIVERS & LAKES

RIVERS

Longest rivers   The longest rivers in the world are the Nile, flowing into the Mediterranean, and the Amazon, flowing into the South Atlantic. Which one is longer is more a matter of definition than of measurement.

The Amazon has several mouths that widen toward the sea, so the exact point where the river ends is uncertain. If the Pará estuary is counted, its length is 4,195 miles. The length of the Nile before the loss of a few miles of meanders due to the construction of the Aswan High Dam was 4,145 miles.

United States   The Mississippi is 2,348 miles long. It flows from its source at Lake Itasca, MN through 10 states to the Gulf of Mexico. The entire Mississippi River system, including the eastern and western tributaries, flows through 25 states.

Shortest rivers   As with the longest river, two rivers could be considered to be the shortest named rivers. The Roe River, which flows into the Missouri River near Great Falls, MT, is fed by a large freshwater spring. It has two forks, measuring 201 feet (East Fork Roe River) and 58 feet (North Fork Roe River). The D River, in Lincoln City, OR, connects Devil's Lake to the Pacific Ocean. Its length is officially quoted as 120 ± 5 feet.

Largest river basin   The Amazon basin covers about 2,720,000 square miles. It has countless tributaries and subtributaries, including the Madeira, which at 2,100 miles is the longest tributary in the world.

Longest estuary   The Ob, in northern Russia, is 550 miles long. It is up to 50 miles wide, and is also the widest river that freezes solid.

Largest delta   The delta created by the Ganges and Brahmaputra in Bangladesh and West Bengal, India covers 30,000 square miles.

United States   The Mississippi River delta has an area of about 10,100 square miles.

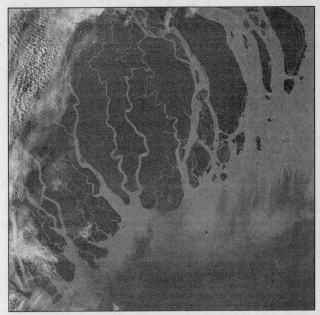

The Ganges Delta covers 30,000 square miles.

Greatest flow   The Amazon discharges an average of 7.1 million cusec into the Atlantic Ocean, increasing to more than 12 million cusec in full flood. The flow of the Amazon is 60 times greater than the flow of the Nile.

Largest submarine river   In 1952, a 190-mile-wide submarine river, known as the Cromwell Current, was discovered flowing eastward below the surface of the Pacific for 4,000 miles along the equator. It flows at depths of up to 1,300 feet, and its volume is 1,000 times the volume of the Mississippi.

Longest waterway   The longest transcontinental waterway is 6,637 miles long and links the Beaufort Sea in northern Canada with the Gulf of Mexico in the United States. It starts at Tuktoyaktuk on the Mackenzie River and ends at Port Eads on the Mississippi delta.

Largest swamp   The world's largest tract of swamp is the Pantanal, in the states of Mato Grosso and Mato Grosso do Sul, Brazil. It is about 42,000 square miles in area.

Largest marsh   The Everglades is a vast plateau of subtropical saw-grass marsh in southern Florida, covering 2,185 square miles. Fed by water from Lake Okeechobee, the Everglades is the largest subtropical wilderness in the continental United States.

Largest river bore   At spring tides, the bore (wave of tidal water) on the Qiantong Jiang in eastern China reaches a height of up to 25 feet and a speed of 13–15 knots. It can be heard advancing at a range of 14 miles.

The annual downstream flood wave on the Mekong, in southeast Asia, can reach a height of 46 feet.

WATERFALLS

Highest waterfall   The highest waterfall (as opposed to vaporized "bridal-veil fall") in the world is the Salto Angel (Angel Falls) in Venezuela, on a branch of the Carrao River, an upper tributary of the Caroni, with a total drop of 3,212 feet; the longest single drop is 2,648 feet.

United States   The tallest continuous waterfall in the United States is Ribbon Falls in Yosemite National Park, CA, with a drop of 1,612 feet. This is a seasonal waterfall and is generally dry from late July to early September.

Yosemite Falls, also in Yosemite National Park, has the greatest total drop at 2,425 feet, but actually consists of three distinct waterfalls. These are the Upper (1,430 feet); Middle (675 feet) and Lower falls (320 feet).

Largest waterfall   On the basis of average annual flow, the greatest waterfall is Boyoma Falls, Congo (formerly Zaire), with 600,000 cusec.

The waterfall with the greatest peak flow was the Guaíra (Salto das Sete Quedas) on the Alto Paraná River between Brazil and Paraguay, which on occasions reached 1.75 million cusec, until the completion of the Itaipú Dam gates in 1982.

Widest waterfall   The Khône Falls in Laos are 6.7 miles wide and 50–70 feet high, with a flood flow of 1.5 million cusec.

LAKES

Largest lake   The Caspian Sea (in Azerbaijan, Russia, Kazakhstan, Turkmenistan and Iran) is the largest inland sea or lake. It is 760 miles long and covers 143,550 square miles. Its maximum depth is 3,360 feet and its surface is 93 feet below sea level.

United States   The largest lake entirely within the United States is Lake Michigan, with a water surface area of 22,300 square miles, a length of 307 miles, a breadth of 118 miles and a maximum depth of 923 feet. Both Lake

Superior and Lake Huron have larger areas, but they straddle the border between Canada and the United States.

Deepest lake   Lake Baikal in Siberia, Russia is 385 miles long and 20–46 miles wide. The deepest part of the lake is 5,371 feet deep.

United States   Crater Lake, a 6-mile-long lake in the Cascade Mountains of Oregon, is 1,932 feet deep at its deepest point, and has an average depth of 1,500 feet. Crater Lake has no inlets or outlets; it is filled by precipitation.

Highest lake   The highest lake in the world is an unnamed lake in Tibet at an altitude of about 19,000 feet above sea level (Lat. 34°16′ N, Long. 85°43′ E). The lake has a maximum length of five miles and a maximum width of three miles. The highest named lake in the world, Burog Co, lies just to the north of it at an altitude of around 18,400 feet above sea level. Burog Co has a maximum length of 11 miles and a maximum width of five miles.

Largest freshwater lake   Measured by surface area, Lake Superior is the largest freshwater lake. It covers 31,800 square miles, of which 20,700 square miles are in Minnesota, Wisconsin and Michigan and 11,100 square miles are in Ontario, Canada.

The freshwater lake with the greatest volume is Lake Baikal in Siberia, Russia, with an estimated volume of 5,500 cubic miles.

Straddling the United States and Canada, Lake Superior is the world's largest freshwater lake.

Largest lagoon   Lagoa dos Patos, located near the seashore in Rio Grande do Sul, Brazil, is 174 miles long and extends over 3,803 square miles, separated from the Atlantic Ocean by long sand strips. It has a maximum width of 44 miles.

Largest underground lake The surface of the lake in the Drachen-hauchloch cave, near Grootfontein, Namibia, is 217 feet underground, and its depth is 276 feet.

United States The Lost Sea in the Craighead Caverns, Sweetwater, TN is 300 feet underground and covers 4½ acres.

Largest lake in a lake The largest lake inside another lake is Manitou Lake (41.09 square miles) on the world's largest lake island, Manitoulin Island (1,068 square miles), in Lake Huron.

DAMS & CANALS

DAMS AND RESERVOIRS

Most massive dam Measured by volume, the largest dam is New Cornelia Tailings, an earth-fill dam on Ten Mile Wash in Arizona, which has a volume of 274.5 million cubic yards.

The Grande Dixence is the world's highest concrete dam, at 935 feet high.

Largest concrete dam   The Grand Coulee Dam on the Columbia River, WA has a crest length of 4,173 feet, is 550 feet high, and contains 285 million cubic feet (21.5 million tons) of concrete.

Highest dam   The 984-foot high Nurek dam, on the River Vakhsh, Tajikistan, is the world's highest dam.

Highest concrete dam   Grande Dixence, on the river Dixence in Switzerland, is the highest concrete dam. It was built between 1953 and 1961 to a height of 935 feet, with a crest length of 2,297 feet.

Strongest dam   The 804-foot-high Sayano-Shushenskaya Dam on the River Yenisey, Russia is designed to bear a load of 20 million tons from a fully filled reservoir of 41 billion cubic yards capacity.

Longest dam   The Kiev Dam across the Dnieper, Ukraine, completed in 1964, has a crest length of 25.6 miles.

Largest tidal river barrier   The Oosterscheldedam, a storm-surge barrier in the southwestern corner of the Netherlands, has 65 concrete piers and 62 steel gates, and covers a total length of 5½ miles.

The largest tidal river barrier is the Oosterscheldedam, a storm-surge barrier in the Netherlands. It has 65 concrete piers and 62 steel gates, and it covers a total length of 5½ miles.

Largest levees The most massive levees ever built were the Mississippi River levees, begun in 1717 but vastly augmented by the federal government after the disastrous floods of 1927. They extended for 1,732 miles along the main river from Cape Girardeau, MO to the Gulf of Mexico and comprised more than a billion cubic yards of earthworks. Levees on the tributaries comprised an additional 2,000 miles.

The most massive levees ever built are the Mississippi River levees.

Longest breakwater The granite South Breakwater protecting the Port of Galveston, TX is 6.74 miles long.

Largest reservoir The largest man-made reservoir in terms of volume is the Bratskoye reservoir, on the Angara River in Siberia, Russia, with a volume of 40.6 cubic miles and an area of 2,111 square miles. It extends for 372 miles with a width of 21 miles.

The world's largest artificial lake measured by surface area is Lake Volta, Ghana, formed by the Akosombo Dam. The lake has an area of 3,275 square miles, with a shoreline 4,505 miles long.

United States The largest wholly artificial reservoir in the United States is Lake Mead in Nevada, formed by the Hoover Dam. It has a capacity of 1,241,445 million cubic feet and a surface area of 28,255,000 acre-feet.

Largest waterwheel The Mohammadieh Noria wheel at Hamah, Syria is 131 feet in diameter and dates from Roman times.

CANALS AND LOCKS

Longest ancient canal The Grand Canal of China was begun in 540 B.C. and not completed until A.D. 1327, by which time it extended (including canalized river sections) for 1,107 miles. The estimated work force *c.* A.D. 600 reached 5 million on the Bian section. The canal is still in use, carrying vessels of up to 2,200 tons.

Longest modern canal   The Belomorsko-Baltiyskiy Canal from Belomorsk to Povenets, Russia is 141 miles long and has 19 locks. The canal cannot accommodate ships of more than 16 feet in draft.

The world's longest big-ship canal is the Suez Canal linking the Red Sea with the Mediterranean, opened on November 17, 1869. It is 100.8 miles long from the Port Said lighthouse to Suez Roads, and ranges from 984 feet to 1,198 feet wide. It took 10 years and a work force of 1.5 million people to build the canal; 120,000 workers died during construction.

Busiest ship canal   Germany's Kiel Canal, linking the North Sea with the Baltic Sea, had more than 43,287 transits in 1995. The busiest in terms of tonnage of shipping is the Suez Canal, with 417,852,000 gross registered tons in the fiscal year 1995.

Longest irrigation canal   The Karakumsky Canal stretches 745 miles from Haun-Khan to Ashkhabad, Turkmenistan. The course length is 500 miles.

Largest canal system   The seawater cooling system associated with the Madinat Al-Jubail Al-Sinaiyah construction project in Saudi Arabia brings 388 million cubic feet of seawater per day to cool the industrial establishments.

Longest artificial seaway   The St. Lawrence Seaway is 189 miles long along the New York State–Canada border from Montreal to Lake Ontario. It enables ships up to 728 feet long and weighing up to 29,100 tons to sail 2,342 miles from the North Atlantic up the St. Lawrence estuary and across the Great Lakes to Duluth, MN.

Largest lock   The Berendrecht lock, which links the River Scheldt with docks in Antwerp, Belgium, is the largest sea lock in the world. It has a length of 1,640 feet, a width of 223 feet and a sill level of 44 feet.

Deepest lock   The Zhaporozhe lock on the River Dniepr, Ukraine can raise or lower barges 123 feet.

United States   The deepest lock in the United States is the John Day dam lock on the River Columbia, in Oregon and Washington. It can raise or lower barges 113 feet.

Highest lock elevator   The lock elevator at Ronquières on the Charleroi–Brussels Canal, Belgium rises to 225 feet.

Largest cut   The Corinth Canal, Greece, opened in 1893, is 3.93 miles long, 26 feet deep, 81 feet wide at the surface and has an extreme depth of cutting of 259 feet.

LAND RECLAMATION

Most reclaimed land   About one half of the Netherlands comprises polders, either former fen or marsh or land reclaimed from the sea. The area of reclaimed land exceeds 6,523 miles.

Since 1958, Monaco's land area has increased by 20 percent with the reclamation of 0.154 square miles of land from the sea.

Largest polder Of the five great polders in the old Zuider Zee, Netherlands, the largest is the East (Oostelijk) Flevoland Polder, at 204 square miles.

The largest would have been the Markerwaard, at 231 square miles, but the project has been abandoned following national debate over environmental issues. The water area remaining after the completion of the 20-mile-long dam in 1932 is called Ijsselmeer and has an area of 487.5 square miles.

Largest artificial island The two Flevoland polders, the East (Oostelijk) Polder and the South (Zuidelijk) Polder, form a continuous land area and are linked to the rest of the Netherlands by dykes, bridges and causeways. Together these two polders make up a single artificial island, the new Dutch province of Flevoland, with an area of 551 square miles and a population of 262,000.

WEATHER

Lowest ozone levels Ozone levels reached a record low between October 9 and 14, 1993 over the South Pole, when an average figure of 91 Dobson units was recorded. The minimum level needed to shield the earth from solar ultraviolet radiation is 300 DU.

Most equable temperature Between 1911 and 1990, the Brazilian offshore island of Fernando de Noronha had a minimum temperature of 63.9°F on February 27, 1980 and a maximum of 90.0°F on March 3, 1968, December 25, 1972 and April 17, 1973, giving an extreme range of 26.1°F.

Greatest temperature range The greatest recorded temperature ranges are around the Siberian "cold pole" in Russia. Temperatures in Verkhoyansk (67° 33′ N, 133° 23′ E) have ranged 188 degrees, from –90°F to 98°F.

The greatest variation recorded in a day is 100 degrees (a fall from 44°F to –56°F) in Browning, MT on January 23–24, 1916. The most freakish rise was 49 degrees in two minutes in Spearfish, SD, from –4°F at 7:30 A.M. to 45°F at 7:32 A.M. on January 22, 1943.

Highest shade temperature The highest shade temperature ever recorded is 136°F at Al'Aziziyah, Libya on September 13, 1922.

Hottest place At Marble Bar, Western Australia (maximum temperature 120.5°F), 160 consecutive days with maximum temperatures of 100°F or higher were recorded between October 31, 1923 and April 7, 1924.

United States The highest temperature recorded in the United States was 134°F at Greenland Ranch, Death Valley, CA on July 10, 1913. In Death Valley, maximum temperatures of over 120°F were recorded on 43 consecutive days, between July 6 and August 17, 1917.

Driest place The annual rainfall on the coast of Chile between Arica and Antofagasta is less than 0.004 inches.

Longest drought The Atacama Desert, in northern Chile, experiences virtually no rain, although several times a century a squall may strike a small area of it.

United States The most intense drought in the United States lasted 57 months, from May 1952 to March 1957, in western Kansas. The Drought Severity Index reached a lowest point ever of –6.2, in September 1956. Below –4.0 on this index indicates extreme drought conditions.

Most sunshine The annual average at Yuma, AZ is 91 percent of the possible hours of sunshine (4,055 hours out of 4,456 possible hours in a year).

St. Petersburg, FL recorded 768 consecutive sunny days from February 9, 1967 to March 17, 1969.

Lowest screen temperature A record low of –128.6°F was registered at Vostok, Antarctica (alt. 11,220 feet) on July 21, 1983.

The coldest permanently inhabited place is the village of Oymyakon, Siberia, Russia, where the temperature reached –90°F in 1933, and an unofficial –98°F has been published more recently.

United States The lowest temperature ever recorded in the United States was –79.8°F on January 23, 1971 in Prospect Creek, AK. The lowest in the conterminous states was –69.7°F in Rogers Pass, MT on January 20, 1954.

Coldest place Polyus Nedostupnosti, Antarctica, at 78° S, 96° E, is the coldest location in the world, with an extrapolated annual mean of –72°F.

United States Langdon, ND had 41 days below 0°F, November 11, 1935 to February 20, 1936. Langdon also holds the record for most consecutive days below 32°F, with 92 days from November 30, 1935 to February 29, 1936.

International Falls, MN has an annual mean temperature of 36.5°F, the lowest in the United States.

Thickest ice The greatest recorded thickness of ice is 2.97 miles, measured by radio echo soundings from a U.S. Antarctic research aircraft at 69° 56′ 17″ S, 135° 12′ 9″ E, 270 miles from the coast of Wilkes Land, Antarctica on January 4, 1975.

Deepest permafrost A permafrost of more than 4,500 feet was reported from the upper reaches of the Viluy River, Siberia, Russia in February 1982.

Greatest rainfall A record 73.62 inches of rain fell in 24 hours in Cilaos (alt. 3,940 feet), Réunion, Indian Ocean on March 15 and 16, 1952. This is equal to 8,327 tons of rain per acre.

For a calendar month, the record is 366 inches, at Cherrapunji, Meghalaya, India in July 1861. The 12-month record was also set at Cherrapunji, with 1,041.8 inches between August 1, 1860 and July 31, 1861.

United States In the United States, the 24-hour record is 43 inches in Alvin, TX, on July 25–26, 1979. Over a 12-month period, 739 inches fell in Kukui, Maui, HI from December 1981 to December 1982. The annual record for the conterminous states is 184.56 inches, in Wynoochee Oxbow, WA in 1931.

Most rainy days   Mt. Wai-'ale-'ale (5,148 feet), Kauai, HI has up to 350 rainy days per year.

Wettest place   By average annual rainfall, the wettest place in the world is Mawsynram, in Meghalaya State, India, with 467½ inches per year.

The wettest state in the U.S. is Louisiana, with an annual rainfall of 56 inches.

Most intense rainfall   The rainfall of 1.5 inches in one minute in Basse Terre, Guadeloupe on November 26, 1970 is the most intense recorded with modern methods.

Longest-lasting rainbow   A rainbow was continuously visible for six hours over Sheffield, England on March 14, 1994.

Deadliest flood   Some 900,000 people died in flooding from the Hwang-ho River, China in October 1887.

The most deaths from a flood in the United States was more than 2,000 people, in Johnstown, PA on May 31, 1889. The water formed a wall 20–30 feet high, rushing through the valley on the way to Johnstown at a rate of 15 mph.

Greatest flood   In 1993, scientists reported the discovery of the largest freshwater flood in history. It occurred *c.* 18,000 years ago when an ancient ice dam lake in the Altay Mountains in Siberia, Russia broke and allowed the water to pour out. The lake was estimated to be 75 miles long and 2,500 feet deep, and the main flow of water was probably about 1,600 feet deep and traveling at 100 mph.

Worst flood damage   In August 1993 it was reported that $12 billion in property and agricultural damage had been caused by the great Midwest flood of 1993. The flood affected parts of nine states and covered an area estimated at twice the size of New Jersey.

Windiest place   Commonwealth Bay, George V Coast, Antarctica, where gales reach 200 mph, is the world's windiest place.

Highest surface wind speed   A surface wind speed of 231 mph was recorded on Mt. Washington (6,288 feet), NH on April 12, 1934. The fastest speed at a low altitude was registered on March 8, 1972 at the U.S.A.F. base in Thule, Greenland, when a peak speed of 207 mph was recorded. The fastest speed measured to date in a tornado is 280 mph in Wichita Falls, TX on April 2, 1958.

Deadliest hurricane   The greatest number of fatalities from an American hurricane is an estimated 6,000 deaths on September 8, 1900 in Galveston Island, TX.

Fastest hurricane winds   The fastest sustained winds in a hurricane in the United States measured 200 mph, with 210-mph gusts, on August 17–18, 1969, when Hurricane Camille hit the Mississippi–Alabama coast at Pass Christian, MS.

Fastest-moving hurricane The greatest forward speed by a hurricane in the United States was in excess of 60 mph, for the Great New England Hurricane on September 21, 1938, when it struck central Long Island at Babylon, NY. The hurricane continued on to landfall at Milford, CT.

Costliest hurricane Hurricane Andrew hit southern Florida on August 24, 1992, crossed the Gulf of Mexico and caused further destruction in Louisiana. The hurricane killed 76 people, left approximately 258,000 people homeless and caused an estimated $46.5 billion in damages, making it the most costly hurricane ever in the United States.

Hurricane Andrew was the costliest hurricane ever to hit the United States. *(See also WEATHER, page 198.)*

Deadliest tornado Approximately 1,300 people were killed by a tornado in Shaturia, Bangladesh on April 26, 1989.

The most deaths from one tornado in the United States is 695, on March 18, 1925 in Missouri, Illinois and Indiana. This tornado also ranks first as the tornado with the longest continuous track on the ground, 219 miles; first with a 3.5-hour continuous duration on the ground; first in total area of destruction, covering 164 square miles; first in dimensions, with the funnel sometimes exceeding one mile wide; and third in forward speed, reaching a maximum of 73 mph, while averaging 62 mph over its duration.

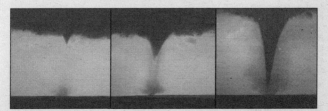

Most tornadoes The state with the most tornadoes recorded in a year is Texas, with 232 in both 1967 and 1995.

Most tornadoes in 24 hours The southern and midwestern United States experienced 148 tornadoes on April 3–4, 1974.

Heaviest hailstones The heaviest hailstones on record, weighing up to 2¼ pounds, are reported to have killed 92 people in Bangladesh on April 14, 1986.

Deadliest hail On April 20, 1888 in Moradabad, Uttar Pradesh, India, 246 people were killed by hailstones.

Greatest snowfall A total of 1,224½ inches of snow fell over a 12-month period from February 19, 1971 to February 18, 1972 at Paradise, Mt. Rainier, WA. The record for a single snowstorm is 189 inches at Mt. Shasta Ski Bowl, CA, February 13–19, 1959, and for a 24-hour period, the record snowfall is 78 inches, at Mile 47 Camp, Cooper River Division, AK on February 7, 1963.

The greatest depth of snow on the ground was 37 ft. 7 in. at Tamarac, CA in March 1911.

Most times struck by lightning Ex-park ranger Roy C. Sullivan was struck seven times. His attraction for lightning began in 1942, when he lost his big toenail. He was hit again in July 1969 (lost eyebrows), in July 1970 (left shoulder seared), on April 16, 1972 (hair set on fire), on August 7, 1973 (hair set on fire again and legs seared), and on June 5, 1976 (ankle injured), and he was sent to Waynesboro Hospital, Waynesboro, VA with chest and stomach burns on June 25, 1977 after being struck while fishing.

Deadliest lightning strike A Boeing 707 was struck by lightning and crashed near Elkton, MD on December 8, 1963, killing 81 people.

Most lightning strike survivors In July 1997, 45 people attending a country music festival in Haverhill, England were simultaneously struck by lightning. Five of them were treated for injuries in a local hospital but discharged soon afterward.

Highest pressure The highest barometric pressure ever recorded was 32 inches at Agata, Siberia, Russia (alt. 862 feet) on December 31, 1968.

Lowest pressure The lowest sea-level barometric pressure was 25.69 inches in Typhoon Tip, 300 miles west of Guam, Pacific Ocean, at Lat. 16° 44′ N, Long. 137° 46′ E, on October 12, 1979.

Foggiest place Sea-level fogs—with visibility less than 0.56 miles—persist for weeks on the Grand Banks, Newfoundland, Canada, with the average being more than 120 days of fog per year.

NATURAL DISASTERS

Greatest explosion There was an explosion of 10–15 megatons in the basin of the Podkamennaya Tunguska River, in Siberia, Russia, on June 30, 1908. The blast devastated an area of 1,500 square miles and the shock was felt 620 miles away. This explosion was probably caused by the disintegration at an altitude of 33,000 feet of a 100-foot-diameter stony asteroid traveling at hypersonic velocity.

EARTHQUAKES

Deadliest earthquake The greatest estimate of the death toll in an earthquake is the 830,000 fatalities in a quake in the Shaanxi, Shanxi and Henan provinces of China on February 2, 1556.

The highest death toll in modern times was the result of the Tangshan earthquake in eastern China on July 28, 1976. On January 4, 1977, the official death toll stood at 655,237, but this figure was later adjusted to 750,000. On November 22, 1979, the New China News Agency inexplicably reduced the official death toll to 242,000.

Strongest earthquake The most commonly used measure of the size of an earthquake is its surface magnitude (Ms), based on amplitudes of surface waves, usually at a period of 20 seconds. The largest reported magnitudes on this scale, known as the Richter scale, are about 8.9, but the scale does not properly represent the size of the very largest earthquakes, above Ms about 8, for which it is better to use the concept of seismic moment, Mo. Moment can be used to derive a "moment magnitude," Mw. The largest recorded earthquake on the Mw scale was the Chilean shock of May 22, 1960, which had Mw = 9.5, but measured only 8.3 on the Ms scale.

The strongest earthquake in American history, measuring 8.4 on the Richter scale and 9.2 on the Mw scale, was near Prince William Sound, AK (80 miles east of Anchorage) on March 27, 1964. It killed 131 people and caused an estimated $750 million in damage; it also caused a 50-foot tsunami that traveled 8,445 miles at 450 mph. The town of Kodiak was destroyed, and tremors were felt in California, Hawaii and Japan.

Most destructive earthquake The greatest physical devastation was in the earthquake on the Kanto plain, Japan, on September 1, 1923 (Mag. Ms = 8.2). In Tokyo and Yokohama, 575,000 dwellings were destroyed. The number of people killed and missing in this quake and the resultant fires was 142,807.

Highest homeless toll More than a million people in a 3,400-square-mile area of Guatemala were made homeless on February 4, 1976 when an earthquake ripped along the Montagua Fault, the boundary between the Caribbean and North American plates.

On February 4, 1976, a giant earthquake left over a million people homeless in Guatemala.

VOLCANOES

Greatest explosion The greatest explosion in historic times occurred on August 27, 1883, with an eruption of Krakatoa, an island (then 18 square miles) in the Sunda Strait, between Sumatra and Java, in Indonesia. The explosion, which was about 26 times as powerful as the largest hydrogen bomb ever tested, wiped out 163 villages, and 36,380 people were killed by the wave it caused. Pumice was thrown 34 miles high and dust fell 3,313 miles away 10 days later. The explosion was recorded four hours later on the island of Rodrigues, 2,968 miles away, as "the roar of heavy guns," and was heard over one-thirteenth of the surface of the globe.

Deadliest volcano Volcanic activity in Tambora, Sumbawa, Indonesia in April 1815 killed about 92,000 people.

United States The most deaths from a volcanic eruption in the United States was 60 people, on May 18, 1980 from the eruption of Mt. St. Helens, WA.

Greatest volume of discharge   The total volume of matter discharged in the eruption of Tambora, a volcano on the Indonesian island of Sumbawa, April 5–10 1815, was 36–43 cubic miles. A crater five miles in diameter was formed and the height of the island was lowered from 13,450 feet to 9,350 feet. More than 92,000 people were killed in the eruption, or died in the subsequent famine.

Most violent eruption   The ejecta in the Taupo eruption in New Zealand *c.* A.D. 130 has been estimated at 33·billion tons of pumice moving at one time at 400 mph. It flattened 6,200 square miles. Less than 20 percent of the 15.4 billion tons of pumice carried up into the air in this most violent of all documented volcanic events fell within 125 miles of the vent.

Longest lava flow   The longest lava flow in historic times was a mixture of ropey lava (twisted cordlike solidifications) and blocky lava resulting from the eruption of Laki in 1783 in southeast Iceland, which flowed 40–43 miles.

   The largest known prehistoric flow is the Roza basalt flow in North America *c.* 15 million years ago, which had an unsurpassed length (190 miles), area (15,400 square miles) and volume (300 cubic miles).

Most active volcano   Kilauea in Hawaii has erupted continuously since 1983. Lava is being discharged at a rate of seven cubic yards per second.

Largest active volcano   Of the 1,343 active volcanoes in the world (many of which are submarine), Mauna Loa in Hawaii is the largest. It has the shape of a broad, gentle dome 75 miles long and 31 miles wide (above sea level), with lava flows that occupy more than 1,980 square miles of the island. It has a total volume of 10,200 cubic miles, of which 84.2 percent is below sea level.

   Its caldera measures four square miles and is 500–600 feet deep. Mauna Loa rises 13,680 feet and erupts approximately every ten years. Its last eruption, however, occurred in 1984.

Highest active volcano   The highest volcano regarded as active is Ojos del Salado, at a height of 22,595 feet, on the Chile–Argentina border.

Northernmost volcano   Mt. Beerenberg (7,470 feet), on the island of Jan Mayen in the Greenland Sea, erupted on September 20, 1970.

Southernmost volcano   The most southerly active volcano is Mt. Erebus (12,447 feet), on Ross Island in the Antarctic Ocean.

Largest volcano crater   The world's largest volcano crater is that of Toba, Sumatra, Indonesia, covering 685 square miles.

AVALANCHES

Greatest avalanche   The greatest natural avalanches occur in the Himalayas, but no estimates of their volume have been published. It was estimated that 120 million cubic feet of snow fell in an avalanche in the Italian Alps in 1885.

Highest death toll   An estimated 40,000–80,000 men died in the Tyrolean Alps during World War I in avalanches triggered by the sounds of war.

Fastest-moving avalanche   The 250-mph avalanche triggered by the Mt. St. Helens eruption in Washington State on May 18, 1980 was estimated to measure 96 billion cubic feet.

GEYSERS

Tallest geyser   The Waimangu geyser in New Zealand erupted to a height of more than 1,500 feet in 1903. Although the ground in the area is still hot, Waimangu itself has not been active since late 1904.

The tallest active geyser is the Steamboat Geyser in Yellowstone National Park, WY. During the 1980s, it erupted at intervals ranging from 19 days to over four years, although there were occasions in the 1960s when it erupted every 4–10 days. Its maximum height is 195–380 feet.

LANDSLIDES

Deadliest landslide   A single landslide of rock debris from Mt. Huascaran, Peru killed over 18,000 people in the town of Yungay in an earthquake on May 31, 1970.

Most destructive landslide $138 million worth of damage was caused in southern California by a series of mudslides caused by nine days of torrential rain in January 1969.

HUMAN WORLD

GEOGRAPHY

COUNTRIES

Largest country   Russia has a total area of 6,592,800 square miles, or 11.5 percent of the world's land area. It is 1.8 times the size of the United States, but had a population of 147,168,000 people in 1995, around 60 percent the size of the U.S. population.

Smallest country   The smallest independent country in the world is the State of Vatican City or Holy See (Stato della Città del Vaticano), an enclave within the city of Rome, Italy. The enclave has an area of 108.7 acres.

Republic   The world's smallest republic is Nauru, in the Pacific Ocean. It has an area of 5,263 acres and a population of 10,600 (1996 estimate).

Colony   Gibraltar has an area of 1,440 acres. However, Pitcairn Island in the South Pacific (population 55 in late 1995) has an area of 960 acres.

Flattest and most elevated countries   The country with the lowest "high point" is Maldives, at eight feet above sea level. Lesotho has the highest "low point," at 4,530 feet above sea level.

Largest political division   The Commonwealth, a free association of 52 independent states and their dependencies, covers an area of 12,294,421 square miles and has a population of 1.5 billion. Almost all members belonged to the former British Empire.

Most national boundaries   There are 319 national land boundaries in the world. The continent with the greatest number is Africa, with 109.

China is the country with the most land frontiers, with 15—Mongolia, Russia, North Korea, Macau, Vietnam, Laos, Myanmar, India, Bhutan, Nepal, Pakistan, Afghanistan, Tajikistan, Kyrgyzstan and Kazakhstan. These extend for 14,900 miles.

The country with the most maritime boundaries is Indonesia, with 19.

Most border crossings   The most frequently crossed frontier is the border between the United States and Mexico, with over 500 million crossings each year.

Longest boundary   The longest boundary in the world is the border between Canada and the conterminous United States, which extends for 3,987 miles.

Maritime   The Greenland–Canada boundary is 1,676 miles long.

Shortest boundary   The land frontier between Gibraltar and Spain at La Linea measures one mile in length.

Longest coastline   Canada has the longest coastline of any country in the world, with 152,100 miles including islands.

Shortest coastline   Monaco has 3½ miles of coastline, excluding piers and breakwaters.

Nearest and farthest capital cities   The nearest capitals of two neighboring countries are the Vatican City and Rome (Italy)—the Vatican is surrounded by Rome. The greatest distance between capitals of countries that share a border is 2,600 miles, for Moscow (Russia) and Pyongyang (Democratic People's Republic of Korea).

STATES

Largest state   The largest state in land area is Alaska, with 591,004 square miles. The largest of the 48 conterminous states is Texas, with 267,017 square miles of land.

Smallest state   The smallest state is Rhode Island, with 1,212 square miles.

Most populous state   The most populous state in the United States as of July 1, 1996 was California, with an estimated 31,878,000 people.

Least populous state   As of July 1, 1996, Wyoming had an estimated 481,000 people.

Longest coastline   Alaska is the state with the longest coastline; it measures 5,580 miles.

COUNTIES

Largest county   The largest in the lower 48 states is San Bernardino County, CA, with an area of 20,062 square miles. The biggest legally established county is the North Slope Borough of Alaska, at 87,860 acres.

Most and fewest counties   The state with the most counties is Texas, with 254, and the state with the fewest is Delaware, with three (Kent, New Castle and Sussex).

CITIES AND TOWNS

Oldest town   The oldest walled town in the world is Ariha (Jericho), which was inhabited by perhaps 2,700 people as early as 7800 B.C. The settlement of Dolní Véstonice, Czech Republic has been dated to the Gravettian culture *c.* 27,000 B.C.

The oldest town of European origin in the United States is St. Augustine, St. John's County, FL. The town was founded on September 8, 1565, on the site of Seloy, by Pedro Menendez de Aviles. Its present population is 11,933.

Oldest city   The oldest capital city in the world is Dimishq (Damascus), Syria. It has been continuously inhabited since *c.* 2500 B.C.

United States   The oldest incorporated city is York, ME (present population 14,000), which received an English charter in March 1642, and was incorporated under the name Georgiana.

Most populous city The 1994 Revision of the United Nations publication *World Urbanization Prospects* lists Tokyo, Japan as the most populous agglomeration, with a population of 26,500,000 in 1994.

United States As of July 1, 1996, New York City had 7,380,906 residents.

Largest city The world's largest city (defined as a densely populated settlement) is Mount Isa, Queensland, Australia. The City Council administers 15,822 square miles.

Highest town The town of Wenzhuan, founded in 1955 on the Qinghai–Tibet road north of the Tangla range, is the highest in the world, at 16,730 feet above sea level.

United States The highest incorporated city in the United States is Leadville, CO, at 10,152 feet. Leadville has a population of 2,629.

Highest capital city The highest capital in the world, before the domination of Tibet by China, was Lhasa, at an elevation of 12,087 feet above sea level. La Paz, administrative and *de facto* capital of Bolivia, stands at an altitude of 11,913 feet above sea level.

Farthest town from the sea The major town most remote from the sea is Urumqi (Wulumuqi) in Xinjiang, the capital of China's Xinjiang Uygur Autonomous Region, at a distance of about 1,500 miles from the nearest coastline.

Highest settlement The settlement on the T'e-li-mo trail in southern Tibet is sited at an altitude of 19,800 feet.

Lowest settlement The Israeli settlement of Ein Bokek on the shores of the Dead Sea is 1,291 feet below sea level.

Lowest city The lowest incorporated city in the United States is Calipatria, CA, at 184 feet below sea level.

Northernmost settlement Ny Ålesund (78° 55′ N) is a coalmining settlement on King's Bay, Vest-Spitsbergen in the Norwegian territory of Svalbard. Its population varies seasonally from 25 to 100.

The northernmost town is Dikson, Russia (73° 32′ N), with a population of 1,400.

United States The northernmost city in the United States is Barrow, AK (71° 17′ N).

Northernmost capital city The northernmost capital is Reykjavik, Iceland (64° 08′ N). Its population was 103,036 in 1994.

Southernmost settlement The world's southernmost village is Puerto Williams (population 1,550) on the north coast of Isla Navarino, Tierra del Fuego, Chile, 680 miles north of Antarctica.

United States The southernmost city in the United States is Hilo, HI (19° 43′ N).

DANGER: POLAR BEARS!

NO VEHICLES BEYOND THIS POINT!

DISTURBING THE BEARS NEAR THE POINT MAY CAUSE
THEM TO RETURN TO BARROW AND THE DUMP AREA

PLEASE HELP REDUCE THE CHANCE OF HUMAN INJURY

The northernmost city in the United States is Barrow, AK. Tourists
are advised to pack warm clothes and to steer clear of polar bears.

Southernmost capital city Wellington, the capital of New Zealand (41° 17′ S), has a population of 331,100.

MAPS

Oldest map A clay tablet depicting the river Euphrates flowing through northern Mesopotamia (Iraq) dates to *c.* 2250 B.C. The earliest printed map in the world is one of western China dated to 1115.

Largest map The largest 2-dimensional map measures 49,000 square feet and was painted by students of O'Hara Park School, Oakley, CA in the summer of 1992.

Relief The Challenger relief map of British Columbia, Canada, measuring 6,080 square feet, was designed and built in the period 1945–52 by the late George Challenger and his son Robert. It is now on display at the Pacific National Exhibition in Vancouver, British Columbia.

Smallest map In 1992, Dr. Jonathon Mamin of IBM's Zurich laboratory used sudden electrical impulses to create a map of the Western Hemisphere from atoms. The map has a scale of one trillion to one, and a diameter of about one micron or $^1/_{100}$th the diameter of a human hair.

POPULATION

Most populous country China had an estimated population of 1.22 billion in mid-1996 and a rate of natural increase of over 12.1 million per year or more than 33,000 per day. Its population is larger than that of the whole world 150 years ago.

Least populous country The independent state with the smallest population is Vatican City, with just under a thousand inhabitants in 1996.

Most densely populated territory The Portuguese province of Macau, with an estimated population of 433,000 (1996) in an area of 7.5 square miles, has a density of 57.733 people per square mile.

Most sparsely populated territory Antarctica became permanently occupied by relays of scientists from 1943 on. The population now reaches 4,000 at times.

Remotest inhabited island The remotest inhabited island is Tristan da Cunha in the South Atlantic. The nearest inhabited land is the island of St. Helena, 1,315 nautical miles away.

Most houses For comparison purposes, a dwelling unit is defined as a structurally separated room or rooms occupied by a private household of one or more people and having separate access or a common passageway to the street. The country with the greatest number of dwelling units is China, with 276,947,962 in 1990.

Most immigrants The country that receives the most legal immigrants is the United States. During fiscal year 1996 (October 1995–September 1996), an estimated 915,900 people legally entered the United States.

In fiscal year 1996, a total of 1,549,876 people were apprehended for immigration violations. The largest group by nationality were 1,487,881 from Mexico.

Most tourists The World Tourism Organization reports that the most popular destination is France, which in 1995 received 60,584,000 foreign tourists.

The World Tourism Organization reports that the country that attracts the most visitors each year is France.

Most and fewest hospitals The country with the greatest number of hospitals is China, with 60,784 in 1993. Monaco has the most hospital beds per person (168 for every 10,000 people); Afghanistan, Bangladesh, Ethiopia and Nepal have the fewest (3 per 10,000).

Most and fewest physicians The country with the greatest number of physicians is China, which had 1,832,000 physicians in 1993, including those practicing dentistry and those practicing traditional Chinese medicine. The United States had 629,815 physicians as of January 1, 1994.

Niger has the highest number of people per physician, with 54,472, while at the other extreme, in Italy there is one physician for every 225 people.

THE MIDDLE OF NOWHERE

The 17th-century English poet John Donne wrote that "no man is an island," expressing the thought that one person cannot live in isolation from another, figuratively speaking. The 280 people who live literally on the remotest inhabited part of the world on the tiny island of Tristan da Cunha might beg to differ.

Discovered by the Portuguese explorer Tristao da Cunha in 1506, the island is located in the South Atlantic, midway between South Africa and South America. The nearest landfall is St. Helena, 1,315 nautical miles away. (St. Helena is 1,200 miles from the southwest coast of Africa and 1,800 miles from the coast of South America.)

Great Britain occupied Tristan da Cunha during Napoleon's exile on St. Helena. The British troops left the island in 1817, but one corporal chose to remain behind with his wife, along with a couple of former members of the Royal Navy. Some shipwrecked sailors joined this group to found Edinburgh, still the only settlement on Tristan da Cunha.

Brendan Dalley is the administrator of the colony. "Big government" keeps the island afloat. "Everything is run by the government because there isn't the market for private enterprise. The government has to provide the services and it is the majority employer." A total of 137 Tristanians work for the government.

Even an island of 280 people needs laws. Tristan da Cunha has a council of eight elected members, one of whom must be a woman by local law.

REMOTEST INHABITED ISLAND

The remotest inhabited island is Tristan da Cunha in the South Atlantic. The nearest inhabited land is the island of St. Helena, 1,315 nautical miles away.

There are also three members appointed by the administrator. What about crime? "We have one full-time policeman and four special constables who serve in their spare time," says Dalley. "We do have a jail, but the last time it was occupied was seven or eight years ago. The inmate was brought in for drunkenness." Dalley is quick to point out that there is only one bar on the island—and two churches.

How do people keep themselves entertained in the middle of the Atlantic Ocean? "Basically, you don't think of yourself as being on a little island. We have dances every Saturday night. There are no movie theaters, but people do have VCRs. We are too far out to get television, but we receive the BBC World Service on the radio," explains Dalley. Communications on the island itself are done the old-fashioned way. "There is no phone here. We send a runner," says Dalley. [Guinness reached Dalley on a satellite line, the kind ordinarily only used by ships.]

There is no airport on Tristan da Cunha, so the people depend on fishing boats and a Royal Mail ship to bring them supplies. "We get the mail every three or four months," Dalley says. What if Tristanians want to take a trip? "Boats leave for Cape Town every three months and occasionally islanders go by boat to St. Helena." There is a doctor on the island, but if surgery is required islanders are evacuated to South Africa. "A dental team visits once a year," says Dalley.

But Tristan da Cunha is not so removed from civilization as to be without *The Guinness Book of World Records*. Dalley has one in his library. "I was looking at it not long ago, looking up something in sports," he says.

Highest and lowest death rates   East Timor had a death rate of 45 per 1,000 in the period of 1975–80, but it subsided to 17.4 in the period 1990–95.

The highest estimated death rate in 1995 was 25.1 per 1,000 in Niger. The lowest estimated rate was 1.9 deaths per 1,000 in Kuwait.

Highest and lowest suicide rates   The country with the highest suicide rate is Sri Lanka, with a rate of 47 per 100,000 population in 1991. The country with the lowest recorded rate is Jordan, with just a single case in 1970 and hence a rate of 0.04 per 100,000.

Most divorces   The country with the most divorces is the United States, with 1,151,000 in 1996. The all-time high rate was 5.3 per 1,000 people, in 1979 and 1981. The lowest rate on record was 0.7 per 1,000 people, in 1900.

Greatest gender ratio imbalance   The country with the largest shortage of women is the United Arab Emirates, where 66.4 percent of the population is male. Latvia has the largest shortage of men; 53.4 percent of the population is female.

Highest and lowest infant mortality rates   The lowest infant mortality rate—the number of deaths at ages under one year per 1,000 live births—is in Guernsey, Channel Islands, Great Britain, with 1.9 per 1,000 in 1995. The sovereign country with the lowest rate is Iceland, with 3.2 per 1,000 in 1995.

The highest infant mortality rate is in Afghanistan, with 152.8 per 1,000 in 1995.

Life expectancy   World life expectancy has risen from 46.4 years in 1950–55 to 64.4 years in 1990–95.

The highest average life expectancy at birth is in the Republic of San Marino, with 85.3 years for women and 77.2 years for men in 1995–96. The lowest life expectancy for 1995–96 was 36.4 years for women and 35.9 years for men in Rwanda.

Highest and lowest birthrates   The crude birthrate—the number of births per 1,000 population—for the whole world was estimated to be 25 per 1,000 in the period 1990–95.

The highest rate estimated by the United Nations for 1995 was 55.2 per 1,000 for Niger.

Excluding Vatican City, where the rate is negligible, the lowest recorded rate for 1995 was 8.6 per 1,000 for Bulgaria.

Highest and lowest natural increase   The rate of natural increase (crude birthrate minus crude death rate) for the whole world was estimated to be 15.7 (25.0 minus 9.3) per 1,000 in the period 1990–95, compared with a peak of 20.4 per 1,000 in 1965–70.

The highest of the latest available recorded rates was 56.8 per 1,000 for Oman in 1995.

The lowest rate of natural increase in any major independent country in recent times was in Latvia, with –6.9 per 1,000.

ACCIDENTS AND DISASTERS

Atomic bomb On the morning of August 6, 1945, a U.S. B-29 dropped an atomic bomb on Hiroshima, Japan, killing over 130,000. Within a year, another 25,200 died from radiation.

Conventional bombing A bomb killed approximately 83,000 people on March 10, 1945 in Tokyo, Japan.

Marine disaster On January 30, 1945, 7,700 people died when the *Wilhelm Gustloff* sank into the Gulf of Danzig. The 25,484-ton German liner was torpedoed by a Russian submarine, leaving only 903 survivors.

Dam burst The Machhu River dam collapsed due to flooding on August 11,1979, claiming 5,000 lives in Morvi, India.

Panic On June 6, 1941, 700 people suffocated in a Chungking underground tunnel where they sheltered during a Japanese air raid.

Smog In London, England in December 1952, 3,500–4,000 people, mainly elderly and children, died from acute bronchitis caused by smog carrying dirt from industrial cities.

Industrial accident The December 3, 1984 methylisocyanate gas leak at a Union Carbide pesticide plant in Bhopal, India killed 3,350 and left 20,000 to suffer from blindness, cancer, and ulcers.

Fire The fire in the Hotel Daeyungak, Seoul, South Korea, December 25, 1971, killed 162 people.

Explosion On December 7, 1917 the French freighter *Mont Blanc,* packed with 5,000 tons of explosives and combustibles, collided with another ship in Halifax Harbour, Nova Scotia, creating a blast felt over 60 miles away and killing 1,635.

Mining accident A coal dust explosion killed 1,549 miners at Honkeiko Colliery, China, April 26, 1942.

Riots On February 28, 1947, Nationalist police in Taiwan beat and arrested an elderly woman selling black market cigarettes, then shot at the crowd that formed in protest. A riot ensued, and approximately 1,400 people were killed.

Mass suicide Rather than submit to the Romans, 960 Jewish zealots committed suicide after a prolonged seige of Massada, their fortress stronghold, during the Roman–Jewish war of A.D. 66–73. In modern times, the greatest mass suicide was on November 18, 1978, when 913 members of the People's Temple cult died of cyanide poisoning near Port Kaituma, Guyana.

The worst industrial accident in U.S. history was the explosion of the French freighter *Grandcamp* in Texas City, TX on April 15, 1947. At least 581 people were killed and 3,500 injured when the ship, loaded with 2,300 tons of ammonium nitrate, caught fire and exploded. The devastating blast threw shrapnel as much as 5,000 feet.

The world's largest airships were the *Hindenburg* (above) and its sister ship, the *Graf Zeppelin II*. On May 6, 1937, the *Hindenburg* exploded while mooring at Lakehurst, NJ. Thirty-six people perished.

The worst midair collision of two aircraft happened on November 12, 1996. Two commercial jets hit each other 50 miles southwest of New Delhi, India, killing 351.

Railroad disaster On June 6, 1981, an overcrowded passenger train travelling in Bihar, India fell off the Bagmati bridge into the river, leaving at least 800 dead.

Underground Approximately 300 people were killed when the underground train they were travelling in caught fire in Baku, Azerbaijan on October 28, 1995.

Aircraft disaster The worst air crash occurred on March 27, 1977, when two Boeing 747s (Pan-Am and KLM) collided on the runway at Tenerife in the Canary Islands, killing 583 people.

The crash of JAL's Boeing 747, flight 123, near Tokyo on August 12, 1985, in which 520 passengers and crew perished, was the worst crash involving a single plane in aviation history.

The worst midair collision occurred on November 12, 1996, when a Saudi Boeing 747 scheduled flight hit a Kazakh Ilushin 76 charter flight 50 miles southwest of New Delhi, India. A total of 351 people died.

Man-eating animal Between 1902 and 1907, 436 people were killed by a man-eating tiger in the Champawat district of India. The tiger was eventually shot by famed hunter Col. Jim Corbett.

Road accident At least 176 Soviet soldiers and Afghani citizens died of carbon monoxide asphyxiation when both ends of the Salang Tunnel in Afghanistan were sealed after a tanker full of petrol collided with the leading Soviet vehicle on November 3, 1982. Western estimates gave the number of deaths at around 1,100.

Latvia has the highest fatality rate in road accidents, with 34.7 deaths per 100,000 population, and Malta the lowest, with 1.6 per 100,000. The worst year for road deaths in the United States was 1972 (56,278).

Offshore oil platform accident A breakdown in production platform communications caused the Piper Alpha oil rig blast, which claimed 167 lives on July 6, 1988 in the North Sea.

Submarine accident The American freighter SS *Thompson Lykes* rammed and sank the Free French submarine *Surcouf*, which was carrying 130 officers and men, in the Caribbean on February 18, 1942. There were no survivors.

Helicopter crash A Russian military helicopter transporting 58 refugees from Abkhaziya on December 14, 1992 was shot down near the Georgian village of Lata. All the refugees and the three crew members died.

Mountaineering accident On July 13, 1990, 43 climbers died when an avalanche triggered by a small earthquake buried their camp on Lenin Peak on the Tajikistan/Kyrgyzstan border.

Fireworks accident The celebration of the Dauphin's wedding on May 16, 1770 in Paris, France ended in disaster when at least 800 people were trampled to death or drowned in the Seine after the fireworks display went wrong.

Ski lift accident On March 9, 1976, 42 skiers fell to their death when their trolley was knocked off its cable, snapping it and causing the car to plummet 250 feet at a resort in northern Italy.

Nuclear reactor disaster Although 31 was the official Soviet total of immediate deaths in the April 26, 1986 Chernobyl disaster, it is not known how many of the *c.* 200,000 people involved in the cleanup died in the 5-year period following the disaster due to radiation exposure, since no systematic records were kept.

Yacht racing accident High seas claimed 19 lives during the 28th Fastnet Race, held August 13–15, 1979, and left 23 boats sunk or abandoned.

Space disaster On January 28, 1986, the U.S. space shuttle *Challenger* exploded just 73 seconds after take-off at Cape Canaveral, Florida, killing the crew of seven.

In the worst accident on the ground, 91 people died when an R-16 rocket exploded during fueling at the Baikonur Space Center, Kazakhstan, on October 24, 1960.

Nuclear waste accident Overheating of a nuclear waste container caused the 1957 explosion at complex i-Kyshtym, Russia, dispersing radioactive compounds over 23,000 square kilometers. More than 30 small communities in a 460-square-mile area were eliminated from maps of the USSR in the years after the accident, with 17,000 people evacuated.

HOUSING

Largest house The 250-room Biltmore House in Asheville, NC is owned by George and William Cecil, grandsons of George Washington Vanderbilt II (1862–1914). The house was built between 1890 and 1895 on an estate of 119,000 acres, at a cost of $4.4 million; it is now valued at $5.5 million, with 12,000 acres.

Most expensive house The most expensive private house ever built is the Hearst Ranch in San Simeon, CA. It was built 1922–39 for William Randolph Hearst (1863–1951), at a cost of over $30 million. It has more than 100 rooms, a 104-foot-long heated swimming pool, an 83-foot-long assembly hall and a garage for 25 limousines. The house was originally maintained by 60 servants.

Largest nonpalatial residence St. Emmeram Castle, Regensburg, Germany, valued at more than $177 million, contains 517 rooms with a floor area of 231,000 square feet. Only 95 rooms are used by the family of the late Prince Johannes von Thurn und Taxis.

Longest continuous house construction Winchester House in San Jose, CA was under construction for 38 years. The original house was an 8-room farmhouse on the 161-acre estate of Oliver Winchester. Sarah Winchester, widowed in 1886, believed that she could balance the ledger for those killed by Winchester firearms by never stopping construction on the estate. She moved to California and transformed the farmhouse into a mansion, which now has 13 bathrooms, 52 skylights, 47 fireplaces, 10,000 windows, 40 staircases, 2,000 doorways and closets opening into blank walls, secret passageways, trapdoors, three elevators and more. The constant remodeling of the house was intended to confuse the resident ghosts.

Largest teepee   The largest teepee measures 42 feet in height and 252 feet in circumference, and utilizes 23 teepee poles. The teepee belongs to Dr. Michael P. Doss of Washington, D.C., a member of Montana's Crow tribe of Native Americans.

Tallest apartment building   The 1,127-foot John Hancock Center in Chicago, IL is 100 stories high; floors 44–92 are residential.

The tallest purely residential apartment house is Lake Point Tower, Chicago, IL, which has 879 units consisting of 70 stories, standing 639 feet high.

Northernmost habitation   The Danish scientific station set up in 1952 in Pearyland, Greenland is more than 900 miles north of the Arctic Circle and is manned every summer.

Southernmost habitation   The United States' Amundsen–Scott South Polar Station was completed in 1957 and replaced in 1975. It is permanently manned.

CASTLES

Oldest castle   The castle at Gomdan, Yemen originally had 20 stories and dates from before A.D. 100.

Largest ancient castle   Hradcany Castle, Prague, Czech Republic dates from the ninth century and covers 18 acres.

Tallest sand castle   A sand castle measuring 21 ft. 6 in. high, constructed only with hands, buckets and shovels, was made by a team led by Joe Maize, George Pennock and Ted Siebert in Harrison Hot Springs, British Columbia, Canada on September 26, 1993.

Longest sand castle   A sand castle 5.2 miles long was made by staff and pupils of Ellon Academy, near Aberdeen, Scotland, on March 24, 1988.

PALACES

Largest palace   The Imperial Palace (Gugong) in the center of Beijing, China covers a rectangle 3,150 by 2,460 feet (an area of 178 acres). The outline survives from the construction of the third Ming emperor, Yongle (1402–24), but most of the five halls and 17 palaces date from the 18th century.

The Palace of Versailles, 14 miles southwest of Paris, France, has a facade 1,903 feet long, with 375 windows. The building, completed in 1682 for Louis XIV (1643–1715), occupied over 30,000 workmen.

AMERICA'S HOUSE

"**W**hy don't the other kids in the neighborhood have to build a dollhouse?" That comment might sound strange coming from most children, but if you're one of miniaturist John Zweifel's six offspring, it's a perfectly normal question.

That's because they, along with more than 100 volunteers, helped their father fashion the world's largest dollhouse, a massive 60-foot replica of the White House.

"It grew out of a patriotic love—out of an individual family trying to show its love for its country," said Zweifel, who spent more than 35 years creating his masterpiece. "I wanted people all over the world to be able to visit America's house."

One peek through the window reveals an attention to detail that is difficult to comprehend. Imagine tiny, hand-blown crystal goblets and lightbulbs the size of a grain of rice. Every object in the White House, from the

rosewood furniture in the Lincoln bedroom to the paintings on the walls, is faithfully recreated in this record-breaking dollhouse. Zweifel and his cadre of volunteers began photographing and cataloguing each White House room in the 1960s so that it could be duplicated for display. Currently, the dollhouse showcases 50 rooms.

Each piece within the dollhouse is handmade to duplicate the original. Rugs are faithfully recreated by painstaking needlework and miniature furniture is whittled by hand. According to Zweifel, the replica is so exacting that even scratches in the furniture are reflected on the reproduction.

To stay current, Zweifel contacts the White House monthly to check for any changes. That means when the Clintons redecorate, so does Zweifel.

He does, however, save each piece for posterity and includes with his exhibit a miniaturization of each president's Oval Office.

The White House replica includes 1,589 feet of electrical wiring, 548 tiny light bulbs and six working television sets. What's more, it weighs over 10 tons. Traveling with this exhibit is no easy feat. It takes four days to set up and another two days to wrap each tiny piece before taking it on the road

LARGEST DOLLHOUSE

The White House Replica, created by John and Jan Zweifel, is 60 feet long and 20 feet wide. The 1:12 scale dollhouse contains authentic and detailed reproductions of each room in the real White House, including rooms that are not open to the public.

again. The dollhouse has toured all 50 states, Europe and Japan, and Zweifel estimates that over 50 million people have seen it. That, says Zweifel, is the payoff.

"The size and scope of this thing is amazing to people," he says. "I just stand there and listen to the people. I see tears in their eyes and hands over their hearts. It's like they're inside the walls and the walls are talking."

To Zweifel, this near life-long project is a "gift to the people," which he hopes will be carried on by his children. "This is not just a dollhouse. It's a history of the past and a project working toward the future."

Residential   Istana Nurul Iman, the palace of the Sultan of Brunei in the capital Bandar Seri Begawan, completed in January 1984 at a reported cost of $350 million, is the largest residence in the world, with 1,788 rooms and 257 bathrooms. The underground garage holds the sultan's 153 cars.

The facade of the Palace of Versailles is 1,903 feet long.

Largest ice palace   The ice palace built by TMK Construction Specialties for the St. Paul, MN Winter Carnival in January 1992 used 18,000 blocks of ice weighing 10.8 million pounds, stood 166 ft. 8 in. tall, and covered an area the size of a football field, making it the largest-ever ice construction.

Largest snow palace   The largest snow construction was a snow palace with a volume of 3,658,310.2 cubic feet and a height of 99 ft. 5 in. unveiled on February 8, 1994 at Asahikawa, Hokkaido, Japan.

Largest moat   From plans drawn by French sources, it appears that the moats surrounding the Imperial Palace in Beijing measure 161 feet wide and have a total length of 10,794 feet.

HOTELS

Oldest hotel   The Hoshi Ryokan in Awazu, Japan dates from A.D. 717, when Garyo Hoshi built an inn near a spring that was said to have miraculous healing powers. The waters are still celebrated for their recuperative effects, and the Ryokan now has 100 bedrooms.

Largest hotel   The MGM Grand Hotel/Casino in Las Vegas, NV consists of four 30-story towers on a 112-acre site. The hotel has 5,005 rooms with suites of up to 6,000 square feet, and the complex also includes a 15,200-seat arena and a 33-acre theme park. The complex was opened in December 1993.

Largest lobby   The lobby at the Hyatt Regency, San Francisco, CA is 350 feet long and 160 feet wide, and with its 170-foot ceiling is as tall as a 17-story building.

Tallest hotel   Measured from the main entrance to the top, the 73-story Westin Stamford in Raffles City, Singapore "topped out" in March 1985 at 742 feet tall. However, the Westin Stamford Detroit Plaza in Detroit, MI is 748 feet tall when measured from the rear entrance.

Most expensive room   The Galactic Fantasy Suite in the Nassau Marriott Resort and Crystal Palace Casino in the Bahamas costs $25,000 per night.

The price includes high-tech toys such as a Lucite piano that produces images as well as music, a rotating sofa and bed, and a thunder and lightning sound and light show.

Most mobile hotel   The 3-story brick Hotel Fairmount in San Antonio, TX, which weighs 1,600 tons, was moved on 36 dollies with pneumatic tires approximately five blocks and over a bridge, which had to be reinforced. The move, by Emmert International of Portland, OR, took six days, March 30–April 4, 1985, and cost $650,000.

Largest fumigation   During the restoration of the Mission Inn complex in Riverside, CA, June 28–July 1, 1987, Fume Masters Inc. of Riverside carried out the largest fumigation ever conducted to rid the buildings of termites. More than 350 tarpaulins were used to cover the 70,000-square-foot site and buildings—domes, minarets, chimneys and balconies, some of which were more than 100 feet high.

GOVERNMENT

WORLD LEGISLATURES

Oldest legislative body   The Althing of Iceland was founded in A.D. 930. This body was abolished in 1800, but restored by Denmark to a consultative status in 1843 and a legislative status in 1874.

The legislative assembly with the oldest *continuous* history is the Tynwald of the Isle of Man, Great Britain, which may have its origins in the late ninth century and possibly predates the Althing.

Largest legislative body   The National People's Congress of the People's Republic of China has 2,978 single-party members who are indirectly elected for a 5-year term.

Highest-paid legislators   The most highly paid of all the world's legislators are the Japanese. The prime minister has an annual salary of 38,463,360 yen ($343,000) including monthly allowances and bonuses.

Members of the House of Representatives and the House of Councilors have annual salaries of 23,633,565 yen ($211,000) including bonuses.

Smallest quorum   The House of Lords in Great Britain has the smallest quorum, expressed as a percentage of members eligible to vote, of any legislative body in the world—less than one-third of 1 percent of 1,205 members. To transact business, there need be only three peers present, including the lord chancellor or his deputy.

Largest petition   The largest petition on record was signed by 21,202,192 people, mainly from South Korea, between June 1, 1993 and October 31, 1994. They were protesting against the forced separation of families since the Korean war, and the division of the country into North and South Korea.

Longest membership The longest span as a legislator was 83 years, by József Madarász (1814–1915). He attended the Hungarian Parliament 1832–38 as *absentium oblegatus* (i.e., on behalf of an absent deputy), and was a full member from 1848 to 1850 and from 1861 until his death on January 31, 1915.

Longest speech Chief Mangosuthu Buthelezi, the Zulu leader, gave an address to the KwaZulu legislative assembly, March 12–29, 1993. He spoke on 11 of the 18 days, averaging nearly 2½ hours on each of those days.

The longest continuous speech made in the United Nations was one of 4 hr. 29 min. on September 26, 1960 by President Fidel Castro of Cuba.

Oldest treaty The oldest treaty still in force is the Anglo-Portuguese Treaty, which was signed in London, England on June 16, 1373.

Oldest constitution The world's oldest national constitution still in uninterrupted use is that of the United States of America, ratified by the necessary ninth state (New Hampshire) on June 21, 1788 and declared to be in effect on March 4, 1789.

The United States Constitution is the world's oldest national uninterrupted constitution.

ELECTIONS

Largest election The elections in April 1996 for the Indian Lok Sabha (Lower House), for 543 elective seats, was the largest election ever to take place. Over 343,350,000 voted in the 537 constituencies, out of a total electorate of 592,600,000. There were nearly 565,000 polling stations manned by 3 million people.

Closest election On January 18, 1961 in Zanzibar (now part of Tanzania), the Afro-Shirazi Party won the general elections by a single seat, after the seat of Chake-Chake on Pemba Island was won by a single vote.

The narrowest percentage win in an election was for the office of Southern District Highway Commissioner in Mississippi on August 7, 1979.

The largest number of votes cast in any election is 343,350,000 in India's national election of April 1996. In 1997 India celebrated its 50th anniversary as an independent nation. Elected leaders of the country have included (clockwise from bottom): Jawaharlal Nehru (1889–1964—seen with Mohandas Gandhi), Indira Gandhi (1917–84), Deve Gowda and Inder Kumal Gujral.

Robert Joiner was declared the winner over W. H. Pyron, with 133,587 votes to 133,582, so the loser obtained more than 49.999 percent of the votes.

Most decisive election   North Korea recorded a 100 percent turnout and a 100 percent vote for the Workers' Party of Korea in the general election of October 8, 1962.

An almost unanimous vote occurred in Albania on November 14, 1982, when a single voter spoiled national unanimity for the official (and only) candidates, who consequently obtained 99.99993 percent of the vote in a reported 100 percent turnout of 1,627,968.

Most crooked election   In the 1927 Liberian presidential election, President Charles D. B. King (1875–1961) was returned with an officially announced majority of 234,000 over his opponent, Thomas J. R. Faulkner of the People's Party. King thus claimed a "majority" more than 15½ times greater than the entire electorate.

Most elections contested   John C. "The Engineer" Turmel of Nepean, Ontario, Canada has contested a record 41 elections as an Independent candidate at a municipal, provincial and federal level since 1979. He founded the federal Abolitionist Party of Canada in 1993.

Longest in power   In Mongolia, the Communists (Mongolian People's Revolutionary Party) have been in power since 1924, although only since July 1990 within a multiparty system. In February 1992, the term "People's Republic" was dropped from the official name of Mongolia.

Highest personal majority   The highest-ever personal majority for any politician was 4,726,112 by Boris Yeltsin, the people's deputy candidate for Moscow, in the parliamentary elections held in the Soviet Union on March 26, 1989. Yeltsin received 5,118,745 votes out of the 5,722,937 that were cast in the Moscow constituency. Yeltsin's closest rival received 392,633 votes.

In the 1990 general election in Pakistan, Benazir Bhutto received 98.48 percent of the vote in the Larkana-III constituency, with 94,462 votes. The next-highest candidate obtained just 718 votes.

Largest political party   The Chinese Communist Party, formed in 1920, had a membership of 55 million in 1995.

Largest field of candidates   There were 301 candidates running to represent one seat, that of Belgaum City, in the State Assembly (Vidhan Sabha) elections in Karnataka, India on March 5, 1985.

Most coups   Statisticians contend that Bolivia, since it became a sovereign country in 1825, has had 191 coups. The latest was on June 30, 1984, when President Hernan Siles Zuazo was temporarily kidnapped from his official residence by a group of more than 60 armed men who were masquerading as police officers.

HEADS OF STATE

Oldest prime minister El Hadji Muhammad el Mokri, Grand Vizier of Morocco, died on September 16, 1957 at a reputed age of 116 Muslim (*Hijri*) years, equivalent to 112½ years.

The oldest age at first appointment was 81, in the case of Morarji Ranchhodji Desai of India (1896–1995) in March 1977.

Philippe Pétain (1856–1951), although not prime minister, became "chief of state" of the French state on July 10, 1940 at age 84.

Youngest head of government Dr. Mario Frick (b. May 8, 1965) became prime minister of Liechtenstein at age 28 on December 15, 1993.

Longest-serving prime minister The longest-serving prime minister of a sovereign state is Khalifa bin Sulman al-Khalifa (b. July 3, 1933) of Bahrain, who took office 1½ years before Bahrain became independent in August 1971.

Marshall Kim Il Sung was head of government or head of state of the Democratic People's Republic of Korea from August 25, 1948 until his death on July 8, 1994.

Woman Indira Gandhi (1917–84) of India was prime minister for 15 years—in two spans, 1966–77 and 1980–84.

Eugenia Charles (b. May 15, 1919) of Dominica is the current record-holder; she took office when her Dominica Freedom Party won the elections in July 1980.

Most women in a cabinet In Sweden, following a general election in March 1996, a new cabinet was formed containing 11 women out of a total 22 ministers.

ROYALTY

Oldest ruling house The Emperor of Japan, Akihito, is the 125th in line from the first Emperor, Jimmu Tenno, whose reign was traditionally from 660 to 581 B.C., but more probably dates from *c.* 40 B.C. to *c.* 10 B.C.

Longest reign The reign of Phiops II, or Neferkare, a Sixth Dynasty pharaoh of Egypt, began *c.* 2281 B.C., when he was six years old, and is believed to have lasted for 94 years.

Current The King of Thailand, Bhumibol Adulyadej (Rama IX), is currently the world's longest-reigning monarch, having succeeded to the throne on June 9, 1946.

Shortest reign Crown Prince Luis Filipe of Portugal was technically king of Portugal (Dom Luis III) for about 20 minutes. He was fatally wounded when his father was assassinated in Lisbon on February 1, 1908.

Youngest monarch King John I of France became sovereign at his birth on November 13 or 14, 1316, but died on November 19. King Alfonso XIII of Spain also became king at birth, on May 17, 1886.

King Hussein of Jordan is the current head of state who ascended to the throne at the youngest age. He became king on August 11, 1952 at age 16 yr. 254 days.

Most prolific royalty   The most prolific monogamous "royal" was Prince Hartmann of Liechtenstein (1613–86), who had 24 children, of whom 21 were born alive, by Countess Elisabeth zu Salm-Reifferscheidt (1623–88). HRH Duke Roberto I of Parma (1848–1907) also had 24 children, but by two wives.

Highest post-nominal number   The highest post-nominal number ever used to designate a member of a royal house was 75, briefly enjoyed by Count Heinrich LXXV Reuss zu Schleiz (1800–1801).

Heaviest monarch   In September 1976, 6-ft.-3-in.-tall King Taufa'ahau of Tonga recorded a weight of 462 pounds. In early 1993, he weighed 280 pounds.

Oldest head of state   The oldest head of state is Nouhak Phoumsavan (b. April 9, 1914), president of Laos. The oldest monarch is King Taufa'ahau of Tonga (b. July 4, 1918).

Largest gathering of world leaders   In honor of the fiftieth anniversary of the United Nations, a Special Commemorative Meeting of the General Assembly was held at United Nations Headquarters, New York City, October 22–24, 1995. The meeting was addressed by 128 heads of state and heads of government.

U.S. GOVERNMENT

PRESIDENTS

Oldest president   Ronald Reagan was 69 yr. 349 days old when he took the oath of office. He was reelected at age 73.

Youngest president   Vice-President Theodore Roosevelt became president at age 42 yr. 10 mo. when President William McKinley was assassinated in 1901. The youngest president ever elected was John Fitzgerald Kennedy, who took the oath of office at age 43 yr. 236 days in 1961.

Longest and shortest terms of office   Franklin D. Roosevelt served in office for 12 yr. 39 days (1933–45).

The shortest term in office was 32 days (March 4–April 4, 1841) by William Henry Harrison.

Longest and shortest inaugural speeches   William Henry Harrison's inaugural speech of 1841 lasted for two hours.

George Washington's second inaugural speech of March 4, 1793 lasted only 90 seconds.

Largest presidential gathering   On December 30, 1834, eight men who had been or would become president gathered together in the old House Chamber of the Capitol: ex-president John Quincy Adams; ex-president Andrew Jackson; Vice-President Martin Van Buren; Senator John Tyler; Senator James Buchanan; and Representatives James K. Polk, Millard Fillmore and Franklin Pierce.

Most handshakes   The most hands shaken by a public figure at an official function was 8,513, by President Theodore Roosevelt at a New Year's Day White House presentation in Washington, D.C. in 1907.

ELECTIONS

Largest popular majority   The greatest majority won was 17,994,460 votes in 1972, when President Richard M. Nixon (Republican) defeated George S. McGovern (Democrat) with 47,165,234 votes to 29,170,774.

Smallest popular majority   The smallest popular majority was 7,023 votes in 1880, when President James A. Garfield (Republican) defeated Winfield Scott Hancock (Democrat) with 4,449,053 votes to 4,442,030.

Largest electoral college majority   Since 1872, the greatest electoral college majority was 515 votes in 1936 when President Franklin D. Roosevelt (Democrat) defeated Alfred M. Landon (Republican) with 523 votes to 8.

VICE-PRESIDENTS

Youngest vice-president   The youngest man to become vice-president was John Cabell Breckinridge (Democrat), who took office on March 4, 1857 at age 36 yr. 1 mo.

Oldest vice-president   Alben William Barkley (Democrat) took office on January 20, 1949 at age 71 yr. 40 days. He served a full 4-year term.

Longest-lived vice-president   John Nance Garner served under Franklin D. Roosevelt from 1933 to 1941. He was born in 1868 and died on November 7, 1967 at age 98.

GOVERNORS

Oldest governor   Walter S. Goodland became governor of Wisconsin in 1943, at age 84.

Youngest governor   Stevens T. Mason was 24 years old when he was elected governor of Michigan in 1835.

CONGRESS

Most expensive election   The Federal Election Commission reported on April 28, 1995 that the 1994 congressional campaign was the most expensive in history. Candidates spent a total of $724 million.

AT THE HELM
OF THE
SHIP OF STATE

"*I*t's great to be the first woman in this job," says Secretary of State Madeleine Albright. "I consider it a major honor, and I'm planning to work very, very hard. It's one of the last big parts of the glass ceiling that have been smashed."

*A*lbright did not follow an easy road in becoming the highest ranking woman government official in the history of the United States. Her family was forced to flee her Czech homeland twice, first from the Nazis and later from the Communists. "I could not say that it had always been my ambition to be secretary of state of the United States," Albright says. "Frankly, I did not think it possible. I arrived in America when I was 11 years old. My ambition at that time was only to speak English well, please my parents, study hard and grow up to be an American."

*A*lbright believes that her appointment reflects the extraordinary opportunities in America, but she downplays the gender issue. "I have been a woman for 60 years; I've never been secretary of state, so now I have to

HIGHEST-RANKING WOMAN IN U.S. GOVERNMENT

Madeleine Albright is the highest-ranking woman in the U.S. government. She was appointed secretary of state by President Bill Clinton and sworn in on January 23, 1997.

see how it goes together. Gender is not the point; the point is to have the opportunity to represent the United States." Albright believes that women offer special skills that can greatly benefit the conduct of diplomacy. "It is sad but true that there are not enough women holding jobs in foreign affairs. At the United Nations, I was one of six female permanent representatives. The other 179 were men," she points out. "Correcting this is not simply about fairness. Today's world needs the unique set of skills and experience that women bring to diplomacy."

*A*lbright has already made her mark in Washington and diplomatic circles with her extraordinarily personal and forthright style. "My goal, and it is causing some culture shock in D.C., is to talk about foreign policy in human terms—and in bipartisan terms. I consider this vital because in our democracy, we cannot pursue policies abroad that are not understood and supported here at home," she says.

The secretary of state considers her job a unique opportunity to try to better the world. "We have a responsibility in our time, as others have had in theirs, not to be prisoners of history, but to shape history. We need to use and defend our own freedom, and to help others who share our aspirations for liberty, peace and the quiet miracle of a normal life. To that end, I pledge my own best efforts."

Longest congressional service   Carl Hayden (1877–1972; D-Arizona) holds the record for the longest congressional service, a total of 57 consecutive years (1912–1969), of which 41 yr. 10 mo. 11 days were spent as a senator and the remainder as a representative.

Longest-serving speaker   The longest time served by any speaker was 17 years, by Sam Rayburn (D-Texas). Rayburn served three terms: 1940–47, 1949–53, and 1955–61.

Shortest term   The shortest term of any speaker was one day, March 3, 1869, served by Theodore Medad Pomeroy (R-New York).

Oldest speaker   Sam Rayburn (D-Texas) was reelected speaker on January 3, 1961 at age 78 yr. 11 mo.

Youngest speaker   Robert Mercer Taliaferro Hunter (D-Virginia) was chosen speaker for the 26th Congress on December 2, 1839 at age 30 yr. 7 mo.

Longest-serving representative   Rep. Jamie L. Whitten (D-Mississippi) began his career on November 4, 1941 and retired on January 3, 1995, after 53 yr. 2 mo.

Youngest representative   The youngest person to serve in the House was William Charles Cole Claiborne (1775–1817; Jeffersonian Democrat-Tennessee), who, in contravention of the 25-year age requirement of the Constitution, was elected in August 1797 at age 22.

Oldest representative   The oldest person elected representative was Claude Pepper (D-Florida), who was reelected on November 8, 1988 at age 88 yr. 2 mo.

Oldest senator   The greatest age at which anyone has been returned as a senator is 87 yr. 11 mo., the age at which Strom Thurmond (R-South Carolina) was reelected in 1990.

Longest-serving senator   The longest-serving member of the Senate is Strom Thurmond (R-South Carolina). As of June 1997, Thurmond had served for 41 yr. 11 mo. He was elected as a Democrat in 1954, but became a Republican in 1964.

Youngest senator   The youngest person elected senator was Brig. Gen. Armistead Thomson Mason (D-Virginia), who was sworn in on January 22, 1816 at age 28 yr. 5 mo. 18 days. The youngest senator was John Henry Eaton (D-Tennessee), who was sworn in on November 16, 1818 at age 28 yr. 4 mo. 29 days.

Most expensive senate race   In 1994, Democratic incumbent Dianne Feinstein and Republican Michael Huffington spent a combined $44,590,675. Despite Huffington's record expenditure of $29,992,884, he lost the race to Feinstein, who spent $14,597,791.

Most consecutive roll calls   Senator William Proxmire (D-Wisconsin) did not miss a single one of the 9,695 roll calls from April 1966 to August 27,

1987. Rep. William H. Natcher (D-Kentucky) cast 18,401 consecutive roll call votes, January 6, 1954–March 3, 1994.

Longest filibuster The longest continuous speech in Senate history was by Senator Wayne Morse (D-Oregon) on April 24–25, 1953, when he spoke on the Tidelands oil bill for 22 hr. 26 min. without resuming his seat.

Interrupted only briefly by the swearing-in of a new senator, Senator Strom Thurmond (R-South Carolina) spoke against a civil rights bill for 24 hr. 19 min., August 28–29, 1957.

MAYORS

Longest mayoralty Edmond Mathis was the mayor of Ehuns, Haute-Saône, France for 75 years, 1878–1953.

The longest-serving mayor in the United States is Robert P. Linn, who took office as mayor of Beaver, PA in January 1946 and had served 51 yr. 217 days as of August 11, 1997.

Youngest mayor The youngest-ever mayor was Shane Mack (b. November 15, 1969), who became mayor of Castlewood, SD at age 18 yr. 169 days on May 3, 1988. He held office until May 6, 1996.

MILITARY & DEFENSE

WAR

Longest continuous war The Thirty Years' War, between various European countries, was fought continuously from 1618 to 1648.

The *Reconquista*—the campaigns in the Iberian Peninsula to recover the region from the Moors—began in 718 and continued intermittently until 1492, when Granada, the last Moorish stronghold, was conquered.

Bloodiest war The most costly war in terms of human life was World War II (1939–45). The total number of fatalities, including battle deaths and civilians, is estimated to have been 56.4 million. The country that suffered most was Poland, with 6,028,000 or 17.2 percent of its population of 35.1 million killed.

Civil The bloodiest civil war in history was the Taiping rebellion, a revolt against the Chinese Qing Dynasty between 1851 and 1864. According to the best estimates, the loss of life was some 20 million.

Most costly war The material cost of World War II far transcended that of all the rest of history's wars put together and has been estimated at $1.5 trillion.

Bloodiest battles The Battle of the Somme, France (July 1–November 19, 1916) produced 1.22 million casualties (dead and wounded); of these, 623,907 were Allied.

The greatest death toll in a battle has been estimated at 1,109,000 in the Battle of Stalingrad, USSR, ending with the German surrender on January 31, 1943. The Germans suffered 200,000 losses. About 650,800 soldiers from the Soviet army were injured but survived. Only 1,515 civilians from a pre-war population of more than 500,000 were found alive after the battle.

The final drive on Berlin, Germany by the Soviet army, and the battle that followed, April 16–May 2, 1945, involved 3.5 million men, 52,000 guns and mortars, 7,750 tanks and 11,000 aircraft.

United States The American Civil War (1861–65) claimed 200,000 lives and left 469,000 wounded. The bloodiest battle was at Gettysburg, PA, July 1–3, 1863, when the Union reported 23,000 killed, wounded and missing, and the Confederacy approximately 28,000 killed, wounded and missing.

Greatest naval battles The greatest number of ships and aircraft ever involved in a sea–air action was 282 ships and 1,996 aircraft in the Battle of Leyte Gulf, in the Philippines, during World War II. It raged from October 22 through October 27, 1944, with 218 Allied and 64 Japanese warships engaged, of which 26 Japanese and 6 U.S. ships were sunk. In addition, 1,280 U.S. and 716 Japanese aircraft were engaged.

The largest airborne invasion was the Anglo-American assault near Arnhem, Netherlands on September 17, 1944.

Greatest invasion   The greatest invasion in military history was the Allied operation against the Normandy coast of France starting on June 6, 1944. Thirty-eight convoys of 745 ships moved in during the first three days, supported by 4,066 landing craft, carrying 185,000 men, 20,000 vehicles and 347 minesweepers.

The air assault comprised 18,000 paratroopers from 1,087 aircraft. The 42 divisions had air support from 13,175 aircraft.

Airborne   The largest airborne invasion was the British–American assault by three divisions (34,000 men), with 2,800 aircraft and 1,600 gliders, near Arnhem, Netherlands, on September 17, 1944.

Longest-range attacks   The longest-range attacks were undertaken by seven B-52G bombers that took off from Barksdale Air Force Base, LA on January 16, 1991 to deliver air-launched cruise missiles against targets in Iraq. Each bomber flew 14,000 miles, with the round-trip mission lasting some 35 hours.

Greatest evacuation   The greatest evacuation in military history was carried out by 1,200 Allied naval and civilian craft from the beachhead at Dunkerque (Dunkirk), France, May 26–June 4, 1940. A total of 338,226 British and French troops were evacuated.

Largest civilian evacuation   Following the Iraqi invasion of Kuwait in August 1990, Air India evacuated 111,711 Indian nationals who were working in Kuwait. Beginning on August 13, 488 flights took the expatriates back to India over a 2-month period.

Longest march   The longest march in military history was the Long March by the Chinese Communists, 1934–35. In 368 days, of which 268 were days of movement, their force of some 100,000 covered 6,000 miles from Ruijin, in Jiangxi, to Yan'an, in Shaanxi. They reached Yan'an with about 8,000 survivors, following continual rearguard actions against Kuomintang (KMT) forces.

Worst sieges   The worst siege in history was the 880-day siege of Leningrad, USSR (now St. Petersburg, Russia) by the German army, from August 30, 1941 through January 27, 1944. The best estimate is that 1.3–1.5 million defenders and citizens died. This included 641,000 people who died of hunger in the city and 17,000 civilians killed by shelling. More than 150,000 shells and 100,000 bombs were dropped on the city.

The longest recorded siege was in Azotus (now Ashdod), Israel, which according to Herodotus was besieged by Psamtik I of Egypt for 29 years, during the period 664–610 B.C.

Chemical warfare   The greatest number of people killed in a single chemical warfare attack were the 4,000 Kurds who died at Halabja, Iraq in March 1988 when President Saddam Hussein used chemical weapons against Iraq's Kurds in revenge for the support they had given to Iran in the Iran–Iraq war.

Biggest demonstration   A figure of 2.7 million was reported from China for a demonstration against the USSR in Shanghai, March 3–4, 1969 following border clashes.

ARMED FORCES

Largest armed force The strength of China's People's Liberation Army in 1995 was estimated to be 2,930,000 troops. Its reserves number 1.2 million.

Largest navy The largest navy in terms of personnel is the United States Navy, with a total of 420,149 active-duty servicemen and servicewomen, plus 174,000 active-duty Marines in mid-1996. As of March 1996, the navy's active strength included 8 nuclear-powered aircraft carriers, 4 conventionally powered aircraft carriers, 16 ballistic missile submarines, 78 nuclear attack submarines, 31 cruisers, 51 destroyers, 34 frigates, and 40 amphibious warfare ships.

Oldest army The 80–90-strong Pontifical Swiss Guard in Vatican City was founded January 21, 1506. Its origins, however, predate 1400.

Largest army The army of the People's Republic of China had a total strength of some 2.2 million in mid-1994.

Oldest soldier John B. Salling of the Army of the Confederate States of America was the last accepted survivor of the Civil War (1861–65). He died in Kingsport, TN on March 16, 1959, aged 112 yr. 305 days.

Tallest soldier Väinö Myllyrinne was conscripted into the Finnish army when he was 7 ft. 3 in.; he later grew to 8 ft. 3 in.

Oldest air force The Royal Air Force can be traced back to 1878, when the British War Office commissioned the building of a military balloon. The Royal Air Force itself came into existence on April 1, 1918. Balloons had also been used for military observation by the French in June 1794 during the French Revolutionary Wars.

The FB-111A can reach speeds of Mach 2.5. The inaugural flight was on July 30, 1967. (See also FLYING, page 109.)

Largest air force   The United States Army Air Corps had 79,908 aircraft in July 1944 and 2,411,294 personnel in March 1944. In mid-1996, the U.S. Air Force, including strategic missile forces, had 387,275 personnel and 6,633 aircraft (plus more in storage).

Longest-serving military pilot   Norman E. Rose (Great Britain) flew military aircraft without a break in service for 47 years from 1942 to 1989, completing 11,539 flying hours in 54 different categories of aircraft.

BOMBS

Heaviest bomb   The heaviest conventional bomb ever used operationally was the Royal Air Force's Grand Slam, weighing 22,000 pounds and measuring 25 ft. 5 in. long, dropped on Bielefeld railroad viaduct, Germany on March 14, 1945.

In 1949, the United States Air Force tested a bomb weighing 42,000 pounds at Muroc Dry Lake, CA.

Nuclear   The heaviest known nuclear bomb was the MK 17, carried by U.S. B-36 bombers in the mid-1950s. It weighed 42,000 pounds and was 24 ft. 6 in. long.

Most powerful thermonuclear device   The most powerful thermonuclear device so far tested has a power equivalent to that of approximately 57 megatons of TNT, and was detonated by the former USSR in the Novaya Zemlya area on October 30, 1961. The largest U.S. H-bomb tested was the 18–22 megaton *Bravo* at Bikini Atoll, Marshall Islands on March 1, 1954.

Largest nuclear weapons   The most powerful ICBM (inter-continental ballistic missile) is the former USSR's SS–18 (Model 5), believed to be armed with 10 750-kiloton MIRVs (multiple independently targetable reentry vehicles). SS–18 ICBMs are located on both Russian and Kazakhstan territory, although the dismantling of those in Kazakhstan has begun.

TANKS

Heaviest tank   The heaviest tank ever constructed was the German Panzer Kampfwagen Maus II, which weighed over 210 tons. By 1945, it had reached only the experimental stage and was not developed further.

The heaviest operational tank used by any army was the 83-ton 13-man French Char de Rupture 2C bis of 1922. It carried a 155-mm howitzer and had two 250-hp engines giving a maximum speed of 7.5 mph.

United States   The heaviest tank in the United States Army is the M1A1 Abrams, which weighs 67 tons when combat loaded, is 32 ft. 3 in. long, and can reach 41.5 mph.

Most heavily armed tank   The most heavily armed tank is the Soviet T-72, which has a 4⁷/₈-inch high-velocity gun and is the only rocket-gun tank with explosive reactive armor.

Fastest tank   The fastest tracked armored reconnaissance vehicle is the British Scorpion, which can reach 50 mph with a 75 percent payload.

The American experimental tank M1936, built by J. Walter Christie, was clocked at 64.3 mph during official trials in Great Britain in 1938.

Most tanks produced   More than 50,000 of the Soviet T-54/55 series tanks were built between 1954 and 1980 in the USSR alone, with further production in the one-time Warsaw Pact countries and China.

GUNS

Largest gun   A gun with a caliber of 31½ inches and a barrel 94 ft. 8½ in. long was used by German forces in the siege of Sevastopol, USSR (now Ukraine) in July 1942. The gun was 141 feet long and weighed 1,481.5 tons, with a crew of 1,500. The range for a 5.3-ton projectile was 29 miles.

Heaviest gun   The heaviest gun in the U.S. Army is the MK19-3 40mm automatic grenade launcher, which weighs 72.5 pounds and has the greatest range of any U.S. Army weapon: about 1,650 yards at point targets, over 2,400 yards at area targets. The bullets can penetrate two inches into armor at 2,400 yards.

Largest cannon   The *Tsar Pushka*, now housed in the Kremlin, Moscow, Russia, was built in the 16th century with a bore of 35 inches and a barrel 17 ft. 6 in. long. It weighs 44 tons.

EDUCATION & AWARDS

EDUCATION

Oldest university   The oldest existing educational institution in the world is the University of Karueein, founded in A.D. 859 in Fez, Morocco.

Largest university   The largest existing university building in the world is the M.V. Lomonosov State University on the Lenin Hills, south of Moscow, Russia. It stands 787 ft. 5 in. tall, and has 32 stories and 40,000 rooms.

Greatest enrollment   The university with the greatest enrollment in the world is the State University of New York, which had 381,568 students at 64 campuses throughout the state in 1995.

The greatest enrollment at a university centered in one city is at the City University of New York, which had 206,500 students in late 1995. It has 21 campuses throughout the city.

Most graduates in a family   Dan and Helen Fagan of Bessemer, AL saw 15 of their 16 children obtain bachelor's degrees from a university or college between 1969 and 1992.

Youngest university student   Michael Kearney started studying for an Associate of Science degree at Santa Rosa Junior College, Santa Rosa, CA in September 1990 at the age of 6 yr. 7 mo.

Youngest graduate   Michael Kearney became the youngest graduate in June 1994, at age 10 yr. 4 mo., when he obtained his BA in anthropology from the University of South Alabama.

Youngest doctorate   On April 13, 1814, mathematician Carl Witte of Lochau was made a Doctor of Philosophy of the University of Giessen, Germany at age 12.

Youngest college president   The youngest president of a major college was Ellen Futter, who was appointed to head Barnard College, New York City in May 1981 at age 31.

Most durable professor   Dr. Joel Hildebrand, Professor Emeritus of Physical Chemistry at the University of California–Berkeley, became an assistant professor in 1913. He published his 275th research paper 68 years later.

Youngest professor   Colin Maclaurin was 19 years old when he was elected to Marischal College, Aberdeen, Scotland as Professor of Mathematics in 1717.

Most schools   The country with the greatest number of primary schools is China, with 857,245 in 1994. San Marino has the lowest pupil-to-teacher ratio, with 5.2 children per teacher.
   At general secondary level, India has the most schools, with 231,670 in 1995, while San Marino has the best pupil-to-teacher ratio, with 5.8 pupils per teacher.

Most expensive school   The annual cost of keeping a pupil at the most expensive school in the United States for the academic year 1997/98 is set at $35,740 at the Oxford Academy in Westbrook, CT.

Worst teacher–student ratio   The Central African Republic has 77 primary school students per teacher and 55.6 secondary school students per teacher.

Most higher education institutions   Mexico has 13,000 higher education students. The United States has the most tertiary-level students, with 14,210,000, while Canada has the highest ratio of tertiary-level students, with 6,980 per 100,000 population.

Largest school   In 1995/96, Rizal High School, Pasig, Manila, Philippines had 19,738 regular students.

Most schools attended   Wilma Williams attended 265 schools from 1933 to 1943 when her parents were in show business traveling around the United States.

Oldest high school graduate   Jean Lefcowitz Bowman received a high school diploma from University-Palisades Community Adult School in the Los Angeles Unified School District on June 30, 1996, when she was 86 yr. 252 days old.

NOW THAT'S A SENIOR

It may have taken Jean Bowman 70 years to finish high school, but when she finally donned her cap and gown, she did it with style. The 87-year-old Los Angeles grandmother not only earned her record as the oldest high school graduate, she gave the valedictory speech as well.

When Bowman dropped out of her junior year of high school in 1926, it was not unusual for a girl of her age to opt for a full-time office job. She married young—at age 19—and then raised three children. Yet throughout her life she harbored a secret wish to obtain her diploma. "Dropping out of school was a big mistake. I will always regret it," Bowman says. "In fact, I was so ashamed that I didn't tell my children I had never graduated from high school until I returned to school." So, some 70 years later, when she saw an ad in the local paper recruiting students interested in finishing their degrees, she picked up the phone and began her record-setting endeavor.

Bowman enrolled in University Palisades Community Adult School in January of 1995 at the age of 85 and attended school four nights a week. She soon found herself entrenched in the

OLDEST HIGH SCHOOL GRADUATE

Jean Lefcowitz Bowman received a high school diploma from University-Palisades Community Adult School in the Los Angeles Unified School District on June 30, 1996, when she was 86 yr. 252 days old.

typical work schedule of a teenager, "loaded down" with four hours of homework a day. The average age of her classmates was close to 20, yet this did not slow her urge to attain her diploma and lifelong dream. "The first day I was a little nervous and subdued, but the other students made me feel comfortable. They accepted me," she says.

Bowman's age did bring her a certain notoriety, however. During Career Night for the school's daytime students, she found it odd, yet endearing, that the daytime students kept trudging up three flights of stairs to interrupt her class and say hello to their history teacher. It was only later that she discovered that "the old lady," not the teacher, was the attraction. "The teacher kept on saying to the class, 'If my 86-year-old student can hand in her work on time, why can't you?'" laughs Bowman, "so they all wanted to get a look."

Her diligence earned her not only a four-point average but national fame to boot. After Bowman graduated at the head of her class, she did the talk show circuit, appearing on programs such as *The Tonight Show* and *The Today Show*. Her walls are lined with plaques and letters from celebrities and politicians congratulating the octogenarian student on her perfect report card. She even received accolades from the community school, which requested that she return to tutor incoming students. "The thing I like about it the most is when people say how proud they are of me. I feel so good about it," she says. "I have to say, though, I did it for myself."

Most durable teacher Medarda de Jesús León de Uzcátegui, alias La Maestra Chucha, has been teaching in Venezuela for 85 years. In 1911, when she was 12, she and her sisters set up a school. Since 1942, La Maestra Chucha has run her own school, which she calls the *Escuela Uzcátegui*, from her home in Caracas.

Highest endowment The greatest single gift in the history of education was $500 million, to the U.S. public education system by Walter Annenberg in December 1993. The gift was intended to help fight violence in schools.

Highest lecture fee Dr. Ronald Dante was paid $3,080,000 for lecturing students on hypnotherapy at a 2-day course held in Chicago in June 1986. He taught for eight hours each day and thus earned $192,500 per hour.

Walter H. Annenberg donated $500 million to the U.S. public education system in 1993.

HONORS, DECORATIONS AND AWARDS

Most lives saved   The greatest number of people saved from death by one person is estimated to be nearly 100,000 Jews in Budapest, Hungary from July 1944 to January 1945, by Swedish diplomat Raoul Wallenberg. After escaping an assassination attempt by the Nazis, he was imprisoned without trial in the Soviet Union. Although officials claimed that Wallenberg died in Lubyanka Jail, Moscow on July 16, 1947, sighting reports within the gulag system persisted for years after his disappearance.

Oldest order   The oldest honor known is the "Gold of Honor" for extraordinary valor, which was awarded in the 18th Dynasty *c.* 1440–1400 B.C. A representative statuette was found at Qan-el-Kebri, Egypt. The oldest true order is the Order of St. John of Jerusalem (the direct descendant of which is the Sovereign Military Order of Malta), legitimized in 1113.

Youngest awardees   Kristina Stragauskaite of Skirmantiskes, Lithuania was awarded a medal "For Courage in Fire" when she was just 4 yr. 252 days old. She had saved the lives of her younger brother and sister in April 1989 when a fire broke out in the family's home while her parents were out. The award was decreed by the Presidium of the then Lithuanian Soviet Socialist Republic.

The youngest person to receive an official gallantry award is Julius Rosenberg of Winnipeg, Canada, who was given the Medal of Bravery on March 30, 1994 for stopping a black bear that attacked his 3-year-old sister on September 20, 1992. Aged five at the time, he saved his sister's life by growling at the bear.

Most titles   The 18th Duchess of Alba, Doña María del Rosario Cayetana Fitz-James Stuart y Silva, is 14 times a Spanish grandee, 5 times a duchess, once a countess-duchess, 18 times a marchioness, 18 times a countess and once a viscountess.

Most valuable annual prize   The most valuable annual prize is the Louis Jeantet Prize for Medicine, which in 1996 was worth SFr2.1 million (equivalent to approximately $1,840,000). It was first awarded in 1986 and is intended to "provide substantial funds for the support of biomedical research projects."

Most statues   The world record for raising statues to oneself was set by Joseph Stalin (1879–1953), leader of the Soviet Union, 1924–53. It is estimated that during the Stalin era there were *c.* 6,000 statues to him throughout the USSR and in many cities in Eastern Europe.

The person to whom the most statues have been raised is Buddha. The 20th-century champion is Vladimir Ilyich Ulyanov, alias Lenin (1870–1924), busts of whom have been mass-produced.

Most honorary degrees   The greatest number of honorary degrees awarded is 131, given to Rev. Father Theodore M. Hesburgh, president of the University of Notre Dame, South Bend, IN. These have been accumulated since 1954.

Most Nobel Prizes   The United States has won 231 Nobel Prizes, outright or shared, including the most for Physiology or Medicine (74), Physics

(62), Chemistry (43), Peace (18), and Economics (23). France has won the most for Literature, with 12.

RELIGION

Largest religion Christianity is the world's largest religion, with some 1.90 billion adherents in 1994, or 33.7 percent of the world's population. Of these, 1.06 billion were Roman Catholics. The largest non-Christian religion is Islam, with some 1.03 billion followers in 1994.

Oldest to be ordained Father Harold Riley was ordained a Roman Catholic priest at age 91 in 1995 by Cardinal Hume.

Oldest chorister Clarissa Lee has been a chorister at St. Mary and St. Andrew Church, Pitminster, England since 1914 and still sings with the choir every week.

BUILDINGS FOR WORSHIP

Oldest church The oldest standing church in the United States is the Newport Parish Church, commonly known as St. Luke's, in Isle of Wight County, VA, four miles south of Smithfield, VA. The church was built *c.* 1632 and was originally called Warrisquioke Parish Church. Its present name was instituted in 1957.

Oldest synagogue The oldest synagogue in the United States is Touro Synagogue, Newport, RI. Construction was started in 1759 and completed in 1763.

Largest synagogue Temple Emanu-El, on Fifth Avenue at 65th Street, New York City, was completed in September 1929. It has a frontage of 150 feet on Fifth Avenue and 235 feet on 65th Street. The sanctuary proper can accommodate 2,500 people, and the adjoining Beth-El Temple seats 350. When all the temple's facilities are in use, 5,800 people can be accommodated.

Largest temple The largest religious structure ever built is Angkor Wat ("City Temple"), enclosing 402 acres in Cambodia. It was built to the Hindu god Vishnu by the Khmer King Suryavarman II in the period A.D. 1113–50. Its population, before it was abandoned in 1432, was 80,000. The whole complex of 72 monuments, begun *c.* A.D. 900, extends over 15 by 5 miles.

Highest temple The Rongbu temple, between Tingri and Shigatse in Tibet, is at an altitude of c. 16,750 feet, just 25 miles from Mt. Everest. It contains nine chapels, and is inhabited by lamas and nuns.

Largest cathedrals The Gothic cathedral church of the Episcopal Diocese of New York, St. John the Divine, in New York City, has a floor area of

121,000 square feet and a volume of 16,822,000 cubic feet. The cornerstone was laid on December 27, 1892, and work on the building was stopped in 1941. Work was restarted in July 1979, but is still not finished. The nave is the world's longest at 601 feet, with a vaulting 124 feet in height.

The cathedral with the largest area is that of Santa María de la Sede in Seville, Spain. It was built between 1402 and 1519, and is 414 feet long, 271 feet wide and 100 feet high to the vault of the nave.

Smallest cathedral The Christ Catholic Church, Highlandville, MO, consecrated in July 1983, measures 14 by 17 feet and seats 18 people.

Largest church The church of the Basilica of Our Lady of Peace (Notre Dame de la Paix) in Yamoussoukro, Ivory Coast was completed in 1989 at a cost of $180 million. It has a total area of 323,000 square feet, with seating for 7,000 people. Including its golden cross, it is 518 feet high.

The elliptical Basilica of St. Pius X (Saint-Pie X) in Lourdes, France was completed in 1957 at a cost of $5.6 million. It is 660 feet long and has a capacity of 20,000.

The tallest cathedral spire sits atop Ulm Cathedral in Germany.

Longest crypt The crypt of the underground Civil War Memorial Church in the Guadarrama Mountains, 28 miles from Madrid, Spain, is 853 feet long. It took 21 years (1937–58) to build, at a reported cost of $392 million, and is surmounted by a cross 492 feet tall.

Smallest church The chapel of Santa Isabel de Hungría is irregular in shape and has a floor area of just 21 1/8 square feet. It is inside the Colomares, a monument to Christopher Columbus, in Benalmádena, Málaga, Spain.

Tallest spire The tallest cathedral spire in the world is that of the Protestant Cathedral of Ulm in Germany. The building is early Gothic and was begun in 1377. The tower was not finally completed until 1890 and is 528 feet high.

The Chicago Temple/First United Methodist Church, Chicago, IL consists of a 22-story skyscraper surmounted by a steeple cross at 568 feet above street level.

Largest mosque The total area of the Shah Faisal Mosque, near Islamabad, Pakistan, is 46.87 acres, with the covered area of the prayer hall being 1.19 acres. It can accommodate 100,000 worshippers in the prayer hall and the courtyard, and a further 200,000 people in the adjacent grounds.

Tallest minaret The minaret of the Great Hassan II Mosque, Casablanca, Morocco measures 656 feet high. The cost of construction of the mosque was $540 million.

Largest Buddhist temple The Borobudur, near Jogjakarta, Indonesia, is 103 feet tall and covers 1,324 square feet.

Largest Mormon temple The largest Mormon temple is the Salt Lake City (Utah) Temple, with a floor area of 5.8 acres.

The world's tallest minaret is the Great Hassan II Mosque in Casablanca, Morocco.

Tallest stupa The Jetavanarama dagoba in the ancient city of Anuradhapura, Sri Lanka is 400 feet high, but is largely ruined.

Oldest stupa The Shwedagon pagoda in Rangoon, Myanmar is built on the site of a pagoda dating from 585 B.C.

Oldest stained glass window The oldest complete stained glass window is in the Cathedral of Augsburg, Germany. It dates from the second half of the 11th century.

Largest stained glass window The stained glass window of the Resurrection Mausoleum in Justice, IL measures 22,381 square feet in 2,448 panels.

The Basilica of Our Lady of Peace (Notre Dame de la Paix) at Yamoussoukro, Ivory Coast contains stained glass windows covering a total area of 80,000 square feet.

Tallest stained glass window The back-lit glass mural installed in 1979 in the atrium of the Ramada Hotel, Dubai is 135 feet high.

The largest statue of Buddha in the United States is located in Carmel, NY and stands 37 feet tall. More statues have been raised to Buddha than to any other person (see MOST STATUES, page 247).

MONUMENTS

Tallest monument The stainless-steel Gateway to the West arch in St. Louis, MO, completed on October 28, 1965, is a sweeping arch spanning 630 feet and rising to 630 feet. It cost $29 million and was designed in 1947 by the Finnish-American architect Eero Saarinen (1910–61).

Tallest menhir The 330-ton Grand Menhir Brisé in Locmariaquer, Brittany, France originally stood 59 feet high, but it is now in four pieces.

Largest trilithons The largest trilithons are at Stonehenge, Salisbury Plain, England, with single sarsen blocks weighing over 50 tons. The blocks would have required at least 550 men to drag them up a 9-degree gradient. The earliest stage of construction is dated to 2950 B.C.

PYRAMIDS

Largest pyramid The largest pyramid, and the largest monument ever constructed, is the Quetzalcóatl Pyramid at Cholula de Rivadabia, 63 miles southeast of Mexico City. It is 177 feet tall and its base covers an area of nearly 45 acres. Its total volume has been estimated at 4.3 million cubic yards.

The largest single block in a pyramid is from the Third Pyramid (Pyramid of Mycerinus) at El Gizeh, Egypt and weighs 320 tons.

Oldest pyramid The Djoser step pyramid in Saqqara, Egypt dates from c. 2630 B.C. It was constructed by Imhotep to a height of 204 feet.

Largest ziggurat The Ziggurat of Choga Zambil, 18.6 miles from Haft Tepe, Iran, had an outer base 344 by 344 feet, and the fifth "box," nearly 164 feet above, measured 92 by 92 feet.

STATUES AND COLUMNS

Tallest monumental column - Constructed 1936–39, the tapering column that commemorates the Battle of San Jacinto (April 21, 1836), on the bank of the San Jacinto River near Houston, TX, is 570 feet tall, 47 feet square at the base, and 30 feet square at the observation tower, which is topped by a star weighing 220 tons.

Tallest columns The 36 fluted marble pillars in the colonnade of the Education Building, Albany, NY are 90 feet tall, with a base diameter of 6 ft. 6 in.

Load-bearing The tallest load-bearing stone columns are in the Hall of Columns of the Temple of Amun at Karnak, Egypt. They are 69 feet tall and were built in the 19th dynasty during the reign of Rameses II c. 1270 B.C.

The Quetzalcóatl Pyramid is the largest monument ever constructed.

Largest monolithic obelisk   The obelisk of Tuthmosis III, brought from Aswan, Egypt by Emperor Constantius in the spring of A.D. 357, was repositioned in the Piazza San Giovanni in Laterano, Rome on August 3, 1588. Once 118 ft. 1 in. tall, it now stands 107 ft. 7 in. and weighs 502 tons.

An unfinished obelisk, probably commissioned by Queen Hatshepsut *c.* 1490 B.C., in situ at Aswan, Egypt is 136 ft. 10 in. long and weighs 1,287 tons.

Tallest statue   A bronze statue of Buddha 394 feet high was completed in Tokyo, Japan in January 1993. It is 115 feet wide and weighs 1,100 tons. The statue took seven years to make, and was a joint Japanese–Taiwanese project.

United States   The Statue of Liberty was designed and built in France to commemorate the friendship of France and the United States. The 152-foot statue was then shipped to New York City, where its copper sheets were assembled. President Cleveland accepted the statue for the United States on October 28, 1886.

EARTHWORKS

Largest earthworks   The largest and most extensive premechanical earthworks were the Linear Earth Boundaries of the Benin Empire, *c.* 1300, and earlier in the Edo state (formerly Bendel), Nigeria. It is estimated that their length was about 10,000 miles, and the volume of earth moved was 100 million cubic yards.

CEMETERIES AND TOMBS

Largest cemetery   Ohlsdorf Cemetery in Hamburg, Germany covers 990 acres, with 972,020 burials and 408,471 cremations as of December 31, 1995. It has been in use since 1877.

The Mount Li tomb contains an army of 8,000 terra-cotta soldiers and horses.

Capsules containing the ashes of 24 people were launched into orbit by the rocket *Pegasus* on April 27, 1997.

Tallest cemetery   The Memorial Necrópole Ecumênica, located in Santos, near São Paulo, Brazil, is 10 stories high, occupying an area of 4.4 acres.

Largest crematorium   The Nikolo-Arkhangelskiy Crematorium, east Moscow, Russia has seven twin cremators. It was completed in March 1972 and covers an area of 519 acres.

Largest artificial mound   The gravel mound on the summit of Nemrud Dagi, Malatya, Turkey measures 197 feet tall and covers 7.5 acres. It was built as a memorial to the Seleucid King Antiochus I (r. 69–34 B.C.).

Largest tomb   The Mount Li tomb, the burial place of Qin Shi Huangdi, the First Emperor of Qin, was built during his reign, 221–210 B.C. and is situated 25 miles east of Xianyang, China. The two walls surrounding the grave measure 7,129 by 3,195 feet and 2,247 by 1,896 feet respectively. The tomb contained an estimated 8,000 terra-cotta soldiers and horses that are life-size and larger.

Largest mass tomb   A tomb housing 180,000 World War II dead in Okinawa, Japan was enlarged in 1985 to accommodate another 9,000 bodies.

Grave digging   Johann Heinrich Karl Thieme, sexton of Aldenburg, Germany, dug 23,311 graves during a 50-year career. In 1826, his apprentice dug his grave.

Highest resting place   The ashes of 24 space pioneers amd enthusiasts, including *Star Trek* creator Gene Roddenberry, rocket scientist Kraffte Ehricke and author Timothy Leary, were sent into orbit on April 27, 1997 on board the rocket *Pegasus*. Held in lipstick-size capsules, the ashes will stay in orbit for 18 months to 10 years.

LANGUAGE

Commonest language   Chinese is spoken by an estimated 1 billion people.

Most widespread language   English is spoken by an estimated 800 million people; more generous estimates put the figure at 1.5 billion. Of these, 310 million are native speakers, including 216 million in the United States and 53 million in the United Kingdom.

Greatest concentration of languages   Papua New Guinea has the greatest concentration of separate languages in the world. Each of the estimated 869 languages has about 4,000 speakers.

Most complex language   The Ample language of Papua New Guinea has over 69,000 finite forms and 860 infinitive forms of the verb. Haida, a North American Indian language, has the most prefixes, with 70. Tabassaran, a language of Daghestan, Azerbaijan, uses the most noun cases, 48.

Inuit uses 63 forms of the present tense, with simple nouns having as many as 252 inflections.

Most irregular verbs   According to *The Morphology and Syntax of Present-day English* by Prof. Olu Tomori, English has 283 irregular verbs, 30 of which are formed merely by adding prefixes.

Rarest sounds   The rarest speech sound is probably that written "ř" in Czech and termed a "rolled post-alveolar fricative." In the southern Bushman language !xo, there is a click articulated with both lips, which is written ☉. This sound, essentially a kiss, is termed a "velaric ingressive bilabial stop."

Commonest sound   No language is known to be without the vowel "a" (as in the English "father").

Largest vocabulary   The English language contains about 616,500 words plus another 400,000 technical terms, the most in any language, but it is doubtful if any individual speaker uses more than 60,000. Shakespeare, for instance, employed a vocabulary of only about 33,000 words.

Most languages spoken   Dr. Harold Williams (1876–1928), a journalist from New Zealand, was reputed to speak 58 languages and many dialects fluently.
   Ziad Fazah (Brazil) speaks and writes 58 languages. He was tested in a live interview in Athens, Greece in July 1991, when he surprised audience members by talking to them in their various native tongues.
   Alexander Schwartz of New York City worked with 31 languages as a translator for the United Nations between 1962 and 1986.

Longest debate   A total of 725 people, including the Rostrum Clubs of Tasmania and other community members, debated the motion "Tasmania's greatest asset is its people" for 29 days 4 hr. 3 min. 20 sec. on the lawn of Hobart's Parliament House, November 3–December 1, 1996.

A record 250 people signed "Somewhere Over the Rainbow" at the Swan Theatre, High Wycombe, England.

Sign language   The greatest number of individuals simultaneously signing was 250 at the Swan Theatre, High Wycombe, England on August 9, 1996. They signed "Somewhere Over the Rainbow" during a performance of *The Wizard of Oz*.

Oldest alphabetic writing   A clay tablet of 32 cuneiform letters was found at Ugarit (now Ras Sharma), Syria, and dated to *c.* 1450 B.C.

Oldest letter   The letter "O" has not changed in shape since its adoption in the Phoenician alphabet *c.* 1,300 B.C.

Longest alphabet   The language with the most letters in its alphabet is Cambodian, with 74.

Shortest alphabet   Rotokas of central Bougainville Island, Papua New Guinea, has the fewest letters, with 11 (a, b, e, g, i, k, o, p, ř, t and u).

Most and fewest consonants   The language with the most distinct consonants was Ubykh, with 80–85. Ubykh speakers migrated from the Caucasus to Turkey in the 19th century and the language is now extinct. The language with the fewest consonants is Rotokas, with six.

Most and fewest vowels   The language with the most vowels is Sedang, a central Vietnamese language with 55 distinguishable vowel sounds. The Caucasian language Abkhazian has the fewest, with two.

WORDS

Longest words   A compound "word" of 195 Sanskrit characters (which transliterates into 428 letters in the Roman alphabet) describes the region near Kanci, Tamil Nadu, India. The word appears in a 16th-century work by Tirumalāmbā, Queen of Vijayanagara.

English   The longest word in the *Oxford English Dictionary* is pneumonoultramicroscopicsilicovolcanoconiosis, which has 45 letters and means "a lung disease caused by the inhalation of very fine silica dust." It is, however, described as "factitious" by the editors of the dictionary.

Spanish   Superextraordinarisimo (22) - extraordinary

Portuguese   Inconstitucionalissimamente (27) - with the highest degree of unconstitutionality

French   Anticonstitutionnellement (25) - anticonstitutionally

Swedish   Nordöstersjökustartilleriflygspaningssimulatoranläggnings-materielunderhåsuppföljningssystemdiskussionsinläggsförberedelsearbeten (130) - preparatory work on the contribution to the discussion on the maintaining system of support of the material of the aviation survey simulator device within the northeast part of the coastartillery of the Baltic

Japanese   Chi-n-chi-ku-ri-n (12) - a very short person (slang)

Italian   Precipitevolissimevolmente (26) - as fast as possible

Russian   Ryentgyenoelyektrokardiografichyeskogo (33 Cyrillic letters) - of the X-ray electrocardiographic

Dutch   Kindercarnavalsoptochtvoorbereidingswerkzaamheden (49) - preparation activities for a children's carnival procession

German   Donaudampfschiffahrtselektrizitaetnhauptbetriebswerkbauunterbeamtengesellschaft (80) - the club for subordinate officials of the head office management of the Danube steamboat electrical services

Longest palindromes   The longest palindromic word (a word that reads the same backward or forward) is saippuakivikauppias (19 letters), Finnish for "a dealer in lye." The longest in English is tattarrattat, with 12 letters, which appears in the *Oxford English Dictionary.*

Longest anagrams   The longest nonscientific English words that can form anagrams are the 17-letter transpositions representationism and misrepresentation.

Longest abbreviation   The initials S.K.O.M.K.H.P.K.J.C.D.P.W.B. stand for the Syarikat Kerjasama Orang-orang Melayu Kerajaan Hilir Perak Kerana Jimat Cermat Dan Pinjam-meminjam Wang Berhad. This is the Malay name for The Cooperative Company of the Lower State of Perak Government's Malay People for Money Savings and Loans Ltd., in Teluk Anson, Perak, West Malaysia (formerly Malaya). The abbreviation for the abbreviation is Skomk.

Shortest abbreviation   The 55-letter full name of Los Angeles (El Pueblo de Nuestra Señora la Reina de los Angeles de Porciuncula) is abbreviated to L.A., or 3.63 percent of its length.

Longest acronym   The longest acronym is NIIOMTPLABOPARMBET-ZHELBETRABSBOMONIMONKONOTDTEKHSTROMONT with 56 letters (54 in Cyrillic) in the *Concise Dictionary of Soviet Terminology, Institutions and Abbreviations* (1969), meaning: the Laboratory for Shuttering, Reinforcement, Concrete and Ferroconcrete Operations for Composite-monolithic and Monolithic Constructions of the Department of the Technology of Building-Assembly Operations of the Scientific Research Institute of the Organization for Building Mechanization and Technical Aid of the Academy of Building and Architecture of the USSR.

Commonest words and letters   The most frequently used words in written English are, in descending order of frequency: the, of, and, to, a, in, that, is, I, it, for and as. The most commonly used in conversation is "I." The commonest letter is "e." More words begin with the letter "s" than with any other, but the most commonly used initial letter is "t" as in "the," "to," "that" or "there."

PERSONAL NAMES

Oldest name   The oldest surviving personal name belongs to a predynastic king of Upper Egypt *ante* 3,050 B.C., who is represented by the hieroglyphic sign for a scorpion. It has been suggested that the name should be read as Sekhen.

Longest personal name   The longest name ever to appear on a birth certificate is Rhoshandiatellyneshiaunneveshenk Koyaanisquatsiuth Williams, born to Mr. and Mrs. James Williams in Beaumont, TX on September 12, 1984. On October 5, 1984, Mr. Williams filed an amendment that expanded his daughter's first name to 1,019 letters and her middle name to 36 letters.

Most first names   A. Lindup-Badarou of Truro, England, formerly known as A. Hicks, had a total of 3,530 first names as of March 1995.

Commonest family name   The commonest surname in the English-speaking world is Smith. There are an estimated 2,382,500 Smiths in the United States.

The most common family name in the English-speaking world is Smith, as in NFL star Emmitt; gossip queen Liz; Howdy Doody star Buffalo Bob; jazz great Bessie; Cure member Robert; Guinness research interns Meghan and Maureen; former British Labour Party leader John; British actress Dame Maggie; Tarheels great Dean; Charlie's Angel Jaclyn; and actor Will.

PLACE-NAMES

Longest place-name   The official name for Bangkok, the capital Thailand, is Krungthep Mahanakhon. However, the city's full name is Krungthep Mahanakhon Bovorn Ratanakosin Mahintharayutthaya Mahadilokpop Noparatratchathani Burirom Udomratchanivet Mahasathan Amornpiman Avatarnsahit Sakkathattiyavisnukarmprasit, which in scholarly transliteration emerges with 175 letters.

The longest place-name now in use is Taumatawhakatangihangakoauauotamateaturipukakapikimaungahoronukupokaiwhenuakitanatahu, the unofficial 85-letter version of the name of a hill in the Southern Hawke's Bay district of North Island, New Zealand. The Maori translation means "The place where Tamatea, the man with the big knees, who slid, climbed and swallowed mountains, known as landeater, played his flute to his loved one."

Most spellings   The spelling of the Dutch town of Leeuwarden has been recorded in 225 versions since A.D. 1046.

LAW

LEGISLATION AND LITIGATION

Oldest statute   The oldest surviving judicial code is the code of King Ur-Nammu, from the third dynasty of Ur, Iraq, *c.* 2250 B.C.

Most protracted litigation   A controversy over the claim of the Prior and Convent (now the Dean and Chapter) of Durham Cathedral in England to administer the diocese during a vacancy in the See grew fierce in 1283. The dispute, with the Archbishop of York, flared up again in 1672 and 1890; an attempt in November 1975 to settle the issue, then 692 years old, was unsuccessful. Neither side admits the legitimacy of writs of appointment issued by the other, even though identical persons are named.

Gaddam Hanumantha Reddi, a civil servant, brought a series of legal actions against the Hyderabad state government and the Indian government covering a total period of 44 years 9 months 8 days from April 1945 to January 1990. The litigation outlasted the entire period of his employment in the Indian Administrative Service. He contended that his results in the entrance examination for the Hyderabad Civil Service entitled him to greater seniority and higher pay. He won the legal battle and received his promotion.

Longest trial Civil   The longest civil case heard before a jury is Kemner vs. Monsanto Co., which concerned an alleged toxic chemical spill in Sturgeon, MO in 1979. The trial started on February 6, 1984, at St. Clair County Court House, Belleville, IL before Circuit Judge Richard P. Goldenhersh, and ended on October 22, 1987. The testimony lasted 657 days, following which the jury deliberated for two months. The residents of Sturgeon were awarded $1 million nominal compensatory damages and $16,280,000 punitive damages, but these awards were overturned by the

Illinois Appellate Court on June 11, 1991 because the jury in the original trial had not found that any damage had resulted from the spill.

Criminal   The longest criminal trial took place in Hong Kong from November 30, 1992 to November 29, 1994. The High Court sat for 398 days to hear murder charges against 14 South Vietnamese boat people accused of murdering 24 North Vietnamese adults and children, who died in a blazing hut during a riot at a refugee camp in Hong Kong, in February 1992. All the defendants were acquitted of murder, but some were convicted of lesser charges.

Greatest damages Civil damages   The largest damages awarded in legal history were $11.12 billion to Pennzoil Company against Texaco Inc., as a result of Texaco's allegedly unethical tactics in January 1984 in attempting to break up a merger between Pennzoil and Getty Oil Company. The verdict was handed down in Houston, TX on December 10, 1985. An out-of-court settlement of $5.5 billion was reached after a 48-hour negotiation on December 19, 1987.

The largest damages awarded against an individual were $2.1 billion. On July 10, 1992, Charles H. Keating, Jr., the former owner of Lincoln Savings and Loan of Los Angeles, CA, was ordered by a federal jury to pay this sum to 23,000 small investors who were defrauded by his company. On July 8, 1993, Keating was sentenced to 12½ years in prison.

Personal injury   Shiyamala Thirunayagam was awarded $163,882,660 by a jury in the Supreme Court of the State of New York on July 27, 1993. She was almost completely paralyzed after the car in which she was traveling hit a broken-down truck in the fast lane of the New Jersey Turnpike on October 4, 1987. Because the defendants would have challenged the jury's verdict in a higher court, Thirunayagam agreed to accept a lump sum of $8,230,000 for pain and suffering and a guarantee that the defendants would pay up to $55,000,000 for her future medical expenses.

The compensation for the disaster on December 2–3, 1984 at the Union Carbide Corporation plant in Bhopal, India was agreed at $470 million. The Supreme Court of India passed the order for payment on February 14, 1989 after a settlement between the corporation and the Indian government, which represented the interests of more than 500,000 claimants, including the families of 3,350 people who died.

Sexual harassment   The record award in a sexual harassment case was $50 million to Peggy Kimzey, a former employee of the Warsaw, MO Wal-Mart. The award of punitive damages was made by a jury in Jefferson City, MO on June 28, 1995. The jury also awarded Kimzey $35,000 for humiliation and mental anguish and $1 in lost wages. Wal-Mart said it would appeal.

Best-attended trial   The greatest attendance at any trial was at that of Major Jesús Sosa Blanco, age 51, for an alleged 108 murders. At one point in the 12½-hour trial (5:30 P.M. to 6 A.M., January 22–23, 1959), 17,000 people were present in the Havana Sports Palace, Cuba. The defendant was found guilty and was executed on February 18, 1959.

Most viewed trial   Between January 24 and October 3, 1995, a daily average of 5.5 million Americans watched live coverage of the O. J. Simpson trial on three major cable networks. Simpson, a pro football Hall of Famer and actor, was on trial for the murder of his ex-wife, Nicole Brown Simpson, and waiter Ronald Goldman on June 12, 1994. He was acquitted when the jury reached a verdict of not guilty on October 3, 1995.

Greatest compensation for wrongful imprisonment Robert McLaughlin, 29, was awarded $1,935,000 in October 1989 for wrongful imprisonment for a murder in New York City in 1979 that he did not commit. He had been sentenced to 15 years in prison and had actually served six years, from 1980 to 1986, when he was released after his foster father succeeded in showing the authorities that he had had nothing to do with the crime.

Defamation On March 20, 1997 the *Wall Street Journal* was ordered to pay $222.7 million to a Houston brokerage firm who claimed an article in the paper contained false information and had contributed to their going out of business. The publisher of the *Wall Street Journal* planned to file an appeal against the decision.

Largest divorce settlement The largest publicly declared settlement, achieved in 1982 by lawyers for Soraya Khashóggi, was £500 million ($950 million) plus property from her husband Adnan.

Largest alimony suit Belgian-born Sheika Dena Al-Fassi filed an alimony claim of $3 billion against her former husband, Sheik Mohammed Al-Fassi of the Saudi Arabian royal family, in Los Angeles, CA in February 1982. Attorney Marvin Mitchelson, explaining the size of the settlement claim, alluded to the Sheik's wealth, which included 14 homes in Florida alone and numerous private aircraft. On June 14, 1983, the claimant was awarded $81 million and declared she would be "very very happy" if she were able to collect.

Largest patent violation case Litton Industries Inc. was awarded $1.2 billion in damages from Honeywell Inc. on August 31, 1993. A jury in Los Angeles, CA decided that Honeywell had violated a Litton patent covering airline navigation systems.

Highest costs The Blue Arrow trial, involving the illegal support of the company's shares during a rights issue in 1987, is estimated to have cost approximately £35 million ($60 million). The trial in London, England lasted a year and ended on February 14, 1992 with four of the defendants being convicted. Although they received suspended prison sentences, they were later cleared on appeal.

Longest lease A lease on a plot for a sewage tank adjoining Columb Barracks, Mullingar, Ireland was signed on December 3, 1868 for 10 million years.

Oldest will The oldest written will dates from 2061 B.C. It was carved on the walls of the tomb of Nek'ure, the son of the Egyptian pharaoh Khafre, and indicated that Nek'ure would bequeath 14 towns, two estates and other property to his wife, another woman and three children.

Shortest will   The shortest valid will consists of four characters in Hindi meaning "All to son." It was written by Bimla Rishi of Delhi, India and is dated February 9, 1995.

Longest will   The will of Frederica Evelyn Stilwell Cook (U.S.) was proved in London, England on November 2, 1925. It consisted of four bound volumes containing 95,940 words, primarily concerning some $100,000 worth of property.

Most codicils   The largest number of codicils (supplements modifying the details) to a will admitted to probate is 21, in the case of the will of J. Paul Getty. The will was dated September 22, 1958 and had 21 codicils dating from June 18, 1960 through March 11, 1976. Getty died on June 6, 1976.

Most durable judge   The oldest recorded active judge was Judge Albert R. Alexander of Plattsburg, MO. He was enrolled as a member of the Clinton County Bar in 1926, and was later the magistrate and probate judge of Clinton County until his retirement at age 105 yr. 8 mo. on July 9, 1965.

Youngest judge   No collated records on the ages of judicial appointments exist. However, David Elmer Ward had to wait until he reached the legal age of 21 before taking office after nomination in 1932 as judge of the County Court in Fort Myers, FL.

Muhammad Ilyas passed the examination enabling him to become a civil judge in July 1952 at the age of 20 yr. 9 mo., although formalities such as medicals meant that it was not until eight months later that he started work as a civil judge in Lahore, Pakistan.

Most lawyers   In the United States there were an estimated 946,499 resident and active lawyers as of June 1996, or one lawyer for every 276 people.

Oldest lawyer   The oldest lawyer was Cornelius Van de Steeg (1889–1994) of Perry, IA. He was a practicing lawyer until April 1991, when he was 101 yr. 11 mo. old.

Most acquittals   Sir Lionel Luckhoo, senior partner of Luckhoo and Luckhoo of Georgetown, Guyana, succeeded in getting 245 successive murder charge acquittals between 1940 and 1985.

THE SUPREME COURT

Longest-serving justice   The longest-serving Supreme Court justice was William O. Douglas, who served for 36 yr. 209 days from April 17, 1939 to November 12, 1975.

The longest-serving woman on the Supreme Court is Sandra Day O'Connor. As of August 7, 1997, she had served for 15 yr. 315 days, since September 25, 1981.

Longest-serving chief justice   John Marshall served for 34 yr. 152 days from February 4, 1801 to July 6, 1835.

Sandra Day O'Connor

Oldest chief justice The oldest chief justice to enter office was Harlan Fiske Stone, who took the oath of office at the age of 68 yr. 261 days on July 3, 1941. He served until his death on April 22, 1946.

The oldest chief justice to leave office was Roger Brooke Taney, at 87 yr. 194 days. Taney served from March 28, 1836 until his death on October 12, 1864.

Harlan Fiske Stone

Youngest chief justice   The youngest chief justice to enter office was John Jay, who took the oath of office at the age of 44 yr. 307 days on October 19, 1789. Jay served until his resignation on June 29, 1795.

Oldest associate justice   The oldest associate justice to enter office was Horace Harmon Lurton, who took the oath of office at the age of 65 yr. 308 days on January 3, 1910. He served until his death on July 12, 1914.

The oldest associate justice to leave office was Oliver Wendell Holmes, at 90 yr. 304 days. Holmes served from December 8, 1902 until his retirement on January 12, 1932.

Youngest associate justice   The youngest associate justice to enter office was William Johnson, who took the oath of office at the age of 32 yr. 130 days on May 7, 1804. Johnson served until his death on August 4, 1834.

Narrowest margin   Judge Clarence Thomas was elected to the Supreme Court in 1991 by the narrowest margin ever recorded, 52 votes to 48.

Clarence Thomas

CRIME

Most assassination attempts   The target of the highest number of failed assassination attempts on an individual head of state in modern times was Charles de Gaulle, president of France from 1958 to 1969. He was reputed to have survived 31 plots against his life between 1944 and 1966, although some plots were foiled and did not culminate in actual attacks.

Most murders committed   It was established at the trial of Behram, the Indian Thug, that he had strangled at least 931 victims in the Oudh district between 1790 and 1840. An estimated 2 million Indians were strangled by Thugs during the reign of the Thuggee cult from 1550 until its suppression by the British raj in 1853.

Twentieth century A total of 592 deaths was attributed to one Colombian bandit leader, Teófilo ("Sparks") Rojas, between 1948 and his death in an ambush near Armenia, Colombia on January 22, 1963. Some sources attribute 3,500 slayings to him during La Violencia of 1945–62.

Worst mass murder Policeman Wou Bom-kon killed 57 people and wounded 35 in a drunken rampage on April 26–27, 1985 in the Kyong Sang-namdo province of South Korea.

Greatest mass arrest The greatest mass arrest reported in a democratic country was of 15,617 demonstrators on July 11, 1988, rounded up by South Korean police to ensure security in advance of the 1988 Olympic Games in Seoul.

Biggest robbery It is estimated that over $3.75 billion (at today's values) was stolen from the Reichsbank following the collapse of Germany at the end of World War II, April–May 1945.

The government of the Philippines announced on April 23, 1986 that it had succeeded in identifying $860.8 million salted away since 1965 by former President Ferdinand Marcos and his wife Imelda. The total wealth taken by the couple was believed to be $5–$10 billion.

Art It is arguable that the Mona Lisa, though never appraised, is the most valuable object ever stolen. The painting disappeared from the Louvre, Paris, France on August 21, 1911. It was recovered in Italy in 1913, when Vincenzo Perugia was charged with its theft.

Armored car The largest robbery of an armored car took place on March 29, 1997 at a Loomis Fargo armored-car warehouse in Jacksonville, FL. The robber, an employee of the firm, escaped with an estimated $20 million in cash, none of which has been recovered.

Bank During the civil disorder prior to January 22, 1976 in Beirut, Lebanon, a guerrilla force blasted the vaults of the British Bank of the Middle East in Bab Idriss and cleared out safe deposit boxes with contents valued by former Finance Minister Lucien Dahdah at $50 million and by another source at an "absolute minimum" of $20 million.

Jewels The greatest recorded theft of jewels was from the Carlton Hotel, Cannes, France on August 11, 1994. Gems with an estimated value of Fr250 million ($48 million) were stolen from the jewelry store by a 3-man gang. A security guard was seriously injured during the raid.

Greatest hijacking ransom The Japanese government paid $6 million to aircraft hijackers for a JAL DC-8 and 38 hostages at Dacca Airport, Bangladesh on October 2, 1977. Six convicted criminals were also exchanged. The Bangladesh government had refused to sanction any retaliatory action.

Greatest kidnapping ransom   Historically, the greatest ransom paid was that for Atahualpa by the Incas to Francisco Pizarro in 1532–33 at Cajamarca, Peru. It constituted a hall full of gold and silver, worth some $1.5 billion on today's market. Pizarro did not keep his side of the bargain; he murdered Atahualpa instead of returning him.

The greatest ransom ever reported in modern times was 1.5 billion pesos ($60 million) for the release of the brothers Jorge and Juan Born of the firm Bunge and Born, paid to the left-wing urban guerrilla group Montoneros in Buenos Aires, Argentina on June 20, 1975.

Largest narcotics haul   In terms of value, the greatest haul in a drug seizure was on September 28, 1989, when cocaine with an estimated street value of $6–7 billion was seized in a raid on a warehouse in Los Angeles, CA.

The heaviest haul was on October 23, 1991, when authorities in Bilo, Pakistan seized 85,846 pounds of hashish and 7,128 pounds of heroin.

Greatest bank note forgery   The German Third Reich's forging operation, code name "Operation Bernhard," was engineered by Major Bernhard Krüger during World War II. It involved more than £130 million worth of British notes produced by 140 Jewish prisoners at Sachsenhausen concentration camp.

Biggest bank fraud   The Banca Nazionale del Lavoro of Italy admitted on September 6, 1989 that it had been defrauded of a huge sum, later estimated to be in the region of $5 billion, with the disclosure that its Atlanta, GA branch had made unauthorized loan commitments to Iraq.

Worst mass killings Cambodia   As a percentage of a nation's total population the worst genocide appears to have taken place in Cambodia during the Khmer Rouge regime of Saloth Sar, alias Pol Pot. According to the foreign minister, Ieng Sary, more than a third of the 8 million Khmers were killed between April 17, 1975, when the Khmer Rouge captured Phnom Penh, and January 1979, when they were overthrown.

Nazi Germany   The most organized extermination campaign against a people was the Holocaust, the genocidal "Final Solution" ordered by Adolf Hitler, starting from the fall of 1941 and continuing into May 1945. Reliable estimates of the number of victims range from 5.1 million to 6 million Jews.

At the SS death camp at Auschwitz-Birkenau in southern Poland, it is estimated that 1,350,000 Jews and 115,000 others were murdered from June 1940 through January 1945. The greatest number killed in a day was 6,000.

Worst terrorist bombing   A bomb exploded on an Air-India Boeing 747, which crashed into the Atlantic southwest of Ireland, killing 329, on June 23, 1985.

Deadliest hijacking   The deadliest hijacking occurred on November 24, 1996, when a hijacked Ethiopian Airlines jet ran out of fuel and crashed into the Indian Ocean near the Comoro Islands. Of the 175 people aboard, 127 died, including one of the three hijackers.

The world's deadliest hijacking claimed 127 lives.

FINES

Heaviest fine   A fine of $650 million was imposed on the U.S. securities firm of Drexel Burnham Lambert in December 1988 for insider trading. This figure represented $300 million in direct fines, with the balance to be put into an account to satisfy claims of parties who could prove they were defrauded by Drexel's actions.

The record for an individual is $200 million, which Michael Milken agreed to pay on April 24, 1990. The payments were in settlement of a racketeering and securities fraud suit brought by the U.S. government in the Drexel Burnham Lambert scandal.

CAPITAL PUNISHMENT

Largest hanging   A Nazi Feldkommandant simultaneously hanged 50 Greek resistance fighters as a reprisal measure in Athens, Greece on July 22, 1944.

The greatest number of people hanged from one gallows was 38 Sioux Indians, by William J. Duly outside Mankato, MN on December 26, 1862 for the murder of unarmed citizens.

Most experienced executioners   The Sanson family of France supplied executioners through several generations, from 1688 to 1847. Charles-Henri Sanson, known as Monsieur de Paris, executed more than 3,000 victims, most of them in 1793–94, including the king, Louis XVI, on January 21, 1793.

Longest stay on death row   Sadamichi Hirasawa (1893–1987) spent 39 years on death row in Sendai Jail, Japan. He was convicted in 1948 of poisoning 12 bank employees with potassium cyanide to effect a theft of $403, and died in prison at age 94.

On October 31, 1987, Liong Wie Tong and Tan Tian Tjoen were executed by firing squad for robbery and murder in Jakarta, Indonesia after 25 years on death row.

IMPRISONMENT

Longest sentences   Chamoy Thipyaso, a Thai woman known as the queen of underground investing, and seven of her associates were each sentenced to serve 141,078 years in jail by the Bangkok Criminal Court, Thailand on July 27, 1989 for swindling the public through a multimillion-dollar deposit-taking business.

Oldest prisoner   Bill Wallace spent the last 63 years of his life in Aradale Psychiatric Hospital, Ararat, Victoria, Australia. He had shot and killed a man at a restaurant in Melbourne, Victoria in December 1925, and having been found unfit to plead, was transferred to the responsibility of the Mental Health Department in February 1926. He remained at Aradale until his death on July 17, 1989, shortly before his 108th birthday.

Longest escape   On December 15, 1923, Leonard T. Fristoe escaped from Nevada State Prison, Carson City, NV, where he was serving time for killing two sheriff's deputies. Fristoe was turned in by his son on November

15, 1969, in Compton, CA, having had nearly 46 years of freedom under the name of Claude R. Willis.

Largest jailbreaks   On February 11, 1979, an Iranian employee of the Electronic Data Systems Corporation led a mob into Gasr prison, Tehran, Iran in an effort to rescue two American employees of EDSC. Some 11,000 other prisoners took advantage of the situation and became part of history's largest-ever jailbreak. Although it was the Iranian employee's actions that allowed the actual jail break to happen, the plan to get the Americans out was masterminded by their employer, H. Ross Perot.

In September 1971, Raúl Sendic and 105 other Tupamaro guerrillas, plus five nonpolitical prisoners, escaped from a Uruguayan prison through a tunnel 298 feet long.

COMMERCE

ECONOMICS

Largest budget   The greatest governmental expenditure ever made was $1.519 trillion by the United States government for the fiscal year 1995. The highest revenue figure was $1.355 trillion in the same year.

Foreign aid   The greatest donor of foreign aid in 1995 was Japan, with aid totaling $14.5 billion.

Lowest taxation rates   The sovereign countries with the lowest income tax in the world are Bahrain and Qatar, where the rate is zero, regardless of income. No tax is levied on the inhabitants of Sark in the Channel Islands, Great Britain.

Highest taxation rates   In Denmark, the highest rate of income tax is 68 percent, but a net wealth tax of 1 percent can result in tax of over 100 percent on income in extreme situations.

Balance of payments   The record balance of payments deficit for any country for a calendar year is $173.4 billion in 1995 by the United States. The record surplus was Japan's $131.5 billion in 1993.

Largest national debt   During fiscal year 1996, the United States had a national debt of $5.129 trillion, and the gross interest paid on the debt was $332.414 billion, with net interest of $202.957 billion.

Largest gross national product   The gross national product of the United States was $7.238 trillion at the end of 1995.

Richest country   The richest country in the world, according to the United Nations Statistical Division, is Liechtenstein, which in 1992 had an average gross national product per capita of $54,607.

According to the Department of Commerce, in 1995, Connecticut enjoyed the highest per capita income level of any state ($30,303), while Mississippi had the lowest ($16,531). Personal income in the United States averaged $23,192 per person for 1995 and set a record high of $6.1 trillion in the same year.

The median household income in the United States in 1994 was $31,241. Alaska enjoyed the highest level, at $42,931, while Mississippi had the lowest, at $22,191.

Poorest country   Mozambique had the lowest gross national product per capita in 1991, with $70, although there are several countries for which the *World Bank Atlas* is not able to include data.

Largest gold reserves   The country with the greatest monetary gold reserves is the United States, whose Treasury held 262 million fine ounces during 1996, worth $100 billion at the June 1996 price of $382 per fine ounce.

Connecticut enjoys the highest per capita income of any U.S. state.
Top to bottom: lighthouse in Stonington; State Capitol building,
Hartford; Litchfield farm; Southport Harbor.

Worst inflation   In Hungary in June 1946, the 1931 gold pengö was valued at 130 million trillion (1.3×10^{20}) paper pengös. Notes were issued for "Egymillard billion" (one sextillion or 1×10^{21}) pengös on June 3 and withdrawn on July 11, 1946. Vouchers for 1 billion trillion (1×10^{27}) pengös were issued for taxation payment only.

The country with the worst inflation in 1995 was Belarus, with 243.96 percent.

The best-known hyperinflationary episode occurred in Germany in 1923. The circulation of the Reichsbank mark reached 400,338,326,350,700,000,000 on November 6 and inflation was 755.7 billion times 1913 levels.

United States   The United States Department of Labor measures changes in the Consumer Price Index (CPI) in 12-month periods ending in December. The Bureau of Labor Statistics first began keeping the CPI in 1913. Since that time, the change of the greatest magnitude was a 20.4 percent increase for the 12-month period ending December 1918, and the largest decline was –10.8 percent in December 1921. The largest peacetime increase, recorded in December 1979, was 13.3 percent.

EMPLOYMENT

Largest labor union   The Professionalniy Soyuz Rabotnikov Agro-Promyshlennogo Kompleksa (Agro-Industrial Complex Workers' Union) in the former Soviet Union had 15.2 million members in 1993.

Smallest labor union   The Jewelcase and Jewelry Display Makers Union, founded in 1894, was dissolved on December 31, 1986 by its general secretary, Charles Evans. The motion was seconded by Fergus McCormack, its only other surviving member.

Longest union name   The union with the longest name is the International Association of Marble, Slate and Stone Polishers, Rubbers and Sawyers, Tile and Marble Setters' Helpers and Marble, Mosaic and Terrazzo Workers' Helpers, or the IAMSSPRSTMSHMMTWH, of Washington, D.C.

Longest strike   The longest recorded strike ended on January 4, 1961, after 33 years. It concerned the employment of barbers' assistants in Copenhagen, Denmark.

Industrial   The longest industrial strike was at the plumbing fixtures factory of the Kohler Co. in Sheboygan, WI, April 1954–October 1962. The strike is alleged to have cost the United Automobile Workers' Union about $12 million to sustain.

Lowest unemployment   In Switzerland (population 6.6 million), the total number of unemployed in 1973 was reported to be 81.

United States   The lowest unemployment average in the United States was 1.2 percent, or 670,000 people, in 1944 during World War II, based on a labor force aged 14 and older.

Highest unemployment   The highest annual unemployment average in United States history was 24.9 percent, or 12,830,000 people, in 1933 during the Great Depression.

Longest working career   Shigechiyo Izumi began work goading draft animals at a sugar mill at Isen, Tokunoshima, Japan in 1872. He retired as a sugar cane farmer in 1970 at the age of 105, after a working career that lasted for 98 years.

Longest in one job   Polly Gadsby started work with Archibald Turner & Co. of Leicester, England at age nine. In 1932, after 86 years' service, she was still at her bench wrapping elastic at age 95.

Largest employment agency   The largest employment services group is Manpower, with worldwide sales of all its brand units of $6.9 billion in 1995.

STOCK EXCHANGES

Oldest stock exchange   The stock exchange in Amsterdam, Netherlands was founded in 1602 with dealings in printed shares of the United East India Company of the Netherlands in the Oude Zijds Kapel.

Largest stock exchange   The largest in trading volume in 1996 was the New York Stock Exchange, with $4.1 trillion.

The market value of stocks listed on the New York Stock Exchange reached an all-time high of $9.25 trillion on July 3, 1997.

The record day's trading was 684,588,000 shares on January 23, 1997.

The largest stock trade in the history of the New York Stock Exchange was a 103,000,000-share block of Occidental Petroleum stock at $10 per share on June 17, 1988.

The highest price paid for a seat on the New York Stock Exchange was $1.48 million on July 31, 1997. The lowest 20th-century price was $17,000, in 1942.

Closing prices   As of August 6, 1997, the highest index figure on the Dow Jones Industrial average of selected stocks at the close of a day's trading was 8,259.31.

The Dow Jones Industrial average, which reached 381.71 on September 3, 1929, plunged 30.57 points on October 29, 1929, on its way to the Depression's lowest point of 41.22 on July 2, 1932. The largest decline in a day, 508 points (22.6 percent), occurred on October 19, 1987.

The total lost in security values from September 1, 1929 to June 30, 1932 was $74 billion. The greatest paper loss in a year was $210 billion in 1974.

The record daily increase, on October 21, 1987, was 186.84 points, to 2,027.85.

Largest flotation   The 1997 flotation of the Halifax Building Society, the United Kingdom's largest mortgage provider, was estimated to be worth £11 billion ($18.5 billion).

The record number of investors for a single issue is 5.9 million in the

Mastergain '92 equity fund floated by the Unit Trust of India, Bombay in April and May 1992.

Longest-listed company   Consolidated Edison Company of New York (ConEd) is reported to be the longest continually listed company on the New York Stock Exchange. First traded under the name New York Gas Light Company in 1824, it formed a merger to create the Consolidated Gas Company of New York in 1884. ConEd took its current name in 1936.

The longest-listed company traded under the same name is the Brooklyn Union Gas Company. Originally listed as the Brooklyn Gas Light Company in the late 1830s, it has been traded under its current name since the mid-1860s.

Most valuable company   The greatest market value of any corporation as of year end 1996 was $169.4 billion for General Electric Co., of Fairfield, CT.

Greatest stockholder attendance   In April 1961, a total of 20,109 stockholders attended the annual general meeting of the American Telephone and Telegraph Co. (AT&T), thereby setting a world record.

Longest-serving current member   As of August 1997, the longest-serving current member of the New York Stock Exchange was David Granger. He became a member on February 4, 1926.

Largest rights issue   The largest recorded rights issue was one of £921 million ($1.57 billion) by Barclays Bank, Great Britain, announced on April 7, 1988.

Highest gold price   The highest closing spot price for gold on the Commodities Exchange (COMEX) in New York City was $875 per fine ounce on January 21, 1980.

Highest silver price   The highest closing spot price for silver on the Commodities Exchange (COMEX) in New York City was $50.35 per fine ounce on January 18, 1980.

Highest par value   The highest denomination of any share quoted in the world is a single share in Moeara Enim Petroleum Corporation, worth 165,000 Dutch florins ($75,500) on April 22, 1992.

BUSINESS

Oldest industry   Flint knapping, involving the production of chopping tools and hand axes, dates from 2.5 million years ago in Ethiopia. Evidence of trading in exotic stone and amber dates from *c.* 28,000 B.C. in Europe.

Oldest company   The oldest existing documented company is Stora Kopparbergs Bergslags of Falun, Sweden, which has been in continuous operation since the 11th century. It is first mentioned in historical records in the year 1288, when a bishop bartered an eighth share in the enterprise, and it was granted a charter in 1347.

Family business   The Hoshi Ryokan, a hotel in Japan, dates back to A.D. 717 and has been run as a family business for 46 generations.

Largest manufacturing company   In terms of revenues and employees, General Motors Corporation of Detroit, MI is the world's largest manufacturing company. It has a workforce of 709,000, and revenues for the company in 1995 totaled $168.8 billion, with assets of $217.1 billion; a profit of $6.88 billion was announced for 1995.

General Motors is the largest manufacturing company in the world.

Largest employer   In 1994–95, Indian Railways had 1,602,000 regular employees.

Greatest sales   The Fortune 500 list of leading industrial corporations in April 1997 was headed by General Motors Corporation, with sales of $168.37 billion for 1996.

Greatest corporate profit   The American Telephone and Telegraph Co. (AT&T) made a record net profit of $7.6 billion in 12 months from October 1, 1981 to September 30, 1982.

Greatest loss   In 1992, General Motors reported an annual net trading loss of $23.5 billion. The bulk of this figure was, however, due to a single charge of some $21 billion for employees' health costs and pensions and was disclosed because of new U.S. accounting regulations.

Largest corporate takeover bid   On October 24, 1988, the Wall Street leveraged buyout firm Kohlberg Kravis Roberts (KKR) bid $21 billion, or $90 a share, for RJR Nabisco Inc., the tobacco, food and beverage company. By December 1, 1988, the bid, led by Henry Kravis, had reached $109 per share, to total $25 billion.

Biggest bankrupt   On September 3, 1992, newspaper heir Kevin Maxwell became the world's biggest bankrupt following the death of his father, Robert Maxwell, with debts of £406.8 million ($813.6 million).

Corporate   The biggest corporate bankruptcy in terms of assets was $35.9 billion, filed by Texaco in 1987.

Largest public auction   In 1995, the Federal Communications Commission (FCC) raised $7.7 billion for the U.S Treasury by auctioning off 99 licenses to provide digital communication services. The auction was conducted by Kennedy-Wilson International.

Greatest barter deal   In July 1984, 30 million barrels of oil, valued at $1.71 billion, were exchanged for 10 Boeing 747s for the Royal Saudi Airline.

COMMERCE

Largest savings and loan association   The world's biggest lender is the Japanese government-controlled House Loan Corporation.

Largest bank   The largest commercial bank is the Bank of Tokyo-Mitsubishi, Ltd. of Tokyo, Japan, with assets of $737 billion as of April 1, 1996.

The International Bank of Reconstruction and Development, also called the World Bank, is the largest multilateral development bank. Based in Washington, D.C., the bank had total assets of $168.7 billion for fiscal year 1995.

Most branches   The State Bank of India had 12,704 outlets on April 1, 1994 and assets of $36 billion.

Most cash machines   The United States had 109,080 ATM (automated teller machine) cash machines as of September 1, 1994. Bank America in San Francisco, CA had 5,700 cash machines, the most of any city in the U.S.

Largest piggy bank   A giant piggy bank called Maximillion, measuring 15 ft. 5 in. long and 8 ft. 8 in. tall, was constructed by the Canadian Imperial Bank of Commerce in Canada in November 1995.

Largest charity food bank   The South Plains Food Bank's Breedlove Dehydration Plant in Lubbock, TX can dehydrate 28 million pounds of surplus fruit and vegetables per year, enough to produce 30,000 meals per day.

Charity fund-raising   The greatest recorded amount raised by a charity walk or run is $Cdn24.7 million by Terry Fox of Canada, who, with an artificial leg, ran from St. John's, Newfoundland to Thunder Bay, Ontario in 143 days, April 12–September 2, 1980. He covered 3,339 miles.

Largest rummage sale   The Cleveland Convention Center, Cleveland, OH White Elephant Sale (instituted 1933) held October 18–19, 1983, raised $427,935.21.

The greatest amount of money raised at a one-day sale was $214,085.99 at the 62nd one-day rummage sale organized by the Winnetka Congregational Church, Winnetka, IL on May 12, 1994.

Largest food company The world's largest food company is Unilever N.V./Unilever PLC, with revenues in 1996 totaling $49 billion.

Largest beverage company The Coca-Cola Company had a total revenue of $18.55 billion in 1996.

The world's most profitable spirits company, and the largest blender and bottler of Scotch whiskey, is United Distillers, the liquor company of Guinness PLC. It made a profit of £673 million ($1.07 billion) in 1995.

Largest insurance companies The company with the highest volume of insurance in force in the world is the Metropolitan Life Insurance Co. of New York City, with $1.27 trillion at year end 1994.

The Prudential Insurance Company of America of Newark, NJ has the greatest volume of consolidated assets, totaling $219.1 billion in 1996.

The largest single insurance association in the world is Blue Cross and Blue Shield Association of Chicago, IL. As of August 14, 1997, it had a membership of 68.6 million. It paid out benefits totaling $75.9 billion in fiscal year 1996.

Largest insurance policies The largest life insurance policy was for $100 million, bought by a major American entertainment corporation on the life of a leading American entertainment industry figure. The policy was sold in July 1990 by Peter Rosengard of London, England and was placed by Albert G. Ruben & Co. Inc. of Beverly Hills, CA and the Feldman Agency, East Liverpool, OH with nine insurance companies to spread the risk.

The highest payout on a single life was reported on November 14, 1970 to be some $18 million to Linda Mullendore, widow of an Oklahoma rancher. Her murdered husband had paid $300,000 in premiums in 1969.

The largest sum claimed for consequential losses was approximately $1.7 trillion against owning, operating and building corporations and Claude Phillips, resulting from the 55-million-gallon oil spill from MT *Amoco Cadiz* off the coast of France in March 1978.

Most expensive land The land around the central Tokyo retail food store Mediya Building was quoted in October 1988 by the Japanese National Land Agency at 358.5 million yen ($248,000) per square foot.

Most expensive offices The world's most expensive office location is Bombay, India. Quoted rents for prime space in the central business district in January 1997 were $145 per square foot, or $159 per square foot with property taxes and service charges.

RETAILERS

Largest restaurant chain McDonald's Corporation is the world's largest food service retailer. At the end of 1996, McDonald's operated 21,022 restaurants in 101 countries. Worldwide sales in 1996 were nearly $31.8 billion.

Largest department store chain Sears Roebuck was the largest operator of department stores in 1996, with sales of $38.24 billion, assets of $36.17 billion and 335,000 employees.

The largest number of visitors to a single department store on one day is an estimated 1.07 million at the Nextage Shanghai, Shanghai, China on December 20, 1995.

Harrods is the largest department store in the United Kingdom, with 25 acres of floor space, compared with 50.5 acres for Macy's, the world's largest.

Largest retailer   The largest retailer in the United States is Wal-Mart, Inc. of Bentonville, AR, with sales of $106.15 billion, net income of $3.06 billion, and 675,000 employees in 1996.

Largest grocery chain   The single largest operator of supermarkets and food stores in the United States is Kroger Co. of Cincinnati, OH, with sales of $25.17 billion in 1996.

Largest drug store chains   The Walgreen Co. of Deerfield, IL had sales totaling $11.8 billion and employed 64,500 people in 1996.

ADVERTISING

Highest TV advertising rate   The highest TV advertising rate was for air time during the transmission of Super Bowl XXXI on January 26, 1997. The 30-second spots sold for an average of $1.2 million, although some spots sold for about $1.3 million.

The highest rate for a regular prime time show was $550,000 for a 30-second spot during *Seinfeld* in the fall of 1996.

Shortest TV commercial   An advertisement lasting only four frames (there are 30 frames in a second) was aired on KING-TV's *Evening Magazine* on November 29, 1993. The ad was for Bon Marche's Frango candies, and cost $3,780 to make.

Fastest production   A 30-second TV advertisement for Reebok Insta-PUMP shoes, starring Emmitt Smith of the Dallas Cowboys, was created, filmed and aired during Super Bowl XXVII on January 31, 1993. Filming continued until the beginning of the fourth quarter, editing began in the the third quarter, and the finished product was aired during the commercial break at the 2-minute warning of the fourth quarter.

Longest-running commercial characters   Jan Miner appeared in U.S. TV commercials as "Madge the Manicurist" from 1965 to 1991, and Dick Wilson, alias "Mr. Whipple," from 1964 to 1989.

Most advertising spending on brand   The most advertising spending by a corporation on a company brand in 1996 was $654 million, for AT&T Telephone Services, by the AT&T Corporation.

SIGNS

Highest advertising sign   The highest advertising sign is the logo "I" at the top of the 73-story, 1,017-foot-tall First Interstate World Center building, Los Angeles, CA.

Most visible advertising sign   The electric Citroën sign on the Eiffel Tower, Paris, France was switched on on July 4, 1925, and could be seen 24 miles

The most expensive TV advertising slots, during Super Bowl XXXI on January 26, 1997, featured commercials for Pepsi (top), Baked Lays (middle) and Nissan (bottom).

away. It was in six colors with 250,000 bulbs and 56 miles of electric cables. The letter "N" in "Citroën" measured 68 ft. 5 in. high. The whole apparatus was dismantled in 1936.

Largest freestanding advertising sign The sign at the Hilton Hotel and Casino in Las Vegas, NV was completed in December 1993. Its two faces had a total area of 2,328 square feet and it was 362 feet high when it was completed, but it was damaged in a storm on July 18, 1994, and part of it fell down. Even after this, it is still both the largest and the tallest sign.

Largest advertising signs The largest advertisement on a building measured 47,385 square feet and was erected to promote the international airline Gulf Air. It was displayed at the side of the M4 motorway near Chiswick, England during May and June 1995.

Airborne Reebok International Ltd. of Massachusetts flew a banner from a single-seater plane that read "Reebok Totally Beachin." The banner measured 50 feet high and 100 feet long, and was flown for four hours each day between March 13–16 and 20–23, 1990, at Daytona Beach, FL.

Animated Topsy the Clown, outside the Circus Circus Hotel, Reno, NV, is 127 feet tall and weighs over 45 tons, with 1.4 miles of neon tubing. Topsy's smile measures 14 feet across.

Billboard The billboard for the Bassat Ogilvy Promotional Campaign for Ford España is 475 ft. 9 in. long and 49 ft. 3 in. high. It is sited at Plaza de Toros Monumental de Barcelona, Barcelona, Spain, and was installed on April 27, 1989.

Largest illuminated advertising signs A sign measuring 210 feet by 55 feet was built for Marlboro cigarettes in Hung Hom, Kowloon, Hong Kong in May 1986. It contains 35,000 feet of neon tubing and weighs approximately 126 tons.

Longest The longest illuminated sign measures 197 by 66 feet. It is lit by 62 400-W metal-halide projectors and was erected by Abudi Signs Industry Ltd. in Ramat Gan, Israel.

A larger such sign, measuring 171 by 138 feet, was displayed throughout 1988 on the Australian Mutual Provident Building in Sydney, New South Wales, Australia. The sign read "1788–1988" and consisted of 4.26 miles of LUMENYTE fiber optics.

Neon The longest neon sign is the letter "M" installed on the Great Mississippi River Bridge, Old Man River at Memphis, TN. It is 1,800 feet long and is made up of 200 high-intensity lamps.

An interior-lit fascia advertising sign in Clearwater, FL completed by the Adco Sign Corp. in April 1983 measured 1,168 ft. 6½ in. long.

COMMERCIAL BUILDINGS

Largest construction project   The Madinat Al-Jubail Al-Sinaiyah project in Saudi Arabia is the largest public works project in modern times. Construction started in 1976 on an industrial city covering 250,705 acres. At the peak of construction, nearly 52,000 workers were employed.

The largest single construction project in the world is the new Hong Kong Airport at Chek Lap Kok. It is built on a 4,127-acre artificial island.

Tallest scaffolding   Regional Scaffolding and Hoisting Co. Inc. of Bronx, NY erected scaffolding with a total height of 650 feet and a volume of 4.8 million cubic feet around the New York City Municipal Building in 1988. The work required 12,000 scaffold frames and 20,000 aluminum planks, and was in place until 1992.

Largest scaffolding   The largest scaffolding was erected by Thyssen Hünnebeck GmbH of Ratingen, Germany around the City Palace in Berlin. The scaffolding, which had a total volume of 6,360,000 feet and stood 102 feet high, was in place from May 1993 until October 1994.

Largest demolition project   The biggest building demolished by explosives was the 21-story Traymore Hotel, Atlantic City, NJ on May 26, 1972 by Controlled Demolition Inc. of Towson, MD. This 600-room hotel had a volume of 6.5 million cubic feet.

The tallest structure ever demolished by explosives was the Matla Power Station chimney, Kriel, South Africa, on July 19, 1981. It stood 902 feet tall and was brought down by the Santon (Steeplejack) Co. Ltd. of Manchester, England.

Largest industrial building   The largest multilevel industrial building that is one discrete structure is the container freight station of Asia Terminals Ltd. at Hong Kong's Kwai Chung container-port. The 15-level building was completed in 1994 and has a total area of 9,320,867 square feet. The building measures 906 by 958 feet, with a height of 359 ft. 3 in. The entire area in each floor is directly accessible by 46-foot container trucks, and the building includes 16.67 miles of roadway and 2,609 container truck parking bays.

Largest brickworks   The Midland Brick Company Pty. Ltd. at Middle Swan Headquarters, WA covers an area of 119 ha and has a weekly production capacity of 7.7 million brick equivalents.

Tallest fountain   The fountain in Fountain Hills, AZ, built for McCulloch Properties Inc., can reach 625 feet when all three pumps are on and weather conditions are favorable.

Largest commercial building   In terms of floor area, the largest commercial building in the world under one roof is the flower auction building Bloemenveiling Aalsmeer (VBA) in Aalsmeer, Netherlands. The floor surface of the building measures 7.6 million square feet.

The world's largest building in terms of volume is the Boeing Company's main assembly plant in Everett, WA. The building had a volume of 196,476,000 cubic feet in 1968, but subsequent expansion programs increased the volume to 472 million cubic feet. The site covers 1,025 acres.

Largest wooden building In 1942–43, 16 wooden blimp hangars for Navy airships were built at various locations throughout the United States. They measure 1,040 feet long, 150 ft. 4 in. high at the crown and 296 ft. 6 in. wide at the base. There are only nine remaining—two each in Tillamook, OR, Moffett Field and Santa Ana, CA and Lakehurst, NJ, and one in Elizabeth City, NC.

Largest kitchen An Indian government field kitchen set up during a famine in April 1973 in Ahmadnagar, Maharashtra provided 1.2 million subsistence meals daily.

Tallest spiral staircase The staircase on the outside of the Bòbila Almirall chimney in Tarrasa, Spain, built by Mariano Masana i Ribas in 1956, is 207 feet high and has 217 steps.

Longest spiral staircase The staircase in the Mapco–White County Coal Mine, Carmi, IL is 1,103 feet deep and has 1,520 steps. It was installed by Systems Control in May 1981.

Longest stairway The service staircase for the Niesenbahn funicular near Spiez, Switzerland rises 5,476 feet. It has 11,674 steps and a banister.

Largest garbage dump Reclamation Plant No. 1, Fresh Kills, Staten Island, NY, opened in March 1948, is the world's largest sanitary landfill. The facility covers 3,000 acres and processes 4,368,000 tons of garbage per year, or 14,000 tons a day, six days a week.

Largest gas tanks In Fontaine-l'Evêque, Belgium, disused mines have been adapted to store up to 17.6 billion cubic feet of gas at normal pressure.

The largest conventional gas tank is in Simmering, Vienna, Austria. It has a height of 275 feet and a capacity of 10.6 million cubic feet.

Largest refuse electrical generation plants The South Meadow, Hartford County, CT plant and the Refuse and Coal Plant, Franklin County, OH, both with a capacity of 90 MW, are the biggest refuse electrical generation plants in the United States.

Largest sewage works The Stickney Water Reclamation Plant (formerly the West–Southwest Sewage Treatment Works) in Stickney, IL began operation in 1939 on a 570-acre site and serves an area containing 2,193,000 people. Its 622 employees treated an average of 802 million gallons of waste per day in 1995.

OFFICES

Largest administrative building The largest ground area covered by any office building is that of the Pentagon, in Arlington, VA. Built to house the

U.S. Defense Department's offices, it was completed on January 15, 1943 and cost an estimated $83 million. Each of the outermost sides is 921 feet long, and the perimeter of the building is about 4,610 feet. Its five stories enclose a floor area of 149.2 acres. The corridors total 17.5 miles in length, and there are 7,754 windows to be cleaned. There are 23,000 people working in the building.

Largest office building   The complex with the largest rentable space is the World Trade Center in New York City, with a total of 12 million square feet of rentable space available in seven buildings, including 4.37 million square feet in each of the twin towers. Each tower has 99 elevators and 43,600 windows containing 600,000 square feet of glass. There are 50,000 people working in the complex and 70,000 visitors daily.

Tallest office building   In March 1996, the Petronas Towers in Malaysia overtook the Sears Tower's 22-year-old record as the world's tallest building. The 241-foot stainless steel pinnacles placed on top of the 88-story towers brought their height to 1,482 ft. 8 in.

Tallest indoor waterfall   The waterfall in the lobby of the International Center Building, Detroit, MI measures 114 feet tall.

WALLS, WINDOWS AND DOORS

Longest wall   The Great Wall of China has a main-line length of 2,150 miles. Completed during the reign of Qin Shi Huangdi (221–210 B.C.), it has a further 2,195 miles of branches and spurs. It is 15–39 feet high and up to 32 feet thick.

Longest fence   The dingo-proof wire fence enclosing the main sheep areas of Australia is six feet high, one foot underground and stretches for 3,437 miles. The Queensland state government discontinued full maintenance in 1982.

Tallest fences   The tallest fences are security screens 65 feet high erected by Harrop-Allin of Pretoria, South Africa in November 1981 to protect fuel depots and refineries at Sasolburg from rocket attack.

Largest windows   The windows in the Palace of Industry and Technology at Rondpoint de la Défense, Paris, France have an extreme width of 715 feet and a maximum height of 164 feet.

Largest sheets of glass   The biggest sheets of glass ever manufactured were 71 feet long and 9 ft. 6 in. wide. They were made by the Saint Gobain Co. in France and installed in their Chantereine-Thourotte factory near Compiègne in August 1966.

Largest doors   The four doors in the Vehicle Assembly Building near Cape Canaveral, FL are 460 feet high.

Heaviest door   The radiation shield door in the National Institute for Fusion Science in Toki, Gifu, Japan weighs 793 tons and is 38 ft. 6 in. high, 37 ft. 5 in. wide and 6 ft. 7 in. thick.

MASTS AND TOWERS

Tallest mast The tallest-ever structure in the world was the guyed Warszawa Radio mast in Konstantynow, Poland. Prior to its fall during renovation work on August 10, 1991, it was 2,120 feet tall. The mast was put into operation on July 22, 1974. It was designed by Jan Polak and weighed 606 tons.

The world's tallest structure is now a stayed television transmitting tower 2,063 feet tall, between Fargo and Blanchard, ND. It was built at a cost of about $500,000 for Channel 11 of KTHI-TV in 30 days (October 2–November 1, 1963) by 11 men from Hamilton Erection, Inc. of York, SC.

The CN Tower rises to 1,815 ft. 5 in.

Tallest tower The tallest freestanding tower (as opposed to a guyed mast) in the world is the $63 million CN Tower in Toronto, Ontario, Canada, which rises to 1,815 ft. 5 in. Excavation began on February 12, 1973 for the erection of the 143,300-ton reinforced, post-tensioned concrete structure, which was completed on April 2, 1975. The 416-seat restaurant revolves in the Sky Pod at 1,150 feet, from which diners can see hills 75 miles away.

Largest cooling tower The cooling tower adjacent to the nuclear power plant in Uentrop, Germany is 590 feet tall and was completed in 1976.

Tallest water tower The Waterspheroid in Edmond, OK rises to a height of 218 feet, and has a capacity of 500,000 gallons. The tower was manufactured by Chicago Bridge and Iron Na-Con Inc.

Tallest chimney The Ekibastuz, Kazakhstan coal power plant No. 2 stack, completed in 1987, is 1,378 feet tall. The chimney tapers from 144 feet in diameter at the base to 46 ft. 7 in. at the top, and it weighs 53,600 tons.

Most massive chimney The 1,148-foot chimney at Puentes de Garcia Rodriguez, northwest Spain, built by M. W. Kellogg Co. for Empresa Nacional de Electricidad S.A., has an internal volume of 6.7 million cubic feet.

The 246-foot towers at the Melbourne Cricket Ground are the world's tallest floodlights.

Tallest flagpole The flagpole at Panmunjon, North Korea, near the border with South Korea, is 525 feet high and flies a flag 98 ft. 6 in. long.

The tallest unsupported flagpole is the 282-foot-tall steel pole erected on August 22, 1985 at the Canadian Expo 86 exhibition in Vancouver, British Columbia. The flagpole supports a gigantic hockey stick 205 feet long.

Tallest totem pole A 180-ft.-3-in.-tall pole known as the Spirit of Lekwammen was raised on August 4, 1994 in Victoria, British Columbia, Canada prior to the Commonwealth Games taking place there. It was a Spirit of Nations project developed by Richard Krentz of Campbell River, also in British Columbia, and took nine months to carve.

Tallest maypole The tallest maypole ever erected was 127 ft. 6 in. tall and was put up in New Westminster, British Columbia, Canada on May 20, 1995.

Tallest lighthouse The 348-foot steel tower near Yamashita Park in Yokohama, Japan has a power of 600,000 candelas and a visibility range of 20 miles.

The lights with the greatest range are 1,089 feet above the ground on the Empire State Building, New York City. Each 4-arc mercury bulb is visible 80 miles away on the ground and 300 miles away from aircraft.

Tallest floodlights The tallest lighting columns are the six towers of the Melbourne Cricket Ground, Melbourne, Victoria, Australia. They are 246 feet high and weigh 132 tons each.

MONEY & WEALTH

PERSONAL WEALTH

Richest person Sir Muda Hassanal Bolkiah Mu'izzaddin Waddaulah, Sultan of Brunei, has a fortune reported to be worth $38 billion by *Forbes* magazine in July 1997.

The richest private individual is Microsoft founder Bill Gates. *Forbes* magazine reported in July 1997 that Gates was worth $36.4 billion. His net worth increased by $18.4 billion in 1996, on top of a $5.1 billion increase the year before.

Richest families The Walton retailing family was worth an estimated $27.6 billion in 1996.

Youngest millionaire The youngest self-made millionaire was the American child film actor Jackie Coogan (1914–84), who co-starred with Charlie Chaplin in *The Kid*, made in 1921.

Youngest billionaire The youngest of the 101 billionaires reported in the United States in 1992 was Bill Gates, cofounder of Microsoft of Seattle, WA, whose MS/DOS operating system runs on an estimated 72 million of the United States' 90 million personal computers. Gates was 20 when he set up his company in 1976 and was a billionaire by 31.

Highest salary Lawrence Coss, CEO of Green Tree Financial, was paid $65.6 million in salary and bonuses in 1995.

Highest income Fund manager George Soros earned at least $1.1 billion in 1993.

Highest personal tax levy The highest recorded personal tax levy is one for $336 million on 70 percent of the estate of Howard Hughes.

Largest golden handshake *Business Week* magazine reported in May 1989 that the largest "golden handshake" ever given was one of $53.8 million, to F. Ross Johnson, who left RJR Nabisco as chairman in February 1989.

Largest dowry In 1929, Don Simón Iturbi Patiño (1861–1947), the Bolivian tin millionaire, bestowed $39 million on his daughter, Elena Patiño. His total fortune was estimated to be worth $607.5 million.

Longest pension Millicent Barclay was born on July 10, 1872, three months after the death of her father, Col. William Barclay, and became eli-

Suzanne Henley scooped up $12,510,549.90 from a one-armed bandit in Las Vegas in 1997.

gible for a Madras Military Fund pension to continue until her marriage. She died unmarried on October 26, 1969, having drawn the pension every day of her life of 97 yr. 3 mo.

Largest return of cash   In May 1994, Howard Jenkins of Tampa, FL, a 31-year-old roofing company employee, discovered that $88 million had been mistakenly transferred into his account. Although he withdrew $4 million, his conscience got the better of him shortly afterward and he returned the $88 million in full.

Largest single bequests   American publisher Walter Annenberg announced on March 12, 1991 that he would be leaving his art collection, worth $1 billion, to the Metropolitan Museum of Art in New York City.

The largest single cash bequest was the $500 million gift, announced on December 12, 1955, to 4,157 educational and other institutions from the Ford Foundation (established 1936) of New York.

Highest lottery sales   In the 1994 fiscal year (July 1–June 30), the United States Lottery netted record total sales of $33,882,158,000 in North America.

Largest lottery jackpot   The largest U.S. lottery jackpot was $118,800,000, in California, on April 17, 1991. Holders of ten tickets shared the prize money.

The highest payout for one ticket was shared by Leslie Robbins and Colleen DeVries of Fond du Lac, WI. The two won $111,200,000 in the Powerball lottery on July 7, 1993; each will receive an annual net sum of $1,500,000 for twenty years.

Largest slot machine jackpot   The biggest beating handed to a "one-armed bandit" was $12,510,549.90, by Suzanne Henley at the New York New York Hotel and Casino, Las Vegas, NV on April 14, 1997.

PAPER MONEY

Oldest paper money   The world's earliest bank notes (banco-sedler) were issued in Stockholm, Sweden in July 1661. The oldest survivor is a 5-daler note dated December 6, 1662.

Largest paper money   The 1-guan note of the Chinese Ming Dynasty issue of 1368–99 measured 9 by 13 inches.

Smallest paper money   The smallest national note ever issued was the 10-bani note of the Ministry of Finance of Romania, in 1917. Its printed area measured $1^{1}/_{16}$ by $1^{1}/_{2}$ inches.

Highest-value paper money   The highest value ever issued by the U.S. Federal Reserve System is a note for $100,000, bearing the head of Woodrow Wilson (1856–1924), which is only used for transactions between the Federal Reserve and the Treasury Department.

The highest-value notes in circulation are U.S. Federal Reserve $10,000 bank notes, bearing the head of Salmon P. Chase (1808–73). It was announced in 1969 that no further notes higher than $100 would be issued, and only 200 $10,000 bills remain in circulation or unretired.

Lowest-value paper money The lowest-value and lowest-denomination legal tender banknote is the one-sen ($^1/_{100}$th of a rupiah) Indonesian note. Its exchange value in June 1996 was 580,970 to the dollar.

Most expensive paper money On February 14, 1991, Richard Lobel paid £240,350 ($478,900) including buyer's premium, on behalf of a consortium, at Phillips, London, England, for a single lot of bank notes. The lot consisted of a cache of British military notes that were found in a vault in Berlin, Germany, and contained more than 17 million notes.

Largest paper money collection Israel Gerber of Ashdod, Israel has accumulated banknotes from 215 different countries since he started collecting in 1962.

CHECKS

Largest check An internal U.S. Treasury check for $4,176,969,623.57 was drawn on June 30, 1954.

The largest check in terms of physical dimensions measured 70 by 31 feet. It was presented by InterMortgage of Leeds, England to Yorkshire Television's 1992 Telephone Appeal on September 4, 1992, and had a value of £10,000 ($19,000).

MINTS

Largest The U.S. Treasury mint was built 1965–1969 on Independence Mall, Philadelphia and covers $11^1/_2$ acres. The mint has an annual production capacity of 12 billion coins.

Fastest The Graebner Press high-speed stamping machine can produce coins at a rate of 42,000 per hour. The record production for coins was in 1982, when 19.5 billion were produced between the Philadelphia and Denver mints.

Smallest issuing The single-press mint belonging to the Sovereign Military Order of Malta, the City of Rome, is housed in one small room and has issued proof coins since 1961.

COINS

Oldest Electrum staters of King Gyges of Lydia, Turkey, *c.* 670 B.C.

Chinese uninscribed "spade" money of the Zhou dynasty has been dated to *c.* 770 B.C.

Oldest dated Samian silver tetradrachm struck in Zankle (now Messina), Sicily, dated year 1, viz. 494 B.C.

Heaviest Swedish 10-daler copper plate, 1644, 43 lb. $7^1/_4$ oz.

Gold Islamic 1,000-muhur, 32 lb., minted in Agra, 1613.

Lightest Nepalese silver ¼ jawa *c*. 1740, 14,000 to the oz.

Most valuable Set $3,190,000 for the King of Siam Proof Set, a set of 1804 and 1834 U.S. coins that had once been given to the King of Siam, purchased by Iraj Sayah and Terry Brand at Superior Galleries, Beverly Hills, CA on May 28, 1990. Included in the set of nine coins was the 1804 silver dollar, which had an estimated value of about $2,000,000.

Individual $1,815,000 for an 1804 silver dollar, at an auction at Bowers and Morena, New York City on April 8, 1997.

Most expensive coin collection The highest price ever paid for a coin collection was $25,235,360 for the Garrett family collection of U.S. and colonial coins, which had been donated to Johns Hopkins University, Baltimore, MD. The sales were made at a series of four auctions held November 28–29, 1979 and March 25–26, 1981 at the Bowers & Ruddy Galleries in Wolfeboro, NH. The collection was put together by members of the Garrett family between 1860 and 1942.

The most valuable column of coins was worth C$85,618 ($62,495).

Column of coins The most valuable column of coins was worth C$85,618 ($62,495) and was 6 ft. 1 in. high. It was built by the British Columbia branch of the Kidney Foundation of Canada at South Surrey on September 8, 1996.

Pile of coins The most valuable pile of coins had a total value of $126,463.61 and consisted of 1,000,298 coins of various denominations. It was constructed by the YWCA of Seattle, King County, WA in Redmond, WA on May 28, 1992.

Line of coins The most valuable line of coins was made up of 1,724,000 quarters with a value of $431,000. It was 25.9 miles long, and was laid at the Atlanta Marriott Marquis Hotel, GA by members of the National Exchange Club on July 25, 1992.

Longest The longest line of coins had a total length of 34.57 miles and comprised 2,367,234 20-sen coins. It was made in Kuala Lumpur, Malaysia and was laid by representatives of WWF (World Wide Fund for Nature) Malaysia and Dumex Sdn Bhd on August 6, 1995.

Coin snatching The greatest number of modern British 10-pence pieces clean-caught from being flipped from the back of a forearm into the same downward palm is 328, by Dean Gould of Felixstowe, England on April 6, 1993.

Coin balancing On November 15, 1995, Aleksandr Bendikov (Belarus) stacked a pyramid of 880 coins on the edge of a coin freestanding vertically on the base of another coin that was on a table.

The tallest single column of coins ever stacked on the edge of a coin was made up of 253 Indian one-rupee pieces on top of a vertical 5-rupee coin, by Dipak Syal of Yamuna Nagar, India on May 3, 1991. Syal also balanced 10 one-rupee coins and 10 10-paise coins alternately horizontally and vertically in a single column on May 1, 1991.

Most valuable hoard The most valuable hoard of coins was one of about 80,000 aurei found in Brescello near Modena, Italy in 1714, and believed to have been deposited *c.* 37 B.C.

GEMS & PRECIOUS METALS

DIAMONDS

Largest diamond The Cullinan, weighing 3,106 carats, was found on January 26, 1905 in the Premier Mine, Pretoria, South Africa. It was later cut into 106 polished diamonds and produced the largest cut fine quality colorless diamond, weighing 530.2 carats.

Largest cut diamond The 545.67-carat gem known as the Golden Jubilee Diamond was made from a 775.5-carat rough into a fire rose cushion cut.

The Golden Jubilee Diamond acted as the forerunner to the Centenary Diamond, the world's largest flawless top color modern fancy cut diamond at 273.85 carats.

The Golden Jubilee Diamond

Smallest brilliant-cut diamond A 0.0000743-carat diamond fashioned by hand by Pauline Willemse at Coster Diamonds B.V., Amsterdam, Netherlands, 1991–94, is 0.0063–0.0067 inches in diameter and 0.0043 inches high.

Highest-priced diamond On May 17, 1995, a 100.1-carat pear-shaped "D" flawless diamond was sold at Sotheby's, Geneva, Switzerland to Sheikh Ahmed Fitaihi (Saudi Arabia) for $16,548,750.

The highest price paid for a rough diamond was $10 million for a 255.1-carat stone from Guinea, by the William Goldberg Diamond Corporation in partnership with the Chow Tai Fook Jewellery Co. Ltd. of Hong Kong, in March 1989.

The record per carat is $926,315 for a 0.95-carat fancy purplish-red stone sold at Christie's, New York on April 28, 1987.

The most expensive diamond sold for $16,548,750.

EMERALDS

Largest cut emerald An 86,136-carat natural beryl was found in Carnaiba, Brazil in August 1974. It was carved by Richard Chan in Hong Kong and valued at $1,120,080 in 1982.

Largest emerald crystal The largest single emerald crystal of gem quality was 7,025 carats. It was found in 1969 at the Cruces Mine, near Gachala, Colombia.

Highest-priced emerald The highest price for a single emerald is $2,126,646, for a 19.77-carat emerald and diamond ring made by Cartier in 1958, which was sold at Sotheby's, Geneva, Switzerland on April 2, 1987.

RUBIES

Largest star ruby The Eminent Star ruby, believed to be of Indian origin, is the largest ruby, at 6,465 carats.

Highest-priced ruby A ruby ring with a stone weighing 15.97 carats was sold at Sotheby's, New York on October 18, 1988 for $227,300.

SAPPHIRES

Largest star sapphire The 9,719.5-carat gem The Lone Star was cut in London, England in November 1989.

Highest-priced sapphire A step-cut stone of 62.02 carats was sold as part of a sapphire and diamond ring at Sotheby's, St. Moritz, Switzerland on February 20, 1988 for $2,791,723.

TOPAZ

Largest topaz The 22,892.5-carat American Golden Topaz has been on display at the Smithsonian Institution, Washington, D.C. since May 4, 1988.

OPALS

Largest opal The largest gem-quality white opal was 26,350 carats, found in July 1989 at the Jupiter Field at Coober Pedy in South Australia.

Largest black opal A stone found on February 4, 1972 at Lightning Ridge, New South Wales, Australia produced a finished gem of 1,520 carats, called the Empress of Glengarry.

Largest rough black opal The largest gem-quality uncut black opal was also found at Lightning Ridge, on November 3, 1986. It weighs 1,982.5 carats and measures 4 by 2⅝ by 2½ inches.

PEARLS

Largest pearl   The 14-lb.-1-oz. Pearl of Lao-tze was found at Palawan, Philippines in May 1934 in the shell of a giant clam.

Largest abalone pearl   A baroque abalone pearl measuring 2¾ by 2 by 1⅛ inches and weighing 469.13 carats was found at Salt Point State Park, CA in May 1990.

Largest cultured pearl   A 1½-inch round, 138.25-carat cultured pearl weighing one ounce was found near Samui Island, off Thailand, in January 1988.

Highest-priced pearl   La Régente, a pearl weighing 302.68 grains and formerly part of the French crown jewels, was sold at Christie's, Geneva, Switzerland on May 12, 1988 for $859,280.

AMBER

Largest piece of amber   Burma Amber weighs 33 lb. 10 oz. and is located in the Natural History Museum, London, England.

JADE

Largest piece of jade   A single lens of nephrite jade weighing 636 tons was found in the Yukon Territory of Canada in 1992.

GOLD

Largest mass of gold   The Holtermann Nugget, found in 1872 in the Beyers & Holtermann Star of Hope mine in New South Wales, Australia, contained 2,640 troy ounces of gold in a 7,560-troy-ounce slab of slate.

Largest pure gold nugget   The Welcome Stranger, found at Moliagul, Victoria, Australia in 1869, yielded 2,248 troy ounces of pure gold from 2,280¼ troy ounces.

PLATINUM

Largest platinum nugget   A 340-ounce nugget of platinum was found in the Ural Mountains in Russia in 1843.

JEWELED OBJECTS

Dress   A wedding outfit created by Hélène Gainville with jewels by Alexander Reza is believed to be worth over $7.3 million. The dress is embroidered with diamonds mounted on platinum and was unveiled in Paris, France on March 23, 1989.

Pen   In May 1997, the 5079 Caran d'Ache solid gold fountain pen, with 4,147 diamonds, sold for $211,900.

Shoes   Emperor Field Marshal Jean Fedor Bokassa of the Central African Empire (now Republic) commissioned pearl-studded shoes at a cost of $85,000 from the House of Berluti, Paris, France for his self-coronation on December 4, 1977.

Wallet   The most expensive wallet ever made is a platinum-cornered, diamond-studded crocodile creation made by Louis Quatorze of Paris, France and Mikimoto of Tokyo, selling in September 1984 for $84,000.

AGRICULTURE

BREWERIES AND VINEYARDS

Oldest brewer   Weihenstephan Brewery, Freising, near Munich, Germany, was founded in A.D. 1040.

Oldest vintners   The world's oldest champagne firm is Ruinart Père et Fils, founded in 1729. The oldest cognac firm is Augier Frères & Cie, established in 1643.

Largest vineyard   The vineyard that extends over the Mediterranean slopes between the Pyrenees and the Rhône in the départements Gard, Hérault, Aude and Pyrénées-Orientales, France covers an area of 2,075,685 acres.

Largest wine cellars   The cellars of the Ko-operatieve Wijnbouwers Vereniging (KWV), Paarl, Cape Province, in the center of the wine-growing district of South Africa, cover an area of 54 acres and have a capacity of 32 million gallons.

FARMS

Largest cattle ranch   The Anna Creek cattle ranch in South Australia, owned by the Kidman family, comprises 11,600 square miles. The biggest component is Strangway, at 5,500 square miles.

Largest dairy farm   The world's largest dairy farm is the Al Safi, near Al Kharj, Saudi Arabia. It has about 24,000 Holsteins and covers 8,600 acres.

Largest egg farm   The Agrigeneral Company L.P. in Croton, OH has 4.8 million hens laying 3.7 million eggs daily.

Largest community garden   The project operated by the City Beautiful Council and the Benjamin Wegerzyn Garden Center in Dayton, OH comprises 1,173 plots, each measuring 812 square feet.

Largest sheep ranch   Commonwealth Hill, South Australia grazes between 50,000 and 70,000 sheep, along with 24,000 uninvited kangaroos, in an area of 4,080 square miles enclosed by 138 miles of dog-proof fencing.

The head count on Sir William Stevenson's 40,970-acre Lochinver station in New Zealand was 127,406 on January 1, 1993.

Combine harvesting   Philip Baker of West End Farm, Merton, England harvested 182.5 tons of wheat in eight hours using a Massey Ferguson MF 38 combine on August 8, 1989.

On August 9, 1990, an international team from CWS Agriculture, led by estate manager Ian Hanglin, harvested 394.73 tons of wheat in eight hours from 108.72 acres at Cockayne Hatley Estate, Sandy, England.

Baling   A rick of 40,400 bales of straw was built between July 22 and September 3, 1982 by Nick and Tom Parsons with a gang of eight at Cuckoo Pen Barn Farm, Birdlip, England. It measured 150 by 30 by 60 feet high and weighed some 784 tons. The team baled, hauled and ricked 24,200 bales in seven consecutive days, July 22–29.

Plowing   The fastest time for plowing an acre by the United Kingdom Society of Ploughmen rules is 9 min. 49.88 sec., by Joe Langcake at Hornby Hall Farm, Brougham, England on October 21, 1989. He used a case IH 7140 Magnum tractor and a Kverneland 4-furrow plow.

Field to loaf   The fastest time for producing 13 loaves of bread (a baker's dozen) from growing wheat is 8 min. 13.6 sec., by Wheat Montana Farms & Bakery, Three Forks, MT on September 19, 1995. They used 13 microwave ovens to bake the loaves.

Using a traditional baker's oven to bake the bread, the record time is 19 min. 14 sec., by a team led by John Haynes and Peter Rix in Alpheton, England on August 22, 1993.

CATTLE

Largest cattle breed   The heaviest breed of cattle is the Val di Chianini. Bulls average 5 ft. 8 in. at the forequarters and weigh 2,865 pounds, but Chianini oxen have been known to attain heights of 6 ft. 2¾ in.

Heaviest bovine   A Holstein–Durham cross named Mount Katahdin, exhibited by A. S. Rand of Maine from 1906 to 1910, frequently weighed in at an even 5,000 pounds. He was 6 ft. 2 in. at the shoulder with a 13-foot girth, and died in a barn fire c. 1923.

Smallest cattle breed   The smallest breed of domestic cattle is the Ovambo of Namibia. Bulls and cows average 496 pounds and 353 pounds respectively.

Oldest bovine   Big Bertha, a Dremon owned by Jerome O'Leary of Blackwatersbridge, County Kerry, Republic of Ireland, died less than three months short of her 49th birthday, on December 31, 1993.

Most reproductive cow   On April 25, 1964, it was reported that a cow named Lyubik had given birth to seven calves in Mogilev, Byelarus. A case of five live calves at one birth was reported in 1928 by T. G. Yarwood of Manchester, England. The lifetime breeding record is 39 in the case of Big Bertha.

Heaviest calf The heaviest recorded live birth weight for a calf is 225 pounds for a British Friesian cow at Rockhouse Farm, Bishopston, Wales in 1961.

Lightest calf The lowest live birthweight for a calf is nine pounds, for a Holstein heifer called Christmas, born on December 25, 1993 on the farm of Mark and Wendy Theuringer in Hutchinson, MN.

Highest milk yields In 1995, the United States produced 155.8 billion pounds of cow's milk. As of June 1996, the state producing the most milk was California, with a monthly total of 2.2 billion pounds.

The highest lifetime yield for a single cow is 465,224 pounds, by the unglamorously named cow No. 289 owned by M. G. Maciel & Son of Hanford, CA, to May 1, 1984.

The greatest yield for one lactation (maximum 365 days) is 59,443 pounds in 1995 by the Friesian cow Acme Goldy 2, owned by Bryce Miller of Woodford Grange Farm, Islip, England.

Hand-milking of cows Joseph Love of Kilifi Plantations Ltd., Kenya milked 117 gallons from 30 cows on August 25, 1992.

GOATS

Largest goat A British Saanen named Mostyn Moorcock, owned by Pat Robinson of Ewyas Harold, England, reached a weight of 400 pounds (shoulder height 44 inches and overall length 66 inches).

Oldest goat A Golden Guernsey–Anglo Nubian cross named Naturemade Aphrodite (1975–93), belonging to Katherine Whitwell of Moulton, Newmarket, England, died on August 23, 1993 aged 18 yr. 1 mo.

Most reproductive goat On January 14, 1980, a nanny goat named Julie, owned by Galen Cowper of Nampah, ID, gave birth to septuplets, but all seven died, along with the mother.

Highest milk yield In 1977, Osory Snow-Goose, owned by Mr. and Mrs. G. Jameson of Leppington, New South Wales, Australia produced 7,714 pounds in 365 days.

PIGS

Largest pig A Poland-China hog named Big Bill weighed 2,552 pounds just before he was put to sleep after suffering a broken leg en route to the Chicago World's Fair for exhibition in 1933. Other statistics included a shoulder height of five feet and a length of nine feet.

Smallest pig After 10 years of experimentation with Vietnamese pot-bellied pigs, Stefano Morini (Italy) developed the Mini Maialino. These pigs weigh 20 pounds at maturity.

Largest litter The highest number of piglets in one litter is 37, farrowed on September 21, 1993 by Sow 570, a Meishan cross Large White–Duroc at

Mr. and Mrs. M. P. Ford's Eastfield House Farm, Melbourne, England. Of the 36 piglets that were born alive, 33 survived.

Highest birth weight A Hampshire–Yorkshire sow belonging to Rev. John Schroeder of Mountain Grove, MO farrowed a litter of 18 on August 26, 1979. Five were stillborn, including one male that weighed 5 lb. 4 oz.

POULTRY

Largest chicken The largest recorded chicken was Big Snow, a rooster weighing 23 lb. 3 oz. on June 12, 1992, with a chest girth of 2 ft. 9 in. and standing 1 ft. 5 in. at the shoulder. Owned and bred by Ronald Alldridge of Deuchar, Queensland, Australia, Big Snow died on September 6, 1992.

Most reproductive chicken A White Leghorn, No. 2988, laid 371 eggs in 364 days in an official test conducted by Prof. Harold V. Biellier ending on August 29, 1979 at the College of Agriculture, University of Missouri.

Largest chicken egg A Black Minorca laid a 5-yolked egg of nearly 12 ounces measuring 12¼ inches around the long axis and nine inches around the short, at Mr. Stafford's Damsteads Farm, Mellor, Lancashire, England in 1896.

Heaviest chicken egg A White Leghorn in Vineland, NJ laid an egg weighing 16 ounces, with double yolk and double shell, on February 25, 1956.

Most-yolked chicken egg In July 1971, a hen's egg was reported by Hainsworth Poultry Farms, Mount Morris, NY to have nine yolks. A hen in Kyrgyzstan was also reported to have nine yolks in August 1977.

Oldest duck Wil Cwac Cwac, owned by Gryfudd Hughes of Pwllheli, Wales, is 25 years old.

Egg shelling Two kitchen hands, Harold Witcomb and Gerald Harding, shelled 1,050 dozen eggs in a 7¼-hour shift at Bowyers, Trowbridge, England on April 23, 1971.

Egg dropping The greatest height from which fresh eggs have been dropped (to the ground) and remained intact is 700 feet, by David Donoghue from a helicopter on August 22, 1994 on a golf course in Blackpool, England.

Longest chicken flight Sheena, a barnyard bantam owned by Bill and Bob Knox, flew 630 ft. 2 in. in Parkesburg, PA in May 1985.

Wil Cwac Cwac celebrates his 25th birthday.

SHEEP

Largest sheep A Suffolk ram named Stratford Whisper 23H weighed 545 pounds and stood 43 inches tall in March 1991. It is owned by Joseph and Susan Schallberger of Boring, OR.

Smallest sheep The Ouessant, from the Ile d'Ouessant, Brittany, France, weighs 29–35 pounds and stands 18–20 inches at the withers.

Oldest sheep A crossbred sheep owned by Griffiths & Davies of Dolclettwr Hall, Taliesin, Wales died on January 24, 1989 just one week before her 29th birthday.

Largest litter A Finnish Landrace ewe owned by the D.M.C. Partnership of Feilding, Manawatu, New Zealand gave birth to eight lambs (five rams and three ewes) at a single birth on September 4, 1991. On April 19, 1994 the record was equaled by 6-year-old ewe "835 Ylva," owned by Birgitta and Kent Mossby of Halsarp Farm, Falkoping, Sweden.

Stratford Whisper 23H weighed 545 pounds.

Heaviest lamb A lamb weighing 38 pounds was born at Clearwater, Sedgwick County, KS in 1975, but neither lamb nor ewe survived. Another lamb of the same weight was born on April 7, 1975 on the Gerald Neises Farm, Howard, SD but died soon afterward.

Lightest lamb The lowest live birthweight for a lamb is 1 lb. 4 oz. for a female named Princess Pippin, born on March 16, 1995 at Howarton Farm, Speldhurst, England, and owned by Ann and Adam Massingham of Fordcombe, England.

Sheep to shoulder At the International Wool Secretariat Development Center, Ilkley, England, a team of eight using commercial machinery produced a sweater—from shearing sheep to the finished article—in 2 hr. 28 min. 32 sec. on September 3, 1986.

Sheep shearing The record for shearing a sheep is held by Godfrey Bowen (New Zealand), who sheared a Cheviot ewe in 46 seconds at the Royal Highland Show, Dundee, Scotland in June 1957.

The highest speed for sheep shearing in a working day was recorded by Alan MacDonald, who machine-sheared 805 lambs in nine hours in Waitnaguru, New Zealand on December 20, 1990.

Peter Casserly (New Zealand) achieved a hand-shearing record of 353 lambs in nine hours on February 13, 1976.

Longest fleece A Merino wether found on K. P. & B. A. Reynolds Company's Willow Springs Station, South Australia in November 1990 produced 65 pounds of wool from a fleece 25 inches long, representing a 7-year growth.

THE LIVING WORLD

PLANTS & TREES

PLANTS

Oldest plant "King's Holly" (*Lomatia tasmania*) found in Tasmania is believed to be 40,000 years old. The shrub was dated using a fossil of an identical specimen found nearby.

Northernmost plant The yellow poppy (*Papaver radicatum*) and the Arctic willow (*Salix arctica*) grow at Lat. 83° N.

Southernmost plant The southernmost flowering plant is the Antarctic hair grass (*Deschampsia antarctica*), which was found at Lat. 68° 21′ S on Refuge Island, Antarctica on March 11, 1981.

Largest cactus (at left) The saguaro (*Cereus giganteus* or *Carnegiea gigantea*) is found in Arizona, southeastern California and Sonora, Mexico. A specimen found in the Maricopa Mountains, near Gila Bend, AZ on January 17, 1988 had candelabra-like branches rising to 57 ft. 11³/₄ in.

An armless cactus 78 feet high was measured in April 1978 by Hube Yates in Cave Creek, AZ. It was toppled in a windstorm in July 1986 at an estimated age of 150 years.

Highest-living plant The flowering plants *Ermania himalayensis* and *Ranunculus lobatus* were found at 21,000 feet on Mt. Kamet in the Himalayas by N. D. Jayal in 1955.

Deepest-living plant Plant life was found underwater at a depth of 884 feet by Mark and Diane Littler off San Salvador Island, Bahamas in October 1984.

Deepest roots The greatest reported depth to which roots have penetrated is a calculated

400 feet for a wild fig tree at Echo Caves, near Ohrigstad, Mpumalanga, South Africa.

Longest roots A single winter rye plant (*Secale cereale*) has been shown to produce 387 miles of roots in 1.8 cubic feet of earth.

Fastest-growing plant Some species of the 45 genera of bamboo have been found to grow up to three feet per day.

FLOWERS

Largest bloom *Rafflesia arnoldi* of southeast Asia has blooms three feet across and weighing as much as 36 pounds.

Inflorescence The world's largest inflorescence is that of *Puya raimondii*. Its panicle (diameter eight feet) emerges to a height of 35 feet, and each panicle bears up to 8,000 white blooms.

Smallest flowering and fruiting plant The floating, flowering aquatic duckweed (*Wolffia angusta*) of Australia is only 0.024 inches long and 0.013 inches wide. It weighs about .00001 ounces and its fruit, which resembles a minuscule fig, weighs .000025 ounces.

Bottom, Rafflesia arnoldi, the largest bloom; top, Amorphophallus titanum, the most pungent-smelling plant, which emits a smell resembling rotting fish and burned sugar.

Fastest-growing flowering plant It was reported from Tresco Abbey, Isles of Scilly, Great Britain in July 1978 that a *Hesperoyucca whipplei* grew 12 feet in 14 days, a rate of about 10 inches per day.

Slowest-flowering plant The panicle of *Puya raimondii* (*see* LARGEST BLOOM, above) emerges after 80–150 years of the plant's life and then dies.

Tallest orchid Specimens of *Grammatophyllum speciosum*, a native of Malaysia, have been recorded up to 25 feet high. There are five species of vanilla orchid that are vines and can spread to almost any length depending on the environment.

Largest orchid flower The petals of *Pathiopedilum sanderianum* are reported to grow up to three feet long in the wild. A specimen grown in Somerset, England in 1991 had three flowers averaging two feet from the top of the dorsal sepal to the bottom of the ribbon petals, giving a record stretched length of four feet.

Largest rose tree A Lady Banks rose tree in Tombstone, AZ has a trunk 163 inches in circumference, stands nine feet high and covers an area of 8,660 square feet. The tree is supported by 77 posts and several thousand feet of piping, which allows 150 people to be seated under the arbor.

Largest leaves The largest leaves of any plant belong to the raffia palm (*Raffia farinifera = R. ruffia*) of the Mascarene Islands in the Indian Ocean, and the Amazonian bamboo palm (*R. taedigera*) of South America, both of which have leaf blades that measure up to 65 ft. 6 in. long, with petioles up to 13 feet.

Most-leafed clovers A 14-leafed white clover (*Trifolium repens*) was found by Randy Farland near Sioux Falls, SD on June 16, 1975. A 14-leafed red clover (*T. pratense*) was reported by Paul Haizlip in Bellevue, WA on June 22, 1987.

SEEDS

Largest seed The single-seeded fruit of the giant fan palm *Lodoicea maldivica* (= *L. callipyge, L. seychellarum*) can weigh 44 pounds. Commonly known as the double coconut or coco de mer, it is found wild only in the Seychelles in the Indian Ocean.

Smallest seed The smallest are those of epiphytic orchids, at 28 billion seeds per ounce (compare with grass pollens at up to 6 billion grains per ounce).

Most durable seed A plausible but inconclusive claim for the longevity of seeds has been made for the Arctic lupine (*Lupinus arcticus*) found in frozen silt at Miller Creek, Yukon, Canada in July 1954 by Harold Schmidt. The seeds were germinated in 1966 and were radiocarbon dated to at least 8000 B.C. and more probably to 13,000 B.C.

GRASSES

Commonest grass Bermuda grass (*Cynodon dactylon*) is native to tropical Africa and the Indo-Malaysian region, but it extends from Lat. 45° N to

45° S. It is possibly the most troublesome weed of the grass family, affecting 40 crops in over 80 countries.

Tallest grass A thorny bamboo culm (*Bambusa arundiancea*) felled at Pattazhi, Travancore, India in November 1904 was 121½ feet tall.

WEEDS

Largest weed The giant hogweed (*Heracleum mantegazzianum*), originally from the Caucasus, reaches 12 feet tall and has leaves three feet long.

Most damaging weed The purple nutsedge, nutgrass or nutsedge (*Cyperus rotundus*) is a land weed native to India. It attacks 52 crops in 92 countries, including the United States, where it is found primarily in the southern states.

Aquatic The most widespread aquatic weed is the water hyacinth *Eichhornia crassipes*), which is a native of the Amazon basin but extends from Lat. 40° N to 45° S.

TREES

Oldest tree species The maidenhair tree (*Ginkgo biloba*), which first appeared about 160 million years ago during the Jurassic era, survives today as a living species. It has been grown since *c.* 1100 in Japan.

Oldest tree A redwood (*Sequoia sempervirens*) named Eternal God is 12,000 years old. This tree, which stands in the Prairie Creek Redwoods State Park in California, has a height of 238 feet and a diameter of 19.6 feet.

Most massive tree General Sherman, a giant sequoia (*Sequoiadendron giganteum*) in Sequoia National Park, CA, is 275 feet tall. In 1991, it had a girth of 102.6 feet, measured 4½ feet above the ground. In terms of total volume, General Sherman, at 52,500 cubic feet, is considered the largest living thing in the world.

Greatest spread The great banyan (*Ficus benghalensis*) in the Indian Botanical Garden, Calcutta, India has 1,775 prop or supporting roots and a circumference of 1,350 feet. It covers some three acres and dates from before 1787.

Greatest girth A circumference of 190 feet was recorded for the European chestnut (*Castanea sativa*) known as the "Tree of the Hundred Horses" (Castagno di Cento Cavalli) on Mount Etna, Sicily, Italy in 1770 and 1780. The tree is now in three parts, widely separated.

Tallest tree An Australian eucalyptus (*Eucalyptus regnans*) at Watts River, Victoria, Australia, was reported in 1872 to measure 435 feet tall. It almost certainly measured over 500 feet at some point in its life.

Living The tallest tree currently standing is the "Mendocino tree," a coast redwood (*Sequoia sempervirens*) in Montgomery State Reserve, Ukiah, CA.

It was measured at 367 ft. 6 in. in December 1996, with a diameter of 10 ft. 4. in. The thousand-year-old tree is still growing.

Fastest-growing tree   Discounting bamboo, which is not classified as a tree but as a woody grass, the fastest rate of growth recorded is 35 ft. 3 in. in 13 months by an *Albizzia falcata* planted on June 17, 1974 in Sabah, Malaysia.

Slowest-growing tree   The slowest-growing tree is a white cedar (*Thuja occidentalis*) located on a cliffside in the Canadian Great Lakes area. At 155 years old, it is less than 4 inches tall.

Most isolated tree   It is believed that the nearest companion to a solitary Norwegian spruce on Campbell Island in the Pacific Ocean is over 120 nautical miles away in the Auckland Islands.

Largest forest   The largest forested areas in the world are the coniferous forests of northern Russia, lying between Lat. 55° N and the Arctic Circle. The total wooded area amounts to 2.7 billion acres (25 percent of the world's forests), of which 38 percent is Siberian larch. In comparison, the largest area of forest in the tropics is the Amazon basin, with some 815 million acres.

PREHISTORIC LIFE

Oldest DNA   The oldest fossil DNA was found in a 125 million-year-old weevil encased in amber in Lebanon.

Oldest flower fossil   A flower believed to be 120 million years old was identified in 1989 by Dr. Leo Hickey and Dr. David Taylor of Yale University from a fossil discovered near Melbourne, Victoria, Australia. The flowering angiosperm, which resembles a modern black pepper plant, had two leaves and one flower and is known as the Koonwarra plant.

Largest protozoan   The largest known protozoans in terms of volume are the extinct calcareous foraminifera (*Foraminiferida*) of the genus *Nummulites*. Individuals up to six inches wide have been found in the Middle Eocene rocks of Turkey.

Oldest land animals   Animals moved from the sea to the land at least 414 million years ago. The first known land animals include two kinds of centipede and a tiny spider found among plant debris. However, all three species were fairly advanced predators—and must therefore have been preying on animals that lived on land even before they did.

Oldest insect fossil   A shrimplike creature found in 1991 in rocks 420 million years old may be the oldest insect. Found in Western Australia, this 5-inch-long euthycarcinoid was a freshwater predator.

Oldest bird fossil Two partial bird skeletons were found in Texas in rocks dating from 220 million years ago. Named *Protoavis texensis* in 1991, the pheasant-sized creature has caused controversy by pushing the age of birds back millions of years from the previous record, that of the more familiar *Archeopteryx lithographica* from Germany.

Oldest reptile fossil *Westlothiana lizziae* is estimated to be 340 million years old, 40 million years older than previously discovered reptiles.

Largest land predator The largest-ever land predator may have been a giant specimen of the alligator *Purussaurus brasiliensis*. It was found on the banks of the Amazon in rocks dated at 8 million years old. Estimates based on the 5-foot-long skull, complete with 4-inch teeth, indicate a total length of 40 feet and a weight of about 19.8 tons, making it larger than *Tyrannosaurus rex*.

Longest snake The python-like *Gigantophis garstini* inhabited what is now Egypt about 38 million years ago. Parts of a spinal column and a small piece of jaw indicate a length of 36 feet—or 3 ft. 3 in. longer than the longest modern snake.

Largest bird Fossil leg bones found in Alice Springs in 1974 indicate that the flightless *Dromornis stirtoni*, a huge emu-like creature that lived in central Australia between 15 million and 25,000 years ago, must have been 10 feet tall and weighed about 1,100 pounds.

The giant moa (*Dinornis maximus*) of New Zealand may have been even taller, possibly reaching a height of 12 feet. It weighed about 500 pounds.

The largest flying bird was the giant teratorn, *Argentavis magnificens*, which lived in Argentina 6–8 million years ago. Fossil remains discovered in 1979 indicate that this gigantic vulture-like bird had a wingspan of at least 19 ft. 8 in. and possibly as much as 25 feet, and weighed about 175 pounds.

Largest land mammal *Indricotherium* was a long-necked, hornless rhinocerotid that roamed across western Asia and Europe about 35 million years ago. A reconstruction in the American Museum of Natural History, New York City measures 17 ft. 9 in. to the top of the shoulder hump and 37 feet in total length. The most likely maximum weight of this gigantic browser is 12–22 tons.

DINOSAURS

Oldest dinosaur The most primitive dinosaur is *Eoraptor lunensis*, named in 1993 from a skeleton found in the foothills of the Andes in Argentina, in rocks dated at 228 million years. This dinosaur was about 3 ft. 3 in. long and is classified as a theropod (a type of meat-eating dinosaur).

Heaviest dinosaur A titanosaurid from Argentina, *Argentinosaurus*, was estimated in 1994 to have weighed up to 110 tons.

Largest dinosaur The sauropod dinosaurs, a group of long-necked, long-tailed, 4-legged plant-eaters, lumbered around the world during the Jurassic and Cretaceous periods, 208–65 million years ago. They ranged in

FOOTSTEPS
FROM THE PAST

Imagine standing in the path of 30 roaming dinosaurs, each weighing several tons. Dr. Martin G. Lockley actually had such an experience in a sparsely populated area of Turkmenistan in Central Asia. But he arrived at the spot 150 million years after the Jurassic-period dinosaurs passed by.

Lockley is a professor of geology, director of the Dinosaur Trackers Research Group at the University of Colorado at Denver and an expert on fossil footprints, which are the most abundant relics of the dinosaurs. British-born Lockley traveled to Turkmenistan in 1995 on an expedition organized by National Geographic.

The expedition's discovery was especially significant because it established the site as the world's longest dinosaur trackway. The trackway—a consecutive series of footprints made by a single animal— measured 1,020 feet. The tracks were made by a carnivorous dinosaur called *Megalosaurus.* Lockley and his team also found four other trackways that surpassed previous world records. "They weren't chasing anything," Lockley notes. "They were probably walking across a mud flat."

In the world of dinosaurs, the brontosaurus takes the title of Big Foot. "There are lots of places in the world where we get large tracks," says Lockley. "The largest known are the rear feet, with several reported from

LONGEST DINOSAUR TRACKWAY

Dr. Martin G. Lockley and other members of a National Geographic expedition found a dinosaur trackway measuring 1,020 feet in length in Turkmenistan in 1995. The tracks were made by a carnivorous dinosaur called *Megalosaurus.*

North America, Korea, Portugal and Switzerland that are approximately 40 inches in diameter." These feet, similar to elephant feet but bigger, had five short toes, some of them barely visible. Brontosaurus feet supported bodies weighing 40 to 50 tons. Dinosaurs had no arch and were flat-footed but apparently had no foot problems.

The largest track of a bipedal dinosaur belonged to a *Tyrannosaurus rex* and measured about 34 inches. "Someone else found it but I identified it [from a mold]," says Lockley. Unlike the brontosaurus foot, this one had three big toes like a bird with a spur sticking out at the back of the foot. The original, on a ranch in New Mexico owned by the Boy Scouts of America, helped support a *T. rex* that weighed five or six tons and lived about 65–70 million years ago.

Asked why people are so intrigued by dinosaurs, which command our attention in every form from movies to toys, Lockley replies, "I suppose the human fascination with these monsters is connected to some primitive state," he says, "when we actually competed with cave bears and cave lions."

length from 80 feet to over 150 feet. Weight estimates range from 15 tons to 100 tons.

Largest predatory dinosaur   In 1995, the largest predatory dinosaur skull was found in Morocco. The 5-ft.-4-in.-long skull belonged to a flesh-eater called *Carcharodontosaurus saharicus*, which is estimated to have been over 40 feet long, larger than *Tyrannosaurus rex* and *Gigantosaurus carolinii*, although the size ranges of these three creatures may have overlapped.

Tallest dinosaur   *Brachiosaurus brancai* ("arm lizard") from the Tendaguru site in Tanzania is dated as Late Jurassic (150–144 million years ago). The site was excavated by German expeditions during the period 1909–11, and a complete skeleton was constructed from the remains of several individuals and put on display at the Humboldt Museum in Berlin in 1937. This is the largest mounted dinosaur skeleton, measuring 72 ft. 9½ in. long and 46 feet tall.

Longest dinosaur   Footprints suggest that the brachiosaurid *Breviparopus* may have attained a length of 157 feet.

In 1991, a sauropod discovered in New Mexico, *Seismosaurus halli*, was estimated to be 128–170 feet long based on comparisons of individual bones.

The longest dinosaur known from a complete skeleton is the diplodocid *Diplodocus carnegii*, assembled from remains found in Wyoming in 1899. The living animal was 86 ft. 6 in. long and weighed about 13 tons.

Widest dinosaur   Ankylosaurs, the most heavily armored dinosaurs, with clubbed tails, bony plates, studs and spikes covering the back and head, were as much as 8 ft. 2 in. wide.

Fastest dinosaur   *Dromiceiomimus*, an ornithomimid, could probably outsprint an ostrich, which has a top speed of 37 mph.

A Late Jurassic trackway in the Morrison formation in Texas, found in 1981, indicated a carnivorous dinosaur moving as fast as 25 mph.

Smallest dinosaur   The chicken-sized *Compsognathus* ("pretty jaw") of southern Germany and southeast France and an undescribed plant-eating fabrosaurid from Colorado both measured 29½ inches from the snout to the tip of the tail and weighed about 15 pounds.

Smartest dinosaur   Troodontids (formerly known as saurornithoidids) had the largest brain to body size ratio of all nonavian dinosaurs.

Most brainless dinosaur   *Stegosaurus* ("plated lizard"), which roamed across Colorado, Oklahoma, Utah and Wyoming about 150 million years ago, was up to 30 feet long but had a 2½-ounce brain. This represented 0.004 of 1 percent of its body weight of 1.9 tons (compare with 0.074 of 1 percent for an elephant and 1.88 percent for a human).

Most teeth   *Pelecanimimus*, an ornithominid (birdlike dinosaur), had more than 220 very sharp teeth.

Largest skull   The long-frilled *Torosaurus*, a caratopsid herbivore that measured about 25 feet in total length, had a skull (including the fringe) of up to 9 ft. 10. in. in length and weighing up to 2.2 tons.

Longest neck   The sauropod *Mamenchisaurus* ("mamenchi lizard") of the Late Jurassic had the longest neck of any animal that has ever lived. The neck measured 36 feet—half the total length of the dinosaur.

Largest claws   The therizinosaurids of the Late Cretaceous had the largest claws. In the case of *Therizinosaurus cheloniformis*, they measured up to three feet along the outside curve (compared with eight inches for *Tyrannosaurus rex*). *T. cheloniformis* had a feeble skull, lacked teeth and probably lived on termites.

Largest dinosaur eggs   *Hypselosaurus priscus* ("high ridge lizard"), a 40-foot-long titanosaurid that lived about 80 million years ago, laid the largest eggs. Examples found in the Durance valley near Aix-en-Provence, France in October 1961 would have had, uncrushed, a length of 12 inches and a diameter of 10 inches (capacity 5.8 pints).

Largest flying creature   The largest flying creature was the pterosaur *Quetzalcoatlus northropi*, which lived 70 million years ago. Partial remains found in Big Bend National Park in Texas indicate that this reptile must have had a wing span of 36–39 feet and weighed 190–250 pounds.

A 65 million-year-old bone found in Jordan in 1943 is thought to be a neck vertebra from a pterosaur called *Arambourgiania philadelphiae*, estimated to have had a wingspan of over 39 feet.

Largest footprints   In 1932, the gigantic footprints of a large bipedal hadrosaurid measuring 53½ inches long and 32 inches wide were found in Salt Lake City, UT, and other reports from Colorado and Utah refer to footprints 37–40 inches wide. Footprints attributed to the largest brachiosaurids also range up to 40 inches wide for the hind feet.

MICROBES & FUNGI

MICROBES

Most dangerous animal   Malarial parasites of the genus *Plasmodium*, carried by mosquitoes of the genus *Anopheles*, have probably been responsible for half of all human deaths, excluding deaths caused by wars and accidents, since the Stone Age.

Smallest free-living entity   *Mycoplasma laidlawii* has a diameter during its early existence of only 0.0000001m. Examples of the strain known as H.39 have a diameter of 0.0000003m and weigh 0.0000000000000001g.

Largest modern protozoan   The largest existing protozoan, a species of *Stannophyllum* (Xenophyophorida), can reach 9¾ inches in length but does not exceed the volume of the extinct calcareous foraminifera of the genus *Nummulites* (*see* LARGEST PROTOZOAN, page 310).

Fastest protozoan *Monas stigmatica* has been found to move a distance equivalent to 40 times its length in a second. Humans cannot cover even seven times their own length in a second.

Largest bacterium *Epulopiscium fishelsoni* inhabits the intestinal tract of the brown surgeonfish (*Acanthurus nigrofuscus*) from the Red Sea and the Great Barrier Reef. Measuring 80 by 600mm or more and therefore visible to the naked eye, it is a million times larger than the human food poisoner *Escherichia coli*.

Fastest bacterium The rod-shaped bacillus *Bdellovibrio bacteriovorus*, which is two micrometers long, can move 50 times its own length in one second, using a polar flagellum rotating 100 times per second. This is equivalent to a human sprinter reaching 200 mph.

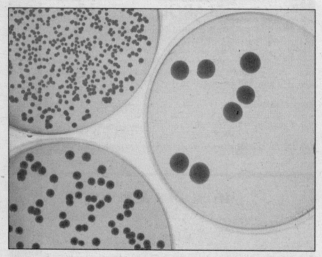

The bacterium *Deinococcus radiodurans* can survive 6,000 times the amount of atomic radiation that would kill a human.

Highest-living bacterium In April 1967, the National Aeronautics and Space Administration (NASA) reported that bacteria had been discovered at an altitude of 25½ miles.

Toughest bacterium The bacterium *Deinococcus radiodurans* (formerly *Micrococcus radiodurans*) is the most radiation-resistant organism ever discovered. It can withstand a dose of atomic radiation of 30,000 grays; by comparison, a dose of 5 grays is fatal to the average human.

In March 1983, John Barras (University of Oregon) reported bacteria from sulfurous seabed vents thriving at 583°F in the East Pacific Rise at Lat. 21° N.

Oldest bacterium Viable bacteria were reported in 1991 to have been recovered from sediments 3–4 million years old from the Sea of Japan.

Living In 1991, live bacteria were found in the flesh of a mastodon from Ohio that died 12,000 years earlier. The bacteria gave the flesh a bad smell even after such a long time.

FUNGI

Largest fungus A single living clonal growth of the underground fungus *Armillaria ostoyae* was reported in May 1992 to cover some 1,500 acres in the forests of Washington State. Estimates based on its size suggest that

LARGEST EDIBLE FUNGUS

The largest edible fungus was a giant puffball (*Calvatia gigantea*) 8 ft. 8 in. in circumference. The 48½ pound monster was found by Jean-Guy Richard of Montreal, Canada in 1987.

For rules, see page 707.

the fungus is 500–1,000 years old, but no attempts have been made to estimate its weight. Also known as the honey or shoestring fungus, it fruits above ground as edible gilled mushrooms.

Largest edible fungus A giant puffball (*Calvatia gigantea*) measuring 8 ft. 8 in. in circumference and weighing 48½ pounds was found by Jean-Guy Richard of Montreal, Canada in 1987.

Largest tree fungus In 1996, the bracket fungus (*Rigidoporus ulmarius*) growing on the grounds of the International Mycological Institute in Kew, England measured 67 by 58 inches, with a circumference of 194 inches.

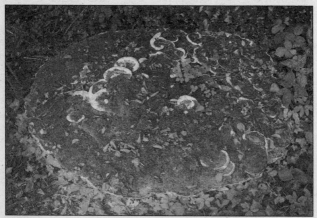

The world's largest tree fungus is growing on the grounds of the International Mycological Institute in Kew, England.

Heaviest fungus A clonal growth of *Armillaria bulbosa* was reported on April 2, 1992 to be covering about 37 acres of forest in Michigan. It was calculated to weigh over 110 tons, which is comparable with the weight of a blue whale. The organism is thought to have originated from a single fertilized spore at least 1,500 years ago.

Heaviest edible fungus A chicken-of-the-woods mushroom (*Laetiporus sulphureus*) weighing 100 pounds was found in the New Forest, England by Giovanni Paba of Broadstone, Dorset, England on October 15, 1990.

Most poisonous fungus The yellowish-olive death cap (*Amanita phalloides*) is responsible for 90 percent of fatal poisonings caused by fungi. The estimated lethal amount for humans, depending on body weight, is about 1¾ ounces of fresh fungus. Six to 15 hours after eating the fungus, the victim experiences vomiting and delirium, followed by collapse and death.

INVERTEBRATES

WORMS

Longest earthworm The species *Microhaetus rappi* (= *M. microhaetus*) is found in South Africa. Around 1937, a giant earthworm measuring 22 feet long when naturally extended and 0.8 inches in diameter was collected in the Transvaal.

Shortest earthworm *Chaetogaster annandalei* measures less than 0.02 inches long.

Worm-charming At the first World Worm Charming Championship held in Willaston, Cheshire, England on July 5, 1980, Tom Shufflebotham charmed a record 511 worms out of the ground (a 9.84-square-foot plot) in 30 minutes. In this contest, garden forks or other implements are vibrated in the soil by the competitors to coax up the worms, but water is banned.

SPONGES

Greatest powers of regeneration The sponges (Porifera) can regrow from tiny fragments of themselves. If a sponge is pushed through a fine-meshed silk gauze, each piece of separated tissue will live as an individual and grow into a full-sized sponge.

Largest sponge The barrel-shaped loggerhead sponge (*Spheciospongia vesparium*) of the West Indies and the waters off Florida can measure 3 ft. 6 in. high and three feet in diameter.

Heaviest sponge In 1909, a wool sponge (*Hippospongia canaliculatta*) measuring six feet in circumference was collected off the Bahamas. When taken from the water it weighed 80–90 pounds, but after it had been cleaned and dried it weighed 12 pounds. This sponge is now kept in the National Museum of Natural History, Washington, D.C.

Smallest sponge The widely distributed *Leucosolenia blanca* measures 0.11 inches in height when fully grown.

Deepest-living sponge Sponges have been recovered from depths of up to 18,500 feet.

MOLLUSKS

Largest animal eye The giant squid has the largest eye of any animal, living or extinct. The squid found in Thimble Tickle Bay (see *LARGEST MOLLUSK*, below) had eyes 15¾ inches wide—almost as wide as this open book.

Largest mollusk The giant squid, *Architeuthis dux*, is the largest invertebrate and the largest mollusk. The heaviest ever recorded was a 2.2-ton specimen that ran aground in Thimble Tickle Bay, Newfoundland, Canada on November 2, 1878. Its body was 20 feet long, and one tentacle measured 35 feet long.

Largest gastropod   The largest known gastropod is the trumpet or baler conch (*Syrinx aruanus*) of Australia. One specimen collected off Western Australia in 1979 and now owned by Don Pisor of San Diego, CA had a shell 30.4 inches long with a maximum girth of 39.75 inches. It weighed nearly 40 pounds when alive.

Largest clam   A marine giant clam (*Tridacna gigas*) found off Okinawa, Japan in 1956 weighed 734 pounds. Its shell was 3 ft. 9¼ in. long.

Longest mollusk   A 57-foot giant *Architeuthis longimanus* was washed up on Lyall Bay, Cook Strait, New Zealand in October 1887. Its two long, slender tentacles each measured 49 ft. 3 in.

Most venomous mollusk   The two closely related species of blue-ringed octopus, *Hapalochlaena masculosa* and *H. lunulata*, found around the coasts of Australia and parts of southeast Asia, carry a neurotoxic venom so potent that their bite can kill in a matter of minutes. It has been estimated that each individual carries sufficient venom to cause the paralysis (or even death) of 10 adult people. Fortunately, blue-ringed octopuses are not considered aggressive and normally bite only when taken out of the water and provoked. These mollusks have a radial spread of just 4–8 inches.

Most venomous gastropods   The most venomous gastropods are cone shells (genus *Conus*), all of which can deliver a fast-acting neurotoxic venom. Several species are capable of killing people, but the geographer cone (*Conus geographus*) of the Indo-Pacific is considered to be one of the most dangerous.

Oldest mollusk   The longest-living mollusk is the ocean quahog (*Arctica islandica*), a thick-shelled clam found in the Atlantic Ocean. A specimen with 220 annual growth rings was found in 1982, but not all biologists accept these growth rings as an accurate measure of age.

Longest suspended animation   In 1846, two specimens of the desert snail (*Eremina desertorum*) were presented to the British Museum (Natural History) in London as dead exhibits. They were placed on display, but four years later, in March 1850, it was found that one of the snails was still alive. This snail lived for another two years before it fell into a torpor and then died.

Slowest animal growth   The deep-sea clam (*Tindaria callistiformis*) of the North Atlantic takes roughly 100 years to reach a length of ⅓rd of an inch.

Snail racing   A garden snail named Archie, owned by Carl Bramham of Pott Row, England, covered a 13-inch course in 2 minutes at the 1995 World Snail Racing Championships, held in Congham, England.

JELLYFISH AND CORALS

Largest jellyfish An Arctic giant jellyfish (*Cyanea capillata arctica*) that washed up in Massachusetts Bay in 1870 had a bell diameter of 7 ft. 6 in. and tentacles stretching 120 feet.

Most venomous jellyfish The Australian sea wasp or box jellyfish (*Chironex fleckeri*) is the most venomous cnidarian in the world. Its cardiotoxic venom has caused the deaths of at least 70 people off the coast of Australia alone in the past century, with some victims dying within four minutes if medical aid is not available.

Largest animal-made structure The largest structure ever built by living creatures is the 1,260-mile-long Great Barrier Reef, off Queensland, Australia, covering 80,000 square miles. It consists of millions of dead and living stony corals (order Madreporaria or Scleractinia). Over 350 species of coral are currently found on this reef, and its accretion is estimated to have taken some 600 million years.

STARFISH

Largest starfish The largest of the 1,600 known species of starfish is the very fragile brisingid *Midgardia xandaras.* One specimen, collected by the Texas A & M University research vessel *Alaminos* in the southern part of the Gulf of Mexico in 1968, measured 4½ feet tip to tip, but the diameter of its disc was only 1.02 inches.

...........sterinid sea star ....

.......ts tracked a swarm of krill (*Euphasia* ...on tons off Antarctica in Ma⎯rch 1981.

.....ed Sea has 12–19 arms and can measure up to 24 inches in diameter. It feeds on coral polyps and can destroy 46–62 square inches of coral in one day. It has been responsible for the destruction of large parts of the Great Barrier Reef off Australia.

CRUSTACEANS

Largest crustacean The takashigani or giant spider crab (*Macrocheira kaempferi*) is the largest, although not the heaviest, of all Crustacea (a category that includes crabs, lobsters, shrimp, crawfish, etc.). It is found in deep waters off the southeastern coast of Japan. One specimen had a claw-span of 12 ft. 1½ in. and weighed 41 pounds.

Freshwater A species of crayfish or crawfish (*Astacopis gouldi*) found in the streams of Tasmania, Australia has been measured up to two feet long and weighing as much as nine pounds. In 1934, an unconfirmed weight of 14 pounds (total length 29 inches) was reported for one specimen caught at Bridport, Tasmania.

Heaviest crustacean The heaviest crustacean, and the largest species of lobster, is the American or North Atlantic lobster (*Homarus americanus*). In 1977, a specimen weighing 44 lb. 6 oz. and measuring 3 ft. 6 in. from the end of the tail fan to the tip of the largest claw was caught off Nova Scotia, Canada. This lobster was later sold to a New York restaurant owner.

The North Atlantic lobster is the world's heaviest crustacean.

Greatest concentration U.S. scientis
superba) estimated to weigh 11 milli

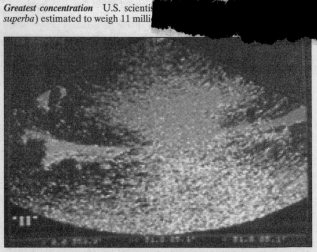

In 1981, U.S. scientists found a swarm of krill estimated to weigh 11 million tons.

INSECTS

Greatest concentration of animals A swarm of Rocky Mountain locusts (*Melanoplus spretus*) that flew over Nebraska on July 20–30, 1874 covered an area estimated at 198,600 square miles. The swarm must have contained at least 12.5 trillion insects with a total weight of about 27.5 million tons.

Fastest animal reproduction One cabbage aphid (*Brevicoryne brassicae*) could theoretically (with unlimited food and no predators) give rise in a year to a mass of descendants weighing 906 million tons.

Most acute sense of smell The male emperor moth (*Eudia pavonia*) has the most acute sense of smell in the animal kingdom. It can detect the sex attractant of the female at a range of 6.8 miles upwind. The chemoreceptors on the male moth's antennae are so sensitive that they can detect a single molecule of scent.

Strongest animal In proportion to their size, the strongest animals are beetles of the family Scarabaeidae. In one test, a rhinoceros beetle (Dynastinae) supported 850 times its own weight on its back (compared with 25 percent of its body weight for an adult elephant). Humans can support 17 times their own body weight in a trestle lift.

The heaviest insect is the goliath beetle.

Most prodigious eater The larva of the Polyphemus moth (*Antheraea polyphemus*) of North America consumes an amount equal to 86,000 times its own birth weight in the first 56 days of its life. In human terms, this would be equivalent to a 7-pound baby taking in 300 tons of nourishment.

Oldest insect The longest-lived insects are the splendor beetles (Buprestidae). On May 27, 1983, a specimen of *Buprestis aurulenta* appeared from the staircase timber in the home of Mr. W. Euston of Prittlewell, England, after 47 years as a larva.

Heaviest insect The heaviest insects are the goliath beetles (family Scarabaeidae) of Equatorial Africa. The largest are *Goliathus regius*, *G. meleagris*, *G. goliathus* (= *G. giganteus*) and *G. druryi*, and in one series of fully grown males (females are smaller) the lengths from the tips of the small frontal horns to the end of the abdomen measured up to 4.33 inches and the weights ranged from 2½ to 3½ ounces.

Longest insect *Pharnacia kirbyi* is a stick insect from the rain forests of Borneo. A specimen in the Natural History Museum, London, England has a body length of 12.9 inches and a total length, including legs, of 20 inches.

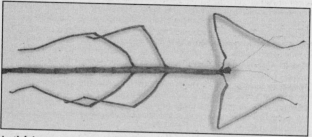

A stick insect specimen in the Natural History Museum in London, England is 20 inches long.

Smallest insect The feather-winged beetles of the family Ptiliidae (= Trichopterygidae) and the battledore-wing fairy flies of the family Mymaridae are smaller than some species of protozoa (single-celled animals).

A colored scanning electron micrograph of the male bloodsucking banded louse, the lightest insect.

Lightest insect   The male bloodsucking banded louse (*Enderleinellus zonatus*) and the parasitic wasp (*Caraphractus cinctus*) may each weigh as little as 5,670,000 to an ounce. Eggs of the latter each weigh 141,750,000 to an ounce.

Loudest insect   At 7,400 pulses per minute, the tymbal organs of the male cicada (family Cicadidae) produce a noise (described by the U.S. Department of Agriculture as "tsh-ee-EEEE-e-ou") detectable more than a quarter of a mile distant.

Fastest-flying insect   A maximum speed of 36 mph has been recorded for the Australian dragonfly *Austrophlebia costalis*.

Fastest wing-beat   The fastest wing-beat of any insect is 62,760 beats per minute by a midge of the genus *Forcipomyia*. The contraction–expansion cycle of 0.00045 seconds is the fastest muscle movement ever measured.

Slowest wing-beat   The slowest wing-beat of any insect is 300 beats per minute by the swallowtail butterfly (*Papilio machaon*).

Fastest-moving insect   The fastest-moving insects are large tropical cockroaches of the family Dictyoptera; the record is 3.36 mph, or 50 body lengths per second, registered by *Periplaneta americana* at the University of California at Berkeley in 1991.

Most legs   The millipede *Illacme plenipes*, which is found in California, has 375 pairs of legs. *(By definition, all insects have six legs; millipedes are officially classed as myriapodous arthropods.)*

Largest egg   The 6-inch-long Malaysian stick insect *Heteropteryx dilitata* lays ½-inch-long eggs. Mantids and cockroaches lay larger egg cases, but these contain up to 200 individual eggs.

Highest g force   The click beetle (*Athous haemorrhoidalis*) endures 400 *g* when "jack-knifing" into the air to escape predators. One specimen measuring half an inch long and weighing 0.00014 ounces that jumped to a height of 11¾ inches was calculated to have endured a peak brain deceleration of 2,300 *g*.

Largest cockroach   A preserved female cockroach (*Megaloblatta longipennis*) in the collection of Akira Yokokura of Yamagata, Japan is 3.81 inches long and 1.77 inches across.

Largest termite mound   A termite mound found in Zaire was 42 feet high, equivalent to the length of 2,000 termite workers laid end to end. In comparison, the 1,454-foot Sears Tower in Chicago is equivalent to 250 people.

Largest grasshopper   An unidentified species of grasshopper from the Malaysia–Thailand border measures 10 inches long and can leap 15 feet.

Largest flea   The largest of the 1,830 recognized flea varieties is *Hystrichopsylla schefferi*, which was described from a specimen taken from the nest of a mountain beaver (*Aplodontia rufa*) in 1913. Females are up to 0.3 inches long.

Longest flea jump The cat flea (*Ctenocephalides felis*) has been known to reach a height of 34 inches in a single jump. The common flea (*Pulex irritans*) is capable of similar feats. In one American experiment carried out in 1910, a specimen performed a long jump of 13 inches and a high jump of 7¾ inches. In jumping 130 times its own height, a flea subjects itself to a force of 200 *g*.

Largest dragonfly *Megaloprepus caruleata* of Central and South America has been measured at 4.72 inches long with a wingspan of 7.52 inches.

Smallest dragonfly The smallest dragonfly is *Agriocnemis naia* of Myanmar. One specimen had a wing spread of 0.69 inches and a body length of 0.71 inches.

Largest butterfly Females of the Queen Alexandra's birdwing butterfly (*Ornithoptera alexandrae*) of Papua New Guinea may have a wingspan of 11 inches and weigh 0.9 ounces.

Smallest moth The micro-moth *Stigmella ridiculosa*, found in the Canary Islands, has a wingspan of 0.079 inches.

Longest butterfly migration A tagged monarch butterfly (*Danaus plexippus*) released by Donald Davis near Brighton, Ontario, Canada in September 1986 was recaptured 2,133 miles away near Angangueo, Mexico in January 1987. This distance was obtained by measuring a line from the release site to the recapture site, but the actual distance traveled could be double this figure.

SPIDERS & SCORPIONS

SPIDERS

Most venomous spider (photo below at left) The most venomous spiders are the Brazilian wandering spiders of the genus *Phoneutria*, and particularly the Brazilian huntsman *P. fera*, which has the most active neurotoxic venom of any living spider. These large and highly aggressive creatures frequently enter human dwellings and hide in clothing or shoes. Hundreds of accidents involving these species are reported annually. When deaths do occur, they are usually in children under the age of seven. Fortunately, an effective antivenin is available.

Largest spider The largest spider is the goliath bird-eating spider (*Theraphosa leblondi*) of the coastal rain forests of Surinam, Guyana, and French Guiana, but specimens have also been reported from Venezuela and Brazil. A male specimen collected by members of the Pablo San Martin Expedition at Rio Cavro, Venezuela in April 1965 had a leg span of 11 inches.

Heaviest spider In February 1985, Charles J. Seiderman of New York City captured a female bird-eating spider near Paramaribo, Surinam that weighed a record peak 4.3 ounces before its death from molting problems in January 1986. Other measurements included a maximum leg span of $10^{1}/_2$ inches, a total body length of four inches, and 1-inch-long fangs.

Strongest spider The Californian trap-door spider (*Bothriocyrtum californicum*), so named because it weaves a silk "door" covering the entrance to its underground burrow, is able to resist a force 38 times its weight attempting to open the trap door.

Fastest spider The long-legged sun spiders of the order Solifugae live in the arid semidesert regions of Africa and the Middle East. They feed on geckos and other lizards and can reach speeds of over 10 mph.

Smallest spider *Patu marplesi* (of the family Symphytognathidae) of Western Samoa in the Pacific is the smallest spider. The type specimen (male), found in moss at *c.* 2,000 feet in Madolelei, Western Samoa in January 1965, measured 0.017 inches overall, which means that it was about the size of a period on this page.

Greatest size difference In some species of the golden orb-web spider (genus *Nephila*), females weigh almost 1,000 times as much as their mates.

Oldest spider Female tarantulas (*Aphonopelma*) can live for up to 30 years.

Noisiest spider The male European buzzing spider (*Anyphaena accentuata*) vibrates its abdomen rapidly against the surface of a leaf, producing a buzzing sound audible to the human ear, as part of courtship behavior. The male of the American species *Lycosa gulosa*, or purring spider, also produces an audible noise by tapping its palps and abdomen on dry leaves.

Most sociable spider Several thousand members of both sexes of the South African species *Anelosimus eximus* live together on light webs that stretch three feet across bushes and small trees.

Most eggs Spiders of the genus *Mygalomorphus* may lay up to 3,000 eggs in a single batch.

Largest eggs The eggs of spiders of the genus *Mygalomorphus* are the size of a small pea.

Strongest web The web made by the American spider *Achaearenea tepidariorum* has been known to trap a small mouse.

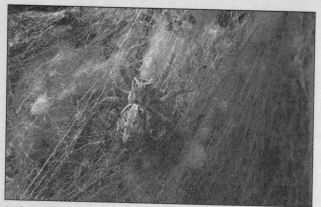

Spiders of the genus *Stegodyphus* can build continuous webs that cover miles of vegetation.

Largest web   The yellow silk constructions of tropical orb-web spiders of the genus *Nephila* can be almost 10 feet long.

Members of the Indian genus *Stegodyphus* build 3-dimensional webs that can cover vegetation in a continuous silken mass stretching out for several miles.

SCORPIONS

Largest scorpion   The largest of the 800 or so species of scorpion is a species called *Heterometrus swannerderdami* from southern India. Males frequently attain a length of more than seven inches from the tips of the pincers to the end of the sting. One specimen found during World War II measured 11½ inches in overall length. The tropical emperor or imperial scorpion (*Pandinus imperator*) of West Africa also grows to seven inches; the largest on record is a male from Sierra Leone that measured nine inches.

Heaviest scorpion   *Pandinus imperator* can weigh up to two ounces.

Smallest scorpion   *Microbothus pusillus*, found on the Red Sea coast, measures about half an inch long.

Most venomous scorpion   The Palestine yellow scorpion (*Leiurus quinquestriatus*) ranges from the eastern part of North Africa through the Middle East to the shores of the Red Sea. Fortunately, the amount of venom it delivers is very small (0.000009 ounces) and adult lives are seldom endangered; however, it has been responsible for a number of fatalities among children under the age of five.

Deepest-living scorpion   *Alacran tartarus* has been found in caves more than 2,625 feet underground.

FISH

Strongest animal bite Experiments carried out with a Snodgrass gnathody-namometer (shark-bite meter) at the Lerner Marine Laboratory, Bimini, Bahamas showed that a 6-ft.-6³⁄₄-in.-long dusky shark (*Carcharhinus obscurus*) could exert a force of 132 pounds between its jaws. This is equivalent to a pressure of 22 tons per square inch at the tips of the teeth. The bites of larger sharks, such as the great white (*Carcharodon carcharias*), must be considerably stronger but have never been measured.

Largest fish The rare plankton-feeding whale shark (*Rhincodon typus*) is found in the warmer areas of the Atlantic, Pacific, and Indian Oceans. The longest specimen to have been scientifically measured was captured off Baba Island near Karachi, Pakistan on November 11, 1949. It measured 41¹⁄₂ feet long, 23 feet around the thickest part of the body and weighed an estimated 16¹⁄₂–23 tons.

Largest predatory fish The largest predatory fish is the great white shark (*Carcharodon carcharias*). Adult specimens average 14–15 feet long and weigh 1,150–1,700 pounds. There are many claims of huge specimens up to 33 feet long and, although few have been properly authenticated, there is plenty of circumstantial evidence to suggest that some great whites grow to more than 20 feet long.

Largest fresh water fish The largest fish that spends its whole life in fresh or brackish water is the rare pla buk or pa beuk (*Pangasianodon gigas*) found only in the Mekong River and its major tributaries in China, Laos, Cambodia and Thailand. The largest specimen, captured in the River Ban Mee Noi, Thailand, was reportedly 9 ft. 10¹⁄₄ in. long and weighed 533¹⁄₂ pounds.

Arapaima gigas of South America is reported to grow to 14 ft. 9 in. in length but weighs only about 440 pounds.

Smallest fish The shortest marine fish—and the shortest vertebrate—is the dwarf goby (*Trimmatom nanus*) of the Chagos Archipelago, central Indian Ocean. In one series of 92 specimens collected by the 1978–79 Joint Services Chagos Research Expedition of the British Armed Forces, the adult males averaged 0.34 inches long and the adult females 0.35 inches.

Lightest fish The lightest of all vertebrates and the smallest possible catch is the dwarf goby of Samoa (*Schindleria praematurus*), which weighs ¹⁄₂₈₀th of an ounce and is ¹⁄₂–³⁄₄ inches long.

Smallest freshwater fish The shortest and lightest freshwater fish is the dwarf pygmy goby (*Pandaka pygmaea*), a colorless and nearly transparent species found in the streams and lakes of Luzon in the Philippines. Adult males measure only 0.28–0.38 inches long and weigh 0.00014–0.00018 ounces.

Fastest fish The cosmopolitan sailfish (*Istiophorus platypterus*) is the fastest species of fish over short distances, although the practical difficulties of measuring make data extremely difficult to secure. In a series of speed trials carried out at the Long Key Fishing Camp, FL, one sailfish took out 300 feet of line in three seconds, which is equivalent to a velocity of 68 mph (compare with 60 mph for the cheetah).

Longest journey by a fish The European eel (*Anguilla anguilla*) spends 7–15 years in fresh water, then begins a marathon journey into the Atlantic Ocean, taking about six months to travel 3,000–4,000 miles.

Piranhas are the world's most ferocious predatory fish.

Contact with the spines of the stonefish can be fatal.

Deepest-living fish Ophidiids of the genus *Bassogigas* are generally regarded as the deepest-living vertebrates. The greatest depth from which a fish has been recovered is 27,230 feet in the Puerto Rico Trench in the Atlantic by Dr. Gilbert L. Voss of the U.S. research vessel *John Elliott*, who caught a 6½-inch-long *Bassogigas profundissimus* in April 1970. It was only the fifth such brotulid ever caught.

Oldest fish In 1948, the death of an 88-year-old female European eel (*Anguilla anguilla*) named Putte was reported by the aquarium at Hälsingborg Museum, Sweden. She was allegedly born in 1860 in the Sargasso Sea, in the North Atlantic, and was caught in a river as a 3-year-old elver.

Oldest goldfish Goldfish (*Carassius auratus*) have been reported to live for over 50 years in China, although there are few authenticated records. A goldfish named Fred, owned by A. R. Wilson of Worthing, England, died on August 1, 1980 at 41 years of age.

Shortest-lived fish Certain species of the family Cyprinodontidae (killifish), found in Africa, the Americas, Asia and the warmer parts of Europe, normally live for about eight months.

Most eggs The ocean sunfish (*Mola mola*) produces up to 30 million eggs at a single spawning, each of them measuring about 0.05 inches in diameter.

Fewest eggs The mouth-brooding cichlid *Tropheus moorii* of Lake Tanganyika, East Africa produces seven eggs or fewer during normal reproduction.

Most valuable fish The Russian sturgeon (*Huso huso*) is the most valuable fish. In 1924, a 2,706-pound female was caught in the Tikhaya Sosna River; it yielded 541 pounds of best-quality caviar, which would be worth $300,000 on today's market.

The 30-inch-long Ginrin Showa koi, which won the supreme championship in nationwide Japanese koi shows in 1976, 1977, 1979 and 1980, was sold two years later for 17 million yen (about $165,000). In March 1986, this 15-year-old ornamental carp was acquired by Derry Evans, owner of the Kent Koi Centre near Sevenoaks, England, for an undisclosed sum, but the fish died five months later.

Most ferocious fish The razor-toothed piranhas of the genera *Serrasalmus* and *Pygocentrus* are generally considered to be the most ferocious freshwater fish in the world. They live in large rivers in South America, and will attack any creature, regardless of size, if it is injured or making a commotion in the water. On September 19, 1981, more than 300 people were reportedly killed and eaten when an overloaded passenger-cargo boat capsized and sank as it was docking at the Brazilian port of Obidos.

Most venomous fish The most venomous fish are the stonefish (Synanceiidae) that live in the tropical waters of the Indo-Pacific, and in particular *Synanceia horrida*, which also has the largest venom glands. Direct contact with the spines of its fins, which contain a strong neurotoxic poison, can prove fatal.

Most electric fish   The electric eel (*Electrophorus electricus*) is found in the rivers of Brazil, Colombia, Venezuela and Peru. An average-sized specimen can discharge one amp at 400 volts, but measurements up to 650 volts have been recorded.

REPTILES & AMPHIBIANS

CROCODILIANS

Largest crocodile   There are four protected estuarine crocodiles at the Bhitarkanika Wildlife Sanctuary, Orissa State, India that measure more than 19 ft. 8 in. long. The largest individual is over 23 feet long.

Smallest crocodilian   The dwarf caiman (*Paleosuchus palpebrosus*) of northern South America is the smallest living crocodilian. Females rarely exceed a length of four feet, and males rarely grow to more than 4 ft. 11 in.

Oldest crocodilian   The greatest age authenticated for a crocodilian is 66 years for a female American alligator (*Alligator mississippiensis*) that arrived at Adelaide Zoo, South Australia on June 5, 1914 as a 2-year-old, and died there on September 26, 1978.

LIZARDS

Largest lizard   Adult male komodo dragons or oras (*Varanus komodoensis*), found on the Indonesian islands of Komodo, Rintja, Padar and Flores, average 7 ft. 5 in. long and weigh about 130 pounds. The largest specimen to be accurately measured was a male presented to an American zoologist in 1928 by the Sultan of Bima. In 1937, this animal was

The spiny-tailed iguana has been clocked at 21.7 mph.

put on display at St. Louis Zoological Gardens, St. Louis, MO for a short period. It then measured 10 ft. 2 in. long and weighed 365 pounds.

Longest lizard The Salvadori or Papuan monitor (*Varanus salvadori*) of Papua New Guinea has been measured at up to 15 ft. 7 in. long, but nearly 70 percent of the total length is taken up by the tail.

Smallest lizard *Sphaerodactylus parthenopion*, a tiny gecko indigenous to the island of Virgin Gorda, British Virgin Islands, is the smallest lizard. It is known from only 15 specimens, including some pregnant females found in August 1964. The three largest females measured 0.70 inches from snout to vent, with a tail of approximately the same length.

Oldest lizard The greatest age recorded for a lizard is over 54 years for a male slow worm (*Anguis fragilis*) kept in the Zoological Museum in Copenhagen, Denmark from 1892 until 1946.

Fastest lizard The highest speed measured for any reptile on land is 21.7 mph for a spiny-tailed iguana (*Ctenosaura*) from Costa Rica, in a series of experiments by Professor Raymond Huey from the University of Washington, Seattle, WA, and colleagues at the University of California, Berkeley, CA.

TURTLES

Largest turtle A male leatherback found dead on the beach at Harlech, Wales on September 23, 1988 measured 9 ft. 5½ in. long from nose to tail, and nine feet across the front flippers. The turtle weighed an astonishing 2,120 pounds.

Smallest turtle The speckled Cape tortoise or speckled padloper (*Homopus signatus*) has a shell length of 2.3–3.7 inches.

The smallest marine turtle is the Atlantic ridley (*Lepidochelys kempii*), which has a shell length of 19.7–27.6 inches and a maximum weight of 175 pounds.

Fastest turtle The fastest speed claimed for any reptile in water is 22 mph by a Pacific leatherback turtle.

Deepest dive In May 1987, it was reported by Dr. Scott Eckert that a leatherback turtle (*Dermochelys coriacea*) fitted with a pressure-sensitive recording device had dived to a depth of 3,973 feet off the Virgin Islands in the West Indies.

Largest tortoise A Galápagos tortoise (*Chelonoidis nigra*) named Goliath, who has lived at the Life Fellowship Bird Sanctuary in Seffner, FL since 1960, measures 54 inches long, 40½ inches wide, and 27½ inches high, and weighs 911 pounds.

Oldest tortoise The greatest age recorded for a tortoise is at least 188 years for a Madagascar radiated tortoise (*Astrochelys radiata*) that was presented to the Tonga royal family by Captain Cook in either 1773 or 1777.

The animal was named Tui Malila and remained in the family's care until its death in 1965.

SNAKES

Longest snake   A reticulated python (*Python reticulatus*) measuring 32 ft. 9½ in. was shot in Celebes, Indonesia in 1912. This species is also found in southeast Asia and the Philippines.

Longest venomous snake   The king cobra (*Ophiophagus hannah*), also called the hamadryad, averages 12–15 feet long and is found in southeast Asia and India. An 18-ft.-2-in. specimen, captured alive near Fort Dickson in the state of Negri Sembilan, Malaysia in April 1937, later grew to 18 ft. 9 in. in London Zoo, England.

Shortest snake   The very rare thread snake (*Leptotyphlops bilineata*) is known only from Martinique, Barbados and St. Lucia. The longest known specimen measured 4¼ inches, and had such a thin body that it could have entered the hole left in a standard pencil after the lead has been removed.

Shortest venomous snake   The namaqua dwarf adder (*Bitis schneider*) of Namibia has an average length of eight inches.

Heaviest snake   The anaconda (*Eunectes murinus*) of tropical South America and Trinidad is nearly twice as heavy as a reticulated python (*Python reticulatus*) of the same length. A female shot in Brazil *c.* 1960 was not weighed, but as it measured 27 ft. 9 in. long with a girth of 44 inches, it must have weighed about 500 pounds. The average adult length is 18–20 feet.

Heaviest venomous snake   The eastern diamondback rattlesnake (*Crotalus adamanteus*) of the southeastern United States is the heaviest venomous snake. One specimen, measuring 7 ft. 9 in. long, weighed 34 pounds.

Oldest snake   The greatest reliable age recorded for a snake is 40 yr. 3 mo. 14 days for a male common boa (*Boa constrictor constrictor*) named Popeye that died at the Philadelphia Zoo, Phildelphia, PA on April 15, 1977.

Most venomous snake   All sea snakes are venomous. *Hydrophis belcheri*, which lives around the Ashmore Reef in the Timor Sea, has a myotoxic venom 100 times as toxic as that of any land snake.

Most venomous land snake   The 5-ft.-7-in. small-scaled or fierce snake (*Oxyuranus microlepidotus*) is found mainly in the Diamantina River and Cooper's Creek drainage basins in Channel County, Queensland, and western New South Wales, Australia. Its venom is several times more toxic than that of the tiger snake (*Notechis scutatus*) of South Australia and Tasmania. One tiger snake yielded 0.00385 ounces of venom after milking, enough to kill 250,000 mice.

Most snakebites   More people die of snakebites in Sri Lanka than in any comparable area in the world. An average of 800 people are killed annually on the island by snakes, and more than 95 percent of the fatalities are caused by the common krait (*Bungarus caeruleus*), the Sri Lankan cobra (*Naja n. naja*), and Russell's viper (*Vipera russelli pulchella*).

The saw-scaled or carpet viper (*Echis carinatus*) bites and kills more than any other species in the world. Its geographical range extends from West Africa to India.

Longest fangs   The highly venomous gaboon viper (*Bitis gabonica*) of tropical Africa has the longest fangs of any snake. In one 6-foot-long specimen, they measured almost two inches long.

Fastest snake   The fastest-moving land snake is probably the aggressive black mamba (*Dendroaspis polylepis*) of the eastern part of tropical Africa. This snake can achieve speeds of 10–12 mph in short bursts over level ground.

Most snakes milked   Over a 10-year period ending in December 1970, Bernard Keyter, a supervisor at the South African Institute for Medical Research in Johannesburg, South Africa, milked 780,000 venomous snakes, obtaining 1,046 gallons of venom. He was never bitten.

FROGS

Largest frog   The rare African giant frog or goliath frog (*Conraua goliath*) is found in Cameroon and Equatorial Guinea. A specimen captured in April 1989 on the Sanaga River, Cameroon by Andy Koffman of Seattle, WA had a snout-to-vent length of 14½ inches (34½ inches overall with legs extended) and weighed 8 lb. 1 oz. on October 30, 1989.

Smallest frog   *Eleutherodactylus iberia* of Cuba measures 0.38–0.41 inches long (snout-to-vent) when fully grown. It is the smallest frog and the smallest amphibian.

Longest jump by a frog   Distances in frog-jumping competitions represent the aggregate of three consecutive leaps. The greatest distance covered by a frog in a triple jump is 33 ft. 5½ in. by a South African sharp-nosed frog (*Ptychadena oxyrhynchus*) named Santjie at a frog derby held in Paulpietersburg, Natal, South Africa on May 21, 1977.

Most poisonous animal   The brightly colored poison-arrow frogs (*Dendrobates* and *Phyllobates*) of South and Central America secrete some of the most deadly biological toxins ever discovered. The skin secretion of the golden poison-arrow frog (*Phyllobates terribilis*) of western Colombia is the most poisonous; this frog is so dangerous that scientists have to wear thick gloves to pick it up in case they have cuts or scratches on their hands.

BIRDS

Largest bird   Male North African ostriches (*Struthio c. camelus*) can reach nine feet in height.

Heaviest flying bird The heaviest flying birds are the Kori bustard (*Ardeotis kori*) of northeast and southern Africa and the great bustard (*Otis tarda*) of Europe and Asia. Weights of 42 pounds have been reported for the Kori bustard, and the heaviest recorded great bustard weighed 39 lb. 11 oz.

Tallest flying bird The tallest flying birds are cranes (members of the family Gruidae), some of which can stand almost 6 ft. 6 in. high.

Heaviest bird of prey An adult male Andean condor (*Vultur gryphus*) has an average weight of 20–27 pounds. An oversized male California condor (*Gymnogyps californianus*) now preserved in the California Academy of

A record-holder both in the air and on the ground, the wandering albatross has the longest wingspan and the longest incubation period.

Sciences in San Francisco weighed 31 pounds. This species rarely exceeds 23 pounds.

Largest wingspan The wandering albatross (*Diomedea exulans*) has the largest wingspan of any living bird. A male with a wingspan of 11 ft. 11 in. was caught in the Tasman Sea in September 1965.

Smallest bird Adult male bee hummingbirds (*Mellisuga helenae*) of Cuba and the Isle of Pines are 2¼ inches long and weigh ¹⁄₁₈th of an ounce (females are slightly larger).

Smallest bird of prey The black-legged falconet (*Microhierax fringillarius*) and the white-fronted or Bornean falconet (*Microhierax latifrons*) each have an average length of 5½–6 inches (excluding a 2-inch tail) and weigh about 1¼ ounces.

Most talkative bird A female gray parrot (*Psittacus erythacus*) named Prudle, cared for by Iris Frost of Seaford, England, won the "Best Talking Parrot-like Bird" title at the National Cage and Aviary Bird Show in London for 12 consecutive years (1965–76). Prudle, who had a vocabulary of nearly 800 words, was taken from a nest in Jinja, Uganda in 1958. She retired undefeated.

Largest vocabulary Puck, a budgerigar owned by Camille Jordan of Petaluma, CA, had a vocabulary estimated at 1,728 words.

The North African ostrich has been known to live for up to 68 years.

Fastest-flying bird Experiments indicate that the peregrine falcon (*Falco peregrinus*) is able to reach a maximum speed of at least 124 mph when swooping during territorial displays or catching prey in midair.

Fastest wing-beat The wingbeat of the horned sungem (*Heliactin cornuta*), a hummingbird found in tropical South America, is 90 beats per second.

Fastest bird on land The ostrich can run at a speed of up to 37 mph.

Fastest swimmer The gentoo penguin (*Pygoscelis papua*) has a maximum burst of speed of about 17 mph.

Slowest-flying bird American woodcocks (*Scolopax minor*) and Eurasian woodcocks (*S.*

The gentoo penguin can swim as fast as 17 mph.

Slowest-flying bird American woodcocks (*Scolopax minor*) and Eurasian woodcocks (*S. rusticola*) can fly at 5 mph.

Oldest bird An 80-year-old male sulfur-crested cockatoo (*Cacatua galerita*) named Cocky died at London Zoo, London, England in 1982.

Domestic Excluding the ostrich, which has been known to live for up to 68 years, the longest-lived domesticated bird is the domestic goose (*Anser a. domesticus*), which can live for 25 years. In December 1976, a gander named George, owned by Florence Hull of Thornton, England, died at the age of 49 yr. 8 mo.

Oldest wild bird The oldest confirmed age for a bird in the wild is 45 years. A fulmar was ringed on Eynhallow Island, Orkney Islands, Great Britain in 1951 and has been seen every year since.

Longest flight A common tern (*Sterna hirundo*) left its nest in Finland in August 1996 and was caught in January 1997 in Victoria, Australia, having covered 16,000 miles.

Highest-flying bird The highest irrefutable altitude recorded for a bird is 37,000 feet for a Ruppell's vulture (*Gyps rueppellii*) that collided with a commercial aircraft over Abidjan, Ivory Coast on November 29, 1973. The impact damaged one of the aircraft's engines, but the plane landed safely. Feather remains allowed the National Museum of Natural History in Washington, D.C. to identify the bird.

Most airborne bird The common swift (*Apus apus*) remains airborne for two to four years, during which time it eats, drinks, sleeps and mates on the wing. A young swift probably completes a non-stop flight of about 310,000 miles between fledging and its first landing.

Longest feathers The longest feathers are those of the Phoenix fowl or Yokohama chicken (a strain of red junglefowl, *Gallus gallus*), which has been bred in southwestern Japan since the mid-17th century. In 1972, a tail covert 34 ft. 9½ in. long was reported for a rooster owned by Masasha Kubota of Kochi, Shikoku, Japan.

Deepest dive In 1990, a depth of 1,584 feet was recorded for an emperor penguin (*Aptenodytes forsteri*) in the Ross Sea, Antarctica.

Sharpest vision It has been calculated that a large bird of prey can detect a target object at a distance three or more times greater than that achieved by humans; thus a peregrine falcon (*Falco peregrinus*) can spot a pigeon at a range of over five miles under ideal conditions.

Greatest field of vision The woodcock (*Scolopax rusticola*) has eyes set so far back on its head that it has a 360-degree field of vision, enabling it to see all around and over the top of its head.

Highest g force The beak of the red-headed woodpecker (*Melanerpes erythrocephalus*) hits the bark of a tree with an impact velocity of 13 mph. When the head snaps back the brain is subject to a deceleration of about 10 *g*.

Longest bill The bill of the Australian pelican (*Pelicanus conspicillatus*) is 13–18½ inches long. The longest bill in relation to overall body length belongs to the sword-billed hummingbird (*Ensifera ensifera*) of the Andes from Venezuela to Bolivia. The bill measures four inches long and is longer than the bird's body.

Largest egg Ostrich eggs are normally six to eight inches long, four to six inches in diameter, and up to 3 lb. 14 oz. in weight, with a volume equivalent to two dozen hen's eggs.

On June 28, 1988, a 2-year-old cross between a northern and a southern ostrich (*Struthio c. camelus* and *Struthio c. australis*) laid an egg weighing a record 5 lb. 2 oz. at the Kibbutz Ha'on collective farm, Israel.

The extinct elephant bird (*Aepyornis maximus*) laid eggs that measured a foot in length and had a liquid capacity of 2¼ gallons, equivalent to seven ostrich eggs.

Smallest egg The vervain hummingbird (*Mellisuga minima*), of Jamaica and nearby islets, lays the smallest eggs. The tiniest specimens are less than ⅖ths of an inch long.

Longest incubation The longest incubation period is that of the wandering albatross (*Diomedea exulans*), with a range of 75–82 days.

Shortest incubation The shortest incubation period is 10 days for the shore lark (*Eremophila alpestris*), lesser whitethroat (*Sylvia curraca*) and a number of other small passerine species.

Largest nest The incubation mounds built by the mallee fowl (*Leipoa ocellata*) of Australia measure up to 15 feet high and 35 feet across, and it has been calculated that their construction may involve the mounding of 8,830 cubic feet of material weighing 330 tons.

Smallest nest The nest of *Mellisuga minima*, the vervain hummingbird, is about half the size of a walnut shell, while the deeper one of the bee hummingbird (*M. helenea*) is thimble-sized.

Most birds ringed The Icelandic Institute of Natural History has been operating the Icelandic Bird Ringing Scheme since its establishment in 1932. Oskar Sigurosson, a lighthouse keeper on Heimaey, Westmann Islands had ringed 65,243 birds as of February 1997.

Bird-watching Since 1965, Phoebe Snetsinger of Webster Groves, MO has seen 8,040 of the 9,700 known bird species, all of the families on the official list and over 90 percent of the genera.

24 hours The greatest number of species spotted in a 24-hour period is 342, by Kenyans Terry Stevenson, John Fanshawe and Andy Roberts on day two of the Birdwatch Kenya '86 event, held November 29–30, 1986.

MAMMALS

Tallest mammal The tallest mammal ever recorded was a male Masai giraffe (*Giraffa camelopardalis tippelskirchi*) named George, received at Chester Zoo, Chester, England on January 8, 1959 from Kenya. His horns almost grazed the roof of the 20-foot-high Giraffe House when he was nine years old. George died in 1969.

Smallest mammal The bumblebee bat or Kitti's hognosed bat (*Craseonycteris thonglongyai*), found in southwest Thailand, is no bigger than a bumblebee. Its head–body length is 1½–1³/₁₀ inches.

The smallest non-flying mammal is Savi's white-toothed pygmy shrew (*Suncus etruscus*), with a head and body length of 1.32–2 inches, a tail length of 0.94–1.14 inches, and a weight 0.05–0.09 ounces. It is found along the Mediterranean coast and southwards to Cape Province, South Africa.

Fastest land mammals Over a short distance (i.e., up to 600 yards) the cheetah (*Acinonyx jubatus*) of the open plains of East Africa, Iran, Turkmenistan and Afghanistan has a probable maximum speed of about 60 mph on level ground.

The pronghorn antelope (*Antilocapra americana*) of the western United States, southwestern Canada, and northern Mexico has been observed to travel at 35 mph for four miles, at 42 mph for one mile, and at 55 mph for half a mile.

Slowest mammal The three-toed sloth of tropical South America (*Bradypus tridactylus*) has an average ground speed of 6–8 feet per minute (0.07–0.1 mph), but in the trees it can accelerate to 15 feet per minute (0.17 mph).

Oldest mammal No other mammal can match the age of 122 years attained by humans, but it is probable that the closest approach is made by the Asiatic elephant (*Elephas maximus*). The greatest age that has been verified with certainty is 78 years in the case of a female named Modoc, which died in Santa Clara, CA on July 17, 1975. Certain whale species are believed to live even longer, although little is known about this. The fin whale (*Balaenoptera physalus*) is probably the longest-lived, with a maximum attainable lifespan estimated at 90–100 years.

Sleepiest mammals Some armadillos (Dasypodidae), opossums (Didelphidae) and sloths (Bradypodidae and Megalonychidae) spend up to 80 percent of their lives sleeping or dozing. The least active are the three species of 3-toed tree sloths in the genus *Bradypus*.

Highest-living mammal By a small margin, the highest-living mammal is the large-eared pika (*Ochotona macrotis*), which has been recorded at a height of 20,106 feet in mountain ranges in Asia.

The yak (*Bos mutus*), of Tibet and the Sichuanese Alps, China, climbs to an altitude of 20,000 feet when foraging.

Largest herds The largest herds on record were those of the springbok (*Antidorcas marsupialis*) during migration across the plains of the western parts of southern Africa in the 19th century. One herd estimated to be 15 miles wide and more than 100 miles long was reported from Karree Kloof, Orange River, South Africa in July 1896.

Largest litter The greatest number of young born to a wild mammal at a single birth is 31 (30 of which survived) in the case of the tailless tenrec (*Tenrec ecaudatus*), found in Madagascar and the Comoro Islands.

Longest gestation period The Asiatic elephant (*Elephas maximus*) has an average gestation period of 650 days (more than 21 months) and a maximum of 760 days.

Shortest gestation period The shortest mammalian gestation period is 12–13 days, which is common in a number of species. These include the Virginia opossum (*Didelphis virginiana*) of North America, and the water opossum or yapok (*Chironectes minimus*) of central and northern South America. On rare occasions, gestation periods of as little as eight days have been recorded for some of these species.

Youngest breeder The female true lemming (*Lemmus lemmus*) of Scandinavia can become pregnant at the age of 14 days. The gestation period is 16–23 days. Lemmings are also prolific animals; one pair reportedly produced eight litters in 167 days.

Largest tusks The longest tusks (excluding prehistoric examples) are a pair from an African elephant (*Loxodonta africana*) preserved in the New York Zoological Society (Bronx Zoo), New York City. The right tusk measures 11 ft. 5½ in. along the outside curve and the left tusk measures 11 feet. The combined weight of the tusks is 293 pounds.

Heaviest A pair of African elephant (*Loxodonta africana*) tusks from a male shot in Kenya in 1897, weighed 240 pounds (length 10 ft. 2½ in.) and 225 pounds (length 10 ft. 5½ in.) respectively, giving a total weight of 465 pounds.

Longest horns The longest horns of any living animal are those of the water buffalo (*Bubalus arnee = B. bubalis*). One male shot in 1955 had horns measuring 13 ft. 11 in. from tip to tip along the outside curve across the forehead.

Domestic animal The largest spread on record is 10 ft. 6 in. for a Texas longhorn steer. The horns are currently on exhibition at the Heritage Museum, Big Springs, TX.

Largest antlers The record antler spread or rack of any living species is 6 ft. 6½ in. from a moose (*Alces alces*) killed near the Stewart River in the Yukon Territory, Canada in October 1897. The antlers are now on display in the Field Museum, Chicago, IL.

A WHALE
OF A TIME

To some, traveling 2,775 miles in 39 days may seem like a snail's pace. At a whale's pace, however, it's a world record.

On January 3, 1988, a 24-year-old male humpback known only to researchers as Number 339 was spotted in the icy waters of Alaska. A little more than a month later, on February 11, Number 339 resurfaced near Hawaii (although it would be more than a decade before scientists made the connection). The same migratory trip from Alaska's feeding grounds to the warmer breeding grounds in the south normally takes a humpback an average of 102 days. Number 339 bettered that mark by 63 days, and raised many interesting questions in the process. First and foremost, according to University of Alaska researcher Janice Straley, is whether this behavior is commonplace, or if Number 339 was simply in a rush.

"It is remarkable, and certainly not all whales do this," Straley explains, "but it does show that they can migrate at a very fast rate if they need to. Some whales might remain in their feeding grounds a little longer, for example, and then have to step on the gas, so to speak, to get to their

breeding grounds in the south. On the other hand, whales are very individualistic, with their own unique quirks and reasons for behavior."

Again, this raises the possibility that Number 339 might have been acting on more than just instinct. University of Hawaii researcher Chris Gabriele, who initially made the identification of Number 339 and recognized his achievement, agrees.

"It was obvious right away that this was a fast transit. What we didn't know was if it was unusual. Now that we're actively searching for other fast migrations, we see that this is relatively uncommon."

Regardless, Number 339 has left other questions in his wake, and Straley and Gabriele will continue to fish for answers. Is this penchant for speed gender related, for example? Might humpbacks travel north just as fast? Or was Number 339 merely anxious to head south to warmer waters? As for his current whereabouts, no one knows for certain. Number 339 was last spotted in waters near Mexico, but given his speed, he could be just about anywhere by now.

WHALES

Largest mammal The largest mammal, and the largest animal ever recorded, is the blue whale (*Balaenoptera musculus*). Newborn calves are 20–26 feet long and weigh up to 6,600 pounds.

Heaviest A female blue whale weighing 190 tons and measuring 90 ft. 6 in. was caught in the Southern Ocean on March 20, 1947.

Longest In 1909, a female blue whale measuring 110 ft. 2½ in. long was landed at Grytviken, South Georgia, Falkland Islands.

Largest toothed mammal A male sperm whale (*Physeter macrocephalus*) 67 ft. 11 in. long was captured in the summer of 1950 off the Kurile Islands, in the northwest Pacific.

Fastest marine mammal In October 1958, a male killer whale (*Orcinus orca*) was timed at 34.5 mph in the North Pacific. Similar speeds have been reported for Dall's porpoise (*Phocoenoides dalli*) in short bursts.

Deepest dive In August 1969, a male sperm whale (*Physeter macrocephalus*) was killed 100 miles south of Durban, South Africa after it surfaced from a dive lasting 1 hr. 52 min. Inside its stomach were two *Scymnodon*, small sharks found only on the sea floor, which suggested that the whale had descended over 9,840 feet.

The deepest measured dive was made in 1991 by a sperm whale off the coast of Dominica. Scientists from the Woods Hole Oceanographic Institute recorded a dive of 6,560 feet, lasting a total of 1 hr. 13 min.

Loudest animal sound The low-frequency pulses made by blue whales have been measured at up to 188 decibels, making them the loudest sounds emitted by any living source. They have been detected 530 miles away.

Greatest animal weight loss During a 7-month lactation period, a 132-ton female blue whale can lose up to 25 percent of her body weight nursing her calf.

Fastest whale migration In 1997, researchers analyzing data on migrating whales discovered that a male humpback (*Megaptera novaeangliae*) called Number 339 had migrated from Alaska to breeding grounds in Hawaii in 39 days. The same trip takes most humpbacks about 102 days to complete.

ELEPHANTS

Largest modern land mammal The largest African bush elephant (*Loxodonta africana africana*) ever recorded was a male shot on November 7, 1974, in Mucusso, Angola. It measured 13 ft. 8 in. in a projected line from the highest point of the shoulder to the base of the forefoot, indicating that its standing height must have been about 13 feet. Its weight was computed to be 13.5 tons.

Tallest The tallest recorded elephant was a male shot in Damaraland, Namibia on April 4, 1978, after it allegedly killed 11 people and caused widespread crop damage. Lying on its side, it measured 14½ feet in a projected line from the shoulder to the base of the forefoot, indicating a height of about 13 ft. 10 in. It weighed an estimated 8.8 tons.

CARNIVORES

Largest carnivore The largest of all carnivores is the polar bear (*Ursus maritimus*). Adult males typically weigh 880–1,300 pounds and have a nose-to-tail length of 95–102 inches.

Smallest carnivore The least or dwarf weasel (*Mustela nivalis*) has a head–body length of 4.3–10.2 inches, a tail length of 0.5–3.4 inches, and a weight of 1–7 ounces. This species varies in size more than any other mammal; the smallest individuals are females from Alaska and southern Canada.

Largest feline Male Siberian tigers (*Panthera tigris altaica*) average 10 ft. 4 in. long from the nose to the tip of the tail, stand 39–42 inches at the shoulder and weigh about 585 pounds. An Indian tiger (*Panthera tigris tigris*) shot in Uttar Pradesh in November 1967 measured 10 ft. 7 in. between pegs (11 ft. 1 in. over the curves) and weighed 857 pounds (compared with 9 ft. 3 in. and 420 pounds for an average adult male).

The rusty-spotted cat is the world's smallest feline.

Smallest feline The rusty-spotted cat (*Prionailurus rubiginosus*) of southern India and Sri Lanka has a head–body length of 13.8–18.9 inches and an average weight of 2 lb. 7 oz. (female) and 3 lb. 5 oz.–3 lb. 8 oz. (male).

SEALS AND SEA LIONS

Largest pinniped The largest of the 34 known species of pinniped is the southern elephant seal (*Mirounga leonina*) of the sub-Antarctic islands. Males average 16½ feet long from the tip of the inflated snout to the tips of the outstretched tail flippers, have a maximum girth of 12 feet, and weigh 4,400–7,720 pounds.

The largest accurately measured specimen was a male weighing at least 4 tons and measuring 21 ft. 4 in. after flensing (stripping of the blubber or skin). Its original length was estimated to be about 22½ feet. The seal was killed in the South Atlantic at Possession Bay, South Georgia on February 28, 1913.

Live   The largest reported live specimen is a male from South Georgia, nicknamed Stalin. It was tranquilized by members of the British Antarctic Survey on October 14, 1989, when it weighed 5,869 pounds and measured 16 ft. 8 in. long.

Smallest pinniped   The smallest pinniped, by a small margin, is the Galápagos fur seal (*Arctocephalus galapagoensis*). Adult females average 47 inches long and weigh about 60 pounds. Males are usually larger, averaging 59 inches long and weighing around 140 pounds.

Oldest pinniped   The greatest authenticated age for a pinniped has been estimated by scientists at the Limnological Institute, Irkutsk, Russia to be 56 years for the female Baikal seal (*Phoca sibirica*) and 52 years for the male.

Fastest swimmer   The maximum swimming speed recorded for a pinniped is a short spurt of 25 mph by a California sea lion (*Zalophus californianus*).

Deepest dive   In May 1989, scientists testing the diving abilities of northern elephant seals (*Mirounga angustirostris*) off the coast of San Miguel Island, CA documented an adult male that reached a maximum depth of 5,017 feet.

BATS

Most acute hearing   Because of their ultrasonic echo-location abilities, bats have the most acute hearing of any terrestrial animal. Most bats use frequencies in the 20–80 kHz range, although some can hear frequencies as high as 120–250 kHz. This compares with a limit of almost 20 kHz for humans, and 280 kHz for common dolphins (*Delphinus delphis*).

Largest bat   The largest bat in terms of wingspan is the Bismarck flying fox (*Pteropus neohibernicus*) of the Bismarck Archipelago and New Guinea. One specimen preserved in the American Museum of Natural History in New York City had a wingspan of 5 ft. 5 in.

Smallest bat   The smallest bat in the United States is the Western pipistrelle (*Pipistrellus hesperus*), found in the western United States. Mature specimens have a wingspan of 7.9 inches.

Oldest bat   The greatest age reliably reported for a bat is 32 years for a banded female little brown bat (*Myotis lucifugus*) in the United States in 1987.

Largest colony   The largest concentration of bats is in Bracken Cave, San Antonio, TX, where up to 20 million Mexican free-tailed bats (*Tadarida brasiliensis*) assemble.

Deepest descent   The little brown bat (*Myotis lucifugus*) has been recorded at a depth of 3,805 feet in a zinc mine in New York State.

RODENTS

Largest colony of animals   The black-tailed prairie dog (*Cynomys ludovicianus*), a rodent of the family Sciuridae found in the western United States and northern Mexico, builds huge colonies. One single "town" discovered in 1901 contained about 400 million individuals and was estimated to cover 24,000 square miles.

A kangaroo rests between record-setting jumps.

Largest rodent   The capybara (*Hydrochoerus hydrochaeris*), of northern South America, has a head and body length of 3¼–4½ feet and can weigh up to 175 pounds, although one exceptional cage-fat specimen attained 250 pounds.

Smallest rodent   The northern pygmy mouse (*Baiomys taylori*), found in Mexico, Arizona and Texas, and the Baluchistan pygmy jerboa (*Salpingotulus michaelis*) of Pakistan both have head–body lengths of as little as 1.42 inches and a tail length of 2.84 inches.

Oldest rodent   The greatest reliable age reported for a rodent is 27 yr. 3 mo. for a Sumatran crested porcupine (*Hystrix brachyura*) that died in the National Zoological Park, Washington, D.C. on January 12, 1965.

Highest density   A population of house mice (*Mus musculus*) numbering 83,000/acre was found in the dry bed of Buena Vista Lake, Kern County, CA in 1926–27.

Longest hibernation   Arctic ground squirrels (*Spermophilus parryi*), found in Canada and Alaska, hibernate for nine months of the year.

DEER

Largest deer   An Alaskan moose (*Alces alces gigas*) standing 7 ft. 8 in. between pegs and weighing an estimated 1,800 pounds was shot on the Yukon River in the Yukon Territory, Canada in September 1897.

Smallest deer   The smallest true deer (family Cervidae) is the southern pudu (*Pudu puda*), which is 13–15 inches tall at the shoulder and weighs 14–18 pounds. It is found in Chile and Argentina.

Oldest deer   A red deer (*Cervus elaphus scoticus*) named Bambi (b. June 8, 1963) died on January 20, 1995, at the advanced age of 31 yr. 8 mo. The deer was owned by the Fraser family of Kiltarlity, Scotland.

KANGAROOS

Largest kangaroo   The male red kangaroo (*Macropus rufus*) of central, southern and eastern Australia measures up to 5 ft. 11 in. tall when standing in its normal position, and up to 9 ft. 4 in. in total length (including the tail). It can weigh up to 198 pounds.

Fastest kangaroo   The fastest speed recorded for a marsupial is 40 mph for a mature female eastern gray kangaroo (*Macropus giganteus*).

Longest kangaroo jump   During a chase in New South Wales, Australia in January 1951, a female red kangaroo made a series of bounds that included one of 42 feet. There is also an unconfirmed report of an eastern gray kangaroo jumping nearly 44½ feet on level ground.

PRIMATES

Noisiest land animal   The male howler monkey (*Alouatta*) of Central and South America makes a sound that has been described as a cross between the bark of a dog and the bray of a donkey, and can be heard clearly for distances of up to 3.1 miles.

Largest primate   The male eastern lowland gorilla (*Gorilla g. graueri*) of the eastern Congo (formerly Zaire) has a bipedal standing height of up to 5 ft. 9 in. and weighs up to 360 pounds.

Tallest   The greatest height (top of crest to heel) recorded for a gorilla in the wild is 6 ft. 5 in. for a male mountain gorilla shot in the eastern Congo (formerly Zaire) on May 16, 1938.

Heaviest   The heaviest gorilla ever kept in captivity was a male of uncertain subspecies named N'gagi, who died in the San Diego Zoo in California on January 12, 1944 at age 18. He weighed 683 pounds at his heaviest in 1943 and was 5 ft. 7¾ in. tall.

Smallest primate   The smallest true primate (excluding tree shrews, which are normally classified separately) is the pygmy mouse lemur (*Microcebus myoxinus*) of Madagascar. It has a head–body length of 2⅕ inches, a tail length of 5⅕ inches, and a weight of 1¹/₁₀ ounces.

Oldest primate   The greatest irrefutable age recorded for a nonhuman primate is 59 yr. 5 mo. for a chimpanzee (*Pan troglodytes*) named Gamma, who died at the Yerkes Primate Research Center in Atlanta, GA on February 19, 1992. Gamma was born at the Florida branch of the Yerkes Center in September 1932.

Monkey The world's oldest monkey, a male white-throated capuchin (*Cebus capucinus*) named Bobo, died on July 10, 1988 at age 53.

PETS & DOMESTIC ANIMALS

HORSES

Largest horse The tallest documented horse was the shire gelding Sampson, bred by Thomas Cleaver of Toddington Mills, England. Foaled in 1846, this horse measured 21.2½ hands (7 ft. 2½ in.) in 1850 and was said to have weighed 3,360 pounds.

Largest mules Apollo (foaled 1977) and Anak (foaled 1976), owned by Herbert L. Mueller of Columbia, IL, are the largest mules on record. Apollo measures 19.1 hands (6 ft. 5 in.) and weighs 2,200 pounds, with Anak at 18.3 hands (6 ft. 3 in.) and 2,100 pounds. Both are the hybrid offspring of Belgian mares and mammoth jacks.

Smallest horse The stallion Little Pumpkin (foaled April 15, 1973), owned by J. C. Williams Jr. of Della Terra Mini Horse Farm, Inman, SC, stood 14 inches tall and weighed 20 pounds on November 30, 1975.

Breed The Falabela was developed by Julio Falabela (Argentina). The smallest example was a 15-inch-tall mare that weighed 26¼ pounds.

Oldest horse The greatest age reliably recorded for a horse is 62 years in the case of Old Billy (foaled 1760), bred by Edward Robinson of Woolston, England. Old Billy died on November 27, 1822.

OLDEST CAGED PETS

Species	Name, Owner, etc.	Age
Bird *Parrot*	*Prudle*, captured 1958, d. Jul. 13, 1994, I. Frost, Seaford, England	35 yr.
Budgerigar	*Charlie*, April 1948–Jun. 20, 1977, J. Dinsey, London, England	29 yr. 2 mo.
Rabbit *Wild*	*Flopsy*, caught Aug. 6, 1964, d. Jun. 29, 1983, L.B. Walker, Tasmania, Australia	18 yr. 10¾ mo.
Guinea pig	*Snowball*, d. Feb. 14, 1979, M. A. Wall, Bingham, England	14 yr. 10½ mo.
Gerbil *Mongolian*	*Sahara*, May 1973–Oct. 4, 1981, A. Milstone, Lathrup Village, MI	8 yr. 4½ mo.
Mouse *House*	*Fritzy*, Sep. 11, 1977–Apr. 24, 1985, B. Beard, West House School, Birmingham, England	7 yr. 7 mo.
Rat *Common*	*Rodney*, January 1983–May 25, 1990, R. Mitchell, Tulsa, OK	7 yr. 4 mo.

Oldest pony   The greatest age reliably recorded for a pony is 55 years, for Teddy E. Bear, owned by Kathy Pennington of Virginia Beach, VA. Teddy can still gallop but no longer takes riders, and his teeth are somewhat worn.

DOGS

Largest dog   The heaviest and longest dog ever recorded is Aicama Zorba of La-Susa (whelped September 26, 1981), an Old English mastiff owned by Chris Eraclides (Great Britain). In November 1989, Zorba weighed 343 pounds, stood 37 inches at the shoulder, and measured 8 ft. 3 in. from nose to tail.

Tallest   Shamgret Danzas (whelped 1975), owned by Wendy and Keith Comley of Milton Keynes, England, was 41½ inches tall, or 42 inches when his hackles were raised, and weighed up to 238 pounds. He died on October 16, 1984.

Smallest dog   The smallest dog on record was a Yorkshire terrier owned by Arthur Marples of Blackburn, England. This dog, which died in 1945 at the age of nearly two years, stood 2½ inches at the shoulder and measured 3¾ inches from its nose to the root of its tail. It weighed four ounces.

The smallest living dog is Big Boss, a Yorkie owned by Dr. Chai Khanchanakom of Bangkok, Thailand. On his first birthday (December 7, 1995) he measured 4⁷/₁₀ inches tall, 5¹/₁₀ inches long and weighed 1 lb. 1 oz.

Oldest dog   An Australian cattle-dog named Bluey, owned by Les Hall of Rochester, Victoria, Australia, was obtained as a puppy in 1910 and worked for nearly 20 years. He was put to sleep on November 14, 1939 at the age of 29 yr. 5 mo.

Longest-serving guide dog   The longest period of active service reported for a guide dog is 14 yr. 8 mo. (August 1972–March 1987) in the case of a Labrador retriever bitch named Cindy-Cleo (1971–87), owned by Aaron Barr of Tel Aviv, Israel.

Hearing   Donna, a hearing guide dog owned by John Hogan of Pyrmont Point, Australia, completed 18 years of active service in New Zealand and Australia before her death in 1995 at age 20 yr. 20 mo.

Most guide dogs placed   The record for the most guide dogs placed with people in a single year is held by Guide Dogs for the Blind, Inc. of San Rafael, CA, with 342 placements in 1996.

The overall record for the most guide dogs placed with people is held by the Seeing Eye of Morristown, NJ, with a total of 11,451 placements as of January 30, 1997.

Most prolific sire   The greatest sire ever was the champion greyhound Low Pressure, nicknamed Timmy (whelped September 1957), owned by Bruna Amhurst of London, England. From December 1961 until his death in November 1969, he fathered over 3,000 puppies.

Highest jump   The canine "high jump" record for a leap and a scramble over a smooth wooden wall (without ribs or other aids) is 12 ft. 2½ in.,

achieved by an 18-month-old lurcher dog named Stag at the annual Cotswold Country Fair in Cirencester, England on September 27, 1993. The dog is owned by Mr. and Mrs. P. R. Matthews of Redruth, England.

The highest freestyle jump is 59 inches by Olive Oyl, a 5-year-old borzoi, during the Chicagoland Family Pet Show at Arlington International Racecourse in Arlington Heights, IL on March 22, 1996.

Champion freestyle jumper Olive Oyl clears 59 inches.

Longest jump A greyhound named Bang jumped 30 feet while chasing a hare at Brecon Lodge, Gloucestershire, England in 1849. He cleared a 4-ft.-6-in. gate and landed on a hard road, damaging his pastern bone.

Best tracker In 1925, a Doberman pinscher named Sauer, trained by Detective-Sergeant Herbert Kruger, tracked a stock thief 100 miles across the Great Karroo, South Africa by scent alone.

Top show dog The greatest number of Best-in-Show awards won by any dog in all-breed shows is 275, by the German shepherd bitch Altana's Mystique (b. May 1987). The dog was formerly owned by Jane Firestone and is now owned and trained by James A. Moses of Alpharetta, GA.

Largest dog show The centennial of the annual Crufts show, held at the National Exhibition Center, Birmingham, England on January 9–12, 1991, attracted a record 22,993 entries.

Most registrations There were 149,505 Labrador retrievers registered in the United States in 1996, according to the American Kennel Club.

Drug sniffing Iowa, a black Labrador retriever used by the Port of Miami, made 155 drug seizures worth a record $2.4 billion. Iowa was trained by Armando Johnson and handled by Chuck Meaders, Chief of Canine Operations for the Port of Miami.

The greatest number of seizures by dogs is 969 (worth $182 million) in 1988 alone by Rocky and Barco, a pair of Malinoises patrolling the Rio Grande Valley ("Cocaine Valley") along the Texas border, where the pair were so proficient that Mexican drug smugglers put a $30,000 price on their heads. The dogs hold the rank of honorary Sergeant Major and always wear their stripes when they are on duty.

Largest dog walk   The 3-mile Pooches on Parade, held on October 5, 1996 at Wickham Park, Manchester, CT involved 1,086 dogs. The event raised money for guide dog charities.

Most petted dog   Josh the Wonder Dog was petted by 478,802 people between 1989 and 1997. Josh, who belonged to author Richard Stack of Glen Burnie, MD, died on July 23, 1997.

CATS

Largest cat   The heaviest domestic cat was a neutered male tabby named Himmy, owned by Thomas Vyse of Redlynch, Queensland, Australia.
Himmy weighed 46 lb. 15¼ oz. (waist 33 inches, length 38 inches).

Smallest cat   A male blue point Himalayan-Persian cat named Tinker Toy, owned by Katrina and Scott Forbes of Taylorville, IL, is just 2¾ inches tall and 7¼ inches long.

Oldest cat   The oldest reliably recorded cat was the female tabby Ma, owned by Alice St. George Moore of Drewsteignton, England. This cat was put to sleep on November 5, 1957 at age 34.

Most registrations   The Cat Fanciers' Association reported that the most popular breed of cat in the United States in 1996 was the Persian, with 42,578 registrations.

Most prolific cat   A tabby named Dusty (b. 1935) of Bonham, TX produced 420 kittens during her life.

Best mouser   A female tortoiseshell named Towser, owned by Glenturret Distillery Ltd. of Crieff, Scotland, killed 28,899 mice.

Most expensive cat   A Californian spangled cat was bought for $24,000 in January 1987. It was the display cat from the Neiman Marcus Christmas Book of 1986.

RABBITS

Largest rabbit   In April 1980, a French lop doe weighing 26.45 pounds was exhibited at the Reus Fair in Spain.

Smallest rabbit   The Netherland dwarf and the Polish dwarf have a weight range of 2–2¼ pounds when fully grown.

Most prolific rabbits   The most prolific domestic breeds are the New Zealand white and the Californian. Does produce 5–6 litters a year, each comprising 8–12 kittens, during their breeding life (compare with five litters and 3–7 young for the wild rabbit).

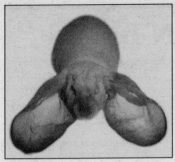

Longest ears "Toby II," a sooty-fawn English lop rabbit owned and bred by Phil Wheeler of Barnsley, England, has ears measuring 2 ft. 5¼ in. long and 7⁷⁄₁₀ inches wide.

Most registrations The American Rabbit Breeders' Association reported that the most popular rabbit in the United States in the year ending June 30, 1996 was the Netherland dwarf, with 2,681 registrations.

Toby II is the rabbit with the longest ears.

LARGEST PET LITTERS

Animal/Breed	No.	Owner	Date
Cat *Burmese/Siamese*	19[1]	V. Gane, Church Westcote, England	Aug. 7, 1970
Dog *American foxhound*	23	W. N. Ely, Ambler, PA	Jun. 19, 1944
St Bernard	23[2]	R. and A. Rodden, Lebanon, MO	Feb. 6–7, 1975
Great Dane	23[3]	M. Harris, Little Hall, England	June 1987
Ferret *Domestic*	15	J. Cliff, Denstone, England	1981
Gerbil *Mongolian*	14[4]	S. Kirkman, Bulwell, England	May 1983
Guinea pig	12	Laboratory specimen	1972
Hamster *Golden*	26[5]	L. and S. Miller, Baton Rouge, LA	Feb. 28, 1974
Mouse *House*	34[6]	M. Ogilvie, Blackpool, England	Feb. 12, 1982
Rabbit *New Zealand white*	24	J. Filek, Cape Breton, Nova Scotia, Canada	1978

[1] Four stillborn.
[2] Fourteen survived.
[3] Sixteen survived.
[4] Litter of fifteen recorded in the 1960s by George Meares, geneticist-owner of gerbil-breeding farm in St Petersburg, FL, using special food formula.
[5] Eighteen killed by mother.
[6] Thirty-three survived.

HUMAN BEING

BIRTH & LIFE

MOTHERHOOD

Most children born to one mother   In a total of 27 confinements, the wife of
Feodor Vassilyev, a peasant from Shuya (near Moscow), Russia, gave birth
to a total of 69 children, comprising 16 pairs of twins, seven sets of triplets
and four sets of quadruplets. The case was reported to Moscow by the
Monastery of Nikolskiy on February 27, 1782. Only two of the children
born to Mme. Vassilyev in the period *c.* 1725–65 died in infancy.

The most prolific living mother is Leontina Albina (née Espinosa) of
San Antonio, Chile, who produced her 55th and last child in 1981. Her
husband, Gerardo Secunda Albina (Alvina), states that they were married
in Argentina in 1943 and had five sets of triplets (all boys) before coming
to Chile. Only 40 children (24 boys and 16 girls) survive.

Oldest mother   Arceli Keh of Highland, CA gave birth to a daughter, Cynthia, at age 63 yr. 9 mo. on November 7, 1996 at Loma Linda University
Medical Center. News of the birth was made public on April 23, 1997.

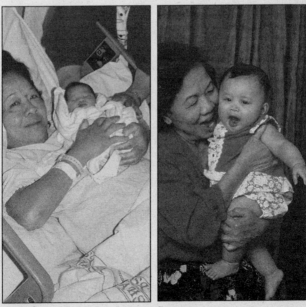

Arceli Keh, 63, gave birth to Cynthia in 1996.

Shortest interval between births   The shortest interval between two children born to the same mother in separate pregnancies is 209 days, by Margaret Blake (Great Britain), who gave birth to Conor William on March 27, 1995 and Bunty Theresa Eileen on October 23, 1995.

BABIES

Heaviest single birth   The heaviest surviving baby was a boy weighing 22 lb. 8 oz. who was born to Carmelina Fedele of Aversa, Italy in September 1955.

Anna Bates (née Swan; 1846–88), a 7-ft.-5½-in. Canadian woman, gave birth to a boy weighing 23 lb. 12 oz. (length 30 inches) in Seville, OH on January 19, 1879, but the baby died 11 hours later.

Heaviest twins   Twins weighing a total of 27 lb. 12 oz. were born to Mrs. J. P. Haskin of Fort Smith, AR on February 20, 1924.

Heaviest quadruplets   Two girls and two boys weighing a total of 22 lb. 15¾ oz., were born to Tina Saunders in Chertsey, England on February 7, 1989.

Heaviest quintuplets   Two sets of quintuplets have been born with a combined weight of 25 pounds, the first on June 7, 1953 to Mrs. Lui Saulian of Zhejiang, China, and the second to Mrs. Kamalammal of Pondicherry, India on December 30, 1956.

Lightest single birth   A 9.9-ounce premature baby girl named Madeline was born at the Loyola University Medical Center, Maywood, IL on June 27, 1989.

Lightest twins   Two sets of twins have been born with a total weight of 30.33 ounces. Roshan Maralyn (17.28 ounces) and Melanie Louise (13.05 ounces) were born to Katrina Gray in Brisbane, Australia on November 19, 1993. Anne Faith Sarah (14.81 ounces) and John Alexander (15.52 ounces) were born to Wendy Kay Morrison in Ontario, Canada, January 14, 1994.

Most-premature baby   James Elgin was born to Brenda and James Gill on May 20, 1987 in Ottawa, Ontario, Canada 128 days premature and weighing 1 lb. 6 oz.

Most-premature twins   Joanna and Alexander Bagwell were born 114 days premature on June 2, 1993 in Oxford, England.

Most-premature triplets   Lewis, Alister and Charlotte Akerman were born 98 days premature on April 23, 1992 in Leeds, England.

Most-premature quadruplets   Tina Piper (Great Britain) had quadruplets after exactly 26 weeks of pregnancy. Oliver, 2 lb. 9 oz. (d. February 1989), Francesca, 2 lb. 2 oz., Charlotte, 2 lb. 4½ oz., and Georgina, 2 lb. 5 oz., were born on April 10, 1988.

MULTIPLE BIRTHS

Most-identical twins The International Twins Association was founded in 1934 and has staged its national "Most Identical Twins" contest annually since 1937. John and William Reiff of Phoenixville, PA have won a record 22 titles, including their current 13-year winning streak, between 1957 and 1996.

Longest-parted twins With the help of New Zealand's television program Missing on April 27, 1989, Iris Johns (born Iris Haughie) and Aro Campbell (born Aro Haughie), who were born on January 13, 1914, were reunited after 75 years' separation.

Longest interval between twins Pegge Lynn gave birth to Hanna on November 11, 1995 in Huntington, PA, but was not delivered of the other twin, Eric, until February 2, 1996, 84 days later.

Highest number at a single birth The highest number reported at a single birth were two boys and eight girls in Bacacay, Brazil on April 22, 1946. Reports of 10 at a single birth were also received from Spain in 1924 and from China on May 12, 1936.

The highest number medically recorded is nine (nonuplets), born to Geraldine Brodrick at Royal Hospital for Women, Sydney, Australia on June 13, 1971. None of the five boys (two stillborn) and four girls lived for more than six days.

The birth of nine children has also been reported on at least two other occasions: in Philadelphia, PA on May 29, 1971; and in Bagerhat, Bangladesh *c.* May 11, 1977; in both cases none of the babies survived.

Most multiple births in a family Quadruplets Four sets, to Mrs. Feodor Vassilyev, Shuya, Russia (b. 1707) (see *MOTHERHOOD*).

Triplets 15 sets, to Maddalena Granata, Italy (1839–*fl.* 1886).

Twins 16 sets, to Mme. Vassilyev (see *above*).

Barbara Zulu of Barbeton, South Africa had three sets of girls and three mixed sets in seven years (1967–73). Anna Steynvaait of Johannesburg, South Africa produced two sets within 10 months in 1960.

DESCENDANTS

Most descendants At his death on October 15, 1992, Samuel S. Mast, age 96, of Fryburg, PA had 824 living descendants: 11 children, 97 grandchildren, 634 great-grandchildren and 82 great-great-grandchildren.

Mrs. Peter L. Schwartz (1902–88) of Missouri had 14 children, 175 grandchildren, 477 great-grandchildren, and 20 great-great-grandchildren.

Seven-generation family Augusta Bunge (née Pagel) of Wisconsin became a great-great-great-great-grandmother at age 109. Her great-great-great-grandson, Christopher John Bollig, was born on January 21, 1989.

Longest lineage The written lineage of K'ung Chia (the great-great-great-great-grandfather of Confucius) extends from the eighth century B.C. to the present. Seven of K'ung Chia's 86th lineal descendants are alive today.

Jewish genealogists and religious leaders have recognized the Lurie (or Luria) family as having traced its genealogy back to the 10th century B.C. In January 1997, Chief Rabbi Lau of Israel concluded that the Lurie family is directly descended from the royal house of the biblical King David. There are now approximately 800 members of the original Lurie family, who arrived in Palestine from Russia and Germany in 1815 and now live throughout the world.

See also MOST DISTANT ANCESTOR, page 136.

LONGEVITY

Oldest person Jeanne Louise Calment was the oldest person who ever lived. Her documented date of birth was February 21, 1875, and she died in Arles, France on August 4, 1997, at the age of 122.

As of August 15, 1997, the oldest living person is Marie Louise Febronie Meilleur (née Chaffe), who was born on August 29, 1880 in Kamouraska, Quebec, Canada and now lives in a nursing home in Corbeil, Ontario.

The oldest person in the world was Jeanne Louise Calment, who died on August 4, 1997 at the age of 122.

Oldest twins Eli Shadrack and John Meshak Phipps were born on February 14, 1803 in Affington, VA. Eli died first, on February 23, 1911 at age 108 yr. 9 days.

Oldest triplets Faith, Hope and Charity Cardwell were born on May 18, 1899 in Elm Mott, TX. Faith died first, on October 2, 1994, at the age of 95 yr. 137 days.

Oldest quadruplets The Ottman quads of Munich, Germany—Adolf, Anne-Marie, Emma and Elisabeth—were born on May 5, 1912. Adolf was the first to die, on March 17, 1992, at the age of 79 yr. 316 days.

Most living ascendants   Megan Sue Austin of Bar Harbor, ME had a full set of grandparents and great-grandparents and five great-great-grandparents, making 19 direct ascendants, when she was born on May 16, 1982.

THE BODY

HANDS AND FEET

Longest fingernails   Fingernails grow at a rate of about 0.02 inches a week—four times faster than toenails.

As of March 1997, the aggregate measurement of the fingernails of Shridhar Chillal of Pune, Maharashtra, India was 20 ft. 1 in. for the five nails on his left hand (thumb 4 ft. 7 in., index finger 3 ft. 7 in., middle finger 3 ft. 10 in., ring finger 4 ft. 1 in., and pinkie 4 feet). Chillal last cut his nails in 1952.

Largest feet   If cases of elephantiasis are excluded, then the biggest feet currently known are those of Matthew McGrory (1973–) of Pennsylvania, who wears size 26 shoes.

Most fingers and toes   An inquest held on a baby boy in Shoreditch, London, England in September 1921 reported that he had 14 fingers and 15 toes.

HAIR AND SKIN

Longest beard   The beard of Hans N. Langseth (Norway) measured 17½ feet at the time of his burial in Kensett, IA in 1927. The beard was presented to the Smithsonian Institution in 1967.

The beard of Janice Deveree, "the bearded lady," of Bracken Co., KY was measured at 14 inches in 1884.

Longest mustache   The mustache of Kalyan Ramji Sain of Sundargarth, India reached a span of 133½ inches (right side 67¾ inches, left side 65¾ inches) in July 1993.

Longest hair   The longest documented hair belongs to Mata Jagdamba of Ujjain, India. Her hair measured 13 ft. 10½ in. in February 1994.

Most tattoos   The ultimate in being tattooed is represented by Tom Leppard of the Isle of Skye, Scotland. He has a leopard-skin design, with the skin between the spots tattooed saffron yellow. Approximately 99.9 percent of his body is covered.

The world's most decorated woman is strip artiste "Krystyne Kolorful" (Canada). Her 95 percent bodysuit took 10 years to complete.

Bernard Moeller of Pennsylvania has the most separate designs, with 14,002 individual tattoos as of April 1, 1996.

The mustache of Kalyan Ramji Sain of Sundargarth, India reached a span of 133½ inches in July 1993.

TEETH

Hardest substance Tooth enamel, the hardest substance in the body, is the only part of the human body that remains basically unchanged throughout life.

Earliest teeth Sean Keaney of Newbury, England was born with 12 teeth on April 10, 1990. The teeth were extracted to prevent possible feeding problems.

Oldest baby tooth Gladys Turner (b. January 4, 1920) of Copthorpe, England has retained a deciduous molar (baby tooth) that her dentists believe dates from 1922, making it 75 years old.

Most dedicated dentist Brother Giovanni Battista Orsenigo of the Ospedale Fatebenefratelli, Rome, Italy, a dentist, saved all the teeth he extracted during the time he practiced his profession from 1868 to 1904. In 1903, the number was found to be 2,000,744 teeth, indicating an average of 185 teeth, or nearly six total extractions, each day.

BONES

Longest bone　The thigh bone or femur is the longest bone in the body. It usually constitutes 27.5 percent of a person's stature, and may be expected to be 19¾ inches long in a 6-foot-tall man.

The longest bone was the 29.9-inch femur of the German giant Constantine, who died in Mons, Belgium on March 30, 1902, at age 30.

Smallest bone　The stapes or stirrup bone, one of the three auditory ossicles in the middle ear, measures 0.10–0.13 inches long and weighs 0.03–0.066 grains.

VISION

Highest acuity　In April 1984, Dr. Dennis M. Levi of the College of Optometry, University of Houston, Houston, TX repeatedly identified the relative position of a thin bright green line within 0.85 seconds of arc, equivalent to a displacement of one fourth of an inch at a distance of one mile.

Light sensitivity　Working in Chicago, IL in 1942, Maurice H. Pirenne detected a flash of blue light of 500 nm in total darkness, when as few as five quanta or photons of light were available to be absorbed by the rod photoreceptors of the retina.

BRAINS

Heaviest brain　In December 1992, Dr. T. Mandybur and Karen Carney of the Department of Pathology and Laboratory Medicine at the University of Cincinnati, Cincinnati, OH reported a brain from a 30-year-old man that weighed 5 lb. 1.1 oz.

Lightest brain　The lightest "normal" or non-atrophied brain on record was one weighing 1 lb. 8 oz. It belonged to Daniel Lyon (Ireland), who died in 1907 at age 46 in New York. He measured just over five feet tall and weighed 145 pounds.

Longest and shortest dreams　Dreaming sleep is characterized by rapid eye movements known as REM. The longest recorded period of REM is one of 3 hr. 8 min. by David Powell at the Puget Sound Sleep Disorder Center, Seattle, WA on April 29, 1994. At the other extreme, in July 1984, the Sleep Research Center, Haifa, Israel recorded no REM in a 33-year-old male with a shrapnel brain injury.

MUSCLES

Largest muscle　The bulkiest of the 639 named muscles in the human body is usually the gluteus maximus or buttock muscle, which extends the thigh.

The uterus, which normally weighs about one ounce, can increase its weight during pregnancy to more than 2.2 pounds.

Smallest muscle   The stapedius, which controls the stapes (see SMALLEST BONE), is less than 0.05 inches long.

Longest muscle   The sartorius, a narrow, ribbonlike muscle, runs from the pelvis across the front of the thigh to the top of the tibia below the knee.

Strongest muscle   The two masseters, one on each side of the mouth, are responsible for the action of biting.

In August 1986, Richard Hofmann of Lake City, FL achieved a bite strength of 975 pounds for about two seconds in a gnatho-dynamometer test at the College of Dentistry, University of Florida. This is more than six times the normal biting strength of these muscles.

Most active muscle   It is estimated that the eye muscles move 100,000 times a day or more. Many of these movements take place during the dreaming phase of sleep.

Longest muscle name   The levator labii superioris alaeque nasi has one branch running to the upper lip and the other to the nostril. It is the muscle that curls the upper lip.

Largest biceps   Denis Sester of Bloomington, MN has a right biceps measuring 30⅝ inches cold.

CHESTS, WAISTS AND NECKS

Largest chest measurement   Robert Earl Hughes (U.S.) had a chest measurement of 124 inches.

Isaac Nesser of Greensburg, PA has the largest muscular chest measurement, at 6 ft. 2 in.

Largest waist   The waist of Walter Hudson (1944–91) of New York measured 10 ft. 11 in. at his peak weight of 1,197 pounds.

Smallest waist   The smallest waist in someone of normal stature was that of Ethel Granger (1905–82) of Peterborough, England, reduced from a natural 22 inches to 13 inches over the period 1929–39. The same measurement was also claimed for the French actress Mlle. Polaire (Emile Marie Bouchand; 1881–1939).

Longest neck   The longest measured extension of the neck by the successive fitting of copper coils, as practiced by the women of the Padaung or Kareni tribe of Myanmar, is 15¾ inches.

VOICE AND BREATHING

Lung power   The inflation of a standard 35-ounce meteorological balloon to a diameter of eight feet in a timed contest was achieved by Nicholas Mason (England) in 45 min. 2.5 sec. for the BBC *Record Breakers* television program on September 26, 1994.

Greatest range   The normal intelligible outdoor range of a man's voice in still air is 600 feet. The silbo, the whistled language of the island of La Gomera in the Canaries, is intelligible across the valleys at five miles under ideal conditions.

There is a recorded case of the human voice being detectable at a distance of 10½ miles across still water at night.

Fastest talker   Few people are able to speak articulately at a sustained speed greater than 300 words per minute.

Steve Woodmore of Orpington, England spoke 595 words in a time of 56.01 seconds, or 637.4 words per minute, on the British TV program *Motor Mouth* on September 22, 1990.

Sean Shannon, a Canadian residing in Oxford, England, recited Hamlet's soliloquy "To be or not to be" (260 words) in a time of 23.8 seconds (equivalent to 650 words per minute) in Edinburgh, Scotland on August 30, 1995.

Talking backwards   Steve Briers of Kilgetty, Wales recited the entire lyrics of Queen's album *A Night at the Opera* backwards at BBC North-West Radio 4 on February 6, 1990 in a time of 9 min. 58.44 sec.

Loudest scream   Simon Robinson of McLaren Vale, South Australia produced a scream of 128 decibels at a distance of 8 ft. 2 in. at The Guinness Challenge in Adelaide, Australia in 1988.

Loudest shout   Annalisa Wray of Comber, Northern Ireland achieved 121.7 decibels when shouting the word "quiet" at the Citybus Challenge, Belfast, Northern Ireland on April 16, 1994.

Loudest whistle   Roy Lomas produced a whistle of 122.5 decibels at a distance of 8 ft. 2 in. in the Deadroom at the BBC studios in Manchester, England on December 19, 1983.

BLOOD

Most common blood group   On a world basis, Group O is the most common (46 percent), but in some areas, for example Norway, Group A predominates.

Rarest blood type   The rarest type in the world is a type of Bombay blood (subtype h-h) found so far only in a Czechoslovak nurse in 1961, and in a brother (Rh positive) and sister (Rh negative) surnamed Jalbert in Massachusetts, reported in February 1968.

Largest vein   The largest is the inferior vena cava, which returns the blood from the lower half of the body to the heart.

Largest artery   The largest is the aorta, which is 1.18 inches in diameter where it leaves the heart. By the time it ends at the level of the fourth lumbar vertebra it is about 0.68 inches in diameter.

Largest blood transfusion   A 50-year-old hemophiliac, Warren C. Jyrich, required 2,400 donor units of blood, equivalent to 1,900 pints of blood, when undergoing open heart surgery at the Michael Reese Hospital, Chicago, IL in December 1970.

Most blood donors   The American Red Cross/University of Missouri blood drive, held in Columbia, MO on April 9, 1997, attracted 3,102 donors, the record for a one-day drive. The drive yielded 2,685 productive units of blood.

CELLS

Largest cell   The megakaryocyte, a blood cell, measures 200 microns. It is found in the bone marrow, where it produces the platelets that play an important role in blood clotting.

Smallest cells   The smallest cells are the brain cells in the cerebellum, which measure about 0.005 mm.

Longest cells   Motor neurons can be $4\frac{1}{4}$ feet long. They have cell bodies in the lower spinal cord with axons that carry nerve impulses down to the big toe.

Fastest turnover of body cells   The body cells with the shortest life are in the lining of the alimentary tract (gut), where the cells are shed every three days.

Longest-living cells   Brain cells last for life. They may be three times as old as bone cells, which live 25–30 years.

Most abundant cell   The body contains approximately 30 billion red blood cells. The function of these cells is to carry oxygen around the body.

HEIGHT & WEIGHT

HEIGHT

Tallest man   The tallest man in medical history of whom there is irrefutable evidence was Robert Pershing Wadlow, born on February 22, 1918 in Alton, IL. When he was last measured, on June 27, 1940, Wadlow was 8 ft. $11\frac{1}{10}$ in. tall. His greatest recorded weight was 491 pounds, on his 21st birthday.

His shoes were size 37AA ($18\frac{1}{2}$ inches) and his hands measured $12\frac{3}{4}$ inches from the wrist to the tip of the middle finger. Wadlow was still growing when he died on July 15, 1940 and may have exceeded 9 feet in height.

Tallest woman   The tallest woman in medical history was Zeng Jinlian (China), who measured 8 ft. $1\frac{3}{4}$ in. when she died on February 13, 1982.

This figure represented her height with assumed normal spinal curvature, because she suffered from severe scoliosis (curvature of the spine) and could not stand up straight. Zeng began to grow abnormally at the age of four months and stood 5 ft. 1½ in. before her fourth birthday. Her hands measured 10 inches and her feet were 14 inches long.

Tallest living man   Ri Myong-hun (North Korea), the tallest living person, is 7 ft. 8½ tall.

Tallest living woman   Sandy Allen, born June 18, 1955 in Chicago, IL, weighed 6½ pounds at birth, but started growing abnormally soon afterward. At 10 years of age she stood 6 ft. 3 in.; by age 16, she had reached 7 ft. 1 in. On July 14, 1977, at 7 ft. 7¼ in., Allen underwent a pituitary gland operation that inhibited further growth. She now weighs 462 pounds and wears a size 16EEE shoe.

Most variable stature   Adam Rainer, born in Graz, Austria (1899–1950), measured 3 ft. 10½ in. at age 21. He then suddenly started growing at a rapid rate, and by 1931 he had reached 7 ft. 1¾ in. He became so weak as a result that he was bedridden for the rest of his life. When Rainer died on March 4, 1950, age 51, he measured 7 ft. 8 in. and was the only person in medical history to have been both a dwarf and a giant.

Tallest married couple   Anna Hanen Swan (1846–88) of Nova Scotia, Canada was said to be 8 ft. 1 in. but actually measured 7 ft. 5½ in. In London, England on June 17, 1871 she married Martin van Buren Bates (1845–1919) of Whitesburg, KY, who stood 7 ft. 2½ in., making them the tallest married couple on record.

Most dissimilar couple   Fabien Pretou, 6 ft. 2 in. tall, married Natalie Lucius, 3 ft. 1 in. tall, in Seyssinet-Pariset, France on April 14, 1990.

Tallest identical twins   Michael and James Lanier (1969–) of Troy, MI measured 7 ft. 1 in. at age 14 and later reached 7 ft. 4 in.

Heather and Heidi Burge (1971–) (U.S.) are 6 ft. 4¾ in. tall. Heidi plays professional basketball with the L.A. Sparks/WNBA team, and Heather recently played professional basketball in Hungary and Spain.

Shortest man   The shortest mature person of whom there is independent evidence is Gul Mohammad of Delhi, India. On July 19, 1990, when he was examined at Ram Manohar Hospital, New Delhi, he was 22½ inches tall and weighed 37½ pounds.

Shortest woman   Pauline Musters was born in Ossendrecht, Netherlands, on February 26, 1876 and measured 12 inches at birth. At nine years of age she was 21.65 inches tall and weighed only 3 lb. 5 oz. She died on March 1, 1895 in New York City at age 19.

Although Musters was billed at 19 inches, a postmortem examination showed her to be exactly 24 inches tall (there was some elongation after death). Her mature weight varied from 7½ to 9 pounds.

Shortest living woman   Madge Bester of Johannesburg, South Africa, is 25½ inches tall. She suffers from osteogenesis imperfecta, a disease characterized by brittle bones and skeletal deformities, and she is confined to a wheelchair. Bester's mother, Winnie, is not much taller, measuring 27½ inches.

DYNAMIC DUO

*M*ost of the time, John Rice is perfectly content to be just under three feet tall. "Life deals you a hand and you just have to play it," says John, who along with his brother Greg holds the record as the world's shortest living twins. "We could have gone through life feeling sorry for ourselves. Instead we've decided to do what we can with what life has given us."

*I*t seems as if everything has been just aces for this small, but very powerful duo. They parlayed their record-breaking qualities into a multimillion-dollar business that has brought them fame and wealth.

*A*bandoned by their natural parents in the hospital, John and Greg were raised by a foster family that instilled the identical twins with a strong sense of self-esteem and confidence that they have carried into their adult lives. "Our parents afforded us the opportunity to experience life as it was," says Greg. "I'm sure there were times when our mother wished we wouldn't try to do certain things, but she always let us try. When we failed, she encouraged us to try again. We were nine or ten before we learned how to ride a bike and then we had to figure out how to jump off a bike that was three times our size," Greg says.

*T*heir perseverance served them well. Their first job—selling cleaning products door to door—was a chance to show their moxie and sense of humor. "It was kind of funny for someone to look through a peephole and not see anyone at the door," Greg laughs. "It was like a Fellini film."

*T*he pair went into the real estate business in the 1970s. They started investing in the Florida market and were successful, breaking sales records for their region. The local newspapers began to run profiles, which were picked up by the national wire services. Soon, companies around the country were calling the twins, asking them to speak at sales seminars. "Obviously, our size is something we use to our advantage," Greg says. "There are 101 reasons why people don't reach their potential. They are either too tall, too fat or too thin. . . The list goes on. John and I could have used that excuse, but our successes came in spite of our physical differences."

When their motivational speaking career blossomed, the two sold off their real estate business and formed Think Big, which today runs seminars on creative problem solving. In addition, the pair produce, write, direct and sometimes star in commercials for their clients.

Their listing in *The Guinness Book of World Records* has brought the pair a new type of fame, says John, who has been stopped by travellers in airports hundreds of times, requesting that he sign their copy of the record book. "We have always been noticed," he says, "but now we are recognized."

SHORTEST LIVING TWINS

The shortest living twins are John and Greg Rice, who stand 34 inches tall.

Shortest twins Matjus and Bela Matina (1903–*c.* 1935) of Budapest, Hungary, who later became United States citizens, were both 30 inches tall.

Shortest living twins The shortest living twins are John and Greg Rice of West Palm Beach, FL (1951–), who stand 34 inches tall.

WEIGHT

Heaviest man The heaviest person in medical history was Jon Brower Minnoch of Bainbridge Island, WA, who had been obese since childhood. The 6-ft.-1-in. former taxi driver weighed 392 pounds in 1963 and 975 pounds in September 1976.

In March 1978, Minnoch was rushed to University Hospital, Seattle, saturated with fluid and suffering from heart and respiratory failure. Consultant endocrinologist Dr. Robert Schwartz calculated that Minnoch must have weighed more than 1,400 pounds when he was admitted.

After nearly 16 months on a 1,200-calorie-a-day diet, Minnoch was discharged at 476 pounds. In October 1981, he had to be readmitted, having put on 197 pounds. When he died on September 10, 1983 he weighed more than 798 pounds.

Heaviest woman The heaviest woman ever recorded is Rosalie Bradford (U.S.; b. 1944), who registered a peak weight of 1,200 pounds in January 1987. In August of that year, she developed congestive heart failure and was rushed to a hospital. She was put on a carefully controlled diet and by February 1994 weighed 283 pounds.

Heaviest twins Billy Leon and Benny Loyd McCrary, alias McGuire, of Hendersonville, NC weighed 743 pounds (Billy) and 723 pounds (Benny) and had 84-inch waists in November 1978. As professional tag-team wrestling performers they were billed at weights up to 770 pounds. Billy died in Niagara Falls, Ontario, Canada on July 13, 1979.

The heaviest known twins were Billy and Benny McCrary. It's even more difficult to tell them apart from this angle.

Greatest weight loss Dieting   The greatest recorded slimming feat by a man was that of Jon Brower Minnoch (see *HEAVIEST MAN*), who had reduced to 476 pounds by July 1979, a weight loss of at least 920 pounds in 16 months.

Rosalie Bradford (see *HEAVIEST WOMAN*) went from a weight of 1,200 pounds in January 1987 to 283 pounds in February 1994, a loss of a record 917 pounds.

Sweating   Ron Allen sweated off 21½ pounds of his weight of 239 pounds in Nashville, TN in 24 hours in August 1984.

Greatest weight gain   The record for weight gain is held by Jon Brower Minnoch (see *HEAVIEST MAN*) at 196 pounds in seven days in October 1981 before his readmission to University Hospital, Seattle, WA.

Arthur Knorr (U.S.; 1916–60) gained 294 pounds in the last six months of his life.

Most dissimilar couple   The greatest weight difference for a married couple is approximately 1,300 pounds, for Jon Brower Minnoch (see *HEAVIEST MAN*) and his 110-pound wife Jeannette in March 1978.

Lightest person   The lightest adult was Lucia Xarate (Mexico, 1863–89). At age 17, she measured 26½ inches and weighed 4.7 pounds. She "fattened up" to 13 pounds by her 20th birthday. At birth she had weighed 2½ pounds.

DISEASE & MEDICINE

MEDICAL EXTREMES

Highest body temperature   Willie Jones, 52, was admitted to Grady Memorial Hospital, Atlanta, GA with heatstroke on July 10, 1980. His temperature was 115.7°F. Jones was discharged 24 days later.

Lowest body temperature   The lowest body temperature was 57.5°F, for Karlee Kosolofski, age two, of Regina, Saskatchewan, Canada on February 23, 1994. She had been accidentally locked out of her house for six hours in a temperature of –8°F. Despite severe frostbite, which required the amputation of her left leg above the knee, she made a full recovery.

Highest blood sugar level   Jonathan Place of Cape Cod, MA was admitted to Falmouth Hospital with a blood sugar level of 1,791 mg/dl while still conscious on February 1, 1997.

Highest blood alcohol level   The University of California Medical School, Los Angeles reported in December 1982 the case of a confused but conscious 24-year-old female, who was shown to have a blood alcohol level of 1,510 mg per 100 ml. After two days, the woman discharged herself.

Cardiac arrest   Norwegian fisherman Jan Egil Refsdahl fell overboard off Bergen on December 7, 1987. His heart stopped for four hours and his body temperature dropped to 77°F, but he recovered after he was connected to a heart–lung machine at Haukeland Hospital.

Longest coma   Elaine Esposito of Tarpon Springs, FL never regained consciousness after an appendectomy on August 6, 1941, when she was age six. She died on November 25, 1978, having been in a coma for 37 yr. 111 days.

Longest without food and water   The longest recorded case of survival without food and water is 18 days, by Andreas Mihavecz of Bregenz, Austria, a passenger in a car crash who was put in a holding cell in Höscht on April 1, 1979 and forgotten by the police until April 18, when he was close to death.

Largest gallbladder   On March 15, 1989 at the National Naval Medical Center in Bethesda, MD, Prof. Bimal C. Ghosh removed a 23-pound gallbladder from a 69-year-old woman. The woman recovered and left the hospital 10 days later.

Largest gallstone   A gallstone weighing 13 lb. 14 oz. was removed from an 80-year-old woman by Dr. Humphrey Arthure at Charing Cross Hospital, London, England on December 29, 1952.

Most gallstones   In August 1987, it was reported that 23,530 gallstones had been removed from an 85-year-old woman by Dr. K. Whittle Martin at Worthing Hospital, Sussex, England.

Highest g force endured   Race car driver David Purley (1945–85) survived a deceleration from 108 mph to zero in a crash at Silverstone, near Towcester, England on July 13, 1977 that involved a force of 179.8 g. He suffered 29 fractures, three dislocations and six heart stoppages.

Hemodialysis   Brian Wilson of Edinburgh, Scotland has suffered from kidney failure since 1964, and has been on hemodialysis since May 30, 1964.

Hiccupping   Charles Osborne (1894–1991) of Anthon, IA began hiccupping in 1922 when he was slaughtering a hog, and hiccupped every 1½ seconds until February 1990.

Longest hospital stay   Martha Nelson was admitted to the Columbus State Institute for the Feeble-Minded in Ohio in 1875 and died in January 1975 at age 103 yr. 6 mo. in the Orient State Institution, OH after spending more than 99 years in hospitals.

Most injections   Samuel L. Davidson of Glasgow, Scotland has had an estimated 78,900 insulin injections since 1923.

Longest in an iron lung   James Firwell of Chichester, England has used a negative pressure respirator since May 1946.

Most artificial joints   Norma Wickwire (U.S.), who has rheumatoid arthritis, had eight out of ten major joints (both hips, both knees, both shoulders, right elbow and left ankle) replaced between 1976 and 1989.

Munchausen's syndrome   The most extreme recorded case of Munchausen's syndrome was Stewart McIlroy (1906–83), who cost Britain's National Health Service an estimated £2.5 million ($4 million). Over 50 years, he had 400 operations and stayed at 100 hospitals using 22 aliases.

Pill-taking The highest recorded total of pills swallowed by a patient is 565,939 between June 9, 1967 and June 19, 1988 by C. H. A. Kilner (1926–88) of Bindura, Zimbabwe.

Sneezing The longest sneezing fit ever recorded is that of Donna Griffiths of Pershore, England. She started sneezing on January 13, 1981 and sneezed an estimated 1 million times in the first 365 days. Griffiths achieved her first sneeze-free day on September 16, 1983—the 978th day.

The fastest speed at which particles expelled by sneezing have ever been measured to travel is 103.6 mph.

Loudest snoring Kåre Walkert of Kumla, Sweden, who suffers from the breathing disorder apnea, recorded peak levels of 93 dBA while sleeping at the Örebro Regional Hospital, Sweden on May 24, 1993.

Swallowing The worst reported case of compulsive swallowing of objects involved a 42-year-old woman who complained of a "slight abdominal pain." She proved to have 2,533 objects, including 947 bent pins, in her stomach. These were removed in June 1927 at the Ontario Hospital, Canada.

The heaviest object extracted from a human stomach was a 5-lb.-3-oz. ball of hair from a 20-year-old female compulsive swallower at the South Devon and East Cornwall Hospital, England in March 1895.

Longest tracheostomy Winifred Campbell (Great Britain) breathed through a silver tube in her throat from the age of four until her death 86 years later in 1992.

Largest tumor An ovarian cyst weighing an estimated 328 pounds was drained and then successfully removed from a patient by Dr. Arthur Spohn in Texas in 1905.

The largest tumor ever removed *intact* was a multicystic mass of the ovary weighing 303 pounds. The 3-foot-diameter growth was removed in October 1991 from the abdomen of an unnamed 35-year-old woman by Prof. Katherine O'Hanlan of Stanford University Medical Center, California. The patient weighed 210 pounds after the 6-hour operation and made a full recovery.

Underwater submergence In 1986, 2-year-old Michelle Funk of Salt Lake City, UT made a full recovery after spending 66 minutes under water.

ILLNESS AND DISEASE

Commonest diseases The commonest noncontagious diseases are periodontal diseases such as gingivitis. Few people completely escape the effects of tooth decay during their lives.

The commonest contagious disease in the world is coryza or acute nasopharyngitis (the common cold).

Highest mortality There are a number of diseases that are considered universally fatal. AIDS and rabies encephalitis are well-known examples.

Pneumonic plague, which caused the Black Death of 1347–51, killed everyone who caught it—some 75 million people worldwide.

Leading cause of death In industrialized countries, roughly half of all deaths are caused by diseases of the heart and blood vessels, including heart attacks, strokes, and gangrene of the lower limbs due to atheroma obstructing the flow of blood.

Most dispensed drug The estrogen replacement drug Premarin was dispensed 44,791,000 times in the United States in 1996, a one percent increase over the previous year.

Greatest drug sales The anti-ulcer drug Zantac was the drug with the highest dollar sales in 1996, at $1,760,726.

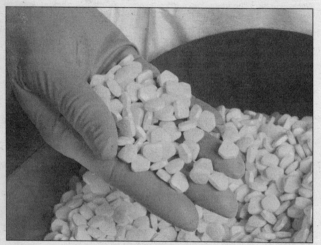

Zantac is the drug with the highest dollar sales.

DOCTORS

Youngest doctor Balamurali Ambati (b. July 29, 1977) of Hollis Hills, NY graduated from the Mount Sinai School of Medicine in New York on May 19, 1995, when he was 17 years old.

Most dedicated doctor Between 1943 and 1993, Dr. M. C. Modi, a pioneer of mass eye surgery in India, performed as many as 833 cataract operations in one day. He visited 46,120 villages and 12,118,630 patients, and performed 610,564 operations.

Dr. Robert B. McClure of Toronto, Ontario, Canada performed 20,423 major operations, 1924–78.

OPERATIONS

Longest operation An operation of 96 hours was performed on Mrs. Gertrude Levandowski from February 4 to February 8, 1951 in Chicago, IL to remove an ovarian cyst. During the operation, her weight fell from 616 pounds to 308 pounds.

Most operations endured From July 22, 1954, to the end of 1994, Charles Jensen of Chester, SD had 970 operations to remove the tumors associated with basal cell nevus syndrome.

Most common inpatient procedure The most frequently performed inpatient procedure is diagnostic ultrasound, which was carried out 1,420,000 times in 1994.

Oldest patient The greatest recorded age at which anyone has undergone an operation is 111 yr. 105 days in the case of James Henry Brett, Jr. (1849–1961) of Houston, TX. He had a hip operation on November 7, 1960.

Longest surviving heart transplant patient Dirk van Zyl of Cape Town, South Africa (1926–94) survived for 23 yr. 57 days, having received an unnamed person's heart in 1971.

Youngest heart transplant patient Olivia Maize of Murphy, NC received a heart transplant at Loma Linda Hospital, Loma Linda, CA on July 1, 1994 at the age of 1 hr. 40 min. She died a month later as a result of rejection complications.

Most kidney transplants From 1954 through 1996, there were 178,031 kidney transplants in the United States. The greatest number performed in one year is 11,788, in 1995.

Longest surviving kidney transplant patients Johanna Leanora Rempel (née Nightingale; b. 1948) of Red Deer, Alberta, Canada was given a kidney from her identical twin sister Lana Blatz on December 28, 1960 at the Peter Bent Brigham Hospital, Boston, MA.

The most frequently performed inpatient procedure is diagnostic ultrasound.

ARTS & ENTERTAINMENT

VISUAL ARTS

PAINTINGS

Largest painting   A painting of the sea measuring 92,419 square feet was completed by ID Cultur in Amsterdam, Netherlands on August 14, 1996.

Most valuable painting   The "Mona Lisa" (*La Gioconda*), by Leonardo da Vinci (1452–1519), in the Louvre, Paris, France was assessed for insurance purposes at $100 million for its move to Washington, D.C. and New York City for exhibition from December 14, 1962 to March 12, 1963. However, insurance was not purchased because the cost of the closest security precautions was less than that of the premiums.

Most prolific painter   Pablo Picasso (1881–1973) was the most prolific of all painters in a career that lasted 78 years. It has been estimated that Picasso produced about 13,500 paintings or designs, 100,000 prints or engravings, 34,000 book illustrations and 300 sculptures or ceramics. The complete body of his work has been valued at over $800 million.

Finest standard paintbrush   The finest standard brush sold is the 000 in Series 7 by Winsor and Newton, known as a "triple goose." It is made of 150–200 Kolinsky sable hairs weighing 0.000529 ounces.

GALLERIES

Largest art gallery   Visitors would have to walk 15 miles to see the 322 galleries of the Winter Palace and the neighboring Hermitage in St. Petersburg, Russia. The galleries house nearly 3 million works of art and objects of archaeological interest.

Most heavily endowed gallery   The J. Paul Getty Museum in Malibu, CA was established with an initial $1.4 billion budget in January 1974 and now has an annual budget of $180 million for acquisitions to stock its 38 galleries.

MOSAICS

Largest mosaic   The mosaic on the walls of the central library of the Universidad Nacional Autónoma de México in Mexico City is the largest in the world. The two largest of the four walls measure 12,949 square feet, and the scenes on each represent the pre-Hispanic past.

MURALS

Largest mural   The Pueblo Levee Project in Colorado produced the world's largest mural, at 178,200 square feet.

Wall hanging   A wall hanging measuring 21,789 square feet and made of 400,000 multicolored plastic chips was hung from the Takamatsu City Hall in Japan for the 50-day Winter Festival, beginning on November 24, 1996.

The largest wall hanging measured 21,789 square feet.

PHOTOGRAPHY

Oldest photograph   In 1827, Joseph Niépce used a camera obscura to photograph the view from his window. The photo is now in the Gernsheim Collection at the University of Texas, Austin, TX.

Most expensive photograph   A photograph by Alfred Stieglitz called *Georgia O'Keeffe: A Portrait—Hands with Thimble*, was sold at Christie's, New York City on October 8, 1993 for a record $398,500.

POSTERS

Largest poster   A poster measuring 236,119 square feet was made by the Community Youth Club of Hong Kong on October 26, 1993. The poster commemorated the International Year of the Family, and was displayed in Victoria Park, Hong Kong.

SCULPTURE

Largest sculpture   The mounted figures of Jefferson Davis (1808–89), Gen. Robert E. Lee (1807–70) and Gen. Thomas "Stonewall" Jackson (1824–63) cover 1.33 acres on the face of Stone Mountain, near Atlanta, GA. They are 90 feet high. Roy Faulkner was on the mountain face for 8 yr. 174 days with a thermo-jet torch, working with sculptor Walker Kirtland Hancock and other helpers, from September 12, 1963 through March 3, 1972.

Sand sculptures   The longest sand sculpture ever made was the 86,535-ft.-6-in.-long sculpture named "The GTE Directories Ultimate Sand Castle" built by over 10,000 volunteers at Myrtle Beach, SC on May 31, 1991.
   The tallest was the "Invitation to Fairyland," which was 56 ft. 2 in. high,

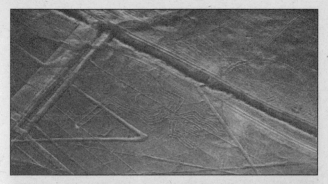

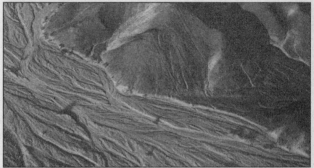

The world's largest ground figures are found in the Nazca Desert, 185 miles south of Lima, Peru. Lines, geometric shapes, plants and animals were drawn on the ground some time between 100 B.C. and A.D. 600.

and was built by 2,000 local volunteers at Kaseda, Japan on July 26, 1989 under the supervision of Gerry Kirk (U.S.) and Shogo Tashiro (Japan).

Largest ground figures In the Nazca Desert, 185 miles south of Lima, Peru, there are straight lines (one more than seven miles long), geometric shapes, and outlines of plants and animals that were drawn on the ground some time between 100 B.C. and A.D. 600. They were first detected from the air around 1928 and have been described as the world's longest works of art.

Modern The painted straw representation of Will the Great Buffalo in northeast Wyoming, completed by Robert Berks in September 1993, is half a mile long.

Largest hill figures A 330-foot-tall figure was found on a hill above Tarapacá, Chile in August 1968.

HIGHEST PRICES

Most expensive painting On May 15, 1990, *Portrait of Dr. Gachet* by Vincent Van Gogh was sold for $82.5 million at Christie's, New York City. The painting depicts Van Gogh's physician and was completed only weeks before the artist's suicide in 1890. The buyer was subsequently identified as Ryoei Saito, Japan's second-largest paper manufacturer.

20th century The record bid at auction for a 20th-century painting is $51.65 million for a painting by Pablo Picasso, at Druout, Binoche and Godeau, Paris, France in November, 1989.

Living artist The highest price paid at auction for a work by an artist who was alive at the time of the sale is $20.68 million for *Interchange*, an abstract by the American painter Willem de Kooning (d. 1997), at Sotheby's, New York City on November 8, 1989. Painted in 1955, it was bought by Japanese dealer–collector "Mountain Tortoise."

Most expensive miniature The record price is £352,000 ($621,600), paid by the Alexander Gallery of New York at Christie's, London, England on November 7, 1988 for a 2⅛-inch-high miniature of George Washington. It was painted by the Irish-American miniaturist John Ramage in 1789.

Most expensive print The record price for a print at auction was £561,600 ($786,000) for a 1655 etching of *Christ Presented to the People* by Rembrandt (1606–69) at Christie's, London on December 5, 1985.

Most expensive drawing On November 14, 1990, at Christie's, New York City, an anonymous buyer paid $8.36 million for the pen-and-ink scene *Jardin de Fleurs*, drawn by Vincent Van Gogh in Arles, France in 1888.

Most expensive poster The record price for a poster is £68,200 ($93,000) for an advertisement for the 1895 Glasgow exhibition by Charles Rennie Macintosh, sold at Christie's, London on February 4, 1993.

Most expensive sculpture Petite danseuse de quatorze ans by Edgar Degas was sold for $11.8 million on November 12, 1996 at Sotheby's, New York.

The highest price paid for the work of a sculptor during his lifetime is $1,265,000 at Sotheby's, New York City on May 21, 1982 for the 75-inch-long elmwood *Reclining Figure by Henry Moore* (Great Britain; 1898–1986).

The highest price paid at auction for a sculpture by an American sculptor is $4.4 million for *Coming Through the Rye*, by Frederic Remington (1861–1909), at Christie's, New York City on May 25, 1989.

ANTIQUES & COLLECTIBLES

HIGHEST PRICES

Unless otherwise stated, all prices quoted are inclusive of the buyer's premium and all records were set at public auction.

Atlas The highest price paid for an atlas is $1,925,000 for a version of Ptolemy's *Cosmographia* dating from 1492, which was sold at Sotheby's, New York City on January 31, 1990.

Art nouveau The highest auction price for any piece of art nouveau is $1.78 million for a standard lamp in the form of three lotus blossoms by the Daum Brothers and Louis Majorelle of France, sold at Sotheby's, New York City on December 2, 1989.

In 1997, Julian Lennon bought this afghan coat, worn by his father John on the cover of *Magical Mystery Tour* in 1967, for £34,999 ($55,998).

Armor The highest auction price paid for a suit of armor was £1,925,000 ($3,657,000), by B. H. Trupin (U.S.) on May 5, 1983 at Sotheby's, London, England, for a suit made in Milan by Giovanni Negroli in 1545 for Henri II of France. It came from the Hever Castle Collection in Kent, England.

Beatles clothing An afghan coat worn by John Lennon on the cover of *Magical Mystery Tour* in 1967 was bought for £34,999 ($55,998) by John Cousins on behalf of Julian Lennon on March 22, 1997.

Blanket A Navajo Churro hand-spun serape dated *c.* 1852 sold for $115,500 at Sotheby's, New York City on October 22, 1983.

Book The highest price paid for any book is £8.14 million ($11.9 million) for the 226-leaf manuscript *The Gospel Book of Henry the Lion,*

Duke of Saxony at Sotheby's, London on December 6, 1983. The book, which measures 13¹/₂ by 10 inches, was illuminated *c*. 1170 by the monk Herimann at Helmershansen Abbey, Germany with 41 full-page illustrations.

Printed Tokyo booksellers Maruzen Co. Ltd. paid $5.39 million for an Old Testament (Genesis to the Psalms) Gutenberg Bible printed in 1455 in Mainz, Germany at Christie's, New York City on October 22, 1987.

Bottle A rare Korean Punch'ong bottle was sold at Christie's, New York City on November 17, 1993 for $376,500.

Box A Cartier jeweled vanity case, set with a fragment of an ancient Egyptian stela, was sold at Christie's, New York City for $189,500 on November 17, 1993.

Broadsheet On June 13, 1991, Donald J. Scheer of Atlanta, GA paid $2,420,000 for one of the 24 known copies of the Declaration of Independence, printed by John Dunlap in Philadelphia, PA in 1776.

Camera The highest auction price for a camera is £55,750 ($86,415) for a rare Enjalbert gun camera, a revolver-shaped spy camera made in France and patented in 1882, sold at Christie's, London, England on August 31, 1995.

A Louis XV Savonnerie carpet was sold at Christie's, London for £1,321,000 ($2,113,600).

Carpet On June 9, 1994, a Louis XV Savonnerie carpet was sold at Christie's, London for £1,321,000 ($2,113,600).

The most expensive carpet ever made was the Spring carpet of Khusraw, made for the Sassanian palace at Ctesiphon, Iraq. It comprised about 7,000 square feet of silk and gold thread, and was encrusted with emeralds. The carpet was cut up as booty by looters in A.D. 635, but from the realization value of the pieces it must have had an original value of some $170 million.

Ceramics The highest auction price for any ceramic is $8.42 million for a Chosan dynasty (early 11th century) dragon jar at Christie's, New York City, on October 31, 1996.

Clock The highest price paid for a clock is $1,652,500 for the Alexander III 25th Wedding Anniversary Clock made by Fabergé, sold on April 18, 1996 at Christie's, New York City.

Dress The most valuable dress sold at auction was a blue silk and velvet gown owned by Diana, Princess of Wales. It sold for $200,000 at Christie's, New York City, on June 26, 1997.

"The Travolta dress," a gown owned by Diana, Princess of Wales (1961–97), sold for $200,000 in 1997.

Furniture The highest price paid for a single piece of furniture is £8.58 million ($15 million) at Christie's, London, on July 5, 1990 for the 18th-century Italian "Badminton Cabinet" owned by the Duke of Beaufort. It was bought by Barbara Piasecka Johnson (U.S.).

The highest price ever paid for a single piece of American furniture is $12.1 million at Christie's, New York City on June 3, 1989 for a mahogany desk-cum-bookcase, made in the 1760s. It was bought by dealer Israel Sack.

Glass The auction record is £520,000 ($1,175,200) for a Roman glass cage-cup of *c.* A.D. 300, measuring seven inches in diameter and four inches in height, sold at Sotheby's, London, on June 4, 1979 to Robin Symes.

Gun An 1873 .45 caliber Colt single-action army revolver, Serial No. 1, was sold for $242,000 at Christie's New York City on May 14, 1987.

Helmet The highest price ever paid for an item of headwear is $66,000 by the Alaska State Museum at an auction in New York City in November 1981 for a native North American Tlingit Kiksadi ceremonial frog helmet dating from *c.* 1600.

Jazz instrument A saxophone owned by Charlie Parker sold for £93,500 ($145,545) at Christie's, London in September 1994.

A saxophone owned by Charlie Parker sold for £93,500 ($145,545) at Christie's, London in September 1994.

Jeans In 1997, Levi Strauss & Co. bought back one of the two oldest surviving pairs of jeans made by the company, dating from the period 1886–1902, for $24,960.

Jewelry The world's largest jewelry auction, which included a Van Cleef and Arpels 1939 ruby and diamond necklace, realized over $50 million when the collection belonging to the Duchess of Windsor (1896–1986) was sold at Sotheby's, Geneva, Switzerland on April 3, 1987.

The highest auction price for individual items of jewelry is $7.79 million for the Begum Blue, a fancy deep blue heart-shaped diamond of 13.78 cts. and a heart-shaped diamond of 16.03 cts., set in a necklace by François Herail, at Christie's of Geneva, Switzerland, November 13, 1995.

A Harry Winston diamond necklace was bought for $4.40 million at Sotheby's, New York City on April 14, 1994 by Saudi Arabian businessman Ahmed Fitahi.

Jigsaw puzzle A dissected map of Europe by John Spilsbury and dated 1767 was bought at Sotheby's, London in July 1984 by Anne Williams (U.S.) for £1,650 ($2,180) plus buyer's premium of 10 percent.

Letter The highest price ever paid on the open market for a single signed autograph letter was $748,000 on December 5, 1991 at Christie's, New York City for a letter written by Abraham Lincoln on January 8, 1863 defending the Emancipation Proclamation. It was sold to Profiles in History of Beverly Hills, CA.

Manuscript An illustrated manuscript by Leonardo da Vinci known as the "Codex Hammer," in which da Vinci predicted the invention of the submarine and the steam engine, was sold for a record $30.8 million at Christie's, New York City on November 11, 1994. The buyer was Bill Gates. It is the only da Vinci manuscript in private hands.

Bill Gates bought da Vinci's Codex Hammer for $30.8 million.

Musical The auction record for a musical manuscript is $4,394,500 at Sotheby's, London, on May 22, 1987 for a 508-page bound volume measuring 8½ by 6½ inches and containing nine complete symphonies in Mozart's hand. The manuscript is owned by Robert Owen Lehman and is on deposit at the Pierpont Morgan Library in New York City.

The record price paid for a single musical manuscript is £1.1 million (c. $2 million), paid at Sotheby's, London, on December 6, 1991 for the autograph copy of the *Piano Sonata in E minor, opus 90*, by Ludwig van Beethoven (1770–1827).

Movie prop In January 1995, the 45-pound statue known as the Maltese Falcon was sold to a secret buyer for a price that cannot be revealed. The Maltese Falcon is described in the 1941 Humphrey Bogart movie of the same name and was sold by Ronald Winston, president of Harry Winston Jewelers, for much more than the $398,500 he paid for it at auction in 1994.

Music box The highest price paid for a music box is £20,900 ($22,990) for a Swiss example made for a Persian prince in 1901 and sold at Sotheby's, London, on January 23, 1985.

Paperweight A mid-1840s Clichy Millefiori basket with no handle sold for $258,500 at Sotheby's, New York on June 26, 1990.

Pen A Japanese collector paid Fr1.3 million ($2,340,000) in February 1988 for the "Anémone" fountain pen made by Réden, France. It was encrusted with 600 precious stones, including emeralds, amethysts, rubies, sapphires and onyx, and took craftsmen over a year to complete.

The most paid for a plastic pen is £6,325 ($9,583) for a Parker prototype Mandarin Yellow Lucky Curve Duofold Senior, sold at Bonhams, London on May 24, 1996.

Playing cards The highest price for a deck of playing cards is $143,352, paid by the Metropolitan Museum of Art, New York City at Sotheby's, London, on December 6, 1983. The cards, dating from *c.* 1470–85, constituted the oldest known complete hand-painted set.

The highest price for a single card was $7,450 for a card dated 1717, which was used as currency in Canada. It was sold by the dealer Yasha Beresiner to Lars Karlson (Sweden) in October 1990.

Silver The record for silver is $3,386,440 for a Hanover chandelier from the collection of M. Hubert de Givenchy, sold at Christie's, Monaco on December 4, 1993.

Song lyrics Paul McCartney's handwritten lyrics for the song "Getting Better" sold for £161,000 ($250,902) in September 1995.

Surgical instrument The record price for a surgical instrument was $34,848 for a 19th-century German mechanical chain saw sold at Christie's, London, on August 19, 1993.

Tapestry The highest auction price for a tapestry is £638,000 ($1,124,794), paid by Swiss dealer Peter Kleiner at Christie's, London, on July 3, 1990 for a fragment of a Swiss example woven near Basle in the 1430s.

Teddy bear A Steiff bear named Teddy Girl was sold for £110,000 ($171,578) by Christie's, London on December 5, 1994 to Japanese businessman Yoshihiro Sekiguchi. The bear was made in 1904, only a year after Steiff made the first jointed plush teddy bear, and had a particularly well documented history.

Toy The most expensive antique toy was sold for $231,000 to an anonymous telephone bidder at Christie's, New York City on December 14, 1991. The work is a hand-painted tinplate replica of the "Charles" hose reel, a piece of fire-fighting equipment pulled by two firemen, measuring 15 by 23 inches and built around 1870 by George Brown & Co. of Forestville, CT.

Watch The record price paid for a watch is SFr4.95 million ($3,315,000) at Habsburg Feldman, Geneva, Switzerland on April 9, 1989 for a Patek Philippe Calibre '89.

The record price for a wristwatch is SFr2.09 million ($1.8 million) for a Patek Philippe "Calatrava" 1939 auctioned at Antiquorium, Geneva, April 20, 1996.

Wine collection Andrew Lloyd Webber's collection of 18,000 bottles of wine sold for a total of $6,056,783 (an average price of about $336 per bottle) at Sotheby's, London, May 20–21, 1997.

Andrew Lloyd Webber's wine collection sold for a total of $6,056,783 at Sotheby's in 1997.

STAMPS

Oldest Put on sale May 6, 1840. 1d Penny Black of Great Britain, Queen Victoria, 68,158,080 printed.

Highest price (auction) $2.27 million. Swedish "Treskilling Yellow," (at left) Zurich, Switzerland, November 11, 1996.

Largest (special) 9¾ by 2¾ in. Express Delivery of China, 1913.

Largest (standard) 6.3 by 4.33 in. Marshall Islands 75-cent issued October 30, 1979.

Smallest 0.31 by 0.37 in. 10-cent and 1-peso Colombian State of Bolivar, 1863–66.

Highest denomination $10,000. Documentary and Stock Transfer stamps, 1952–58.

Lowest denomination 3,000 pengö of Hungary. Issued 1946 when 604.5 trillion pengö = 1 cent.

Rarest Unique examples include British Guiana 1-cent black on magenta, 1856 (last on the market in 1980) and Swedish 3-skilling-banco yellow color error, 1855.

LITERATURE

Oldest book The oldest handwritten book still intact is a Coptic Psalter dated to about 1,600 years ago, found in 1984 at Beni Suef, Egypt.

Oldest mechanically printed work The oldest surviving printed work is the Dharani scroll or sutra from wooden printing blocks found in the foundations of the Pulguk Sa pagoda, Kyongju, South Korea on October 14, 1966. It has been dated to no later than A.D. 704.

Smallest book The smallest marketed bound and printed book is printed on 22-gsm paper and measures ¹/₂₅ by ¹/₂₅ inches. It contains the children's story *Old King Cole!* and was published in 85 copies in March 1985 by The Gleniffer Press of Paisley, Scotland. The pages can be turned only by using a needle.

Largest publication   The *Yongle Dadian* (the great thesaurus of the Yongle reign) comprises 22,937 manuscript chapters (370 of which still survive) in 11,095 volumes. It was written by 2,000 Chinese scholars between 1403 and 1408.

The largest publication on CD-ROM is the British Library's *General Catalog of Printed Books*, published by Saztec Europe Ltd. on three CD-ROMs. It contains the equivalent of 178,000 catalog pages.

Largest dictionary   *Deutsches Wörterbuch*, started by Jacob and Wilhelm Grimm in 1854, was completed in 1971 and consists of 34,519 pages and 33 volumes.

English language   The second edition of the 20-volume *Oxford English Dictionary*, published in March 1989, comprises 21,543 pages and over 231,000 main entries. The longest entry is for the verb *set*, with over 60,000 words of text.

Largest encyclopedia   The Chinese *Yongle Dadian* (see LARGEST PUBLICATION) was the largest encyclopedia ever compiled.

Currently, the largest encyclopedia is *La Enciclopedia Universal Ilustrada Europeo-Americana* (J. Espasa & Sons, Madrid and Barcelona), totaling 105,000 pages, with an annual supplement of 165.2 million words.

BEST-SELLING BOOKS

Most copies sold   The world's best-selling and most widely distributed book is the Bible, with an estimated 2.5 billion copies sold, 1815–1975. By the end of 1995, the whole Bible had been translated into 349 languages; 2,123 languages have translations of at least one book of the Bible.

Excluding noncopyright books, such as the Bible and the Koran, the all-time best-selling book is *The Guinness Book of World Records*, first published in October 1955 by the Guinness Brewery. Global sales in 37 languages reached 80 million in July 1997.

Most weeks on the best-seller list   The longest duration on the *New York Times* best-seller list was *The Road Less Traveled* by M. Scott Peck, which had its 598th week on the list as of April 14, 1995. Over 5 million copies of the book, which is published by Touchstone, are currently in print.

PUBLISHERS AND PRINTERS

Largest printer   The largest printer in 1994 was Bertelsmann in Germany. In 1993, the company had sales of $10,956 million with profits of $289 million. It employed 14,696 people.

The largest printer under one roof is the United States Government Printing Office (founded 1861) in Washington, D.C. Encompassing 34.4 acres of floor space, the central office processes an average of 1,464 print orders daily, and uses 93.2 million pounds of paper annually.

Highest printings   It is believed that in the United States, Van Antwerp Bragg and Co. printed some 60 million copies of the 1879 edition of *The McGuffey Reader*, compiled by Henry Vail in the pre-copyright era for distribution to public schools.

NO STRANGER TO THE BESTSELLER LIST

MOST BOOKS ON THE BEST-SELLER LIST

All six parts of *The Green Mile* by Stephen King appeared simultaneously in the *New York Times* paperback best-seller list the weeks of September 15 and 22, 1996.

The only gas station was closed. There were no lights on at the 24-hour deli-mart. The stranger straddled his Harley Davidson and waited in the red glow of the town's only traffic light. He wondered what force held this eerie place in thrall. He didn't linger. As he roared away towards the black horizon, the stranger was destined never to know the truth: Everyone was home reading the latest record-breaking Stephen King novel.

When it comes to breaking records, Stephen King went into overdrive in 1996, publishing *The Green Mile* (a series of six paperbacks), and two hardcover titles: *Desperation* and *The Regulators* (written under the pseudonym Richard Bachman). The *New York Times* best-seller list included all six installments of *The Green Mile* for the weeks of September 15 and 22. King himself couldn't be happier: "I think everybody dreams of being the most successful in their field."

A serial comprising six books, *The Green Mile* raised a question about the best-seller list: should the serial be counted as six individual titles or a single book? The *New York Times* changed its policy: Now, any serialized novel will only count as one book. "Their argument was that Stephen King just monopolized too many spots on the best seller list. My view is, if you don't like it, it's tough, too bad," King says. "It was a tremendous risk. No one had tried to do a serial novel in modern times.

I thought it would be a real stinker and that I'd be stuck with the copies. Luckily, it did sell."

Paradoxically, the author has also been criticized for writing too much. "Dickens worked faster than me. At his prime, he wrote much more than I do," responds King. "Thomas Wolfe and Anthony Trollope wrote 10,000 words a day. Wolfe, in his prime, wrote the equivalent of two novels a week."

Reading is the key to King's love of writing. "My mother read to me. I became a writer by becoming a reader. I love imaginative fiction. I'll just sit in my office at night and kick back and read a book. The dog lies down by the footstool." King urges young people to experience the joy of reading: "If you read, then you are never bored," he says.

Few have been bored by King's writing, but popularity doesn't sway some detractors who pan horror writing as well as mass-marketable works. Does King classify himself as a horror writer? "I don't know what I am and I don't care," he declares. "There is an urge in people to put others in categories. I sometimes think of people as demon postmen putting all this stuff in a post box." King has little patience for literary critics. "Critics are not creative. There is an assumption made that writing fiction is an analytical, contemplative occupation. It's the opposite," says King. "It's intuitive. It happens as fast as it happens or as slow as it happens."

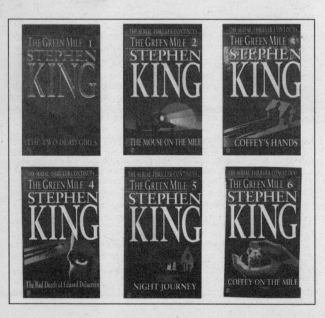

The highest order for an initial print-run of a work of fiction is 2.8 million, ordered by Doubleday for John Grisham's sixth novel, *The Rainmaker*.

Oldest publisher   Cambridge University Press has a continuous history of printing and publishing since 1584. The University received a Royal Letters Patent to print and sell all manner of books on July 20, 1534.

The firm of Williams and Wilkins (formerly Lea and Febiger) of Baltimore, MD has a continuous history of publishing since 1785.

Most prolific publisher   At its peak in 1989, Progress Publishers (founded in 1931 as the Publishing Association of Foreign Workers in the former USSR) of Moscow, Russia printed over 750 titles in 50 languages annually.

Fastest publishing   Two thousand bound copies of *The Book Fair Book*, published by the Zimbabwe International Book Fair Trust and printed by Print Holdings (Pvt) Ltd., were produced from raw disk in 5 hr. 23 min. at the Zimbabwe International Book Fair in Harare on August 5, 1993. The time for 1,000 copies was 4 hr. 50 min. Braille, large print, CD-ROM, and audiotape formats were produced simultaneously.

AUTHORS

Top-selling fiction author   The world's top-selling writer of fiction is Agatha Christie (1890–1976), whose 78 crime novels have sold an estimated 2 billion copies in 44 languages. Royalty earnings from her works are estimated to be worth $4.25 million per year.

Brazilian author Jorge Amado has had his 32 novels published in 48 different languages in 60 countries. His first book, *O País do Carnaval*, appeared in 1931; his most recent book, *A Descoberta da América pelos Turcos*, was published in 1994.

Oldest author   Sarah Louise Delaney's second book, *The Delaney Sisters' Book of Everyday Wisdom*, was published by Kodansha America in October 1994, when she was 105 years old. Her sister and co-author, A. Elizabeth Delaney (who died in September 1995), was 103.

Longest poem   The longest poem ever published was the Kirghiz folk epic *Manas*, which appeared in printed form in 1958 but has never been translated into English. According to the Dictionary of Oriental Literatures, this 3-part epic runs to about 500,000 lines.

English language   A poem on the life of King Alfred by John Fitchett (1766–1838) of Liverpool, England ran to 129,807 lines and took 40 years to write. His editor, Robert Riscoe, added the concluding 2,585 lines.

DIARIES AND LETTERS

Longest-kept diary   Col. Ernest Loftus of Harare, Zimbabwe began his daily diary on May 4, 1896 at age 12 and continued it until his death on July 7, 1987 at the age of 103 yr. 178 days. George C. Edler of Bethesda, MD kept a hand-written diary continuously from September 20, 1909 until his death in 1987, a total of 78 years.

Longest and most letters From July 1961 until the death of his bedridden wife, Mitsu, in March 1985, Uichi Noda wrote her 1,307 letters, amounting to 5 million characters, during his overseas trips. The letters were published in 25 volumes totaling 12,404 pages.

Rev. Canon Bill Cook and his fiancée/wife Helen of Diss, England exchanged 6,000 love letters during their 4¼-year separation from March 1942 to May 1946.

Most presidential signatures The only known document that bears eleven U.S. presidential signatures is a letter sent by President Franklin Delano Roosevelt to Richard C. Corbyn, then of Dallas (now of Amarillo), TX, dated October 26, 1932. It was later signed by Herbert Hoover, Harry S. Truman, Dwight D. Eisenhower, Gerald Ford, Lyndon Johnson, Jimmy Carter, Ronald Reagan, George Bush and Bill Clinton. Richard Nixon's first signature was signed with an auto-pen but he later re-signed it.

Most Christmas cards The most personal Christmas cards sent by an individual is believed to be 62,824, by Werner Erhard of San Francisco, CA in December 1975.

NEWSPAPERS & MAGAZINES

NEWSPAPERS

Most newspaper readers The country with the most newspaper readers is Sweden, where 580 newspapers are sold for every 1,000 people.

Highest circulation The highest circulation for any newspaper was for *Komsomolskaya Pravda* (founded 1925), the youth paper of the former Soviet Communist Party, which reached a peak daily circulation of 21,975,000 copies in May 1990.

The 8-page weekly newspaper *Argumenty i Fakty* (founded 1978) of Moscow, Russia attained a figure of 33,431,100 copies in May 1990, when it had an estimated readership of over 100 million.

The highest circulation for any currently published newspaper is that of *Yomiuri Shimbun*, founded 1874, which publishes morning and evening editions, and had a combined daily circulation of 14,565,474 in January 1996.

Oldest newspaper A copy has survived of a news pamphlet published in Cologne, Germany in 1470.

The oldest existing newspaper in the world is the Swedish official journal *Post och Inrikes Tidningar*, founded in 1645 and published by the Royal Swedish Academy of Letters.

The oldest existing commercial newspaper is the *Haarlems Dagblad/ Oprechte Haarlemsche Courant*, published in Haarlem, Netherlands, first issued as the *Weeckelycke Courante van Europa* on January 8, 1656. A copy of issue No. 1 survives.

Largest newspaper   The most massive single issue of a newspaper was the September 14, 1987 edition of the Sunday *New York Times*, which weighed 12 pounds and had 1,612 pages.

The largest page size ever used was 55.9 by 39.2 inches for the June 14, 1993 edition of *Het Volk*, which was published in Ghent, Belgium.

Smallest newspaper   A Bengali newspaper called "Bireswar-Smriti," which has appeared monthly since 1991 and is published by Kuntal Saha, measures $1^{15}/_{16}$ by $^9/_{16}$ inches.

Longest editorship   Sir Etienne Dupuch of Nassau, Bahamas was editor-in-chief of *The Tribune* from April 1, 1919 to 1972, and a contributing editor until his death on August 23, 1991—a total of 72 years.

Most belated apology   The *Hartford Courant* issued an apology to Thomas Jefferson 193 years late. In 1800, the newspaper ran a vehement editorial opposing his election, and expounding on the ways in which the country would be irrevocably damaged as a result. At the 250th anniversary of his birth, in 1993, the *Courant* finally admitted the error of its judgment with a formal apology, and the words: "It's never too late to admit a mistake."

Most Pulitzer prizes   The *New York Times* has won 74 Pulitzer prizes, more than any other news organization.

Most durable feature   Mary MacArthur of Port Appin, Scotland has contributed a regular feature to *The Oban Times* and *West Highland Times* since 1926.

Most durable advertiser   The Jos Neel Co., a clothing store in Macon, GA, ran an ad in the *Macon Telegraph* in the upper-left-hand corner of page two every day from February 22, 1889 to August 16, 1987. This constituted 35,291 consecutive advertisements.

Most widely syndicated columnist   Ann Landers appears in over 1,200 newspapers with an estimated readership of 90 million.

PERIODICALS

Oldest periodical   The oldest continuing periodical in the world is *Philosophical Transactions of the Royal Society*, published in London, England, which first appeared on March 6, 1665.

The oldest continuously published periodical in the United States is *The Old Farmer's Almanac*, started in Massachusetts by Robert Thomas, a teacher and amateur astronomer, in 1792.

Largest circulations   The total dispersal through non-commercial channels by Jehovah's Witnesses of *The Truth that Leads to Eternal Life*, published by the Watchtower Bible and Tract Society of New York City on May 8, 1968, reached 107,686,489 in 117 languages by June 1996.

The world's highest-circulation periodical is *TV Guide*, with a circulation of 13,171,025 as of June 30, 1997.

The largest circulation of a free magazine is 2.49 million by the Danish quarterly *Ide-nyt*.

In its 48 basic international editions, *Reader's Digest* (established February 22, 1922) circulates more than 27 million copies monthly in 19 languages. In the United States, the magazine sells 15,213,370 copies per month.

Reader's Digest **circulates more than 27 million copies monthly in 19 languages.**

Largest consumer magazine The January 1992 issue of *Hong Kong Toys*, published by the Hong Kong Trade Development Council, ran to 1,356 pages.

Most advertising pages The greatest number of pages of advertisements sold in a single issue of a periodical is 829.54 in the October 1989 issue of *Business Week*.

COMIC STRIPS

Most durable comic strip The longest-lived newspaper comic strip is "The Katzenjammer Kids" (Hans and Fritz), created by Rudolph Dirks and first published in the *New York Journal* on December 12, 1897. The strip, currently drawn by cartoonist Hy Eisman, has been taken over by King Features Syndicate and is now syndicated in approximately 50 Sunday newspaper publications.

Most widely syndicated cartoon strip Charles Schulz's comic strip *Peanuts*, which first appeared in October 1950, currently appears in 2,620 newspapers in 75 countries and 26 languages.

Political cartoons Ranan R. Lurie (U.S.) is the most widely syndicated political cartoonist in the world. As of July 1997, his work was published in

"Happy Birthday" is the most frequently sung song in the English-speaking world.

LOTS OF PLOTS!

Paul S. Newman knows that comic books are not just for kids. He has worked the better part of a lifetime writing them and has been declared the most prolific comic book writer in history. "I've written 4,121 comic book stories," he says. "That's about 36,000 comic book pages, the equivalent of over 100 detective novels. And I'm still writing comic books."

Newman, the father of two grown children and grandfather of two youngsters, has immersed himself in the dramas and misadventures of such personages as "Superman," "Doctor Solar," "Mighty Mouse," "The Lone Ranger," "Prince Valiant," "Jungle Jim," "Tweety and Sylvester" and "Turok, Son of Stone."

His distinction as the most prolific writer of comic books was established by Randall W. Scott, comic book bibliographer at Michigan State University and reported in Robin Snyder's *History of the Comics*, the trade publication of the industry. Told that he would be entering *The Guinness Book of World Records*, Newman, who is 73, had a childlike reaction. "You mean it's okay to tell the grandchildren?"

Newman, who lives in Columbia, MD, explains his method of working: He makes up the entire story, panel by panel, describing the drawing and action for the artist to follow, submits the plot to an editor, then writes the dialogue to suit the action. "To get my 4,000-plus stories approved," he says, "I had to submit another 5,000 plots that were not approved." His profuse output—no one is even close, he says—has not made him rich. "In the old days, you wrote a comic book for about $10 a page or about $300 an issue. I'm not a millionaire but I made a very good living."

Like many high achievers, Newman never planned his ultimate career. "I always wanted to be a playwright. But I needed the money to afford to write plays. So my bread and butter made me famous." He has not given up on his early ambitions, however. He has sold four screenplays, so far unproduced. Four plays written for Broadway remain under option.

eing the inventor of so many stories, he has intimate knowledge of the characters' histories and personalities. How about the relationship between the Lone Ranger and Tonto? "Nothing but respect. Tonto saved the Ranger's life when the rest of the Rangers were ambushed by a gang of outlaws. The Lone Ranger rescued Tonto as a youth. 'Kemo Sabe' means faithful companion. But," says Newman, "it's not Native American, it's made-up language." He should know.

MOST PROLIFIC COMIC BOOK WRITER

Paul S. Newman has written more than 4,000 published stories for 360 different comic book titles, including *Superman*, *Mighty Mouse*, *Prince Valiant*, *Fat Albert*, *Tweety and Sylvester*, and *The Lone Ranger*.

103 countries in 1,105 newspapers with a total circulation of 104 million copies.

Most prolific comic book writer   Paul S. Newman has written more than 4,000 published stories for 360 different comic book titles, including *Superman*, *Mighty Mouse*, *Prince Valiant*, *Fat Albert*, *Tweety and Sylvester*, and *The Lone Ranger*.

MUSIC & INSTRUMENTS

SONGS

Oldest song   The *shaduf* chant has been sung since time immemorial by irrigation workers on the Nile in Egypt.

The oldest known harmonized music performed today is the English song "Sumer Is Icumen In," which dates from *c*. 1240.

Oldest national anthem   The words of the "Kimigayo" of Japan date from the ninth century, although the music was written in 1881. The oldest music belongs to the anthem of the Netherlands, "Vilhelmus," which was written *c*. 1570.

Shortest national anthems   The anthems of Japan, Jordan and San Marino each have four lines.

Longest rendering of a national anthem   "God Save the King" was played nonstop 16 or 17 times by a German military band on the platform of Rathenau railroad station, Brandenburg, Germany on the morning of February 9, 1909. The reason was that King Edward VII was struggling to put on a German field-marshal's uniform inside the train before he could emerge.

Most renditions of the national anthem   Susan R. Jeske sang "The Star-Spangled Banner" live at 17 official events in California, attended by approximately 60,000 people, within a 24-hour period, July 3–4, 1992. She traveled to the functions by automobile, helicopter and boat.

Most frequently sung songs   The most frequently sung songs in English are, in order, "Happy Birthday to You" by Mildred Hill and Patty Smith Hill (written in 1893 and under copyright from 1935 to 2010); "For He's a Jolly Good Fellow" (originally the French "Malbrouk"), known at least as early as 1781; and "Auld Lang Syne" (originally the strathspey "I Fee'd a Lad at Michaelmass"), some words of which were written by Scottish poet Robert Burns (1759–96).

Most successful songwriters   In terms of number-one singles, the most successful songwriters are John Lennon and Paul McCartney. McCartney is credited as writer on 32 number-one hits in the United States to Lennon's 26 (with 23 co-written), whereas Lennon authored 29 British number-ones to McCartney's 28 (25 co-written).

Oldest hymns The music and parts of the text of a hymn in the Oxyrhynchus Papyri from the second century are the oldest known hymnody. The oldest exactly datable hymn is the "Heyr Himna Smíóur (Hear, the Maker of Heaven)" from 1208 by the Icelandic bard and chieftain Kolbeinn Tumason (1173–1208).

Longest published hymn "Sing God's Song," a hymn by Carolyn Ann Aish of Inglewood, New Zealand, is 754 verses or 3,016 lines long, with an additional 4-line refrain to each verse.

Most prolific hymnist Frances (Fanny) Jane van Alstyne (née Crosby, 1820–1915) of the United States wrote 8,500 hymns.

Highest and lowest voices Madeleine Marie Robin (1918–60), the French operatic coloratura, could produce and sustain the B above high C in the Lucia mad scene in Donizetti's *Lucia di Lammermoor*.

Ivan Rebroff (Russia) has a voice that extends easily over four octaves, from low F to high F, one and a quarter octaves above C.

Dan Britton of Branson, MO can produce the note E-flat$_1$ (18.84 Hz).

The highest note put into song is g_4, occurring in Mozart's *Popoli di Tessaglia*. The lowest vocal note in the classical repertoire is in Mozart's *Die Entführung aus dem Serail* in Osmin's aria, which calls for a low D (73.4 Hz).

Oldest choral society The oldest active choral society in the United States is the Old Stoughton Musical Society of Stoughton, MA, founded in 1786.

Largest choir Excluding sing-alongs in stadiums, the greatest choir was one of 60,000 that sang in unison as a finale to a choral contest held in Breslau, Germany on August 2, 1937.

Fastest rapper Rebel X.D. of Chicago, IL rapped 674 syllables in 54.9 seconds at the Hair Bear Recording Studio, Alsip, IL on August 27, 1992.

INSTRUMENTS

Smallest musical instrument In 1997, scientists Harold Craighead and Dustin Carr of Cornell University sculpted the "nanoguitar" out of a single crystal of silicon to demonstrate the possibilities of building electromechanical devices at the nanometric level. The guitar measures 10 micrometers long, about the size of a human blood cell, and has six strings that can be plucked with the tip of an atomic force microscope, but at an inaudible frequency.

Largest organ The largest and loudest musical instrument ever constructed is the now only partially functional Auditorium Organ in Atlantic City, NJ. Completed in 1930, this instrument had two consoles, 1,477 stop controls and 33,112 pipes.

The largest fully functional organ is the 6-manual 30,067-pipe Grand Court Organ in the Wanamaker Department Store, Philadelphia, PA. The organ has a 64-foot tone gravissima pipe.

Loudest organ stop The Ophicleide stop of the Grand Great in the Solo Organ in the Atlantic City Auditorium has a pure trumpet note of more than six times the volume of a locomotive whistle.

Grandest piano The grandest weighed 1.4 tons and was 11 ft. 8 in. long. It was made by Chas H. Challen & Son Ltd. of London, England in 1935. Its longest string measured 9 ft. 11 in.

Most expensive piano On March 26, 1980, a non-pianist paid $390,000 for a *c.* 1888 Steinway grand piano sold by the Martin Beck Theater at Sotheby Parke Bernet, New York City.

Largest brass instrument A contrabass tuba standing 7½ feet tall, with 39 feet of tubing and a bell 3 ft. 4 in. across, was constructed for a world tour by the band of American composer John Philip Sousa, *c.* 1896–98.

Largest movable stringed instrument A pantaleon with 270 strings stretched over 50 square feet was used by George Noel in 1767.

Largest double bass A double bass measuring 14 feet tall was built in 1924 in Ironia, NJ by Arthur K. Ferris. It weighed 1,301 pounds, and its low notes could be felt rather than heard.

The largest playable guitar is 38 ft. 2 in. long.

Largest playable guitar Students of Shakamak High School in Jasonville, IN made a guitar measuring 38 ft. 2 in. tall, 16 feet wide and weighing 1,865 pounds. It was unveiled on May 17, 1991.

An acoustic guitar 28 ft. 5 in. long and 3 ft. 2 in. deep is on display at the Stradivarium exhibition in The Exploratory, Bristol, England. Its dimensions were enlarged from the proportions of a Stradivarius classical guitar.

Most expensive guitar A Fender Stratocaster belonging to legendary rock guitarist Jimi Hendrix (1942–70) was sold by his former drummer Mitch Mitchell to an anonymous buyer for £198,000 ($338,580) at Sotheby's, London on April 25, 1990.

Most valuable violin The highest price paid at auction for a violin is £902,000 ($1.7 million) for the 1720 "Mendelssohn" Stradivarius. It was sold to a mystery buyer at Christie's, London on November 21, 1990.

Largest cello Master violinmaker Christian Urbista of Cordes, France built the world's largest playable cello. The instrument is 24.4 feet tall.

Most valuable cello   The highest auction price for a cello is £682,000 ($1.2 million) at Sotheby's, London on June 22, 1988 for a Stradivarius known as "The Cholmondeley," which was made in Cremona, Italy c. 1698.

Largest drum   A drum with a 13-foot diameter was built by the Supreme Drum Co., London, England and played at the Royal Festival Hall, London on May 31, 1987.

Largest drum kit   A drum kit consisting of 308 pieces—153 drums, 77 cymbals, 33 cowbells, 12 hi-hats, 8 tambourines, 6 wood blocks, 3 gongs, 3 bell trees, 2 maracas, 2 triangles, 2 rain sticks, 2 bells, 1 ratchet, 1 set of chimes, 1 xylophone, 1 afuche, and 1 doorbell—was built by Dan McCourt of Pontiac, MI in 1994.

Most drums played   Rory Blackwell played 400 separate drums in 16.2 seconds at Finlake Leisure Park, Chudleigh, England on May 29, 1995.

Longest alphorn   An alphorn 154 ft. 8 in. long (excluding mouthpiece) and weighing 227 pounds was made by Swiss-born Peter Wutherich of Boise, ID in December 1989.

Highest and lowest notes   The extremes of orchestral instruments (excluding the organ) range from a handbell tuned to g_5 (6,272 cycles per second, or 6,272 Hz) to the sub-contrabass clarinet, which can reach C4 (16.4 Hz). In 1873, a sub-double bassoon able to reach B4 (14.6 Hz) was made, but no surviving specimen is known. The extremes for the organ are g6 (12,544 cycles per second, or 12,544 Hz) and C5 (8.12 Hz), obtainable from ¾-inch and 64-foot pipes respectively.

COMPOSERS & PERFORMERS

COMPOSERS

Most prolific composer   Georg Telemann (1681–1767) of Germany composed 12 complete sets of services for a year, 78 services for special occasions, 40 operas, 600 to 700 orchestral suites, 44 passions, plus concertos, sonatas and other chamber music.

Longest symphony   The symphony *Victory at Sea*, written by Richard Rodgers (1902–79) and arranged by Robert Russell Bennett in 1952 for the NBC television series of the same name, lasted 13 hours.

Longest solo piano composition   The longest continuous and nonrepetitious piano piece ever published is *The Well-Tuned Piano* by La Monte Young, first presented by the Dia Art Foundation at the Concert Hall, Harrison St., New York City on February 28, 1980. The piece lasted 4 hr. 12 min. 10 sec.

Longest silence   The longest interval between the known composition of a piece by a major composer and its performance in the manner intended is from March 3, 1791 until October 9, 1982, in the case of Mozart's *Organ Piece for a Clock*, a fugue fantasy in F minor (K 608), arranged by the organ builders Wm. Hill & Son and Norman & Beard Ltd. at Glyndebourne, England.

BANDS AND ORCHESTRAS

Oldest orchestra The oldest existing symphony orchestra, the Gewandhaus Orchestra of Leipzig, Germany, was established in 1743.

Largest orchestra On June 17, 1872, Johann Strauss the younger (1825–99) conducted a 987-piece orchestra supported by a choir of 20,000, at the World Peace Jubilee in Boston, MA. The number of first violinists was 400.

On December 14, 1991, the 2,000-piece "Young People's Orchestra and Chorus of Mexico," consisting of 53 youth orchestras from Mexico plus musicians from Venezuela and the former USSR, gave a full classical concert conducted by Fernando Lozano and others in Mexico City, Mexico.

Most prolific conductor Herbert von Karajan (Austria; 1908–89), principal conductor of the Berlin Philharmonic Orchestra for 35, made over 800 recordings of all the major works.

Longest-serving conductor Dr. Aloys Fleischmann (1910–92) conducted the Cork Symphony Orchestra (Cork, Ireland) for 58 seasons, ending in 1991–92.

Longest-serving society orchestra leader Lester Lanin has directed and played over 12,480 engagements around the world over six decades.

Largest band The most massive band was one of 20,100 players at the Ullevaal Stadium, Oslo, Norway from Norges Musikkorps Forbund bands on June 28, 1964.

Most pianists The largest number of pianos played at one time is 44, by 88 pianists at The Settlement Music School, Philadelphia, PA on April 27, 1996.

Largest one-man band Rory Blackwell (Great Britain), aided by his double left-footed perpendicular percussion-pounder, plus his 3-tier right-footed horizontal 22-pronged differential beater, and his 12-outlet bellow-powered horn-blower, played 108 different instruments simultaneously in Dawlish, England on May 29, 1989.

Largest marching band On June 27, 1993, a marching band of 6,017 people, including 927 majorettes and standard-bearers, marched 3,084 feet at Stafsberg Airport, Hamar, Norway.

Longest musical march The North Allegheny Marching Tiger Band, from Wexford, PA, marched 50.1 miles in 14 hr. 41 min. on May 26, 1996 at the Ross Park Mall in Pittsburgh, PA.

Bottle orchestra The Brighton Bottle Orchestra—consisting of Terry Garoghan and Peter Miller—performed a musical medley on 444 Gordon's Gin bottles at the Brighton International Festival, England on May 21, 1991.

Musical chairs   The largest game of musical chairs started with 8,238 participants. It was held at the Anglo-Chinese School, Singapore, August 5, 1989.

Baton twirling   The greatest number of complete spins done between tossing a baton into the air and catching it is 10, by Donald Garcia, on December 9, 1986. The women's record is eight spins, by Danielle Novakowski, in South Bend, IN on July 24, 1993.

CONCERTS

Classical concert   An estimated 800,000 people attended a free open-air concert by the New York Philharmonic conducted by Zubin Mehta, on the Great Lawn of Central Park, New York City on July 5, 1986.

Rock/pop festival   Steve Wozniak's 1983 US Festival in San Bernardino, CA attracted an audience of 670,000.

Solo performer   The largest paying audience ever attracted by a solo performer was an estimated 180,000–184,000 in the Maracaña Stadium, Rio de Janeiro, Brazil to hear Paul McCartney on April 21, 1990.

Rod Stewart's free concert at Copacabana Beach, Rio de Janeiro, Brazil on New Year's Eve, 1994 attracted an audience of 3.5 million.

Most successful concert tour   The Rolling Stones' 1989 "Steel Wheels" North American tour earned an estimated $310 million and was attended by 3.2 million people in 30 cities.

Most rock concerts performed   The Grateful Dead performed 2,317 documented rock concerts, 1965–95. They played live in front of an estimated 25 million Deadheads and played 454 different songs and jams.

Three continents in a day   Def Leppard played concerts on three continents on October 23, 1995. Each concert lasted at least one hour and was attended by 200 or more people. The first concert began at 12:23 A.M. in Morocco. The band flew to London for the second concert and finished their tour in Vancouver at 11:33 P.M.

Most durable musicians   The Romanian pianist Cella Delavrancea (1887–1991) gave her last public recital, receiving six encores, at the age of 103.

The career of Yiannis Pipis of Nicosia, Cyprus, a professional folkloric violinist, lasted from 1912 to 1997.

The world's oldest active musician is Jennie Newhouse (b. July 12, 1889) of High Bentham, England, who has been the regular organist at the Church of St. Boniface in Bentham since 1920.

The Singing Webers began performing publicly as a group in 1926 and are still performing after a record 70 years. Brothers Ralph (84), Clayton (85), Paul (86) and Jacob (92) were recently joined by another brother, Henry (91).

Most successful concert series   Michael Jackson sold out for seven nights at Wembley Stadium, London, England in the summer of 1988. A total of 504,000 people saw Jackson perform July 14–16, 22–23, and August 26–27, 1988.

Largest concert   On July 21, 1990, Potsdamer Platz, straddling East and West Berlin, was the site of the largest rock concert in terms of participants. Roger Waters' production of Pink Floyd's *The Wall* had 600 people performing on stage. An estimated 200,000 people gathered for the symbolic building and demolition of a wall made of 2,500 styrofoam blocks.

The Singing Webers have been performing for 70 years.

OPERA

Longest opera   *The Heretics* by Gabriel von Wayditch (1888–1969) is orchestrated for 110 pieces and lasts 8½ hours. The longest commonly performed opera is *Die Meistersinger von Nürnberg* by Richard Wagner (1813–83) of Germany. A normal performance entails 5 hr. 15 min. of music.

Shortest opera   *The Sands of Time* by Simon Rees and Peter Reynolds was first performed by Rhian Owen and Dominic Burns on March 27, 1993 at The Hayes, Cardiff, Wales; it lasted 4 min. 9 sec. An even shorter performance, lasting only 3 min. 34 sec., was directed by Peter Reynolds at BBC Television Centre, London, England on September 14, 1993.

Largest opera house   The Metropolitan Opera House, Lincoln Center, New York City completed in September 1966 at a cost of $45.7 million, has a standing and seating capacity of 4,065 with 3,800 seats in an auditorium 451 feet deep.

Longest aria   The longest single aria, in the sense of an operatic solo, is Brünnhilde's immolation scene in Wagner's *Götterdämmerung*. It has been timed at 14 min. 46 sec.

Oldest opera singers   Ukrainian bass Mark Reizen (b. July 3, 1895) sang the substantial role of Prince Gremin in Tchaikovsky's *Eugene Onegin* at the Bolshoi Theatre in Moscow on his 90th birthday. Danshi Toyotake (b. Yoshie Yokota, 1891–1989) of Hyogo, Japan sang traditional Japanese narrative for 91 years from age seven. Her career spanned 81 years.

Most curtain calls   On February 24, 1988, Luciano Pavarotti received 165 curtain calls and was applauded for 1 hr. 7 min. after singing the part of Nemorino in Gaetano Donizetti's *L'Elisir d'amore* at the Deutsche Oper in Berlin, Germany.

Longest applause   On July 30, 1991, Placido Domingo was applauded through 101 curtain calls for 1 hr. 20 min. after a performance of *Otello* at the Vienna Staatsoper, Vienna, Austria.

Oldest opera company   The oldest opera company in the United States is the Metropolitan Opera Company of New York City; its first season was in 1883.

Longest operatic encore   The Austro-Hungarian emperor Leopold II (*r.* 1790–92) ordered an encore

The oldest opera house in the United States that stages only original musical theater productions is the Goodspeed Opera House, East Haddam, CT, which opened on October 24, 1877.

of the entire opera *Il Matrimonio Segreto* by Cimarosa at its premiere in 1792.

Most roles performed   Placido Domingo has performed 109 different roles, the most of any tenor.

TELEVISION & RADIO

TELEVISION

Most durable shows   The most durable TV show is NBC's *Meet the Press*, first transmitted on November 6, 1947 and broadcast weekly since September 12, 1948. As of August 4, 1997, 2,555 shows had been broadcast.

The last televised broadcast of the *Joe Franklin Show* aired in August 1993. Starting in 1951, Franklin hosted 31,015 episodes of the show and conducted 309,136 interviews.

Stock Market Observer is the longest-running television show in terms of total hours of air time. Since August 1967, it has broadcast more than 39,779 hours of New York Stock Exchange floor trading.

Most episodes   Since 1949, over 150,000 individual episodes of the TV show *Bozo the Clown*, by Larry Harmon Pictures, have been aired daily on 150 stations in the United States and abroad.

Most hours on camera   The most hours on camera on U.S. national television is 10,511 hours by TV personality Hugh Downs in 50 years up to August 5, 1997.

Most spinoffs   The U.S. television series with the most spinoffs is *Star Trek*, which has evolved into five syndicated programs: *Star Trek* (1966–69), *Star Trek* cartoon (1973–75), *Star Trek: The Next Generation* (1987–94), *Star Trek: Deep Space Nine* (1993–present) and *Star Trek: Voyager* (1995–present). It has also spawned seven feature films.

Greatest audience   On January 28, 1996, 138.5 million viewers watched Super Bowl XXX.

The program that attracted the highest-ever rating share was the final episode of *M*A*S*H*, transmitted by CBS on February 28, 1983 to 60.2 percent of households in the United States. An estimated 125 million people tuned in, taking a 77 percent share of all viewing.

Longest uninterrupted broadcast   The state-owned Swiss television station Suisse 4 broadcast the 1996 Olympic Games around the clock for 16 days 22 hr. 45 min. The transmission began on July 19 and ended on August 5.

Longest running prime-time cartoon   On February 9, 1997, the 167th episode of *The Simpsons* aired on the Fox network, making it the longest running prime-time animated show in television history. As of July 31, 1997, 178 original episodes of *The Simpsons* had been broadcast.

THE 51ST STATE

Meet the Press first aired on November 6, 1947. Now a Sunday morning staple for millions of news junkies, the show then aired on Thursday evening at 8:00 p.m. The show's first moderator was its founder, Lawrence Spivak. His introduction described the show as "America's press conference of the air." By the '60s, *Meet the Press* was much more. "President Kennedy called the program 'the 51st State,'" recalls Tim Russert, today's moderator.

"*T*he mission hasn't changed all that much. You need to understand the guest's position on issues and challenge that position. If you do that, people will hear both sides of the debate. It will show the necessary balance in terms of dueling philosophies," says Russert.

*T*ime slots and moderators have changed over the years (Russert is the show's ninth moderator) but *Meet the Press* still makes as much news as it covers. "It is extraordinary to see the amount of news that has been made on the show," says Russert. "Whittaker Chambers accused Alger Hiss of being a communist, President Carter announced the boycott of the Moscow Olympics, and more recently lawyers for Paula Jones laid out their position for a settlement with President Clinton."

*T*he media and coverage of politics has changed dramatically since the program made its debut. "There has been an explosion of these shows, but I think ours is still the truest to the original form," says Russert. "The key is to follow the news closely and stay in touch with the newsmakers." Guests are rarely selected until Thursdays. "Sunday's show is usually the topic of discussion for the President's press secretary on Monday."

*I*n accepting the moderator's job in 1991, Russert knew he was taking custody of a national treasure. "If you're looking for a food fight, you won't find it on *Meet the Press*," laughs Russert. The newsman points to another national institution, Cal Ripken Jr., as the record holder he most admires: "I was there with my son the night Ripken set the record. The beauty of his record is that it isn't a naturally endowed talent." It's hardly surprising that Russert admires staying power. "It's not a question of running the fastest or throwing the longest, but it's the discipline to get up every day and do the job. Hard work does pay off."

MOST DURABLE SHOW

The most durable TV show is NBC's *Meet the Press*, first transmitted on November 6, 1947 and broadcast weekly since September 12, 1948. As of August 4, 1997, 2,555 shows had been broadcast.

HEY, MAN, HOMER'S NUMBER ONE

*E*veryone loves cartoons. At least that's what Matt Groening was betting on when he created the animated sitcom *The Simpsons*. Now, 178 episodes (and counting) after its premier in December 1989, Groening's weekly show has snagged the record for the longest running prime time cartoon, topping *The Flintstones*.

*T*he show began as a short cartoon segment on *The Tracey Ullman Show*. After 50 cartoons aired on the show, Groening was offered his own series. "That's how I got my feet wet with animation. We did this show without a pilot and it was a pretty huge hit right out of the gate," says Groening. Originally Groening designed the show for adults but knew that kids would probably be his biggest fans. "I truly believe kids can handle content that's considered to be for adults. I knew children would love this show because it's a cartoon—but I didn't think adults would give it a

LONGEST-RUNNING PRIME-TIME CARTOON

On February 9, 1997, the 167th episode of *The Simpsons* aired on the Fox network, making it the longest running prime-time animated show in television history. As of July 31, 1997, 178 original episodes of *The Simpsons* had been broadcast.

chance because it can be so silly. Once the show started, I think parents heard their kids laughing so hard from the TV room, they had to come watch for themselves."

*O*ne of the most popular features of the show is Groening's "freeze-frame" jokes—little gags which are only noticed if the viewer is watching the show closely. "I like to reward people for paying attention," says Groening. "You can get into *The Simpsons* at any level you're up to. But if you really pay attention, there's a lot going on...subtle background jokes on signs and the like. For me, that's partly from watching TV and taking great delight when people put that extra effort into their shows."

*G*roening doesn't pretend that Homer, Marge, Bart, Lisa and Maggie are role models for America, but he feels his creation is a tribute to the American family—at its wildest. "They're having a great time—and we're having a great time telling these stories. I also think it's an opportunity for people to tune into a TV show and see a family everyone knows they're better than," he says.

YADA, YADA, YADA

"All I ever wanted to be was a stand-up comedian. Just work at nightclubs with a suit on," Jerry Seinfeld claims. "Actually, that's still what I'd like to be." Maybe so, but for the past nine years, Seinfeld has been writing and starring in his own top-rated television show.

How has this show become so hugely popular, given its creator's alleged lack of ambition? "We try to keep the show quirky and original," says Seinfeld. "We work hard for this every week and although we don't always succeed, you'll usually be surprised by what you see. I think this is a very big part of its appeal."

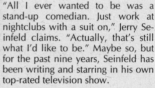

But how did it all begin? One day, Seinfeld's manager sent a note to the late Brandon Tartikoff, then president of NBC, which Seinfeld paraphrases: "Call me a crazy guy, but I have a feeling that someday Jerry Seinfeld will be doing a television show for NBC." Following the meeting with NBC, Seinfeld bumped into Larry David in New York. "We talked about the meeting a bit and then went to get something to eat at one of those late night Korean delis, where we just started making fun of the food. And sud-

MOST EXPENSIVE TV SERIES RENEWAL

In 1997, NBC renewed its contract to produce *Seinfeld* at a reported cost of $120 million for the 1997/98 season. *Seinfeld* also commands the most money in television history for advertising, at more than $1 million per minute.

denly, it hit us . . . this is what the show should be about—just two comedians walking around New York, making fun of stuff."

Originally, Seinfeld admits, the show was to consist only of himself and the character of George Costanza, who would also be a comedian. But later on, the other characters of Cosmo Kramer and Elaine Benes were admitted, and the wacky circle of friends was formed. "I think people relate to these characters' self-interest because everyone has a strong self-interest themselves," Seinfeld explains. "And because these characters kind of wear this on the outside and the actors play it so well, it's funny. It's just relatable." He also acknowledges that New Yorkers are not the only people who associate with the show. "It's funny. And funny crosses over cultural lines."

How does Seinfeld feel about breaking a Guinness record? Pretty well satisfied. "Of course I read the book as a kid. In fact, one of the routines that got me started as a comedian was about the fattest man in the world," Seinfeld says. "It was something about how he weighed 1,400 pounds and even if he managed to lose 200 pounds, what, as a friend of his, could you say? 'You look great'? 'You're a rail'? And he would say, of course, 'Well, I feel fantastic! I'm 1,100 pounds. I've never felt so great.' "

Highest-paid performer   Oprah Winfrey reportedly earned $146 million in 1994–95.

Most expensive television rights   In November 1991, a group of U.S. and European investors, led by CBS, paid $8 million for the television rights to *Scarlett*, the sequel to Margaret Mitchell's *Gone With the Wind*, written by Alexandra Ripley.

Most Emmy Awards   The most Emmys won by any individual is 17, by television producer Dwight Arlington Hemion. He also holds the record for most nominations, with 46.

Sesame Street (PBS) has won the most awards for a series, with 64 between 1970 and 1996. *Cheers* has received the most nominations, with 117 (winning 27) between 1983 and 1993. The most Emmys awarded to a miniseries was 9, to *Roots* (ABC) in 1977. In 1977, *Eleanor and Franklin: The White House Years* (ABC) received the most Emmys, 11, for a television movie.

Nielsen Top 10 (CBS)   The television show that has appeared the most times as a Top 10 rated prime-time show is *60 Minutes*. The CBS newsmagazine graced the Top 10 for 19 consecutive seasons, 1978–96. The show broke its streak when it ranked 11th in 1997.

Most expensive TV production   *War and Remembrance* was the most expensive TV production, costing $110 million. The 14-episode ABC miniseries won the 1989 Emmy for best miniseries.

Most prolific TV scriptwriter   The most prolific television writer in the world was the Rt. Hon. Lord Willis (1918–92). He created 41 series, 37 stage plays and 39 feature films, and had 29 plays produced.

Most prolific TV producer   The most prolific producer was game show producer Mark Goodson. Goodson produced over 39,000 episodes totaling more than 21,240 hours of airtime.

Aaron Spelling has produced more than 3,097 TV episodes totaling more than 3,099 hours of airtime.

Largest TV set   The Sony Jumbo Tron color TV screen at the Tsukuba International Exposition '85 near Tokyo, Japan measured 80 by 150 feet.

Smallest TV set   The Seiko TV-Wrist Watch has a 1.2-inch screen and weighs 2.8 ounces. Including the receiver unit and headphones, the black and white system, costing 108,000 yen ($1,038), weighs 1.3 ounces.

The smallest single-piece set is the Casio-Keisanki TV-10, weighing 11.9 ounces with a 2.7-inch screen.

The smallest and lightest color set is the Casio CV-1, with dimensions of 2.4 by 0.9 by 3.6 inches, weighing, with batteries, only six ounces. It has a screen size of 1.4 inches and retails in Japan for 40,000 yen (about $350).

Most TV sets   The United States has the most homes with television sets, with 95.4 million households as of May 1996. Of these, 62.9 million households had cable television.

Best-selling video The world's best-selling video is Walt Disney's animated feature *The Lion King*, which had sold over 55 million copies worldwide through August 15, 1997.

RADIO

Most durable programs *Rambling with Gambling*, the early morning program on WOR, New York City, was first broadcast in March 1925 and celebrated its 22,583rd show on July 29, 1997. The show has been hosted by three generations of the Gambling family: John B. Gambling (1925–59), John A. Gambling (1959–89) and John R. Gambling (1985–present). The show currently airs six days a week, year-round.

The Grand Ole Opry has broadcast continuously since November 1925.

Most hours broadcast per week Larry King's radio and television programs were broadcast a combined 36 hours per week from 1985 through May 27, 1994. Since May 30, 1994, King's television show has aired simultaneously on radio and television six hours per week in 210 countries.

Most radio stations The United States had 12,177 authorized broadcast stations as of June 30, 1997, more than any other country.

Largest audience Surveys carried out in over 100 countries showed that the global estimated audience for the British Broadcasting Corporation World Service was 140 million regular listeners in 1995—greater than any other international broadcaster. The World Service is now broadcast in 41 languages.

Largest response The largest recorded response to a radio show occurred June 21–27, 1993, when FM Osaka 85.1 in Osaka, Japan received a total of 8,091,309 calls in response to a phone-in lottery. The prize was 100,000 yen (around $1,500), and a chance to win it was offered for a 20-minute period every hour, for 10 hours each day. The maximum call count in one day of phone-ins (3 hr. 20 min.) was 1,540,793 on June 23, 1993.

Biggest radio prize Mary Buchanan, 15, won a prize of $25,000 for 40 years (or $1 million) on WKRQ Cincinnati on November 21, 1980.

Most assiduous radio ham The late Richard C. Spenceley of KV4AA in St. Thomas, VI built his contacts (QSOs) to a record level of 48,100 in 365 days in 1978.

Most listened-to network radio personality An estimated 21.58 million people listened to Paul Harvey news programs as of the fall of 1996. Harvey's weekly morning program was the top program in network radio, with 5.3 million listeners, during the fall of 1996.

RECORDED MUSIC

Oldest recordings   The oldest existing recording was made in 1878 by Augustus Stroh, but it remains on the mandrel of his machine and has never been played.

The oldest playable record is believed to be an engraved metal cylinder made by Frank Lambert in 1878 or 1879 and voicing the hours on the clock. The recording is owned by Aaron Cramer of New York City.

Smallest recorder   In April 1983, Olympic Optical Industry Co. of Japan marketed a micro-cassette recorder measuring $4\frac{1}{5}$ by 2 by $\frac{1}{2}$ inches and weighing 4.4 ounces.

Smallest cassette   The NT digital cassette made by the Sony Corporation of Japan for use in dictating machines measures just $1\frac{1}{5}$ by $\frac{4}{5}$ by $\frac{4}{5}$ inches.

Smallest functional record   Six titles of $1\frac{5}{16}$-inch diameter were recorded by HMV's studio at Hayes, England on January 26, 1923 for Queen Mary's Doll House. Some 92,000 of these miniature records were pressed, including 35,000 of "God Save the King."

Largest record store   HMV opened the world's largest record store at 150 Oxford Street, London, England on October 24, 1986. Its selling area measures 36,684 square feet.

"The Devil Glitch" is the longest commercially released pop song, at 68 min. 53 sec.

Longest recorded pop song   The longest continuous pop song ever recorded and commercially released is "The Devil Glitch" (Future Fossil Music, 1996), written by Chris Butler in collaboration with others, at 68 min. 53 sec.

TOP RECORDING ARTISTS

Most successful solo recording artist   Although no independently audited figures have ever been published for Elvis Presley, he had over 170 hit singles and over 80 top-selling albums, 1956–77. Aretha Franklin is the female solo artist with the most million-selling singles, with 14, 1967–97.

Most successful group   The singers with the greatest sales of any group were the Beatles. The group, from Liverpool, England, comprised George Harrison, John Lennon, Paul McCartney and Ringo Starr. The all-time Beatles sales have been estimated by EMI at over a billion discs and tapes.

416   ● **Arts & Entertainment**

Most gold, platinum, and multiplatinum discs　The only audited measure of gold, platinum and multiplatinum singles and albums within the United States is certification by the Recording Industry Association of America (RIAA), introduced on March 14, 1958.

The Beatles have the most certified gold discs for any group, with 60 (38 albums, 22 singles). The group with the most multiplatinum albums is the Beatles, with 20.

The recording artist with the most certified titles ever is Elvis Presley. Of his 61 gold albums, 29 went platinum, and 25 of his 50 gold singles went platinum. The female solo artist to receive the most gold discs is Barbra Streisand, with 44 (36 albums, 8 singles).

The Beatles holds the record for most platinum albums, with 33. The solo artist with the most platinum albums is Elvis Presley, with 29 (including 10 short form albums). Elton John and George Strait share the record for the most full length platinum albums, with 20.

Elvis Presley holds the record for the most multiplatinum albums for an individual, with 12 (including 2 short form albums). The record for the most full length multiplatinum albums is 11, held by Billy Joel. Barbra Streisand holds the platinum record for a female solo artist, with 23. Streisand shares the record for most multiplatinum albums by a female recording artist (10) with Madonna.

Most recordings　A set of 180 compact discs containing the complete works of Mozart was produced by Philips Classics for release in 1990/91 to commemorate the bicentennial of the composer's death. The complete set comprises over 200 hours of music and would occupy $6^1/_2$ feet of shelving.

Most Grammy Awards　An all-time record 32 awards to an individual (including a special Trustees' award presented in 1967 and a lifetime achievement award presented in 1996) have been won by the Hungarian-born British conductor Sir Georg Solti.

The most won by a solo pop performer is 18 (including a lifetime achievement award), by Stevie Wonder. The most won by a group is eight, by Manhattan Transfer. The greatest number won in one year is eight, by Michael Jackson, in 1984.

Longest recording contract　Yehudi Menuhin signed a contract with the Gramophone Company (now EMI) on March 24, 1931. He has remained under contract with EMI ever since.

BIGGEST SELLERS

Singles　The greatest seller of any phonograph record to date is "White Christmas" by Irving Berlin, recorded by Bing Crosby on May 29, 1942. It is estimated that global sales exceed 30 million.

The highest claim for any rock record is an unaudited 25 million for "Rock Around the Clock," copyrighted in 1953 by James E. Myers under the name Jimmy De Knight and Max C. Freedmann and recorded on April 12, 1954 by Bill Haley and the Comets.

The highest certified singles, at 4 million copies, are "I Will Always Love You" by Whitney Houston; "Whoomp! (There It Is)" by Tag Team; "We Are The World" by USA for Africa; "Bambi" by Disney; and "Macarena" by Los Del Rio.

The fastest-selling single is "We Are the World," by USA for Africa, which reportedly sold 800,000 copies in three days in March 1985. Band Aid's "Do They Know It's Christmas?" sold 1.6 million copies in its first week on sale in December 1984.

Albums The best-selling album of all time is *Thriller* by Michael Jackson, with global sales of 47 million and domestic sales (as reported by RIAA) of

Jagged Little Pill by Alanis Morissette has sold over 27 million copies worldwide, making it the best-selling debut album of all time.

over 25 million. The best-selling album by a group is the Eagles' *Their Greatest Hits, 1971–75* with over 24 million sold.

Jagged Little Pill by Alanis Morissette has sold over 27 million copies worldwide, making it the best-selling debut album of all time.

Soundtrack The best-selling movie soundtrack is *Saturday Night Fever*, with sales of over 30 million.

Classical album The best-selling classical album is *In Concert*, with worldwide sales of 5 million to date. It was recorded by José Carreras, Placido Domingo and Luciano Pavarotti at the 1990 Soccer World Cup Finals in Rome, Italy.

The fastest-selling album of all time is *John Fitzgerald Kennedy—A Memorial Album*, recorded on November 22, 1963, the day of Kennedy's assassination, which sold 4 million copies in six days, December 7–12, 1963.

THE CHARTS

U.S. singles "One Sweet Day" by Mariah Carey and Boyz II Men spent 16 weeks at Number 1 in 1995–96.

The Beatles have had the most No. 1 singles (22), Conway Twitty the most Country No. 1's (40) and Aretha Franklin and Stevie Wonder the most Rhythm and Blues No. 1's (20 each). Elvis Presley has had the most hit singles on Billboard's Hot 100—149 from 1956 to 1983.

Bing Crosby's "White Christmas" spent a total of 86 weeks on the charts between 1942 and 1962. "Tainted Love" by Soft Cell stayed on the charts for 43 consecutive weeks from January 1982.

The Spice Girls—Geri Halliwell (Ginger Spice), Victoria Adams (Posh Spice), Melanie Brown (Scary Spice), Emma Bunton (Baby Spice), and Melanie Chisholm (Sporty Spice)—entered the U.S. charts at number five with their single "Say You'll Be There" in May 1997, becoming the highest new entry by a British act.

Albums *South Pacific* was No. 1 for 69 weeks (nonconsecutive) from May 1949. *Dark Side of the Moon* by Pink Floyd was on the Billboard charts for 741 weeks to October 1988.

The Beatles had the most No. 1 albums (18). Elvis Presley was the most successful male soloist (9). Presley has had the most hit albums (93 from 1956 to January 1995).

DANCING

Largest dance   An estimated 72,000 people took part in a Chicken Dance held during the Canfield Fair in Canfield, OH on September 1, 1996.

Longest dance   The most taxing marathon dance staged as a public spectacle was by Mike Ritof and Edith Boudreaux, who logged 214 days 12 hr. 28½ min. to win $2,000 at Chicago's Merry Garden Ballroom, Belmont and Sheffield, IL, August 29, 1930–April 1, 1931. Rest periods were progressively cut from 20 to 10 to 5 to zero minutes per hour, with 10-inch steps and a maximum of 15 seconds for closure of eyes.

Tap dancing   The longest distance tap danced by one person was 23.219 miles, by David Meenan, who tap-danced for 6 hr. 12 min. 53 sec. in Red Bank, NJ on June 30, 1996.
   Rosie Radiator led 12 tap dancers through the streets of San Francisco, CA in a routine covering 9.61 miles on July 11, 1994.

Ballet Fastest entrechat douze   In the entrechat, the starting and finishing position each count as one, so that in an entrechat douze there are five

David Meenan tap danced 23.219 miles on June 30, 1996.

crossings and uncrossings. This feat was performed by Wayne Sleep for the British Broadcasting Corporation *Record Breakers* TV program on January 7, 1973. He was in the air for 0.71 seconds.

Grands jetés   On November 28, 1988, Wayne Sleep completed 158 grands jetés along the length of Dunston Staiths, Gateshead, England in two minutes.

Most turns   The greatest number of spins called for in classical ballet choreography is 32 fouettés rond de jambe en tournant in *Swan Lake* by Piotr Ilyich Tchaikovsky (1840–93). Delia Gray (Great Britain) achieved 166 such turns at The Playhouse, Harlow, England on June 2, 1991.

Most curtain calls   Dame Margot Fonteyn and Rudolf Nureyev received 89 curtain calls after a performance of *Swan Lake* at the Vienna Staatsoper, Austria in October 1964.

Most successful ballroom dancers   The professional ballroom dancing champions Bill and Bobbie Irvine won 13 world titles between 1960 and 1968.

Oldest ballroom dancer   The oldest competitive ballroom dancer was Albert J. Sylvester (1889–1989) of Corsham, England, who retired at age 94.

The oldest competitive ballroom dancer in the United States is Lorna S. Lengfeld, who was still competing at age 90.

Over 3,500 hula dancers danced on Waikiki Beach, Honolulu, HI on September 21, 1996.

Longest conga line   The Miami Super Conga, held in conjunction with Calle Ocho—a party to which Cuban-Americans invite the rest of Miami for a celebration of life—consisted of 119,986 people. The event was held on March 13, 1988.

Largest country line dance   A total of 3,770 people danced for five minutes to "T-R-O-U-B-L-E" by Travis Tritt in Redwood City, CA on July 4, 1996.

Largest hula dance   Over 3,500 hula dancers danced to "Waikiki" by Andy Cummings on Waikiki Beach, Honolulu, HI on September 21, 1996 to celebrate the 50th anniversary of Aloha Festivals.

Longest dancing dragon   On November 3, 1996, a total of 2,431 people brought to life a dancing dragon measuring 6,200 feet from nose to tail. The event took place at Shatin Horse Racecourse in Hong Kong, China.

Fastest flamenco dancer   Solero de Jerez attained 16 heel taps per second in Brisbane, Australia in September 1967.

Lowest limbo dancer   Dennis Walston, alias King Limbo, passed under a bar that was just six inches off the floor in Kent, WA on March 2, 1991.

The record for a performer on roller skates is $4^7/_{10}$ inches, achieved by Syamala Gowri at Hyderabad, Andhra Pradesh, India on May 10, 1993.

Square dance calling   Alan Covacic called for 26 hr. 2 min. for the Wheelers and Dealers Square Dance Club at Halton Royal Air Force Base, Aylesbury, England, November 18–19, 1988.

Tap dancing Fastest tap dancer   The fastest rate for tap dancing is 32 taps per second, by Stephen Gare (Great Britain) in Birmingham, England on March 28, 1990.

Most taps   Roy Castle achieved one million taps in 23 hr. 44 min. at the Guinness World of Records Exhibition, London, England, October 31–November 1, 1985.

Most tap dancers in a routine   On August 18, 1996, 6,554 tap dancers tapped through a single routine outside Macy's department store at 34th Street and Sixth Avenue, New York City.

Longest chorus lines   The longest chorus line numbered up to 120 in some of the early Ziegfeld Follies. In the finale of *A Chorus Line* on the night of September 29, 1983, when it broke the record as the longest-running Broadway show ever, 332 top-hatted "strutters" performed on stage.

On March 28, 1992 in Eastleigh, England, 543 members of the cast of *Showtime News*, a production by Hampshire West Guides, performed a routine choreographed by professional dancer Sally Horsley.

THE CIRCUS

Oldest circus The oldest circus building is Cirque d'Hiver (originally Cirque Napoléon), which opened in Paris, France on December 11, 1852.

Largest circus The most performers in a circus act was 263 people plus 175 animals, in the 1890 Barnum & Bailey Circus tour of the United States.

The record for an animal-free circus is 61, for Cirque du Soleil's tour of Japan in 1992.

Largest circus tent The traveling circus tent of Ringling Bros. and Barnum & Bailey, used on tours in the United States from 1921 to 1924, covered 91,415 square feet. It consisted of a round top 200 feet in diameter with five middle sections, each 60 feet wide.

Largest circus audience An audience of 52,385 attended the Ringling Bros. and Barnum & Bailey Circus at the Superdome, New Orleans, LA on September 14, 1975.

The largest audience in a tent was 16,702, also for Ringling Bros. and Barnum & Bailey, in Concordia, KS on September 13, 1924.

Aerial acts The highest trapeze act was performed by Mike Howard (Great Britain) at heights of 19,600 to 20,300 feet, suspended from a hot-air balloon between Glastonbury and Street, England on August 10, 1995.

Janet May Klemke (U.S.) performed 305 1-arm planges at Medina Shrine Circus, Chicago, IL on January 21, 1938.

Flexible pole The only publicly performed quadruple back somersault on the flexible pole was accomplished by Maksim Dobrovitsky (USSR) of the Yegorov Troupe at the International Circus Festival of Monte Carlo in Monaco on February 4, 1989.

Corina Colonelu Mosoianu (Romania) performed a triple full twisting somersault, at Madison Square Garden, New York City, on April 17, 1984.

Flying return trapeze The back somersault record is a quadruple back, by Miguel Vasquez (Mexico) to Juan Vasquez at Ringling Bros. and Barnum & Bailey Circus, Tucson, AZ on July 10, 1982. The most consecutive triple back somersaults is 135, by Jamie Ibarra (Mexico) to Alejandro Ibarra, between July 23 and October 12, 1989, at various locations in the United States.

High diving Col. Harry A. Froboess (Switzerland) jumped 394 feet into the Bodensee from the airship *Graf Hindenburg* on June 22, 1936.

The greatest height reported for a dive into an air bag is 326 feet, by stuntman Dan Koko, who jumped from the top of Vegas World Hotel and Casino onto a 20 by 40 by 14-foot target on August 13, 1948.

High wire A 7-person pyramid was achieved by the Great Wallendas (Germany) at Wallenda Circus in 1947. The highest high-wire feat (ground

Cirque du Soleil, the world's largest animal-free circus, is a mix of circus arts and street entertainment that features colorful costumes, dramatic lighting and original music. The artists and workers are committed to breaking down old ideas and preconceptions of the traditional big-top circus. At present, Cirque du Soleil has three running shows, one of which is in Las Vegas, NV. The troupe is planning for an upcoming tour of Europe and Asia.

supported) was at a height of 1,350 feet by Philippe Petit (France) between the towers of the World Trade Center, New York on August 7, 1974.

Horseback riding James Robinson (U.S.) performed 23 consecutive somersaults on horseback at Spalding & Rogers Circus, Pittsburgh, PA in 1856. Willy, Beby, and Rene Fredianis (Italy) performed a 3-high column at Nouveau Cirque, Paris, France in 1908. "Poodles" Hanneford (Ireland; b. England) holds the record for running leaps on and off, with 26 at Barnum & Bailey Circus, New York in 1915.

Human arrow "Ariana" (Vesta Gueschkova; Bulgaria) was fired 75 feet from a crossbow at Ringling Bros. and Barnum & Bailey Circus, Tampa, FL on December 27, 1995.

Human cannonball Emanuel Zacchini (Italy) was fired a record 175 feet from a cannon in the United States in 1940.

Human pyramid The weight record is 1,700 pounds, when Tahar Douis supported 12 members of the Hassani Troupe in Birmingham, England on December 17, 1979. The height record is 39 feet, when Josep-Joan Martinez Lozano of the Colla Vella dels Xiquets mounted a 9-high pyramid at Valls, Spain on October 25, 1981.

Plate spinning The greatest number of plates spun simultaneously is 108, by Dave Spathaky of London, England for the *Tarm Pai Du* television program in Thailand on November 23, 1992.

Stilt-walking Speed Roy Luiking covered 328 feet on 1-foot-high stilts in 13.01 seconds in Didam, Netherlands on May 28, 1992.
  In 1892, M. Garisoain (France) walked 4.97 miles from Bayonne to Biarritz on stilts in 42 minutes, at an average speed of 7.10 mph.

Distance Joe Bowen walked 3,008 miles on stilts from Los Angeles, CA to Bowen, KY, February 20–July 26, 1980.

Tallest and heaviest stilts Eddy Wolf ("Steady Eddy") of Loyal, WI mastered stilts measuring 40 ft. 9½ in. from ground to ankle and weighing 57 pounds each when he walked 25 steps without touching his safety handrail wires on August 3, 1988.

Teeter board The Shanghai Acrobats achieved a 6-person-high unaided column in Shanghai, China in 1993.

Trampoline Marco Canestrelli (U.S.) performed a septuple twisting back somersault to bed at Ringling Bros. and Barnum & Bailey Circus, St. Petersburg, FL on January 5, 1979. He also managed a quintuple twisting back somersault to a 2-high column at Ringling Bros. and Barnum & Bailey Circus, New York City on March 28, 1979.

THEATER

Oldest indoor theater   The Teatro Olimpico in Vicenza, Italy was designed in the Roman style by Andrea di Pietro, alias Palladio (1508–80). It was begun three months before his death and finished in 1583. The theater is preserved today in its original form.

Largest theater   The Perth Entertainment Center, Western Australia is the largest theater measured by capacity. It was completed in November 1976 and has 8,003 seats. The stage area is 12,000 square feet.

   The highest-capacity theater in use on Broadway is the Gershwin Theater, with 1,933 seats. Designed by Ralph Alswang, the theater opened in November 1972.

Largest amphitheater   The Colosseum in Rome, Italy, completed in A.D. 80, covers five acres and has a capacity of 87,000. It has a maximum length of 612 feet and a maximum width of 515 feet.

Smallest theater   The smallest regularly operated professional theater in the world is the Piccolo in Juliusstrasse, Hamburg, Germany. It was founded in 1970 and has a maximum capacity of 30 seats.

Largest stage   The Hilton Theater at the Reno Hilton, Reno, NV measures 175 by 241 feet. The stage has three main elevators each capable of raising 40 tons, two $62\frac{1}{2}$-foot-circumference turntables and 800 spotlights.

Longest runs   *The Mousetrap* by Agatha Christie opened on November 25, 1952 at the Ambassador Theatre, London, England and later moved to the St. Martin's Theatre. The 18,503rd performance was on May 9, 1997, and the show has grossed more than £20 million ($36 million).

   The Vicksburg Theater Guild, Vicksburg, MS has been playing the melodrama *Gold in the Hills* by J. Frank Davis discontinuously but every season since 1936.

Revue   The greatest number of performances of any theatrical presentation is 47,250, by *The Golden Horseshoe Revue*, a show staged at Disneyland, Anaheim, CA. It started on July 16, 1955 and closed on October 12, 1986.

Musicals   The off-Broadway musical show *The Fantasticks* by Tom Jones and Harvey Schmidt opened on May 3, 1960. As of August 5, 1997, the show had been performed a record 15,429 times at the Sullivan Street Playhouse, Greenwich Village, New York City.

   Cats is the longest-running musical in the history of the West End, London, England. It opened on May 12, 1981 at the New London Theatre, Drury Lane, where the 6,925th show was performed on July 25, 1997.

   Cats is also the longest running musical in the history of Broadway, New York City. *Cats* made its Broadway debut on October 7, 1982, and had been performed 6,190 times as of August 4, 1997.

CATS 6138

Cats opened on Broadway on October 7, 1982, before many of its most enthusiastic fans were born. On June 19, 1997, with its 6,138th performance, *Cats* became the longest-running Broadway show. *Cats* is the record-holder in London, too, where it has been playing at the New London Theatre in Drury Lane since May 12, 1981.

CATS: PAST

Q. How did the poems of T.S. Eliot come to be the subject of a musical?

Lord Andrew Lloyd Webber, composer: "I've always loved T.S. Eliot's *Old Possum's Book of Practical Cats.* I have always had a special affinity with cats. We always had cats in my home when I was a boy and I've always had cats in all my houses as an adult."

Q. Why was bringing Cats to the stage so difficult initially?

Cameron Mackintosh, producer: "Everybody thought this was the worst idea in the world. When I tried to raise money for the show, people practically held my hand and said, 'There, there, you really should see a doctor.' Some of my oldest investors refused to put money into it on the grounds that they were dog lovers. The interesting thing was that Andrew had had phenomenal success at this point, and had difficulty raising his half. Trevor Nunn, the director, was the artistic director of the Royal Shakespeare Company, and people scoffed at him doing a musical. Everything seemed against it."

Q. But cats are the most popular pets in Britain and America. What was the big problem?

Trevor Nunn, director: "When we were preparing the show, friends of mine were trying outright not to snicker. They thought it was a very unfortunate choice of subject. I was only hoping and praying it would run for six months in London. Then it wouldn't be a complete disgrace and Andrew Lloyd Webber wouldn't have to forfeit the mortgage on his house."

CATS: NOW

Q. Why is Cats *such a success?*

Mackintosh: "The show is a wonderful mixture of dance, irreverence, and theatrical magic. Trevor embraced every theatrical form and put it into the show. That's why the show just exploded in surprise. It was completely different from anything anyone has ever seen or will see again."

Marlene Daniel, *Cats* actress since 1982: "There is no one thing. All the elements contribute. We just go out there and have a ball every time."

Nunn: "*Old Possum's Book of Practical Cats* was written to celebrate the birthdays of children of Eliot's friends. Apparently the parents read over the children's shoulders. We picked up on this in the production. We hoped children of all ages would respond, whether they be 95-year-old children or 5-year-old children. There is no barrier to any person having a delightful experience with *Cats*, because cats themselves are common to all cultures."

Webber: "It's not for me to question or answer why *Cats* was a success. I think the main thing is to enjoy it."

CATS: FOREVER

Q. How has Cats *changed your view of theater?*

Mackintosh: "I dreamed that one day I would have a success in London and one day, perhaps, if I was very lucky, I might have a show open on Broadway. For me to have the longest show in the history of Broadway is slightly mind-boggling."

Nunn: "It continues to amaze and delight me. I believe it does give great pleasure to people. It gives me satisfaction that a new generation of people now has access to the show."

Daniel: "This show has good songs and good dancing. It's not too serious, and not too demanding. The people who come to the show are so enthusiastic about it."

Q. How long will Cats *go on?*

Webber: "Obviously I'm hopeful that it will run as long as possible. It somehow has found a universal appeal with families and particularly children."

CATS HAS SEEN . . .

6,138 performances (as of June 19, 1997)
$2.2 billion in box office receipts
8.25 million audience members
7 Tony Awards
4 national tours
42 road productions
231 performers
1.5 million pounds of dry ice
2,706 pounds of yak hair

AND THE WINNER IS . . .

The Last Night of Ballyhoo won the 1997 Tony Award for Best Play. The award earned the play's author, Alfred Uhry, the distinction of being the third artist to win an Academy Award, a Tony Award and a Pulitzer Prize. The honor took the playwright by surprise. "I was not aware of it until my producer's husband said to me at the ceremony that if I won this Tony, I would have won the triple crown," says Uhry.

Frank Loesser and Stephen Sondheim are the other triple crown winners. Ironically, Uhry got his first start in show business writing lyrics and jingles for a music company owned by Loesser. "I got weekly tutorials from Frank Loesser for three or four years. He said, 'Every syllable counts. Don't put one syllable into your work that you can't defend.' " Adds Uhry, "That's why my work is a little shorter than most. I don't want to waste the audience's time. I want to make sure my work is clear."

"The Tony was the one I always dreamed about when I was a kid in Atlanta," says Uhry. The other two awards were for his work Driving Miss Daisy. "Winning the Oscar was like entering Wonderland," Uhry recalls. "When people like Jack Nicholson and Warren Beatty come over to congratulate you, it's just like a fantasy. It was surreal and amazing. I still don't quite believe it." The Pulitzer was a less giddy experience, but one of tremendous significance to Uhry: "The Pulitzer is the acme of awards for anyone."

Entertainment award shows are very popular, but their merits are the subject of debate and controversy. Uhry is not one of the critics. "I think my awards have a dual significance. Recognition by your peers and your colleagues is terribly important. First, it's a tribute to your own work and second, it's always good for business." Uhry adds, "There is not a big budget to advertise straight plays on Broadway. But since we won the Tony, everyone knows who we are."

Now that he's had television experience, what's next? The Emmys? "Miss America is next," Uhry quips.

ON THE RECORD

MULTIPLE AWARD WINNERS

Three people have won an Oscar, a Tony and a Pulitzer Prize award: Frank Loesser, Stephen Sondheim and Alfred Uhry.

SECOND TO NONE: WILLIAM SHAKESPEARE

*H*e is the world's most famous playwright. He was born on either April 22 or 23, 1564, and lived 52 years. In that time he wrote 37 solo plays, as well as play collaborations and poetry. From *Two Gentlemen of Verona* to *Henry VIII*, every line has become a treasure of the English language. Four centuries later, William Shakespeare lives on through his words, in stage productions, films, and the printed page. And he has never been so popular in America. The Shakespeare Association of America reports a membership increase of one third since 1990. With 60 percent of colleges and universities teaching Shakespeare, he is the most studied author of all.

"Shakespeare is an icon of Anglo-American heritage. There are very few white Anglo-Saxon Protestants in my classes. The children of immigrants want to study an assured canonical figure."
—*Maurice Charney, Rutgers University*

Hamlet is Shakespeare's longest play, with words. Kenneth Branagh's *Hamlet* was the most recent film edition of the play. Other film Hamlets have ranged from Laurence Olivier to Mel Gibson. As written, the part of Hamlet is Shakespeare's longest speaking part: at 11,610 words, memorizing it—not to mention performing it—takes some doing.

By the Book

The biggest-ever edition of *The Norton Shakespeare* was published in 1997. At 3,420 pages, it boasts all Shakespeare's works, including three versions of *King Lear*.

Marathon Man

The Joseph Papp Public Theater/New York Shakespeare Festival began its Shakespeare Marathon in 1987 with *A Midsummer Night's Dream* and wrapped it up in 1997 with *Henry VIII*. In between, the Marathon featured the complete canon of Shakespeare's plays. "The glaring thing about Shakespeare is that he is contemporary," says George C. Wolfe, director of the New York Shakespeare Festival. "His plays pulse with an intimacy and urgency that resonate one hundred percent with contemporary American audiences.

"New York City for some ridiculous reason acts like it's a cultural colony of Great Britain. 'We lowly Americans; we can't do the classics like the Brits.' By feeding on a steady diet of wonderful, brilliant, erotic, messy, exhilarating classical work by casts of primarily American actors, both audiences and artists have surrendered a significant portion of that inferiority thought process."

"The Shakespeare Marathon proclaims Shakespeare alive." —*Joseph Papp, director of the New York Public Theater*

Emma Thompson as Regan and Sir John Gielgud as King Lear.

The World's Best-Known Theater Company

The Royal Shakespeare Company plays to audiences of more than a million a year, and is blessed with the largest performing arts sponsorship in Great Britain. In operation since 1879, the Company has staged hundreds of versions of Shakespeare's plays. The most widely produced Shakespeare play, according to the Company, is *Twelfth Night.*

"If you are rehearsing a Shakespeare play, it's inevitable with intelligent directors and a good team of actors that the issues that are debated in the rehearsal room are quite extraordinary: love, life, death, war, peace, rage, religion, God, hell, everything." —*Ben Kingsley, actor*

The oldest complete U.S. feature film was found in 1997 in the Portland, Oregon, basement of William Buffum. The 1912 movie version of *Richard III* is a silent film featuring Frederick C. Warde in the title role. The film was shown at the American Film Institute Film Festival in October, along with *Looking for Richard*, a film about making a film of *Richard III*, starring Al Pacino.

Favorite Line

"When, we are born, we cry, that we are come to this great stage of fools."—*Lear 4.6 182-183* Kenneth Branagh, actor/director

Speedy Shakespeare

Sean Shannon recited Hamlet's soliloquy ("To be or not to be...") in 24 seconds.

Shakespeare's Around

Nobody is sure exactly when London's first Globe Theatre was built, only that by 1599 Shakespeare was performing there and writing plays for its stage. The Globe was destroyed by fire in 1613, during a performance of *Henry VIII*. Replicas of The Globe have been built in several places, including Stratford, Connecticut and Stratford, Ontario, but the most famous (and newest) stands on the banks of the Thames in London. It opened in 1997. Since it's open to the sky, like the original, audiences come with their raincoats—umbrellas are not allowed.

Is Shakespeare Accessible? or Fighting the "Cringe Factor"

What is the greatest challenge of bringing a Shakespeare play to the silver screen? Actor/director Kenneth Branagh (*Henry V, Much Ado About Nothing, Hamlet*) gives a succinct answer: "Making it real." Branagh's films have helped bring the bard to a wide cinema audience. "We all owe Ken Branagh a debt of gratitude," says Adrian Noble, artistic director of The Royal Shakespeare Company.

Just how accessible is Shakespeare to the general public? "So much of Shakespeare is in the language," says Noble. He gives examples: "'The play's the thing.' 'To be or not to be.' 'The course of true love never did run smooth.' 'Now is the winter of our discontent.' " Yet, if you ask many people if they want to read Shakespeare, they'll shun the idea. How do you explain that paradox?

"I think the education system has a lot to answer for. There is a fear of Shakespeare because of how it is taught in school. In Australia they call it the cringe factor. People feel humbled by what they think is culturally superior."

Can Shakespeare's language appeal to today's sound-bite-oriented audiences? "One film has been more successful than all the others—Baz Luhrman's *William Shakespeare's Romeo and Juliet*," says director Trevor Nunn (*Twelfth Night*). *William Shakespeare's Romeo and Juliet* hit number one at the box office when it opened in 1997, and it grossed nearly $50 million—impressive for a writer whose works are usually confined to smaller art theaters. "While the film is inventive visually, it is almost overnumbered with the small amounts of Shakespeare language the director has allowed to stay in. Shakespeare's text was cut by 75 percent."

"*Henry VIII* seems like it was written about politicians of today." —*Julie Harris, actor*

Leonardo DiCaprio and Claire Danes as Romeo and Juliet.

Most ardent theatergoer Dr. H. Howard Hughes, Prof. Emeritus of Texas Wesleyan College, Fort Worth, TX attended 6,136 shows in the period 1957–87.

Greatest loss The greatest loss sustained by a theatrical show was by the American producers of the Royal Shakespeare Company's musical *Carrie*, which closed after five performances on Broadway on May 17, 1988 at a cost of $7 million.

Tony Awards Hal Prince has won 17 Tonys—the awards of the American Theater Wing—the most for any individual. Prince has won a total of 9 awards as a producer and 8 as a director.

Three plays have won five Tonys: *A Man for All Seasons* (1962), *Who's Afraid of Virginia Woolf?* (1963) and *Amadeus* (1981).

The only person to win five Tonys in starring roles is Julie Harris, in *I Am a Camera* (1952), *The Lark* (1956), *Forty Carats* (1969), *The Last of Mrs. Lincoln* (1973) and *The Belle of Amherst* (1977).

Multiple award winners Three people have won an Oscar, a Tony and a Pulitzer Prize award: Frank Loesser, Stephen Sondheim and Alfred Uhry.

One-man shows The longest run of one-man shows is 849, by Victor Borge (Denmark) in his *Comedy in Music* from October 2, 1953 through January 21, 1956 at the Golden Theater, Broadway, New York City.

The aggregate record for one-man shows is 1,700 performances of *Brief Lives* by Roy Dotrice (Great Britain), including 400 straight at the Mayfair Theatre, London, England ending on July 20, 1974. He was on stage for more than 2½ hours per performance of this 17th-century monologue and required three hours for makeup and an hour for removal of makeup, thus totaling 40 weeks in the chair.

Most durable performer Kanmi Fujiyama played the lead role in 10,288 performances by comedy company Sochiku Shikigeki from November 1966 to June 1983.

Most durable understudy In 1994, Nancy Seabrooke, age 79, retired from the company of *The Mousetrap* in London, England, having understudied the part of "Mrs. Boyle" for 15 years or 6,240 performances.

Greatest advance sales *Miss Saigon*, produced by Cameron Mackintosh, opened on Broadway in April 1991 after generating record advance sales of $36 million.

Most roles The greatest recorded number of theatrical, film and television roles portrayed is 3,395 since 1951 by Jan Leighton (U.S.).

Theatrical roles Kanzaburo Nakamura performed in 806 Kabuki titles from November 1926 to January 1987. Since each title in this classical Japanese theatrical form lasts 25 days, he gave 20,150 performances.

Longest Shakespeare play *Hamlet* is the longest of Shakespeare's 37 plays. Written in 1604, it has 4,042 lines or 29,551 words. The longest of Shakespeare's 1,277 speaking parts is the role of Hamlet, with 11,610 words.

Largest arts festival   The largest arts festival is the annual Edinburgh Fringe Festival, held in Edinburgh, Scotland (instituted in 1947). In 1993, its record year, 582 groups gave 14,108 performances of 1,643 shows between August 15 and September 4.

The largest arts festival is the annual Edinburgh Fringe Festival.

MOVIES

Highest box office gross   The box office champion of first-run films is Universal's *Jurassic Park*, which had earned over $913 million worldwide up to June 1997.

In May 1997, Steven Spielberg's *The Lost World* (Universal) passed the $100 million mark in 5½ days, faster than any other movie.

The Lost World also brought in the highest opening-day box office gross and highest single-day gross by bringing in $22 million on May 23, 1997.

Biggest opening weekend (re-released movie)   To celebrate the 20th anniversary of its original release in 1977, *Star Wars* was re-released in North American theaters on January 31, 1997. With 4½ minutes of extra footage and digitally enhanced images, the two-decade-old space adventure generated a record $36.2 million in box office earnings over its opening weekend.

Highest-grossing foreign language film   The highest-grossing foreign language film in the United States is Michael Radford's *Il Postino* ("The Postman"), which had earned a domestic gross of $21,845,977 as of May 28, 1997.

Best budget to box office ratio   The $350,000 Australian production *Mad Max* (1980) had a record budget to box office ratio of 1:285, grosssing $100 million in its first two years of international distribution.

Most profitable series   The most successful movie series is the *Star Wars* trilogy. As of August 1997, its worldwide gross, including special editions, was $1.776 billion.

On May 23, 1997, *The Lost World* smashed the records for both opening day and single-day box office gross.

Largest loss MGM's *Cutthroat Island* (1995) cost over $100 million to produce, promote and distribute. It grossed $2.3 million in its first weekend, and by May 1996, it had reportedly earned back just $11 million.

Largest output India's production of feature-length movies was a record 948 in 1990, and its annual output has exceeded 700 every year since 1979.

Longest movie The longest movie commercially released in its entirety was Edgar Reitz's 25-hr.-32-min. *Die Zweite Heimat* (Germany, 1992), premiered in Munich, September 5–9, 1992.

Largest movie premiere *A Few Good Men*, starring Tom Cruise, Demi Moore and Jack Nicholson, was simultaneously released in over 50 countries by Columbia Pictures in 1992.

Tom Cruise's 1996 *Jerry Maguire* was his fifth consecutive movie to gross over $100 million, the longest streak for any actor.

Twenty years on, the force is still with *Star Wars*. The anniversary
re-release set box office records worldwide.

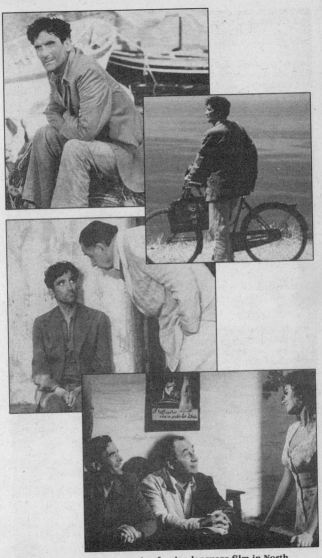

Il Postino is the highest-grossing foreign language film in North America.

Longest first run   The longest first run of a movie in the same theater was by *Emmanuelle* (France, 1974), which was seen by 3,268,874 people during the 10 yr. 32 weeks it played at the Paramount City Cinema, Paris, France between June 1974 and February 1985.

Longest directorial career   The directorial career of King Vidor lasted for 67 years, beginning with the 2-reel comedy *Hurricane in Galveston* (1913) and culminating in another short, a documentary called *The Metaphor* (1980).

Oldest director   The Dutch director Joris Ivens (1898–1989) made the Franco-Italian co-production *Une Histoire de Vent* in 1988 at age 89. He made his directorial debut with the Dutch movie *De Brug* in 1928.

Hollywood   George Cukor (1899–1983) made his 50th and final movie, MGM's *Rich and Famous*, in 1981 at age 81.

Youngest director   The movie *Lex the Wonderdog* was written, produced, and directed by Sydney Ling (b. 1959) when he was 13 years old. Ling was therefore the youngest director of a professionally made feature-length movie.

Most successful director   Steven Spielberg is the most successful filmmaker ever. Collectively, his movies had grossed more than $4.93 billion as of August 15, 1997.

Youngest producer   Steven Paul was 20 years old when he produced and directed *Falling in Love Again* (1980), starring Elliott Gould and Susannah York.

Most durable performers   The record for the longest screen career is 83 years, held by German actor Curt Bois (1900–91), who made his debut in *Der Fidele Bauer* at age eight. His last movie was *Wings of Desire* (1988).
   American actress Helen Hayes (1900–93) first appeared on screen at age 10 in *Jean and the Calico Doll*, with much of her later work being for television. Her last screen role was in *Divine Mercy, No Escape* (1988) in a career lasting 78 years.

Oldest performer   The oldest screen performer in a speaking role was Jeanne Louise Calment (1875–1997), who portrayed herself in the 1990 Canadian movie *Vincent and Me*. (*See also* OLDEST PERSON.)

Most leading roles   John Wayne appeared in 153 movies from *The Drop Kick* (1927) to *The Shootist* (1976). In all but 11 he played the lead.

Greatest age span portrayed   Dustin Hoffman was 33 years old when he played the title role in *Little Big Man* (1970) from age 17 to age 121.

Most generations of screen actors   There are four generations of screen actors in the Redgrave family. Roy Redgrave made his screen debut in 1911 and continued to appear in Australian movies until 1920. His son, Sir Michael Redgrave, married actress Rachel Kempson, and their two daughters Vanessa and Lynn and son Corin are all actors. Vanessa's two daughters Joely and Natasha and Corin's daughter Jemma are also actresses.

Longest contract to one studio Lewis Stone, best known for his portrayal of Judge Hardy in the Andy Hardy films, became an MGM contract artist at the studio's inception in 1924 and remained with them until his death in 1953, for a total of 29 years.

Most portrayed character The character most frequently recurring on the screen is Sherlock Holmes, created by Sir Arthur Conan Doyle (1859–1930). The Baker Street sleuth has been portrayed by 75 actors in 211 movies since 1900.

In horror movies, the character most often portrayed is Count Dracula, created by the Irish writer Bram Stoker (1847–1912). Representations of the Count or his immediate descendants outnumber those of his closest rival, Frankenstein's monster, by 161 to 117.

The cartoon character most often portrayed is Zorro, with 68 movies to date.

Most movies seen Gwilym Hughes of Dolgellau, Wales had seen 22,990 movies as of February 28, 1997. He saw his first movie in 1953 while in the hospital.

Most costumes The largest number of costumes used for any one movie was 32,000 for the 1951 movie *Quo Vadis*.

Most costume changes Madonna appeared in 85 different costumes in her role as Eva Perón in *Evita* (1996). The costumes were designed by Penny Rose

Madonna wore 85 different costumes in *Evita*. Accessories included 39 hats, 45 pairs of shoes, 56 pairs of earrings and 42 hairstyles.

and were based on Evita's own clothes, many of which lie in an Argentinian bank vault.

Most expensive costume   Constance Bennett's sable coat in *Madame X* was valued at $50,000.

The most expensive costume made for a movie was Edith Head's mink-and-sequin dance costume worn by Ginger Rogers in *Lady in the Dark*. It cost Paramount $35,000.

The ruby slippers worn by Judy Garland in *The Wizard of Oz* were sold on June 2, 1988 to a mystery buyer at Christie's, New York City for $165,000.

Largest studios   The largest complex of movie studios in the world is the one at Universal City, Los Angeles, CA. The back lot contains 479 buildings and there are 31 sound stages on the 420-acre site.

Largest studio stage   The 007 stage at Pinewood Studios, Buckinghamshire, England was built in 1976 for the James Bond movie *The Spy Who Loved Me*. It measures 336 by 139 by 41 feet and can accommodate 1.2 million gallons of water, a full-scale 672,000-ton oil tanker and three scaled-down nuclear submarines.

Largest movie set   Veniero Colosanti and John Moore designed a Roman Forum measuring 1,312 by 754 feet for Samuel Bronston's production of *The Fall of the Roman Empire* (1964). It was built on a 55-acre site outside Madrid, Spain. It took 1,100 workers seven months to lay 170,000 cement blocks, erect 22,000 feet of stairways, 601 columns and 350 statues, and construct 27 buildings.

Largest number of extras   It is believed that over 300,000 extras appeared in the funeral scene of Sir Richard Attenborough's *Gandhi* (1982).

Most animals in a movie   *Around the World in Eighty Days* (1956) had a total of 8,552 animals: 3,800 sheep, 2,448 buffalo, 950 donkeys, 800 horses, 512 monkeys, 17 bulls, 15 elephants, 6 skunks and 4 ostriches.

Most expensive prop   The most expensive single prop used for a movie was the full-scale replica of a Spanish galleon built for Roman Polanski's *Pirates* (1986) at a cost of $10.2 million. Its construction kept 2,000 Maltese shipyard workers in jobs for a whole year.

The paintings and sculptures assembled for the art gallery scenes in Universal's *Legal Eagles* (1986) were worth $10 million. They included works by Picasso, Willem de Kooning and Roy Lichtenstein.

THE OSCARS

Most Oscars   Walt Disney (1901–66) won more Oscars than any other person. The physical count comprises 20 statuettes and 12 other plaques and certificates, including posthumous awards.

Katharine Hepburn won four Oscars in starring roles, for *Morning Glory* (1932/33), *Guess Who's Coming to Dinner* (1967), *The Lion in Winter* (1968) and *On Golden Pond* (1981).

Six actors have won two Oscars for Best Actor. Spencer Tracy won for

Captains Courageous (1937) and *Boys Town* (1938); Fredric March for *Dr. Jekyll and Mr. Hyde* (1932) and *The Best Years of Our Lives* (1946); Gary Cooper for *Sergeant York* (1941) and *High Noon* (1952); Marlon Brando for *On the Waterfront* (1954) and *The Godfather* (1972); Dustin Hoffman for *Kramer vs. Kramer* (1979) and *Rain Man* (1988); and Tom Hanks for *Philadelphia* (1993) and *Forrest Gump* (1994).

Most Oscars (movie) The movie with the most awards is *Ben-Hur* (1959) with 11.

Most nominations The most nominations, 14, went to *All About Eve* (1950), which won 6 awards.

Aardman Animation of Bristol, England has received six consecutive Oscar nominations since 1991.

Youngest winners The youngest winner in competition was Tatum O'Neal, who was 10 when she received the award in 1974 for Best Supporting Actress in *Paper Moon* (1973). Shirley Temple was awarded an honorary Oscar at age five in 1934.

Oldest winner The oldest recipient of an Oscar was Jessica Tandy, who won Best Actress for *Driving Miss Daisy* in 1990 at the age of 80.

Aardman Animation has received six consecutive Oscar nominations for films featuring its animated creations, including Wallace and Gromit.

Longest acceptance speech   Greer Garson's speech on receiving the Best Actress award for *Mrs. Miniver* (1942) lasted 5 min. 30 sec.

MOVIE THEATERS

Largest movie theater   Radio City Music Hall, New York City, opened on December 27, 1932, with 5,945 (now 5,910) seats.

Kinepolis, in Brussels, Belgium, has 26 theaters with seating for 160–70 people. It also has an IMAX theater, with a screen measuring 65 ft. 7 in. by 98 ft. 5 in., that can seat 450 people. The total seating capacity of the complex is around 6,000.

Largest movie theater attendance   China had a peak mainland movie theater attendance figure of 21.8 billion in 1988.

Largest movie screen   The largest permanent movie screen is in the Panasonic IMAX theater at Darling Harbour, Sydney, Australia. The screen measures 117 feet by 97 feet.

The Six Flags Great America Pictorium, Gurnee, IL has a 3D screen of 96 by 70$\frac{1}{2}$ feet.

Largest image wall   The European Park of the Moving Image contains a wall of 850 video screens with a total surface area of 1,744 square feet.

SPORTS

BASEBALL

THE MAJOR LEAGUES

Hitting

Highest batting average (career)   Ty Cobb, Detroit Tigers (AL), 1905–26; Philadelphia Athletics (AL), 1927–28 holds the all-time mark for highest batting average at .367. Cobb compiled his record from 4,191 hits in 11,429 at-bats.

Highest batting average (season)   The highest batting average single-season record is .438, by Hugh Duffy, Boston Beaneaters (NL) in 1894. Duffy compiled 236 hits in 539 at-bats. The modern record is .424, by Rogers Hornsby, St. Louis Cardinals (NL), in 1924. Hornsby compiled 227 hits in 536 at-bats.

The Yankees' Tino Martinez and Mariners' Ken Griffey Jr. got off to record-breaking starts in 1997. Martinez set a new record for the most RBI's in April, and Griffey gained the equivalent mark for most home runs.

Most hits (career) The career record for the most hits is 4,256, by Pete Rose, Cincinnati Reds (NL), 1963–78, 1984–86; Philadelphia Phillies (NL), 1979–83; Montreal Expos (NL), 1984. Rose compiled his record hits total in 14,053 at-bats.

Most hits (season) George Sisler of the St. Louis Browns (AL) achieved a record 257 hits in 1920, in 631 at-bats.

Most hits (game) The most hits in a single game is nine, by John Burnett, Cleveland Indians (AL), during an 18-inning game on July 10, 1932. The record for a nine-inning game is seven hits, by two players: Wilbert Robinson, Baltimore Orioles (NL), on June 10, 1892; Rennie Stennett, Pittsburgh Pirates (NL), on September 16, 1975.

Most home runs (career) Hank Aaron holds the major league career record with 755 home runs—733 for the Milwaukee/Atlanta Braves (NL) 1954–74 and 22 for the Milwaukee Brewers (AL) 1975–76.

Most home runs (season) The major league record for home runs in a season is 61, by Roger Maris for the New York Yankees (AL) in 162 games in 1961.

Most home runs (game) The record for the most home runs in a game is four, achieved by 12 players: Bobby Lowe, Boston (NL), May 30, 1894; Ed Delahanty, Philadelphia Phillies (NL), July 13, 1896; Lou Gehrig, New York Yankees (AL), June 3, 1932; Chuck Klein, Philadelphia Phillies (NL), July 10, 1936; Pat Seerey, Chicago White Sox (AL), July 18, 1948; Gil Hodges, Brooklyn Dodgers (NL), August 31, 1950; Joe Adcock, Milwaukee Braves (NL), July 31, 1954; Rocky Colavito, Cleveland Indians (AL), June 10, 1959; Willie Mays, San Francisco Giants (NL), April 30, 1961; Mike Schmidt, Philadelphia Phillies (NL), April 17, 1976; Bob Horner, Atlanta Braves (NL), July 6, 1986; and Mark Whiten, St. Louis Cardinals (NL), September 7, 1993. Klein, Schmidt and Seerey matched the record in extra-inning games.

Longest home run The longest measured home run in a major league game was 643 feet, by Mickey Mantle for the New York Yankees vs. Detroit Tigers on September 10, 1960 at Briggs Stadium in Detroit.

Most RBI's (career) The career record for the most RBI's is 2,297, by Hank Aaron, Milwaukee/Atlanta Braves (NL), 1954–74; Milwaukee Brewers (AL), 1975–76.

Most RBI's (season) The most RBI's in one season is 190 achieved by Hack Wilson of the Chicago Cubs (NL) in 1930.

Most RBI's (game) The most RBI's in a single game is 12, achieved by two players: Jim Bottomley, St. Louis Cardinals (NL), on September 16, 1924; and Mark Whiten, St. Louis Cardinals (NL), on September 7, 1993.

Most runs scored (career) The career record for the most runs scored is 2,245, by Ty Cobb, Detroit Tigers (AL), 1905–26; Philadelphia Athletics (AL), 1927–28.

CATCHING THE
RECORDS

"I became aware of the record around late July when I hit my 30th home run," says Todd Hundley, the New York Mets catcher. "Someone told me that the record for home runs by a catcher was 40. I thought I could hit 11 more."

As Hundley gained on former Brooklyn Dodger Roy Campanella's mark, the New York City press zeroed in on the home run chase. The catcher

ON THE RECORD

MOST HOME RUNS IN ONE SEASON

The most home runs hit by a catcher in one season is 41, hit by Todd Hundley of the New York Mets in 1996.

admits that the media spotlight made his quest more difficult: "It was distracting. I'd be lying if I didn't say that. I had to start getting to the ballpark an hour earlier than usual to give interviews. But it didn't really hit me until we went into Los Angeles and Roy Campanella's widow was there."

Hundley credits his father, Randy, a former Chicago Cubs catcher, with helping him stay focused: "He always pounded into me, 'Have fun, don't get caught up in the pressure, don't take it too seriously.'" Former Mets manager Dallas Green's philosophy helped Hundley during his home run spree. "Dallas taught me how to play a kid's game like a man," says Hundley. "He'd say, 'No excuses, I don't want to hear excuses. Just get the job done. Get the hit.'"

At 28, Hundley has earned a reputation as one of baseball's most durable catchers. He was behind the plate for 150 games during his record-setting season, no mean feat itself. "You have to take care of yourself off the field. Eat right and be sure to work in the weight room. Build the muscles around the knees and hips because you are going to squat 200 to 250 times a game."

The great baseball sluggers are renowned for launching moonshot home runs over the outfield fence. Hundley wants to go a step further and go into outer space himself: "I would love to be an astronaut and go into a different world. I've gone down to see the shuttle launch. It's just such an unbelievable experience." And his ambitions back down on terra firma? "I would love nothing more than to win a World Series in New York City," he says.

Most runs scored (season) The most runs scored in a single-season is 196, by Billy Hamilton, Philadelphia Phillies (NL), in 1894. The modern-day record is 177 runs, scored by Babe Ruth, New York Yankees (AL), in 1921.

Most runs scored (game) The most runs scored in a game is seven, by Guy Hecker, Louisville Colonels (American Association), on August 15, 1886. The modern-day record is six runs scored, achieved by 12 players, 10 in the National League and two in the American League.

Most total bases (career) The career record for total bases is 6,856, by Hank Aaron, Milwaukee/Atlanta Braves (NL), 1954–74; Milwaukee Brewers (AL),1975–76. Aaron's record includes 2,294 singles, 624 doubles, 98 triples and 755 home runs.

Most total bases (season) The record for the most bases in a single season is 457, by Babe Ruth of the New York Yankees (AL) in 1921. Ruth's total comprised 85 singles, 44 doubles, 16 triples and 59 home runs.

Most total bases (game) The record for the most total bases is 18, by Joe Adcock, Milwaukee Braves (NL) on July 31, 1954. Adcock hit four home runs and a double.

Most grand slams (career) Lou Gehrig of the New York Yankees (AL) hit 23 grand slams from 1923 to 1939.

Most grand slams (season) Don Mattingly of the New York Yankees (AL) hit six grand slams in 1987.

Most grand slams (game) The record for the most grand slams hit in a game is two, achieved by eight players: Tony Lazzeri, New York Yankees (AL), May 24, 1936; Jim Tabor, Boston Red Sox (AL), July 4, 1939; Rudy York, Boston Red Sox (AL), July 27, 1946; Jim Gentile, Baltimore Orioles (AL), May 9, 1961; Tony Cloninger, Atlanta Braves (NL), July 3, 1966; Jim Northrup, Detroit Tigers (AL), June 24, 1968; Frank Robinson, Baltimore Orioles (AL), June 26, 1970; and Robin Ventura, Chicago White Sox (AL), September 4, 1995. Cloninger is the only player from the National League to achieve this feat, and he was a pitcher.

Most walks (career) The career record for the most walks is 2,056, by Babe Ruth, Boston Red Sox (AL), 1914–19; New York Yankees (AL), 1920–34; Boston Braves (NL), 1935.

Most walks (season) Babe Ruth of the New York Yankees (AL) walked 170 times in 1923.

Most strikeouts (career) The record for the most strikeouts in a career is 2,597, by Reggie Jackson, Kansas City/Oakland Athletics (AL), 1967–75, 1987; Baltimore Orioles (AL), 1976; New York Yankees (AL), 1977–81; California Angels (AL), 1982–86.

Most strikeouts (season) Bobby Bonds of the San Francisco Giants (NL) holds the record for the most strikeouts (189) in 1970.

Most consecutive hits The record for the most consecutive hits is 12, achieved by two players: Pinky Higgins, Boston Red Sox (AL), over four games, June 19–21, 1938; and Walt (Moose) Dropo, Detroit Tigers (AL), over three games, July 14–15, 1952.

Most consecutive hits (games) Joe DiMaggio of the New York Yankees (AL) hit in 56 consecutive games from May 15 through July 16, 1941. During the streak, DiMaggio added 91 hits in 223 at-bats: 56 singles, 16 doubles, 4 triples and 15 home runs.

Most consecutive home runs (game) The record for the most consecutive home runs is four, achieved by five players: Bobby Lowe, Boston (NL), May 30, 1894; Lou Gehrig, New York Yankees (AL), June 3, 1932; Rocky Colavito, Cleveland Indians (AL), June 10, 1959; and Mike Schmidt, Philadelphia Phillies (NL), April 17, 1976.

Most consecutive home runs (games) Three players hit home runs in a record eight games in a row: Dale Long, Pittsburgh Pirates (NL), May 19–28, 1956; Don Mattingly, New York Yankees (AL), July 8–18, 1987; Ken Griffey Jr., Seattle Mariners (AL), July 20–28, 1993.

PITCHING

Most wins (career) The career record for the most wins is 511, by Cy Young, Cleveland Spiders (NL), 1890–98; St. Louis Cardinals (NL), 1899–1900; Boston Red Sox (AL), 1901–08; Cleveland Indians (AL), 1909–11; Boston Braves (NL), 1911.

Most wins (season) The all-time record for the most single-season wins is 60, by "Old Hoss" Radbourn, Providence Grays (NL), in 1884. The modern-day record is 41, by Jack Chesbro, New York Yankees (AL), in 1904.

Most strikeouts (career) The record for the most strikeouts is 5,714, by Nolan Ryan, New York Mets (NL), 1966–71; California Angels (AL), 1972–79; Houston Astros (NL), 1980–88; Texas Rangers (AL), 1989–93.

Most strikeouts (season) The all-time record for the most strikeouts in a season is 513, by Matt Kilroy, Baltimore (American Association), in 1886. The modern-day record is 383, by Nolan Ryan, California Angels (AL), in 1973.

Roger Clemens tied his own mark for most strikeouts in a game (20) on September 18, 1996.

Most strikeouts (game—extra innings) Tom Cheney of the Washington Senators (AL) pitched 21 strikeouts on September 12, 1962 in a 16-inning game.

Most strikeouts (game—nine innings)   Roger Clemens of the Boston Red Sox (AL) pitched 20 strikeouts on April 29, 1986 and on September 18, 1996.

Most innings pitched (career)   The career record for the most innings pitched is 7,356, by Cy Young, Cleveland Spiders (NL), 1890–98; St. Louis Cardinals (NL), 1899–1900; Boston Red Sox (AL), 1901–08; Cleveland Indians (AL), 1909–11; Boston Braves (NL), 1911.

Most innings pitched (season)   Will White of the Cincinnati Reds (NL) pitched 680 innings in 1879. The modern-day record is 464, by Ed Walsh, Chicago White Sox (AL), in 1908.

Most shutouts (career)   The career record for the most shutouts is 110, by Walter Johnson, Washington Senators (AL), 1907–27.

Most shutouts (season)   The most shutouts in one season is 16, achieved by two pitchers: George Bradley, St. Louis (NL), in 1876; and Grover Alexander, Philadelphia Phillies (NL), in 1916.

Lowest earned run average (career, min. 2,000 innings)   The lowest ERA is 1.82, by Ed Walsh, Chicago White Sox (AL), 1904–16; Boston Braves (NL), 1917.

Widest ERA differential (min. 200 innings)   In 1994, Greg Maddux, Atlanta Braves (NL) had an ERA of 1.56, 2.56 below the league's overall average.

Most losses (career)   The career record for the most losses is 315, by Cy Young, Cleveland Spiders (NL), 1890–98; St. Louis Cardinals (NL), 1899–1900; Boston Red Sox (AL), 1901–08; Cleveland Indians (AL), 1909–11; Boston Braves (NL), 1911.

Most losses (season)   The all-time single-season record for the most losses is 48, by John Coleman, Philadelphia Phillies (NL), in 1883. The modern-day record is 29, by Vic Willis, Boston Braves (NL), in 1905.

Most walks (career)   The career record for the most walks is 2,795, by Nolan Ryan of the New York Mets (NL), 1966–71; California Angels (AL), 1972–79; Houston Astros (NL), 1980–88; and Texas Rangers (AL), 1989–93.

Most walks (season)   The all-time single-season record for the most walks is 289, by Amos Rusie, New York Giants (NL), in 1890. The modern-day record is 208, by Bob Feller, Cleveland Indians (AL), in 1938.

Most walks (game)   The most walks given up in a game is 16, by two pitchers: Bruno Haas, Philadelphia Athletics (AL), on June 23, 1915 in a nine-inning game; Tom Byrne, St. Louis Browns (AL) on August 22, 1951 in a 13-inning game.

Most complete games (career)   The career record for the most complete games is 749, by Cy Young, Cleveland Spiders (NL), 1890–98; St. Louis Cardinals (NL), 1899–1900; Boston Red Sox (AL), 1901–08; Cleveland Indians (AL), 1909–11; Boston Braves (NL), 1911. The modern-day record is 531, by Walter Johnson, Washington Senators (AL), 1907–27.

Most complete games (season)   The all-time record for the most complete games in a season is 75, by Will White of the Cincinnati Reds (NL) in 1879. The modern-day record is 48, by Jack Chesbro, New York Yankees (AL), in 1904.

Most saves (career)   The career record for the most saves is 478, by Lee Smith, Chicago Cubs (NL), 1980–87; Boston Red Sox (AL), 1988–90; St. Louis Cardinals (NL), 1990–93; New York Yankees (AL), 1993; Baltimore Orioles (AL), 1994; California Angels (AL), 1995–96; Cincinnati Reds (NL), 1996; and Montreal Expos (NL), 1997.

Most saves (season)   Bobby Thigpen of the Chicago White Sox (AL) made a record 57 saves in 1990.

Most no-hitters (career)   The career record for the most no-hitters is seven, by Nolan Ryan: California Angels vs. Kansas City Royals (3–0), May 15, 1973; California Angels vs. Detroit Tigers (6–0), July 15, 1973; California Angels vs. Minnesota Twins (4–0), September 28, 1974; California Angels vs. Baltimore Orioles (1–0), June 1, 1975; Houston Astros vs. Los Angeles Dodgers (5–0), September 26, 1981; Texas Rangers vs. Oakland Athletics (5–0), June 11, 1990; and Texas Rangers vs. Toronto Blue Jays (3–0), May 1, 1991.

Most no-hitters (season)   Four players hold the single-season record of two no-hitters: Johnny Vander Meer, Cincinnati Reds (NL), 1938; Allie Reynolds, New York Yankees (AL), 1951; Virgil Trucks, Detroit Tigers (AL) 1952; and Nolan Ryan, California Angels (AL), 1973.

Most consecutive games won   Carl Hubbell of the New York Giants (NL) won 24 consecutive games; 16 in 1936 and eight in 1937.

Most consecutive scoreless innings   Orel Hershiser of the Los Angeles Dodgers (NL) achieved a record 59 scoreless innings: from the sixth inning of August 30 through the tenth inning of September 28, 1988.

Most consecutive strikeouts   Tom Seaver of the New York Mets (NL) holds the mark of the most consecutive strikeouts at 10 on April 22, 1970.

Most consecutive shutouts   Don Drysdale of the Los Angeles Dodgers (NL) holds the record for the most consecutive shutouts with six from May 14 through June 4, 1968.

BASERUNNING

Most stolen bases (career)   As of August 24, 1997 the career record for the most stolen bases is 1,222, achieved by Rickey Henderson, Oakland Athletics (AL), 1979–84, 1989–92, 1994–95; New York Yankees (AL), 1985–89;

Toronto Blue Jays (AL), 1993; San Diego Padres (NL), 1996–97; Anaheim Angels (AL), 1997.

Most stolen bases (season)   Rickey Henderson of the Oakland Athletics (AL) stole 130 bases in 1982.

Most stolen bases (game)   The record for the most bases stolen in one game is seven, stolen by two players: George Gore, Chicago Cubs (NL), on June 25, 1881; Billy Hamilton, Philadelphia Phillies (NL), on August 31, 1894. The modern-day record is six, by three players: Eddie Collins, Philadelphia Athletics (AL), on September 11, 1912; Otis Nixon, Atlanta Braves (NL), on June 17, 1991; Eric Young, Colorado Rockies (NL), on June 30, 1996.

40/40 club   Two players have stolen at least 40 bases and hit at least 40 home runs in one season: Jose Canseco, Oakland Athletics (AL), 40 stolen bases and 42 home runs, 1988; and Barry Bonds, San Francisco Giants (NL), 40 stolen bases and 42 home runs, 1996.

PLAYING THE GAME

Most games played   The record for the most games played is 3,562, by Pete Rose, Cincinnati Reds (NL), 1963–78, 1984–86; Philadelphia Phillies (NL), 1979–83; Montreal Expos (NL), 1984.

Giants outfielder Barry Bonds is one of two players to hit at least 40 home runs and steal at least 40 bases in a season.

Most consecutive games played   As of August 24, 1997, the record for the most games played in a row was 2,441, by Cal Ripken Jr., Baltimore Orioles (AL). The streak started on May 30, 1982.

Most games pitched (career)   The career record for the most games pitched is 1,070, by Hoyt Wilhelm, New York Giants (NL), 1952–56; St. Louis Cardinals (NL), 1957; Cleveland Indians (AL), 1957–58; Baltimore Orioles (AL), 1958–62; Chicago White Sox (AL), 1963–68; California Angels (AL), 1969; Atlanta Braves (NL), 1969–70; Chicago Cubs (NL), 1970; Atlanta Braves (NL), 1971; Los Angeles Dodgers (NL), 1971–72.

Most games pitched (season)   The record for the most games pitched in one season is 106, by Mike Marshall of the Los Angeles Dodgers (NL) in 1974.

Longest game (elapsed time)   The Chicago White Sox (AL) played the longest major league ballgame in elapsed time, 8 hr. 6 min., beating the Milwaukee Brewers, 7–6, in the 25th inning on May 9, 1984 in Chicago. The game started on Tuesday night and was still tied at 3–3 when the 1 a.m. curfew caused suspension until Wednesday night.

Longest game (most innings)   The most innings in a major league game were 26, when the Brooklyn Dodgers (NL) and the Boston Braves (NL) played to a 1–1 tie on May 1, 1920.

Longest 9-inning game (elapsed time)   The New York Yankees (AL) played the longest 9-inning game, 4 hr. 21 min., beating the Baltimore Orioles 13–10 on April 30, 1996.

Longest 1–0 game   The longest 1–0 game was 3 hr. 20 min., won by the Milwaukee Brewers against the Oakland Athletics, on May 7, 1997.

Shortest game (elapsed time)   In the shortest major league game on record, the New York Giants (NL) beat the Philadelphia Phillies (NL), 6–1, in nine innings in 51 minutes on September 28, 1919.

Youngest player   The youngest major league player was the Cincinnati Reds (NL) pitcher Joe Nuxhall, who played one game on June 10, 1944, at age 15 yr. 314 days. He did not play again in the National League until 1952.

Oldest player   Satchel Paige pitched for the Kansas City A's (AL) at 59 yr. 78 days on September 25, 1965.

Shortest player   The shortest major league player was Eddie Gaedel, who measured 3 ft. 7 in. and weighed 65 pounds. Gaedel pinch-hit for the St. Louis Browns (AL) vs. the Detroit Tigers (AL) on August 19, 1951; wearing number $1/8$, the batter with the smallest-ever major league strike zone walked on four pitches.

Tallest player   The tallest major leaguers of all time are two pitchers measuring 6 ft. 10 in.: Randy Johnson, Seattle Mariners (AL) who played in his first game for the Montreal Expos (NL) on September 15, 1988, and Eric Hillman, who debuted for the New York Mets (NL) on May 18, 1992.

Most generations There are two three-generation families in Major League history. On August 19, 1992, Bret Boone made his major league debut for the Seattle Mariners (AL), making the Boone family the first three-generation family. Boone's father Bob Boone played 18 seasons in the majors, 1972–89, and his grandfather Ray Boone played from 1948 to 1960. On May 5, 1995 David Bell made his Major League debut for the Cleveland Indians (AL), making the Bell family the second three-generation family. David's father, Buddy Bell, played 18 seasons in the majors, 1972–89, and his grandfather, Gus Bell, played 15 seasons, 1950–64.

Most generations on the same team On August 31, 1990, Ken Griffey Sr. and Ken Griffey Jr., of the Seattle Mariners (AL), became the first father and son to play for the same major league team at the same time. In 1989 the Griffeys had been the first father/son combination to play in the major leagues at the same time. Griffey Sr. played for the Cincinnati Reds (NL) during that season.

MANAGERS

Most games managed 7,755, by Connie Mack, Pittsburgh Pirates (NL), 1894–96; Philadelphia Athletics (AL), 1901–50. Mack's career record was 3,731 wins, 3,948 losses, 75 ties and one no-decision.

Most wins 3,731, by Connie Mack, Pittsburgh Pirates (NL), 1894–96; Philadelphia Athletics (AL), 1901–50.

Most losses 3,948, by Connie Mack, Pittsburgh Pirates (NL), 1894–96; Philadelphia Athletics (AL), 1901–50.

Highest winning percentage .615, by Joe McCarthy, Chicago Cubs (NL), 1926–30; New York Yankees (AL), 1931–46; Boston Red Sox (AL), 1948–50. McCarthy's career record was 2,125 wins, 1,333 losses, 26 ties and three no-decisions.

AWARDS

Most MVP Awards The most selections in the annual vote (instituted in 1931) of the Baseball Writers' Association for Most Valuable Player of the Year (MVP) in the major leagues is three, won by: *National League*: Stan Musial (St. Louis), 1943, 1946, 1948; Roy Campanella (Brooklyn), 1951, 1953, 1955; Mike Schmidt (Philadelphia), 1980–81, 1986; Barry Bonds (Pittsburgh/San Francisco), 1990, 1992-1993; *American League*: Jimmie Foxx (Philadelphia), 1932–33, 1938; Joe DiMaggio (New York), 1939, 1941, 1947; Yogi Berra (New York), 1951, 1954–55; Mickey Mantle (New York), 1956–57, 1962.

Most Cy Young Awards The Cy Young Award has been given annually since 1956 to the outstanding pitcher in the major leagues. The most wins is four, by Steve Carlton (Philadelphia Phillies), 1972, 1977, 1980 and 1982, and Greg Maddux (Chicago Cubs, Atlanta Braves, NL), 1992–95. Maddux is the only pitcher to win four times in a row.

LEAGUE CHAMPIONSHIP SERIES

Games played

Most series   The record for the most series played is 11, achieved by Reggie Jackson, Oakland Athletics (AL), 1971–75; New York Yankees (AL), 1977–78, 1980–81; California Angels (AL), 1982, 1986.

Most games   Reggie Jackson holds the mark for the most games played at 45, Oakland Athletics (AL), 1971–75; New York Yankees (AL), 1977–78, 1980–81; California Angels (AL), 1982, 1986.

Hitting (career)

Highest batting average   The highest batting average (minimum 50 at-bats) is .392, by Devon White, California Angels (AL), 1986; Toronto Blue Jays (AL), 1991–93. White collected 29 hits in 74 at-bats in 21 games.

Most hits   The record for the most hits is 45, by Pete Rose, Cincinnati Reds (NL), 1970, 1972–73, 1975–76; Philadelphia Phillies (NL), 1980, 1983.

Most home runs   Nine, by George Brett of the Kansas City Royals (AL) hit a record nine home runs in 1976–78, 1980, and 1984–85.

Most RBI's   The most RBI's is 21, by Steve Garvey, Los Angeles Dodgers (NL), 1974, 1977–78, 1981; San Diego Padres (NL), 1984.

Most runs scored   George Brett of the Kansas City Royals (AL) scored a record 22 runs in 1976–78, 1980, and 1984–85.

Most walks   The record for the most walks is 23, by Joe Morgan, Cincinnati Reds (NL), 1972–73, 1975–76, 1979; Houston Astros (NL), 1980; Philadelphia Phillies (NL), 1983.

Most stolen bases   Rickey Henderson stole a record 16 bases, Oakland Athletics (AL) in 1981, 1989–90, and 1992; and Toronto Blue Jays (AL), 1993.

Pitching (career)

Most series   The record for the most series pitched is eight, by Bob Welch of the Los Angeles Dodgers (NL), 1978, 1981, 1983, 1985; and Oakland Athletics (AL), 1988–90, 1992;

Most games   The most games pitched in a career is 20, by Rick Honeycutt, Los Angeles Dodgers (NL), 1983, 1985; Oakland Athletics (AL), 1988–90, 1992; St. Louis Cardinals, 1996.

Most wins   The most wins in a League Championship Series is eight. This feat was achieved by Dave Stewart: Oakland Athletics (AL), 1988–90, 1992; Toronto Blue Jays (AL), 1993.

Most losses   The most losses recorded is seven, by Jerry Reuss, Pittsburgh Pirates (NL), 1974–75; Los Angeles Dodgers (NL), 1981, 1983, 1985.

Most innings pitched   The record for the most innings pitched is 75, by Dave Stewart, Oakland Athletics (AL), 1988–90, 1992; Toronto Blue Jays (AL), 1993.

Most complete games   Jim Palmer of the Baltimore Orioles (AL) pitched five complete games, 1969–71, 1973–74, 1979.

Most strikeouts   John Smoltz of the Atlanta Braves (NL) holds the record for the most strikeouts with 58, 1991–1993, 1995–1996.

Most saves   The record for the most saves is 11, achieved by Dennis Eckersley, Chicago Cubs (NL), 1984; Oakland Athletics (AL), 1988–90, 1992; St. Louis Cardinals (NL), 1996.

Relief pitcher Dennis Eckersley has recorded more saves in LCS playoff games than any other pitcher.

WORLD SERIES

Team Records

Most wins The New York Yankees (AL), have won the World Series a record 23 times in 1923, 1927–28, 1932, 1936–39, 1941, 1943, 1947, 1949–53, 1956, 1958, 1961–62, 1977–78, and 1996.

Most appearances The New York Yankees (AL) appeared in a record 34 World Series: 1921–23, 1926–28, 1932, 1936–39, 1941–43, 1947, 1949–53, 1955–58, 1960–64, 1976–78, 1981, and 1996.

Hitting

Highest batting average (career) Lou Brock of the St. Louis Cardinals (NL), 1964, 1967–68, holds the career record for the highest batting average with .391. Brock collected 34 hits in 87 at-bats over 21 games.

Highest batting average (series) Billy Hatcher of the Cincinnati Reds (NL) holds the single-series record for the highest batting average with .750 in 1990. Hatcher collected nine hits in 12 at-bats in four games.

Most home runs (career) The career record for the most home runs is 18, by Mickey Mantle of the New York Yankees (AL), 1951–53, 1955–58, 1960–64. Mantle hit his record 18 homers in 230 at-bats in 65 games.

Most home runs (series) Reggie Jackson of the New York Yankees (AL) hit five home runs in 1977.

Most home runs (game) The most home runs ever scored in a single game is three, achieved by two players: Babe Ruth of the New York Yankees (AL) did it twice: on October 6, 1926 vs. St. Louis Cardinals, and on October 9, 1928 vs. St. Louis Cardinals; and Reggie Jackson of the New York Yankees (AL) on October 18, 1977 vs. Los Angeles Dodgers.

Andruw Jones' long blast over the fence in Game 1 of the '96 World Series made him the youngest player to hit a home run in the Fall Classic.

Most RBI's (career) Mickey Mantle holds the career mark for the most RBI's, at 40, for the New York Yankees (AL), 1951–53, 1955–58, 1960–64.

Most RBI's (series) Bobby Richardson had 12 RBI's for the New York Yankees (AL) in 1960.

Most RBI's (game) Bobby Richardson had six RBI's for the New York Yankees (AL) on October 8, 1960 vs. Pittsburgh Pirates.

Pitching

Perfect game The only perfect game in World Series history was hurled by Don Larsen, New York Yankees (AL), on October 8, 1956 vs. Brooklyn Dodgers.

Most wins (career) Whitey Ford of the New York Yankees (AL) holds the career record of 10 wins in 11 series, 1950–64. Ford's career record was 10 wins, 8 losses in 22 games.

Most wins (series) The record for the most wins in a series is three, achieved by 12 pitchers. Only two pitchers have won three games in a five-game series: Christy Mathewson, New York Giants (NL) in 1905; and Jack Coombs, Philadelphia Athletics (AL) in 1910.

Most strikeouts (career) Whitey Ford of the New York Yankees (AL) holds the record for the most strikeouts with 94 in 11 series, 1950–64.

Most strikeouts (series) Bob Gibson of the St. Louis Cardinals (NL) holds the mark for the most strikeouts in a series at 35, from seven games in 1968.

Most strikeouts (game) Bob Gibson of the St. Louis Cardinals (NL) struck out 17 players on October 2, 1968 vs. Detroit Tigers.

Most innings pitched (career) Whitey Ford of the New York Yankees (AL) pitched a record 146 innings in 11 series, 1950, 1953, 1955–58, 1960–64.

Most innings pitched (series) In 1903, Deacon Phillippe of the Pittsburgh Pirates (NL), pitched 44 innings in an eight-game series.

Most innings pitched (game) On October 9, 1916, Babe Ruth of the Boston Red Sox (AL) pitched a record 14 innings vs. Brooklyn Dodgers.

Most saves (career) Rollie Fingers of the Oakland Athletics (AL) holds the mark at six saves from 1972 to 1974.

Most saves (series) In 1996, John Wetteland of the New York Yankees (AL) achieved four saves in a six-game series.

Games played

Most series Yogi Berra of the New York Yankees (AL) played in a record 14 series: 1947, 1949–53, 1955–58, 1960–63.

Most series (pitcher)   Whitey Ford of the New York Yankees (AL) has pitched in a record 11 series: 1950, 1953, 1955–58, 1960–64.

Most games played   Yogi Berra played 75 games for the New York Yankees (AL): 1947, 1949–53, 1955–58, 1960–63.

Most games (pitcher)   Whitey Ford of the New York Yankees (AL) pitched in a record 22 games: 1950, 1953, 1955–58, 1960–64.

Managers

Most series (career)   The record for the most series is 10, by Casey Stengel, New York Yankees (AL), 1949–53, 1955–58, 1960. Stengel's record was seven wins, three losses.

Most wins (career)   The career record for the most wins is seven, set by two managers: Joe McCarthy, New York Yankees (AL), 1932, 1936–39, 1941, 1943; and Casey Stengel, New York Yankees (AL), 1949–53, 1956, 1958.

Most losses (career)   John McGraw of the New York Giants (NL) holds the career record at six losses, 1911–13, 1917, 1923–24.

Yankees skipper Joe Torre waited longer than any other player and/or manager to reach the World Series, 4,268 games.

Wins, both leagues   The only manager to lead a team from each league to a World Series title is Sparky Anderson, who skippered the Cincinnati Reds (NL) to championships in 1975–76, and the Detroit Tigers (AL) in 1984.

COLLEGE BASEBALL

NCAA Division I

Most home runs (career)   The record for the most home runs is 100, achieved by Pete Incaviglia, Oklahoma State, 1983–85.

Most hits (career)   Phil Stephenson, of Wichita State holds the record for the most hits with 418, 1979–82.

Most wins (career)   Don Heinkel of Wichita State pitched a record 51 wins from 1979 to 1982.

Most strikeouts (career)　The career record for the most strikeouts pitched is 602, by John Powell, Auburn University, 1990–94.

COLLEGE WORLD SERIES

Most championships　The most wins is 11, by Southern Cal., in 1948, 1958, 1961, 1963, 1968, 1970–74 and 1978.

Hitting

Most home runs (career)　J. D. Drew of Florida State University hit a record five home runs, 1995–96.

Most hits (career)　Keith Moreland of Texas holds the record for the most hits, at 23, 1973–75.

Florida State's J.D. Drew holds the record for the most home runs in the College World Series.

Pitching

Most wins (career) The record for the most career wins is four, set by nine players: Bruce Gardner, Southern Cal., 1958, 1960; Steve Arlin, Ohio State, 1965–66; Bert Hooten, Texas at Austin, 1969–70; Steve Rogers, Tulsa, 1969, 1971; Russ McQueen, Southern Cal., 1972–73; Mark Bull, Southern Cal., 1973–74; Greg Swindell, Texas, 1984–85; Kevin Sheary, Miami (FL), 1984–85; Greg Brummett, Wichita State, 1988–89.

Most strikeouts (career) Carl Thomas of Arizona holds the record for the most strikeouts with 64 from 1954 to 1956.

BIG PLAYS

Fastest time circling the bases The fastest time for circling the bases is 13.3 seconds, by Ernest Swanson in Columbus, OH in 1931, at an average speed of 18.45 mph.

Largest baseball bat The largest baseball bat, made from a solid cypress log, measures 12 ft. 2 in. long, has a diameter of 11¼ inches at the handle and 14 inches at the barrel, and weighs 280 pounds. The bat, completed in 1996, was made by Thomas Timm, his father Russ, and his son Joshua of Custom Woodcrafter in Summerville, SC.

Longest baseball throw Glen Gorbous (Canada) threw a baseball 445 ft. 10 in. on August 1, 1957.

Most games watched (elapsed time) Wayne Zumwalt of Colorado Springs, CO attended a major league baseball game at all 28 major league stadiums in 28 consecutive days, from June 10 to July 7, 1993.

Longest game The longest game was a minor league game in 1981 that lasted 33 innings. At the end of nine innings the score was tied 1–1, with the Rochester (NY) Red Wings battling the home team Pawtucket (RI) Red Sox. After 21 innings it was tied 2–2, and at the end of 32 innings, the score was still 2–2, at which point the game was suspended. Two months later, play was resumed, and 18 minutes later, Pawtucket scored one run and won. The winning pitcher was the Red Sox's Bob Ojeda.

BASKETBALL

NATIONAL BASKETBALL ASSOCIATION (NBA)

Team Records

Most points (one team) The record for the most points is 186, by the Detroit Pistons, defeating the Denver Nuggets, 186–184, at Denver, on December 13, 1983 after three overtimes.

Most points, regulation (one team)   The record for the most points by two teams is 173: Boston Celtics vs. Minneapolis Lakers (139 points), at Boston, on February 27, 1959; Phoenix Suns vs. Denver Nuggets (143 points), at Phoenix, on November 10, 1990.

Highest-scoring game (aggregate)   The highest scoring game totalled 370 points,when the Detroit Pistons defeated the Denver Nuggets, 186–184, at Denver, on December 13, 1983 after three overtimes.

Highest-scoring game (aggregate), regulation   The highest scoring regulation game totalled 320 points, when the Golden State Warriors defeated the Denver Nuggets, 162–158, at Denver, on November 2, 1990.

Lowest-scoring game (aggregate)   The lowest scoring game totalled 37 points, when the Fort Wayne Pistons defeated the Minneapolis Lakers, 19–18, at Minneapolis, on November 22, 1950.

Greatest margin of victory   The greatest margin of victory is 68 points, by the Cleveland Cavaliers, defeating the Miami Heat, 148–80, on December 17, 1991.

Most wins (season)   The Chicago Bulls won a record 72 games,1995–96.

Most consecutive wins   The most consecutive wins is 33, by the Los Angeles Lakers. The Lakers' streak began with a 110–106 victory over the Baltimore Bullets on November 5, 1971 in Los Angeles, and ended on January 9, 1972 when they were beaten 120–104 by the Milwaukee Bucks in Milwaukee.

Most losses (season)   The Philadelphia 76ers lost a record 73 games, 1972–73.

Most consecutive losses   The record for the most losses is 24, by the Cleveland Cavaliers. The Cavs' undesirable roll started on March 19, 1982 when they lost to the Milwaukee Bucks, 119–97, in Milwaukee, and ended on November 10, 1982 when they defeated the Golden State Warriors 132–120 in overtime on November 10, 1982. During the streak the Cavs lost the last 19 games of the 1981–82 season, and the first five of the 1982–83 season.

Individual Records

Youngest player   The youngest NBA player was Jermaine O'Neal, who made his debut for the Portland Trail Blazers on December 5, 1996 at 18 years 53 days.

Oldest player   The oldest NBA player is Robert Parish of the Chicago Bulls, who was 43 yr. 286 days (at the end of the 1996–1997 season) on June 13, 1997.

Tallest basketball player   Gheorghe Muresan, 7 ft. 7 in., is the tallest player in NBA history. He made his pro debut for the Washington Bullets in 1994.

Most consecutive games played
Randy Smith played in a record 906 consecutive games, from February 18, 1972 to March 13, 1983. During his streak, Smith played for the Buffalo Braves, San Diego Clippers (twice), Cleveland Cavaliers, and New York Knicks.

Most consecutive 50+ point scores
The record for the most 50+ point scores is seven, by Wilt Chamberlain, Philadelphia Warriors, December 16–29, 1961.

Most consecutive 10+ point scores
The record for the most 10+ point scores is 787, by Kareem Abdul-Jabbar, Los Angeles Lakers, from December 4, 1977 through December 2, 1987.

Most consecutive free throws The record for the most free throws is 97, by Michael Williams, Minnesota Timberwolves, from March 24 through November 9, 1993.

Number 00 Robert Parish is the oldest player to play in the NBA.

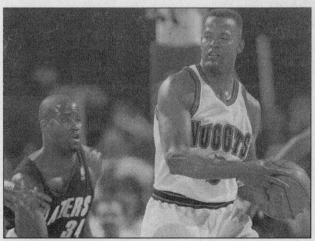

Dale Ellis holds the NBA mark for most three-point field goals scored in a career.

NBA INDIVIDUAL RECORDS

Games Played *Season*   88, Walt Bellamy, New York Knicks, Detroit Pistons, 1968–69

Career   1,611, Robert Parish, Golden StateWarriors, Boston Celtics, Charlotte Hornets, Chicago Bulls, 1976–97

Points *Game*   100, Wilt Chamberlain, Philadelphia Warriors vs. New York Knicks, March 2, 1962

Season   4,029, Wilt Chamberlain, Philadelphia Warriors, 1961–62

Career   38,387, Kareem Abdul-Jabbar, Milwaukee Bucks, Los Angeles Lakers, 1969–89

Field Goals *Game*   36, Wilt Chamberlain, Philadelphia Warriors vs. New York Knicks, March 2, 1962

Season   1,597, Wilt Chamberlain, Philadelphia Warriors, 1961–62

Career   15,837, Kareem Abdul-Jabbar, Milwaukee Bucks, Los Angeles Lakers, 1969–89

Three-Point Field Goals *Game*   11, Dennis Scott, Orlando Magic vs. Atlanta Hawks, April 18, 1996

Season   267, Dennis Scott, Orlando Magic, 1995–96

Career   1,461, Dale Ellis, Dallas Mavericks, Seattle SuperSonics, Milwaukee Bucks, San Antonio Spurs, Denver Nuggets, 1983–97

Free Throws *Game*   28, Wilt Chamberlain, Philadelphia Warriors vs. New York Knicks, March 2, 1962; Adrian Dantley, Utah Jazz vs. Houston Rockets, January 4, 1984

Season   840, Jerry West, Los Angeles Lakers, 1965–66

Career   8,531, Moses Malone, Buffalo Braves, Houston Rockets, Philadelphia 76ers, Washington Bullets, Atlanta Hawks, Milwaukee Bucks, Philadelphia 76ers, San Antonio Spurs, 1976–95

Assists *Game*   30, Scott Skiles, Orlando Magic vs. Denver Nuggets, December 30, 1990

Season   1,164, John Stockton, Utah Jazz, 1990–91

Career   12,170, John Stockton, Utah Jazz, 1984–97

Rebounds *Game*   55, Wilt Chamberlain, Philadelphia Warriors vs. Boston Celtics, November 24, 1960

Season   2,149, Wilt Chamberlain, Philadelphia Warriors, 1960–61

Career   23,924, Wilt Chamberlain, Philadelphia/San Francisco Warriors, Philadelphia 76ers, Los Angeles Lakers, 1959–73

Steals Game   11, Larry Kenon, San Antonio Spurs vs. Kansas City Kings, December 26, 1976

Season   301, Alvin Robertson, San Antonio Spurs, 1985–86

Career   2,531, John Stockton, Utah Jazz, 1984–97

Blocked Shots *   *Game*   17, Elmore Smith, Los Angeles Lakers vs. Portland Trail, Blazers October 28, 1973

Season   456, Mark Eaton, Utah Jazz, 1984–85

Career   3,363, Hakeem Olajuwon, Houston Rockets, 1984–97

Personal Fouls Game   8, Don Otten, Tri-Cities vs. Sheboygan, November 24, 1949

Season   386, Darryl Dawkins, New Jersey Nets, 1983–84

Career   4,657, Kareem Abdul-Jabbar, Milwaukee Bucks, Los Angeles Lakers, 1969–89

Disqualifications Season   26, Don Meineke, Fort Wayne Pistons, 1952–53

Career   127, Vern Mikkelsen Minneapolis Lakers, 1950–59

* *Compiled since 1973–74 season.*

Dennis Scott holds the NBA three-point marks for most goals scored in a game and in a season.

NBA PLAYOFF RECORDS

		Player(s)	Team(s)	Date(s)
Points				
Game	63	Michael Jordan	Chicago Bulls vs. Boston Celtics	April 20, 1986 (2 OT)
	61	Elgin Baylor	Los Angeles Lakers vs. Boston Celtics	April 14, 1962
Series	284	Elgin Baylor	Los Angeles Lakers vs. Boston Celtics	1962
Career	5,762	Kareem Abdul-Jabbar	Milwaukee Bucks, Los Angeles Lakers	1969–89
Field Goals				
Game	24	Wilt Chamberlain	Philadelphia Warriors vs. Syracuse Nationals	March 14,1960
		John Havlicek	Boston Celtics vs. Atlanta Hawks	April 1, 1973
		Michael Jordan	Chicago Bulls vs. Cleveland Cavaliers	May 1, 1988
Series	113	Wilt Chamberlain	San Francisco Warriors vs. St. Louis Hawks	1964
Career	2,356	Kareem Abdul-Jabbar	Milwaukee Bucks, Los Angeles Lakers	1970–89
Free Throws				
Game	30	Bob Cousy	Boston Celtics vs. Syracuse Nationals	March 21, 1953 (4 OT)
	23	Michael Jordan	Chicago Bulls vs. New York Knicks	May 14,1989
Series	86	Jerry West	Los Angeles Lakers vs. Baltimore Bullets	1965
Career	1,213	Jerry West	Los Angeles Lakers	1960–74
Assists				
Game	24	Magic Johnson	Los Angeles Lakers vs. Phoenix Suns	May 15, 1984
		John Stockton	Utah Jazz vs. Los Angeles Lakers	May 17, 1988
Series	115	John Stockton	Utah Jazz vs. Los Angeles Lakers	1988
Career	2,346	Magic Johnson	Los Angeles Lakers	1979–91, 1995–96

Rebounds

Game	41	Wilt Chamberlain	Philadelphia 76ers vs. Boston Celtics	April 5, 1967
Series	220	Wilt Chamberlain	Philadelphia 76ers vs. Boston Celtics	1965
Career	4,104	Bill Russell	Boston Celtics	1956–69

Steals

Game	8	Rick Barry	Golden State Warriors vs. Seattle SuperSonics	April 14, 1975
		Lionel Hollins	Portland Trail Blazers vs. Los Angeles Lakers	May 8, 1977
		Maurice Cheeks	Philadelphia 76ers vs. New Jersey Nets	April 11, 1979
		Craig Hodges	Milwaukee Bucks vs. Philadelphia 76ers	May 9, 1986
		Tim Hardaway	Golden State Warriors vs. Los Angeles Lakers	May 8, 1991
		Tim Hardaway	Golden State Warriors vs. Seattle SuperSonics	April 30, 1992
		Mookie Blaylock	Atlanta Hawks vs. Indiana Pacers	April 29, 1996
Series	28	John Stockton	Utah Jazz vs. Los Angeles Lakers	1988
Career	358	Magic Johnson	Los Angeles Lakers	1979–91, 1995–96

Source: NBA

Most consecutive free throws (game) Dominique Wilkins shot a record 23 free throws for the Atlanta Hawks, December 8, 1992.

Coaches

Lenny Wilkens has the most wins of any NBA coach.

Most wins Lenny Wilkens won a record 1,070 games through the 1996–97 season: Seattle Super-Sonics (1969–72), Portland Trail Blazers (1974–76), Seattle Super-Sonics (1977–85), Cleveland Cavaliers (1986–93) and Atlanta Hawks (1994–97).

Most wins (playoffs) Pat Riley has won a record 145 playoff games, 102 with the Los Angeles Lakers (1981–90), 35 with the New York Knicks (1992–95) and eight with the Miami Heat (1997).

Highest winning percentage The highest winning percentage is .736, by Phil Jackson, Chicago Bulls, 1989–97. Jackson's record is 483 wins, 173 losses.

Most games The record for the most games coached is 1,968, achieved by Bill Fitch, Cleveland Cavaliers, 1970–79; Boston Celtics, 1979–83; Houston Rockets, 1983–88; New Jersey Nets, 1989–92; Los Angeles Clippers, 1994–97. Fitch's career totals are 927 wins and 1,041 losses.

NBA FINALS

Most titles The Boston Celtics have won 16 NBA titles: 1957, 1959–66, 1968–69, 1974, 1976, 1981, 1984, 1986.

Consecutive titles The Boston Celtics won eight consecutive titles, 1959–66.

Most titles (coach) Nine, by Red Auerbach of the Boston Celtics has won a record nine titles, 1957 and 1959–66.

Most minutes played Kevin Johnson played for 62 minutes for the Phoenix Suns vs. the Chicago Bulls on June 13, 1993. The game went to three over-times.

Most points scored The record for the most points scored is 61, by Elgin Baylor, Los Angeles Lakers vs. Boston Celtics on April 14, 1962 in Boston.

Most field goals made The most field goals made is 22, achieved by two players: Elgin Baylor, Los Angeles Lakers vs. Boston Celtics on April 14, 1962 in Boston; and Rick Barry, San Francisco Warriors vs. Philadelphia 76ers on April 18, 1967 in San Francisco.

Most free throws made   Bob Pettit made 19 free throws for the St. Louis Hawks vs. the Boston Celtics on April 9, 1958 in Boston.

Most assists   The record for the most assists is 21, set by Magic Johnson, Los Angeles Lakers vs. Boston Celtics on June 3, 1984.

Most rebounds   40, by Bill Russell of the Boston Celtics has performed 40 rebounds on two different occasions: vs. St. Louis Hawks on March 29, 1960; and vs. Los Angeles Lakers on April 18, 1962, in an overtime game.

Most steals   Seven, by Robert Horry, Houston Rockets vs. Orlando Magic, June 9, 1995.

Most points (one team)   The Boston Celtics scored 148 points vs. Los Angeles Lakers (114 points) on May 27, 1985.

Highest-scoring game   The highest-scoring game in NBA history totalled 276 points, when the Philadelphia 76ers defeated the San Francisco Warriors, 141–135, in overtime, on April 14, 1967.

Highest-scoring game, regulation   The highest-scoring regulation game totalled 263 points, when the Los Angeles Lakers defeated the Boston Celtics, 141–122, on June 4, 1987.

Greatest margin of victory   The Washington Bullets shot down the Seattle SuperSonics, 117–82, on June 4, 1978, setting the record for the greatest margin of victory with 35 points.

Three players hold the mark for most blocked shots in an NBA Finals game: Bill Walton, Patrick Ewing (left) and Hakeem Olajuwon (right).

THE STUFF
OF DREAMS

MOST POINTS IN A PLAYOFF GAME

Michael Jordan scored 63 points in the Bull's victory over the Boston Celtics on April 20, 1986.

"*F*or me, it's all about driving myself and being my best. I am competitive by nature," says Michael Jordan, the greatest basketball player of his generation. In the 1990's Jordan has led the Chicago Bulls to five NBA championships and set numerous NBA regular season and playoff records.

Thanks to a combination of grace, acrobatic athleticism and charisma, Jordan has transcended his sport. The Air Jordan sneaker line is the most sought-after in the shoe industry and replica Bulls shirts are the biggest sellers in the apparel industry. When Jordan took a sabbatical from basketball to play professional baseball, NBA television ratings plummeted.

But it wasn't always so easy for Jordan. At Emsley A. Laney High School in Wilmington, N.C., Jordan failed to make the freshman basketball team. Jordan learned a lesson from that disappointment. "It's not always about ability. It's about attitude, hard work and heart. Those are the keys to success." Adds Jordan, "I received some very good advice when I was young, 'Don't accept not trying.' To me, that's so important for young basketball players and young people in general."

Besides his individual records, Jordan was the leader of the Bulls team that set the NBA record for most victories in a season, 72, during the 1995/96 season. Jordan takes more pride in the team record than in his individual efforts. "We went through the season meeting all of the challenges and winning the games. That says a lot about the teamwork during that season. It was a very special season."

At 34, does Jordan think he can top Bill Russell's 11 NBA titles? "I would love to be able to do that, but at my age, it probably isn't going to happen," says Jordan. So what are his basketball goals? "I would love to win another championship for Chicago."

BASKETBALL DRIBBLING (24 HOURS)

The greatest distance "traveled" while continuously dribbling a basketball in 24 hours is 96.57 miles. Ashrita Furman performed this feat by dribbling around Victory Field Track in Forest Park, Queens, New York from 9:32 A.M. on May 17, 1997 to 9:32 A.M. the following day. He completed 371 laps of the track. A very competitive Guinness category, this record has bounced back and forth between Furman, Jamie Borges (above), and Terry Cole, who have each set and reset this record in recent years.

For rules, see page 707.

OLYMPIC GAMES

Most gold medals (team—men)   The United States has won 11 gold medals in Olympic basketball competition: 1936, 1948, 1952, 1956, 1960, 1964, 1968, 1976, 1984, 1992 and 1996.

Most gold medals (team—women)   In the women's basketball tournament the gold medal has been won three times by two teams: the USSR/Unified Teams in 1976, 1980 and 1992; and the United States in 1984, 1988 and 1996.

Most gold medals (men)   The record for the most Olympic gold medals is two, achieved by 11 men: Bob Kurland in 1948 and 1952; Bill Houghland in 1952 and 1956; Burdette Eliele Haldorson in 1956 and 1960; Michael Jordan, Patrick Ewing, and Chris Mullin, all in 1984 and 1992; and Charles Barkley, John Stockton, David Robinson, Karl Malone and Scottie Pippen, all in 1992 and 1996.

Most gold medals (women)   The record for the most gold medals is three, by Theresa Edwards, in 1984, 1988 and 1996.

BIG PLAYS

Basketball-spinning   On July 18, 1994, Bruce Crevier balanced and spun 18 balls across his body.

Dribbling (24 hours)   Ashrita Furman (U.S.) dribbled a basketball a distance of 96.57 miles in 24 hours on May 17–18, 1997.

Longest field goal (men)   Christopher Eddy scored a field goal measured at 90 ft. 2³/₄ inches for Fairview High School in Erie, PA on February 25, 1989.

Longest field goal (women)   Nikki Fierstos scored a field goal of approximately 79 feet on January 2, 1993 at Huntington North High School, Huntington, IN.

Most valuable basket   Don Calhoun, a spectator randomly picked from the stands at a Chicago Bulls home game on April 14, 1993, sank a basket from the opposite foul line—a distance of 75 feet—and won $1 million.

Vertical dunk height   Joey Johnson of San Pedro, CA successfully dunked a basketball at a rim height of 11 ft. 7 in. at the One-on-One Collegiate Challenge on June 25, 1990 at Trump Plaza Hotel and Casino in Atlantic City, New Jersey.

Most free throws (consecutive)   The greatest goal-shooting demonstration was by Thomas Amberry (U.S.), who scored 2,750 consecutive free throws in Seal Beach, CA in November 1993.

Most free throws (one minute)   In one minute, Jeff Liles scored 25 out of 29 attempts in Bethany, OK on September 18, 1994.

Most free throws (10 minutes) On June 11, 1992, Jeff Liles scored 231 out of 240 attempts in 10 minutes at Southern Nazarene University, Bethany, OK. He repeated this total of 231 (241 attempts) on June 16. This speed record is achieved using one ball and one rebounder.

Most free throws (24 hours) In 24 hours, Fred Newman scored 20,371 free throws from a total of 22,049 taken (92.39 percent) at Caltech, Pasadena, CA, September 29–30, 1990.

Most points (one minute) Steve Bontrager (U.S.) of the British team Polycell Kingston scored 21 points in one minute from seven positions in a demonstration on October 29, 1986.

NCAA (MEN)

Individual Records (All Divisions)

Most points scored (career) Travis Grant of Kentucky State (Division II) scored a record 4,045 points, 1969–72.

Most points scored (season) Pete Maravich of Louisiana State (Division I) scored 1,381 points in 1970. Pistol Pete hit 522 field goals and 337 free throws in 31 games.

Most points scored (game) Clarence "Bevo" Francis scored 113 points for Rio Grande (Division II) vs. Hillsdale on February 2, 1954.

Most field goals (career) Travis Grant of Kentucky State (Division II) scored a career record of 1,760 points from 1969–72. Grant achieved his career record from 2,759 attempts.

Most field goals (season) The single-season record for the most field goals is 539, achieved by Travis Grant of Kentucky State (Division II) in 1972. Grant's season record was gained from 869 attempts.

Most field goals (game) The single-game record for the most field goals is 41, set by Frank Selvy, Furman (Division I), vs. Newberry on February 13, 1954. Selvy amassed his record total from 66 attempts.

UMass center Marcus Camby set the NCAA tournament mark for most blocked shots during his 3-year college career.

NCAA MEN'S DIVISION I RECORDS

Career Records

Points	3,667	Pete Maravich: Louisiana State	1968–70
Field goals	1,387	Pete Maravich: Louisiana State	1968–70
Best percentage	690	Ricky Need: Appalachian State	1991–94
3-point field goals	401	Doug Day: Radford	1990–93
Free throws	905	Dickie Hemric: Wake Forest	1952–55
Rebounds	2,201	Tom Gola: La Salle	1952–55
Assists	1,076	Bobby Hurley: Duke	1990–93
Blocked shots	453	Alonzo Mourning: Georgetown	1989–92
Steals	376	Eric Murdock: Providence	1988–91

Season Records

Points	1,381	Pete Maravich: Louisiana State	1970
Field goals	522	Pete Maravich: Louisiana State (from 1,168 attempts)	1970
Best percentage	746	Steve Johnson: Oregon State	1981
3-point field goals	158	Darrin Fitzgerald: Butler (in 362 attempts)	1987
Free throws	355	Frank Selvy: Furman (in 444 attempts)	1954
Best percentage	959	Craig Collins: Penn State	1985
Rebounds	734	Walt Dukes: Seton Hall (in 33 games)	1953
Assists	406	Mark Wade: Nevada–Las Vegas	1987
Blocked shots	207	David Robinson: Navy (in 35 games)	1986
Steals	150	Mookie Blaylock: Oklahoma	1988

Game Records

Points	100	Frank Selvy: Furman (vs. Newberry)	Feb. 13, 1954
Field goals	41	Frank Selvy: Furman	Feb. 13, 1954
3-point field goals	14	Dave Jamerson: Ohio (vs. Charleston)	Dec. 21, 1989
	14	Askia Jones: Kansas State (vs. Fresno State)	Mar. 24, 1994
Free throws	30	Pete Maravich: Louisiana State (vs. Oregon State)	Dec. 22, 1969
Rebounds	51	Bill Chambers: William and Mary (vs. Virginia)	Feb. 14, 1953
Assists	22	Tony Fairly: Baptist (vs. Armstrong State)	Feb. 9, 1987
	22	Avery Johnson: Southern–B.R. (vs. Texas Southern)	Jan. 25, 1988
	22	Sherman Douglas: Syracuse (vs. Providence)	Jan. 28, 1988
Blocked shots	14	David Robinson: Navy (vs. North Carolina–Wilmington)	Jan. 4, 1986
	14	Shawn Bradley: BYU (vs. Eastern Kentucky)	Dec. 7, 1990
Steals	13	Mookie Blaylock: Oklahoma (vs. Centenary)	Dec. 12, 1987
	13	Mookie Blaylock: Oklahoma (vs. Loyola Marymount)	Dec. 17, 1988

THE DEAN OF

COACHING

"I wish they didn't keep records," says University of North Carolina head coach Dean Smith. "I am just interested in how each team does, and I go from there. What each team does is the most important thing to me."

A modest man, Dean Smith is a member of a vanishing breed in sports—a coach who prepares his players for life both on and off the basketball court. During the 1997 NCAA tournament, his 36th campaign with the Tarheels, Smith surpassed the long-standing record for wins in college basketball, set by the legendary Adolph Rupp of the University of Kentucky. In addition to this record, Smith has won two NCAA championships, in 1982 and 1993, and coached such great players as Michael Jordan, James Worthy, Bob McAdoo, Phil Ford and Jerry Stackhouse.

MOST WINS—NCAA

Dean Smith of North Carolina holds the mark for the most wins, with 879 from 1962 to 1997.

Smith's original career goal was to be a high school teacher and coach. Teaching runs in the Smith family. "My dad was a high school football, basketball and baseball coach. I thought I'd be teaching math and coaching sports at the high school level. But it worked out that I became a basketball coach," says Smith. He graduated from the University of Kansas in 1953 and stayed on as an assistant basketball coach to Phog Allen.

One year later he left the Jayhawks to join the Air Force. "When I was in the Air Force, I was invited to be the assistant coach at the Air Force Academy. I was also a golf coach there. After I got out of the Air Force, Frank McGuire asked me to be an assistant at UNC in 1958. It just happened that I went back to college coaching and not high school," recalls Smith. He has been in Chapel Hill ever since.

In the nineties, an era clouded by recruiting scandals and low graduation rates, Smith's program stands out as an example of the finest qualities of collegiate athletics. Both Smith and the University of North Carolina set rigorous academic performance targets for the players. "The best way to show the importance I place on academics is to look at the players I've coached and their degrees. Ninety-seven percent have received their bachelor's degrees and nearly half have gone on to some kind of graduate work. The University of North Carolina demands good students," the coach says proudly.

Most assists (career)   Bobby Hurley of Duke (Division I) made 1,076 assists from 1990–93. During his record-setting career Hurley played in 140 games.

Most assists (season)   Mark Wade of UNLV (Division I) made 406 assists in 1987. Wade played in 38 games.

Most assists (game)   On March 11, 1989, Robert James of Kean (Division III) made 26 assists vs. New Jersey Tech.

Most rebounds (career)   The career record for the most rebounds is 2,334, set by Jim Smith, Steubenville (Division II), 1955–58. Smith amassed his record total from 112 games.

Most rebounds (season)   Elmore Smith, Kentucky State (Division II), set the record with 799 rebounds in 1971. Smith played in 33 games.

Most rebounds (game)   Bill Chambers of William & Mary (Division I) had 51 rebounds vs. Virginia on February 14, 1953.

Team Records (Division I)

Most points (one team)   Loyola Marymount (CA) scored 186 points vs. U.S. International (140 points) on January 5, 1991.

Highest-scoring game   The highest-scoring game totalled 331 points, when Loyola Marymount (CA) defeated U.S. International, 181–150, on January 31, 1989.

Fewest points scored (one team)   The record for the fewest points scored is six, set by two teams: Temple vs. Tennessee (11 points), on December 15, 1973; Arkansas State vs. Kentucky (75 points), on January 8, 1945.

Lowest-scoring game   The lowest-scoring game totalled 17 points, when Tennessee defeated Temple, 11–6, on December 15, 1973.

Widest margin of victory   The widest margin of victory is 97 points: Southern-Baton Rouge vs. Patten, 154–57, on November 26, 1993.

Most wins (season)   The record for the most wins in a single season is 37, achieved by two teams: Duke in 1986 (37 wins, 3 losses); and UNLV in 1987 (37 wins, 2 losses).

Most consecutive wins   UCLA set the NCAA mark for consecutive victories (including the playoffs) at 88 games. The streak started on January 30, 1971 and ended on January 19, 1974, when the Bruins were defeated by Notre Dame, 71–70.

Most losses (season)   In 1992, Prairie View finished the season with zero wins and 28 losses.

NCAA MEN'S CHAMPIONSHIP RECORDS

Points Game   61, Austin Carr, Notre Dame vs. Ohio, 1st round, 1970

Tournament   184, Glen Rice, Michigan (6 games), 1989

Career   401, Christian Laettner, Duke (23 games), 1989–92

Field Goals Game   25, Austin Carr, Notre Dame vs. Ohio, 1st round, 1970

Tournament   75, Glen Rice, Michigan (6 games), 1989

Career   152, Elvin Hayes, Houston (13 games), 1966–68

Three-Point Field Goals Game   11, Jeff Fryer, Loyola Marymount vs. Michigan, 2nd round, 1990

Tournament   27, Glen Rice, Michigan (6 games), 1989

Career   42, Bobby Hurley, Duke (20 games), 1990–93

Free Throws Game   23, Bob Carney, Bradley vs. Colorado, 2nd round, 1954; 23, Travis Mays, Texas vs. Georgia, 1st round, 1990

Tournament   55, Bob Carney, Bradley (5 games), 1954

Career   142, Christian Laettner, Duke (23 games), 1989–92

Assists Game   18, Mark Wade, UNLV vs. Indiana, National semi-final, 1987

Tournament   61, Mark Wade, UNLV (5 games), 1987

Career   145, Bobby Hurley, Duke (20 games), 1990–93

Rebounds Game   34, Fred Cohen, Temple vs. UConn, Regional Semifinal, 1956

Tournament   97, Elvin Hayes, Houston (5 games), 1968

Career   222, Elvin Hayes, Houston (13 games), 1966–68

Blocked Shots Game   11, Shaquille O'Neal, LSU vs. BYU, 1st round, 1992

Tournament   23, David Robinson, Navy (4 games), 1986

Career   43, Marcus Camby, UMass (11 games), 1994–96

Steals Game   8, Darrell Hawkins, Arkansas vs. Holy Cross, 1st round, 1993; 8, Grant Hill, Duke vs. California, 2nd round, 1993

Tournament   23, Mookie Blaylock, Oklahoma (6 games), 1988

Career   39, Grant Hill, Duke (20 games), 1991–94

Coaches

Most wins Dean Smith of North Carolina holds the mark for the most wins at 879, 1962–97.

Highest winning percentage The highest winning percentage is .822, set by Adolph Rupp, Kentucky, 1931–52, 1954–72. Rupp's career record was 876 wins, 190 losses.

Most games The record for the most games is 1,105, by Henry Iba, Northwest Missouri State, 1930–33; Colorado, 1934; Oklahoma State, 1935–70. Iba's career record was 767 wins, 338 losses.

NCAA Championship

Most wins (team) UCLA has won a record 11 NCAA Championships, 1964–65, 1967–73, 1975, 1995.

Most wins (coach) John Wooden coached UCLA to 10 wins, 1967–73, 1975.

Championship Game

Most points Bill Walton scored 44 points for UCLA vs. Memphis State in 1973.

Most field goals Bill Walton also holds the record for the most field goals with 21 for UCLA vs. Memphis State in 1973.

Most rebounds The record for the most rebounds is 27, set by Bill Russell for San Francisco vs. Iowa in 1956.

Most assists The record for the most assists is 11, achieved by Rumeal Robinson, Michigan vs. Seton Hall, 1989.

Grant Hill's stellar college career at Duke was highlighted by two NCAA titles. He also set the NCAA tournament career mark for most steals.

Most points (team)   The most points in a Championship game is 103, achieved by UNLV vs. Duke (73) in 1990.

Highest scoring game   The highest scoring game totalled 181, when UCLA defeated Duke, 98–83, in 1964.

Widest margin of victory   The widest margin of victory is 30 points, achieved by UNLV (103) vs. Duke (73) in 1990.

NCAA (WOMEN)

Individual Records (Divisions I, II, III)

Most points (game)   Jackie Givens, of Fort Valley State (Division II), scored 67 points vs. Knoxville on February 22, 1991. Givens hit 19 field goals, six three-point field goals, and 11 free throws.

Most points (season)   The record for the most points in one season is 1,075, achieved by Jackie Givens, Fort Valley State (Division II), in 1991. Givens' record-setting season consisted of 249 field goals, 120 three-point field goals, and 217 free throws in 28 games.

Most points (career)   The career record for the most points is 3,171, by Jeannie Demers, Buena Vista (Division III), 1983–87. Demers' career totals are 1,386 field goals and 399 free throws in 105 games.

The career record for the most points before the NCAA compiled statistics for women's basketball is 3,649 points, by Lynette Woodard, Kansas, 1978–81. In 139 games, Woodard's career totals are 1,572 field goals and 505 free throws.

Most field goals (game)   The record for the most field goals in a single game is 28, by Ann Gilbert, Oberlin (Division III), vs. Allegheny, February 6, 1991.

Most field goals (season)   The single-season record is 392, by Barbara Kennedy, Clemson (Division I) in 1982. Kennedy set her record total from 760 attempts.

Most field goals (career)   Jeannie Demers, Buena Vista (Division III), made 1,386 field goals from 1984–87. Demers made her record total from 2,838 attempts.

Most assists (game)   The most assists in a game is 24, performed by Joanna Bernabei, West Liberty State (Division II) vs. West Virginia State, February 8, 1997.

Most assists (season)   Suzie McConnell had 355 assists for Penn State (Division I) in 1987.

Most assists (career)   The career record for the most assists is 1,307, by Suzie McConnell, Penn State (Division I), 1984–88.

NCAA DIVISION I WOMEN'S RECORDS

		Player(s)	Team(s)	Date(s)
Points				
Game	60	Cindy Brown	Long Beach State vs. San Jose State	Feb. 16, 1987
Season	974	Cindy Brown	Long Beach State	1987
Career	3,122	Patricia Hoskins	Mississippi Valley	1985–89
Field Goals				
Game	27	Lorri Bauman	Drake vs. Southwest Missouri State	Jan. 6, 1984
Season	392	Barbara Kennedy	Clemson	1982
Career	1,259	Joyce Walker	Louisiana State	1981–84
Free Throws				
Game	23	Shaunda Greene	Washington vs. Illinois	Nov. 30, 1991
Season	275	Lorri Bauman	Drake	1982
Career	907	Lorri Bauman	Drake	1981–84
Assists				
Game	23	Michelle Burden	Kent vs. Ball State	Feb. 6, 1991
Season	355	Suzie McConnell	Penn State	1987
Career	1,307	Suzie McConnell	Penn State	1984–88
Rebounds				
Game	40	Deborah Temple	Delta State vs. Alabama–Birmingham	Feb. 14, 1983
Season	534	Wanda Ford	Drake	1985
Career	1,887	Wanda Ford	Drake	1983–86

Blocked Shots				
Game	15	Amy Lundquist	Loyola (Cal.) vs. Western Illinois	Dec. 20, 1992
Season	151	Michelle Wilson	Texas Southern	1989
Career	428	Genia Miller	Cal. St. Fullerton	1987–91
Steals				
Game	14	Natalie White	Florida A&M vs. South Alabama	Dec.13, 1991
	14	Heidi Caruso	Lafayette vs. Kansas St.	Dec. 5, 1992
	14	Stephanie Wine	Marshall vs. Western Carolina	Jan. 23, 1995
	14	Keisha Anderson	Wisconsin vs. Cleveland State	Feb. 11, 1997
Season	191	Natalie White	Florida A&M	1995
Career	624	Natalie White	Florida A&M	1991–95

Most rebounds (game) The most rebounds in a game is 40, by Deborah Temple, Delta State (Division I), vs. Alabama–Birmingham, on February 14, 1983.

Most rebounds (season) The most rebounds in a season is 635, by Francine Perry, Quinnipiac (Division II), in 1982.

Most rebounds (career) Wanda Ford of Drake (Division I) had 1,887 rebounds, 1983–86.

Team Records (Division I)

Most points scored (team) Long Beach State scored 149 points vs. San Jose State (69 points), on February 16, 1987.

Highest-scoring game The highest recorded score is 252 when Southern Methodist defeated Texas Christian, 127–125, after four overtimes, on January 25, 1997.

Fewest points scored (team) The fewest points scored is 12, by Bennett vs. North Carolina A&T (85 points), on November 21, 1990.

Lowest-scoring game The lowest recorded score is 72 points when Virginia defeated San Diego State, 38–34, on December 29, 1981.

Rebecca Lobo was a member of the winning team in 102 consecutive games. During the streak she played for the University of Connecticut, the U.S. Olympic team and the New York Liberty of the WNBA.

Most wins (season)   The record for the most wins in a season is 35, achieved by four teams: Texas, 1982; Louisiana Tech., 1982; Tennessee, 1989; and Connecticut, 1995.

Most losses (season)   Charleston Southern lost a record 28 times in 1991.

Coaches

Most wins   As of February 24, 1997, Jody Conradt coached Texas to a record 697 wins, beginning in 1970.

Highest winning percentage   The highest recorded winning percentage is .865 by Leon Barmore of Louisiana Tech. His career record from 1983 through the 1996–97 season is 428 wins, 67 losses.

Undefeated Seasons

Most undefeated seasons   Two teams have completed Division I seasons without losing: the University of Texas in 1986 (34–0) and the University of Connecticut in 1995 (35–0).

NCAA Championships

Most wins   Tennessee has captured five NCAA titles: 1987, 1989, 1991 and 1996–97.

Most wins (coach)   Pat Summitt coached Tennessee to all five NCAA titles.

Tennessee coach Pat Summitt (left) celebrates her fifth NCAA title. Her 1997 championship team was led by Chamique Holdsclaw (right), who set an NCAA tournament mark for most field goals.

Championship Game

Most points Sheryl Swoopes scored 47 points for Texas Tech vs. Ohio State, 1993.

Most field goals Sheryl Swoopes made 16 field goals for Texas Tech vs. Ohio State in 1993.

Most rebounds The most rebounds in a Championship game is 23, by Charlotte Smith for North Carolina vs. Louisiana Tech in 1994.

Most assists The most assists in a championship game is 10, by two players: Kamie Ethridge, Texas vs. Southern Cal, in 1986; Melissa McCray, Tennessee vs. Auburn, in 1989.

NCAA WOMEN'S CHAMPIONSHIP RECORDS

Points Game 50, Lorri Bauman, Drake vs. Maryland, 1982

Tournament 177, Sheryl Swoopes, Texas Tech (5 games), 1993

Career 388, Bridgette Gordon, Tennessee, 1986–89

Field Goals Game 21, Lorri Bauman, Drake vs. Maryland, 1982

Tournament 59, Chamique Holdsclaw, Tennessee (6 games), 1997

Career 155, Bridgette Gordon, Tennessee, 1986–89

Free Throws Game 17, Bridgette Gordon, Tennessee vs. Long Beach State, 1989

Tournament 57, Sheryl Swoopes, Texas Tech (5 games), 1993

Career 91, Cheryl Miller, Southern California, 1983–86

Rebounds Game 23, Cheryl Taylor, Tennessee Tech vs. Georgia, 1985; 23, Charlotte Smith, North Carolina vs. Louisiana Tech, 1994

Tournament 72, Tracy Claxton, Old Dominion (5 games), 1985

Career 170, Cheryl Miller, Southern California, 1983–86

Assists Game 17, Suzie McConnell, Penn State vs. North Carolina, 1985; 17, Suzie McConnell, Penn State vs. Rutgers, 1986

Tournament 42, Teresa Weatherspoon, Louisiana Tech (5 games), 1987

FOOTBALL

NATIONAL FOOTBALL LEAGUE (NFL)

Team Records

Most consecutive games won   The Chicago Bears won 17 straight regular-season games, 1933–34.

Most games won in a season   Two teams have compiled 15-win seasons: the San Francisco 49ers in 1984, and the Chicago Bears in 1985.

Perfect season   The only team to win all its games in one season was the 1972 Miami Dolphins. The Dolphins won 14 regular-season games and then won three playoff games, including Super Bowl VII.

Most consecutive games lost   This most undesirable of records is held by the Tampa Bay Buccaneers, who lost 26 straight games, 1976–77.

Most points scored   The Washington Redskins scored 72 points vs. the New York Giants on November 27, 1966 to set the single-game NFL regular-season record for most points scored by one team.

Highest scoring game   On November 27, 1966, the Washington Redskins defeated the New York Giants 72–41 in Washington, D.C. The Redskins' total was an NFL record for most points (*see above*).

Largest deficit overcome   On January 3, 1993, the Buffalo Bills, playing at home in the AFC Wild Card game, trailed the Houston Oilers 35–3 with 28 minutes remaining. The Bills rallied to score 35 unanswered points and take the lead with 3:08 left. The Bills eventually won the game in overtime, overcoming a deficit of 32 points—the largest in NFL history.

Coaches

Most seasons   40, George Halas, Decatur/Chicago Staleys/Chicago Bears: 1920–29, 1933–42, 1946–55, 1958–67.

Most wins (including playoffs)   Don Shula holds the mark for most wins at 347 for the Baltimore Colts, 1963–69; and the Miami Dolphins, 1970–95.

Longest Plays

Run from scrimmage   Tony Dorsett, Dallas Cowboys, ran through the Minnesota Vikings defense for a 99-yard touchdown on January 3, 1983.

Pass completion   The longest pass completion, all for touchdowns, is 99 yards, performed by eight quarterbacks: Frank Filchock (to Andy Farkas), Washington Redskins vs. Pittsburgh Steelers, October 15, 1939; George

Izo (to Bobby Mitchell), Washington Redskins vs. Cleveland Browns, September 15, 1963; Karl Sweetan (to Pat Studstill), Detroit Lions vs. Baltimore Colts, October 16, 1966; Sonny Jurgensen (to Gerry Allen), Washington Redskins vs. Chicago Bears, September 15, 1968; Jim Plunkett (to Cliff Branch), Los Angeles Raiders vs. Washington Redskins, October 2, 1983; Ron Jaworski (to Mike Quick), Philadelphia Eagles vs. Atlanta Falcons, November 10, 1985; Stan Humphries (to Tony Martin), San Diego Chargers vs. Seattle Seahawks, September 18, 1994; Brett Favre (to Robert Brooks), Green Bay Packers vs. Chicago Bears, September 11, 1995.

Field goal   The longest was 63 yards, by Tom Dempsey, New Orleans Saints vs. Detroit Lions, on November 8, 1970.

Punt   Steve O'Neal, New York Jets, boomed a 98-yard punt on September 21, 1969 vs. Denver Broncos.

Interception return   The longest interception return for a touchdown is 104 yards, by James Willis and Troy Vincent, both of the Philadelphia Eagles, vs. Dallas Cowboys, November 3, 1996. Willis returned the ball 14 yards, then lateraled the ball to Vincent, who returned it for the remaining 90 yards.

The longest interception return for a touchdown by an individual player is 103 yards, shared by two players: Venice Glenn, San Diego Chargers vs. Denver Broncos, November 29, 1987; and Louis Oliver, Miami Dolphins vs. Buffalo Bills, October 4, 1992.

Kickoff return   Three players share the record for a kickoff return at 106 yards: Al Carmichael, Green Bay Packers vs. Chicago Bears, October 7, 1956; Noland Smith, Kansas City Chiefs vs. Denver Broncos, December 17, 1967; and Roy Green, St. Louis Cardinals vs. Dallas Cowboys, October 21, 1979. All three players scored touchdowns.

Punt return   The longest punt return in an NFL regular-season game is 103 yards by Robert Bailey, Los Angeles Rams vs. New Orleans Saints on October 23, 1994.

Streaks

Scoring (games)   206, Morten Andersen, New Orleans Saints, 1982–94; Atlanta Falcons, 1995–96.

Scoring touchdowns (games)   Lenny Moore of the Baltimore Colts scored 18 touchdowns, 1963–1965.

PATs, consecutive kicked   Tommy Davis of the San Francisco 49ers kicked 234 PATs, 1959–65.

Field goals, consecutive kicked   Minnesota Viking Fuad Reveiz kicked a record 31 consecutive field goals, 1994–95.

Field goals (games)   Fred Cox of the Minnesota Vikings kicked field goals in 31 games, 1968–70.

In 1996, Marcus Allen broke the NFL record for most touchdowns scored rushing.

Touchdown passes (games) Johnny Unitas of the Baltimore Colts completed at least one touchdown pass in 47 consecutive games, 1956–60.

Touchdown rushes (games) Touchdown rushes were performed by two players in a record 13 games: John Riggins, Washington Redskins, 1982–83; and George Rogers, Washington Redskins, 1985–86.

Touchdown receptions (games) Jerry Rice of the San Francisco 49ers holds the record for touchdown receptions in the most games, with 13, 1986–87.

Pass receptions (games) Pass receptions were completed in a record 183 games by Art Monk, Washington Redskins, 1980–93; New York Jets, 1994; and Philadelphia Eagles, 1995.

NFL CHAMPIONSHIP

Most NFL titles The Green Bay Packers have won 12 NFL championships: 1929–31, 1936, 1939, 1944, 1961–62, 1965, and Super Bowls I, II and XXXI (1966, 1967 and 1996 seasons).

THE SUPER BOWL

Team Records

Most wins Two teams have won five Super Bowls. The San Francisco 49ers won Super Bowls XVI, XIX, XXIII, XXIV and XXIX. The Dallas Cowboys won Super Bowls VI, XII, XXVII, XXVIII and XXX.

Consecutive wins Five teams have won Super Bowls in successive years: the Green Bay Packers, I and II; the Miami Dolphins, VII and VIII; the Pittsburgh Steelers (twice), IX and X, and XIII and XIV; the San Francisco 49ers, XXIII and XXIV; and the Dallas Cowboys, XXVII and XXVIII.

Most appearances The Dallas Cowboys have played in eight Super Bowls: V, VI, X, XII, XIII, XXVII, XXVIII and XXX. The Cowboys have won five games and lost three.

Most points scored The San Francisco 49ers scored 55 points vs. the Denver Broncos in Super Bowl XXIV.

Highest scoring game The record for the highest score is 75 points, set when the San Francisco 49ers beat the San Diego Chargers 49–26, in Super Bowl XXIX.

The Green Bay Packers' victory in Super Bowl XXXI set several records. The team's victory was a record 12th NFL championship. Brett Favre threw the longest touchdown pass in Super Bowl history (to Antonio Freeman); and Desmond Howard's record 99-yard kickoff return sealed the win.

Greatest margin of victory   The greatest margin of victory is 45 points, set by the San Francisco 49ers when they defeated the Denver Broncos 55–10 in Super Bowl XXIV.

Narrowest margin of victory   The narrowest margin of victory is one point, set by the New York Giants when they defeated the Buffalo Bills 20–19 in Super Bowl XXV.

Individual Records

Most points (game)   The record for the most points in a single game is 18, achieved by three players: Roger Craig, San Francisco 49ers vs. Denver Broncos (Super Bowl XXIV); Jerry Rice, San Francisco 49ers vs. Denver Broncos (Super Bowl XXIV) and vs. San Diego Chargers (Super Bowl XXIX); and Ricky Watters, San Francisco 49ers vs. San Diego Chargers (Super Bowl XXIX).

NFL RECORDS

Most points
Career 2,002, George Blanda (Chicago Bears, Baltimore Colts, Houston Oilers, Oakland Raiders), 1949–75. *Season* 176, Paul Hornung (Green Bay Packers), 1960. *Game* 40, Ernie Nevers (Chicago Cardinals), November 28, 1929.

Most touchdowns
Career 165, Jerry Rice (San Francisco 49ers), 1985–96. *Season* 25, Emmitt Smith (Dallas Cowboys), 1995. *Game* 6, Ernie Nevers (Chicago Cardinals), November 28, 1929; 6, William "Dub" Jones (Cleveland Browns) November 25, 1951; 6, Gale Sayers (Chicago Bears), December 12, 1965.

Most yards gained rushing
Career 16,726, Walter Payton (Chicago Bears), 1975–87. *Season* 2,105, Eric Dickerson (Los Angeles Rams), 1984. *Game* 275, Walter Payton (Chicago Bears), November 20, 1977.

Highest career average
5.22 yd. per game (12,352 yd. from 2,359 attempts), Jim Brown (Cleveland Browns), 1957–65

Most yards gained receiving
Career 16,377 Jerry Rice (San Francisco 49ers), 1985–96. *Season* 1,848, Jerry Rice (San Francisco 49ers), 1995. *Game* 336, Willie Anderson (Los Angeles Rams), November 26, 1989.

Most yards gained passing
Career 51,636, Dan Marino (Miami Dolphins), 1983–96. *Season* 5,084, Dan Marino (Miami Dolphins), 1984. *Game* 554, Norm Van Brocklin (Los Angeles Rams), September 28, 1951.

Most net yards gained
Career 21,803 Walter Payton (Chicago Bears), 1975–87. *Season* 2,535, Lionel James (San Diego Chargers), 1985. *Game* 373, Billy Cannon (Houston Oilers), December 10, 1961.

Passing attempts
Career 6,904 Dan Marino (Miami Dolphins), 1983–96. *Season* 691, Drew Bledsoe (New England Patriots), 1994. *Game* 70, Drew Bledsoe (New England Patriots), November 13, 1994.

Most passes completed
Career 4,134, Dan Marino (Miami Dolphins), 1983–96. *Season* 404, Warren Moon (Houston Oilers), 1991. *Game* 45 (from 70 attempts), Drew Bledsoe (New England Patriots, overtime), November 13, 1994. *Consecutive* 22, Joe Montana (San Francisco 49ers), November 29, 1987 vs. Cleveland Browns (5); December 6, 1987 vs. Green Bay Packers (17).

Pass receptions
Career 1,050, Jerry Rice (San Francisco 49ers), 1985–96. *Season* 123, Herman Moore (Detroit Lions), 1995. *Game* 18, Tom Fears (Los Angeles Rams), December 3, 1950.

Field goals
Career 383, Nick Lowery (New England Patriots, Kansas City Chiefs, New York Jets), 1978, 1980–96. *Season* 37, John Kasay (Carolina Panthers), 1996. *Game* 7, Jim Bakken (St. Louis Cardinals), September 24, 1967; Rich Karlis (Minnesota Vikings), November 5, 1989; Chris Boniol (Dallas Cowboys), November 18, 1996.

Punting
Career 1,154, Dave Jennings (New York Giants, New York Jets), 1974–87. *Season* 114, Bob Parsons (Chicago Bears), 1981. *Game* 15, John Teltschik (Philadelphia Eagles vs. New York Giants), December 6, 1987.

Sacks
Career 165.5, Reggie White (Philadelphia Eagles, Green Bay Packers), 1985–96. *Season* 22, Mark Gastineau (New York Jets), 1984. *Game* 7, Derrick Thomas (Kansas City Chiefs vs. Seattle Seahawks), November 11, 1990.

Most Interceptions
Career 81, Paul Krause (Washington Redskins, Minnesota Vikings), 1964–79. *Season* 14, Dick Lane (Los Angeles Rams), 1952. *Game* 4, by 16 players.

MO(O)RE
CATCHES

"**I** never thought I'd be able to catch so many passes. It's something I never envisioned," declares Herman Moore, the Detroit Lions' wide receiver. "I felt a lot of satisfaction."

The Lions play indoors where there are no swirling winds or freezing temperatures. Moore, however, doesn't think that playing conditions have much bearing on the record. "I catch just as many outside as inside," he says. "Ultimately you have to play a team whose goal is to stop your team. It's still the same game, but a different atmosphere."

The route to NFL glory was anything but a simple post pattern. "In high school, in Danville, VA, I started out as a place-kicker. From there I moved to tight end." Notes Moore, "I eventually got moved over to wide receiver but I got recruited by the University of Virginia as a defensive back first and a receiver second." An outstanding high jumper in college, Moore credits his agility and ball catching skills as the key to his success on the football field. "I have very good coordination and the ability to catch the ball in my hands. That is my security," he says.

A standout receiver at the University of Virginia, Moore also holds NCAA career reception marks. In Detroit, however, Moore plays in the shadow of his teammate, Barry Sanders, the great running back. Sanders' presence doesn't make Moore's job easier: "Although I know the concentration of the defense is on stopping Barry, I still have to line up against one or two defenders. It's seldom that I get one-on-one coverage. I still have to do my job and defeat the man in front of me." Adds Moore, "We help each other out. I take pressure off him, and he takes pressure off me."

A reader of *The Guinness Book of World Records,* the 6'4" receiver admires record-breakers who live on the edge: "I have a need for speed. I admire the fastest recorded nonstop flight around the world. I also admire the fastest cars." Moore's next Guinness record? "I want to outlive everybody," he says.

MOST PASS RECEPTIONS IN A SEASON

Herman Moore caught a record 123 passes for the Detroit Lions during the 1995 season.

Most points (career)   Jerry Rice holds the mark for the most career points at 42 for the San Francisco 49ers (Super Bowls XXII, XXIV, and XXIX).

Most touchdown passes (game)   The most touchdowns thrown is six, by Steve Young, San Francisco 49ers vs. San Diego Chargers (Super Bowl XXIX).

Most touchdown passes (career)   The career record for touchdowns thrown is 11, by Joe Montana, San Francisco 49ers (Super Bowls XVI XIX, XXIII, XXIV).

Most touchdowns scored (game)   The most touchdowns scored is three, by three players: Roger Craig, San Francisco 49ers vs. Denver Broncos (Super Bowl XXIV); Jerry Rice, San Francisco 49ers vs. Denver (Super Bowl XXIV) and vs. San Diego Chargers (Super Bowl XXIX); and Ricky Watters, San Francisco 49ers vs. San Diego Chargers (Super Bowl XXIX)..

Most touchdowns scored (career)   A career record of seven touchdowns has been achieved by Jerry Rice of the San Francisco 49ers (Super Bowls XXII, XXIV, XXIX).

Most yards gained rushing (game)   The most yards gained rushing is 204, by Timmy Smith, Washington Redskins vs. Denver Broncos (Super Bowl XXII).

Most yards gained rushing (career)   The career record for the most yards gained rushing is 354, by Franco Harris, Pittsburgh Steelers (Super Bowls IX, X, XIII, XIV).

Most pass completions (game)   The most completions thrown is 31, by Jim Kelly, Buffalo Bills vs. Dallas Cowboys (Super Bowl XXVIII).

49ers wide receiver Jerry Rice has scored more touchdowns in the Super Bowl than any other player.

Most pass completions (career)   The career record for the most pass completions is 83, by Joe Montana, San Francisco 49ers (Super Bowls XVI, XIX, XXIII, XXIV).

Highest pass completion percentage (game)   The highest pass completion mark is 88 percent (22–25) by Phil Simms, New York Giants vs. Denver Broncos (Super Bowl XXI).

Highest pass completion percentage (career)   The career record for highest pass completion is 70 percent (56–80), by Troy Aikman, Dallas Cowboys (Super Bowls XXVII, XXVIII, XXX).

Most receptions (game)   The most receptions is 11, by two players: Dan

Ross, Cincinnati Bengals vs. San Francisco 49ers (Super Bowl XVI); and Jerry Rice, San Francisco 49ers vs. Cincinnati Bengals (Super Bowl XXIII).

Most receptions (career)   The career record for the most receptions is 28, by Jerry Rice, San Francisco 49ers (Super Bowls XXIII, XXIV, XXIX).

Most field goals (game)   The most field goals kicked in a game is four, by two players: Dan Chandler, Green Bay Packers (Super Bowl II); and Ray Wersching, San Francisco 49ers (Super Bowl XVI).

Most field goals (career)   The career record for most field goals is five, by Ray Wersching, San Francisco 49ers (Super Bowls XVI, XIX).

Longest Plays

Run from scrimmage   The longest run from scrimmage is 74 yards, performed by Marcus Allen, Los Angeles Raiders (Super Bowl XVIII).

Pass completion   Brett Favre (Green Bay Packers) holds the pass completion mark at 81 yards, to Antonio Freeman (Super Bowl XXXI).

Field goal   The longest field goal kick is 54 yards, by Steve Christie, Buffalo Bills, XXVIII).

Kickoff return   The record for the longest kickoff return is 99 yards, by Desmond Howard, Green Bay Packers (Super Bowl XXXI).

Punt   The longest punt is 63 yards by Lee Johnson, Cincinnati Bengals (Super Bowl XXIII).

Coaches

Most wins   Chuck Noll led the Pittsburgh Steelers to four Super Bowl titles, IX, X, XIII and XIV.

Most appearances   Don Shula has been the head coach of six Super Bowl teams: the Baltimore Colts, III; the Miami Dolphins, VI, VII, VIII, XVII and XIX. He won two games and lost four.

Awards

Most MVPs   Joe Montana, quarterback of the San Francisco 49ers, has been voted the Super Bowl MVP on a record three occasions, XVI, XIX and XXIV.

(NCAA) FOOTBALL

Career Records
(All Divisions)

Most points scored (game)   Four players have scored 48 points in an NCAA game: Junior Wolf, Panhandle State (Div. II), November 8, 1958 vs. St.

Mary's (Kans.); Paul Zaeske, North Park (Div. II), October 12, 1968 vs. North Central; Howard Griffith, Illinois (Div. I-A), September 22, 1990 vs. Southern Illinois; and Carey Bender, Coe College (Div. III), November 12, 1994 vs. Beloit.

Most points scored (season)   The season record is 234, by Barry Sanders, Oklahoma State (Div. I-A) in 1988, all from touchdowns, 37 rushing and two receptions.

Most points scored (career)   The career record is 528, by Carey Bender, Coe College (Div. III), 1991–94. Bender scored 86 touchdowns, 70 rushing, 16 receptions and 12 extra points.

Most yards gained rushing (game)   A. J. Pittorino, Hartwick (Div. III) rushed for an NCAA single-game record 443 yards vs. Waynesburg on November 2, 1996.

Most yards gained rushing (season)   The most yards gained in a season is 2,628, by Barry Sanders, Oklahoma State (Div. I-A), in 1988. Sanders played in 11 games and carried the ball 344 times for an average gain of 7.64 yards per carry.

Most yards gained rushing (career)   The record for most yards gained is 6,320, by Johnny Bailey, Texas A&M–Kingsville (Div. II), 1986–89. Bailey carried the ball 885 times for an average gain of 7.14 yards per carry.

Most yards gained passing (game)   David Klingler, Houston (Div. I-A) threw for a single-game record 716 yards vs. Arizona State on December 2, 1990.

Most yards gained passing (season)   The single-season mark is held by Ty Detmer, BYU, who threw for 5,188 yards in 1990.

Most yards gained passing (career)   The career passing record is 15,031 yards, set by Ty Detmer, BYU (Div. I-A), 1988–91.

Most yards gained receiving (game)   The most yards gained from pass receptions in a single game is 370, by two players: Barry Wagner, Alabama A&M (Div. II), vs. Clark Atlanta on November 4, 1989; Michael Lerch, Princeton (Div. 1-AA), vs. Brown on October 12, 1991.

Most yards gained receiving (season)   The single-season NCAA record is 1,876 yards, by Chris George, Glenville State (Div. II). George caught 117 passes for an average gain of 16.0 yards in 1993.

In 1996, Wyoming's Marcus Harris set the NCAA Division I-A mark for career yards gained by a receiver.

Most yards gained receiving (career) The career receiving record is 4,693 yards, set by Jerry Rice, Mississippi Valley (Division I-AA), 1981–84.

NCAA (DIVISION I-A)

Longest Plays

Run from scrimmage The record for the longest run from scrimmage is 99 yards, by four players: Gale Sayers (Kansas vs. Nebraska), 1963; Max Anderson (Arizona State vs. Wyoming), 1967; Ralph Thompson (West Texas State vs. Wichita State), 1970; Kelsey Finch (Tennessee vs. Florida), 1977.

Pass completion The longest pass completion is 99 yards, on nine occasions, performed by eight players (Terry Peel and Robert Ford did it twice): Fred Owens (to Jack Ford), Portland vs. St. Mary's, CA, 1947; Bo Burris (to Warren McVea), Houston vs. Washington State, 1966; Colin Clapton (to Eddie Jenkins), Holy Cross vs. Boston U, 1970; Terry Peel (to Robert Ford), Houston vs. Syracuse, 1970; Terry Peel (to Robert Ford), Houston vs. San Diego State, 1972; Cris Collingsworth (to Derrick Gaffney), Florida vs. Rice, 1977; Scott Ankrom (to James Maness), TCU vs. Rice, 1984; Gino Torretta (to Horace Copeland), Miami vs. Arkansas, 1991; John Paci (to Thomas Lewis), Indiana vs. Penn State, 1993.

Field goal The longest field goal is 67 yards, by three players: Russell Erxleben (Texas vs. Rice), 1977; Steve Little (Arkansas vs. Texas), 1977; Joe Williams (Wichita State vs. Southern Illinois), 1978.

Punt The longest punt is 99 yards, by Pat Brady, Nevada-Reno vs. Loyola Marymount in 1950.

Team Records

Most wins Michigan has won 764 games out of 1,054 played, 1879–1996.

Highest winning percentage The highest winning percentage in college football history is .759 by Notre Dame. The Fighting Irish have won 746, lost 222 and tied 42 out of 1,010 games played, 1887–1996.

The most storied team in college football, Notre Dame, has the highest winning percentage in Division I-A football.

NCAA DIVISION 1-A INDIVIDUAL RECORDS

Points Game 48, Howard Griffith (Illinois vs. Southern Illinois; 8 touchdowns), September 22, 1990

Season 234, Barry Sanders (Oklahoma State; 39 touchdowns in 11 games), 1988

Career 423, Roman Anderson (Houston; 70 field goals; 213 point-after-touchdowns), 1988–91

Total yardage Game 732, David Klingler (Houston vs. Arizona State; 716 passing, 16 rushing), December 2, 1990

Season 5,221, David Klingler (Houston; 5,140 passing, 81 rushing), 1990

Career 14,665, Ty Detmer (Brigham Young; 15,031 passing, 366 rushing), 1988–91

Yards gained rushing Game 396, Tony Sands (Kansas vs. Missouri; 58 rushes), November 23, 1991

Season 2,628, Barry Sanders (Oklahoma State; 344 rushes in 11 games, record av. 238.9), 1988

Career 6,082, Tony Dorsett (Pittsburgh), 1,074 rushes, 1973–76

Yards gained passing Game 716, David Klingler (Houston vs. Arizona State; completed 41 of 70), December 2, 1990

Season 5,188, Ty Detmer (Brigham Young; completed 361 of 562), 1990

Career 15,031, Ty Detmer (Brigham Young; completed 958 of 1,530), 1988–91

Pass completions Game 55, Rusty LaRue (Wake Forest vs. Duke; 78 attempts), October 28, 1995

Season 374, David Klingler (Houston; 643 attempts), 1990

Career 958, Ty Detmer (Brigham Young; 1,530 attempts), 1988–91

Touchdown passes Game 11, David Klingler (Houston vs. Eastern Washington), November 17, 1990

Season 54, David Klingler (Houston; 11 games), 1990

Career 121, Ty Detmer (Brigham Young), 1988–91

Pass receptions Game 23, Randy Gatewood (UNLV vs. Idaho), September 17, 1994

Season 142, Emmanuel Hazard (Houston), 1989

Career 266, Aaron Turner (Pacific), 1989–92

Yards gained receiving Game 363, Randy Gatewood (UNLV vs. Idaho), September 17, 1994

Season 1,854, Alex Van Dyke (Nevada), 1995

Career 4,518, Marcus Harris (Wyoming), 1993–96

Pass interceptions Game 5, Dan Rebsch (Miami [Ohio] vs. Western Michigan), [three others with less yards], November 4, 1972

Season 14, Al Worley (Washington; 130 yards in 10 games), 1968

Career 29, Al Brosky (Illinois; 356 yards, 27 games), 1950–52

Touchdowns (receiving) Game 6, Tim Delaney (San Diego State vs. New Mexico State), November 15, 1969

Season 22, Emmanuel Hazard (Houston), 1989

Career 43, Aaron Turner (Pacific), 1989–92

Field Goals Game 7, Mike Prindle (West Michigan vs. Marshall), September 29, 1984; 7, Dale Klein (Nebraska vs. Missouri), October 19, 1985

Season 29, John Lee (UCLA), 1984

Career 80, Jeff Jaeger (Washington), 1983–86

Consecutive 30, Chuck Nelson (Washington), 1981–82

Touchdowns Game 8, Howard Griffith (Illinois vs. Southern Illinois; all rushing), September 22, 1990

Season 39, Barry Sanders (Oklahoma State; all rushing), 1988

Career 65, Anthony Thompson (Indiana; 64 rushing, one pass reception), 1986–89

Longest winning streak   The longest winning streak in Division I-A football, including bowl games, is 47 games by Oklahoma, 1953–57. Oklahoma's streak was stopped on November 16, 1957, when Notre Dame defeated them 7–0 in Norman.

Most points scored   Wyoming crushed Northern Colorado 103–0 on November 5, 1949 to set the Division I-A mark for most points scored by one team in a single game. The Cowboys scored 15 touchdowns and converted 13 PATs.

Highest-scoring game   The most points scored in a Division I-A game is 124, when Oklahoma defeated Colorado 82–42 on October 4, 1980.

Bowl Games

Most wins   Alabama has won a record 28 bowl games: Sugar Bowl, eight times, 1962, 1964, 1967, 1975, 1978–80, 1992; Rose Bowl, four times, 1926, 1931, 1935, 1946; Orange Bowl, four times, 1943, 1953, 1963, 1966; Sun Bowl (now John Hancock Bowl), three times, 1983, 1986, 1988; Cotton Bowl, twice, 1942, 1981; Liberty Bowl, twice, 1976, 1982; Aloha Bowl, once, 1985; Blockbuster Bowl, once, 1991; Gator Bowl, once, 1993; Florida Citrus Bowl, once, 1995; Outback Bowl, once, 1997.

Alabama has won a record 28 bowl games, including its 1997 Outback Bowl win.

Most consecutive seasons   Florida State won a bowl game for 11 consecutive seasons: Gator Bowl, 1985; All-American Bowl, 1986; Fiesta Bowl, 1988; Sugar Bowl, 1989; Fiesta Bowl, 1990; Blockbuster Bowl, 1990; Cotton Bowl, 1992; Orange Bowl, 1993–94; Sugar Bowl, 1995; Orange Bowl, 1996.

Most appearances   Alabama has played in 48 bowl games.

National Championship

Most selections   The most wins in the national journalists' poll, established in 1936 to determine the college team of the year, is eight, by Notre Dame, 1943, 1946–47, 1949, 1966, 1973, 1977 and 1988.

Coaches

Most wins (all divisions)   In overall NCAA competition, Eddie Robinson, holds the mark for most victories with 405. Robinson coached at Grambling (Division I-AA), 1941–42, 1945–1997.

Most wins (Division I-A)   Paul "Bear" Bryant has won more games than any other coach, with 323 victories over 38 years. Bryant coached four teams: Maryland, 1945 (6–2–1); Kentucky, 1946–53 (60–23–5); Texas A&M, 1954–57 (25–14–2); and Alabama, 1958–82 (232–46–9). His completed record was 323 wins–85 losses–17 ties, for a .780 winning percentage.

Highest winning percentage (Division I-A)   The highest winning percentage in Division I-A competition is .881, held by Knute Rockne of Notre Dame. Rockne coached the Irish from 1918 to 1930, for a record of 105 wins, 12 losses and 5 ties.

Fans

Most games attended   Giles Pellerin had attended 775 consecutive University of Southern California games, home and away, from the start of the 1926 season through the end of the 1996 season.

Roger and Doris Goodridge of Baldwinsville, NY have attended every Colgate University football game since 1940, both at home and away. During this streak, they have cheered for the Red Raiders through 529 games.

Largest crowd   It has been estimated that crowds of 120,000 were present for two Notre Dame games played at Soldier Field, Chicago, IL: vs. Southern Cal. (November 26, 1927); and vs. Navy (October 13, 1928). Attendance records have been kept by the NCAA since 1948. The highest official crowd for a regular-season NCAA game was 107,608 Volunteers fans at Neyland Football Stadium, Knoxville, TN on September 21, 1996 for the Tennessee vs. Florida game.

Largest crowd (Bowl games)   The record attendance for a bowl game is 106,869 people at the 1973 Rose Bowl, where Southern Cal. defeated Ohio State 42–17.

Awards

Most Heisman Trophy wins   The only double winner of the Heisman Trophy was Archie Griffen of Ohio State, 1974–75. The University of Notre Dame has had more Heisman Trophy winners than any other school, with seven selections.

CANADIAN FOOTBALL LEAGUE (CFL)

Team Records

Longest winning streak   The Calgary Stampeders won 22 consecutive games between August 25, 1948 and October 22, 1949 to set the CFL mark.

Longest winless streak   The Hamilton Tiger-Cats hold the dubious distinction of being the CFL's most unsuccessful team, amassing a 20-game winless streak (0–19–1), from September 28, 1948 to September 2, 1950.

Highest-scoring game   The Toronto Argonauts defeated the B.C. Lions 68–43 on September 1, 1990 to set a CFL combined score record of 111 points.

Highest score (one team)   The Montreal Alouettes rolled over the Hamilton Tiger-Cats 82–14 on October 20, 1956 to set the CFL highest-score mark.

Most points in a season   The Edmonton Eskimos tallied 32 points in the 1989 season. The team's season record was 16 wins and two losses.

THE GREY CUP

Most wins (team)   The Toronto Argonauts won 13 Grey Cup championships, 1914, 1921, 1933, 1937–38, 1945–47, 1950, 1952, 1983, 1991, 1996.

Most consecutive wins (team)   The Edmonton Eskimos won five consecutive Grey Cup championships from 1978 to 1983.

Individual Records

Most points (game)   The most points scored in a Grey Cup game is 23, by Don Sweet for Montreal vs. Edmonton, November 27, 1977.

CFL record holder Doug Flutie led the Toronto Argonauts to the 1996 Grey Cup title.

Most points (career)   The career record for the most points in a Grey Cup game is 72, achieved by Dave Cutler of Edmonton, 1969–84.

Most touchdowns (game)   A record three touchdowns have been scored by four players: Ross Craig, Hamilton vs. Toronto, November 29, 1913; Red Storey, Toronto vs. Winnipeg, December 10, 1938; Jackie Parker, Edmonton vs. Montreal, November 24, 1956; and Tommy Scott, Edmonton vs. Hamilton, November 23, 1980.

Most touchdowns (career)   The career record for most touchdowns is five, shared by two players: Hal Patterson (Montreal, Hamilton), 1954–1967; and Brian Kelly (Edmonton), 1979–1987.

Most converts (game)   The record for the most converts is six, performed by two players: Dave Cutler, Edmonton vs. Hamilton, November 23, 1980; Trevor Kennerd, Winnipeg vs. Edmonton, November 25, 1990.

CFL INDIVIDUAL RECORDS

Games Played Most   336, Lui Passaglia, B.C. Lions, 1976–96

Consecutive   293, Bob Cameron, Winnipeg Blue Bombers, 1980–96

Points Scored Game   36, Bob McNamara, Winnipeg Blue Bombers vs. B.C. Lions, October 13,1956

Season   236, Lance Chomyc, Toronto Argonauts, 1991

Career   3,316, Lui Passaglia, B.C. Lions, 1976–96

Touchdowns Scored Game   6, Eddie James, Winnipegs vs. Winnipeg St. Jonns, September 28, 1932; Bob McNamara, Winnipeg Blue Bombers vs. B.C. Lions, October 13, 1956

Season   22, Cory Philpot, B.C. Lions, 1995

Career   137, George Reed, Saskatchewan Rough Riders, 1963–75

Passing

Yards Gained Game   713, Matt Dunigan, Edmonton Eskimos vs. Winnipeg Blue Bombers, July 14, 1994

Season   6,619, Doug Flutie, B.C. Lions, 1991

Career   50,535, Ron Lancaster, Ottawa Roughriders/Saskatchewan Rough Riders, 1960–78

Touchdowns Thrown Game   8, Joe Zuger, Hamilton Tiger-Cats, October 15, 1962

Season   48, Doug Flutie, Calgary Stampeders, 1994

Career   333, Ron Lancaster, Ottawa/Saskatchewan Rough Riders, 1960–78

Completions Game   41, Dieter Brock, Winnipeg Blue Bombers vs. Ottawa Rough Riders, October 3, 1981; Kent Austin, Saskatchewan Rough Riders vs. Toronto Argonauts, October 31, 1993

Season   466, Doug Flutie, B.C. Lions, 1991

Career   3,384, Ron Lancaster, Ottawa Rough Riders/Saskatchewan Rough Riders, 1960–78

Pass Receiving

Receptions Game   16, Terry Greer, Toronto Argonauts vs. Ottawa Rough Riders, August 19, 1983, Brian Wiggins, Calgary Stampeders vs. Saskatchewan Rough Riders, October 23, 1993

Season   126, Allen Pitts, Calgary Stampeders, 1994

Career   830, Ray Elgaard, Saskatchewan Rough Riders, 1983–96

Yards Gained Game   338, Hal Patterson, Montreal Alouettes vs. Hamilton Tiger-Cats, September 29, 1956

Season   2,036, Allen Pitts, Calgary Stampeders, 1984

Career   13,198, Ray Elgaard, Saskatchewan Rough Riders, 1983–96

Most converts (career)   The career record for the most converts is 17, achieved by Don Sutherin (Hamilton, Ottawa, Toronto), 1958–1970.

Most yards gained rushing (game)   Johnny Bright gained a record 171 yards for Edmonton vs. Montreal on November 24, 1956.

Most yards gained rushing (career)   Leo Lewis of Winnipeg holds the record with 359 yards, 1955–1966.

Most receptions (game)   The most pass receptions is 13, achieved by Red O'Quinn for Montreal vs. Edmonton, November 27, 1954.

Most receptions (career)   Hal Patterson (Montreal, Hamilton) made 29 receptions from 1954–1967.

Most field goals (game)   A record six field goals were achieved by three players: Don Sweet, Montreal vs. Edmonton, November 27, 1977; Paul Osbaldiston, Hamilton vs. Edmonton, November 30, 1986; and Sean Fleming, Edmonton vs. Winnipeg, November 28, 1993.

Most field goals (career)   Dave Cutler of Edmonton holds the mark for the most field goals in a career at 18, 1969–1984.

Most singles (game)   The record for the most singles in a game is eight, held by Hugh Gall for U. of T. vs. Toronto–Parkdale, December 4, 1909.

Most singles (career)   The career record for most singles is 12, by Hugh Gall (U. of T. Parkdale), 1908–1912.

ARENA FOOTBALL

Team Records

Most ArenaBowl Championships   The record for the most championship titles is four, by the Detroit Drive (II, III, IV, VI) and the Tampa Bay Storm (V, VII, IX, X).

Most wins (season)   The record for the most wins in a single season is 15, achieved by the Tampa Bay Storm, 1996; and the Arizona Rattlers, 1997.

Longest consecutive winning streak   The Arizona Rattlers and the Iowa Barnstormers both had a 9–0 undefeated winning streak in 1997.

Highest scoring game   The highest scoring game in Arena Football history was on June 20, 1997, when the New Jersey Red Dogs gained a 91–62 victory over the Texas Terror.

Individual Records

Most points (game)   Eddie Brown scored a record 54 points for the Albany Firebirds vs. the Minnesota Fighting Pike on May 18, 1996.

Most points (season)   The single-season record for the most points is 308, achieved by Eddie Brown for the Albany Firebirds in 1996.

Most points (career)   The record for the most points scored in one career is 1,016, by Barry Wagner of the Orlando Predators, 1992–1996.

Most touchdowns (game)   Eddie Brown holds the single-game record for the most touchdowns with nine for the Albany Firebirds vs. the Minnesota Fighting Pike on May 18, 1996.

Most touchdowns (season)   Eddie Brown also holds the single-season record for the most touchdowns with 51 for the Albany Firebirds in 1996.

Most touchdowns (career)   Barry Wagner of the Orlando Predators holds the career record for the most touchdowns with 165, 1992–1996.

Most yards gained passing (game)   The record for the most yards gained passing in a single game is 455, set by Mike Pawlawski for the Albany Firebirds in their 76–64 loss to the Iowa Barnstormers, August 2, 1997.

Most yards gained passing (season)   Mike Perez of the Albany Firebirds gained a record 4,153 yards passing in 1996.

Most yards gained passing (career)   Jay Gruden gained a record 15,514 yards for the Tampa Bay Storm, 1991–96.

Most touchdown passes (game)   The record for the most touchdown passes completed is 10, shared by two players: Whit Taylor, Denver Dynamite vs. Washington Commandos, July 3, 1987; and Clint Dolezel, Texas Terror vs. Iowa Barnstormers, July 26, 1997.

Most touchdown passes (season)   Mike Perez of the Albany Firebirds holds the single-season record for the most touchdown passes with 84 in 1996.

Most touchdown passes (career)   Jay Gruden (Tampa Bay Storm, 1991–96) successfully completed a record 280 touchdown passes.

Most receptions (game)   Dwayne Dixon holds the mark for the most receptions in a single game at 20 for the Washington Commandos vs. the Chicago Bruisers, July 16, 1987.

Barry Wagner holds several Arena Football career records, including most points and touchdowns scored.

Most receptions (season) Andre Langley holds the mark for the most receptions in one season at 124, Charlotte Rage, 1996.

Most receptions (career) George LaFrance (Detroit Drive, 1988–89, 1991–93; Tampa Bay Storm, 1994–96) holds the mark for the most receptions in one career at 393.

Most yards gained receiving (game) The record for the most yards gained receiving is 264, by Dwayne Dixon for the Washington Commandos vs. Chicago Bruisers, July 16, 1987.

Most yards gained receiving (season) Eddie Brown gained 1,685 yards for the Albany Firebirds during the 1996 season.

Most yards gained receiving (career) George LaFrance (Detroit Drive, 1988–89, 1991–93; Tampa Bay Storm, 1994–96) gained a record 5,800 yards during his career.

Most yards gained rushing (game) The single-game record for the most yards gained rushing is 95, achieved by Major Harris for the Columbus T'Bolts vs. Denver Dynamite, July 6, 1991.

Most yards gained rushing (season) Major Harris of the Columbus T'Bolts gained a record 429 yards rushing during the 1991 season.

Most yards gained rushing (career) The career record for the most yards gained rushing is 837, achieved by Major Harris (Columbus T'Bolts, 1991; Cleveland Thunderbolts, 1992, 1994).

Most touchdowns gained rushing (game) The most touchdowns gained rushing in a game is five, achieved three times by two players: Barry Wagner, Orlando Predators vs. Miami Hooters, June 17, 1995; and Bernard Hall, St. Louis Stampede vs. Minnesota Fighting Pike, May 10, 1996 and vs. Memphis Pharoahs, May 17, 1996.

Most touchdowns gained rushing (season) In the 1996 season, Bernard Hall of the St. Louis Stampede gained a record 30 touchdowns.

Most touchdowns gained rushing (career) Barry Wagner (Orlando Predators, 1992–96) holds the career record for the most touchdowns gained rushing with 45.

Most 3-point field goals (game) Kenny Stucker made a record six 3-point field goals for the Milwaukee Mustangs vs. the Cleveland Thunderbolts on July 22, 1994.

Most 3-point field goals (season)   The single-season record for the most 3-point field goals is 23, achieved by Mike Black of the Charlotte Rage in 1993.

Most 3-point field goals (career)   Mike Black (Charlotte Rage, 1993–94; Iowa Barnstormers, 1995–96) holds the all-time record for the most field goals in a career with 66.

HOCKEY

NATIONAL HOCKEY LEAGUE (NHL)

Team Records

Most wins (season)   The Detroit Red Wings won 62 games during the 1995–96 season. In 82 games, the Red Wings won 62, lost 13 and tied 7.

Highest winning percentage (season)   The 1929–30 Boston Bruins set an NHL record .875 winning percentage. The Bruins' record was 38 wins, 5 losses and 1 tie.

Most points, wins and ties (season)   The Montreal Canadiens accumulated 132 points during their record-setting campaign of 1976–77, when they won a record 60 games.

Longest winning streak   The Pittsburgh Penguins won 17 consecutive games from March 9 through April 10, 1993.

Longest undefeated streak   The longest undefeated streak in one season is 35 games by the Philadelphia Flyers. The Flyers won 25 games and tied 10 from October 14, 1979–January 6, 1980.

Most goals (game)   The NHL record for goals in one game is 21, which has occurred on two occasions. The mark was set on January 10, 1920, when the Montreal Canadiens defeated the Toronto St. Patricks, 14–7, at Montreal. This record was matched on December 11, 1985, when the Edmonton Oilers beat the Chicago Blackhawks, 12–9, at Chicago.

Highest scoring game   The Montreal Canadiens pounded the Quebec Bulldogs 16–3 on March 3, 1920 to set the single-game scoring record. To make matters worse for Quebec, the game was on home ice.

Most goals (season)   The Edmonton Oilers scored 446 goals in 80 games during the 1983–84 season.

Most assists (season)   The Edmonton Oilers recorded 737 assists in the 1985–86 season.

Most points (season)   The Edmonton Oilers amassed 1,182 points (446 goals, 736 assists) during the 1983–84 season.

Most power-play goals scored (season)   The Pittsburgh Penguins scored 119 power-play goals during the 1988–89 season.

Most shorthanded goals scored (season)   The Edmonton Oilers scored 36 shorthand goals during the 1983–84 season.

Most penalty minutes (game)   At the Boston Garden on February 26, 1981, the Boston Bruins and the Minnesota North Stars received a combined 406 penalty minutes, a record for one game. The Bruins received 20 minors, 13 majors, three 10-minute misconducts and six game misconducts for a total of 195 penalty minutes; the North Stars received 18 minors, 13 majors, four 10-minute misconducts and seven game misconducts for a total of 211 penalty minutes. It is reported that a hockey game broke out between the fights, which the Bruins won 5–1.

Longest game   The longest game was played between the Detroit Red Wings and the Montreal Maroons at the Forum Montreal and lasted 2 hr. 56 min. 30 sec. The Red Wings won when Mud Bruneteau scored the only goal of the game in the sixth period of overtime at 2:25 A.M. on March 25, 1936. Norm Smith, the Red Wings goaltender, turned aside 92 shots for the NHL's longest shutout.

Individual Records

Most games played   Gordie Howe played 1,767 games over a record 26 seasons for the Detroit Red Wings (1946–71) and Hartford Whalers (1979–80). The most games played by a goaltender is 971, by Terry Sawchuk, who played 21 seasons for five teams: Detroit Red Wings, Boston Bruins, Toronto Maple Leafs, Los Angeles Kings and New York Rangers (1949–70).

Most consecutive games played   Doug Jarvis played 964 consecutive games from October 8, 1975 to October 10, 1987. During the streak, Jarvis played for three teams: the Montreal Canadiens, Washington Capitals and Hartford Whalers.

Fastest goals   The fastest goal from the start of a game is five seconds, a feat performed by three players: Doug Smail (Winnipeg Jets) vs. St. Louis Blues at Winnipeg on December 20, 1981; Bryan Trottier (New York Islanders) vs. Boston Bruins at Boston on March 22, 1984; and Alexander Mogilny (Buffalo Sabres) vs. Toronto Maple Leafs at Toronto on December 21, 1991. The fastest goal from the start of any period was after four seconds, achieved by two players: Claude Provost (Montreal Canadiens) vs. Boston Bruins in the second period at Montreal on November 9, 1957, and by Denis Savard (Chicago Blackhawks) vs. Hartford Whalers in the third period at Chicago on January 12, 1986.

Most goals (period)   Ten players hold the record for the most goals (four) scored in a single period: Busher Jackson, Toronto Maple Leafs vs. St. Louis Eagles, November 20, 1934; Max Bentley, Chicago Blackhawks vs.

New York Rangers, January 28, 1943; Clint Smith, Chicago Blackhawks vs. Montreal Canadiens, March 4, 1945; Red Berenson, St. Louis Blues vs. Philadelphia Flyers, November 7, 1968; Wayne Gretzky, Edmonton Oilers vs. St. Louis Blues, February 18, 1981; Grant Mulvey, Chicago Blackhawks vs. St. Louis Blues, February 3, 1982; Bryan Trottier, New York Islanders vs. Philadelphia Flyers, February 13, 1982; Al Secord, Chicago Blackhawks vs. Toronto Maple Leafs, January 7, 1987; Joe Nieuwendyk, Calgary Flames vs. Winnipeg Jets, January 11, 1989; and Peter Bondra, Washington Capitals vs. Tampa Bay Lightning, February 5, 1994.

Most goals (game)   Joe Malone holds the record for the most goals scored in one game. Malone scored seven goals for the Quebec Bulldogs vs. Toronto St Patricks on January 31, 1920.

Most goals (season)   The most goals scored in a season in the NHL is 92, in the 1981/82 season by Wayne Gretzky for the Edmonton Oilers.

Most goals (career)   Wayne Gretzky scored a record 862 goals (Edmonton Oilers, Los Angeles Kings, St. Louis Blues, New York Rangers), 1979–97.

Most assists (period)   The record number of assists in one period is five, by Dale Hawerchuk, for the Winnipeg Jets vs. the Los Angeles Kings on March 6, 1984.

Most assists (game)   The most assists in an NHL game is seven, once by Billy Taylor for Detroit, 10–6 vs. Chicago on March 16, 1947, and three times by Wayne Gretzky for Edmonton, 8–2 vs. Washington on February 15, 1980, 12–9 vs. Chicago on December 11, 1985, and 8–2 vs. Quebec on February 14, 1986.

Most assists (season)   Wayne Gretzky holds the record for the most assists in one season with 163 for the Edmonton Oilers in 1985/86.

Most assists (career)   The record number of assists in one career is 1,843, by Wayne Gretzky (Edmonton Oilers, Los Angeles Kings, St. Louis Blues, New York Rangers), 1979–97.

Wayne Gretzky dominates the NHL record book. He leads all players in goals scored, assists credited and points amassed.

Most points (period)   The most points scored in a single period is six, by Bryan Trottier, for the New York Islanders vs. the New York Rangers on December 23, 1978.

Most points (game)   Darryl Sittler holds the record for the most points in a game. Sittler scored ten points for the Toronto Maple Leafs vs. the Boston Bruins on February 7, 1976

Most points (season)   The most points scored in a season is 215, in 1985/86 by Wayne Gretzky of the Edmonton Oilers.

Most points (career)   Wayne Gretzky (Edmonton Oilers, Los Angeles Kings, St. Louis Blues, New York Rangers) holds the mark of most career points at 2,705 from 1979 through 1997.

Most shutouts (season)   The most shutouts in a season is 22, in 1928/29 by George Hainsworth of the Montreal Canadiens.

Most shutouts (career)   Terry Sawchuk (Detroit Red Wings, Boston Bruins, Toronto Maple Leafs, Los Angeles Kings, New York Rangers) holds the career record of shutouts with 103 from 1949 to 1970.

Most wins, goalie (season)   The goaltender with the most wins is Bernie Parent of the Philadelphia Flyers with 47 in the 1973/74 season.

Most wins, goalie (career)   The record number of wins in a career is 447, by Terry Sawchuk (Philadelphia Flyers, Detroit Red Wings, Boston Bruins, the Toronto Maple Leafs, Los Angeles Kings, New York Rangers) from 1949 to 1970.

Most hat tricks (season)   Wayne Gretzky holds the record for most hat tricks in a season, 10, in both the 1981–82 and 1983–84 seasons for the Edmonton Oilers.

Most hat tricks (career)   The most hat tricks (three or more goals in a game) in a career is 49, by Wayne Gretzky (Edmonton Oilers, Los Angeles Kings, St. Louis Blues, New York Rangers) from 1979 through February 24, 1997.

Longest goal-scoring streak   The most consecutive games scoring at least one goal in a game is 16, by Harry (Punch) Broadbent (Ottawa Senators) in the 1921–22 season. Broadbent scored 25 goals during the streak.

Longest assist-scoring streak   The record for most consecutive games recording at least one assist is 23 games, by Wayne Gretzky (Los Angeles Kings) in 1990–91. Gretzky was credited with 48 assists during the streak.

Longest point-scoring streak   The most consecutive games scoring at least one point is 51, by Wayne Gretzky (Edmonton Oilers) between October 5, 1983 and January 27, 1984. During the streak, Gretzky scored 61 goals, 92 assists for 153 points.

Longest shutout streak (goalie)   Alex Connell (Ottawa Senators) played 461 min. 29 sec. without conceding a goal in the 1927–28 season.

Longest undefeated streak (goalie)   Gerry Cheevers (Boston Bruins) went 32 games (24 wins, 8 ties) undefeated during the 1971–72 season.

Most goals, defensemen (season) Paul Coffey holds the single-season record for goals scored by a defenseman, 48, which he scored in 1985–86 when he played for the Edmonton Oilers.

Most goals, defensemen (career) Paul Coffey (Edmonton Oilers, 1980–87; Pittsburgh Penguins, 1987–91; Los Angeles Kings, 1991–93; Detroit Red Wings, 1993–96; Hartford Whalers, 1996; Philadelphia Flyers, 1996–1997) scored a record 381 goals, 1980–97.

Paul Coffey leads all NHL defensemen in career goals, assists and points. Here he leaves former Edmonton teammate Mark Messier in his wake.

Most assists, defensemen (season) Bobby Orr (Boston Bruins) holds the single-season record for the most assists (102) in the 1970–71 season.

Most assists, defensemen (career) Paul Coffey (Edmonton Oilers, 1980–87; Pittsburgh Penguins, 1987–91; Los Angeles Kings, 1991–93; Detroit Red Wings, 1993–96; Hartford Whalers, 1996; Philadelphia Flyers, 1996–1997) holds the record for the most assists in a single career with 1,063, 1980–97.

Most points, defensemen (season) The single-season record for the most points scored by a defenseman is 139, by Bobby Orr of the Boston Bruins, in the 1970–71 season.

Most points, defensemen (career) Paul Coffey (Edmonton Oilers, 1980–87; Pittsburgh Penguins, 1987–91; Los Angeles Kings, 1991–93; Detroit Red Wings, 1993–96; Hartford Whalers, 1996; Philadelphia Flyers, 1996–1997) holds the record for the most points scored by a single defenseman in a career with 1,444, 1980–97.

Coaches

Most wins Scotty Bowman has coached his teams to 1,013 victories (110 wins, St. Louis Blues, 1967–71; 419 wins, Montreal Canadiens, 1971–79; 210 wins, Buffalo Sabres, 1979–87; 95 wins, Pittsburgh Penguins, 1991–93; 179 wins, Detroit Red Wings, 1993–97).

Most games coached   Scotty Bowman has coached a record 1,736 games with five teams: St. Louis Blues, 1967–71; Montreal Canadiens, 1971–79; Buffalo Sabres, 1979–87; Pittsburgh Penguins, 1991–93; Detroit Red Wings, 1993–97. Bowman's career 1,013 wins, 461 losses, 262 ties.

Awards

Hart Trophy (most wins)   The Hart Trophy, awarded annually starting with the 1923/24 season by the Professional Hockey Writers Association as the Most Valuable Player award of the NHL, has been won a record nine times by Wayne Gretzky, 1980–87 and 1989.

Ross Trophy (most wins)   Wayne Gretzky won the Art Ross Trophy a record 10 times, 1981–87, 1990–91 and 1994; this trophy has been awarded annually since 1947/48 to the NHL season's leading scorer.

Norris Trophy (most wins)   Bobby Orr of Boston won the James Norris Memorial Trophy, awarded annually starting with the 1953/54 season to the league's leading defenseman, a record eight times, 1968–75.

Vezina Trophy   Jacques Plante won the Vezina Trophy, awarded annually since 1926/27 to the NHL season's leading goalkeeper, a record seven times, for Montreal, 1956–60, 1962; and for St. Louis, 1969.

STANLEY CUP

Most championships   The Montreal Canadiens have won the Stanley Cup a record 24 times: 1916, 1924, 1930–31, 1944, 1946, 1953, 1956–60, 1965–66, 1968–69, 1971, 1973, 1976–79, 1986, 1993.

Most consecutive wins   The Montreal Canadiens won the Stanley Cup for five consecutive years, 1956–60.

Individual Records

Most games played   Mark Messier has played in 236 Stanley Cup playoff games for the Edmonton Oilers (1979–91, 166 games) and the New York Rangers (1992–97, 70 games).

Fastest goal   The fastest goal from the start of any playoff game was scored by Don Kozak (Los Angeles Kings) past Gerry Cheevers (Boston Bruins) with six seconds elapsed. The Kings went on to win 7-4; the game was played on April 17, 1977. Kozak's goal shares the mark for fastest goal from the start of any period with one scored by Pelle Eklund (Philadelphia Flyers). Eklund scored in the second period of a game against the Pittsburgh Penguins in Pittsburgh on April 25, 1989; his effort was in vain, however, as the Penguins won 10–7.

Most goals (period)   The record for the most goals scored in one period (4) is held by two players: Tim Kerr, Philadelphia Flyers vs. New York Rangers, April 13, 1985; and Mario Lemieux, Pittsburgh Penguins vs. New York Rangers, April 25, 1989.

Most goals (game) Five goals in a Stanley Cup game were scored by five players: Newsy Lalonde, Montreal Canadiens vs. Ottawa Senators, March 1, 1919; Maurice Richard, Montreal Canadiens vs. Toronto Maple Leafs, March 23, 1944; Darryl Sittler, Toronto Maple Leafs vs. Philadelphia Flyers, April 22, 1976; Reggie Leach, Philadelphia Flyers vs. Boston Bruins, May 6, 1976; and Mario Lemieux, Pittsburgh Penguins vs. Philadelphia Flyers, April 25, 1989.

Most goals (season) The record for the most single-season goals (19) is held by Reggie Leach of the Philadelphia Flyers in 1976 and Jari Kurri of the Edmonton Oilers in 1985.

Most goals (career) Wayne Gretzky (Edmonton Oilers, Los Angeles Kings, St. Louis Blues, New York Rangers) holds the record for the most goals scored in one career with 122, 1979–97.

Most assists (period) The feat of three assists in one period has been achieved 64 times.

Most assists (game) A record six assists were achieved by Mikko Leinonen (Finland) for the New York Rangers (7) vs. Philadelphia Flyers (3), on April 8, 1982 and by Wayne Gretzky, Edmonton Oilers (13) vs. Los Angeles Kings (3), on April 9, 1987.

Most assists (season) The most assists attained in a season in the NHL is 31, in the 1988 season by Wayne Gretzky for the Edmonton Oilers.

Most assists (career) Wayne Gretzky (Edmonton Oilers, Los Angeles Kings, St. Louis Blues, New York Rangers) holds the career record of 260 assists from 1979 to 1997.

Most points (period) The record for most points scored in one period (4) has been achieved eleven times by ten players: Maurice Richard, Montreal Canadiens vs. Toronto Maple Leafs, March 29, 1945; Dickie Moore, Montreal Canadiens vs. Boston Bruins, March 25, 1954; Barry Pederson, Boston Bruins vs. Buffalo Sabres, April 8, 1982; Peter McNab, Boston Bruins vs. Buffalo Sabres, April, 11, 1982; Tim Kerr, Philadelphia Flyers vs. New York Rangers, April 13, 1985; Ken Linseman, Boston Bruins vs. Montreal Canadiens, April 14, 1985; Wayne Gretzky, Edmonton Oilers vs. Los Angeles Kings, April 12, 1987; Glenn Anderson, Edmonton Oilers vs. Winnipeg Jets, April 6, 1988; and Dave Gagner, Minnesota North Stars vs. Chicago Blackhawks, April 8, 1991. Mario Lemieux has achieved a record four points on two occasions: Pittsburgh Penguins vs. Philadelphia Flyers, April 25, 1989 and Pittsburgh Penguins vs. Washington Capitals, April 23, 1992.

Most points (game) The most points in one game is eight, by Patrik Sundstrom (Sweden) for the New Jersey Devils (10) vs. Washington Capitals (4), April 22, 1988, and by Mario Lemieux for the Pittsburgh Penguins (10) vs. Philadelphia Flyers (7) on April 25, 1989.

Most points (season) The most points scored in a season in the NHL is 47, in the 1985 season by Wayne Gretzky for the Edmonton Oilers.

Most points (career) Wayne Gretzky (Edmonton Oilers, Los Angeles Kings, St. Louis Blues, New York Rangers) scored a record 382 points, 1979–97.

Most power-play goals (period) The record for the most power-play goals in one period is three, achieved by Tim Kerr for the Philadelphia Flyers vs. the New York Rangers on April 13, 1985.

Most power-play goals (season) Nine power-play goals were scored by Mike Bossy of the New York Islanders in 1981 and by Cam Neely of the Boston Bruins in 1991.

Most power-play goals (career) Mike Bossy of the New York Islanders scored a record 35 power-play goals from 1977 to 1987.

Most shutouts, goalie (season) The record for the most shutouts by a goaltender in one season is four, achieved by eight players on nine occasions: Clint Benedict, Montreal Maroons, 1926 and 1928; Dave Kerr, New York Rangers, 1937; Frank McCool, Toronto Maple Leafs, 1945; Terry Sawchuk, Detroit Tigers, 1952; Bernie Parent, Philadelphia Flyers, 1975; Ken Dryden, Montreal Canadiens, 1977; Mike Richter, New York Rangers, 1994; and Kirk McLean, Vancouver Canucks, 1994.

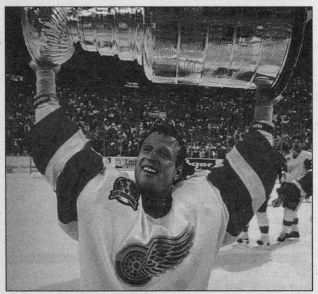

Red Wings goalie Mike Vernon celebrates Detroit's 1997 Stanley Cup title. Vernon tended the goal in all 16 Red Wing victories during the playoffs, tying the NHL mark.

Most shutouts, goalie (career)   Clint Benedict (Ottawa Senators, Montreal Maroons) holds the mark for career shutouts by a goaltender at 15, 1917–30.

Most wins, goalie (season)   The record for the most single-season wins is 16, achieved by seven players on nine occasions: Grant Fuhr, Edmonton Oilers, 1988; Mike Vernon, Calgary Flames, 1989, Detroit Red Wings, 1997; Bill Ranford, Edmonton Oilers, 1990; Tom Barrasso, Pittsburgh Penguins, 1992; Patrick Roy, Montreal Canadiens, 1993, Colorado Avalanche, 1996; Mike Richter, New York Rangers, 1994; and Martin Brodeur, New Jersey Devils, 1995.

Most wins, goalie (career)   Patrick Roy (Montreal Canadiens, Colorado Avalanche) holds the record for career wins by a goaltender with 96, 1985–97.

Most goals, goalie (career)   The record for the most goals scored by a goalie is one, achieved by two players in the playoff: Ron Hextall for Philadelphia Flyers vs. Washington Capitals, April 11, 1989; and Martin Brodeur for New Jersey Devils vs. Montreal Canadiens, April 12, 1997.

Most goals, defensemen (game)   The most goals scored by a defenseman in a playoff game is three, by nine players: Bobby Orr, Boston Bruins vs. Montreal Canadiens, April 11, 1971; Dick Redmond, Chicago Blackhawks vs. St. Louis Blues, April 4, 1973; Denis Potvin, New York Islanders vs. Edmonton Oilers, April 17, 1981; Paul Reinhart, Calgary Flames, who performed the feat twice, vs. Edmonton Oilers, April 14, 1983; vs. Vancouver Canucks, April 8, 1984; Doug Halward, Vancouver Canucks vs. Calgary Flames, April 7, 1984; Al Ioufrate, Washington Capitals vs. New York Islanders, April 26, 1993; Eric DesJardins, Montreal Canadiens vs. Los Angeles Kings, June 3, 1993; Gary Suter, Chicago Black Hawks vs. Toronto Maple Leafs, April 24, 1994; and Brian Leetch, New York Rangers vs. Philadelphia Flyers, May 22, 1995.

Most goals, defenseman (season)   Paul Coffey (Edmonton Oilers) scored 12 goals in 18 games during the 1985 playoffs.

Most goals, defenseman (career)   Paul Coffey (Edmonton Oilers, 1980–87; Pittsburgh Penguins, 1987–91; Los Angeles Kings, 1991–93; Detroit Red Wings, 1993–96; Philadelphia Flyers, 1997) has scored a playoff record 59 goals.

Most assists, defenseman (game)   The most assists in a game is five, by two players: Paul Coffey, Edmonton Oilers vs. Chicago Blackhawks on May 14, 1985; and Risto Siltanen, Quebec Nordiques vs. Hartford Whalers on April 14, 1987.

Most assists, defenseman (season)   The most assists in one playoff year is 25 in 18 games, by Paul Coffey, Edmonton Oilers in 1985.

Most assists, defenseman (career)   The most assists by a defenseman in a career is 136, by Paul Coffey (Edmonton Oilers, 1980–87; Pittsburgh Penguins, 1987–91; Los Angeles Kings, 1991–93; Detroit Red Wings, 1993–96; Philadelphia Flyers, 1997). Coffey played in 189 games.

Most points, defenseman (game)   Paul Coffey earned a record six points on one goal and five assists, for the Edmonton Oilers vs. the Chicago Blackhawks on May 14, 1985.

Most points, defenseman (season)   Paul Coffey also holds the record for most points by a defenseman in a season, with 37 in 1985 for the Edmonton Oilers. Coffey's total comprised 12 goals and 25 assists in 18 games.

Most points, defenseman (career)   Paul Coffey (Edmonton Oilers, 1980–87; Pittsburgh Penguins, 1987–91; Los Angeles Kings, 1991–93; Detroit Red Wings, 1993–96; Philadelphia Flyers, 1997) has scored a playoff record 195 points. Coffey scored 59 goals and 136 assists in 189 games.

Longest point-scoring streak   Bryan Trottier (New York Islanders) scored a point in 27 consecutive playoff games over three seasons (1980–82), scoring 16 goals and 26 assists for 42 points.

Longest goal-scoring streak   Reggie Leach (Philadelphia Flyers) scored at least one goal in nine consecutive playoff games in 1976. The streak started on April 17 vs. the Toronto Maple Leafs, and ended on May 9 when he was shut out by the Montreal Canadiens. Overall, Leach scored 14 goals during his run.

Longest shutout streak   In the 1936 semi-final contest between the Detroit Red Wings and the Montreal Maroons, Norm Smith, the Red Wings goaltender, shut out the Maroons for 248 min. 32 sec. The Maroons failed to score in the first two games (the second game lasted 116 min. 30 sec., the longest overtime game in playoff history), and finally breached Smith's defenses at 12:02 of the first period in game three. The Red Wings swept the series 3–0.

Awards

Most Conn Smythe Trophies   The Conn Smythe Trophy for the most valuable player has been awarded annually since 1965. It has been won twice by Bobby Orr (Boston), 1970, 1972; Bernie Parent (Philadelphia), 1974–75; Wayne Gretzky (Edmonton), 1985, 1988; Mario Lemieux (Pittsburgh), 1991–92; and Patrick Roy (Montreal), 1986, 1993.

Coaches

Most championships   Toe Blake coached the Montreal Canadiens to eight Stanley Cups, 1956–60, 1965–66, 1968.

Most playoff wins   Through the 1996–97 season the record for playoff wins is 178 games, by Scotty Bowman, St. Louis Blues, 1967–71 (26 wins), Montreal Canadiens, 1971–79 (70 wins), Buffalo Sabres, 1979–87 (18 wins), Pittsburgh Penguins, 1991–93 (23 wins), Detroit Red Wings, 1993–97 (41 wins).

Most games   Scotty Bowman holds the mark for most games coached, at 283 with five teams: St. Louis Blues, 1967–71; Montreal Canadiens, 1971–79; Buffalo Sabres, 1979–87; Pittsburgh Penguins, 1991–93; Detroit Red Wings, 1993–97.

OLYMPIC GAMES

Most gold medals (country) The USSR/Unified Team has won eight Olympic titles, in 1956, 1964, 1968, 1972, 1976, 1984, 1988 and 1992.

Most gold medals (player) The most gold medals won by any player is three, achieved by Soviet players Vitaliy Davydov, Anatoliy Firsov, Viktor Kuzkin and Aleksandr Ragulin in 1964, 1968 and 1972, and by Vladislav Tretyak in 1972, 1976 and 1984.

NCAA CHAMPIONSHIPS

Most wins Michigan has won the title eight times: 1948, 1951–53, 1955–56, 1964 and 1996.

The winning goal in Michigan's 1996 NCAA championship win. The team has won the most NCAA titles.

SOCCER

FIFA WORLD CUP (MEN)

Team Records

Most wins Brazil has won four World Cups, 1958, 1962, 1970 and 1994.

MARACANA MAGIC

"The pressure of coaching Brazil is unbelievable. Brazil is the only country in the world that is already in 'World Cup mode.' It's one year until the competition and it dominates the news," says Carlos Alberto Parreira.

He should know. Parreira, head coach of the New York/New Jersey MetroStars, led Brazil to its record-breaking fourth World Cup victory in 1994.

In a tournament played every four years, Brazil won the World Cup three times between 1958 and 1970. Soccer-besotted Brazilians had come to expect victory, and the media condemned successive failures. Parreira coached the national team briefly in 1983; his reinstatement in 1991 was not a popular choice. But he refused to be intimidated: "It was the greatest challenge of my life. I had to convince the federation that I needed time, but I wanted the opportunity to lead the team in the World Cup," he says.

Brazilian soccer players are renowned for their brilliant passing and dribbling skills. But teams packed with all-time greats (such as Zico and Socrates) had failed to win the World Cup for 24 years. Parreira insisted that the traditional flamboyant playing style must be balanced with discipline. The critics labeled Parreira's tactics as defensive, tantamount to treason in Brazil. "It is a big misconception that we were a defensive

MOST WORLD CUP WINS

Brazil holds the record for the most World Cup wins, with four, in 1958, 1962, 1970 and 1994.

team. When we had the ball, we had all the freedom in the world to go forward and be creative. But to win the World Cup, we needed to be organized when we didn't have the ball," says Parreira.

Brazil did play with its usual flair on offense during the World Cup tournament, winning the final in a penalty shootout over Italy. Parreira maintains that the strategy on defense was the key to the victory: "We allowed only three goals in seven World Cup games. We were well-organized." After living under such scrutiny, how did Parreira feel at the end of the championship game? "At the moment we won, I only felt relief. I let out a huge breath," he says.

Parreira resigned as Brazil coach following the World Cup, a decision that stunned the soccer world. "When you coach the Brazilian national team, there is no chance to relax. You breathe soccer every minute you are awake. No man can keep up that pace," explains Parreira. In 1997, he joined the MetroStars, a coup for Major League Soccer. "I believe that soccer has a great future in the United States. We see crowds of 10,000 and 15,000 almost every night and the league is just a baby. The quality of the league will improve drastically in five to ten years. It will be a great league," he says.

But coaching his country to World Cup victory will always be Parreira's greatest moment: "I only played in the second division myself, and yet I coached a world champion. I think that says it all."

Most qualifications Brazil is the only country to qualify for all 15 World Cup tournaments.

Most goals (qualifying game) The record for the most goals in one game was set in a qualifying match on June 2, 1997 when Iran beat the Maldives, 17–0.

Most goals (finals game) Hungary holds the record for most goals in a finals game. The Mighty Magyars defeated El Salvador 10–1 in Elche, Spain on June 15, 1982.

Most goals (finals tournament) In 1954, Hungary tallied their record total of 27 goals in five games, but lost in the Final to Germany, 3–2.

Most goals (all finals tournaments) Brazil achieved a record 159 goals in 73 games over 15 tournaments.

Eric Wynalda is the United States' leading career goal-scorer in international play.

Individual Records

Most appearances (finals) Goalkeeper Antonio Carbajal (Mexico) played in 11 games in five (1950, 1954, 1958, 1962 and 1966) finals tournaments.

Most games (finals) A record 21 finals games have been played by four players: Uwe Seeler (West Germany), 1958–70; Wladyslaw Zmuda (Poland), 1974–86; Diego Maradona (Argentina), 1982–94; and Lothar Matthaus (West Germany/Germany), 1982–94.

Most goals (game) Oleg Salenko (Russia) scored a record five goals in a 6–1 defeat of Cameroon in 1994.

Most goals (tournament) In 1958, Just Fontaine (France) scored 13 goals in six games.

Most goals (career) Gerd Muller of West Germany scored a career record 14 goals; 10 in 1970 and four in 1974.

Most goals (World Cup Final) Geoff Hurst (England) scored a record three goals in a 4–2 defeat of West Germany on July 30, 1966.

FIFA WORLD CUP (WOMEN)

Most wins The record for most wins (one) is shared by two countries: the United States in 1991 and Norway in 1995.

Three record breakers from South America: Marco Etcheverry (left) of D.C. United and Bolivia led the MLS in assists in 1996. Ronaldo (right) of Brazil was traded from Barcelona (Spain) to Internazionale of Milan (Italy) for a record cash payment in 1997. Claudia Martini (top) of Brazil juggled a soccer ball for 7 hr. 5 min. 25 sec. on July 12, 1996.

MAJOR LEAGUE SOCCER (MLS)

Team records

Most goals (game)   The record for the most goals scored in a single game is six, achieved by three teams on four occasions: Kansas City Wiz(zards) (6) vs. Columbus Crew (4), May 2, 1996; D.C United (6) vs. Dallas Burn (1), July 7, 1996; San Jose Clash (6) vs. New England Revolution (1), August 11, 1996; and Kansas City Wiz(zards) (6) vs. D.C. United, June 21, 1997.

Highest scoring game   The highest scoring game was played on May 2, 1996 when the Kansas City Wiz(zards) won a 6–4 victory over the Columbus Crew on May 2, 1996.

Longest shootout   On April 21, 1996, the Kansas City Wiz(zards) played a 2–2 tie with the San Jose Clash. The subsequent shootout to decide the game lasted a record 16 rounds. 32 players, including both goalkeepers, participated in the shootout. Kansas City's Alan Prampin shot the winning goal to seal a 3–2 win for the Wiz(zards).

Individual Records

Most goals (season)   Roy Lassiter of the Tampa Bay Mutiny holds the mark for single-season goals at 27 in 1996.

Most assists (season)   The record for the most single season assists is 19, by Marco Etcheverry in 1996 for D.C. United.

Most points (season)   Roy Lassiter of the Tampa Bay Mutiny scored a record 58 points (27 goals, four assists) in 1996.

NCAA DIVISION I

Most titles (men)   The University of St. Louis achieved a record 10 titles, including one tie game, in 1959–60, 1962–63, 1965, 1967, 1969–70, and 1972–73.

Most titles (women)   The record for most titles is 13, by the University of North Carolina in 1982–84, 1986–94, 1996.

OLYMPIC GAMES

Most wins (men)   The record for most wins by a men's Olympic team is three, by Hungary, in 1952, 1964 and 1968.

Most wins (women)   The United States won the inuagural 1996 women's tournament, defeating China 2–1 in sudden-death overtime.

BIG PLAYS

Ball juggling (duration) Ricardinho Neves (Brazil) juggled a regulation soccer ball nonstop with his feet, legs and head, without the ball touching the ground, for 19 hr. 5 min. 31 sec. at the Los Angeles Convention Center, July 15–16, 1994. The women's record is 7 hr. 5 min. 25 sec. by Claudia Martini (Brazil) at Caxias do Sul, Brazil on July 12, 1996.

Heading (duration) Godzerzi Maakharadze (Georgia) headed a ball for 8 hr. 12 min. 25 sec. on May 26, 1996 in Tbilisi, Georgia.

Marathon The fastest time for completing a marathon while juggling a soccer ball is 7 hr. 18 min. 55 sec. by Jan Skorkovsky (Czechoslovakia) on July 8, 1990 when he "ran" the Prague Marathon.

Most red cards On June 1, 1993 in a league soccer game between Sportivo Ameliano and General Caballero in Paraguay, referee William Weiler ejected 20 players. Trouble flared after two Sportivo players were thrown out, a 10-minute fight ensued and Weiler then dismissed a further 18 players, including the rest of the Sportivo team. Not surprisingly, the game was abandoned.

Most peripatetic fan Ken Ferris of Redbridge, Essex, England, watched a League match at all the League grounds in England and Wales (including Berwick Rangers) in 237 days from 1994 to 1995.

Largest crowd The biggest recorded crowd at a soccer game was the 199,854 spectators at the Brazil vs. Uruguay World Cup game in the Maracana Municipal Stadium, Rio de Janeiro, Brazil, in July 1950.

OTHER TEAM SPORTS

FIELD HOCKEY

Olympic Games

Most gold medals (team, men) In the men's competition, India has won eight gold medals: 1928, 1932, 1936, 1948, 1952, 1956, 1964 and 1980.

Most gold medals (team, women) In the women's competition, no team has won the event more than once.

Most medals (player) Six members of the India team have won three gold medals. Of those gold medalists, two have also won a silver medal: Leslie Walter Claudius, in 1948, 1952, 1956 and 1960 (silver); and Udham Singh, in 1952, 1956, 1964, and 1960 (silver).

Most international appearances Alison Ramsay has made 257 international appearances, 150 for Scotland and 107 for Great Britain, 1982–95.

World Cup

Most wins (men)   The most wins in the men's competition is four by Pakistan in 1971, 1978, 1982 and 1994.

Most wins (women)   The most wins in the women's competition is five by Netherlands in 1974, 1978, 1983, 1986 and 1990.

Scoring Records

Highest scoring game   The highest score in an international game was India's 24–1 defeat of the United States in Los Angeles, CA, in the 1932 Olympic Games. In women's competition, England hammered France 23–0 in Merton, England, February 3, 1923.

Most goals (career)   Paul Litjens (Netherlands) holds the record for most goals by one player in international play. He scored 267 goals in 177 games.

Fastest goal   The fastest goal scored in an international game was netted only seven seconds after the bully by John French for England vs. West Germany in Nottingham, England on April 25, 1971.

No country has won the Olympic women's hockey tourney more than once. Australia won the '96 title. Another Aussie leads the way in Rugby; David Campese has scored more tries in international competition than any other player.

NCAA Division I (Women)

Most titles   Old Dominion has won the most championships, with seven titles: 1982–84, 1988 and 1990–92.

LACROSSE

World Championships

Most titles (men)   The United States men's team has won six world titles, 1967, 1974, 1982, 1986, 1990 and 1994.

Most titles (women)   The United States women's team has won four world titles, 1974, 1982, 1989 and 1993.

NCAA Championships (Division I)

Most titles (men)   Johns Hopkins University has the most wins overall: seven NCAA titles between 1974 and 1987, and six wins and five ties between 1941 and 1970.

Most titles (women)   Maryland has won the most titles, with five: 1986, 1992, and 1995–97.

RUGBY

World Cup

Most wins   No team has won more than one World Cup in either men's or women's events.

Most points (game)   The most points in a Rugby World Cup finals tournament game is 145, scored by New Zealand against Japan (17 points) in Bloemfontein, South Africa on June 4, 1995.

Highest scoring game   The highest aggregate score in a Rugby World Cup finals tournament is 162 points, New Zealand defeating Japan 145–17 (*see above*).

Individual Records

Most points (game)   Simon Culhane (New Zealand) scored 45 points (one try and 20 conversions) vs. Japan in Bloemfontein, South Africa, June 4, 1995.

Most points (tournament)   Grant Fox (New Zealand) scored 126 points in 1987.

Most points (career)   Gavin Hastings (Scotland) scored 227 points in three finals, 1987, 1991 and 1995.

International Records

Highest scoring game   The highest score by a team in a full international game is 164, by Hong Kong against Singapore in Kuala Lumpur, Malaysia on October 27, 1994.

Most points (game)   Ashley Billington (Hong Kong) scored 50 points (10 tries) on October 27, 1994.

Most points (career)   Michael Lynagh (Australia) scored a record 911 points in international rugby competition, 1984–95.

Most tries (game)   Ashley Billington (Hong Kong) scored 10 tries, October 27, 1994.

Most tries (career)   David Campese (Australia) scored 64 tries in international competition, 1982–97.

Most penalty goals (game)   The record for the most penalty goals in a game is eight, tied by five players: Mark Wyatt (Canada) vs. Scotland in St. John, New Brunswick, May 25, 1991; Neil Jenkins (Wales) vs. Canada in Cardiff, Wales, November 10, 1993; Santiago Meson (Argentina) vs. Canada in Buenos Aires, Argentina, March 12, 1995; Gavin Hastings (Scotland) vs. Tonga in Pretoria, South Africa, May 30, 1995; Thierry Lacroix (France) vs. Ireland in Durban, South Africa, June 10, 1995.

Most internationals   Philippe Sella (France) played a record 111 international matches, 1982–95.

Most consecutive internationals   Sean Fitzpatrick (New Zealand) played in 63 consecutive games, 1986–95.

Big Plays

Tallest posts   The world's highest Rugby Union goal posts are 33.54 m (110 ft. ½ in.) high, and are situated at the Roan Antelope Rugby Union Club, Luanshya, Zambia.

SOFTBALL

Most world titles (men)   The United States has won five world titles: 1966, 1968, 1976 (tied), 1980 and 1988.

Most world titles (women)   The United States has won five world titles: 1974, 1978, 1986, 1990 and 1994.

Most ASA National titles (men)   The Clearwater (FL) Bombers won 10 championships between 1950 and 1973.

Most ASA National titles (women)   The Raybestos Brakettes (Stratford, CT) won 23 women's fast pitch titles from 1958 through 1992.

Most NCAA titles (women)   UCLA has won eight titles: 1982, 1984–85, 1988–90, 1992 and 1995.

Olympic Games

Most titles   Women's fast pitch softball made its first appearance in the 1996 Olympic Games in Atlanta, Georgia. The United States defeated China 3–1 on June 30, 1996.

Big Plays

Perfect game   Carol Christ Hampton, pitcher for Les's Legacy, Seattle, WA, pitched an entire game with all strikes except for three balls called at the ASA Class C Women's National Softball Championship, St. Augustine, FL on September 25, 1994.

TEAM HANDBALL

Olympic Games

Most wins (men)   In men's competition the USSR/Unified Team has won the Olympic gold medal three times—1976, 1988 and 1992.

Most wins (women)   In women's competition, introduced in 1976, two countries have won the gold medal twice: USSR, 1976, 1980; and South Korea, 1988, 1992.

World Championship

Most titles (indoors, men)   Indoor team handball is the most popular form of the game. The most world titles won is four by Romania, 1961, 1964, 1970 and 1974.

Most titles (indoors, women)   Three women's world titles have been won by two teams: East Germany, 1971, 1975 and 1978; and the USSR, 1982, 1986 and 1990.

Teams from the former Soviet Union have won the most Olympic team handball titles. However, in 1996, Croatia snagged the gold.

Most titles (outdoors) The most titles won is five by Germany/West Germany, 1938–66. In women's competition the most outdoor championships won is two by Romania, 1956 and 1960.

Big Plays

Highest scoring game The highest score in an international match was recorded when the USSR beat Afghanistan 86–2 in the 'Friendly Army Tournament' at Miskolc, Hungary, in August 1981.

VOLLEYBALL (INDOOR)

Olympic Games

Most wins (men, team) The USSR has won three men's titles in 1964, 1968, and 1980.

Most wins (women, team) The USSR has also won four women's titles in 1968, 1972, 1980 and 1988.

Most medals (individual) Inna Ryskal (USSR) has won four medals in Olympic competition: two gold, 1968, 1972; and two silver, 1964, 1976. The men's record is three, won by three players: Yuriy Poyarkov (USSR), two golds, 1964, 1968, one bronze, 1972; Katsutoshi Nekoda (Japan), one gold, 1972, one silver, 1968, and one bronze, 1964; and Steve Timmons (U.S.), two gold, 1984, 1988, and one bronze, 1992.

World Championships

Most titles (men) The USSR has won six men's titles in 1949, 1952, 1960, 1962, 1978 and 1982.

Most titles (women) The USSR won five women's titles, 1952, 1956, 1960, 1970 and 1990.

BEACH VOLLEYBALL

AVP Tour

Most wins (team) Sinjin Smith and Randy Stoklos have earned 115 wins, 1982–1993.

Most wins (individual) Sinjin Smith has won 139 tour events, 1977–1994.

Highest earnings Karch Kiraly had earned a career record $2,578,840 as of March 16, 1997.

Beach volleyball was an official Olympic sport for the first time at the '96 Atlanta Games. The Brazilian team of Jackie Silva Cruz and Sandra Pires Tavares won the inaugural women's gold.

BOWLING

PROFESSIONAL BOWLERS ASSOCIATION (PBA)

Most titles (career)   Earl Anthony of Dublin, CA has won a career record 41 PBA titles, 1970–83.

Most titles (season)   The record number of titles won in one PBA season is eight, by Mark Roth of North Arlington, NJ, in 1978.

Most perfect games (career)   Since 1977, when the PBA began to keep statistics on perfect games, Wayne Webb has bowled 37 in tournament play.

Most perfect games (season)   Three bowlers have bowled eight perfect games in one season: Kelly Coffman, 1994; Dave D'Entremont, 1995; and Eric Forkel, 1995.

Most perfect games (tournament)   Two bowlers have bowled four perfect games in one tournament: Walter Ray Williams Jr., Mechanicsburg, PA, 1993; and Dave D'Entremont, Peoria, IL, 1995.

Highest score (6 games)   Norm Duke of Peoria, IL scored a record 1,635 points in 1994.

Highest score (8 games)   Billy Hardwick of Toyko, Japan scored 2,165 points in 1968.

Highest score (12 games)   Mike Aulby of Baltimore, MD scored a record 3,083 points in 1996.

Highest score (16 games)   John Mazza of Las Vegas, NV scored a record 4,019 points in 1996.

Highest score (18 games)   Norm Duke of Peoria, IL scored a record 4,696 points in 1994.

Highest score (24 games)   Pete Weber of Las Vegas, NV scored a record 6,019 points in 1996.

Highest earnings (career)   Walter Ray Williams Jr. has won a career record $2,002,373 in PBA competitions through July 1, 1997.

Highest earnings (season)   Mike Aulby of Indianapolis, IN set a single-season earnings mark of $298,237 in 1989.

LADIES PROFESSIONAL BOWLERS TOUR (LPBT)

Most titles (career)   Lisa Wagner has won 30 tournaments in her 18-year career, 1980–97.

Most titles (season) Patty Costello won a season record seven tournaments in 1976.

Most perfect games (career) Tish Johnson has bowled an LPBT-approved record 39 perfect games.

Most perfect games (season) The most perfect games in a season is seven, by Tish Johnson in 1993.

Highest earnings (career) Aleta Sill won a career record $821,462 in prize money through December 31, 1996.

Highest earnings (season) Aleta Sill also had the season high record in 1994, with $126,325 in earnings.

AMERICAN BOWLING CONGRESS (ABC)

Highest individual score (three games) The highest individual score for three games is 900, by Jeremy Sonnenfeld in Lincoln, NE, February 2, 1997.

Highest team score (one game) The all-time ABC-sanctioned two-man single-game record is 600, held jointly by nine teams: John Cotta and Steve Larson, May 1, 1981 in Manteca, CA; Jeff Mraz and Dave Roney, November 8, 1987 in Canton, OH; William Gruner and Dave Conway, February 27, 1990 in Oceanside, CA; Scott Williams and Willie Hammar, June 7, 1990 in Utica, NY; Darrell Guertin and George Tignor, February 20, 1993 in Rutland, VT; Ken Mayo and Mike Mayo, January 22, 1995 in Peoria, IL; Keith Nusbaum and Dale Ellis, February 5, 1995 in Toledo, OH; Ryan Boyd and Clayton Hicks, July 27, 1995 in Miami, FL; and Duke Matties and Dave Frascatore, November 27, 1995 in Albany, NY.

The youngest person to bowl a perfect game is Scott Owsley of Fontana, CA.

MR. 900

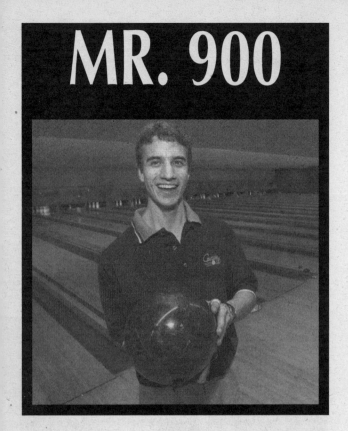

In the 101 years the American Bowling Congress has been keeping records, no one had ever accomplished what Jeremy Sonnenfeld made look so easy on February 2, 1997. The 20-year-old bowler from Sioux Falls, South Dakota rolled 36 consecutive strikes in a sanctioned competition, becoming the first to post a perfect 900-pin score. "The Bowling Congress tells me that's out of about 10 billion estimated games since they started keeping track," Sonnenfeld adds quietly.

Still enrolled at the University of Nebraska, and still graciously humble about his achievement, Sonnenfeld recalls the satisfaction he felt after bowling the first of his three perfect games that day. It was not for himself, but for the young children bowling with him in the Junior Husker Tournament. "We were paired up with little kids, kind of like a pro-am event,

HIGHEST INDIVIDUAL SCORE
(THREE GAMES)

The highest individual score for three games is 900, by Jeremy Sonnenfeld in Lincoln, NE on February 2, 1997.

and I thought it would be great to bowl a 300 for them." Which he did, and in short order began another: "I just kept striking," Sonnenfeld says. "I couldn't do anything wrong." When the second perfect score went up, "I thought, 'Now there's something I've never done before!'"

Sonnenfeld then went on to do what no one had ever done before, and as the pins continued to fall, interested onlookers continued to gather. "The crowd kept getting a little bit bigger behind me," he recalls. "I've had other successes in competition and had other crowds around watching the event, but never before just watching me. This crowd was so supportive, and really great. They cheered after every strike, and the kids were giving me high fives, and I think that's really what helped me stay relaxed more than anything. They were great."

Before his 36th strike, Sonnenfeld remembers very clearly a distinct feeling of relief. "I told myself, 'You've come this far, and all you have left is one shot.' When the ball came off my hand, it felt good, and I saw it cross the marks I was looking for. But anybody can throw a perfect shot and not get the strike. So I kind of ran to my left as the ball hit the pocket, and when they all fell, the entire place went nuts. This was something I thought was unattainable, impossible. It took a while to sink in."

The ball he used that day has been retired, Sonnenfeld says. "It served its purpose," he explains, his humility cracking just slightly. "Its last ball was a strike."

Highest team score (three games) The highest three-game team score is 3,868, by Hurst Bowling Supplies, of Luzerne, PA on February 23, 1994.

Highest season average The highest season average attained in sanctioned competition is 251.0, by Ross Hunt of Odgen, UT, in the 1995–96 season.

Consecutive strikes The record for consecutive strikes in sanctioned play is 36, by Jeremy Sonnenfeld on February 2, 1997, in Lincoln, NE.

Most perfect games (career) The highest number of sanctioned 300 games is 54, by Bob Learn, Jr. of Erie, PA.

Oldest 300 bowler The oldest person to bowl a perfect game is Joe Norris of San Diego, CA. He performed the feat on December 14, 1994 aged 86 yr. 10 mo. 6 days.

Youngest 300 bowler The youngest person to bowl a perfect game is Scott Owsley of Fontana, CA, on March 26, 1994, aged 10 yr. 9 mo. 6 days.

WOMEN'S INTERNATIONAL BOWLING CONGRESS (WIBC)

Highest individual score (three games) The highest individual score for three games is 865, by Anne Marie Duggan in Edmond, OK, on July 18, 1993.

Highest team score (one game) Pamela Beach and Cindy Fry bowled the all-time two-woman single-game highest score of 578 in Lansing, MI on November 21, 1992.

Highest team score (three games) The highest three-game team score is 3,536 by Contour Power Grips of Detroit, MI on August 29, 1994.

Highest season average The highest season average attained in sanctioned WIBC competition is 234, by Elizabeth Johnson of Niagara Falls, NY in the 1993/94 season.

Consecutive strikes Jeanne Naccarato bowled a record 40 consecutive strikes on November 23, 1986 in Sodon, OH.

Most perfect games (career) The highest number of WIBC-sanctioned perfect games (300) is 25, by Tish Johnson.

The highest score for three games bowled by a woman is 865, by Anne Marie Duggan.

Oldest 300 bowler   The oldest woman to bowl a perfect game is Myrt Kressin of Bremerton, WA, on February 8, 1997. She performed this feat at age 71 yr. 5 mo. 7 days old.

Youngest 300 bowler   The youngest girl to roll a 300 game is Nicole Long of Columbia, MO, at age 12 yr. 5 mo. on May 27, 1995.

BIG PLAYS

Consecutive spares and splits   Mabel Henry of Winchester, KY had 30 consecutive spares in the 1986–87 season.

Highest score in 24 hours   A team of six scored 242,665 at Dover Bowl, Dover, DE on March 18–19, 1995. During this attempt a member of the team, Richard Ranshaw, set an individual record of 51,064.

Largest bowling center   The Fukuyama Bowl, Osaka, Japan has 144 lanes. The Tokyo World Lanes Center, Japan, now closed, had 252 lanes.

GOLF

THE MAJORS (MEN)

Most grand slam titles   Jack Nicklaus has won the most majors, with 18 professional titles (six Masters, four U.S. Opens, three British Opens, five PGA Championships).

THE MASTERS

Most wins   Jack Nicklaus has won the coveted green jacket a record six times (1963, 1965–66, 1972, 1975, 1986).

Lowest 18-hole total (any round)   The record for the lowest 18-hole total is 63, achieved by two players: Nick Price (Zimbabwe) in 1986; and Greg Norman (Australia) in 1996.

Lowest 72-hole total   Tiger Woods scored 270 (70, 66, 65, 69) in 1997.

Oldest champion   The oldest player to win the Masters is Jack Nicklaus at 46 yr. 81 days in 1986.

Youngest champion   Tiger Woods set the record for the youngest player to win the Masters at 21 yr. 104 days in 1997.

U.S. OPEN

Most wins   The record for the most wins is four, set by four players: Willie Anderson (1901, 1903–05); Bobby Jones (1923, 1926, 1929–30); Ben Hogan (1948, 1950–51, 1953); Jack Nicklaus (1962, 1967, 1972, 1980).

Lowest 18-hole total (any round)   The lowest 18-hole total is 63, achieved by three players: Johnny Miller at Oakmont Country Club, PA, on June 17, 1973; Jack Nicklaus and Tom Weiskopf at Baltusrol Country Club, Springfield, NJ, June 12, 1980.

Lowest 72-hole total   The lowest 72-total is 272, achieved by two players: Jack Nicklaus (63, 71, 70, 68), at Baltusrol Country Club, Springfield, NJ, in 1980; and Lee Janzen (67, 67, 69, 69), also at Baltusrol, in 1993.

Oldest champion   The oldest golfer to win the U.S. Open is Hale Irwin at 45 yr. 15 days in 1990.

Youngest champion   The youngest player to win the U.S. Open is John J. McDermott at 19 yr. 317 days in 1911.

Golf's Year of the Tiger began in January 1997 at the Mercedes Championships. Woods' win pushed his career earnings past $1 million—the fastest any player had reached that milestone. In April he became the youngest winner of the Masters ((and won by the widest margin). In May he won the GTE Byron Nelson Classic, career earnings now $2 million—the fastest to that mark. In July Tigermania moved to the UK, where Woods tied the British Open 18-hole mark, when he shot a 63 in the 3rd round.

THE BRITISH OPEN

Most wins   Harry Vardon won six titles, 1896, 1898–99, 1903, 1911, 1914.

Lowest 18-hole total (any round)   The lowest 18-hole total is 63, achieved by seven players: Mark Hayes, at Turnberry, Scotland, July 7, 1977; Isao Aoki (Japan) at Muirfield, Scotland, July 19, 1980; Greg Norman (Australia) at Turnberry, Scotland, July 18, 1986; Paul Broadhurst (Great Britain) at St. Andrews, Scotland, July 21, 1990; Jodie Mudd at Royal Birkdale, England, July 21, 1991; Nick Faldo (Great Britain) July 16, 1993 at Royal St. Georges; and Payne Stewart, July 18, 1993 at Royal St. Georges.

Lowest 72-hole total   Greg Norman (Australia) scored 267 (66, 68, 69, 64) at Royal St. George's, England in 1993.

Oldest champion   Tom Morris Sr. (Great Britain) is the oldest player to win the British Open at 46 yr. 99 days in 1867.

Youngest champion   In 1868, Tom Morris Jr. (Great Britain) is the youngest player to win the British Open at 17 yr. 249 days in 1868.

PGA CHAMPIONSHIP

Most wins   Two players have won the title five times: Walter Hagen (1921, 1924–27); and Jack Nicklaus (1963, 1971, 1973, 1975, 1980).

Lowest 18-hole total (any round)   The lowest 18-hole total is 63, achieved by six players: Bruce Crampton (Australia) at Firestone Country Club, Akron, OH, in 1975; Ray Floyd at Southern Hills, Tulsa, OK, in 1982; Gary Player (South Africa) at Shoalcreek Country Club, Birmingham, AL in 1984; Vijay Singh (Fiji) at the Inverness Club, Toledo, OH in 1993; Michael Bradley and Brad Faxon at Riviera Country Club, Pacific Palisades, CA in 1995.

Lowest 72-hole total   The lowest 72-hole total is 267, achieved by Steve Elkington (Australia) (68, 67, 68, 64) and by Colin Montgomerie (Great Britain) (68, 67, 67, 65) at the Riviera Country Club, Pacific Palisades, CA in 1995. Elkington defeated Montgomerie in a playoff.

Oldest champion   In 1968, Julius Boros became the oldest player to win a PGA Championship at 48 yr. 140 days.

Youngest champion   Gene Sarazen became the youngest PGA champion at 20 yr. 173 days in 1922.

PGA TOUR RECORDS

Most wins (season)   Byron Nelson won a record 18 tournaments in 1945.

Most wins (career)   Sam Snead won 81 official PGA tour events, 1936–65.

Oldest champion   Sam Snead became the oldest winner at the 1965 Greater Greensboro Open at 52 yr. 10 mo.

Youngest champion   In 1911, Johnny McDermott set the record for the youngest winner of the U.S. Open at 19 yr. 10 mo.

Widest winning margin   The widest winning margin is 16 strokes, achieved by two players: Joe Kirkwood Sr., 1924, Corpus Christi Open; and Bobby Locke (South Africa), 1948 Chicago Victory National Championship.

Lowest score (9 holes)   The lowest score for nine holes is 27, achieved by two players: Mike Souchak, at the Brackenridge Park Golf Course, San Antonio, TX, on the back nine of the first round of the 1955 Texas Open; Andy North, at the En-Joie Golf Club, Endicott, NY, on the back nine of the first round of the 1975 B.C. Open.

Lowest score (18 holes)   The record for the lowest score in 18-holes is 59, set by two players: Al Geiberger at the Colonial Country Club, Memphis, TN, during the second round of the 1977 Danny Thomas Memphis Classic; Chip Beck at the Sunrise Golf Club, Las Vegas, NV, during the third round of the 1991 Las Vegas Invitational.

Lowest score (36 holes)   Four players scored a record 125: Gay Brewer at the Pensacola Country Club, Pensacola, FL, during the second and third rounds of the 1967 Pensacola Open; Ron Streck at the Oak Hills Country Club, San Antonio, TX, during the third and fourth rounds of the 1978 Texas Open; Blaine McCallister at the Oakwood Country Club, Coal Valley, IL, during the second and third rounds of the 1988 Hardee's Golf Classic; John Cook at the Tournament Players Club at Southwind, Germantown, TN during the second and third rounds of the 1996 FedEx St. Jude Classic.

Lowest score (54 holes)   The lowest score recorded is 189, achieved by two players: Chandler Harper at the Brackenridge Park Golf Course, San Antonio, TX, during the last three rounds of the 1954 Texas Open; and John Cook at the Tournament Players Club at Southwind, Germantown, TN during the first three rounds of the 1996 FedEx St. Jude Classic.

Lowest score (72 holes)   Mike Souchak scored a record 257 at the Brackenridge Park Golf Course, San Antonio, TX, at the 1955 Texas Open.

Lowest score (90 holes)   The record for the lowest score in 90 holes (four courses) is 325, set by Tom Kite at the 1993 Bob Hope Chrysler Classic in La Quinta, CA.

Most shots under par   Tom Kite also set the record for the most shots under par (35) at the 90-hole 1993 Bob Hope Chrysler Classic. The most shots under par in a 72-hole tournament is 27, shared by two players: Mike Souchak, at the 1955 Texas Open; and Ben Hogan, at the 1945 Portland Invitational.

Highest earnings (season)   As of August 18, 1997, Tiger Woods had earned a season record $1,835,520, beating the all-time season record held by Tom Lehman in 1996.

Highest earnings (career)   As of August 18, 1997, Greg Norman (Australia) had career earnings of $11,254,981.

THE MAJORS (WOMEN)

Most grand slam titles   Patty Berg has won the most majors, with 15 titles (one U.S. Open, seven Titleholders, seven Western Open) at Indianwood Golf and Country Club, Lake Orion, MI in 1994.

THE U.S. OPEN

Most wins   Two players have won the title four times: Betsy Rawls (1951, 1953, 1957, 1960); Mickey Wright (1958–59, 1961, 1964).

Lowest 18-hole total   In 1994, Helen Alfredsson (Sweden) scored a record 63 at the Indianwood Golf and Country Club in Lake Orion, MI.

Lowest 72-hole total   Liselotte Neumann (Sweden) scored 277 at the Baltimore (MD) Country Club in 1988.

Oldest champion   In 1955, Fay Croker became the oldest champion at 40 yr. 11 mo.

Youngest champion   In 1967, Catherine Lacoste (France) became the youngest champion at 22 yr. 5 days.

LPGA CHAMPIONSHIP

Most wins   Mickey Wright has won the LPGA Championship a record four times: 1958, 1960–61, 1963.

Lowest 18-hole total   Patty Sheehan scored a record 63 at the Jack Nicklaus Golf Course, Kings Island, OH, in 1984.

Lowest 72-hole total   In 1992, Betsy King scored 267 at the Bethesda (MD) Country Club.

NABISCO DINAH SHORE

Most wins   The record for the most wins is three, achieved by two players: Amy Alcott (1983, 1988 and 1991); Betsy King (1987, 1990 and 1997).

Lowest 18-hole total   Two players set the record for the lowest 18-hole total at 64: Nancy Lopez in 1981; Sally Little in 1982.

Lowest 72-hole total   The lowest 72-hole total is 273, set by Amy Alcott in 1991.

DU MAURIER CLASSIC

Most wins   Pat Bradley has won this event three times, 1980, 1985–86.

Lowest 18-hole total   The lowest recorded 18-hole total is 64, achieved by three players: Jo-Anne Carner at St. George's Country Club, Toronto in 1978; Jane Geddes at Beaconsfield Country Club, Montreal in 1985; Dawn Coe-Jones at London (Ontario) Hunt and Country Club in 1993.

Lowest 72-hole total　Jody Rosenthal scored a record 272 at the Islesmere Golf Course, Laval, Quebec in 1987.

LPGA TOUR RECORDS

Most wins (career)　Kathy Whitworth set the career record for the most wins with 88 from 1959 to 1991.

Most wins (season)　The single-season career for the most wins is 13, achieved by Mickey Wright in 1963.

Oldest winner　JoAnne Carner became the oldest LPGA winner at the 1985 Safeco Classic at 46 yr. 5 mo. 9 days.

Youngest winner　Marlene Hagge finished in first place at 18 yr. 14 days at the 1952 Sarasota Open.

Widest margin of victory　The record for the widest margin of victory is 14, set by two players: Louise Suggs in the 1949 U.S. Open; Cindy Mackey in the 1986 Mastercard International.

Lowest score (9 holes)　Five players achieved a record score of 28 in nine holes: Mary Beth Zimmerman at the Rail Golf Club, Springfield, IL, during the 1984 Rail Charity Golf Classic; Pat Bradley at the Green Gables Country Club, Denver, CO, during the 1984 Columbia Savings Classic; Muffin Spencer-Devlin at the Knollwood Country Club, Elmsford, NY, during the 1985 MasterCard International Pro-Am; Peggy Kirsch at the Squaw-Creek Country Club, Vienna, OH during the 1991 Phar-Mar in Youngstown; Renee Heiken at the Highland Meadows Golf Club, Sylvania, OH during the 1996 Jamie Farr Kroger Classic.

Lowest score (18 holes)　Four players hold the record for the lowest score in 18 holes, at 62: Mickey Wright at Hogan Park Golf Club, Midland, TX, in the first round of the 1964 Tall City Open; Vicki Fergon at Alamaden Golf & Country Club, San Jose, CA, in the second round of the 1984 San Jose Classic; Laura Davies (Great Britain) at the Rail Golf Club, Springfield, IL, during the first round of the 1991 Rail Charity Golf Classic; and Hollis Stacy at the Meridian Valley Country Club, Kent, WA, during the second round of the 1992 Safeco Classic.

Lowest score (36 holes)　Judy Dickinson scored 129 at Pasadena Yacht & Country Club, St. Petersburg, FL, during the first and second rounds of the 1985 S&H Golf Classic.

Lowest score (54 holes)　Pat Bradley scored 197 during all three rounds of the 1991 Rail Charity Golf Classic at the Rail Golf Club in Springfield, IL.

Lowest score (72 holes)　Betsy King scored a record 267 at the Bethesda Country Club, MD, in the 1992 Mazda LPGA Championship.

Highest earnings (season)　Karrie Webb (Australia) earned a record $1,002,000 in 1996.

Highest earnings (career)   As of August 18, 1997, Betsy King had earned $5,894,927.

SENIOR PGA TOUR

Most wins (career)   Lee Trevino has won a record 27 Senior PGA Tours between 1990 and 1997.

Most wins (season)   Peter Thomson holds the single-season record for the most wins with nine in 1985.

Senior Tour/Regular Tour win   Ray Floyd (U.S.) is the only player to win a Senior Tour event and a PGA Tour event in the same year. He won the Doral Open PGA event in March 1992 and the GTE Northern in September 1992.

Highest earnings (season)   Jim Colbert earned a record $1,627,890 in 1996.

Highest earnings (career)   As of August 18, 1997, Bob Charles (New Zealand) had career earnings of $7,146,619.

RYDER CUP

Most individual wins   Arnold Palmer has won the most matches in Ryder Cup competition with 22 victories out of 32 played.

Most selections   The most contests played is 10, by two players: Christy O'Connor Sr. (Great Britain and Ireland), 1955–73; and Nick Faldo (Great Britain and Ireland/Europe), 1977–95. The record in the United States is eight, held by three players: Billy Casper, 1961–75; Ray Floyd, 1969–93; and Lanny Wadkins, 1977–93.

Nick Faldo has played in more Ryder Cup contests than any other golfer.

AMATEUR GOLF

Most wins (men)   Bobby Jones won a record five United States Amateur Championships: 1924–25, 1927–28, 1930.

Most wins (women)   The women's record for the most wins is six, set by Glenna Collette Vare: 1922, 1925, 1928–30, 1935.

NCAA CHAMPIONSHIP

Most titles (team)   Yale has won the most team championships with 21 victories (1897–98, 1902, 1905–13, 1915, 1924–26, 1931–33, 1936, 1943).

Most titles (individual)   Two golfers have won three individual titles: Ben Crenshaw (Texas), 1971–73; Phil Mickelson (Arizona State), 1989–90, 1992.

BIG PLAYS

Longest holes in one   The longest hole ever sunk in one shot was the "dog-leg" 496-yard 17th at Teign Valley Golf Course, Exeter, England, by Shaun Lynch on July 24, 1995. The women's record is 393 yards, by Marie Robie on the first hole of the Furnace Brook Golf Club, Wollaston, MA on September 4, 1949.

Consecutive holes in one   There are at least 20 cases of "aces" being achieved in consecutive holes, of which the greatest was Norman L. Manley's unique "double albatross" on the par-4 330-yard seventh and par-4 290-yard eighth holes on the Del Valle Country Club course, Saugus, CA on September 2, 1964.

Youngest ace   The youngest golfer recorded to have shot a hole in one is Coby Orr (5 years) of Littleton, CO on the 103-yard fifth at the Riverside Golf Course, San Antonio, TX in 1975.
　　The youngest girl is Nicola Mylonas (10 yr. 64 days) on the 133-yard 1st at South Course, Nudgee, Australia on September 18, 1993.

Oldest ace   Otto Bucher (Switzerland) was 99 yr. 244 days old when he sank the 130-yard 12th hole at La Manga Golf Club, Spain on January 13, 1985.

Most rewarding ace   On November 1, 1992, Jason Bohn (U.S.) won $1 million when he made a hole in one in a charity contest. He aced the 136-yard second hole at the Harry S. Pritchett Gold Course, Tuscaloosa, AL using a 9-iron.

Throwing a golf ball   The lowest recorded score for throwing a golf ball around 18 holes (over 6,000 yards) is 82, by Joe Flynn (U.S.), 21, at the 6,228-yard Port Royal course, Bermuda on March 27, 1975.

Golf ball balancing   Lang Martin balanced seven golf balls vertically on a flat surface without adhesive in Charlotte, NC on February 9, 1980.

Longest drive (general)   Niles Lied (Australia) drove a golf ball 2,640 yards (1½ miles) across an ice cap at Mawson Base, Antarctica in 1962.

The greatest recorded carry of a golf ball is 458 yards, by Jack Hamm at Highlands Ranch, CO, July 20, 1993.

The greatest carry below 1,000 meters altitude is 364.8 yards, by Karl Woodward (Great Britain) at the Boca Raton (FL) Country Club, June 28, 1996.

Longest drive (regulation course)   Michael Hoke Austin holds the record for longest recorded drive on a standard course. On September 25, 1974, Austin hit a golf ball 515 yards in the U.S. National Seniors Open Championship in Las Vegas, NV.

Longest putt (tournament)   The longest recorded holed putt in a professional tournament is 110 feet, by Jack Nicklaus in the 1964 Tournament of Champions; and by Nick Price in the 1992 United States PGA Championship.

Most balls hit in one hour   The most balls driven in one hour—at least 100 yards and into a target area—is 2,146, by Sean Murphy at Wifts Practice Range, Carlisle, England on June 30, 1995.

Fastest round (individual)   With wide variations in the lengths of courses, speed records, even for rounds under par, are of little comparative value. The fastest round played with the golf ball coming to rest before each new stroke is 27 min. 9 sec., by James Carvil at Warrenpoint Golf Course, County Down, Northern Ireland, 18 holes 6,154 yards on June 18, 1987.

Fastest round (team)   The Fore Worcester's Children team of golfers completed 18 holes in 9 min. 28 sec. at the Tatnuck Country Club, Worcester, MA on September 9, 1996. They scored 70.

Most holes, 24 hours (on foot)   Ian Colston, 35, played 22 rounds plus five holes (401 holes in all) at Bendigo Golf Club, Victoria, Australia (par-73, 6,061 yards), November 27–28, 1971.

Members of the team that played the fastest round of golf celebrate their new record.

GOLF BALL BALANCING

The most golf balls stacked vertically without the use of adhesives is seven. Lang Martin performed the feat in Charlotte, NC on February 9, 1980.

For rules, see page 707.

Most holes, 24 hours (using golf cart) David Cavalier played 846 holes at Arrowhead Country Club, North Canton, OH (9 holes, 3,013 yards), August 6–7, 1990. The women's record is held by Cyndy Lent (U.S.), who played 509 holes at Twin Lakes Country Club, Twin Lakes, WI on August 7–8, 1994.

Most holes in 12 hours Doug Wert played 440 holes in 12 hours on the 6,044-yard course at Tournament Players Club, Coral Springs, FL on June 7, 1993.

Most holes played in a week Steve Hylton played 1,128 holes at the Mason Rudolph Golf Club (6,060 yards), Clarksville, TN, August 25–31, 1980. Using a golf cart, Leroy Kilpatrick (U.S.) completed 1,363 holes at Jack Gaither Golf Course, Tallahassee, FL, October 23–29, 1995.

Lowest score, one club (18 holes) Thad Daber (U.S.), with a 6-iron, played the 6,037-yard Lochmore Golf Club course, Cary, NC in 70 to win the 1987 World One-Club Championship.

Lowest score, men (18 holes) At least four players have played a long course (over 6,561 yards) in a score of 58—most recently Monte Carlo Money (U.S.), at the par-72, 6,607-yard Las Vegas Municipal Golf Club, NV on March 11, 1981.

Lowest score, women (18 holes) The lowest score on an 18-hole course over 5,000 yards is 60 (31+29) by Wanda Morgan, on the Westgate and Birchington Golf Club course, Kent, England, on July 11, 1929.

Lowest score, men (72 holes) Horton Smith scored 245 (63, 58, 61 and 63) for 72 holes on the 4,700-yard course (par-64) at Catalina Country Club, CA to win the Catalina Open, December 21–23, 1928.

Lowest score, women (72 holes) Trish Johnson (Great Britain) scored 242 (64, 60, 60, 58; 21 under par) in the Bloor Homes Eastleigh Classic at the Fleming Park Course (4,402 yards) in Eastleigh, England, July 22–25, 1987.

Oldest player to score his age The oldest player to achieve a score equal to his age is C. Arthur Thompson (1869–1975) of Victoria, British Columbia, Canada, who scored 103, on the Uplands course of 6,215 yards in 1973.

Oldest club The oldest club of which there is written evidence is the Gentlemen Golfers (now the Honourable Company of Edinburgh Golfers) formed in March 1744. The Royal Burgess Golfing Society of Edinburgh, Scotland claims to have been founded in 1735.

Two golf clubs claim to be the first established in the United States: the Foxburg Golf Club, Clarion Co., PA (1887) and St. Andrews Golf Club of Yonkers, NY (1888).

Largest tournament The Volkswagen Grand Prix Open Amateur Championship in Great Britain attracted a record 321,778 (206,820 men and 114,958 women) competitors in 1984.

Longest course   The world's longest course is the par-77 8,325-yard International Golf Club in Bolton, MA from the "Tiger" tees, remodeled in 1969 by Robert Trent Jones.

Transcontinental golf   Floyd Satterlee Rood used the entire United States as a course, when he played from the Pacific surf to the Atlantic surf from September 14, 1963 to October 3, 1964 in 114,737 strokes. He lost 3,511 balls on the 3,397.7-mile trail.

Largest green   Probably the largest green in the world is that of the par-6 695-yard fifth hole at International Golf Club, Bolton, MA with an area greater than 28,000 square feet.

Longest hole   The seventh hole (par-7) of the Satsuki Golf Club, Sano, Japan measures 964 yards.
   The longest hole in the United States is the 12th hole at Meadows Farm Golf Course in Locust Grove, VA, at a distance of 841 yards.

Biggest bunker   The biggest bunker is Hell's Half Acre on the 585-yard seventh hole of the Pine Valley course, Clementon, NJ, built in 1912 and generally regarded as the world's most trying course.

TENNIS

GRAND SLAM

Most singles   The most singles championships won in grand slam tournaments is 24, by Margaret Court (née Smith; Australia): 11 Australian, five French, three Wimbledon, five U.S. Open between 1960 and 1973. The men's record is 12, by Roy Emerson (Australia): six Australian, two French, two Wimbledon, two U.S. Open between 1961 and 1967.

Most doubles   The most wins by a doubles partnership is 20, by two teams: Louise Brough (U.S.) and Margaret Du Pont (U.S.), who won three French, five Wimbledon and 12 U.S. Open, 1942–57; and by Martina Navratilova (U.S.) and Pam Shriver (U.S.). They won seven Australian, four French, five Wimbledon, four U.S. Open,1981–89.

AUSTRALIAN OPEN CHAMPIONSHIPS

Most titles (overall)   Margaret Court (née Smith) won 21 Australian Open titles, 1960–73: 11 singles, eight doubles and two mixed doubles.

Most singles (men)   The most wins is six, by Roy Emerson (Australia), 1961, 1963–67.

Most singles (women)   The most wins is 11, by Margaret Court (née Smith) of Australia, 1960–66, 1969–71, 1973.

Most doubles (men) The most wins by one pair is eight, by John Bromwich and Adrian Quist (both Australia), 1938–40, 1946–50. Quist also holds the record for most wins by one player with 10, winning in 1936–37 with Don Turnbull, to add to his triumphs with Bromwich.

Most doubles (women) The most wins by one pair is 10, by Nancye Bolton (née Wynne) and Thelma Long (née Coyne), both Australian. Their victories came in 1936–40, 1947–49, 1951–52. Long also holds the record for most wins, with 12, winning in 1956 and 1958 with Mary Hawton.

Most mixed doubles The most wins by one pair is four, by two teams: Harry Hopman and Nell Hopman (née Hall; Australia), 1930, 1936–37, 1939; Colin Long and Nancye Bolton (née Wynne; Australia), 1940, 1946–48. Thelma Long (Australia) shares the women's record of four wins, 1951–52, 1954–55.

Oldest champion (singles) Ken Rosewall (Australia) was 37 yr. 2 mo. old when he captured the singles championship in 1972.

Youngest champion (singles) The youngest singles champion is Martina Hingis (Switzerland), who won the 1997 event at age 16 yr. 117 days. The youngest male to win the Australian Open was Rodney Heath (Australia) in 1905, at age 17 yr. 11 mo.

FRENCH OPEN

Most titles (overall) Margaret Court (née Smith) has won a record 13 French Open titles, 1962–73: five singles, four doubles and four mixed doubles.

Most singles (women) Chris Evert has won a record seven French titles: 1974–75, 1979–80, 1983, 1985–86.

Most singles (men) Bjorn Borg (Sweden) has won the French title a record six times: 1974–75, 1978–81.

Most doubles (men) The most wins by one pair is three, by Henri Cochet and Jacques Brugnon (both France). They won in 1927, 1930 and 1932. The most wins

Gustavo Kuerten raises the French Open trophy. He is the lowest-ranked player to win the event.

WUNDERKIND

The 1997 year in sports will be remembered as the year of the prodigy. More championships were won by younger athletes than ever before. The trend began with Martina Hingis. In January, at 16 years old, she won the Australian Open.

"It was an unbelievable feeling to stand on the podium at the prize-giving ceremony," recalls Hingis. "I was proud of myself that I was the youngest player ever to win the Australian Open. It was like a dream come true."

Hingis was born in the former Czechoslovakia and is now a Swiss citizen. Her mother was a professional tennis player and named Hingis after the legendary Czech-born tennis champion, Martina Navratilova. Hingis acknowledges her mother, who is also her coach, as "the person who has influenced me the most." The tennis ace insists that such early success

YOUNGEST AUSTRALIAN OPEN CHAMPION (SINGLES)

The youngest singles champion is Martina Hingis (Switzerland), who won the 1997 event at age 16 years 117 days.

was not part of her career plan: "It was not my goal to break age records. They came automatically, but it is very nice."

By mid-summer 1997, Hingis had notched up more tennis records. She became the youngest to be ranked number one and was the youngest Wimbledon singles champion in the 20th century. She is not the first tennis prodigy, though, and most of the others burned out quickly. The Wimbledon champion insists that she is different from her predecessors. "I am not afraid of losing interest in tennis. With success comes the motivation." Hingis varies her practice routines to maintain her enthusiasm for the game. She advises aspiring players to do the same: "It's important to have fun. Practice different things every day so that it won't be boring," she says.

Off the court, Hingis has little time to be bored. Too busy to attend high school full-time, she travels with a private tutor. When she isn't keeping up with her studies, Hingis enjoys watching movies and listening to music. She also plays a number of other sports, including skiing, mountain biking and inline skating. Although a fall from a horse in spring kept her out of tennis for several weeks, horses remain Hingis' second greatest passion. "I would love to leap the highest horse jump," she says.

Back on the solid ground of the tennis court, she has set her sights higher: "I want to win the whole Grand Slam." That task will start for Hingis in January 1998 when she defends her Australian title.

by one player is six, by Roy Emerson (Australia), 1960–65, with five different partners.

Most doubles (women)   Three teams have won the doubles title four times: Doris Hart and Shirley Fry (both U.S.), 1950–53; Martina Navratilova and Pam Shriver (both U.S.), 1984–85, 1987–88; and Gigi Fernandez (U.S.) and Natasha Zvereva (Belarus), 1992–95. The most wins by an individual player is seven, by Martina Navratilova—four times with Pam Shriver, 1984–85, 1987–88; and with three other players, in 1975, 1982 and 1986.

Most mixed doubles   Two teams have won the mixed title three times: Ken Fletcher and Margaret Smith (Australia), 1963–65; Jean-Claude Barclay and Francoise Durr (France), 1968, 1971, 1973. Margaret Court (née Smith) has won the title the most times, with four wins, winning with Marty Riessen (U.S.) in 1969, in addition to her wins with Fletcher. Fletcher and Barclay share the men's record of three wins.

Oldest champion   The oldest singles champion at the French Open was Andrés Gimeno (Spain) in 1972, at age 34 yr. 301 days.

Youngest champion   The youngest singles champion at the French Open was Monica Seles (Yugoslavia) in 1990, at 16 yr. 169 days. The youngest men's winner was Michael Chang (U.S.), who was 17 yr. 109 days when he won the 1989 title.

WIMBLEDON

Most titles (overall)   Billie Jean King (U.S.) won 20 Wimbledon titles from 1961–79: six singles, 10 doubles and four mixed doubles.

Most singles (men)   Overall, the most titles is seven, by William Renshaw (Great Britain), 1881–86, 1889. Since the abolition of the Challenge Round in 1922, the most wins is five, by Bjorn Borg (Sweden), 1976–80.

Mark Woodfoode and Todd Woodbridge celebrate their 1997 Wimbledon doubles win. It was their fifth consecutive win, tying the Wimbledon mark.

Most singles (women)   Martina Navratilova has won a record nine titles: 1978–79, 1982–87, 1990.

Most doubles (men)   Lawrence and Reginald Doherty (Great Britain) won the doubles title eight times: 1897–1901, 1903–05.

Most doubles (women)   Suzanne Lenglen (France) and Elizabeth Ryan (U.S.) won the doubles six times: 1919–23, 1925. Elizabeth Ryan was a winning partner on 12 occasions: 1914, 1919–23, 1925–27, 1930, 1933–34.

Most mixed doubles   The team of Ken Fletcher and Margaret Court (née Smith), both of Australia, won the mixed doubles four times: 1963, 1965–66, 1968. Fletcher's four victories tie him for the men's record for wins, which is shared by two other players: Vic Seixas (U.S.), 1953–56; Owen Davidson (Australia), 1967, 1971, 1973–74. Elizabeth Ryan (U.S.) holds the women's record with seven wins: 1919, 1921, 1923, 1927–28, 1930, 1932.

Oldest champion   The oldest champion is Arthur Gore (Great Britain) who won Wimbledon at age 41 yr. 6 mo.

Youngest champion   The youngest champion was Lottie Dod (Great Britain), who was 15 yr. 285 days when she won in 1887. The youngest men's champion was Boris Becker (Germany), who was 17 yr. 227 days when he won in 1985.

U.S. OPEN

Most titles (overall)   Margaret Du Pont (née Osborne) won a record 25 U.S. Open titles, 1941–60—three singles, 13 doubles, and nine mixed doubles.

Most singles (men)   The most wins is seven, by three players: Richard Sears (U.S.), 1881–87; William Larned (U.S.), 1901–02, 1907–11; Bill Tilden (U.S.), 1920–25, 1929.

Most singles (women)   Molla Mallory (née Bjurstedt; U.S.) won a record eight titles: 1915–18, 1920–22, 1926.

Most doubles (men)   The most wins by one pair is five, by Richard Sears and James Dwight (U.S.), 1882–84, 1886–87. The most wins by an individual player is six, by two players: Richard Sears, 1882–84, 1886–87 (with Dwight) and 1885 (with Joseph Clark); Holcombe Ward, 1899–1901 (with Dwight Davis), 1904–06 (with Beals Wright).

Most doubles (women)   The most wins by a pair is 12, by Louise Brough and Margaret Du Pont (née Osborne), both of the U.S. They won in 1942–50 and in 1955–57. Margaret Du Pont holds the record for an individual player with 13 wins; adding to her victories with Brough was the 1941 title with Sarah Fabyan (née Palfrey).

Most mixed doubles   The most wins by one pair is four, by William Talbert and Margaret Osborne (U.S.), who won in 1943–46. The most titles won by any individual is nine, by Margaret Du Pont (née Osborne). She won in 1943-46, 1950, 1956, 1958-60. The most titles won by a man is four, accomplished by six players: Edwin Fischer (U.S.), 1894–96, 1898; Wallace Johnson (U.S.), 1907, 1909, 1911, 1920; Bill Tilden (U.S.), 1913–14, 1922–23; William Talbert (U.S.), 1943–46; Owen Davidson (Australia), 1966–67, 1971, 1973; and Marty Riessen (U.S.), 1969–70, 1972, 1980.

Oldest champion   The oldest singles U.S Open champion was Bill Larned (U.S.) in 1911, at age 38 yr. 8 mo.

Youngest champion   The youngest singles champion was Tracy Austin (U.S.), who was 16 yr. 271 days when she won the women's singles in 1979. The youngest men's champion was Pete Sampras (U.S.), who was 19 yr. 28 days old when he won the 1990 title.

MEN'S PROFESSIONAL TOUR RECORDS
(ATP TOUR)

Most singles titles (career)   Jimmy Connors (U.S.) has won 109 singles titles, 1972–89.

Most singles titles (season)   Guillermo Vilas (Argentina) won 16 titles in 1977.

Most consecutive match wins   Bjorn Borg (Sweden) won 49 consecutive matches in 1978.

Most consecutive weeks ranked number one   Jimmy Connors (U.S.) held the number one ranking on the ATP computer from July 29, 1974 to August 23, 1977, a total of 160 weeks.

Highest earnings (career)   Pete Sampras (U.S.) has won a record $25,562,347, 1988–96.

Highest earnings (season)   Pete Sampras (U.S.) earned $5,415,066 in 1995.

1997 Wimbledon champion Pete Sampras is the all-time money leader in tennis.

WOMEN'S PROFESSIONAL TOUR RECORDS (WTA)

Most singles titles (career)   Martina Navratilova (U.S.) won 167 titles, 1975–94.

Most singles titles (season)   Martina Navratilova won 16 titles in 1983.

Most consecutive matches won   Martina Navratilova won 74 consecutive matches in 1984.

Most consecutive weeks ranked number one   Steffi Graf (Germany) held the number one computer ranking from August 17, 1987 to March 11, 1991, a total of 186 weeks.

Highest earnings (career)   Martina Navratilova (U.S.) won a career record $20,344,061, 1972–94.

Highest earnings (season)   Arantxa Sánchez Vicario (Spain) won $2,943,665 in 1994.

TEAM COMPETITIONS

Davis Cup

Most wins   The U.S. team has won the Davis Cup a record 31 times, 1900–96.

Most matches (career)   Nicola Pietrangeli (Italy) played a record 163 matches (66 ties), 1954 to 1972, winning 120. He played 109 singles (winning 78) and 54 doubles (winning 42).

The longest Davis Cup Final was decided in the fifth set of the fifth match, 10-8. Arnaud Boetsch defeated Nicklas Kulti to give France a 3–2 victory over Sweden.

Most matches (season)   The most wins is 18, by two players: Manuel Santana (Spain), 11 of 12 singles matches and seven of eight doubles matches in 1965; and Ilie Nastase (Romania), 13 of 14 singles matches and five of six doubles matches in 1971.

Longest final   In 1996, Arnaud Boetsche secured France's 3–2 victory over Sweden as he defeated Nicklas Kulti 10–8 in the fifth set of the fifth match, making it the longest final in the history of the Davis Cup.

Most selections (U.S.)   John McEnroe has played for the U.S. team on 31 occasions, 1978–92.

Most wins (U.S.)   John McEnroe has won 60 matches in Davis Cup competition—41 singles and 19 doubles.

Fed Cup

Most wins (country)   The United States has won the Fed Cup 15 times.

Most wins (overall)   Virginia Wade (Great Britain) holds the career mark for the most Fed Cup wins with a record of 66–33 (36–20 singles and 32–5 doubles), 1967–83.

Most singles wins (overall)   Helena Sukova (Czech Republic) holds the mark for the best singles record at 45–11. Sukova has played in 54 ties including five finals for Czechoslovakia winning in 1983–85 and 1988.

Most singles wins (U.S.)   Chris Evert (U.S.) holds the record for the most singles wins for an American with 40–2 played over 42 ties.

Most matches (career)   The career record for the most matches played is 99, set by Virginia Wade (Great Britain), 1967–83.

Olympic Games

Most gold medals   Max Decugis (France) won four gold medals: men's singles, 1906; men's doubles, 1906; mixed doubles, 1906 and 1920.

Most medals   Max Decugis (France) won a record six medals in Olympic competition: four gold (*see above*), one silver and one bronze, 1900–20. Kitty McKane (Great Britain) won a women's record five medals: one gold, two silver and two bronze, 1920–24.

Big Plays

Longest match   The longest match in the history of tennis lasted 6 hr. 22 min., when John McEnroe (U.S.) defeated Mats Wilander (Sweden) in the 1982 World Group Quaterfinal Round in St. Louis, MO.

Longest game   The longest singles game was one of 37 deuces (80 points) between Anthony Fawcett (Rhodesia) and Keith Glass (Great Britain) in the first round of the Surrey Championships in Surbiton, England on May 26, 1975. It lasted 31 minutes. Noëlle van Lottum and Sandra Begijn

Mark Philippoussis has set new standards for the fastest serve in tennis. He hit the 142-mph mark twice in 1997.

played a 52-minute game in the semifinals of the 1984 Dutch Indoor Championships.

Longest tie break The longest tie break was 26–24 for the fourth set of a first round men's doubles at the Wimbledon Championships on July 1, 1985. Jan Gunnarsson (Sweden) and Michael Mortensen (Denmark) defeated John Frawley (Australia) and Victor Pecci (Paraguay) 6–3, 6–4, 3–6, 7–6.

Fastest service (men) Mark Philippoussis (Australia) completed a serve of 142.3 mph at the ATP Toure World Team Championships in Düsseldorf, Germany, May 25, 1997.

Fastest service (women) The women's record is 121.8 mph, by Brenda Schultz-McCarthy (Netherlands) at the Australian Open in Melbourne, January 22, 1996.

Most aces (match) Goran Ivanisevic (Croatia) achieved a record 46 aces against Magnus Norman (Sweden) during the second round at Wimbledon, June 28, 1997.

"Golden set" The only known example of a "golden set" (winning a set 6–0 without dropping a single point, i.e., winning 24 consecutive points) in professional tennis was achieved by Bill Scanlon (U.S.) against Marcos Hocevar (Brazil) in the first round of the WCT Gold Coast Classic in Del Ray, FL on February 22, 1983. Scanlon won the match, 6–2, 6–0.

OTHER RACQUET SPORTS

BADMINTON

Olympic games

Most medals Gil Young-ah (South Korea) has won three medals: one bronze, women's doubles, 1992; one gold, mixed doubles, 1996; and one silver, women's doubles, 1996.

World Championships

Most titles (overall) Park Joo-bong (South Korea) has won a record five world titles: men's doubles in 1985 and 1991; mixed doubles in 1985, 1989 and 1991. Three women have won three titles: Lin Ying (China), doubles in 1983, 1987 and 1989; Li Lingwei (China), singles in 1983 and 1989, doubles in 1985; Guan Weizhan (China), doubles in 1987, 1989 and 1991.

Most titles (singles) Yang Yang (China) is the only man to have won two world singles titles, in 1987 and 1989. Two women have won two singles titles: Li Lingwei (China), 1983 and 1989; Han Aiping (China), 1985 and 1987.

United States National Championships

Most titles Judy Hashman (née Devlin) has won 31 titles, including a record 12 singles titles: 12 women's singles, 1954, 1956–63 and 1965–67; 12 women's doubles, 1953–55, 1957–63 and 1966–67 (10 with her sister Susan); and seven mixed doubles, 1956–59, 1961–62 and 1967. Wynn Rogers won a record 18 men's titles: 10 men's doubles, 1948–53, 1955, 1961–62 and 1964; eight mixed doubles, 1949–52, 1955 and 1961–62. David G. Freeman has won a record seven men's singles titles: 1939–42, 1947–48 and 1953.

Big Plays

Longest rally In the men's singles final of the 1987 All-England Championships between Morten Frost (Denmark) and Icuk Sugiarto (Indonesia), there were two successive rallies of over 90 strokes.

Longest game In the World Championship men's singles final at Glasgow, UK, on June 1, 1997, Peter Rasmussen (Denmark) beat Sun Jun (China) 16–17, 18–13, 15–10, in a match that lasted 2 hr. 4 min.

Shortest game Ra Kyung-min (South Korea) beat Julia Mann (England) 11–2, 11–1 in six minutes during the 1996 Uber Cup in Hong Kong on May 19, 1996.

The shortest game in international badminton competition was Ra Kyung-min's (left) 6-minute defeat of Julia Mann (right) on May 19, 1996.

JAI ALAI

World Championships

Most titles (pair)   The most successful pair has been Roberto Elias and Juan Labat (Argentina), who won the Trinquete Share four times, 1952, 1958, 1962 and 1966.

Most titles (any player)   Two players, both from Argentina, won seven world titles: Juan Labat, 1952–1966; and Riccardo Bizzozeroalso, in various *Trinquete* and *Frontón corto* events, 1970–82.

The most wins in the long court game Cesta Punta is three, by José Hamuy (Mexico; 1934–83), with two different partners, 1958, 1962 and 1966.

Longest domination   The longest domination as the world's No. 1 player was enjoyed by Chiquito de Cambo (France; born Joseph Apesteguy) from the beginning of the century until 1938.

Big Plays

Fastest speed   An electronically measured ball velocity of 188 mph was recorded by José Ramon Areitio (Spain) at the Newport (RI) Jai Alai on August 3, 1979.

Largest frontón   The world's largest frontón (enclosed stadium) is the Palm Beach Jai Alai, West Palm Beach, which has a seating capacity of 6,000 and covers three acres.

Largest crowd   The record attendance for a jai alai contest was 15,052 people at the World Jai Alai in Miami, FL on December 27, 1975. The frontón has seating capacity for only 3,884.

RACQUETBALL

World Championships

Most titles (team)   The United States has won all eight team titles, in 1981, 1984, 1986 (tie with Canada), 1988, 1990, 1992, 1994 and 1996.

Most titles (women)   Michelle Gilman-Gould (U.S.) has won three singles titles, in 1992, 1994 and 1996.

Most titles (men)   Egan Inoue (U.S.) has won two singles titles, in 1986 and 1990.

United States Championships

Most titles (women)   A record seven women's open titles have been won by Michelle Gilman-Gould, 1989–93 and 1995–96.

Most titles (men)   Four men's open titles have been won by Ed Andrews of California, 1980–81 and 1985–86.

SQUASH

World Open Championships

Most titles (men) Jansher Khan (Pakistan) has won eight titles, 1987, 1989–90, and 1992–96.

Most titles (women) Susan Devoy (New Zealand) holds the mark in the women's event with four victories, 1985, 1987, 1990 and 1992.

Most titles (team, men) Australia (1967, 1969, 1971, 1973, 1989 and 1991) and Pakistan (1977, 1981, 1983, 1985, 1987 and 1993) have each won six men's world team titles.

Most titles (team, women) The women's world team title has been won four times, by England (1985, 1987, 1989 and 1990) and by Australia (1981, 1983, 1992 and 1994).

Susan Devoy has won a record four world championships.

United States Amateur Championships

Most titles G. Diehl Mateer won 11 men's doubles titles between 1949 and 1966 with five different partners. Joyce Davenport won eight women's doubles titles with two different partners, 1969–90.

Most titles (singles) Alicia McConnell has won seven women's singles titles, 1982–88. Stanley Pearson won a record six men's titles, 1915–17, 1921–23.

Longest game The longest recorded competitive match was one of 2 hr. 45 min. when Jahangir Khan beat Gamal Awad (Egypt) 9–10, 9–5, 9–7, 9–2, the first game lasting a record one hr. 11 min., in the final of the Patrick International Festival in Chichester, England on March 30, 1983.

Shortest game Philip Kenyon (England) beat Salah Nadi (Egypt) in 6 min. 37 sec. (9–0, 9–0, 9–0) in the British Open at Lamb's Squash Club, London, England on April 9, 1992.

TABLE TENNIS

Olympic Games

Most gold medals Deng Yapin (China) has won four gold medals, 1992–96.

Most medals Two players have won four medals in Olympic competition: Yoo Nam-kyu (South Korea), one gold, three bronze, 1988–96; and Deng Yapin (*see above*).

World Championships

Most men's singles The most victories in singles is five, by Viktor Barna (Hungary), 1931, 1932–35.

Most women's singles The most victories is six, by Angelica Rozeanu (Romania), 1950–55.

Most men's doubles The most victories is eight, by Viktor Barna (Hungary), 1929–35, 1939. The partnership that won the most titles is Viktor Barna and Miklos Szabados (Hungary), 1929–33, 1935.

The most successful table tennis Olympian is Deng Yapin. She has won four gold medals, 1992–96.

Most women's doubles The most victories is seven, by Maria Mednyanszky (Hungary), 1928, 1930–35. The team that won the most titles is Maria Mednyanszky and Anna Sipos (Hungary), 1930–35.

Most mixed doubles Maria Mednyanszky (Hungary) won a record six mixed doubles titles: 1927–28, 1930-31, 1933 (twice). The pairing of Miklos Szabados and Maria Mednyanszky (Hungary) won the title a record three times: 1930–31, 1933.

Swaythling Cup

Most titles The most wins is 12, by Hungary (1926, 1928–31, 1933 [two events were held that year, with Hungary winning both times], 1935, 1938, 1949, 1952, 1979).

Corbillon Cup

Most titles China has won the most titles, with 11 wins (1965, 1975, 1977, 1979, 1981, 1983, 1985, 1987, 1989, 1993 and 1995).

United States National Championships

Most titles Leah Neuberger (née Thall) won a record 21 titles between 1941 and 1961: nine women's singles, 12 women's doubles. Richard Mills won a record 10 men's singles titles between 1945 and 1962.

Big Plays

Most hits   The record number of hits in 60 seconds is 173, by Jackie Bellinger and Lisa Lomas (née Bellinger) in Great Britain on February 7, 1993.

With a paddle in each hand, S. Ramesh Babu (India) completed 5,000 consecutive volleys over the net in 41 min. 27 sec. on April 14, 1995.

Youngest championship player   Joy Foster (Jamaica) was eight years old when she played at the West Indies Championships in Port of Spain, Trinidad in August 1988.

HORSE RACING

TRIPLE CROWN

Most wins (trainer)   The record for the most wins is two, achieved by two trainers: J.E. Fitzsimmons, 1930 and 1935; and Ben A. Jones, 1941 and 1948.

Most wins (jockey)   Eddie Arcaro has won the Triple Crown twice, riding Whirlaway in 1941 and Citation in 1948.

The Triple Crown has been won by 11 horses. In 1997 Silver Charm (seen here winning the Kentucky Derby) won the first two legs of the famous series, but failed in his bid to land the Triple Crown.

KENTUCKY DERBY

Most wins (jockey)   The record for the most wins is five, by two jockeys: Eddie Arcaro, 1938, 1941, 1945, 1948, 1952; and Bill Hartack, 1957, 1960, 1962, 1964, 1969.

Most wins (trainer)   Trainer Ben Jones won a record six Kentucky Derby races, 1938, 1941, 1944, 1948–49, and 1952.

Fastest time   The fastest recorded time in a Kentucky Derby race is 1 min. 59 ²/₅ sec., achieved by Secretariat in 1973.

Largest field   A record 23 horses participated in the Kentucky Derby in 1974.

PREAKNESS STAKES

Most wins (jockey)   Eddie Arcaro won a record six Preakness Stakes in 1941, 1948, 1950–51, 1951, and 1957.

Most wins (trainer)   The record for the most wins by a trainer is seven, by Robert Wyndham Walden in 1875, 1878–82, and 1888.

Fastest time   The record for the fastest time in a Preakness Stakes race is 1 min. 53²/₅ sec., achieved by two horses: Tank's Prospect, 1985; and Louis Quatorze, 1996.

Largest field   A record 18 horses participated in the Preakness Stakes in 1928.

BELMONT STAKES

Most wins (jockey)   The most wins is six, by two jockeys: Jim McLaughlin, 1882–84, 1886–88; and Eddie Arcaro, 1941–42, 1945, 1948, 1952, 1955.

Most wins (trainer)   Trainer James Rowe Sr. holds the mark for the most wins at eight in 1883–84, 1901, 1904, 1907–08, 1910, 1913.

Fastest time   The fastest time recorded at the Belmont Stakes is 2 min. 24 sec., by Secretariat in 1973.

Largest field   A record 15 horses participated in the Belmont Stakes in 1983.

BREEDERS' CUP SERIES

Most series wins (horse)   Three horses have won two Breeders' Cup races: Bayakoa, which won the Distaff, in 1989 and 1990; Miesque, which won the Mile, in 1987 and 1988; and Lure, which won the Mile in 1992 and 1993.

Most series wins (jockey)   Two jockeys have ridden seven winners in the Breeders' Cup Championship: Laffit Pincay Jr., Juvenile (1985, 1986, 1988), Classic (1986), Distaff (1989, 1990), Juvenile Fillies (1993); and Eddie Delahoussaye, Distaff (1984, 1993), Turf (1989), Juvenile Fillies (1991), Sprint (1992, 1993).

Highest earnings (horse)   Alysheba has won a record $2,133,000 in Breeders' Cup races, from three starts, 1986–88.

Highest earnings (jockey)   Pat Day has won a record $13,503,000 in Breeders' Cup racing, 1984–96.

Highest earnings (trainer)   D. Wayne Lukas holds the mark for the highest earnings at $12,456,000, 1984–1996.

BREEDERS' CUP CLASSIC

Most wins (jockey)   Jerry Bailey has won the Classic three times: 1991, 1993 and 1995.

JOCKEYS

Most wins, career (men)   Bill Shoemaker rode 8,833 winners from 40,350 mounts. "The Shoe" made his debut aboard Waxahachie on March 19, 1949, and raced for the last time on Patchy Groundfog on February 3, 1990. His first victory came on April 20, 1949 aboard Shafter V, his last on January 20, 1990 aboard Beau Genius at Gulfstream Park, FL.

Most wins, career (women)   Julie Krone has won 3,158 races from 1980 through 1996.

Most wins, season (men)   Kent Desormeaux rode 598 winners, from 2,312 mounts, in 1989.

Most wins, season (women)   Gwen Jocson rode 376 winners, from 2,007 mounts in 1991.

Most wins (single day)   The most winners ridden in one day is nine, by Chris Antley on October 31, 1987. Antley rode four winners in the afternoon at Aqueduct, NY and five in the evening at The Meadowlands, NJ.

The most successful female jockey is Julie Krone. She heads the career tables in earnings and victories, and is the only woman to ride a Triple Crown winner.

Most wins (one card)   The most winners ridden on one card is eight, achieved by four jockeys: Hubert Jones, from 13 rides, in Caliente, CA, June 11, 1944; Dave Gall, from 10 rides, at Cahokia Downs, East St. Louis, IL, October 18, 1978; Robert Williams, from 10 rides, in Lincoln, NE, September 29, 1984; and Pat Day, from nine rides, in Arlington, IL, September 13, 1989.

Consecutive wins   The longest winning streak by a jockey is nine races, by two jockeys: Albert Adams won nine races at Marlboro Racetrack, MD, over three days, September 10–12, 1930. He won the last two races on September 10, all six races on September 11, and the first race on September 12. Tony Black won nine races on July 30–31, 1993. He won three races at Atlantic City Racecourse on July 30, two at Philadelphia Park on July 31 and four at Atlantic City on July 31.

Highest earnings, career (men)   Laffit Pincay Jr. has won a record $190,538,811 from 1964 through the end of 1996.

Highest earnings, career (women)   Julie Krone has won a record $70,560,436 from 1980 through the end of 1996.

Highest earnings, season (men)   The greatest prize money earned in a season is $19,465,376, by Jerry Bailey in 1996.

Highest earnings, season (women)   The greatest prize money earned by a female jockey in one season is $9,220,824 by Julie Krone in 1992.

HORSES

Most wins, career   The most wins is 89, by Kingston, from 138 starts, 1986–94.

Most wins (graded stakes races)   John Henry won 25 graded stakes races, including 16 Grade I races, 1978–84.

Most wins, year   Lenoxbar won 46 races in one year, 1940, in Puerto Rico from 56 starts.

Most consecutive wins   Camarero, foaled in 1951, was undefeated in 56 races in Puerto Rico from April 19, 1953 to his first defeat on August 17, 1955 (in his career to 1956, he won 73 of 77 races).

Highest earnings, career   The career record for earnings is $9,999,815, by Cigar, 1992–96. Cigar's career record was 19 wins, four seconds and five thirds from 33 races.

Highest earnings, year   The highest earnings in one year is $4,910,000, by Cigar, in 1996, from eight starts (five wins, two seconds and one third).

Highest earnings, race   The one-race earnings record is $2.6 million by Spend A Buck for the Jersey Derby, Garden State Park, NJ, on May 27, 1985.

TRAINERS

Most wins, career   The career record is 6,362, by Dale Baird (U.S.), 1962–1993.

Most wins, year   Jack Charles Van Berg (U.S.) had a record 496 wins in 1976.

Highest earnings, career   D. Wayne Lukas has won $140,024,750 in his career.

Highest earnings, year   The greatest amount won in a year is $17,842,358, by D. Wayne Lukas (U.S.) in 1988.

BIG PLAYS

Oldest thoroughbred   The greatest age recorded for a thoroughbred race-horse is 42 years, in the case of the chestnut gelding Tango Duke (foaled 1935), owned by Carmen J. Koper of Barongarook, Victoria, Australia. The horse died on January 25, 1978.

Oldest winner (horse)   The oldest winning horses are 18-year-old Revenge at Shrewsbury, England, 1790; Marksman at Ashford, Kent, England,1826; and Jorrocks at Bathurst, Australia, 1851. At the same age, Wild Aster won three hurdle races in 1919, and Sonny Somers won two steeplechases in February 1980.

Isitingood ran the fastest mile in thoroughbred racing history on February 5, 1997 at Santa Anita Park. He was timed at 1:32.05.

Fastest horse   Big Racket reached 43.26 mph in a ¼-mile race in Mexico City, Mexico on February 5, 1945. Onion Roll reached the same speed at Thistledown, Cleveland, OH on September 27, 1993.

The record for 1½ miles is 37.82 mph, by 3-year-old Hawkster (carrying

121 pounds) at Santa Anita Park, Arcadia, CA on October 14, 1989, with 2 min. 22.8 sec.

Biggest payout   Anthony A. Speelman and Nicholas John Cowan (both Great Britain) won $1,627,084.40, after federal income tax of $406,768.00 was withheld, on a $64 9-horse accumulator at Santa Anita Racetrack, Arcadia, CA on April 19, 1987. Their first seven selections won, and the payout was for a jackpot accumulated over 24 days.

Highest purse, race   The largest single race purse is $4 million including a record first prize of $2.4 million for the Dubai World Cup; won by Cigar on March 27, 1996 and Singspiel on April 3, 1997.

OTHER EQUESTRIAN SPORTS

SHOW JUMPING

Olympic Games

Most gold medals (rider)   Hans-Gunther Winkler (West Germany) has won five titles, 1956, 1960, 1964 and 1972 in the team competition, and the individual championship in 1956. The only rider to win two individual titles is Pierre Jonqueres d'Oriola (France), in 1952 and 1964.

At the Third Royal Equestrian Show held in the Sultanate of Oman in 1995, there were 510 horses, 170 camels and a marching band of 1,000 musicians.

Most gold medals (horse)   The most successful horse is Halla, ridden by Hans-Gunther Winkler during his individual and team wins in 1956, and during the team win in 1960.

Most medals (rider)   Hans-Gunther Winkler has won a record seven medals: five gold (*see above*), one silver and one bronze in the team competition in 1976 and 1968.

World Championships

Most titles Two riders share the record for most men's championships with two victories: Hans-Gunther Winkler (West Germany), 1954–55, and Raimondo d'Inzeo (Italy), 1956 and 1960. The women's title was won twice by Janou Tjssot (née Lefebvre) of France, in 1970 and 1974. No rider has won the integrated competition more than once.

Big Plays

Highest jump The record for the highest jump is 8 ft. 1¼ in., by Huasó, ridden by Capt. Alberto Larraguibel Morales (Chile) at Viña del Mar, Santiago, Chile on February 5, 1949.

Longest jump The record for the longest jump over water is 27 ft. 6¾ in., by Something, ridden by André Ferreira (South Africa) in Johannesburg, South Africa on April 25, 1975.

THREE-DAY EVENT

Olympic Games

Most gold medals (rider) Charles Pahud de Mortanges (Netherlands) has won four gold medals—the individual title in 1928 and 1932, and the team event in 1924 and 1928. Mark Todd (New Zealand) is the only other rider to have won the individual title twice, in 1984 and 1988.

Most gold medals (horse) Marcroix was ridden by Charles Pahud de Mortanges in three of his four medal rounds, 1928–32.

Most medals (rider) Charles Pahud de Mortanges has won five medals: four gold (*see above*) and one silver in the 1932 team event.

World Championships

Most titles (rider) Two riders have won three world titles: Bruce Davidson (U.S.), individual title in 1974 and 1978, team title in 1974; and Virginia Leng (Great Britain), individual in 1986 and team in 1982 and 1986. Davidson is the only rider to have won two individual championships.

Most titles (country) Great Britain has won the team title a record three times, 1970, 1982 and 1986. The United States won the team event in 1974.

DRESSAGE

Olympic Games

Most gold medals (rider) Reiner Klimke (West Germany) has won six gold medals: one individual in 1984, and five team in 1964, 1968, 1976, 1984 and 1988. Henri St. Cyr (Sweden) is the only rider to have won two individual titles, in 1952 and 1956. Two riders have won the individual title on two occasions: Henri St. Cyr (Sweden), 1952 and 1956; and Nicole Uphoff (Germany), 1988 and 1992.

Most gold medals (horse)   Rembrandt was ridden by Nicole Uphoff in all four of her medal-winning rounds—two individual titles and two team titles, both in 1988 and 1992.

Most medals (rider)   Reiner Klimke won eight medals: six gold (*see p. 573*), and two bronze in the individual event in 1968 and 1976.

World Championships

Most titles (rider)   Reiner Klimke (West Germany) is the only rider to have won two individual titles, on Mehmed in 1974 and on Ahlerich in 1982.

Most titles (country)   West Germany has won six times: 1966, 1974, 1978, 1982, 1986 and 1990.

CARRIAGE DRIVING

World Championships

Most titles (driver)   The most World Championships titles is two, achieved by three drivers: György Bárdos (Hungary), 1978 and 1980; Tjeerd Velstra (Netherlands), 1982 and 1986; and Ijsbrand Chardon (Netherlands), 1988 and 1992.

Most titles (country)   The record for the most titles is three, achieved by Great Britain, 1972, 1974, 1980; Hungary, 1976, 1978, 1984; and Netherlands, 1982, 1986, 1988.

Big Plays

Most animals in a hitch   Willard McWilliams of Navan, Ontario, Canada drove 50 horses in a single hitch at the 50th Navan Fair on August 13, 1995. The lead horses were on reins 168 feet long.
   Floyd Zopfi of Stratford, WI has driven 52 llamas in a hitch on several occasions since 1990, with the lead llamas on 150-foot reins.

Longest horse-drawn procession   The longest horse-drawn procession was a cavalcade of 68 carriages that measured 3,018 feet "nose to tail," organized by the Spies Traveling Company of Denmark on May 7, 1986. It carried 810 people through the woods around Copenhagen to celebrate the coming of spring.

POLO

World Championships

Most titles   The record for the most Polo World Championship titles is two, by Argentina in Buenos Aires, 1987; and in Chile, 1992.

Scoring/Handicap

Highest scoring game The highest aggregate number of goals scored in an international match is 30, when Argentina beat the U.S. 21–9 at the Meadow Brook Club, Westbury, NY in September 1936.

Highest handicap Polo players are assigned handicaps based on their skill, with a 10 handicap being the highest level of play. Only 56 players have been awarded the 10-goal handicap.

40-goal games There have only been three games staged between two 40-goal handicap teams. These games were staged in Argentina in 1975, the United States in 1990 and Australia in 1991.

Big Plays

Most chukkas The greatest number of chukkas played on one ground in a day is 43. This was achieved by the Pony Club in Kirtlington Park, England on July 31, 1991.

RODEO

World Championships (PRCA)

Most titles (overall) Jim Shoulders has won 16 rodeo world championship events: all-around, 1949, 1956–59; bareback riding, 1950, 1956–58; bull riding, 1951, 1954–59.

Saddle bronc riding Casey Tibbs won six saddle bronc titles, in 1949, 1951–54 and 1959.

Bareback riding Two cowboys have won five titles: Joe Alexander, 1971–75; and Bruce Ford, 1979–80, 1982–83, 1987.

Bull riding Don Gay has won eight bullriding titles: 1975–81 and 1984.

Calf roping Dean Oliver has won eight titles: 1955, 1958, 1960–64 and 1969.

Steer roping Guy Allen has won 11 titles: 1977, 1980, 1982, 1984, 1989, 1991–96.

Steer wrestling Homer Pettigrew has won six titles: 1940, 1942–45 and 1948.

Team roping The team of Jake Barnes and Clay O'Brien Cooper has won seven titles, 1985–89, 1992 and 1994.

Women's barrel racing Charmayne Rodman has won 10 titles, 1984–93.

Oldest world champion Ike Rude won the 1953 steer roping title at age 59 to became the oldest rodeo titleholder.

Youngest champion   The youngest winner of a world title is Anne Lewis, who won the WPRA barrel racing title in 1968 at 10 years of age. Ty Murray, 20, became the youngest cowboy to win the PRCA World Champion All-Around Cowboy title in 1989.

Riding Records

Bull riding   Wade Leslie scored 100 points riding Wolfman Skoal at Central Point, OR in 1991.

Saddle bronc riding   Two riders have scored 95 points: Doug Vold, riding Transport, in Meadow Lake, Saskatchewan, Canada in 1979; and Glen O'Neill, riding Skoal's Airwolf, in Innisfail, Alberta, Canada in June 1996.

Glen O'Neill is one of two cowboys to score a record 95 points in saddle bronc riding.

Bareback riding   Joe Alexander scored 93 points riding Marlboro in Cheyenne, WY in 1974.

Fastest Times

Calf roping   The fastest time in this event is 5.7 seconds, by Lee Phillips in Assinobia, Saskatchewan, Canada in 1978.

Steer wrestling   Without a barrier, the fastest time is 2.2 seconds by Oral Zumwalt in the 1930s. With a barrier, the record time is 2.4 seconds, achieved by three cowboys: Jim Bynum, Marietta, OK, 1955; Gene Melton, Pecatonia, IL, 1976; and Carl Deaton, Tulsa, OK, 1976.

Team roping   The team of Bob Harris and Tee Woolman performed this feat in a record 3.7 seconds in Spanish Fork, UT in 1986.

Steer roping   The fastest time in this event is 8.1 seconds, by Guy Allen in Coffeyville, KS in 1996.

Highest Earnings

Career   Roy Cooper holds the career PRCA earnings mark at $1,742,278, 1976–96.

Season   The single-season PRCA mark is $297,896 by Ty Murray in 1993.

Big Plays

Texas skips   Vince Bruce (U.S.) performed 4,001 Texas skips (jumping back and forth through a large, vertical spun hoop) on July 22, 1991 in New York City.

Largest loop   Kalvin Cook spun a 95-foot loop in Las Vegas, NV on March 27, 1994.

HARNESS RACING

Horses (Trotters)

Most victories (career)   Goldsmith Maid won an all-time record 350 races (including dashes and heats) from 1864 through 1877.

Most victories (season)   Make Believe won a record 53 races in 1949.

Highest earnings (career)   The greatest career earnings for any harness horse is $4,907,307, by Peace Corps, 1988–93.

Highest earnings (season)   The single-season record for a trotter is $1,610,608, by Prakas in 1985.

Highest earnings (race)   The richest race in the trotting calendar is the Hambletonian. The richest Hambletonian was the 1992 event, with a total purse of $1,380,000. The record first-place prize was $673,000 for the 1990 race, won by Harmonious.

Horses (Pacers)

Most victories (career)   Single G won 262 races (including dashes and heats), 1918–26.

Most victories (season)   Victory Hy won a record 65 races in 1950.

Highest earnings (career)   The all-time earnings record for a pacer is $3,225,653, by Nihilator, 1984–85.

Highest earnings (season)   The season record for a pacer is $2,264,714, by Cam's Card Shark in 1994.

Highest earnings (race)   The richest race in harness racing history was the 1984 Woodrow Wilson, which carried a total purse of $2,161,000. The winner, Nihilator, earned $1,080,500.

Drivers

Most wins (career)   Hervé Filion (Canada) had won 14,783 harness races as of February 25, 1997.

Most wins (season)   Tony Morgan won a record 853 races in 1996.

Most wins (day)   Mike Lachance won 12 races at Yonkers Raceway, NY on June 23, 1987.

Highest earnings (career)   John Campbell has won a career record $147,101,299 in prize money, 1972–February 25, 1997.

Highest earnings (season)   John Campbell won a season record $11,620,878 in 543 races in 1990.

Oldest winning driver   Eighty-three-year-old George McCandless of Vineland, NJ guided Kehm's Scooter to victory at Freehold Raceway in 1994.

AUTOMOTIVE SPORTS

NASCAR

Most championships   Two drivers have won seven NASCAR titles: Richard Petty, 1964, 1967, 1971–72, 1974–75 and 1979; and Dale Earnhardt, 1980, 1986–87, 1990–91, and 1993–94.

Mark Martin ran the fastest-ever Winston Cup race in 1997.

Most consecutive titles   Cale Yarborough is the only driver to "threepeat" as NASCAR champion, winning in 1976–78.

Most wins (career)   Richard Petty has won 200 NASCAR Winston Cup races of 1,185 in which he competed, 1958–92.

Most wins (season)   Richard Petty won a record 27 races in 1967.

Fastest average speed   The fastest average speed in a Winston Cup race is 188.354 mph, set by Mark Martin at Talladega Superspeedway, AL on May 10, 1997.

Highest earnings (season)   Jeff Gordon earned a single-season record $4,347,343 in 1995.

Highest earnings (career)   Dale Earnhardt holds the career earnings mark at $29,229,195, from 1975 to July 22, 1997.

DAYTONA 500

Most wins   Richard Petty has won seven times: 1964, 1966, 1971, 1973–74, 1979 and 1981.

Most consecutive wins   Richard Petty and Cale Yarborough are the only drivers to have repeated as Daytona 500 winners in consecutive years. Petty's double was in 1973–74 and Yarborough's in 1983–84.

Oldest winner   Bobby Allison became the oldest person to win in 1988 at age 50 yr. 2 mo. 11 days.

Youngest winner   Jeff Gordon won in 1997 at age 25 yr. 6 mo.

Indy Car Racing

Most championships   A. J. Foyt Jr. has won seven Indy Car National Championships: 1960–61, 1963–64, 1967, 1975 and 1979.

Most consecutive championships   Ted Horn won three consecutive national titles, 1946–48.

Most wins (career)   A. J. Foyt Jr. has won a career record 67 Indy Car races, 1957–92. Foyt's first victory came at the DuQuoin 100 in 1960 and his last at the Pocono 500 in 1981.

Most wins (season)   The record for most victories in a season is 10, shared by two drivers: A.J. Foyt Jr. in 1964 and Al Unser in 1970.

Closest races   The closest margin of victory in an Indy Car race using electronic timing was Mark Blundell's 0.027-second victory in the Budweiser/ GI Joe's 200 at Portland, OR on June 22, 1997.
The closest finish in a 500-mile event was Al Unser Jr.'s 0.043-second victory in the 1992 Indianapolis 500.
Mario Andretti pulled off the closest finish in an Indy road race, when

A MAN IN A HURRY

As the popularity of NASCAR racing increases, Jeff Gordon is leading the way—literally. He and his team continue to dominate the Winston Cup Series, highlighted by Gordon's victory at the 1997 Daytona 500, a race that helped him to establish himself as a dual record holder in *The Guinness Book of World Records*. At the age of 25 years 6 months, Gordon became the youngest driver ever to win the prestigious NASCAR trophy at Daytona. Earlier successes helped him to set the highest single-season winnings total of $4,347,343 in 1995. And he will undoubtedly own several more records before his final victory lap.

Though many would think his is a solitary endeavor, Gordon insists that racing is as much a team sport as baseball or basketball, and that his success has as much to do with those around him as it does with his passion for the thrill of the race. "I think it's definitely a combination. You've got to have good equipment and a good race team, and you've got to have a good driver. I'm always the first one to admit that we've got great race cars and a great race team. I've been very fortunate to enjoy this kind of success. We've got a great package."

Experience lends a hand as well. Gordon has been racing (and winning) since the age of five, and shows no signs of slowing down. "I'm young, and I hope that I can stay competitive for many more years, and also that we can keep a great team together for a good long time."

The Winston Cup Series is the only place Gordon sees himself for now, though he admits that the idea of racing in the Indianapolis 500 does hold some appeal. "If I did anything, I would love to try out a Formula One

ON THE RECORD

YOUNGEST WINNER
(DAYTONA 500)

Jeff Gordon won the Daytona 500 in 1997 at age 25 yr. 6 mo.

car, but in order to do that there would be so many things that I would have to do or give up right now. I'd hate to leave NASCAR when I have such a great team and such fan support, and in the midst of the success we're experiencing."

Gordon confides that he sees himself racing for another 15 years or so, and that he genuinely enjoys what he does regardless of the outcome. But before he turns in his keys, he admits that setting a few more records might be something worth gunning for.

One in particular draws his attention: "There's a gentleman by the name of Richard Petty who owns the record for most wins. That one certainly wouldn't be too bad!"

he won the Portland 200 by 0.07 seconds on June 15, 1986. The loser in this showdown was Andretti's son, Michael.

Oldest winner On April 4, 1993 Mario Andretti won the Valvoline 200 at the Phoenix International Raceway. At 53 yr. 52 days, Andretti became the oldest driver to win an Indy Car race.

Youngest winner Greg Moore's (Canada) win in the 1997 Miller 200 at age 22 yr. 1 mo. 10 days is the youngest age any driver has won an Indy Car race.

The closest PPG-CART race ever was won by Mark Blundell (top) by 0.027 seconds on June 22, 1997. Greg Moore (center) became the youngest Indy Car winner with his victory at the Milwaukee Mile on June 22, 1997. In Formula One, Ferrari extended its lead as the most successful team, posting a victory at the 1997 Monaco Grand Prix (bottom).

Highest earning (season)   The single-season earnings record is $3,535,813, set in 1994 by Al Unser Jr.

Highest earnings (career)   Through the 1996 season, Al Unser Jr. had the highest career earnings for Indy drivers with $17,735,906.

INDIANAPOLIS 500

Most wins   Three drivers have won the Indy 500 four times: A. J. Foyt Jr., in 1961, 1964, 1967 and 1977; Al Unser, in 1970–71, 1978 and 1987; and Rick Mears, in 1979, 1984, 1988 and 1991.

Most consecutive wins   Four drivers have won the race in consecutive years: Wilbur Shaw, 1939–40; Mauri Rose, 1947–48; Bill Vukovich, 1953–54; and Al Unser, 1970–71.

Fastest average speed   The record time is 2 hr. 41 min. 18.404 sec. (185.981 mph) by Arie Luyendyk (Netherlands), in a 1990 Lola-Chevrolet on May 27, 1990.

Closest race   The closest margin of victory was 0.043 seconds in 1992 when Al Unser Jr. edged Scott Goodyear (Canada).

Oldest winner   Al Unser became the oldest winner when he won the 1987 race at age 47 yr. 11 mo.

Youngest winner   Troy Ruttman became the youngest winner when he won the 1952 race at age 22 yr. 2 mo.

Highest earnings   The record prize fund is $8,642,450 awarded in 1997. The individual prize record is $1,568,150, by Arie Luyendyk (Netherlands) in 1997. Luyendyk also leads the field in career earnings at $5,224,829 from 13 starts, 1985–97.

Fastest qualifier   The record average speed for four laps qualifying is 236.986 mph by Arie Luyendyk (Netherlands) in a Reynard-Ford-Cosworth on May 12, 1996. On the same day he set the one-lap record of 237.498 mph.

FORMULA ONE

Most championships   Juan-Manuel Fangio (Argentina) has won the drivers' championship five times, 1951 and 1954–57. He also holds the record for consecutive titles with four straight, 1954–57.

Oldest champion   Juan-Manuel Fangio is the oldest world champion, winning the 1957 title at age 46 yr. 41 days.

Youngest champion   Emerson Fittipaldi (Brazil) became the youngest champion in 1972, at age 25 yr. 273 days.

Most wins (career)   Alain Prost (France) has won 51 Formula One races (from 200), between 1980 and 1993.

Most wins (season) The most victories in a season is nine, by two drivers: Nigel Mansell (Great Britain) in 1992, and Michael Schumacher (Germany) in 1995.

Oldest winner The oldest driver to win an official race was Luigi Fagioli (Italy), who was 53 years 22 days old when he won the 1951 French Grand Prix.

Youngest winner The youngest driver to win an official race was Troy Ruttman, who was 22 yr. 80 days old when he won the 1952 Indianapolis 500, which counted in the World Drivers' Championship that year.

Closest finish The narrowest margin of victory in a Formula One race was when Ayrton Senna (Brazil) held off Nigel Mansell by 0.014 seconds to win the Spanish Grand Prix on April 13, 1986.

Most successful manufacturer Ferrari of Italy have won a record eight manufacturers' World Championships (1961, 1964, 1975–77, 1979 and 1982–83).

As of August 1997, Ferrari also holds the record for the most race wins, at 111.

Fastest average speed The fastest overall average speed for a Grand Prix race is 242.623 km/h (150.759 mph), by Peter Gethin (Great Britain) in a BRM in the Italian Grand Prix at Monza on September 5, 1971.

Fastest qualifying lap Keke Rosberg (Finland) set the fastest qualifying lap in Formula One history, when he qualified for the British Grand Prix at Silverstone with an average speed of 160.817 mph on July 20, 1985.

LE MANS (24 HOURS)

Most wins (driver) The most wins by a driver is six, by Jacky Ickx (Belgium), 1969, 1975–77 and 1981–82.

Most wins (manufacturer) The race has been won by Porsche cars a record 14 times (1970–71, 1976–77, 1979, 1981–87, 1993 and 1996).

Greatest distance The greatest distance covered in the 24-hour *Grand Prix d'Endurance* (first held May 26–27, 1923) on the old Sarthe circuit at Le Mans, France is 3,315.203 miles, by Dr. Helmut Marko (Austria) and Gijs van Lennep (Netherlands) in a 4,907-cc flat-12 Porsche 917K Group 5 sports car, June 12–13, 1971.

The record for the greatest distance covered for the current circuit is 3,313.150 miles (average speed 137.047 mph) by Jan Lammers (Netherlands), Johnny Dumfries and Andy Wallace (both Great Britain) in a Jaguar XRJ9 on June 11–12, 1988.

Fastest lap (race) The race lap record (now 8.411-mile lap) is 3 min. 21.27 sec. (average speed 150.429 mph) by Alain Ferté (France) in a Jaguar XRJ-9 on June 10, 1989.

Fastest lap (qualifying) Hans Stück (West Germany) set the practice lap speed record of 156.377 mph.

The most famous automobile endurance race is the Le Mans 24 hours. The most successful team is Porsche, with 14 victories.

RALLYING

World Championship

Most titles (driver)　The World Drivers' Championships (instituted 1979) have been won four times by Juha Kankkunen (Finland), 1986–87, 1991, 1993.

Most titles (manufacturer)　A record 11 manufacturers' titles were won by Lancia between 1972 and 1992.

Most wins (career)　The career record for the most wins in World Championship races is 21, achieved by Juha Kankkunen.

Most wins (season)　The most wins in a season is six, by Didier Auriol (France) in 1992.

Youngest World Champion　Colin McRae (Great Britain) was 27 yr. 89 days old when he won in 1995.

Monte Carlo Rally

Most wins　The Monte Carlo rally has been won a record four times by two drivers: Sandro Munari (Italy) in 1972, 1975, 1976 and 1977; and Walter Röhrl (West Germany), in 1980, 1982, 1983 and 1984.

DRAG RACING (NHRA)

Top Fuel

Shortest elapsed time   The shortest elapsed time recorded by a Top Fuel dragster from a standing start for 440 yards is 4.564 seconds by Joe Amato of Old Forge, PA, in Pomona, CA, February 1997.

Fastest top speed   The fastest speed recorded in a Top Fuel race is 317.57 mph by Joe Amato at the 1997 Slick 50 Nationals, Baytown, TX.

Most NHRA titles   Joe Amato has won a record five national titles: 1984, 1988 and 1990–92.

The most successful top fuel driver is Joe Amato, the winner of five NHRA titles.

Most wins (season)   The record for the most wins in a single-season is six, achieved by six drivers: Don Garlits, 1985; Darrel Gwynn, 1988; Gary Ormsby, 1989; Joe Amato, 1990; Kenny Bernstein, 1991; and Eddie Hill, 1993.

Most wins (career)   The record for the most wins in a career is 36, achieved by Joe Amato, 1982–96.

Funny Car

Shortest elapsed time   The shortest elapsed time is 4.889 seconds, by John Force on July 7, 1996 in Topeka, KS.

Fastest top speed   Whit Bazemore of Indianapolis, IN, was timed at 313.04 mph in Baytown, TX , March 1997.

Most NHRA titles   John Force has won a record six national titles, in 1990–91 and 1993–96.

Most wins (season)   John Force won a record 13 races in 1996.

Most wins (career)   John Force has won a record 61 Funny Car races (1975–96).

Pro Stock

Shortest elapsed time   The shortest elapsed time in the Pro Stock class is 6.883 seconds, by Warren Johnson, of Duluth, GA, in Dinwiddie, VA, April 1997.

Fastest top speed   The fastest speed achieved in a Pro Stock race is 200.53 mph by Warren Johnson, of Duluth, GA, in Dinwiddie, VA, April 1997.

Most NHRA titles   Bob Glidden has won a record 10 national titles, in 1974–75, 1978–80 and 1985–89.

Most wins (season)   Darrell Alderman won a record 11 races in 1991.

Most wins (career)   Bob Glidden has won a record 85 races (1972–96), the most victories of any driver in NHRA events.

BIG PLAYS

Oldest auto race   The oldest auto race still regularly run is the Royal Automobile Club (RAC) Tourist Trophy, first staged on September 14, 1905 on the Isle of Man, Great Britain.

Oldest winner   The oldest winner of a professionally sanctioned race is Charles F. Grabiak, M.D. (U.S.; b. March 9, 1920), who was 72 years old when he finished first in a nationally sanctioned auto race in 1992 at Watkins Glen, NY.

Fastest circuits   The highest average lap speed attained on any closed circuit is 250.958 mph, in a trial by Dr. Hans Liebold (Germany), who lapped the 7.85-mile high-speed track at Nardo, Italy in 1 min. 52.67 sec. in a Mercedes-Benz C111-IV on May 5, 1979. It was powered by a V8 engine with two KKK turbochargers, with an output of 500 hp at 6,200 rpm.

Fastest race   The fastest race is the Busch Clash at Daytona, FL over 50 miles on a 31-degree banked track 2½ miles long. In 1987, Bill Elliott (U.S.) averaged 197.802 mph in a Ford Thunderbird.

Fastest Race (500 miles)   Al Unser Jr. (U.S.) set the world record for a 500-mile race when he won the Michigan 500 on August 9, 1990 at an average speed of 189.727 mph.

Longest rally (distance)   The Singapore Airlines London–Sydney Rally was held over 19,329 miles from Covent Garden, London, England on August 14, 1977 to Sydney Opera House, Australia. It was won on September 28,

1977 by Andrew Cowan, Colin Malkin and Michael Broad in a Mercedes 280E.

MOTORCYCLE RACING

World Championships

Most titles (125 cc) Angel Nieto (Spain) won a total of seven World Championships: 1971–72, 1979, 1981–84.

Most titles (250cc) Phil Read (Great Britain) won four World Championship titles: 1964–65, 1968, 1971.

Most titles (500cc) The record for 500 cc titles is eight, achieved by Giacomo Agostini (Italy), 1966–72, 1975.

The first motorcycle race was staged in 1896. No doubt the riders in the first race would jump at the chance to ride on these machines.

Most titles (sidecar) Rolf Biland (Switzerland), won seven world sidecar titles, 1978–79, 1981, 1983 and 1992–94.

Multiple titles The only rider to win more than one world championship in one year is Freddie Spencer (U.S.), who won the 250cc and 500cc titles in 1985.

Youngest champion Loris Capirossi (Italy) was 17 yr. 165 days old when he won the 125 cc title on September 16, 1990.

Oldest champion Hermann-Peter Müller (West Germany) won the 250 cc title in 1955 at age 46.

Most Grand Prix wins (125 cc) Angel Nieto (Spain) won 62 Grand Prix titles.

Most Grand Prix wins (250 cc) Anton Mang (West Germany) won 33 Grand Prix titles.

Most Grand Prix wins (500cc) Giacomo Agostini (Italy) won a record eight Grand Prix titles.

Oldest race The oldest continuous motorcycle races in the world are the Auto-Cycle Union Tourist Trophy (TT) series, first held on the 15.81-mile "Peel" (St. John's) course in the Isle of Man, Great Britain in 1907, and still run on the "Mountain" circuit.

Fastest circuits The highest average lap speed attained on any closed circuit is 160.288 mph, by Yvon du Hamel (Canada) on a modified 903 cc 4-cylinder Kawasaki Z1 at the 31-degree banked 2.5-mile Daytona International Speedway, FL in March 1973. His lap time was 56.149 seconds.

The fastest road circuit used to be Francorchamps circuit near Spa, Belgium, then 8.77 miles long. It was lapped in 3 min. 50.3 sec. (average speed 137.150 mph) by Barry Sheene (Great Britain) on a 495 cc 4-cylinder Suzuki during the Belgian Grand Prix on July 3, 1977. On that occasion he set a record time for this 10-lap (87.74-mile) race of 38 min. 58.5 sec. (average speed 135.068 mph).

Longest circuit The 37.73-mile "Mountain" circuit on the Isle of Man, over which the Tourist Trophy (TT) races have been run since 1911, has 264 curves and corners and is the longest used for any motorcycle race.

MOTO-CROSS

World Championships

Most titles Joel Robert (Belgium) won six 250cc Motocross World Championships (1964, 1968–72). He won a record fifty 250cc Grand Prix between April 25, 1964 and June 18, 1972.

Multiple titles Eric Geboers (Belgium) has uniquely won all three categories of the Motocross World Championships, at 125cc in 1982 and 1983, 250cc in 1987 and 500cc in 1988 and 1991.

Youngest champion The youngest motocross world champion was Sébastien Tortelli (France), who won the 125cc title at the age of 17 yr. 343 days on July 28, 1996.

CYCLING

TOUR DE FRANCE

Most wins Four riders have each won the event five times: Jacques Anquetil (France), 1957, 1961–64; Eddy Merckx (Belgium), 1969–72, 1974; Bernard Hinault (France), 1978–79, 1981–82, 1985; Miguel Indurain (Spain), 1991–95.

Longest race   The 1926 Tour de France race was 3,569 miles long.

Closest race   The closest race ever was in 1989, when, after 2,030 miles over 23 days (July 1–23), Greg LeMond (U.S.), who completed the Tour in 87 hr. 38 min. 35 sec., beat Laurent Fignon (France) in Paris by only eight seconds.

Fastest average speed   The fastest average speed was 24.547 mph, by Miguel Indurain (Spain) in 1992.

Longest stage   The longest-ever stage was the 486 kilometers (302 miles) from Les Sables d'Olonne to Bayonne in 1919.

Most participants   The most participants was 210 starters in 1986.

Most finishers   The most riders to finish the Tour de France race is 151, in 1988.

Most races   Joop Zoetemilk (Netherlands) participated in a record 16 tours, 1970–86. Zoetemilk won the race in 1980 and finished second a record six times.

Most stage wins   Eddy Merckx (Belgium) won a record 35 individual stages in just seven races, 1969–75.

OLYMPIC GAMES

Most gold medals   Four men have won three gold medals: Paul Masson (France), 1,000 meter time-trial, 1,000 meter sprint, 10,000 meter track in 1896; Francesco Verri (Italy), 1,000 meter time-trial, 1,000 meter sprint, 5,000 meter track in 1906; Robert Charpentier (France), individual road race, team road race, 4,000 meter team pursuit in 1936; Daniel Morelon (France), 1,000 meter sprint in 1968 and 1972, 2,000 meter tandem in 1968.

Most medals   Daniel Morelon (France) won five Olympic medals: three gold (*see above*); one silver, 1,000 meter sprint, 1972; one bronze, 1,000 meter sprint, 1964.

WORLD CHAMPIONSHIPS

Most titles (one event)   The most wins in a single event is 10, by Koichi Nakano (Japan), professional sprint 1977–86. The most wins in a men's amateur event is seven, by two cyclists: Daniel Morelon (France), sprint, 1966–67, 1969–71, 1973, 1975; and Leon Meredith (Great Britain), 100 kilometer motor-paced, 1904–05, 1907–09, 1911 and 1913. The most women's titles is 11, by Jeannie Longo (France), individual pursuit, 1986 and 1988–89; road race, 1985–87,1989 and 1995; points race, 1989; and individual time trial, 1995–96.

RACE ACROSS AMERICA

Most wins (men)   Rob Kish has won three men's titles, in 1992 and 1994–95.

Most wins (women)   Seana Hogan has won four women's titles, in 1992–93 and 1994–95.

Fastest time (men)   Michael Secrest cycled from Huntington Beach, CA to New York, NY in 7 days 23 hr. 16 min., at an average speed of 15.24 mph, in 1990.

Fastest time (women)   Seana Hogan cycled from Irvine, CA to Savannah, GA in a record 9 days 4 hr. 2 min., at an average speed of 13.21 mph, in 1995.

Fastest average speed   The fastest average speed by a transcontinental cyclist is 15.40 mph, by Pete Penseyres who cycled from Huntington Beach, CA to Atlantic City, NJ in 8 days 9 hr. 47 min., in 1986.

Fastest time (tandem, men)   Lon Haldeman and Pete Penseyres cycled from Huntington Beach, CA to Atlantic City, NJ in 7 days 14 hr. 15 min., at an average speed of 15.97 mph, in 1987.

Fastest time (tandem, women)   Estelle Grey and Cheryl Marek cycled from Santa Monica, CA to New York, NY in 10 days 22 hr. 48 min., at an average speed of 11.32 mph, in 1984.

BIG PLAYS

Circumnavigation   Tal Burt (Israel) circumnavigated the world (13,523 road miles) from Place du Trocadero, Paris, France in 77 days 14 hr., from June 1 to August 17, 1992.

Cycling the Americas   Christopher "Spike" Ramsden and Wayne N. Ross left Prudhoe Bay, AK on bicycles on June 12, 1996. Ramsden cycled to Cape Horn, Argentina, a distance of 15,654 miles, arriving on March 3, 1997. (Ross was seriously injured in a road accident and could not complete the trip.)

Cross-Canada   The trans-Canada record is 13 days 9 hr. 6 min., by Bill Narasnek (Canada), cycling 3,751 miles from Vancouver to Halifax, Nova Scotia, July 5–18, 1991.

Greatest distance (one year)   Thomas Godwin (Great Britain), cycling every day during the 365 days of 1939, covered 75,065 miles, or an average of 205.65 miles per day. Continuing his effort, he went on to complete 100,000 miles in 500 days to May 14, 1940.

Greatest distance (one hour-paced)   The greatest distance covered in one hour is 122.28 km, by Leon Vanderstuyft (Belgium) on the Montlhéry Motor Circuit, France, on September 30, 1928, from a standing start paced by a motorcycle.

Longest race (one-day)   The longest single-day "massed start" road race is the Bordeaux–Paris, France event of 342–385 miles. The highest average speed was 29.32 mph, by Herman van Springel (Belgium) for 363.1 miles in 13 hr. 35 min. 18 sec., in 1981.

CYCLING (ONE YEAR)

The greatest mileage cycled in one calendar year is 75,065 miles. This feat was performed by Thomas Godwin (Great Britain), who cycled every day during the 365 days of 1939, averaging 205.65 miles per day.

For rules, see page 707.

Greatest mileage From 1922 to December 25, 1973, Tommy Chambers of Glasgow, Scotland rode a verified total of 799,405 miles.

Longest cycle tour (tandem) Ronald and Sandra Slaughter hold the U.S. record for tandem bicycling, having traveled 18,077.5 miles around the world from December 30, 1989 to July 28, 1991.

Cycle tour (most participants) It has been estimated that more than 45,000 people participated in the 46-mile Tour de I'lle de Montréal, Canada, on June 7, 1992.

High altitude cycling Canadians Bruce Bell, Philip Whelan and Suzanne MacFadyen cycled at an altitude of 22,834 feet on the peak of Mt. Aconcagua, Argentina in January 1991. This feat was matched by Mozart Hastenreiter Catão (Brazil) in March 1993 and by Tim Sumner (Great Britain) and Jonathan Greene (Great Britain) in January 1994.

Fastest speed The fastest speed achieved on a bicycle is 166.944 mph, by Fred Rompelberg (Netherlands) behind a windshield at Bonneville Salt Flats, UT on October 3, 1995.

Fastest speed (24 hours) The 24-hour record behind pace is 1,216.8 miles, by Michael Secrest at Phoenix International Raceway, AZ, April 26–27, 1990.

Richard Virenque (polka dots) won the "King of the Mountains" title in the Tour de France for a record-equaling fourth consecutive time in the 1997 race. The race winner was Jan Ullrich (behind Virenque), the first German rider to win the race.

CYCLING RECORDS

These records are those recognized by the Union Cycliste Internationale (UCI). From January 1, 1993, its severely reduced list no longer distinguished between those set by professionals and amateurs, indoor and outdoor, at altitude and at sea level.

MEN

Unpaced Standing Start

	min : sec	Name and Country	Place	Date
1 km	1:02.091	Maic Malchow (East Germany)	Colorado Springs,CO	Aug. 28, 1986
4 km	4:20.894	Graeme Obree (Great Britain)	Hamar, Norway	Aug. 19, 1993
4 km team	4:03.840	Australia	Hamar, Norway	Aug. 20, 1993

Unpaced Flying Start

	min : sec	Name and Country	Place	Date
200 meters	0:10.099	Vladimir Adamashvili (Russia)	Moscow, Russia	Aug. 6, 1990
500 meters	0:26.649	Aleksandr Kirichenko (Russia)	Moscow, Russia	Oct. 29, 1988

		Name and Country	Place	Date
Unpaced—One Hour	55.291 km	Tony Rominger (Switzerland)	Bordeaux, France	Nov. 6, 1994

WOMEN

Unpaced Standing Start

	min : sec	Name and Country	Place	Date
500 m	0:33.438	Galina Yenyukhina (Russia)	Moscow, Russia	Apr. 29, 1993
3 km	3:31.924	Antonella Bellutti (Italy)	Cali, Colombia	Apr. 6, 1996

Unpaced Flying Start

	min : sec	Name and Country	Place	Date
200 meters	0:10.831	Olga Slyusareva (Russia)	Moscow, Russia	Aug. 6, 1990
500 meters	0:29.655	Erika Salumäe (Russia)	Moscow, Russia	Aug. 6, 1987

		Name and Country	Place	Date
Unpaced—One Hour	47.112 km	Catherine Marsal (France)	Bordeaux, France	Apr. 29, 1995

Fastest speed (rollercycling)   James Baker (U.S.) achieved a record speed of 153.2 mph at El Con Mall, Tucson, AZ on January 28, 1989.

EXTREME SPORTS

AEROBATICS

World Championships

Most titles (team)   The USSR won the men's title six times, 1964, 1966, 1976, 1982, 1986, and 1990.

Most titles (individual)   Petr Jimus (Czechoslovakia) has won two men's world titles: 1984 and 1986. Betty Stewart (U.S.) has won two women's world titles, 1980 and 1982.

AIR RACING

National Championship Air Races (NCAR)

Staged annually in Reno, NV since 1964, the NCAR has been held at its present site, the Reno/Stead Airport, since 1986. Races are staged in four categories: Unlimited class, AT-6 class, Formula One class and Biplane class.

Unlimited Class

In this class the aircraft must use piston engines, be propeller driven and be capable of pulling six gs. The planes race over a pylon-marked 9.128 mile course.

Most titles   Darryl Greenmyer has won seven unlimited NCAR titles: 1965–69, 1971 and 1977.

Fastest average speed (race)   Lyle Shelton won the 1991 NCAR title recording the fastest average speed at 481.618 mph in his Rare Bear.

Fastest qualifying speed   The one-lap NCAR qualifying record is 482.892 mph, by Lyle Shelton in 1992.

AT-6 CLASS

Only World War II Advanced Trainers (AT), complying with the original stock configuration, are allowed to compete. Seats can be removed and the engines stripped and reassembled, but the cubic inch displacement of the 650-horsepower 1340-R Pratt & Whitney engine cannot exceed the original level.

Most titles   Eddie Van Fossen has won seven AT-6 NCAR titles: 1986–88, 1991–94.

Fastest average speed (race)   Eddie Van Fossen won the 1992 NCAR title recording the fastest average speed at 234.788 mph in Miss TNT.

Fastest qualifying speed   The one-lap NCAR qualifying record is 235.223 mph, by Eddie Van Fossen in 1992.

Big Plays

Inverted flight   The duration record is 4 hr. 38 min. 10 sec. by Joann Osterud (U.S.) from Vancouver to Vanderjoof, Canada on July 24, 1991.

The duration record for continuously flying upside down in an aircraft is 4 hr. 38 min. 10 sec.

BUNGEE JUMPING

Longest bungee cord   Gregory Riffi used an 820-foot-long bungee cord when he jumped from a helicopter above the Loire Valley, France in February 1992. The cord stretched 2,000 feet during the jump.

HANG GLIDING

Flexible Wing—Single Place Distance Records (Men)

Straight line   Larry Tudor (U.S.) piloted a Ram-Air 154 for a straight-line distance of 307.696 miles from Rock Springs, WY to Stoneham, CO on June 30, 1994.

Single turnpoint Larry Tudor (U.S.) piloted his Ram-Air 154 a single turnpoint (dogleg) record 307.773 miles from Rock Springs, WY to Stoneham, CO on June 30, 1994.

Triangular course James Lee Jr. (U.S.) piloted a Willis Wing HPAT 158 for a triangular course record 121.79 miles over Wild Horse Mesa, CO on July 4, 1991.

Out and return The out and return goal distance record is 192.818 miles, set by two pilots on the same day, July 26, 1988, over Lone Pine, CA: Larry Tudor, Wills Wing HPAT 158; and Geoffrey Loyns (Great Britain), Enterprise Wings.

Altitude gain Larry Tudor set a height gain record of 14,250.69 feet flying a G2-155 over Horseshoe Meadows, CA on August 4, 1985.

The official altitude record for hang gliding is 14,250.69 feet.

Flexible Wing—Single Place Distance Records (Women)

Straight line Kari Castle (U.S.) piloted a Wills Wing AT 145 a straight-line distance of 208.63 miles over Lone Pine, CA on July 22, 1991.

Single turnpoint Kari Castle piloted a Pacific Airwave Magic Kiss a single-turnpoint distance of 181.47 miles over Hobbs, NM on July 1, 1990.

Triangular course Judy Leden (Great Britain) flew a triangular course record 70.173 miles over Austria on June 22, 1991.

Out and return The out and return goal distance record is 81.99 miles, set by Tove Buas-Hansen (Norway), piloting an International Axis over Owens Valley, CA on July 6, 1989.

Altitude gain The record for height gain is 13,025 feet by Judy Leden (Great Britain), flying over Kuruman, South Africa on December 1, 1992.

Rigid Wing—Single Place Distance Records (Men)

Straight line   The straight-line distance record is 139.07 miles, set by William Reynolds (U.S), piloting a Wills Wing over Lone Pine, CA on June 27, 1988.

Out and return   The out and return goal distance is 47.46 miles, set by Randy Bergum (U.S.), piloting an Easy Riser over Big Pine, CA on July 12, 1988.

Altitude gain   Rainer Scholl (South Africa) set an altitude gain record of 12,532.80 feet on May 8, 1985.

Flexible Wing—Multiplace Distance Records (Men)

Straight line   The straight line distance record is 100.60 miles, set by Larry Tudor and Eri Fujita, flying a Comet II-185 on July 12, 1985.

Out and return   The out and return goal distance record is 81.99 miles, set by Kevin and Tom Klinefelter (U.S.) on July 6, 1989.

Altitude gain   Tom and Kevin Klinefelter set an altitude record of 10,997.30 feet on July 6, 1989 over Bishop Airport.

INLINE SKATING (ROLLERBLADING)

World Championships

Most wins   The United States has dominated the sport thus far. Derek Parra (U.S.) was the overall world track champion in 1993 and the overall individual road champion for 1994. No woman inline skater has won more than one overall title.

Speed records   In the 1994 Championships in Gujan Mestras, France, Derek Parra broke two records: the 1,500 meter, 2 min. 4.26 sec.; and the 42k marathon, 1 hr. 4 min. 27.986 sec.

The greatest distance traveled on inline skates in a day is 283.07 miles. Not all inline skaters confine themselves to the road.

INLINE SKATING RECORDS

Skater (Country)	Distance	Place	Date
One hour (track)			
Haico Bauma (Netherlands)	22.11 miles	Groningen, Netherlands	August 16, 1994
One hour (road)			
Eddy Matzger (U.S.)	21.64 miles	Long Beach, CA	February 2, 1991
Six hours (road)			
Jonathan Seutter (U.S.)	91.35 miles	Long Beach, CA	February 2, 1991
Twelve hours (road)			
Jonathan Seutter (U.S.)	177.63 miles	Long Beach, CA	February 2, 1991
Twenty-four hours (road)			
Kimberly Ames (U.S.)	283.07 miles	Portland, OR	October 2, 1994

Source: International Inline Skating Association

MOUNTAIN BIKE RACING

Olympic Games

Mountain Bike Racing made its first appearance as an official Olympic sport on June 30, 1996 at the Olympic Games in Atlanta, GA. The men's cross-country event was won by Bart Brentjens (Netherlands) in 2hr. 17 min. 38 sec. The women's cross-country event was won by Paola Pezza (Italy) in 1 hr. 50 min. 51 sec.

World Championships

The Mountain Bike Racing World Championships were first held in Durango, CO in 1990. This competition includes both cross-country and downhill racing and is held annually at different venues around the world.

Most gold medals (overall, men)   The record for the most gold medals is three, achieved by Hienrik Djernis (Denmark) in the cross-country event, 1992–94.

Most gold medals (overall, women)   The women's record for the most gold medals is three, set by Allison Sydor (Canada) in the cross-country event, 1994–96.

Most medals (overall, men)   Thomas Frischknecht won a record four medals (all silver) in the cross-country event, 1990–92 and 1996.

Most medals (overall, women)   The record for the most medals is four, achieved by three women: Allison Sydor (Canada) in cross-country, gold, 1994–96 and silver, 1992; Ruthie Matthes (U.S.) in cross-country, gold, 1991, silver, 1996, and bronze, 1990, 1992; and Giovanna Bonazzi (Italy) in downhill, gold, 1991, 1993, and bronze, 1994–95.

WORLD CUP

The Grundig/UCI World Cup was first staged at Bassano del Grappa, Italy in 1991. This competition is held annually at different venues around the world.

Most wins (overall, men)   Thomas Frischknecht (Switzerland) won a record four World Cup championships in the cross-country event, 1992, 1993, 1995–96.

Most wins (overall, women)   Juliana Furtado won a record four World Cup titles in the cross-country event, 1992–95.

PARACHUTING

The oldest person to parachute jump was Hildegarde Ferrera. She completed a tandem jump on her 99th birthday on February 17, 1996.

World Championships

Most wins (team)   The USSR won the men's team title in 1954, 1958, 1960, 1966, 1972, 1976 and 1980, and the women's team title in 1956, 1958, 1966, 1968, 1972 and 1976.

Most wins (individual)   Nikolay Ushamyev (USSR) has won the individual title twice, in 1974 and 1980.

Greatest accuracy   Dwight Reynolds scored a record 105 daytime dead centers, and Bill Wenger and Phil Munden tied with 43 nighttime dead centers, competing as members of the U.S. Army Golden Knights in Yuma, AZ, in March 1978.

With electronic measuring, the official *Fédération Aeronautique Internationale* (FAI) record is 50 dead centers, by Linger Abdurakhmanov (USSR) in Fergana in 1988, when the women's record was set at 41, by Natalya Filinkova (USSR).

The oldest (former) President of the United States to complete a parachute jump was George Bush. He was 72 years old when he completed his first parachute jump on March 25, 1997.

The Men's Night Accuracy Landing record on an electronic score pad is 31 consecutive dead centers, by Vladimir Buchenev (USSR) on October 30, 1986. The women's record is 21, by Inessa Stepanova (USSR) in Fergana, October 18, 1988.

PARAGLIDING

Greatest distance (men)   The greatest distance flown is 176.4 miles by Alex François Louw (South Africa) from Kuruman, South Africa on December 31, 1992.

Greatest distance (women)   The women's record is 113.2 miles, by Kat Thurston (Great Britain) from Cabo Paquica, Chile on November 19, 1994.

Greatest height gain (men)   The men's height gain record is 14,849 feet by Robby Whittal (Great Britain), in Brandvlei, South Africa on January 6, 1993.

Greatest height gain (women)   The women's record is 14,190 feet by Kat Thurston (Great Britain) in Kuruman, South Africa on January 1, 1996. All these records were tow launched.

Parachuting Records

Longest-Duration Fall • Lt. Col. Wm H. Rankin (USMC) 40 min. due to thermals, North Carolina, Jul. 26, 1956.

Longest-Delayed Drop • Capt. Joseph W. Kittinger, 84,700 ft. (16.04 miles), from balloon at 102,800 ft., Tularosa, NM, Aug. 16, 1960.

Women's Record • Elvira Fomit-cheva (USSR), 48,556 ft. over Odessa, USSR (now Ukraine), Oct. 26, 1977.

Highest Base Jump • Nicholas Feteris and Dr. Glenn Singleman from the "Great Trango Tower" at 19,300 ft. in Karakoram, Pakistan, Aug. 26, 1992.
Jumps from buildings and claims for lowest base jumps will not be accepted.

Lowest Mid-Air Rescue • Eddie Turner saved Frank Farnan (unconscious), who had been injured in a collision after jumping out of an aircraft at 13,000 ft. He pulled his ripcord at 1,800 ft.—less than 10 seconds from impact—over Clewiston, FL on Oct. 16, 1988.

Highest Escape • Flt. Lt. J. de Salis (RAF) and Fg. Off. P. Lowe (RAF), 56,000 ft., Monyash, Derby, England, Apr. 9, 1958.

Lowest Escape • S/Ldr. Terence Spencer (DFC, RAF), 30–40 ft., Wismar Bay, Baltic, Apr. 19, 1945.

Highest Landing • Ten USSR parachutists (of whom four were killed), 23,405 ft., Lenina Peak, USSR (now Tajikistan/Kyrgyzstan border), May 1969.

Cross-Channel (lateral fall) • Sgt. Bob Walters with three soldiers and two British Royal Marines, 22 miles from 25,000 ft., Dover, Great Britain to Sangatte, France, Aug. 31, 1980.

Total Sport Parachuting Descents • Don Kellner (U.S.), 25,500, various locations, up to Mar. 17, 1997.

Women's Record • Cheryl Stearns (U.S.), 10,100, various locations, up to Aug. 2, 1995.

24-Hour Total • Jay Stokes (U.S.), 331 (in accordance with United States Parachute Association rules), Raeford, NC, May 30–31, 1995.

Women's Record • Cheryl Stearns (U.S.), 352 at Lodi, CA, Nov. 8–9, 1995.

Most Traveled • Kevin Seaman from a Cessna Skylane (pilot Charles E. Merritt), 12,186 miles, jumps in all 50 states, Jul. 26–Oct. 15, 1972.

Heaviest Load • Space shuttle *Columbia*, booster rocket retrieval, 80-ton capacity, triple array, each 120 ft. in diameter, Atlantic, off Cape Canaveral, FL, Apr. 12, 1981.

Highest Canopy Formation • 37, a team of French parachutists at Brienne le Chateau, Troyes, France, held for 13 sec. on Aug. 16, 1992.

Largest Free-fall Formation • 216, from 23 countries, held for 8.21 seconds from 21,000 ft. over Bratislava, Slovakia, Aug. 19, 1994 (unofficial). 200, from 10 countries, held for 6.47 sec. from 16,500 ft., Myrtle

Beach, SC, Oct. 23, 1992 (record recognized by FAI).

Women's Record • 100, from 20 countries, held for 5.97 sec., from 17,000 ft., Aéreodrome du Cannet des Maures, France, Aug. 14, 1992.

Oldest • Edwin C. Townsend (d. Nov. 7, 1987), 89 years, Vermillion Bay, LA, Feb. 5, 1986.

Women's Record • Sylvia Brett (Great Britain), 80 yr. 166 days, Cranfield, England, Aug. 23, 1986.

Oldest Tandem • Hildegarde Ferrera (U.S.), 99 years, Mokuleia, HI, Feb. 17, 1996.

Men's Record • Edward Royds-Jones, 95 yr. 170 days, Dunkeswell, England, Jul. 2, 1994.

Survival from Longest Fall without Parachute • Vesna Vulovic (Yugoslavia), flight attendant on DC–9 that blew up at 33,330 ft. over Srbská Kamenice, Czechoslovakia (now Czech Republic), Jan. 26, 1972.

Most dead centers   Nigel Horder scored four successive dead centers at the 1983 Dutch Open, Flevhof, Netherlands, flying a Moyes Delta Glider.

ROLLER HOCKEY

Most titles   Portugal has won most titles, with 14: 1947–50, 1952, 1956, 1958, 1960, 1962, 1968, 1974, 1982, 1991, and 1993.

SKATEBOARDING

Big Plays

Farthest distance   Eleftherios Argiropoulos covered 271.3 miles in 36 hr. 33 min. 17 sec. in Ekali, Greece on November 4–5, 1993.

Fastest speed (prone)   The fastest speed recorded on a skateboard is 78.37 mph by Roger Hickey (US), on a course near Los Angeles, CA on March 15, 1990.

Fastest speed (standing)   The stand-up record is 55.43 mph, achieved by Roger Hickey, in San Demas, CA on July 3, 1990.

Highest jump   The high jump record is 5 ft. $5^3/_4$ in. by Trevor Baxter (England), in Grenoble, France on September 14, 1982.

Longest jump   At the World Professional Championships in Long Beach, CA on September 25, 1977, Tony Alva jumped over 17 barrels for a distance of 17 feet.

SNOWBOARDING

World Championships

There have been two FIS (International Ski Federation) Snowboarding World Championships in 1996 and 1997.

Most wins (overall) Karine Ruby (France) has won a record two World Championship titles, giant slalom in 1996 and board cross in 1997. No man has won more than one title.

Grundig FIS World Cup

Grundig FIS World Cup competitions were first staged during the 1995/1996 season. They are held annually at different venues around the world.

Most wins (overall, men) Mike Jacoby (U.S.) holds the record for the most overall wins at the 1996 Grundig Snowboard FIS World Cup in the slalom, parallel slalom, and giant slalom events with total score of 1243.22.

At the 1998 Winter Games in Nagano, Japan, snowboarding will be included as an official Olympic sport for the first time.

Most wins (overall, women)   Karine Ruby (France) holds the record for the most overall wins at the 1996 Grundig Snowboard FIS World Cup in the slalom, parallel slalom, and giant slalom events with a score totalling 1760.60.

SOARING

World Championships

Most individual titles   The most individual titles won is four, by Ingo Renner (Australia) in 1976 (Standard class), 1983, 1985 and 1987 (Open).

Longest straight distance (single-seater)   Hans-Werner Grosse (Germany) soared a record 907.7 miles from Lubeck, Germany to Biarritz, France, April 25, 1972.

Longest declared goal distance (single-seater)   The record for the longest declared goal distance in a single-seater is 779.4 miles, by three pilots: Bruce Drake, David Speight and Dick Georgeson (all New Zealand), who each flew from Te Anau to Te Araroa, New Zealand, January 14, 1978.

Longest goal and return (single-seater)   Tom Knauff (U.S.) soared a record 1,023.2 miles from Williamsport, PA to Knoxville, TN, April 25, 1983.

Absolute altitude   The highest absolute altitude achieved 49,009 feet, achieved by Robert R. Harris (U.S.), over California, February 17, 1986. The women's record is 41,449 feet, by Sabrina Jackintell (U.S.) on February 14, 1979.

Height gain   The greatest height gain is 42,303 feet, by Paul Bikle (U.S.), Mojave, CA, February 25, 1961. The women's record is 33,506 feet, by Yvonne Loader (New Zealand) in Omarama, New Zealand on January 12, 1988.

Fastest speed, triangular course (100 km)   The record for the fastest speed in a triangular course of 100 km is 121.35 mph, set by Ingo Renner (Australia), December 14, 1982.

Fastest speed, triangular course (300 km)   The fastest speed in a distance of 300 km is 105.32 mph, by Jean-Paul Castel (France), November 15, 1986.

Fastest speed, triangular course (500 km)   The record for a distance of 500 km is 105.67 mph, achieved by Beat Bunzli (Switzerland), January 9, 1988.

Fastest speed, triangular course (750 km)   The record for 750 km is 98.43 mph, Hans-Werner Grosse (Germany), January 8, 1985.

Fastest speed, triangular course (1,000 km)   The record for the fastest speed in 1,000 km is 105.4 mph, Helmut H. Fischer (Germany), January 5, 1995.

Fastest speed, triangular course (1,250 km)   The record for 1,250 km is 82.79 mph, Hans-Werner Grosse (Germany), January 9, 1980.

ULTRALIGHTING

Landplanes, Solo

Distance in a straight line without landing The record for the farthest distance in a straight line without landing is 850.68 miles, set by Bernard d'Otreppe (Belgium), Frejus la Palud, France to Teesside, England, September 6, 1988.

Distance in a closed circuit without landing The record for the farthest distance in a closed circuit is 665.58 miles, achieved by Michel Serane (France), in Besancon-Thise, France, August 5, 1991.

Highest altitude The highest altitude achieved was 31,889 feet, by Serge Zin (France), in Saint Auban, France, September 18, 1994.

Speed over a 50 km closed circuit Serge Ferrari (France) travelled at a record 97.82 mph over a 50 km closed circuit in Belleville sur Saone, France, June 30, 1995.

Landplanes, Multiplace

Distance in a closed circuit without landing The farthest distance is 312.79 miles, Robert Mair and Dietmar Spekking (Germany), in Griesau, Germany, September 29, 1996.

Highest altitude Walter Mauri and Heike Goettlicher (Italy) reached a record of 23,434 feet in Udine, Italy, April 16, 1993.

Speed over a 500 km closed circuit The record for the fastest speed over a 500 km closed circuit is 51.00 mph, set by Robert Mair and Dietmar Spekking (Germany), in Griesau, Germany, September 29, 1996.

X GAMES

The X Games were first held in 1995. Extreme Sports featured in the Olympic-style tournament staged by the ESPN television network includes bicycle stunt riding, skysurfing and street luge.

Most gold medals (men) The record for the most X Games gold medals is four, achieved by two athletes: Tony Hawk of Carlsbad, CA won the gold in skateboarding vert, 1995 and 1997, in vert doubles in 1997, and the silver in skateboarding vert, 1997; and Michael Sherlock of Pacific Beach, CA won the gold in street luge (mass discipline), 1996, the gold in both dual and mass street luge, 1997, and the silver in super mass street luge, 1997.

Most gold medals (women) The most gold medals won by a female athlete is two, set by three women: Gypsy Tidwell of Waco, TX won the gold in women's downhill inline skating, 1996 and 1997; Katie Brown of Lafayette, GA won the gold in women's sportclimbing, 1996 and 1997; and Fabiola da Silva of Sao Paulo, Brazil won the gold in women's aggressive inline vert, 1996 and 1997.

Most medals (men) Dennis Derammelaere of Novato, CA, won six medals in the dual and mass street luge competition: two gold and two silver in 1997 and two bronze in 1996.

Most medals (women) The record for the most medals is two, shared by three athletes: Gypsy Tidwell of Waco, TX, won the gold in women's downhill inline skating, 1996 and 1997; Katie Brown of Lafayette, GA won the gold in women's sportclimbing, 1996 and 1997; and Fabiola da Silva of Sao Paulo, Brazil won the gold in women's aggressive inline vert, 1996 and 1997.

Youngest medalist (men) Parks Bonifay of Lake Alfred, FL, won the gold medal at the 1996 X Games in the men's wakeboarding competition at age 15.

Youngest medalist (women) Ayumi Kawasaki of Osaka, Japan, won the bronze medal at the 1997 X Games in the aggressive inline vert competition at age 12.

Big Plays

Highest scoring run (skateboarding vert) Tony Hawk of Carlsbad, CA, posted a record 97.50 out of a possible 100 points at the 1997 X Games during a run in which he pulled four consecutive five forties (one and a half rotations in midair) while utilizing a different grab on each one.

Most jumps (skysurfing) Eric Fradet of Le Tignet, France, has logged the most jumps in the sport of skysurfing; he has jumped more than 14,700 times.

Tallest competitor Ryan Brennan of Costa Mesa, CA, competed in the bicycle stunt competition at the 1997 X Games at 6 ft. 6 in.

Shortest competitor Shane Bonifay of Lake Alfred, FL, was the shortest competitor at the 1997 X Games at 4 ft. 10 in. Bonifay competed in the wakeboarding competition.

SWIMMING

OLYMPIC GAMES

Most gold medals (men) The most Olympic gold medals won is nine, by Mark Spitz (U.S.): 100-meter and 200-meter freestyle, 1972; 100-meter and 200-meter butterfly, 1972; 4 × 100-meter freestyle, 1968 and 1972; 4 × 200-meter freestyle, 1968 and 1972; 4 × 100-meter medley, 1972.

Most gold medals (women) The most gold medals won by a woman is six, by Kristin Otto (East Germany) at Seoul, South Korea in 1988: 100-meter freestyle, backstroke and butterfly, 50-meter freestyle, 4 × 100-meter freestyle and 4 × 100-meter medley.

Most medals (men) The most medals won by a swimmer is 11, by two competitors: Mark Spitz (U.S.): nine gold (*see above*), one silver and one bronze, 1968–72; and Matt Biondi (U.S.), eight gold, two silver and one bronze, 1984–92.

Most medals (women) The most medals won by a woman is eight, by three swimmers: Dawn Fraser (Australia), four gold, four silver, 1956–64; Kornelia Ender (East Germany), four gold, four silver, 1972–76; Shirley Babashoff (U.S.), two gold, six silver, 1972–76.

Most medals (one Games—men) The most medals won at one Games is seven, by two swimmers: Mark Spitz (U.S.), seven golds in 1972; and Matt Biondi (U.S.), five gold, one silver and one bronze in 1988.

Penny Heyns set the world record for the 100-meter breaststroke at the '96 Olympic Games.

Most medals (one Games—women)   Kristin Otto (East Germany) won six gold medals at the 1988 Games, the most for a female swimmer.

WORLD CHAMPIONSHIPS

Most gold medals (women)   Kornelia Ender (East Germany) won eight gold medals, 1973–75.

Most gold medals (men)   Jim Montgomery (U.S.) won six gold medals, 1973–75, the most by a male swimmer.

Most medals (men)   Michael Gross (West Germany) has won 13 medals: five gold, five silver and three bronze, 1982–90.

Most medals (women)   The most medals won by a female swimmer is 10, by Kornelia Ender, who won eight gold and two silver, 1973–75.

Most medals (one championship—men)   Matt Biondi (U.S.) won seven medals—three gold, one silver and three bronze—in 1986 in Madrid, Spain.

Most medals (one championship—women)   Two swimmers share the women's record of six medals: Shirley Babashoff (U.S.), two gold, three silver, one bronze, 1975; and Tracy Caulkins (U.S.), five gold, one silver in 1978.

BIG PLAYS

Fastest swimmer (men)   In a 25-yard pool, Tom Jager (U.S.) achieved an average speed of 5.37 mph for 50 yards in 19.05 seconds in Nashville, TN on March 23, 1990.

Fastest swimmer (women)   The fastest speed ever achieved by a female swimmer is 4.48 mph, by Yang Wenyi (China), during her world record swim in the 50-meter sprint.

Greatest distance   The greatest recorded distance ever swum is 1,826 miles down the Mississippi River between Ford Dam near Minneapolis, MN and Carrollton Ave., New Orleans, LA, by Fred P. Newton of Clinton, OK from July 6 to December 29, 1930. He was in the water for 742 hours.

Greatest distance (24 hours–men)   Anders Forvass (Sweden) swam 63.3 miles at the 25-meter Linköping public swimming pool, Sweden, October 28–29, 1989.

Greatest distance (24 hours—women)   The women's record is 58.17 miles, by Susie Maroney (Australia) at Carss Park, Sydney, Australia, April 21–22, 1995.

Greatest distance (24 hours—20-person relay)   The New Zealand national relay team of 20 swimmers swam a record 113.59 miles in Lower Hutt, New Zealand in 24 hours, passing 100 miles in 20 hr. 47 min. 13 sec., December 9–10, 1983.

Greatest distance (24 hours—5-person relay [men])　The 24-hour club record by a team of five is 100.99 miles, by the Portsmouth Northsea SC at the Victoria Swimming Centre, Portsmouth, England, March 4–5, 1993.

Greatest distance (24 hours—5-person relay [women])　The 24-hour women's team record is 88.93 miles by the City of Newcastle ASC, December 16–17, 1986.

Most participants (relay)　The most participants in a one-day swim relay is 2,375, each swimming a length, at Liverpool High School, Liverpool, NY, May 20–21, 1994.

Largest sponsored swim　The greatest amount of money raised for charity at an event staged at several pools was £548,006.14, by "Penguin Swimathon '88." A total of 5,482 swimmers participated at 43 pools throughout London, England, on February 26–28, 1988.

Largest sponsored swim (one pool)　The greatest amount of money collected in a charity swim was £122,983.19 (*c.* $350,000) in "Splash '92," organized by the Royal Bank of Scotland Swimming Club and held at the Royal Commonwealth Pool, Edinburgh, Scotland on January 25–26, 1992 with 3,218 participants.

Greatest underwater swim (24 hours)　Paul Cryne (Great Britain) and Samir Sawan al Awami (Qatar) swam 49.04 miles in 24 hours from Doha, Qatar to Umm Said and back, February 21–22, 1985, using sub-aqua equipment. They were underwater 95.5 percent of the time.

Greatest underwater swim (24 hours–6-person relay)　A relay team of six swam 94.44 miles in a swimming pool in Olomouc, Czechoslovakia, October 17–18, 1987.

Largest swimming pool　The world's largest swimming pool is the seawater Orthlieb Pool, Casablanca, Morocco. It is 480 meters (1,574 feet) long and 75 meters (246 feet) wide, and has an area of 3.6 ha (8⁹/₁₀ acres).

LONG DISTANCE SWIMMING

English Channel

Fastest time (men)　Chad Hundeby (Irvine, CA) swam the English Channel in a record time of 7 hr. 17 min. on September 27, 1994.

Fastest time (women)　The official women's record is 7 hr. 40 min. by Penny Dean (U.S.).

Fastest time (France–England)　The fastest France–England time is 8 hr. 5 min., by Richard Davey (Great Britain) in 1988.

Fastest time (relay)　The fastest crossing by a relay team is 6 hr. 52 min. (England to France), by the U.S. National Swim Team on August 1, 1990. They went on to complete the fastest two-way relay in 14 hr. 18 min.

SWIMMING RECORDS (set in 50-meter pools)

Event	Time	Name and Country	Place	Date
MEN				
Freestyle				
50 meters	0:21.81	Tom Jager (U.S.)	Nashville, TN	Mar. 24, 1990
100 meters	0:48.21	Aleksandr Popov (Russia)	Monte Carlo, Monaco	Jun. 18, 1994
200 meters	1:46.69	Giorgis Lamberti (Italy)	Bonn, Germany	Aug. 15, 1989
400 meters	3:43.80	Kieren Perkins (Australia)	Rome, Italy	Sep. 9, 1994
800 meters	7:46.00	Kieren Perkins (Australia)	Victoria, Canada	Aug. 24, 1994
1,500 meters	14:41.66	Kieren Perkins (Australia)	Victoria, Canada	Aug. 24, 1994
4 × 100 meter relay	3:15.11	United States (David Fox, Joe Hudpohi, Jon Olsen, Gary Hall, Jr.)	Atlanta, GA	Aug. 12, 1995
4 × 200 meter relay	7:11.95	EUN (Dmitry Lepikov, Vladimir Pychenko, Veniamin Taianovich, Yevgeniy Sadoviy)	Barcelona, Spain	Jul. 27, 1992
Breaststroke				
100 meters	1:00.60	Frederik Deburghgraeve (Belgium)	Atlanta, GA	Jul. 20, 1996
200 meters	2:10.16	Michael Barrowman (U.S.)	Barcelona, Spain	Jul. 29, 1992
Butterfly				
100 meters	0:52.27	Denis Pankratov (Russia)	Atlanta, GA	Jul. 24, 1996
200 meters	1:55.22	Denis Pankratov (Russia)	Canet-en-Roussillon, France	Jun. 14, 1995
Backstroke				
100 meters	0:53.86	Jeff Rouse (U.S.—relay leg)	Barcelona, Spain	Jul. 31, 1992
200 meters	1:56.57	Martin Lopez-Zubero (Spain)	Tuscaloosa, AL	Nov. 23, 1991
Medley				
200 meters	1:58.16	Jani Nikanor Sievenen (Finland)	Rome, Italy	Sep. 11, 1994
400 meters	4:12.30	Tom Dolan (U.S.)	Rome, Italy	Sep. 6, 1994
4 × 100 meter relay	3:34.84	United States (Jeff Rouse, Jeremy Linn, Mark Henderson, Gary Hall, Jr.)	Atlanta, GA	Jul. 26, 1996

WOMEN

Freestyle

50 meters	0:24.51	Le Jingyi (China)	Rome, Italy	Sep. 11, 1994
100 meters	0:54.01	Le Jingyi (China)	Rome, Italy	Sep. 5, 1994
200 meters	1:56.78	Franziska van Almsick (Germany)	Rome, Italy	Sep. 6, 1994
400 meters	4:03.85	Janet B. Evans (U.S.)	Seoul, South Korea	Sep. 22, 1988
800 meters	8:16.22	Janet B. Evans (U.S.)	Tokyo, Japan	Aug. 20, 1989
1,500 meters	15:52.10	Janet B. Evans (U.S.)	Orlando, FL	Mar. 26, 1988
4 × 100 meter relay	3:37.91	China (Le Jingyi, Shan Ying, Le Ying, Lu Bin)	Rome, Italy	Sep. 10, 1994
4 × 200 meter relay	7:55.47	East Germany (Manuela Stellmach, Astrid Strauss, Anke Möhring, Heike Friedrich)	Strasbourg, France	Aug. 18, 1987

Breaststroke

100 meters	1:07.02	Penny Heyns (South Africa)	Atlanta, GA	Jul. 21, 1996
200 meters	2:24.76	Rebecca Brown (Australia)	Brisbane, Australia	Mar. 16, 1994

Butterfly

100 meters	0:57.93	Mary T. Meagher (U.S.)	Milwaukee, WI	Aug. 16, 1981
200 meters	2:05.96	Mary T. Meagher (U.S.)	Milwaukee, WI	Aug. 13, 1981

Backstroke

100 meters	1:00.16	He Cihong (China)	Rome, Italy	Sep. 10, 1994
200 meters	2:06.62	Krizstina Egerszegi (Hungary)	Athens, Greece	Aug. 26, 1991

Medley

200 meters	2:11.65	Li Lin (China)	Barcelona, Spain	Jul. 30, 1992
400 meters	4:36.10	Petra Schneider (East Germany)	Guayaquil, Ecuador	Aug. 1, 1982
4 × 100 meter relay	4:01.67	China (He Cihong, Dai Guohong, Liu Limin, Le Jingyi)	Rome, Italy	Sep. 11, 1994

SHORT-COURSE SWIMMING RECORDS

(set in 25-meter pools)

Event	Time	Name & Country	Place	Date
MEN				
Freestyle				
50 meters	0:21.50	Aleksandr Popov (Russia)	Desenzano, Italy	Mar. 13, 1994
100 meters*	0:46.74	Aleksandr Popov (Russia)	Gelsenkirchen, Germany	Mar. 19, 1994
200 meters	1:43.64	Giorgio Lamberti (Italy)	Bonn, Germany	Feb. 11, 1990
400 meters	3:40.46	Danyon Loader (New Zealand)	Sheffield, England	Feb. 11, 1995
800 meters	7:34.90	Kieren Perkins (Australia)	Sydney, Australia	Jul. 25, 1993
1,500 meters	14:26.52	Kieren Perkins (Australia)	Auckland, New Zealand	Jul. 15, 1993
4 × 50 meters	1:27.62	Sweden	Stavanger, Norway	Dec. 2, 1994
4 × 100 meters	3:12.11	Brazil	Palma de Mallorca, Spain	Dec. 5, 1993
4 × 200 meters	7:02.74	Australia	Gothenburg, Sweden	Apr. 18, 1997
Backstroke				
50 meters	0:24.25	Chris Renaud (Canada)	St. Catherine's, Canada	Mar. 1, 1997
100 meters	0:51.43	Jeff Rouse (U.S.)	Sheffield, England	Apr. 11, 1993
200 meters	1:52.51	Martin Lopez-Zubero (Spain)	Gainesville, FL	Apr. 10, 1991
Breaststroke				
50 meters	0:26.97	Mark Warnecke (Germany)	Paris, France	Feb. 8, 1997
100 meters	0:59.02	Frédéric Deburghgraeve (Belgium)	Bastogne, Belgium	Feb. 17, 1996
200 meters	2:07.66	Ryan Mitchell (Australia)	Melbourne, Australia	Dec. 21, 1996
Butterfly				
50 meters	0:23.35	Denis Pankratov (Russia)	Paris, France	Feb. 8, 1997
100 meters	0:51.78	Denis Pankratov (Russia)	Paris, France	Feb. 9, 1997
200 meters	1:52.34	Denis Pankratov (Russia)	Paris, France	Feb. 3, 1996
Medley				
100 meters	0:53.10	Jani Sievinen (Finland)	Malmö, Sweden	Jan. 30, 1996
200 meters	1:54.65	Jani Sievinen (Finland)	Kuopio, Finland	Jan. 19, 1996
400 meters	4:05.41	Marcel Wouda (Netherlands)	Paris, France	Feb. 8, 1997
4 × 50 meters	1:36.69	Auburn University	Auburn, AL	Apr. 16, 1996
4 × 100 meters	3:30.66	Australia		

614 ● Sports

WOMEN

Freestyle

50 meters	0:24.23	Le Jingyi (China)	Palma de Mallorca, Spain	Dec. 3, 1993
100 meters	0:53.01	Le Jingyi (China)	Palma de Mallorca, Spain	Dec. 2, 1993
200 meters	1:54.17	Claudia Poll (Costa Rica)	Gothenburg, Sweden	Apr. 18, 1997
400 meters	4:00.03	Claudia Poll (Costa Rica)	Gothenburg, Sweden	Apr. 19, 1997
800 meters	8:15.34	Astrid Strauss (East Germany)	Bonn, Germany	Feb. 6, 1987
1,500 meters	15:43.31	Petra Schneider (East Germany)	Gainesville, FL	Jan. 10, 1982
4 × 50 meters	1:40.63	Germany	Espoo, Finland	Nov. 22, 1992
4 × 100 meters	3:34.55	China	Gothenburg, Sweden	Apr. 19, 1997
4 × 200 meters	7:51.92	China	Gothenburg, Sweden	Apr. 17, 1997

Backstroke

50 meters	0:27.64	Bai Xiuyu (China)	Desenzano, Italy	Mar. 12, 1994
100 meters	0:58.50	Angel Martino (U.S.)	Palma de Mallorca, Spain	Dec. 3, 1993
200 meters	2:06.09	He Chong (China)	Palma de Mallorca, Spain	Dec. 5, 1993

Breaststroke

50 meters	0:30.77	Xue Han (China)	Gelsenkirchen, Germany	Feb. 2, 1997
100 meters	1:05.70	Samantha Riley (Australia)	Rio de Janeiro, Brazil	Dec. 1, 1995
200 meters	2:20.85	Samantha Riley (Australia)	Rio de Janeiro, Brazil	Dec. 1, 1995

Butterfly

50 meters	0:26.55	Misty Hyman (U.S.)	Gothenburg, Sweden	Apr. 19, 1997
100 meters**	0:57.79	Jenny Thompson (U.S.)	Gothenburg, Sweden	Apr. 19, 1997
200 meters	2:05.65	Mary T. Meagher (U.S.)	Gainesville, FL	Jan. 2, 1981

Medley

100 meters	1:01.03	Louise Karlsson (Sweden)	Espoo, Finland	Nov. 22, 1992
200 meters	2:07.79	Allison Wagner (U.S.)	Palma de Mallorca, Spain	Dec. 5, 1993
400 meters	4:29.00	Dai Guohong (China)	Palma de Mallorca, Spain	Dec. 2, 1993
4 × 50 meters	1:52.44	Germany	Espoo, Finland	Nov. 21, 1992
4 × 100 meters	3:57.73	China	Palma de Mallorca, Spain	Dec. 5, 1993

*Hand timed for first leg.
**Slower than long-course bests.

Fastest double crossing (men)   Philip Rush (New Zealand) completed a double crossing in 16 hr. 10 min. on August 17, 1987.

Fastest double crossing (women)   The women's record is 17 hr. 14 min., by Susie Maroney (Australia) on July 23, 1991.

Fastest triple crossing   Philip Rush (New Zealand) completed a triple crossing in 28 hr. 21 min., August 17–18, 1987.

Most Channel crossings (women)   The greatest number of Channel conquests is 32, by Alison Streeter (Great Britain), from 1982 to September 1995 (including a record seven in one year in 1992).

Most Channel crossings (men)   The most Channel crossings by a man is 31, by Michael Read (Great Britain), between August 24, 1969 and August 19, 1984.

Oldest Channel swimmer (men)   Bertram Clifford Batt (Australia) was 67 yr. 241 days old when he swam from Cap Gris-Nez, France to Dover, England in 18 hr. 37 min. on August 19–20, 1987.

Oldest Channel swimmer (women)   Susan Fraenkel (South Africa) was 46 yr. 93 days old when she swam the Channel in 12 hr. 5 min. on July 24, 1994.

Manhattan Island

Fastest time (men)   The fastest swim around Manhattan Island in New York City was in 5 hr. 53 min. 57 sec., by Kris Rutford (U.S.) on August 29, 1992.
   Kris Rutford also holds the record for swimming clockwise around Manhattan, at 17 hr. 48 min. 30 sec.

Fastest time (women)   Shelley Taylor-Smith (Australia) swam around the island of Manhattan in a record 5 hr. 45 min. 25 sec. on July14, 1995.

Oldest swimmer (men)   Dextor Woodford swam around the island of Manhattan at 77 years old in 1991.

Oldest swimmer (women)   In 1995, Vicki Altomonte swam around the island of Manhattan in 9 hr. 19 min. 22 sec. at age 45.

Most circumnavigations (men)   Christopher Green (Great Britain) swam around the island of Manhattan a record total of 14 times.

Most circumnavigations (women)   Shelley Taylor-Smith (Australia) swam around the island of Manhattan a record seven times.

Golden Gate Strait

Most crossings   Joseph Bruno has crossed the Golden Gate Strait 61 times. He first performed the feat on September 17, 1933.

Oldest swimmer   Joseph Bruno crossed the Golden Gate Strait on September 11, 1993, two months shy of his 81st birthday.

Youngest swimmer   Emma Macchiarini (b. July 28, 1980) swam across the Golden Gate Strait, from Fort Point to Lime Point–1⅛ miles, on July 12, 1989. At age 8 yr. 349 days, Macchiarini was the youngest person to swim the strait. It took her 1 hr. 51 min. 8 sec. to complete the swim. Throughout the swim, she was accompanied by her father, swimming in the water, and a boat was near at hand for safety reasons.

Cuba–Florida

Fastest crossing   On May 12, 1997, Susie Maroney (Australia) swam from Havana, Cuba to Fort Zachary Taylor State Park in the Florida Keys in 24 hr. 30 min. Maroney swam the 118 miles inside a 28- by 8-foot cage that protected her from sharks.

SYNCHRONIZED SWIMMING

Olympic Games

Most gold medals   Two swimmers have won two gold medals: Tracie Ruiz-Conforto (U.S.), solo and duet, 1984; and Carolyn Waldo (Canada), solo and duet, 1988.

Most medals   Two swimmers have won three medals: Tracie Ruiz-Conforto (U.S.), two gold and one silver, 1984–88; and Carolyn Waldo (Canada), two gold and one silver, 1984–88.

World Championships

Most titles   The solo title has been won by a different swimmer on each occasion.

Most titles (team)   The United States has won five team titles, 1973, 1975, 1978, 1991 and 1994.

DIVING

Olympic Games

Most gold medals   Two divers have won four gold medals: Pat McCormick (U.S.), who won both the women's springboard and the platform events in 1952 and 1956; and Greg Louganis (U.S.), who performed the platform/springboard double in 1984 and 1988.

Most medals   Two divers have won five medals: Klaus Dibiasi (Italy), three golds, platform in 1968, 1972 and 1976, and two silver, platform in 1964 and springboard in 1968; and Greg Louganis, four golds (*see above*) and one silver, platform in 1976.

At 33 years old, Mary Ellen Clark became the oldest diver to win an Olympic medal when she won a bronze medal in the platform event in the '96 Atlanta Games.

World Championships

Most titles   Greg Louganis (U.S.) won a record five world titles—platform in 1978 and the platform/springboard double in 1982 and 1986. Philip Boggs (U.S.) is the only diver to win three gold medals at one event, springboard, in 1973, 1975 and 1978.

Scoring

Highest score (men–highboards)   The record for the highboard is 723.45 points, awarded to Dmitry Sautin at the 1996 Southern Cross Invitational.

Highest score (men–Olympics)   Greg Louganis achieved a record 710.91 points for the highboard event at the 1984 Olympic Games in Los Angeles, CA.

Highest score (men–springboard)   In non-Olympic competitions, Mark Lenzi set the record for the springboard, with 764.52 points at the 1996 U.S. Olympic team trials in Atlanta, GA.

Highest score (men–Olympics)   Greg Louganis achieved record scores at the 1984 Olympic Games in Los Angeles, CA, with 754.41 points for the 11-dive springboard event.

Highest score (women–springboard)   In 1988, Gao Min (China) won 614.07 points in a 10-dive springboard event at Dive Canada, in Québec, Canada.

Highest score (women–highboard)   Since 1995, the women's highboard event has required nine dives instead of eight. Chi Bin (China) holds the women's highboard record for her nine dives at the 1995 China Open, which earned 549.81 points.

Big Plays

Highest dives (cliffs)   The highest regularly performed head-first dives are those of professional divers from La Quebrada in Acapulco, Mexico, a height of 87½ feet. The base rocks necessitate a leap of 27 feet out. The water is 12 feet deep.

Highest dives (diving board)   The highest dive from a diving board is 176 ft. 10 in., by Olivier Favre (Switzerland) in Villers-le-Lac, France on August 30, 1987. The women's record is 120 ft. 9 in., by Lucy Wardle (U.S.) in Ocean Park, Hong Kong on April 6, 1985.

SAILING

AMERICA'S CUP

Most wins (skipper) Three skippers have won the cup three times: Charlie Barr (U.S.), who defended in 1899, 1901 and 1903; Harold S. Vanderbilt (U.S.), who defended in 1930, 1934 and 1937; and Dennis Conner (U.S.), who defended in 1980, challenged in 1987, and defended in 1988.

Most races (any crew) There have been 29 challenges since August 8, 1870, and the United States has won on every occasion except 1983 and 1995, when it lost to Australia and New Zealand respectively.

In individual races sailed, American boats have won 81 races and foreign challengers have won 13.

Closest race The closest finish in a race for the cup was on October 4, 1901, when *Shamrock II* (Great Britain) finished two seconds ahead of the American *Columbia*.

Largest yacht The largest yacht to have competed in the America's Cup was the 1903 defender, the gaff-rigged cutter *Reliance*, with an overall length of 144 feet, a record sail area of 16,160 square feet and a rig 175 feet high.

OLYMPIC GAMES

Most gold medals Paul Elvstrom (Denmark) won a record four gold medals in yachting, and in the process became the first competitor in Olympic history to win individual gold medals in four successive Games. Elvstrom's titles came in the Firefly class in 1948, and in the Finn class in 1952, 1956 and 1960.

Most medals Paul Elvstrom's four gold medals are also the most medals won by any Olympic yachtsman.

CIRCUMNAVIGATION

It is not possible to make a simple circumnavigation of the world by sea, which would be along the equator. The World Sailing Speed Record Council gives the following rules: the vessel must start and return to the same point, must cross all meridians of longitude and must cross the Equator. It may cross some, but not all, meridians more than once. The vessel must cover at least 21,600 nautical miles in the course of the circumnavigation.

A non-stop circumnavigation is self-maintained; no water supplies, provisions, equipment or replacements of any sort may be taken aboard en route. Vessels may anchor but no physical help may be accepted apart from communications.

Longest race (nonstop) The world's longest nonstop sailing race is the Vendée Globe Challenge, the first of which started from Les Sables d'Olonne, France on November 26, 1989. The distance circumnavigated without stopping was 22,500 nautical miles. The race is for boats of between 50 and 60 feet, sailed single-handed. The record time on the course is 105 days 20 hr. 31 min., by Christophe Auguin (France) in the sloop *Geodis*, which finished at Les Sables on February 17, 1997.

Longest race (total distance)   The longest and oldest regular sailing race around the world is the quadrennial Whitbread Round the World race (instituted August 1973), organized by the Royal Naval Sailing Association (Great Britain). It starts in England, and the course around the world and the number of legs with stops at specified ports vary from race to race. The distance for 1993–94 was 32,000 nautical miles. The record time for the race is 120 days 5 hr. 9 min., by *New Zealand Endeavour*, skippered by Grant Dalton (New Zealand) on June 3, 1994.

The longest and oldest regularly staged sailing event is the quadrennial Whitbread Round the World Race. The record time is 120 days 5 hr. 9 min.

Fastest circumnavigation *Sport-elec.*, a 90-foot Tamarin, skippered by Olivier Kersauson (France), completed the fastest nonstop circumnavigation at Ushart, France on May 19, 1997. The voyage took 71 days 14 hr. 22 min. 8 sec.

Fastest circumnavigation (solo) The record for the fastest solo circumnavigation is 105 days 20 hr. 31 min., achieved by Christophe Auguin (France) in the sloop *Geodis*, which finished at Les Sables d'Olonne, France, on February 17, 1997.

Fastest east–west (solo, nonstop) *Group 4*, a 67-foot sloop skippered by Mike Golding (Great Britain), holds the record for the fastest east–west solo nonstop journey at 161 days 16 hr. 32 min. *Group 4* began its journey at Southampton, England on November 21, 1993 and finished in Southampton on May 7, 1994.

Smallest vessel *Acrohc Australis*, an 11-ft.-10-in. sloop skippered by Serge Testa (Australia), is the smallest vessel to sail around the world. *Acrohc Australis* left Brisbane, Australia in 1984 and returned to Brisbane 500 days later in 1987.

ATLANTIC OCEAN

Fastest solo crossing (east–west, sailing) The fastest solo crossing from east to west is 10 days 9 hr. (11.6 knots smg), achieved by *Fleury Michon (IX)*, a 60-foot trimaran skippered by Philippe Poupon (France). *Fleury Michon (IX)* left Plymouth, Devon, England on June 5 and arrived at Newport, RI on June 15, 1988.

Fastest solo crossing (west–east, sailing) Laurent Bourgnon (France) sailed *Primagaz*, a 60-foot trimaran, from Ambrose Light Tower on June 27 to Lizard Point, Cornwall, England on July 4, 1994, in 7 days 2 hr. 34 min. 42 sec. (17.15 knots).

Fastest crewed crossing (east–west, sailing) Laurent Bourgnon (France) and Cam Lewis (U.S.) sailed *Primagaz* from Plymouth, Devon, England to Newport, RI from June 5 to June 14, 1994, in 9 days 8 hr. 58 min. 20 sec. (12.49 knots).

Fastest crewed crossing (west–east, sailing) *Jet Services 5*, a 75-foot catamaran sloop skippered by Serge Madec (France), crossed the Atlantic in 6 days 13 hr. 3 min. 32 sec. (18.4 knots smg). *Jet Services 5* left Ambrose Light Tower on June 2 and arrived at Lizard Point, Cornwall, England on June 9, 1990.

Youngest solo crossing The youngest person to sail solo across the Atlantic was David Sandeman (Great Britain), who was 17 yr. 176 days old when he made the crossing in a time of 43 days in 1976.

Oldest solo crossing The oldest person to sail singlehandedly across the Atlantic was Michael Richey (Great Britain), in 55 days at the age of 79 yr. 36 days in 1996.

DURATION AND DISTANCE

Longest journey (nonstop)   Skipper Jon Sanders (Australia) sailed around the world three times aboard the Bermudan sloop *Parry Endeavour*. Sanders covered a record 71,000 miles (4.5 knots), beginning in Fremantle, West Australia on May 25, 1986 and ending in Fremantle on March 13, 1988.

Most miles, solo (24 hours)   The record for the most miles covered in 24 hours is 540 miles (22.5 knots) by *Primagaz*, a 60-foot trimaran skippered by Laurent Bourgnan (France), beginning and ending in the North Atlantic, June 28–29, 1994.

Most miles, crew (24 hours)   *Intrum Justitia*, a 64-foot monohull skippered by Lawrie Smith (Great Britain), covered 428 1/10 miles of the Southern Ocean on February 20–21, 1994.

SPEED

Fastest speed (yacht)   The fastest speed by a true yacht is 36.22 knots (41.68 mph), by Jean Saucet (France) in *Charante Maritime* on the Bassin de Thau, near Sete, on October 5, 1992.

Fastest speed (boat)   The record for a boat is 43.55 knots (80.65 kilometers per hour) by *Longshot*, steered by Russell Long (U.S.) in Tarifa, Spain in July 1992.

Fastest sea passage (under sail)   *Piere 1er*, skippered by Florence Arthaud (France), holds the record for the fastest sea passage under sail with 458 miles in 22 hr. 9 min. 56 sec. (20.66 knots) from Marseille, France to Carthage, Tunisia, August 26–27, 1991.

Fastest San Francisco-to-Boston sail   Richard B. Wilson and Bill Biewenga sailed from San Francisco to Boston via Cape Horn in 69 days 19 hr. 44 min. They left San Francisco in the 53-foot trimaran *Great American II* on January 27 and arrived in Boston on April 7, 1993.

WINDSURFING

Olympic Games

Most medals   The record for the most Olympic medals is two, achieved by two men: Bruce Kendall (New Zealand) won the bronze in 1984 and the gold in 1988 (both Board Sailing events); and Mike Gebhardt (U.S.) won the bronze in 1988 (Board Sailing event) and the silver in 1992 (Lechner event). The women's record is held by Barbara Kendall (New Zealand) who won two medals in the Board Sailing event: the gold in 1992, and the bronze in 1996.

World Championships

Most titles   Stephan van den Berg (Netherlands) has won five world titles, 1979–83.

Lai Shan Lee won the women's mistral event at the '96 Atlanta Games. She is the only Hong Kong athlete to win a gold medal at the Olympic Games.

Big Plays

Longest sailboard   A sailboard of 165 feet was constructed in Fredrikstad, Norway. It was first sailed on June 28, 1986.

Longest snake of sailboards   The longest snake of sailboards was made by 70 windsurfers in a row at the Sailboard Show '89 event in Narrabeen Lakes, Manly, Australia on October 21, 1989.

Fastest speed   The fastest speed reached under sail on water by any craft over a 500-meter timed run is 46.25 knots, by Simon McKeon and Tim Daddo (Australia) in the trifoiler *Yellow Pages Endeavour c.* October 26, 1993 in Shallow Inlet near Melbourne. The women's record is held by boardsailer Babethe Coquelle (France), who achieved 40.38 knots in Tarifa, Spain on July 7, 1995.

Most miles (24 hours)   Françoise Canetos (France) sailed *Fanatic board*, a Gaastra sailboard, a record 227 miles in 24 hours (9.46 knots) in Séte, France on July 13–14, 1988.

OTHER AQUATIC SPORTS

CANOEING

Olympic Games

Most gold medals Gert Fredriksson (Sweden) won a record six Olympic gold medals: 1,000 meter Kayak Singles (K1), 1948, 1952 and 1956; 10,000 meter K1, 1948 and 1956; 1,000 meter Kayak Pairs (K2), 1960. In women's competition, Birgit Schmidt (née Fischer; East Germany/Germany) has won five golds: 500 meter K1, 1980 and 1992; 500 meter K2, 1988; 500 meter K4, 1988 and 1996.

World Championships

Most titles Birgit Schmidt (East Germany/ Germany) has won a record 26 titles, 1979–96. The men's record is 13, by three canoeists: Gert Fredriksson (Sweden), 1948–60; Rudiger Helm (East Germany), 1976–83; and Ivan Patzaichin (Romania), 1968–84.

Big Plays

Fastest speed (men) The German 4-man kayak Olympic champions in 1992 in Barcelona, Spain covered 1,000 meters in 2 min. 52.17 sec. in a heat on August 4. This represents an average speed of 12.98 mph. At the 1988 Olympics in Seoul, South Korea, the Norwegian four achieved a 250 m split of 42.08 seconds between 500 m and 750 m for a speed of 13.29 mph.

Fastest speed (women) The Hungarian four won the 200-m title at the 1995 World Championships in 31.227 seconds, at an average speed of 14.32 mph.

Longest journey Father and son Dana and Donald Starkell paddled from Winnipeg, Manitoba, Canada by ocean and river to Belem, Brazil, a distance of 12,181 miles, from June 1, 1980 to May 1, 1982. All portages were human-powered. Without portages or aid of any kind, the longest journey is one of 6,102 miles, by Richard H. Grant and Ernest "Moose" Lassy, circumnavigating the eastern United States via Chicago, New Orleans, Miami, New York City and the Great Lakes, September 22, 1930 to August 15, 1931.

Most miles (24 hours) Zdzislaw Szubski paddled 157.1 miles in a Jaguar K1 canoe on the Vistula River, Wockawek to Gdansk, Poland, September 11–12, 1987.

Most miles, flatwater (24 hours) Marinda Hartzenberg (South Africa) paddled, without benefit of current, 137.13 miles on Loch Logan, Bloemfontein, South Africa, December 31, 1990–January 1, 1991.

Most miles, open sea (24 hours)   Randy Fine (U.S.) paddled 120.6 miles along the Florida coast, June 26–27, 1986.

Most miles (career)   Fritz Lindner of Berlin, Germany totaled 64,278 miles of canoeing from 1928 to 1987.

Eskimo rolls (1,000)   Ray Hudspith achieved 1,000 rolls in 34 min. 43 sec. at the Elswick Pool, Newcastle-upon-Tyne, England on March 20, 1987.

Eskimo rolls (100)   Ray Hudspith also completed 100 rolls in 3 min. 7.25 sec. at Killingworth Leisure Centre, Tyne & Wear, England on March 3, 1991.

Eskimo rolls (consecutive)   Randy Fine (U.S.) completed 4,109 continuous rolls on Bambi Lake, Hialeah, FL on April 20, 1997.

Hand rolls (1,000)   The fastest time recorded for completing 1,000 hand rolls is 31 min. 55.62 sec., by Colin Brian Hill in Consett, England on March 12, 1987.

Hand rolls (100)   Colin Brian Hill achieved 100 rolls in 2 min. 39.2 sec. in London, England on February 22, 1987.

Hand rolls (consecutive)   Colin Brian Hill also completed 3,700 continuous rolls at Durham City Swimming Baths, Durham, England on May 1, 1989.

Largest canoe raft   A raft of 582 kayaks and canoes, organized by Cleveland Metroparks, was held together by hands only for 30 seconds while free floating on Hinckley Lake, Cleveland, OH on May 21, 1995.

The largest canoe raft consisted of 582 canoes and kayaks held together by hands only.

Longest race   The Canadian Government Centennial Voyageur Canoe Pageant and Race from Rocky Mountain House, Alberta to the Expo 67 site in Montreal, Quebec was 3,283 miles. Ten canoes represented Canadian provinces and territories. The winner of the race, which lasted from May 24 to September 4, 1967, was the Province of Manitoba canoe *Radisson*.

Fastest Rhine crossing   The fastest time to paddle the length of the River Rhine is 10 days 12 hr. 9 min. by Frank Palmer (Great Britain), May 15–25, 1988.

Fastest Rhine crossing (with support team)   The supported team record is 7 days 23 hr. 31 sec. by the RAF Laarbruch Canoe Club, led by Andy Goodsell (Great Britain), May 17–24, 1989.

ROWING

Olympic Games

Most gold medals   Steven Redgrave (Great Britain) won four gold medals: coxed fours, 1984, coxless pairs, 1988, 1992 and 1996.

Most medals   Two oarsmen have won five medals in rowing competition: Jack Beresford (Great Britain), three gold (single sculls, 1924, coxless fours, 1932, and double sculls, 1936) and two silver (single sculls, 1920, and eights, 1928); and Steven Redgrave (Great Britain), four gold (*see* MOST GOLD MEDALS) and one bronze (coxed pairs, 1988).

Steven Redgrave (rear of the scull) is the most successful Olympic rower, with four gold medals.

World Championships

Most titles   Steven Redgrave (Great Britain) has won 10 titles: coxed fours, 1984; coxed pairs, 1986; coxless pairs, 1987–88 and 1991–96. Yelena Tereshina (USSR) won seven titles: eights, 1978–79, 1981–83 and 1985–86.

Single sculls   Three oarsmen have won five single sculls titles: Peter-Michael Kolbe (West Germany), 1975, 1978, 1981, 1983 and 1986; Pertti Karppinen (Finland), 1976, 1979–80 and 1984–85; and Thomas Lange

(Germany), 1988–92. Christine Hahn (née Scheiblich; East Germany) has won five women's titles, 1974–78.

Eights   Since 1962, East German crews have won seven men's eights titles—1970, 1975–80. In women's competition the USSR has won seven titles—1978–79, 1981–83, 1985–86.

Collegiate Championships

Most wins (men)   Cornell has won 24 titles: 1896–97 (includes two wins in 1897), 1901–03, 1905–07, 1909–12, 1915, 1930, 1955–58, 1962–63, 1971, 1977, and 1981. Since 1982, Harvard has won six titles, 1983, 1985, 1987–89, and 1992.

Most wins (women)   Washington has won seven titles—1981–85, 1987–88.

Big Plays

Longest race   The longest annual rowing race is the annual Tour du Lac Leman, Geneva, Switzerland for coxed fours (the 5-man crew taking turns as cox) over 99 miles. The record winning time is 12 hr. 22 min. 29 sec., by RG Red Bull, Bonn, Germany on October 2, 1994.

Fastest speed   (eights, men)   The record time for 2,187 yards on non-tidal water is 5 min. 24.28 sec. (13.79 mph) by an eight from Hansa Dortmund (Germany), in Essen, Germany on May 17, 1992.

Fastest speed   (eights, women)   The women's record is 5 min. 58.50 sec., by Romania in Duisburg, Germany, on May 18, 1996.

Fastest speed   (single sculls, men)   The men's record speed for single sculls is 6 min. 37.03 sec. (11.26 mph), by Juri Jaanson (Estonia) in Lucerne, Switzerland, on July 9, 1995.

Fastest speed   (single sculls, women)   On July 17, 1994, Silken Laumann (Canada) set a women's record of 7 min. 17.09 sec. in Lucerne, Switzerland.

Greatest distance (24 hours)   The greatest distance rowed in 24 hours (upstream and downstream) is 141.26 miles, by six members of Dittons Skiff & Punting Club on the River Thames between Hampton Court and Teddington, England on June 3–4, 1994.

Longest solo ocean row   Peter Bird spent 304 days 14 hr. nonstop rowing at sea during a trans-Pacific voyage, which began on May 12, 1993 and was ended prematurely on March 12, 1994.

POWERBOAT RACING

APBA Gold Cup

Most wins (driver)   The most wins by a driver is 10, by Chip Hanauer, 1982–88, 1992–93 and 1995.

POWERBOAT SPEED RECORDS

One Kilometer

Type	Class	Speed (mph)	Driver	Location	Year
Inboard	GP	170.024	Kent MacPhail	Decatur, IL	1979
Inboard	KRR	146.649	Gordon Jennings	Lincoln City, OR	1989
Offshore	Super Boat	158.452	Dennis Kaiser	Sarasota, FL	1995
Offshore	Open	157.428	Tom Gentry	San Diego, CA	1994
PR Outboard	500ccH	121.940	Daniel Kirts	Moore Haven, FL	1987
PR Outboard	700ccH	118.769	Billy Rucker Jr.	Waterford, CA	1992
Performance	Champ Boat	143.716	Todd Bowden	Parker, AZ	1996
Performance	Mod U	142.968	Bob Wartinger	Moore Haven, FL	1989
Special Event	World Outboard Assault	176.556	Bob Wartinger	Parker, AZ	1989
Special Event	Jet	317.600	Ken Warby	Tumut, Australia	1976

Unlimited in Competition

Type	Distance	Speed (mph)	Driver	Location	Year
Qualifying Lap	2 miles	165.975	Chip Hanauer	Evansville, IN	1993
Lap	2 miles	156.713	Chip Hanauer	Evansville, IN	1993
Qualifying Lap	2.5 miles	172.166	Chip Hanauer	San Diego, CA	1995
Lap	2.5 miles	166.236	Steve David	Honolulu, HI	1992

Source: APBA

Most wins (owner)   Bernie Little, the owner of *Miss Budweiser* (registered at Hydroplane, Inc.), holds the record with 10 wins, driven by Bill Sterett Sr. in 1969; by Dean Chenoweth in 1970, 1973 and 1980–81; by Tom D'Eath in 1989–90; and by Chip Hanauer in 1992–93 and 1995. Little is sponsored by Budweiser Brewing Company.

Most consecutive wins   Chip Hanauer has won a record seven successive victories, 1982–88.

Highest average speed   The highest average speed for the race is 147.943 mph by Mark Tate, piloting *Smokin' Joe's* in June 1994.

Big Plays

Fastest speed (electric powerboat)   David Mischke set the APBA electric powerboat speed record of 70.597 mph in a 14-foot outboard hydroplane with a 48-volt motor at Kilometer Speed Trials, Devil's Lake, Lincoln City, OR on October 14, 1995.

Fastest speed (unofficial)   Kenneth Peter Warby achieved 300 knots (345.48 mph) on Blowering Dam Lake, New South Wales, Australia on November 20, 1977 in his unlimited hydroplane *Spirit of Australia*.

Fastest speed (official)   The official world water speed record is 275.8 knots (511.11 kilometers per hour) set on October 8, 1978 by Kenneth Peter Warby on Blowering Dam Lake.

Fastest speed   (unofficial, women)   Mary Rife set a women's unofficial record of 206.72 mph in her blown fuel hydro *Proud Mary* in Tulsa, OK on July 23, 1977.

Fastest speed   (official, women)   The official speed record is 197 mph, achieved by Mary Rife of Flint, TX.

Fastest Atlantic crossing   Under the rules of the Hales Trophy, which recognizes the highest average speed rather than the shortest duration, the record is held by the 222-foot Italian powerboat *Destriero*, with an average speed of 53.09 knots between the Nantucket Light Buoy and Bishop Rock Lighthouse, Isles of Scilly, Great Britain, August 6–9, 1992, in a time of 58 hr. 34 min. 4 sec.

Longest jet-ski journey   Gary Frick (U.S.) traveled 5,040 miles along the United States coastline on a stand-up Kawasaki 650sx Jet Ski. He left Lubec, ME on May 8, 1993 and arrived in Seattle, WA on September 16, 1993.

SURFING

World Amateur Championships

Most titles   The women's title has been won twice by two surfers: Joyce Hoffman (U.S.), 1965–66; and Sharon Weber (Hawaii), 1970 and 1972. The men's title has been won by a different surfer each time.

World Professional Championships

Most titles (men)   Two surfers have won four titles: Mark Richards (Australia), in 1979–82; and Kelly Slater (U.S.), in 1992 and 1994–96.

Most titles (women)   The women's record is also four, by two surfers: Frieda Zamba (U.S.), 1984–86, 1988; Wendy Botha (Australia), 1987, 1989, 1991–92.

Youngest champion (women)   The youngest surfing world champion was Frieda Zamba, who was 19 years old when she won in 1984.

Youngest champion (men)   The youngest men's champion was Kelly Slater, who won the 1992 crown at age 20.

Kelly Slater is the youngest world surfing champion.

Prize Money

Highest earnings (season)   Kelly Slater holds the season earnings mark, with $140,400 in 1996. The women's record is $55,510, by Lisa Anderson in 1996.

Highest earnings (career)   Barton Lynch (Australia) has the highest career earnings with $582,787. The women's leader is Pam Burridge (Australia) with $227,375.

WATERSKIING

World Championships

Most titles (overall)   Sammy Duvall (U.S.) has won four overall titles, in 1981, 1983, 1985 and 1987. Two women have won three overall titles: Willa McGuire (née Worthington; U.S.), 1949–50 and 1955; Liz Allan-Shetter (U.S.), 1965, 1969 and 1975.

WATERSKIING RECORDS

Slalom

Men: 4 buoys on a 10.25 m line, Andrew Mapple (Great Britain) in Charleston, SC on September 4, 1994.
Women: 2.25 buoys on a 10.75-m line, Susi Graham (Canada) in Santa Rosa, FL on September 25, 1994.

Tricks

Men: 11,590 points, Aymeric Benet (France) in West Palm Beach, FL on October 30, 1994.
Women: 8,580 points, Tawn Larsen (U.S.) in Groveland, FL on July 4, 1992.

Jumping

Men: 220 ft., Sammy Duvall (U.S.) in Santa Rosa Beach, FL on October 10, 1993.
Women: 156 ft., Deena Mapple (née Brush; U.S.) in Charlotte, MI on July 9, 1988.

Most titles (individual)   Liz Allan-Shetter has won eight individual championship events and is the only person to win all four titles—slalom, jumping, tricks, and overall—in one year, in Copenhagen, Denmark in 1969. Patrice Martin (France) has won a men's record seven titles: three overall, 1989, 1991, 1993, and four tricks, 1979, 1985, 1987 and 1991.

Fastest speed (men)   The fastest waterskiing speed recorded is 143.08 mph, by Christopher Michael Massey (Australia) on the Hawkesbury River, Windsor, New South Wales, Australia on March 6, 1983.

Fastest speed (women)   Donna Patterson Brice set a women's record of 111.11 mph in Long Beach, CA on August 21, 1977.

BAREFOOT WATERSKIING

World Championships

Most titles   The most overall titles is four, by Kim Lampard (Australia), 1980, 1982, 1985, 1986; and the men's record is three, by Brett Wing (Australia), 1978, 1980, 1982.

Most titles (team)   The team title has been won five times by Australia in 1978, 1980, 1982, 1985, and 1986.

Fastest speed (men)   The official barefoot speed record is 135.74 mph, by Scott Michael Pellaton over a ¼-mile course in Chandler, CA, in November 1989.

The fastest speed for barefoot waterskiing is 135.74 mph. Traveling backwards, the record is 62 mph.

Fastest speed (women)   The fastest by a woman is 73.67 mph, by Karen Toms (Australia) on the Hawkesbury River, Windsor, New South Wales on March 31, 1984.

Fastest speed (backwards)   The fastest official speed backwards barefoot is 62 mph, by Robert Wing (Australia) on April 3, 1982.

Longest jump (men)   The barefoot jump record is 90 ft. 3 in., by Richard Mainwaring in Thurrock, England on August 20, 1994.

Longest jump (women)   The women's record for the longest jump is 54 ft. 5 in., by Sharon Stekelenberg (Australia) in 1991.

Big Plays

Most skiers towed   A record 100 waterskiers were towed on double skis over a nautical mile by the cruiser *Reef Cat* in Cairns, Queensland, Australia on October 18, 1986. This feat, organized by the Cairns and District Powerboat and Ski Club, was then repeated by 100 skiers on single skis.

Longest duration (barefoot)   The barefoot duration record is 2 hr. 42 min. 39 sec., by Billy Nichols (U.S.) on Lake Weir, FL on November 19, 1978.

Longest duration (backwards barefoot)   The backwards barefoot record is 1 hr. 27 min. 3.96 sec., by Steve Fontaine in Jupiter, FL, on August 31, 1989.

Longest distance (walking on water)   Rémy Bricka of Paris, France "walked" across the Atlantic Ocean on waterskis 13 ft. 9 in. long in 1988. Leaving Tenerife, Canary Islands on April 2, 1988, he covered 3,502 miles, arriving in Trinidad on May 31, 1988.

Fastest speed (walking on water)   Bricka also set a speed record of 7 min. 7.41 sec. for 1,094 yards in the Olympic pool in Montreal, Canada on August 2, 1989.

Wearing 11-foot waterski shoes, called Skijaks, and using a twin-bladed paddle, David Kiner walked 155 miles on the Hudson River from Albany, NY to Battery Park, New York City. His walk took him 57 hours, June 22–27, 1987.

WATER POLO

Most gold medals (country)   Hungary has won six Olympic titles, 1932, 1936, 1952, 1956, 1964 and 1976.

Most gold medals (players)   Five players have won three gold medals: George Wilkinson (Great Britain), 1900, 1908, 1912; Paul Radmilovic (Great Britain), 1908, 1912, 1920; Charles Smith (Great Britain), 1908, 1912, 1920; Deszo Gyarmati (Hungary), 1952, 1956, 1964; Gyorgy Karpati (Hungary), 1952, 1956, 1964.

World Championships

Most titles (men)   Two countries have won two men's titles: USSR, 1975 and 1982; Yugoslavia, 1986 and 1991.

Most titles (women)   The women's competition was won by Australia in 1986, and by the Netherlands in 1991.

Big Plays

Most goals (game)   The greatest number of goals scored by an individual in an international match is 13, by Debbie Handley for Australia (16) vs. Canada (10) at the World Championship in Guayaquil, Ecuador in 1982.

Most international appearances   The greatest number of international appearances is 412, by Aleksey Stepanovich Barkalov (USSR), 1965–80.

SKIING

ALPINE SKIING

Olympic Games

Most gold medals   In men's competition, the most gold medals won is three, by three skiers: Anton Sailer (Austria), who won all three events, downhill, slalom and giant slalom, in 1956; Jean-Claude Killy (France), who matched Sailer's feat in 1968; and Alberto Tomba (Italy), who won the slalom and giant slalom in 1988 and the giant slalom in 1992. For women the record is also three golds, by Vreni Schneider (Switzerland), who won the giant slalom and slalom in 1988 and the slalom in 1994.

Moguls was introduced as an Olympic sport at the '92 Games.

Most medals   Two men have won five Olympic medals: Alberto Tomba (Italy), three gold and two silver, 1988–94; Kjetil Andre Aamodt (Norway), one gold, two silver and two bronze, 1992–94. The most by a woman is also five, by Vreni Schneider (Switzerland): three gold, one silver and one bronze, 1994.

World Championships

Most gold medals   Christel Cranz (Germany) won 12 titles: four slalom, 1934, 1937–39; three downhill, 1935, 1937, 1939; five combined, 1934–35, 1937–39. Anton Sailer (Austria) holds the men's record with seven titles: one slalom, 1956; two giant slalom, 1956, 1958; two downhill, 1956, 1958; two combined, 1956, 1958.

World Cup

Most overall titles   The record for the most overall World Cup titles is six, achieved by Annemarie Moser-Pröll (Austria) in 1971–75, 1979. The men's record is five, achieved by Marc Girardelli (Luxembourg), 1985–86, 1989, 1991, and 1993.

Most downhill titles   Annemarie Moser-Pröll (Austria) has won a record seven downhill titles in 1971–75, and 1978–79. Franz Klammer (Austria) has won five downhill titles, 1975–78, and 1983.

Most slalom titles   The record for the most World Cup slalom titles is eight, set by In-gemar Stenmark (Sweden) in 1975–81, and 1983. The women's record is six, by Vreni Schneider (Switzerland), 1989–90 and 1992–95.

Yelena Valbe (Russia, left) won a record five World Cup titles. Bjorn Daehlie (Norway, right), has won a record five Olympic titles.

Most giant slalom titles Ingemar Stenmark (Sweden) also holds the record for the most World Cup giant slalom titles with seven, in 1975–76, 1978–81, and 1984. The women's record is five, by Vreni Schneider (Switzerland) in 1986–87, 1989, 1991, and 1995.

Most super giant slalom titles The record for the most super giant slalom titles is four, achieved by three skiers: Pirmin Zurbriggen (Switzerland), 1987–1990; Carole Merle (France), 1989–92; and Katja Seizinger (Germany), 1993–96.

Most titles (one season) The record for the most titles in one season is four, achieved by two skiers: Jean-Claude Killy (France) won all four possible disciplines (downhill, slalom, giant slalom and overall) in 1967; and Pirmin Zurbriggen (Switzerland) won four of the five possible disciplines (downhill, giant slalom, super giant slalom [added 1986] and overall) in 1987.

Most race wins (men) Ingemar Stenmark (Sweden) won a record 86 races (46 giant slalom, 40 slalom) from 287 contested, 1974–89.

Most race wins (women) Annemarie Moser-Pröll (Austria) won a record 62 races, 1970–79.

Most wins (season) Ingemar Stenmark (Sweden) won 13 races in 1978–79 to set the men's mark. Vreni Schneider (Switzerland) won 13 races in 1988–89 to set the women's mark.

Most consecutive wins Ingemar Stenmark (Sweden) won 14 successive giant slalom races from March 18, 1978 to January 21, 1980. The women's record is 11 wins by Annemarie Moser-Pröll (Austria) in the downhill from December 1972 to January 1974.

NCAA Championships

Most titles (team) Denver has won 14 titles, 1954–57, 1961–67, and 1969–71.

Most titles (individual) Chiharu Igaya of Dartmouth won a record six NCAA titles: Alpine, 1955–56; downhill, 1955; slalom, 1955–57.

CROSS-COUNTRY SKIING

Olympic Games

Most gold medals The most gold medals won in Nordic events is six, by Lyubov Yegorova (Unified Team/Russia), 15 km, 4 × 5 km relay and 5 × 10 km relay, 1992; 5 km, 4 × 5 km relay and 10 km pursuit, 1994. Bjorn Daehlie (Norway) holds the men's record with five gold medals: 50 km, 15 km pursuit, and 4 × 10 km relay, 1992; 10 km and 15 km pursuit, 1994.

Most medals The most medals won in Nordic events is 10, by Raisa Smetanina (four gold, five silver and one bronze, 1976–92). Sixteen Jernberg (Sweden) holds the men's record with nine (four gold, three silver, two bronze, 1956–64).

World Cup

Most titles The record for the most overall titles is five, set by Yelena Valbe (USSR/Russia), 1989, 1991–92, 1995 and 1997; and Bjorn Daehlie (Norway), 1992–93 and 1995–97.

SKI JUMPING

Olympic Games

Most gold medals Matti Nykanen (Finland) has won four gold medals: 70-meter hill, 1988; 90-meter hill, 1984 and 1988; 90-meter team, 1988.

Most medals Matti Nykanen has won five medals in Olympic competition: four gold (*see above*) and one silver, 70-meter hill, 1984.

World Cup

Most titles Matti Nykanen (Finland) has won four World Cup titles, 1983, 1985–86 and 1988.

MOGULS

Olympic Games

Most medals No skiier has won an Olympic medal more than once.

World Championships

Most wins (men) Edgar Grospiron (France) has won the event three times, in 1989, 1991 and 1995.

Most wins (women) No skier has won the women's event more than once.

AERIALS

World Championships

Most wins (men) Two men have won the title twice: Lloyd Langlois (Canada), 1986 and 1989; and Philippe Laroche (Canada), 1991 and 1993.

Most wins (women) No skier has won this event more than once.

ACRO-SKIING

World Championships

Most wins (men)   No skier has won more than once.

Most wins (women)   Two women have won the event twice: Jan Bucher (U.S.), 1986 and 1989; and Ellen Breen (U.S.), 1991 and 1993.

GRASS SKIING

World Championships

Most titles (women)   Ingrid Hirschhofer (Austria) has won 14 titles, 1979–93.

Most titles (men)   The most by a man is seven, by Erwin Gansner (Switzerland), 1981–87, and Rainer Grossman, 1985–93.

Most titles (one season)   The feat of winning all four titles in one season has been achieved by (*men*) Erwin Gansner, 1987, and Rainer Grossman, 1991, and by (*women*) Katja Krey (West Germany), 1989, and Ingrid Hirschhofer, 1993.

Big Plays

Fastest speed (men)   The official world record is 150.028 mph by Jeffrey Hamilton (U.S.), April 14, 1995.

Fastest speed (women)   The fastest speed by a woman is 140.864 mph, by Karine Dubouchet (France) on April 20, 1996.

Fastest speed—one-legged   On April 16, 1988 Patrick Knaff set a one-legged record of 115.306 mph.

Fastest speed—cross-country   The world record time for a 50 km race is 1 hr. 54 min. 46 sec. by Aleksei Prokurorov (Russia) at Thunder Bay, Canada on March 19, 1994 at an average speed of 16.24 mph.

Fastest speed—grass-skiing   Klaus Spinka (Austria) set a record of 57.21 mph in Waldassen, Germany on September 24, 1989.

Fastest speed—snowmobile   The fastest speed attained by a snowmobile is 103.1 mph, by Erich Brenter (Austria), in Cervinia, Italy in 1964.

Longest ski-jump   The longest ski-jump ever recorded is 686 feet, by Espen Bredesen (Norway) in Planica, Slovenia on March 18, 1994. The women's record is 367 feet, by Eva Ganster (Austria), in Bischofshofen, Austria on January 7, 1994.

Most miles, cross-country (24 hours)   Seppo-Juhani Savolainen skied 258.2 miles at Saariselka, Finland on April 8–9, 1988.

Most miles, cross-country (48 hours)   In 48 hours, Bjørn Løkken (Norway) covered 319 mi. 205 yd., March 11–13, 1982.

Most miles, alpine (one year)   During calendar year 1994, Lucy Dicker and Arnie Wilson (both Great Britain) skied every day in an around-the-world expedition. They skied a total of 3,678 miles and 472,050 feet at 237 resorts in 13 countries on five continents.

Longest race (cross-country)   The longest Nordic ski race is the Vasaloppet, at 55.3 miles. There were a record 10,934 starters on March 6, 1977 and a record 10,650 finishers on March 4, 1979. The fastest time is 3 hr. 48 min. 55 sec., by Bengt Hassis (Sweden) in 1986.

   The 1984 Finlandia Ski Race, 46.6 miles from Hämeenlinna to Lahti, had 13,226 starters and 12,909 finishers.

Longest race (downhill)   The longest downhill race is the Inferno in Switzerland, 9.8 miles from the top of the Schilthorn to Lauterbrunnen. The record number of entries was 1,401 in 1981, and the record time was 13 min. 53.40 sec. by Urs von Allmen (Switzerland) in 1991.

Longest ski lift   The longest gondola ski lift is 3.88 miles long, in Grindel-wald-Männlichen, Switzerland (in two sections, but one gondola).

OTHER WINTER SPORTS

FIGURE SKATING

Olympic Games

Most gold medals   Three skaters have won three gold medals: Gillis Grafstrom (Sweden) in 1920, 1924 and 1928; Sonja Henie (Norway) in 1928, 1932 and 1936; Irina Rodnina (USSR), with two different partners, in the pairs in 1972, 1976 and 1980.

World Championships

Most titles (individual)   The greatest number of men's individual world figure skating titles is 10, by Ulrich Salchow (Sweden), in 1901–05 and 1907–11. The women's record (instituted 1906) is also 10 individual titles, by Sonja Henie (Norway) between 1927 and 1936.

Most titles (pairs)   Irina Rodnina (USSR) has won 10 pairs titles (instituted 1908), four with Aleksey Ulanov, 1969–72, and six with her husband, Aleksandr Zaitsev, 1973–78.

Most titles (ice dance)   The most ice dance titles (instituted 1952) won is six, by Lyudmila Pakhomova and her husband, Aleksandr Gorshkov (USSR), 1970–74 and 1976.

Tara Lipinski became the youngest world figure skating champion when she won the 1997 title at age 14.

Youngest champion (women)   Tara Lipinski (U.S.) won the 1997 World Figure Skating Championships at the age of 14.

Youngest champion (men)   Donald MacPherson (Canada) won the World Figure Skating Championships at age 18 in 1963.

Scoring

Highest marks (event)   The record for the highest tally of a maximum six marks in an international championship is 29, awarded to Jayne Torvill and Christopher Dean (Great Britain) in the World Ice Dance Championships in Ottawa, Canada on March 22–24, 1984.

Most 6.0's awarded (career)   Jayne Torvill and Christopher Dean (Great Britain) hold the career record for the most sixes, with 136.

Most 6.0's awarded (solo skater)   The highest tally by a soloist is seven, by Donald Jackson (Canada) in the World Men's Championship in Prague,

Czechoslovakia, 1962; and by Midori Ito (Japan) in the World Ladies' Championships in Paris, France in 1989.

Big Plays

Longest jump   Robin Cousins (Great Britain) achieved 19 ft. 1 in. in an axel jump and 18 feet with a back flip in Richmond, England in 1983.

Longest barrel jump   The official distance record is 29 ft. 5 in. over 28 barrels, by Yvon Jolin in Terrebonne, Québec, Canada on January 25, 1981. The women's record is 22 ft. 5¼ in. over 11 barrels, by Marie Josée Houle in Lasalle, Québec, Canada on March 1, 1987.

Largest skating rink   The world's largest indoor ice rink is in the Moscow Olympic Arena, which has an ice area of 86,800 square feet. The five rinks at Fujikyu Highland Skating Center in Japan total 285, 243 square feet.

SPEED SKATING

Olympic Games

Most gold medals (women)   Lydia Skoblikova (USSR) has won six gold medals: 500-meter, 1964; 1,000-meter, 1964; 1,500-meter, 1960, 1964; 3,000-meter, 1960, 1964.

Most gold medals (men)   The men's record for the most gold medals is five, shared by two skaters: Clas Thunberg (Finland), 500-meter, 1928; 1,500-meter, 1924, 1928; 5,000-meter, 1924; all-around title, 1924; and Eric Heiden (U.S.), 500-meter, 1,000-meter, 1,500-meter, 5,000-meter, and 10,000-meter, all in 1980.

Most gold medals (one Olympiad)   Eric Heiden (U.S.) achieved five gold medals at the Olympic Games in 1980: 500-meter, 1,000-meter, 1,500-meter, 5,000-meter, and 10,000-meter.

World Championships

Most titles (men)   Oscar Mathisen (Norway) and Clas Thunberg (Finland) have won a record five overall world titles. Mathisen won titles in 1908–09 and 1912–14; Thunberg won in 1923, 1925, 1928–29 and 1931.

Most titles (women)   Karin Enke-Kania (East Germany) holds the women's mark, also at five. She won in 1982, 1984 and 1986–88.

Big Plays

Longest race   The "Elfstedentocht," which originated in the 17th century, was held in the Netherlands, 1909–63, and again in 1985 and 1986, covering 200 km (124 miles 483 yards).

As the weather does not permit an annual race in the Netherlands, alternative "Elfstedentocht" have taken place on Lake Vesijärvi, Finland; Ottawa River, Canada; and Lake Weissensee, Austria. The record time for

200 km is: (*men*) 5 hr. 40 min. 37 sec., by Dries van Wijhe (Netherlands); and (*women*) 5 hr. 48 min. 8 sec., by Alida Pasveer (Netherlands), both on Lake Weissensee (altitude 3,609 feet), Austria on February 11, 1989. Jan-Roelof Kruithof (Netherlands) won the race nine times—1974, 1976–77, 1979–84. An estimated 16,000 skaters took part in 1986.

Greatest distance (24 hours) Martinus Kuiper (Netherlands) skated 339.67 miles in 24 hours in Alkmaar, Netherlands, December 12–13, 1988.

The longest speed skating race is the "Elfstedentocht."

SHORT TRACK SPEED SKATING

Olympic Games

Most gold medals Kim Ki-hoon (South Korea) won three gold medals: 1,000 meters and 5,000 meter relay, 1992; 1,000 meters, 1994.

World Championships

Most wins (men) Mark Gagnon (Canada) has won three titles, 1994–96.

Most wins (women) Sylvie Daigle (Canada) has won four world titles, 1983, 1988–90.

BOBSLEDDING

Olympic Games

Four-man bob Switzerland has won a record five Olympic titles: 1924, 1936, 1956, 1972 and 1988.

Two-man bob Switzerland has won a record four Olympic titles: 1948, 1980, 1992 and 1994.

Most gold medals Meinhard Nehmer and Bernhard Germeshausen (both East Germany) have both won a record three gold medals. They were both members of the 1976 2-man and 4-man winning crews and the 1980 4-man winning crew.

Most medals   Eugenio Monti (Italy) has won six medals: two gold, two silver and two bronze, 1956–68.

Oldest gold medalist   The oldest age at which a gold medal has been won in any Winter Olympic sport is 49 yr. 7 days, for James Jay O'Brien (U.S.) in 4-man bob in 1932.

World Championships

Four-man bob   Switzerland has won the world title a record 20 times: 1924, 1936, 1939, 1947, 1954–57, 1971–73, 1975, 1982–83, 1986–90 and 1993.

Two-man bob   Italy has won the world title 14 times: 1954, 1956–63, 1966, 1968–69, 1971 and 1975.

Most titles   Eugenio Monti (Italy) has won 11 bobsled world championships: eight in the two-man, 1957–61, 1963, 1966 and 1968; three in the four-man, 1960–61 and 1968.

LUGE

Olympic Games

Most gold medals   Thomas Kohler, Hans Rinn, Norbert Hahn and Steffi Martin-Walter (all East Germany) and George Hackl (West Germany; Germany) have each won two Olympic titles: Kohler won the single-seater in 1964 and the two-seater in 1968; Rinn and Hahn won the two-seater in 1976 and 1980; Martin-Walter won the women's single-seater in 1984 and 1988; Hackl won the single-seater in 1992 and 1996.

World Championships

Most titles   Thomas Kohler and Hans Rinn (both East Germany) have both won six world titles: Kohler won the single-seater in 1962, 1964 and 1966–67, and the two-seater in 1967–68; Rinn won the single-seater in 1973 and 1977, and the two-seater in 1976–77 and 1980 (two world championships were held in 1980, with Rinn winning each time). Margit Schumann (East Germany) holds the women's mark with five world titles, 1973–77.

Big Plays

Fastest speed (luge)   The fastest recorded photo-timed speed is 85.38 mph, by Asle Strand (Norway) in Tandådalens Linbana, Sälen, Sweden on May 1, 1982.

Highest-altitude luge run   Michael Coyne and Michael Daly luged down the north face of Mount Chacaltaya in the Bolivian Andes at 17,200 feet on

July 18, 1996. As members of the Expedition Outreach team, Coyle and Daly accomplished this feat in an effort to raise awareness about AIDS.

Michael Coyne and Michael Daly luged down the north face of Mount Chacaltaya in the Bolivian Andes on July 18, 1996. At a height of 17,200 feet, it was the highest luge run.

CURLING

World Championships

Most titles (men) Canada has dominated this event, winning 24 titles: 1959–64, 1966, 1968–72, 1980, 1982–83, 1985–87, 1989–90, and 1993–96. Ernie Richardson (Canada) has been a winning skip a record four times, 1959–60, 1962–63.

Most titles (women) Canada has won 10 championships, in 1980, 1984–87, 1989, 1993–94, and 1996–97. Three women have been skips of two winning teams: Djordy Nordby (Norway), 1990–91; Sandra Peterson (Canada), 1993–94; and Elisabet Gustafson (née Johanssen; Sweden), 1992 and 1995.

Labatt Brier

Most titles The most wins is 25, by Manitoba (1928–32, 1934, 1936, 1938, 1940, 1942, 1947, 1949, 1952–53, 1956, 1965, 1970–72, 1979, 1981, 1984, 1992 and 1995–96).

United States Championships

Most titles (men) Bud Somerville of the Superior (WI) Curling Club has been the skip on five championship teams, in 1965, 1968–69, 1974 and 1981.

Most titles (women)   In this competition, Nancy Langley of the Granite Curling Club, Seattle, WA has been the skip of a record four championship teams: 1979, 1981, 1983 and 1988.

Scoring

Perfect games   Stu Beagle, of Calgary, Alberta, played a perfect game (48 points) against Nova Scotia in the Canadian Championships (Brier) in Fort William (now Thunder Bay), Ontario on March 8, 1960. Andrew McQuiston skipped the Scotland team to a perfect game vs. Switzerland at the Uniroyal Junior Men's World Championship at Kitchener, Ontario, Canada in 1980.

Bernice Fekete, of Edmonton, Alberta, Canada, skipped her rink to two consecutive eight-enders on the same ice at the Derrick Club, Edmonton on January 10 and February 6, 1973.

Two eight-enders in one bonspiel were scored at the Parry Sound Curling Club, Ontario, Canada from January 6–8, 1983.

SLED DOG RACING

Iditarod Trail

Most wins   Rick Swenson has won the event five times: 1977, 1979, 1981–82, 1991. The most wins by a woman is four, by Susan Butcher, in 1986–88, 1990.

Fastest time   The fastest time was set by Doug Swingley (U.S.) in 1995, with 9 days 2 hr. 42 min. 19 sec.

GYMNASTICS

OLYMPIC GAMES

Most gold medals (all events)   Larissa Latynina (USSR) has won nine gold medals: six individual—all-around title, 1956 and 1960; floor exercise, 1956, 1960 and 1964; vault, 1956; and three team titles—1956, 1960 and 1964.

Most gold medals (men)   In men's competition, Sawao Kato (Japan) has won eight gold medals: five individual—all-around title, 1968 and 1972; floor exercise, 1968; and parallel bars, 1972 and 1976; and three team titles—1968, 1972 and 1976.

Most gold medals (individual events)   Vera Caslavska (Czechoslovakia) has won a record seven individual gold medals: all-around title, 1964 and 1968; uneven bars, 1968; beam, 1964; floor exercise, 1968; and vault, 1964 and 1968.

Most gold medals (men)   In men's competition, Boris Shakhlin and Nikolai Andrianov (both USSR) have each won six individual titles. Shakhlin won the all-around title, 1960; parallel bars, 1960; pommel horse, 1956, 1960; horizontal bar, 1964; vault, 1960. Andrianov won the all-around title, 1976; floor exercise, 1972, 1976; rings, 1976; and vault, 1976 and 1980.

Most gold medals (one Olympiad)   Vitaliy Scherbo (Belarus) won a record six golds at one Games in 1992: four individual titles, the all-around and the team gold that he won with the Unified Team.

Most medals (women)   Larisa Latynina won six individual gold medals and was on three winning teams, 1956–64, earning nine gold medals. She also won five silver and four bronze, 18 in all—an Olympic record.

The United States women's gymnastics team celebrating their victory at the '96 Games. Shannon Miller (far right) is the most successful American gymnast in Olympic competition, winning seven medals, 1992–96.

Most medals (men)   The most medals for a male gymnast is 15, by Nikolay Andrianov (USSR)—seven gold, five silver and three bronze, 1972–80.

Most medals (one Olympiad)   Aleksandr Dityatin (USSR) is the only man to win a medal in all eight categories in the same Games, with three gold, four silver and one bronze in Moscow in 1980.

WORLD CHAMPIONSHIPS

Most titles (women)   Larissa Latynina (USSR) won 17 world titles: five team and 12 individual, 1956–64.

Most titles (men)   In the men's competition, Boris Shakhlin (USSR) has won 13 titles: three team and 10 individual, 1954–64.

NCAA CHAMPIONSHIPS (MEN)

Most team titles The most team championships won is nine, by two colleges: Illinois, 1939–42, 1950, 1955–56, 1958, 1989; Penn State, 1948, 1953–54, 1957, 1959–61, 1965, 1976.

Most titles, individual (one year) The record for the most individual titles in a year is four, set by two gymnasts: Jean Cronstedt, Penn State, won the all-around title, parallel bar, horizontal bar and floor exercise in 1954; Robert Lynn, Southern Cal., won the all-around title, parallel bar, horizontal bar and floor exercise in 1962.

Most titles, individual (career) The career record for the most individual titles is seven, by two gymnasts: Joe Giallombardo, Illinois, won the tumbling, 1938–40; all-around title, 1938–40; and flying rings, 1938; Jim Hartung, Nebraska, won the all-around title, 1980–81; rings, 1980–82; and parallel bar, 1981–82.

NCAA CHAMPIONSHIPS (WOMEN)

Most team titles The most team championships won is nine, by Utah, 1982–86, 1990, 1992, 1994–95.

Most titles, individual (one year) The record for the most titles in one year is four, achieved by two gymnasts: Missy Marlowe, Utah, won the all-around, balance beam, uneven bars and floor exercise in 1992; and Jenny Hansen, Kentucky, won the all-around, vault, balance beam and floor exercise in 1995.

Most titles, individual (career) The record for the most titles in a career is eight, by Jenny Hansen, Kentucky. She won the all-around, 1993–95, vault, 1994–95, balance beam, 1994–95 and floor exercise, 1995.

RHYTHMIC SPORT GYMNASTICS

Olympic Games

Most gold medals Alexandra Timoshenko (USSR/CIS) won a record two Olympic medals in the Rhythmic Sport Gymnastics competition: the bronze at the 1988 games in Seoul and the gold at the 1992 games in Barcelona.

Bulgaria has dominated Rhythmic Sport Gymnastics, winning nine world team titles.

EXERCISES

Records are for the most repetitions within the given time span.

Chins—consecutive 370, Lee Chin-yong (South Korea) at Backyon Gymnasium, Seoul, South Korea on May 14, 1988.

Chins—consecutive, one arm, from a ring 22, Robert Chisnall at Queen's University, Kingston, Ontario, Canada on December 3, 1982. (Also 18 2-finger chins, 12 1-finger chins).

Parallel bar dips—1 hour 3,726, Kim Yang-ki (South Korea) at the Rivera Hotel, Seoul, South Korea on November 28, 1991.

Push-ups—24 hours 46,001, Charles Servizio (U.S.) at Fontana City Hall, Fontana, CA on April 24–25, 1993.

Push-ups—one arm, 5 hours 8,794, Paddy Doyle (Great Britain) at Stamina's Kickboxing Self Defence Gym, Birmingham, England on February 12, 1996.

Push-ups—fingertip, 5 hours 7,011, Kim Yang-ki (South Korea) at the Swiss Guard Hotel, Seoul, South Korea on August 30, 1990.

Push-ups—consecutive, one finger 124, Paul Lynch (Great Britain) at the Hippodrome, London, England on April 21, 1992.

Push-ups in a year Paddy Doyle (Great Britain) achieved a documented 1,500,230 push-ups, October 1988–October 1989.

Leg lifts—12 hours 41,788, Lou Scripa Jr. at Jack La Lanne's American Health & Fitness Spa, Sacramento, CA on December 2, 1988.

Somersaults Ashrita Furman performed 8,341 forward rolls in 10 hr. 30 min. over 12 miles 390 yd., Lexington to Charleston, MA on April 30, 1986.

Backwards somersaults—Shigeru Iwasaki somersaulted backwards 54.68 yd. in 10.8 sec. in Tokyo, Japan on March 30, 1980.

Squats—1 hour 4,289, Paul Wai Man Chung at the Yee Gin Kung Fu of Chung Sze Health (HK) Association, Kowloon, Hong Kong on April 5, 1993.

Squat thrusts—1 hour 3,552, Paul Wai Man Chung at the Yee Gin Kung Fu of Chung Sze Kung Fu (HK) Association, Kowloon, Hong Kong on April 21, 1992.

Burpees—1 hour 1,840, Paddy Doyle at the Bull's Head, Polesworth, England on February 6, 1994.

Pummel horse double circles—consecutive 97, Tyler Farstad (Canada) at Surrey Gymnastic Society, Surrey, British Columbia on November 27, 1993.

Static wall sit (Samson's chair) 11 hr. 5 min., Rajikumar Chakraborty (India) at Panposh Sports Hostel, Rourkel, India on April 22, 1994.

MOST PUSH-UPS (24 HOURS)

The most push-ups performed in one day is 46,001. This feat was performed by Charles Servizio in Fontana, CA on April 24–25, 1993.

For rules, see page 707.

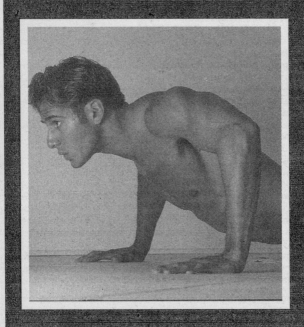

World Championships

Most titles (individual)   The most overall individual world championships is three, by two gymnasts: Maria Gigova (Bulgaria), 1969, 1971 and 1973 (tied); and Maria Petrova (Bulgaria), 1993–95.

Most titles (country)   Bulgaria has won nine team championships: 1969, 1971, 1981, 1983, 1985, 1987, 1989 (tie), 1993 and 1995.

Big Plays

Largest aerobics display   The largest number of participants was 30,517 for the Great Singapore Workout at The Padang, Singapore on August 27, 1995.

TRAMPOLINING

World Championships

Most titles   Judy Wills (U.S.) has won a record five individual world titles, 1964–68. The men's record is two, shared by six trampolinists: Wayne Miller (U.S.), 1966 and 1970; Dave Jacobs (U.S.), 1967–68; Richard Tisson (France), 1974 and 1976; Yevgeniy Yanes (USSR), 1976 and 1978; Lionel Pioline (France), 1984 and 1986; and Alexander Moskalenko (USSR/Russia), 1990 and 1992.

Most somersaults (consecutive)   Christopher Gibson performed 3,025 consecutive somersaults in Shipley Park, Derbyshire, England on November 17, 1989.

Most somersaults (one minute)   The most complete somersaults in one minute is 75, by Richard Cobbing of Lightwater, England, in London, England on November 8, 1989.

Most baranis (one minute)   The most baranis in a minute is 78, by Zoe Finn of Chatham, England in London, England on January 25, 1988.

TRACK & FIELD

OLYMPIC GAMES

Most gold medals (career—men)   Ray Ewry (U.S.) holds the all-time record for most appearances atop the winners' podium, with 10 gold medals: standing high jump (1900, 1904, 1906, 1908); standing long jump (1900, 1904, 1906, 1908); standing triple jump (1900, 1904).

Most gold medals (career—women)   The women's record is four, shared by four athletes: Fanny Blankers-Koen (Netherlands): 100 m, 200 m, 80 m hurdles and 4 × 100 m relay in 1948; Betty Cuthbert (Australia): 100 m,

200 m, 4 × 100 m relay in 1956, and 400 m in 1964; Barbel Wockel (née Eckert; East Germany): 200 m and 4 × 100 m relay in both 1976 and 1980; and Evelyn Ashford (U.S.): 100 m and 4 × 100 m relay in 1984, 4 × 100 m relay in 1988, 4 × 100 m relay in 1992.

Most gold medals (one Games) Paavo Nurmi (Finland) won five gold medals at the 1924 Games. His victories came in the 1,500 m, 5,000 m, 10,000 m cross-country, 3,000 m team, and cross-country team. The most wins at individual events (not including relay or other team races) is four, by Alvin Kraenzlein (U.S.) in 1900 at 60 m, 110 m hurdles, 200 m hurdles and the long jump.

Most medals won (career—men) Paavo Nurmi (Finland) won 12 medals (nine gold, three silver) in 1920, 1924 and 1928.

Most medals won (career—women) The women's record is seven, shared by three athletes: Shirley de la Hunty (Australia), three gold, one silver, three bronze in the 1948, 1952 and 1956 Games; Irena Szewinska (Poland), three gold, two silver, two bronze in the 1964, 1968, 1972 and 1976 Games; and Merlene Ottey (Jamaica), two silver, five bronze in the 1980, 1984, 1992 and 1996 Games.

Oldest champion (men) The oldest athlete to win an Olympic title was Irish-born Babe McDonald (b. McDonnell; U.S.), who was age 42 yr. 26 days when he won the 56 lb. weight throw in Antwerp, Belgium on August 21, 1920.

Oldest champion (women) The oldest female champion was Lia Manoliu (Romania), age 36 yr. 176 days when she won the discus in Mexico City on October 18, 1968.

Youngest champion (women) The youngest gold medalist was Barbara Pearl Jones (U.S.), who at 15 yr. 123 days was a member of the winning 4 × 100 m relay team, in Helsinki, Finland on July 27, 1952.

Youngest champion (men) The youngest male champion was Bob Mathias (U.S.), age 17 yr. 263 days when he won the decathlon at the London Games, August 5–6, 1948.

Oldest medalist (men) The oldest Olympic medalist was Tebbs Lloyd Johnson (Great Britain), age 48 yr. 115 days when he was third in the 1948 50,000-m walk.

Oldest medalist (women) The oldest woman medalist was Dana Zátopková (Czechoslovakia), age 37 yr. 348 days when she was second in the javelin in 1960.

WORLD CHAMPIONSHIPS

Most gold medals (men) The record for the most gold medals is eight, achieved by Carl Lewis (U.S.) in three events: 100 meter, long jump, 4 × 100 meter relay, in 1983 and 1987; and 100 meter, 4 × 100 meter relay in 1991.

Most gold medals (women)   The most gold medals won by a woman is four, by Jackie Joyner-Kersee (U.S.)—long jump 1987, 1991; heptathlon 1987, 1993.

Most medals (women)   The most medals won is 14, by Merlene Ottey (Jamaica)—three gold, four silver and seven bronze, 1983–97.

Most medals (men)   The most medals won by a man is 10, by Carl Lewis (U.S.)—a record eight gold, one silver and one bronze, 1983–93.

Jamaica's Merlene Ottey has won more medals at the World Championships than any other athlete.

TRACK AND FIELD RECORDS—Women

World records for the women's events scheduled by the International Amateur Athletic Federation.

Running	Time	Name and Country	Place	Date
100 meters	0:10.49	Florence Griffith Joyner (U.S.)	Indianapolis, IN	Jul. 16, 1988
200 meters	0:21.34	Florence Griffith Joyner (U.S.)	Seoul, South Korea	Sep. 29, 1988
400 meters	0:47.60	Marita Koch (East Germany)	Canberra, Australia	Oct. 6, 1985
800 meters	1:53.28	Jarmila Kratochvílová (Czechoslovakia)	Munich, Germany	Jul. 26, 1983
1,000 meters	2:29.34	Maria Mutola (Mozambique)	Brussels, Belgium	Aug. 25, 1995
1,500 meters	3:50.46	Qu Yunxia (China)	Beijing, China	Sep. 11, 1993
1 mile	4:12.56	Svetlana Masterkova (Russia)	Zurich, Switzerland	Aug. 14, 1996
2,000 meters	5:25.36	Sonia O'Sullivan (Ireland)	Edinburgh, Scotland	Jul. 8, 1994
3,000 meters	8:06.11	Wang Junxia (China)	Beijing, China	Sep. 13, 1993
5,000 meters	14:36.45	Fernanda Ribeiro (Portugal)	Hechtel, Belgium	Jul. 22, 1995
10,000 meters	29:31.78	Wang Junxia (China)	Beijing, China	Sep. 8, 1993

Hurdling

100 meters (2' 9")	0:12.21	Yordanka Donkova (Bulgaria)	Stara Zagora, Bulgaria	Aug. 20, 1988
400 meters (2' 6")	0:52.61	Kim Batten (U.S.)	Gothenburg, Sweden	Aug. 11, 1995

Relays

4 × 100 meters	0:41.37	East Germany	Canberra, Australia	Oct. 6, 1985
		(Silke Gladisch, Sabine Rieger, Ingrid Auerswald, Marlies Göhr)		
4 × 200 meters	1:28.15	East Germany	Jena, Germany	Aug. 9, 1980
		(Marlies Göhr, Romy Müller, Bärbel Wöckel, Marita Koch)		
4 × 400 meters	3:15.17	USSR	Seoul, South Korea	Oct. 1, 1988
		(Tatyana Ledovskaya, Olga Nazarova, Maria Pinigina, Olga Bryzgina)		
4 × 800 meters	7:50.17	USSR	Moscow, USSR	Aug. 5, 1984
		(Nadezhda Olizarenko, Lyubov Gurina, Lyudmila Borisova, Irina Podyalovskaya)		

Field Events

	m	ft.	in.			
High jump	2.09	6	10¼	Stefka Kostadinova (Bulgaria)	Rome, Italy	Aug. 30, 1987
Pole vault	4.55	14	11	Emma George (Australia)	Melbourne, Australia	Feb. 20, 1997
Long jump	7.52	24	8¼	Galina Chistyakova (USSR)	Leningrad, USSR	Jun. 11, 1988
Triple jump	15.50	50	10¼	Inessa Kravets (Ukraine)	Göteborg, Sweden	Aug. 10, 1995
Shot 8 lb. 13 oz.	22.63	74	.3	Natalya Lisovskaya (USSR)	Moscow, USSR	Jun. 7, 1987
Discus 2 lb. 3 oz.	76.80	252	.0	Gabriele Reinsch (East Germany)	Neubrandenburg, Germany	Jul. 9, 1988
Javelin 24 lb. 7 oz.	80.00	262	.5	Petra Felke (East Germany)	Potsdam, Germany	Sep. 9, 1988
Heptathlon	7,291 points			Jacqueline Joyner-Kersee (U.S.)	Seoul, South Korea	Sep. 23–24, 1988

TRACK AND FIELD RECORDS—Men

World records for the men's events scheduled by the International Amateur Athletic Federation. Fully automatic electric timing is mandatory for events up to 400 meters.

Running	Time	Name & Country	Place	Date
100 meters	0:9.84*	Donovan Bailey (Canada)	Atlanta, GA.	Jul. 27, 1996
200 meters	0:19.32	Michael Johnson (U.S.)	Atlanta, GA.	Aug. 1, 1996
400 meters	0:43.29	Butch Reynolds Jr. (U.S.)	Zurich, Switzerland	Aug. 17, 1988
800 meters	1:41.11	Wilson Kipketer (Denmark)	Cologne, Germany	Aug. 24, 1997
1,000 meters	2:12.18	Sebastian Coe (Great Britain)	Oslo, Norway	Jul. 11, 1981
1,500 meters	3:27.37	Noureddine Morceli (Algeria)	Nice, France	Jul. 12, 1995
1 mile	3:44.39	Noureddine Morceli (Algeria)	Rieti, Italy	Sep. 5, 1993
2,000 meters	4:47.88	Noureddine Morceli (Algeria)	Paris, France	Jul. 13, 1995
3,000 meters	7:20.67	Daniel Komen (Kenya)	Rieti, Italy	Sep. 1, 1996
5,000 meters	12:39.74	Daniel Komen (Kenya)	Brussels, Belgium	Aug. 22, 1997
10,000 meters	26:27.85	Paul Tergat (Kenya)	Brussels, Belgium	Aug. 22, 1997
20,000 meters	56:55.6	Arturo Barrios (Mexico)	La Flèche, France	Mar. 30, 1991
25,000 meters	1 hr. 13:55.8	Toshihiko Seko (Japan)	Christchurch, New Zealand	Mar. 22, 1981
30,000 meters	1 hr. 29:18.8	Toshihiko Seko (Japan)	Christchurch, New Zealand	Mar. 22, 1981
1 hour	13.111 miles	Arturo Barrios (Mexico)	La Flèche, France	May 30, 1991

* Ben Johnson (Canada) ran 100 m in 9.79 seconds in Seoul, South Korea on Sep. 24, 1988, but was subsequently disqualified when he tested positive for steroids. He later admitted to having taken drugs over many years, and this also invalidated his 9.83 sec. in Rome, Italy on Aug. 30, 1987.

Hurdling				
110 meters (3' 6")	0:12.91	Colin Jackson (Great Britain)	Stuttgart, Germany	Aug. 20, 1993
400 meters (3' 0")	0:46.78	Kevin Young (U.S.)	Barcelona, Spain	Aug. 6, 1992
3,000 meter steeplechase	7:55.72	Bernard Barmasai (Kenya)	Cologne, Germany	Aug. 24, 1997

Relays

4 × 100 meters	0:37.40	United States	Barcelona, Spain	Aug. 8, 1992
		(Mike Marsh, Leroy Burrell, Dennis Mitchell, Carl Lewis)		
	0:37.40	United States	Stuttgart, Germany	Aug. 22, 1993
		(John Drummond, Andre Cason, Dennis Mitchell, Leroy Burrell)		
4 × 200 meters	1:18.68	Santa Monica Track Club	Walnut, CA	Apr. 17, 1994
		(Mike Marsh, Leroy Burrell, Floyd Heard, Carl Lewis)		
4 × 400 meters	2:54.29	United States	Stuttgart, Germany	Aug. 22, 1993
		(Andrew Valmon, Quincy Watts, Butch Reynolds, Michael Johnson)		
4 × 800 meters	7:03.89	Great Britain	London, England	Aug. 30, 1982
		(Peter Elliott, Garry Peter Cook, Steven Cram, Sebastian Coe)		
4 × 1,500 meters	14:38.8	Germany	Cologne, Germany	Aug. 17, 1977
		(Thomas Wessinghage, Harald Hudak, Michael Lederer, Karl Fleschen)		

Field Events

	m	ft.	in.			
High jump	2.45	8	0½	Javier Sotomayor (Cuba)	Salamanca, Spain	Jul. 27, 1993
Pole vault	6.14*	20	1¾	Sergey Bubka (Ukraine)	Sestriere, Italy	Jul. 31, 1994
Long jump	8.96	29	4½	Mike Powell (U.S.)	Tokyo, Japan	Aug. 30, 1991
Triple jump	18.29	60	¼	Jonathan Edwards (Great Britain)	Göteborg, Sweden	Aug. 7, 1995
Shot 16 lb.	23.12	75	10¼	Randy Barnes (U.S.)	Los Angeles, CA	May 20, 1990
Discus 4 lb. 8 oz.	74.08	243	0	Jürgen Schult (East Germany)	Neubrandenburg, Germany	Jun. 6, 1986
Hammer 16 lb.	86.74	284	7	Yuriy Sedykh (USSR)	Stuttgart, Germany	Aug. 30, 1986
Javelin	98.48	323	1	Jan Zelezny (Czech Republic)	Jena, Germany	May 25, 1996
Decathlon	8,891 points			Dan O'Brien (U.S.)	Talence, France	Sep. 4–5, 1992

*This record was set at high altitude. Best mark at low altitude: 20 ft. 1¼ in. by Sergey Bubka, Tokyo, Japan, Sep. 19, 1992.

THE *FASTEST MAN* ALIVE

Canadian Donovan Bailey rocketed into the record books when he set a new world mark at 9.84 seconds for the 100 meter dash at the Atlanta Olympics. "I had been training really hard and knew I was capable of breaking the record from the times I was doing in practice sessions. But I was very surprised that I did it in Atlanta," says Bailey. "It was the biggest stage to do it on. I was very elated."

Bailey was born in Jamaica and was fast from an early age. "We start school at three and have a 'Sports Day' where you test your skills against your friends. In Jamaica you start participating in track and field when you are four years old," he says. The sprinter moved to Ontario, Canada when he was 12. He ran track and played basketball in high school and college, but then abandoned the track for six years. "I really got bored. The moti-

ON THE RECORD

100 METER WORLD RECORD

Donovan Bailey (Canada) ran the 100-meter dash in 9.84 seconds at the Olympic Games in Atlanta, GA on July 27, 1996.

vation wasn't there for track," declares Bailey. His time was occupied by his studies. At 20 years old, he graduated from college with a degree in economics and then formed his own marketing company.

In 1991 Bailey was playing in a Toronto recreational basketball league when he got the urge to try track again. "One day, I went with spikes I still had from high school to a track meet. I got into the meet and won the 60-meter race," recalls Bailey. By the end of the year Bailey was ranked as one of Canada's top three sprinters. But Bailey's road to the record had another detour. In 1992, he failed to make Canada's Olympic team due to an injury. "It was devastating. Guys I had beaten several times were there and I wasn't," says Bailey. But four years later, he made up for missing Barcelona.

In the wake of his Olympic triumph, Bailey didn't gain the normally automatic title of "world's fastest human" that goes to the 100-meter world record holder. With his record-setting feat in the 200 meters, American sprinter Michael Johnson sparked a debate about who was the fastest runner. "No one has ever run as fast as I have, running 27 mph," declares Bailey. "But I don't know if it's an apt description anyway. In setting the record, I still made major mistakes and I think I can get better."

BIG PLAYS

Most track records (one day)   Jesse Owens (U.S.) set six world records in 45 minutes in Ann Arbor, MI on May 25, 1935, with a 9.4-second 100 yards, a 26-ft.-8¼-in. long jump, a 20.3-second 220 yards (and 200 m), and a 22.6-second 220 yards (and 200 m) low hurdles.

Highest jump   The greatest height cleared above an athlete's own head is 23¼ inches, by Franklin Jacobs (U.S.), 5 ft. 8 in. tall, who jumped 7 ft. 7¼ in. in New York City, on January 27, 1978. The women's record is 12¾ inches, by Yolanda Henry (U.S.), 5 ft. 6 in. tall, who jumped 6 ft. 6¾ in. in Seville, Spain on May 30, 1990.

Highest standing jump   The best high jump from a standing position is 6 ft. 2¾ in., by Rune Almen (Sweden) in Karlstad, Sweden on May 3, 1980. The women's best is 4 ft. 11¾ in., by Grete Bjørdalsbakka (Norway) in Flisa, Norway in 1984.

Longest standing jump   The best long jump from a standing position is 12 ft. 2 in., by Arne Tvervaag (Norway) in 1968. The women's record is 9 ft. 7 in., by Annelin Mannes (Norway) in Flisa, Norway on March 7, 1981.

Oldest record breaker   Gerhard Weidner (Germany) set a 20-mile walk record on May 25, 1974, at age 41 yr. 71 days, thus becoming the oldest to set an official world record recognized by an international governing body.

Youngest record breaker   The youngest individual record breaker is Wang Yan (China), who set a women's 5,000 m walk record at age 14 yr. 334 days with 21 min. 33.8 sec. in Jian, China on March 9, 1986. The youngest male is Thomas Ray (Great Britain) at 17 yr. 198 days when he pole-vaulted 11 ft. 2¾ in. on September 19, 1879 (prior to IAAF ratification).

Svetlana Masterkova of Russia is the world record–holder in the mile.

Longest winning sequence Iolanda Balas (Romania) won 150 consecutive competitions in high jump, 1956–67. The record in a track event is 122, in 400 m hurdles, by Edwin Moses (U.S.) between his loss to Harald Schmid (West Germany) in Berlin, Germany on August 26, 1977 and his loss to Danny Lee Harris (U.S.) in Madrid, Spain on June 4, 1987.

Mass relay (100 miles) The record for 100 miles by 100 runners from one club is 7 hr. 53 min. 52.1 sec., by the Baltimore Road Runners Club, Towson, MD on May 17, 1981. The women's record is 10 hr. 15 min. 29.5 sec. on July 29, 1995, by the Dolphin South End Runners, Los Altos Hills, CA.

Jan Zelezny of the Czech Republic is the world record–holder in the javelin.

Mass relay (100 × 100m) The record for 100 × 100 m is 19 min. 14.19 sec., by a team from Antwerp in Merksem, Belgium on September 23, 1989.

Mass relay (24 hours) The greatest distance covered in 24 hours by a team of 10 is 302.281 miles, by Puma Tyneside RC at Monkton Stadium, Jarrow, England, September 10–11, 1994.

MARATHONS

Olympic Games

Most gold medals The most wins in the men's race is two, by two runners: Abebe Bikila (Ethiopia), 1960 and 1964; Waldemar Cierpinski (East Germany), 1976 and 1980. The women's event has been run four times, with different winners each time.

World Championships

Most wins No athlete in either the men's or women's division has won the world title more than once.

Boston Marathon

Most wins (men) Clarence De Mar (U.S.) won the race seven times— 1911, 1922–24, 1927–28, 1930.

ULTRA LONG DISTANCE RECORDS

Event	Time	Name and Country	Place	Date
MEN				
Track				
50 km	2:48:06	Jeff Norman (Great Britain)	Manchester, England	Jun. 7, 1980
100 km	6:10:20	Don Ritchie	London, England	Oct. 28, 1978
200 km	15:11:10	Yiannis Kouros (Greece)	Montauban, France	Mar. 15–16, 1985
500 km	60:23:00	Yiannis Kouros	Colac, Australia	Nov. 26–29, 1984
1,000 km	136:17:00	Yiannis Kouros	Colac, Australia	Nov. 26–Dec. 1, 1984
Kilometers				
24 hours	293.704	Yiannis Kouros (Greece; now Australia)	Coburg, Australia	Apr. 13–14, 1996
48 hours	473.496	Yiannis Kouros (Greece; now Australia)	Surgères, France	May 3–5, 1996
WOMEN				
Track				
50 km	3:18.52	Carolyn Hunter-Rowe	Barry, Wales	Mar. 3, 1996
100 km	7:50:09	Ann Trason (U.S.)	Hayward, CA	Aug. 3–4, 1991
200 km	19:28:48*	Eleanor Adams (Great Britain)	Melbourne, Australia	Aug. 19–20, 1989
500 km	77:53:46	Eleanor Adams (Great Britain)	Colac, Australia	Nov. 13–15, 1989
Kilometers				
24 hours	240.169	Eleanor Adams (Great Britain)	Melbourne, Australia	Aug. 19–20, 1989
48 hours	366.512	Hilary Walker (Great Britain)	Blackpool, England	Nov. 5–7, 1988

No stopped time known.

TOP THIS

FASTEST MARATHON TOSSING A PANCAKE

The fastest time for completing an official marathon while continuously flipping a pancake is 3 hr 6 min. 22 sec., by Dominic Cuzzacrea in the Buffalo Nissan Marathon on May 6, 1990.

For rules, see page 707.

Most wins (women)   The women's division has been won three times by two women: Rosa Mota (Portugal), 1987–88, 1990, and Uta Pippig (Germany), 1994–96. Prior to 1972, when the marathon was opened to women, two women "unofficially" won the women's division three times each: Roberta Gibb (U.S.) 1966–68; and Sarah Mae Berman (U.S.) in 1969–71.

Fastest time   The course record for men is 2 hr. 7 min. 15 sec., by Cosmas Ndeti (Kenya) in 1994. The women's record is 2 hr. 21 min. 45 sec., by Uta Pippig (Germany) in 1994.

Most races   John A. Kelley (U.S.) finished the Boston Marathon 62 times through 1993, winning twice, in 1933 and 1945.

New York City Marathon

Most wins (women)   Grete Waitz (Norway) has won nine times—1978–80, 1982–86 and 1988.

Most wins (men)   Bill Rodgers has a men's record four wins—1976–79.

Fastest time   The course record for men is 2 hr. 8 min. 1 sec., by Juma Ikangaa (Tanzania) in 1989, and for women, 2 hr. 24 min. 40 sec., by Lisa Ondieki (Australia) in 1992.

Big Plays

Fastest time   The following are the best times recorded, all on courses with verified distances: for men, 2 hr. 6 min. 50 sec., by Belayneh Dinsamo (Ethiopia) in Rotterdam, Netherlands on April 17, 1988; for women, 2 hr. 21 min. 6 sec., by Ingrid Kristiansen (née Christensen; Norway) in London, England on April 21, 1985.

Highest altitude   The highest start for a marathon is the biennially held Everest Marathon, first run on November 27, 1987. It begins at Gorak Shep at 17,100 feet and ends at Namche Bazar, 11,300 feet. The fastest times to finish this race are (*men*) 3 hr. 59 min. 4 sec., by Jack Maitland in 1989; (*women*) 5 hr. 32 min. 43 sec., by Cath Proctor in 1993.

Most competitors   The record number of confirmed finishers in a marathon is 38,706 in the centennial Boston race on April 15, 1996.

Most marathons   As of May 29, 1996, Horst Preisler (Germany) had run 631 races of 26 mi. 385 yd. or longer, starting in 1974. Henri Girault (France) has run 330 races of 100 km (an IAAF-recognized distance) from 1979 to June 1996 and has completed a run on every continent except Antarctica.

Triple marathons   The fastest combined time for three marathons in three days is 8 hr. 22 min. 31 sec., by Raymond Hubbard (Belfast, Northern Ireland: 2 hr. 45 min. 55 sec.; London, England: 2 hr. 48 min. 45 sec.; and Boston: 2 hr. 47 min. 51 sec.), April 16–18, 1988.

The highest altitude at which any marathon race is started is 17,100 feet for the beginning of the Everest Marathon.

Oldest finisher (men) Dimitrion Yordanidis (Greece) was aged 98 when he completed a marathon in Athens, Greece on October 10, 1976 in 7 hr. 33 min.

Oldest finisher (women) The women's record was set by Thelma Pitt-Turner (New Zealand) in August 1985 when she completed the Hastings, New Zealand Marathon in 7 hr. 58 min. at age 82.

Pancake tossing Dominic M. Cuzzacrea (U.S.) of Lockport, NY ran the Buffalo, New York Nissan Marathon (26.2 miles) while flipping a pancake in a time of 3 hr. 6 min. 22 sec. on May 6, 1990.

Baby carriage-pushing Tabby Puzey pushed a baby buggy while running the Abingdon half marathon in Abingdon, England, on April 13, 1986 in 2 hr. 4 min. 9 sec.

Running backwards Bud Badyna (U.S.) ran the fastest backwards marathon in 3 hr. 53 min. 17 sec. in Toledo, OH on April 24, 1994.

Joggling with three balls Ashrita Furman (U.S.) juggled during a 26 mi. 385 yd. marathon in 3 hr. 22 min. 32.5 sec in 1998.

Half marathon The world best time on a properly measured course is 58 min. 31 sec. by Paul Tergat (Kenya) in Milan, Italy on March 30, 1996.

Ingrid Kristiansen (Norway) ran 66 min. 40 sec. in Sandes, Norway on April 5, 1987, but the course measurement has not been confirmed. Liz McColgan ran 67 min. 11 sec. in Tokyo, Japan on January 26, 1992, but the course was 33 m downhill, a little more than the allowable 1-in-1,000 drop.

LONG DISTANCE RUNNING

Big Plays

Greatest mileage Ron Hill, the 1969 European and 1970 Commonwealth marathon champion, has not missed a day's training since December 20, 1964. His meticulously compiled training log shows a total of 131,585 miles from September 3, 1956 to May 20, 1996. He has finished 115 marathons, all sub 2:52 (except his last one) and has raced in 57 nations.

Longest run The longest run by an individual is one of 11,134 miles around the United States, by Sarah Covington-Fulcher (U.S.), starting and finishing in Los Angeles, CA, from July 21, 1987 to October 2, 1988.

Around Australia In 1983 Ron Grant (Australia) ran around Australia, covering 8,316 miles in 217 days 3 hr. 45 min.

Trans-Americas The fastest time for the cross-America run is 46 days 8 hr. 36 min., by Frank Giannino, Jr. (U.S.) for the 3,100 miles from San Francisco to New York, September 1 to October 17, 1980. The women's record is 69 days 2 hr. 40 min., by Mavis Hutchinson (South Africa), March 12 to May 21, 1978.

Trans-Canada   Al Howie (Great Britain) ran across Canada, from St. Johns, Newfoundland to Victoria, British Columbia, a distance of 4,533.2 miles, in 72 days 10 hr. 23 min., from June 21 to September 1, 1991.

Across the United States   The fastest time for the cross-America run is 46 days 8 hr. 36 min., by Frank Giannino, Jr. (U.S.) for the 3,100 miles from San Francisco to New York, September 1 to October 17, 1980. The women's record is 69 days 2 hr. 40 min., by Mavis Hutchinson (South Africa), March 12 to May 21, 1978.

Roof of the world   Ultra runner Hilary Walker ran from Lhasa, Tibet to Kathmandu, Nepal, a distance of 590 miles, in 14 days 9 hr. 36 min. from September 18 to October 2, 1991. The run was made at an average altitude of 13,780 feet.

1,000-hour distance   Ron Grant (Australia) ran 1.86 miles within an hour, every hour, for 1,000 consecutive hours in New Farm Park, Brisbane, Queensland, Australia from February 6 to March 20, 1991.

Longest running race   The longest race staged annually is the New York 1,300 Mile race, held in Ward Island Park, NY. The fastest time to complete the race is 16 days 14 hr. 28 min. 19 sec. by Georg Jermolajevs (Latvia), September 11–28, 1995.

CROSS-COUNTRY RUNNING

World Championships

Most wins (team)   England has won the men's team event a record 45 times, 1903–14, 1920–21, 1924–25, 1930–38, 1951, 1953–55, 1958–60, 1962, 1964–72, 1976, 1979–80. The women's competition has been won eight times by two countries: United States, 1968–69, 1975, 1979, 1983–85, 1987; USSR, 1976–77, 1980–82, 1988–90.

Most wins (individual)   Two women have won five titles: Doris Brown (U.S.), 1967–71, and Grete Waitz (Norway), 1978–81 and 1983. John Ngugi (Kenya) has won the men's title a record five times, 1986–89 and 1992.

Greatest margin   The greatest margin of victory is 56 seconds or 390 yards by Jack Holden (England) at Ayr Racecourse, Strathclyde, Scotland on March 24, 1934.

Greatest team victory   The greatest team domination was by Kenya in Auckland, New Zealand on March 26, 1988. Kenya's senior men's team finished eight men in the first nine, with a low score of 23 (six to score), and its junior men's team set a record low score 11 (four to score) with six in the first seven. Kenya won the men's senior team title for a record 10th time in succession at the 1995 World Cross-Country Championships.

NCAA Championships

Most titles (men)   Three athletes have won the men's individual title three times: Gerry Lindgren (Washington State), 1966–67 and 1969; Steve Prefontaine (Oregon), 1970–71 and 1973; and Henry Rono (Washington State), 1976–77 and 1979.

Most titles (team—men)   Two teams have won the men's team title a record eight times: Michigan State, 1939, 1948–49, 1952, 1955–56, 1958–59; and Arkansas, 1984, 1986–87, 1990–93, 1995.

Most titles (women)   Three runners have won the title twice: Betty Springs (North Carolina State), 1981 and 1983; Sonia O'Sullivan (Villanova), 1990 and 1991; and Carole Zajac (Villanova), 1992–93.

Most titles (team—women)   In women's competition, Villanova has won the team title six times, 1989–94.

WALKING

Olympic Games

Most gold medals   The only walker to win three gold medals has been Ugo Frigerio (Italy) with the 3,000 m in 1920, and 10,000 m in 1920 and 1924.

Most medals   The record for the most medals is four, achieved by Ugo Frigerio (Italy),who won three gold medals (*see above*) and the bronze in the 50,000 m event in 1932; and Vladimir Stepanovich Golubnichiy (USSR), who won gold medals for the 20,000 m in 1960 and 1968, the silver in 1972 and the bronze in 1964.

Big Plays

Longest race   The race from Paris to Colmar (until 1980 from Strasbourg to Paris) in France (instituted 1926 in the reverse direction), now about 325 miles, is the world's longest annual race walk.

The fastest performance is by Robert Pietquin (Belgium), who walked 315 miles in the 1980 race in 60 hr. 1 min. 10 sec. (after deducting 4-hour compulsory stops). This represents an average speed of 5.25 mph. Roger Quémener (France) has won a record seven times, 1979, 1983, 1985–89.

Most miles (24 hours)   Jesse Castenada (U.S.) walked 142 mi. 440 yd. in Albuquerque, NM, September 18–19, 1976. The best 24-hour distance by a woman is 131.27 miles, by Annie van der Meer-Timmerman (Netherlands) in Rouen, France, May 10–11, 1986.

Most miles (walking on hands)   The distance record is 870 miles, by Johann Hurlinger (Austria), who averaged 1.58 mph from Vienna, Austria to Paris, France in 1900.

Fastest mile, relay (walking on hands)   The 4-man relay team of David Lutterman, Brendan Price, Philip Savage and Danny Scannell covered one mile in 24 min. 48 sec. on March 15, 1987 in Knoxville, TN.

TRACK WALKING RECORDS

The International Amateur Athletic Federation recognizes men's records at 20 km, 30 km, 50 km and 2 hours, and women's at 5 km and 10 km.

Event	Time	Name and Country	Place	Date
MEN				
20 km	1:17:25.6	Bernardo Segura (Mexico)	Bergen, Norway	May 7, 1994
30 km	2:01:44.1	Maurizio Damilano (Italy)	Cuneo, Italy	Oct. 4, 1992
50 km	3:40:57.9	Thierry Toutain (France)	Hericourt, France	Sept. 29, 1996
2 hours	29,572 m	Maurizio Damilano (Italy)	Cuneo, Italy	Oct. 4, 1992
WOMEN				
5 km	20:13.26	Kerry Saxby-Junna (Australia)	Hobart, Australia	Feb. 25, 1996
10 km	41:56.23	Nadezhda Ryashkina (USSR)	Seattle, WA	Jul. 24, 1990

Fastest 50 meters (walking on hands)   Mark Kenny (U.S.) completed a 50 meter inverted sprint in 16.93 seconds in Norwood, MA on February 16, 1994.

GOING BACKWARDS

Backwards Running

Fastest 100 yards   Ferdie Ato Adoboe (Ghana) ran 100 yards backwards in 12.7 seconds at Smith College, Northampton, MA on July 25, 1991.

Fastest mile   Donald Davis (U.S.) ran one mile in 6 min. 7.1 sec. at the University of Hawaii on February 21, 1983.

Fastest 10 km   Bud Badyna ran 10 km backwards in 45 min. 37 sec. in Toledo on July 13, 1991.

Fastest marathon   (*see* RUNNING BACKWARDS, *page 666*)

Longest distance   Arvind Pandya (India) ran backwards across the U.S., Los Angeles to New York, in 107 days, August 18–December 3, 1984.
     He also ran backwards from John O'Groat's to Land's End in 26 days 7 hr., April 6–May 2, 1990.

Walking Backwards

Greatest distance   Plennie L. Wingo walked backwards 8,000 miles from Santa Monica, CA to Istanbul, Turkey from April 15, 1931 to October 24, 1932.

Most miles (24 hours)   The longest distance recorded for walking backwards in 24 hours is 95.40 miles, achieved by Anthony Thornton (U.S.) in Minneapolis, MN, December 31, 1988 to January 1, 1989.

JUGGLING

3 Objects Aloft

Fastest 100 meters   Owen Morse (U.S.) juggled three objects a distance of 100 m in 11.68 seconds in 1989.

Fastest 400 meters   Owen Morse also juggled three objects a distance of 400 m in 57.32 seconds in 1990.

Fastest mile   Kirk Swenson (U.S.) juggled three objects a distance of one mile in 4 min. 43 sec. in 1986.

Fastest 5,000 meters   The record for the fastest time in 5,000 meters (3.1 miles) is 16 min. 55 sec., by Kirk Swenson in 1986.

Fastest marathon   (*see* JOGGLING WITH 3 BALLS, *PAGE 285*)

Fastest 50 miles   The record for the fastest time juggling three objects for 50 miles is 8 hr. 52 min. 7 sec. in 1989, achieved by Ashrita Furman (U.S.).

Fastest 110-m hurdles   Albert Lucas (U.S.) juggled a distance of 110 m over hurdles in 18.58 seconds in April 1997.

Fastest 400-m hurdles   Albert Lucas (U.S.) juggled a distance of 400 m over hurdles in 1 min. 7 sec. in 1993.

Fastest mile, relay   Owen Morse, Albert Lucas, Tuey Wilson and John Wee (all U.S.) juggled a one mile relay in 3 min. 57.38 sec. in 1990.

5 Objects Aloft

Fastest 100 meters   The record for the fastest time juggling five objects aloft for 100 meters is 13.8 seconds, by Owen Morse (U.S.).

Fastest mile   Bill Gillen (U.S.) juggled five objects a distance of one mile in 7 min. 41.01 sec. in 1989.

Fastest 5 km   Barry Goldmeier (U.S.) juggled five objects over a distance of 3.1 miles (5 km) in 27 min. 53 sec. in 1996.

Albert Lucas holds the world record for the 110m hurdles while juggling 3 objects.

INDOOR TRACK AND FIELD RECORDS

Track performances around a turn must be made on a track of circumference no longer than 200 meters.
World Championships: The most individual titles is four, shared by Stefka Kostadinova (Bulgaria), highjump 1985, 1987, 1989, 1993; by Mikhail Schennikov (Russia), 5,000 m walk 1987, 1989, 1991, 1993; and by Sergey Bubka (Ukraine), pole vault 1985, 1987, 1991, 1995.

Event	Time	Name and Country	Place	Date
MEN				
Running				
50 meters	0:5.56*	Donovan Bailey (Canada)	Reno, NV	Feb. 9, 1996
60 meters	0:6.41	Andre Cason (U.S.)	Madrid, Spain	Feb. 14, 1992
200 meters	0:19.92	Frank Fredericks (Namibia)	Liévin, France	Feb. 18, 1996
400 meters	0:44.63	Michael Johnson (U.S.)	Atlanta, GA	Mar. 4, 1995
800 meters	1:42.67	Wilson Kipketer (Denmark)	Paris, France	Mar. 9, 1997
1,000 meters	2:15.26	Noureddine Morceli (Algeria)	Birmingham, England	Feb. 22, 1992
1,500 meters	3:31.18	Hicham-el Guerroj (Morocco)	Stuttgart, Germany	Feb. 2, 1997
1 mile	3:48.45	Hicham-el Guerroj (Morocco)	Ghent, Belgium	Feb. 12, 1997
3,000 meters	7:35.15	Moses Kiptanui (Kenya)	Ghent, Belgium	Feb. 12, 1995
5,000 meters	12:59.04	Haile Gebrselassie (Ethiopia)	Stockholm, Sweden	Feb. 20, 1997
50 meter hurdles	0:6.25	Mark McKoy (Canada)	Kobe, Japan	Mar. 5, 1986
60 meter hurdles	0:7.30	Colin Jackson (Great Britain)	Sindelfingen, Germany	Mar. 6, 1994

* Set at high altitude; best at low altitude: 5.61 sec. by Manfred Kokot (GDR) in Berlin, Germany on Feb. 4, 1973 and James Sanford (U.S.) in San Diego, CA on Feb. 20, 1981.

Relays				
4 × 200 meters	1:22.11	United Kingdom	Glasgow, Scotland	Mar. 3, 1991
		(Linford Christie, Darren Braithwaite, Ade Mafe, John Regis)		
4 × 400 meters	3:03.05	Germany	Seville, Spain	Mar. 10, 1991
		(Rico Lieder, Jens Carlowitz, Karsten Just, Thomas Schönlebe)		

Walking

5,000 meters	18:07.08	Mikhail Schennikov (Russia)	Moscow, Russia	Feb. 14, 1995

Field Events

	m	ft.	in.			
High jump	2.43	7	11½	Javier Sotomayor (Cuba)	Budapest, Hungary	Mar. 4, 1989
Pole vault	6.15	20	2¼	Sergey Nazarovich Bubka (Ukraine)	Donetsk, Ukraine	Feb. 21, 1993
Long jump	8.79	28	10¼	Carl Lewis (U.S.)	New York, NY	Jan. 27, 1984
Triple jump	17.77	58	3½	Leonid Voloshin (Russia)	Grenoble, France	Feb. 6, 1994
Shot	22.66	74	4¼	Randy Barnes (U.S.)	Los Angeles, CA	Jan. 20, 1989
Heptathlon	6,476 points			Dan O'Brien (U.S.)	Toronto, Canada	Mar. 13–14, 1993

WOMEN
Running

50 meters	0:5.96	Irina Privalova (Russia)	Madrid, Spain	Feb. 9, 1995
60 meters	0:6.92	Irina Privalova	Madrid, Spain	Feb. 11, 1993
	0:6.92	Irina Privalova	Madrid, Spain	Feb. 9, 1995
200 meters	0:21.87	Merlene Ottey (Jamaica)	Liévin, France	Feb. 13, 1994
400 meters	0:49.59	Jarmila Kratochvílová (Czechoslovakia)	Milan, Italy	Mar. 7, 1982
800 meters	1:56.40	Christine Wachtel (East Germany)	Vienna, Austria	Feb. 13, 1988
1,000 meters	2:31.23	Maria Mutola (Mozambique)	Stockholm, Sweden	Feb. 25, 1996
1,500 meters	4:00.27	Doina Melinte (Romania)	East Rutherford, NJ	Feb. 9, 1990
1 mile	4:17.14	Doina Melinte	East Rutherford, NJ	Feb. 9, 1990
3,000 meters	8:33.82	Elly van Hulst (Netherlands)	Budapest, Hungary	Mar. 4, 1989
5,000 meters	15:03.17	Elizabeth McColgan (Great Britain)	Birmingham, England	Feb. 22, 1992
50 meter hurdles	0:6.58	Cornelia Oschkenat (East Germany)	Berlin, Germany	Feb. 20, 1988
60 meter hurdles	0:7.69*	Lyudmila Narozhilenko (USSR)	Chelyabinsk, Russia	Feb. 4, 1993

*Narozhilenko recorded a time of 7.63 in Seville, Spain on November 4, 1993, but was disqualified on a positive drugs test.

Event	Time			Name and Country	Place	Date
Relays						
4 × 200 meters	1:32.55			S. C. Eintracht Hamm (West Germany) (Helga Arendt, Silke-Beate Knoll, Mechthild Kluth, Gisela Kinzel)	Dortmund, Germany	Feb. 19, 1988
4 × 400 meters	3:26.84			Russia (Tatyana Chebykina, Olga Goncharenko, Olga Kotylarova, Tatyana Alekseyeva)	Paris, France	Mar. 9, 1997
Walking						
3,000 meters	11:44.00			Alina Ivanova (Ukraine)	Moscow, Russia	Feb. 7, 1992
Field Events	**m**	**ft.**	**in.**			
High jump	2.07	6	9½	Heike Henkel (Germany)	Karlsruhe, Germany	Feb. 9, 1992
Pole vault	4.40	14	5	Emma George (Australia)	Melbourne, Australia	Dec. 10, 1996
	4.40	14	5	Stacy Dragila (U.S.)	Paris, France	Mar. 9, 1997
Long jump	7.37	24	2¼	Heike Dreschler (East Germany)	Vienna, Austria	Feb. 13, 1988
Triple jump	15.03	49	3½	Yolanda Chen (Russia)	Barcelona, Spain	Mar. 11, 1995
Shot	22.50	73	10	Helena Fibingerová (Czechoslovakia)	Jablonec, Czechoslovakia	Feb. 19, 1977
Pentathlon	4,991 points			Irina Belova (Russia)	Berlin, Germany	Feb. 14-15, 1992

MULTI-EVENT SPORTS

BIATHLON

Olympic Games

Most gold medals (men) Aleksandr Tikhonov (USSR) won four gold medals as a member of the Soviet relay team that won the 4 × 7.5 km races in 1968, 1972, 1976 and 1980.

In individual events, a record two gold medals have been won by two men: Magnar Solberg (Norway), 20 km in 1968 and 1972; and Franz-Peter Rotsch (East Germany), 10 km and 20 km in 1988.

Most gold medals (women) The record for the most gold medals is two, achieved by two women: Anfisa Reztsova (Unified Team/Russia), who won the 75 km event in 1992 and was a member of the winning team in the 4 × 7.5 km relay race in 1994; and Myriam Bedard (Canada), who won a women's record two gold medals in individual events, the 7.5 km and 15 km events, in 1994.

Anfisa Reztsova is one of two women biathletes to win two Olympic gold medals.

Most medals Aleksandr Tikhonov has won a record five medals in Olympic competition. In addition to his four gold medals (*see above*), he won the silver medal in the 20 km in 1968.

World Championships

Most titles (overall—men) Aleksandr Tikhonov (USSR) has won 11 world titles: 6 in the 4 × 7.5 km relay, 1969–74 and 1989; five individual events, 10 km in 1976–77 and 20 km in 1969–70 and 1973.

Most titles (overall—women) In women's events, Petra Schaaf (Germany) has won a record nine gold medals: four in individual events, 15 km in 1989, 1991, 1993, and 10 km in 1988; three in the 4 × 7.5 km relay, 1995–97; and two in the team competition, 1992, 1996.

Most titles (individual—men) Frank Ullrich (East Germany) won a record five individual titles: the 10 km in 1978–79, 1981 and the 20 km in 1982–83.

Most titles (individual—women) The most women's individual titles is four, by Petra Schaaf (Germany) in the 15 km in 1989, 1991, 1993 and the 10 km in 1988.

MODERN PENTATHLON

Olympic Games

Most gold medals (overall) András Balczó (Hungary) has won three gold medals in Olympic competition: team event, 1960 and 1968; individual title, 1972.

Most gold medals (individual event) The only person to win a gold medal in an individual event is András Balczó (Hungary) in 1972.

Most gold medals (team event) Two countries have won the team event four times: Hungary, 1952, 1960, 1968 and 1988; USSR, 1956, 1964, 1972 and 1980.

Most medals (individual) Pavel Lednev (USSR) has won a record seven medals in Olympic competition: two gold—team event, 1972 and 1980; two silver—team event, 1968; individual event, 1976; and three bronze—individual event, 1968, 1972 and 1980.

World Championships

Most titles (overall—men) András Balczó (Hungary) has won a record 13 world titles, including a record six individual titles: seven team, 1960, 1963, 1965–68 and 1970; and six individual, 1963, 1965–67, 1969 and 1972.

Most titles (team event—men) The USSR has won 17 world championships: 1956–59, 1961–62, 1964, 1969, 1971–74, 1980, 1982–83, 1985 and 1991.

Most titles (individual event—women)   Eva Fjellerup (Denmark) is the only woman to win the individual title four times, in 1990, 1991, 1993 and 1994.

Most titles (team event—women)   Poland has won five world titles: 1985, 1988–91.

ORIENTEERING

World Championships

Most titles (relay)   The men's relay has been won a record seven times by Norway: 1970, 1978, 1981, 1983, 1985, 1987, and 1989. Sweden has won the women's relay 10 times—1966, 1970, 1974, 1976, 1981, 1983, 1985, 1989, 1991, 1993.

Most titles (individual) Three women's individual titles have been won by Annichen Kringstad (Sweden), in 1981, 1983 and 1985. The men's title has been won twice by four men: Age Hadler (Norway), in 1966 and 1972; Egil Johansen (Norway), in 1976 and 1978; Oyvin Thon (Norway), in 1979 and 1981; Jörgen Mårtensson (Sweden), in 1991 and 1995.

Orienteering requires cross-country running and map-reading skills. Norway and Sweden are the dominant powers in the sport.

Ski Orienteering

Most world titles (relay) Sweden has won the men's relay six times (1977, 1980, 1982, 1984, 1990 and 1996) and Finland has won the women's relay five times (1975, 1977, 1980, 1988 and 1990).

Most world titles (individual) The most individual titles is four, by Ragnhild Bratberg (Norway), Classic 1986, 1990, Sprint 1988, 1990. The men's record is three, shared by Anssi Juutilainen (Finland), Classic 1984, 1988, Sprint 1992 and Nicolo Corradini (Italy), Classic 1994, 1996 and Sprint 1994.

TRIATHLON

World Championships

Most titles (men) Simon Lessing (Great Britain) has won a record three times, 1992–95.

Most titles (women) The women's race has been won twice by Michellie Jones (Australia), 1992–93 and by Karen Smyers (U.S.), 1990 and 1995.

Hawaii Ironman

Most titles (women) The women's event has been won a record eight times by Paula Newby-Fraser (Zimbabwe/U.S.) in 1986, 1988–89, 1991–94 and 1996.

Most titles (men) Two men have won the Ironman a record six times: Dave Scott (U.S.), 1980, 1982–84, 1986–87; and Mark Allen (U.S.), 1989–93 and 1995.

Fastest time (men) Luc Van Lierde (Belgium) set the course record at 8 hr. 4 min. 8 sec. in 1996.

Fastest time (women) Paula Newby-Fraser set the women's record at 8 hr. 55 sec. in 1992.

Big Plays

Fastest time (men) The fastest time recorded over the Ironman

Luc Van Lierde holds the record for the Ironman Triathlon.

distances is 8 hr. 1 min. 32 sec., by Dave Scott (U.S.) at Lake Biwa, Japan on July 30, 1989.

Fastest time (women)   The fastest time record for a woman is 8 hr. 55 min., by Paula Newby-Fraser (Zimbabwe), in Roth, Germany on July 12, 1992.

Oldest triathlete   The oldest triathlete to finish the Ironman Triathlon was 73-year-old Walt Stack in 1981. Stack completed the course in a time of 26 hr. 20 min., the longest elapsed time ever.

Largest field   The most competitors to finish a triathlon race were the 5,030 who completed the 1995 Mrs. T's Chicago Triathlon in Chicago, IL.

TARGET SPORTS

ARCHERY

Olympic Games

Most gold medals   Hubert van Innis (Belgium) has won six gold medals (au cordon dore—33 meters, au chapelet—33 meters, 1900; moving bird target, 28 meters, 33 meters, moving bird target [team], 33 meters, 50 meters, 1920).

Archer Justin Huish won two gold medals at the 1996 Olympics making him the first American to achieve a Games double.

Most medals   Hubert van Innis has won nine medals in all: six gold (*see* MOST GOLD MEDALS), and three silver (au cordon dore—50 meters, 1900; moving bird target, 50 meters, moving bird target [team] 28 meters, 1920).

WORLD ARCHERY RECORDS

Men

FITA   Kyo-Moon Oh, South Korea, 1,368, 1995

90 m   Vladimir Esheev, USSR, 330, 1990

70 m   Hiroshi Yamamoto, Japan, 344, 1990

50 m   Seung Hun Han, South Korea, 348, 1994

30 m   Seung Hun Han, South Korea, 360, 1994

Women

FITA   Jung-Rye Kim, South Korea, 1,377, 1995

70 m   Elif Altinkaynak, Turkey, 339, 1996

60 m   He Ying, China, 349, 1995

50 m   Kim Moon-sun, South Korea, 345, 1996

30 m   Joanne Edens, Great Britain, 357, 1990

Source: U.S. National Archery Association

World Championships

Most titles, outdoor (archer)   The most titles won is seven, by Janina Spychajowa-Kurkowska (Poland) in 1931–34, 1936, 1939 and 1947. The most titles won by a man is four, by Hans Deutgen (Sweden) in 1947–50.

Most titles, outdoor (country)   The United States has a record 13 men's (1959, 1961, 1963, 1965, 1967, 1969, 1971, 1973, 1975, 1977, 1979, 1981, 1983) and nine women's (1952, 1957, 1958, 1959, 1961, 1963, 1965, 1977, 1995 [Compound Bow]) team titles.

Most titles, indoor (archer)   The most titles is two, by Natalia Valeeva (Moldova) in 1991 and 1993.

Most titles, indoor (country)   The United States has won two men's team titles, 1991 and 1993.

Big Plays

Longest arrow flight   The furthest an arrow has been shot is 2,047 yd. 2 in. by Harry Drake (U.S.), using a crossbow at the Smith Creek Flight Range near Austin, NV on July 30, 1988.

Greatest draw on a longbow   Gary Sentman of Roseberg, OR drew a longbow weighing a record 176 pounds to the maximum draw on the arrow of $28\frac{1}{4}$ inches at Forksville, PA on September 20, 1975.

Highest score in 24 hours   The highest recorded score over 24 hours by a pair of archers is 76,158, during 70 Portsmouth Rounds (60 arrows per round at 20 yards at 2-foot FITA targets) by Simon Tarplee and David Hathaway in Evesham, England on April 1, 1991. During this attempt Tarplee set an individual record of 38,500.

DARTS

World Championships

Most titles   Eric Bristow of England has won the title a record five times (1980–81, 1984–86).

Scoring Records (24 Hours)

Highest score (individual)   Kenny Fellowes (Great Britain) scored 567,145 points at The Prince of Wales, Cashes Green, England on September 28–29, 1996.

Team (8-man)   The Broken Hill Darts Club of New South Wales, Australia scored 1,722,249 points in 24 hours from September 28–29, 1985.

Team (8-woman)   A team from the Lord Clyde of Leyton, England scored 744,439 points on October 13–14, 1990.

Bulls and 25s (8-man team)   An 8-member team scored 526,750 points at the George Inn, Morden, England, July 1–2, 1994.

Scoring Records (10 Hours)

Highest score (pair)   The pair of Jon Archer and Neil Rankin (Great Britain) scored 465,919, retrieving their own darts, at the Royal Oak, Cossington, England on November 17, 1990.

Most bulls   Jim Damore (U.S.) hit 1,321 bulls in 10 hours at the Parkside Pub, Chicago IL on June 29, 1996.

Most trebles   The record for the most trebles is 3,056, achieved by Paul Taylor (Great Britain) at the Woodhouse Tavern, Leytonstone, England on October 19, 1985.

Most doubles   Paul Taylor also holds the record for the most doubles with 3,265 at the Lor Brooke, Walthamstow, England on September 5, 1987.

Fewest Darts

501 score   On March 9, 1987, Roy Blowes (Canada) achieved a 501 in nine darts, "double-on, double-off," at the Widgeions Pub, Calgary, Canada. His scores were: bull, treble 20, treble 17, five treble 20s and a double 20 to finish.
   This feat was equaled by Steve Draper (Great Britain) at the Ex-Service-men's Club in Wellingborough, England on November 10, 1994. His scores were: double 20, six treble 20s, treble 17 and bull.

1,001 score   The lowest number of darts thrown for a score of 1,001 is 19, by Cliff Inglis (Great Britain) (160, 180, 140, 180, 121, 180, 40) at the Bromfield Men's Club, Devon, England on November 11, 1975; and by Jocky Wilson (Great Britain) (140, 140, 180, 180, 180, 131, Bull) at The London Pride, Bletchley, England on March 23, 1989.

2,001 score   A score of 2,001 in 52 darts was achieved by Alan Evans in Ferndale, Wales on September 3, 1976.

3,001 score   A score of 3,001 in 73 darts was thrown by Tony Benson at the Plough Inn, Gorton, England on July 12, 1986. Linda Batten set a women's 3,001 record of 117 darts at the Old Wheatsheaf, London, England on April 2, 1986.

100,001 score   A score of 100,001 was achieved in 3,579 darts by Chris Gray at the Dolphin, Cromer, England on April 27, 1993.

1,000,001 score (men)   A team of eight at Buzzy's Pub and Grub, Lynn, MA, scored 1,000,001 in a record 36,583 darts on October 19–20, 1991.

1,000,001 score (women)   The Delinquents darts team at the Top George Pub, Combe Martin, England achieved 1,000,001 in 70,019 darts on September 11–13, 1987.

Speed Records

Around-the-board   The record for around-the-board in numerical order is 14.5 seconds by Jim Pike at the Craven Club, Newmarket, England, March 1944.

Around-the-board (retrieving darts)   The record for around-the-board at the 9-foot throwing distance, retrieving own darts, is 2 min. 13 sec. by Bill Duddy at The Plough, London, England on October 29, 1972.

MILLION AND ONE UP

The fewest darts thrown to accumulate a million and one score in darts is 36,583 darts. This feat was performed by an 8-man team at Buzzy's Pub and Grub in Lynn, MA, October 19–20, 1991.

For rules, see page 707.

Doubles　The record time for going around the board clockwise in "doubles" at arm's length is 9.2 seconds, by Dennis Gower at the Millers Arms, Hastings, England, October 12, 1975.

Three games of 301　The fastest time taken to complete three games of 301, finishing on doubles, is 1 min. 38 sec., by Ritchie Gardner on the British TV show *Record Breakers*, on September 12, 1989.

SHOOTING

Olympic Games

Most gold medals (men)　Seven marksmen have won five gold medals: Konrad Staheli (Switzerland), 1900–1906; Louis Richardet (Switzerland), 1900–06; Alfred Lane (U.S.), 1912–20; Carl Osburn (U.S.), 1912–24; Ole Lilloe-Olsen (Norway), 1920–24; Morris Fisher (U.S.), 1920–24; and Willis Lee (U.S.), 1920.

Most gold medals (women)　Marina Logvinenko (Unified Team) is the only woman to win two gold medals: sport pistol and air pistol, both in 1992.

Most medals (men)　Carl Osburn (U.S.) won 11 medals: five gold, four silver and two bronze.

Most medals (women)　The greatest tally by a woman competitor is three medals, by Jasna Sekaric (Yugoslavia/Independent Olympic Participant). She won one gold and one bronze in 1988, and one silver in 1992.

Youngest champion　Kimberly Rhode of El Monte, CA, succeeded in becoming the youngest Olympic shooting champion at 17 years old. Rhode won a gold medal in the women's double trap event at the 1996 Olympic Games in Atlanta, GA.

Oldest champion　The oldest Olympic shooting champion was Oscar Swahn (Sweden) at 60 yr. 264 days old. Swahn won the gold medal in the running dear event in 1908.

NCAA Championships

Most titles (team)　West Virginia has won 11 NCAA team titles, 1983–84, 1986, 1988–93, 1995–96.

Most titles (individual)　Eight competitors have won two individual titles: Rod Fitz-Randolph, Tennessee Tech, smallbore and air rifle, 1980; Kurt Fitz-Randolph, Tennessee Tech, smallbore, 1981–82; John Rost, West Virginia, air rifle, 1981–82; Pat Spurgin, Murray State, air rifle, 1984, smallbore, 1985; Web Wright, West Virginia, smallbore, 1987–88; Michelle Scarborough, South Florida, air rifle, 1989, smallbore, 1990; Ann-Marie Pfiffner, West Virginia, air rifle, 1991–92; Trevor Gathman, West Virginia, air rifle, 1993, 1996.

SHOOTING (INDIVIDUAL WORLD RECORDS)

The table below shows the world records for the 13 Olympic shooting disciplines, giving in parentheses the score for the number of shots specified plus the score in the additional round.

MEN

Event	Points	Marksman (Country)	Date
Free rifle 50 m 3 × 40 shots	1,287.9 (1,186 + 101.9)	Rajmond Debevec (Slovenia)	August 29, 1992
Free rifle 50 m 60 shots prone	704.8 (600 + 104.8)	Christian Klees (Germany)	July 25, 1996
Air rifle 10 m 60 shots	699.4 (596 + 103.4)	Rajmond Debevec (Yugoslavia)	June 7, 1990
Free pistol 50 m 60 shots	675.3 (580 + 95.3)	Taniu Kirlakov (Bulgaria)	April 21, 1995
Rapid-fire pistol 25 m 60 shots	699.7 (596 + 107.5)	Ralf Schumann (Germany)	June 8, 1994
Air pistol 10 m 60 shots	695.1 (593 + 102.1)	Sergey Pyzhyanov (USSR)	October 13, 1989
Running target 10 m 30 + 30 shots	687.9 (586 + 101.9)	Ling Yang (China)	June 6, 1996
Traps 125 targets	150 (125 + 25)	Marcello Tittarelli (Italy)	June 11, 1996
Skeet 125 targets	150 (125 + 25)	Jan Henrik Heinrich (Germany)	June 5, 1996

WOMEN

Event	Points	Markswoman (Country)	Date
Standard rifle 50 m 3 × 20 shots	689.7 (592 + 97.7)	Vessela Letcheva (Bulgaria)	June 15, 1995
Air rifle 10 m 40 shots	501.5 (398 + 103.5)	Vessela Letcheva (Bulgaria)	April 12, 1996
Sport pistol 25 m 60 shots	696.2 (594 + 102.2)	Diana Jorgova (Bulgaria)	May 31, 1994
Air pistol 10 m 40 shots	492.7 (392 + 100.7)	Jasna Sekaric (Yugoslavia)	September 22, 1996

Big Plays

Highest score (24 hours) The Easingwold Rifle and Pistol Club (Yorkshire, England) team of John Smith, Edward Kendall, Phillip Kendall and Paul Duffield scored 120,242 points (averaging 95.66 per card), August 6–7, 1983.

Smallest group (500 meters) The smallest at 500 meters (546 yards) is 1.5 inches, by Ross Hicks (Australia) using a .30–06 rifle of his own design in Canberra, Australia on March 12, 1994.

Smallest group (1,000 yards) The smallest group on record at 1,000 yards is 3.960 inches, by Frank Weber (U.S.) with a .308 Baer Magnum in Williamsport, PA on November 14, 1993.

Most clay birds (one hour) The record number of clay birds shot in an hour is 4,551, by John Cloherty (U.S.) in Seattle, WA on August 31, 1992.

MARTIAL ARTS

JUDO

Olympic Games

Most gold medals Four men have won two gold medals: Willem Ruska (Netherlands), open class and over 93 kilograms class, in 1972; Hiroshi Saito (Japan), over 95 kilograms class, in 1984 and 1988; Peter Seisenbacher (Austria), up to 86 kilograms class, in 1984 and 1988; and Waldemar Legien (Poland), up to 78 kilograms class, in 1988 and up to 86 kilograms class, in 1992.

Most medals Angelo Parisi has won a record four Olympic medals, while representing two countries. In 1972 Parisi won a bronze medal in the open class, representing Great Britain. In 1980 Parisi represented France and won a gold, over 95 kilograms class, and a silver, open class; and won a second silver in the open class in 1984.

World Championships

Most titles (women) Ingrid Berghmans (Belgium) has won a record six world titles: open class, 1980, 1982, 1984 and 1986; under 72 kilograms class, 1984 and 1989.

Most titles (men) Three men have won four world titles: Yasuhiro Yamashita (Japan), open class, 1981; over 95 kilograms class, 1979, 1981, 1983; Shozo Fujii (Japan), under 80 kilograms class, 1971, 1973, 1975; under 78 kilograms class, 1979; and Naoya Ogawa (Japan), open class, 1987, 1991 and over 95 kilograms class, 1989.

Three martial arts disciplines have been included in the Olympic Games: judo (bottom), karate (center) and taekwondo (top).

The fastest time to demolish a 10-room house by a 15-person team using feet and bare hands is 3 hr. 6 min. 50 sec.

Big Plays

Most Judo throws Brian Woodward and David Norman completed 33,681 judo throws in 10 hours in Rainham, England on April 10, 1994.

House demolition Fifteen members of the Aurora Karate Do demolished a 10-room house in Prince Albert, Saskatchewan, Canada in 3 hr. 6 min. 50 sec., using only feet and bare hands, on May 11, 1996.

KARATE

World Championships

The first men's world championships were staged in Tokyo, Japan in 1970; a women's competition was first staged in 1980. Both tournaments are now staged biennially. The competition consists of two types: kumite, in which combatants fight each other, and kata events, in which contestants perform routines.

Kumite Championships

Most titles (team, men) Great Britain has won six kumite world team titles, in 1975, 1982, 1984, 1986, 1988 and 1990.

Most titles (individual, men) Four men have won two world titles: Pat McKay (Great Britain) in the under 80 kilograms class, 1982, 1984; Emmanuel Pinda (France), in the open class, 1984, and the over 80 kilograms class, 1988; Thierry Masci (France), in the under 70 kilograms class, 1986, 1988; Jose Manuel Egea (Spain), in the under 80 kilograms class, 1990, 1992.

Most titles (individual, women) Guus van Mourik (Netherlands) has won four world titles in the over 60 kilograms class, in 1982, 1984, 1986 and 1988.

Kata Championships

Most titles (team, men) Japan has won four kata world team titles, in 1986, 1988, 1992 and 1994.

Most titles (individual, men) Tsuguo Sakumoto (Japan) has won three world titles, in 1984, 1986 and 1988.

Most titles (individual, women) Two women have won three world titles: Mie Nakayama (Japan), 1982, 1984 and 1986; and Yuki Mimura (Japan), 1988, 1990 and 1992.

TAEKWONDO

World Championships

Most titles (men) Chung Kook-hyun (South Korea) has won a recor~~ur~~ world titles: light middleweight, 1982–83; welterweight 1985, 1987.

Most titles (women) The women's record is three titles, achieved by Lynette Love (U.S.), 1985, 1987 and 1991.

COMBAT SPORTS

FENCING

Olympic Games

Most gold medals Aladar Gerevich (Hungary) has won a record seven gold medals, all in saber: individual, 1948; team, 1932, 1936, 1948, 1952, 1956 and 1960. In individual events, two fencers have won three titles: Ramon Fonst (Cuba), épée, 1900 and 1904, and foil, 1904; Nedo Nadi (Italy), foil, 1912 and 1920, and saber, 1920. The most golds won by a woman is four, by Yelena Novikova (née Belova; USSR), all in foil: individual, 1968; team, 1968, 1972 and 1976.

Most medals Edoardo Mangiarotti (Italy) has won a record 13 medals in fencing: six gold, five silver and two bronze in foil and épée events from 1936 to 1960.

World Championships

Most titles The most individual world titles won is five, by Aleksandr Romankov (USSR), at foil, 1974, 1977, 1979, 1982 and 1983. Five women foilists have won three world titles: Hélène Mayer (Germany), 1929, 1931 and 1937; Ilona Schacherer-Elek (Hungary), 1934–35, 1951; Ellen Müller-Preis (Austria), 1947, 1949–50; Cornelia Hanisch (West Germany), 1979, 1981 and 1985; and Anja Fichtel (West Germany), 1986, 1988 and 1990.

NCAA CHAMPIONSHIPS

Most wins (Division I, team) Penn State has won the most championships, with four titles: 1990–91 and 1995–96.

Most titles (fencer) The most titles won in a career is four, by Michael Lofton, New York University, with four victories in saber, 1984–87; and by Olga Kalinovskaya, Penn State, with four victories in foil, 1993–96.

WRESTLING

Olympic Games

Most gold medals Four wrestlers won three Olympic titles: Carl Westergren (Sweden) in 1920, 1924 and 1932; Ivar Johansson (Sweden) in 1932 and 1936; Aleksandr Medved (USSR) in 1964, 1968 and 1972; and ...ndr Karelin (USSR/Unified Team/Russia) 1988–96.

Aleksandr Karelin (left) is one of four wrestlers to win three Olympic titles.

Most medals (individual)   Wilfried Dietrich (Germany) won five medals in Olympic competition: one gold, two silver and two bronze, 1956–68. The most Olympic medals won by a U.S. wrestler is four, by freestyler Bruce Baumgartner: two gold, one silver and one bronze, 1984–96.

World Championships

Most titles (individual, men)   The freestyler Aleksandr Medved (USSR) won a record seven world championships, 1962–63, 1966–67 and 1969–71, in three weight categories. The most world titles won by any U.S. wrestler is four, by the freestyler John Smith, 1987 and 1989–91.

Most titles (individual, women)   Yayoi Urano (Japan) has won five titles, 1990–91, 1993–94 and 1996.

Most titles (team, women)   Japan has won all six women's world titles (1989–94) since 1989, when women first competed.

NCAA Division I Championships

Most titles   Including five unofficial titles, Oklahoma State has won a record 30 NCAA titles, in 1928–31, 1933–35, 1937–42, 1946, 1948–49, 1954–56, 1958–59, 1961–62, 1964, 1966, 1968, 1971, 1989–90 and 1994.

Most consecutive titles   The University of Iowa has won the most consecutive titles, with nine championships from 1978 to 1986.

Big Plays

Heaviest Olympic wrestler   The heaviest wrestler in Olympic history was Chris Taylor (U.S.), bronze medalist in the super-heavyweight class in 1972, who stood 6 ft. 5 in. tall and weighed over 420 pounds.

FILA introduced an upper weight limit of 286 pounds for international competition in 1985.

Most wins   In international competition, Osamu Watanabe (Japan), the 1964 Olympic freestyle 63 kg champion, was unbeaten and did not concede a score in 189 consecutive matches.

Outside of FILA sanctioned competition, Wade Schalles (U.S.) won 821 bouts from 1964 to 1984, with 530 of these victories by pin.

SUMO WRESTLING

Most Emperor's Cup wins   *Yokozuna* Koki Naya, known as Taiho, won the Emperor's Cup 32 times up to his retirement in 1971.

Most wins, yokozuna   Mitsugu Akimoto, known as Chiyonofuji, set a record for domination of one of the six annual tournaments by winning the Kyushu Basho for eight years, 1981–88. He also holds the record for most career wins, with 1,045, and Makunoiuchi (top division) wins, with 807.

Most bouts, yokozuna   Kenji Hatano, known as Oshio, contested a record 1,891 bouts in his 26-year career, 1962–88, the longest in modern sumo history.

Youngest yokozuna   The youngest of the 64 men to attain the rank of *yokozuna* was Toshimitsu Ogata, alias Kitanoumi, in July 1974 at age 21 yr. 2 mo. He set a record in 1978, winning 82 of the 90 bouts that top *rikishi* fight annually.

Heaviest yokozuna   The heaviest yokozuna in sumo history was Hawaiian-born Chad Rowan, known as Akebono, who stood 6 ft. 8 in. tall and weighed 467$\frac{1}{2}$ pounds.

Longest sumo bout   The longest recorded wrestling bout was 11 hr. 40 min., when Martin Klein (Russia) beat Alfred Asikáinen (Finland) for the Greco-Roman 75-kg "A" event silver medal in the 1912 Olympic Games in Stockholm, Sweden.

BOXING

Heavyweight Division

Longest reign   Joe Louis was champion for 11 yr. 252 days, from June 22, 1937, when he knocked out James J. Braddock in the eighth round in Chicago, IL, until announcing his retirement on March 1, 1949. During his reign, Louis defended his title a record 25 times.

Shortest reign   Tony Tucker (U.S.) was IBF champion for 64 days, May 30–August 2, 1987, the shortest duration of a title won and lost in the ring.

Most recaptures   Two boxers have regained the heavyweight championship twice: Muhammad Ali and Evander Holyfield. Ali first won the title on February 25, 1964, defeating Sonny Liston. He defeated George Foreman on October 30, 1974, having been stripped of the title by the world boxing authorities on April 28, 1967. He won the WBA title from Leon Spinks on September 15, 1978, having previously lost to him on February 15, 1978. Holyfield won the title on October 20, 1990, defeating James "Buster"

Douglas. He regained the WBA and IBF titles from Riddick Bowe on November 6, 1993, having lost to him previously on November 13, 1992. After losing to Michael Moorer on April 22, 1994, Holyfield regained the WBA title on November 9, 1996, when he beat Mike Tyson.

Evander Holyfield has had three bites at the world heavyweight title. He defeated Buster Douglas to win the title in 1990, regained the crown in 1992 from Riddick Bowe, and regained the title again from Mike Tyson in 1996. Boxing fans will have to wait to see if Holyfield will give Tyson the chance to have a third bite at him.

Undefeated champion Rocky Marciano is the only world champion at any weight to have won every fight of his entire professional career (1947–56); 43 of his 49 fights were by knockouts or stoppages.

Oldest champion The oldest heavyweight boxing champion was George Foreman, at 45 yr. 287 days old. He knocked out former WBA/IBF champion Michael Moorer in the tenth round on November 5, 1994. Foreman was Moorer's senior by 19 years, and he outweighed him by 28 pounds. It had been 21 years since Foreman lost the crown; he defeated Joe Frazier for the title in 1973, but lost it the following year to Muhammad Ali. Foreman defended the IBF version on April 22, 1995 at 46 yr. 104 days when he knocked out Axel Schulz.

Youngest champion Mike Tyson was 20 yr. 144 days when he beat Trevor Berbick to win the WBC title in Las Vegas, NV on November 22, 1986. He added the WBA title when he beat James "Bone-crusher" Smith on March 7, 1987 at 20 yr. 249 days. He became the youngest undisputed champion on August 1, 1987 when he defeated Tony Tucker for the IBF title at 21 yr. 59 days.

Lightest champion Bob Fitzsimmons (Great Britain) weighed 167 pounds when he won the title by knocking out James J. Corbett in Carson City, NV on March 17, 1897.

Heaviest champion Primo Carnera (Italy) weighed in at 270 pounds for the defense of his title vs. Tommy Loughran on March 1, 1934. Carnera won a unanimous point decision.

Greatest weight difference Primo Carnera (Italy) outweighed his opponent, Tommy Loughran, by 86 pounds (270 pounds to 184 pounds) when they fought for the heavyweight title on March 1, 1934 in Miami, FL. Surprisingly, the bout went the distance, with Carnera winning on points.

Quickest knockout   The quickest knockout in a heavyweight title fight was 55 seconds, by James J. Jeffries over Jack Finnegan in Detroit, MI on April 6, 1900.

World Champions (All Divisions)

Longest reign   Joe Louis's heavyweight duration record of 11 yr. 252 days stands for all divisions.

Shortest reign   Tony Canzoneri (U.S.) was world light-welterweight champion for 33 days, May 21 to June 23, 1933, the shortest period for a boxer to have won and lost the world title in the ring.

Most recaptures   The only boxer to win a world title five times at one weight is Sugar Ray Robinson, who beat Carmen Basilio in Chicago Stadium, Chicago, IL on March 25, 1958 to regain the world middleweight title for the fourth time.

Youngest champion   Wilfred Benitez of Puerto Rico was 17 yr. 176 days old when he won the WBA light-welterweight title in San Juan, Puerto Rico on March 6, 1976.

Oldest champion   Archie Moore, recognized as a light-heavyweight champion up to February 10, 1962, when his title was removed, was then believed to be between 45 and 48 years old.

Longest title fight   The longest world title fight (under Queensberry Rules) was that between the lightweights Joe Gans (U.S.) and "Battling" Nelson, the "Durable Dane," in Goldfield, NV on September 3, 1906. It was terminated in the 42nd round when Gans was declared the winner on a foul.

Olympic Games

Most gold medals   Two boxers have won three gold medals: Laszlo Papp (Hungary) won the middleweight title in 1948, and the light middleweight in 1952 and 1956; Teofilo Stevenson (Cuba) won the heavyweight division in 1972, 1976 and 1980. The only man to win two titles at the same Games was Oliver L. Kirk, who won both the bantamweight and featherweight titles in 1904. It should be noted that Kirk only had to fight one bout in each class.

Oldest gold medalist   Richard Gunn (Great Britain) won the Olympic featherweight gold medal on October 27, 1908 in London, England at age 37 yr. 254 days.

Youngest gold medalist   The youngest Olympic boxing champion was Jackie Fields (born Finkelstein; U.S.), who won the 1924 featherweight title at age 16 yr. 162 days. The minimum age for Olympic boxing competitors is now 17.

Big Plays

Longest fight (gloves) The longest recorded fight with gloves was between Andy Bowen and Jack Burke in New Orleans, LA on April 6–7, 1893. It lasted 110 rounds, 7 hr. 19 min. and was declared a no contest (later changed to a draw).

Longest fight (bare-knuckle) The longest bare-knuckle fight was 6 hr. 15 min. between James Kelly and Jack Smith in Fiery Creek, Dalesford, Victoria, Australia on December 3, 1855.

Most fights without loss Of boxers with complete records, Packey McFarland had 97 fights (five draws) from 1905 to 1915 without a defeat.

Consecutive wins Pedro Carrasco (Spain) won 83 consecutive fights, April 22, 1964–September 3, 1970.

Most knockouts The greatest number of finishes classified as "knockouts" in a career is 145 (129 in professional bouts), by Archie Moore, 1936–63.

Greatest "tonnage" The highest aggregate weight recorded in a fight is 699 pounds, when Claude "Humphrey" McBride (Oklahoma), 339½ pounds, knocked out Jimmy Black (Houston, TX), 359½ pounds, in the third round in Oklahoma City, OK on June 1, 1971.

WEIGHTLIFTING

OLYMPIC GAMES

Most gold medals Naim Suleymanoglu (Turkey), featherweight, won three gold medals, in 1988, 1992 and 1996.

Most medals Norbert Schemansky (U.S.) won four medals: one gold, one silver and two bronze, 1960–64.

WORLD CHAMPIONSHIPS

Most titles (men) The record for most titles is eight, held by three lifters: John Davis (U.S.), 1938, 1946–52; Tommy Kono (U.S.), 1952–59; and Vasiliy Alekseyev (USSR), 1970–77.

Chinese women have dominated the sport of women's weightlifting. Shown here is Ding Meiyuan at a meet held in 1997.

Andrei Chemerkin (left) and Naim Suleymanoglu (right) set world weightlifting records while winning their respective Olympic divisions in 1996.

WEIGHTLIFTING RECORDS

From January 1, 1993, the International Weightlifting Federation (IWF) introduced modified weight categories, thereby making the then world records redundant. This is the current list for the new weight categories.

Men

Bodyweight	Lift.	kg	Name and Country	Place	Date
54 kg (119 lb.)	Snatch	132.5	Halil Mutlu (Turkey)	Atlanta, GA	July 20, 1996
	Clean and Jerk	160	Halil Mutlu (Turkey)	Istanbul, Turkey	Nov. 18, 1994
	Total	290	Halil Mutlu (Turkey)	Istanbul, Turkey	Nov. 18, 1994
59 kg (130 lb.)	Snatch	140	Hafiz Suleymanoglu (Turkey)	Warsaw, Poland	May 3, 1995
	Clean and Jerk	170	Nikolai Pershalov (Bulgaria)	Warsaw, Poland	May 3, 1995
	Total	307.5	Tang Ninsheng (China)	Atlanta, GA	July 21, 1996
64 kg (141 lb.)	Snatch	150	Guohau Wang (China)	Pusan, South Korea	May 5, 1997
	Clean and Jerk	187.5	Valerios Leonidis (Greece)	Atlanta, GA	July 22, 1996
	Total	335	Naim Suleymanoglu (Turkey)	Atlanta, GA	July 22, 1996
70 kg (154 lb.)	Snatch	163	Jianhui Wan (China)	Yangzhou, China	July 9, 1997
	Clean and Jerk	195	Zhan Xugang (China)	Atlanta, GA	July 23, 1996
	Total	357.5	Zhan Xugang (China)	Atlanta, GA	July 23, 1996
76 kg (167 lb.)	Snatch	170	Ruslan Savchenko (Ukraine)	Melbourne, Australia	Nov. 16, 1993
	Clean and Jerk	208	Pablo Lara (Cuba)	Szekszard, Hungary	Apr. 20, 1996
	Total	372.5	Pablo Lara (Cuba)	Szekszard, Hungary	Apr. 20, 1996
83 kg (183 lb.)	Snatch	180	Pyrros Dimas (Greece)	Atlanta, GA	July 26, 1996
	Clean and Jerk	214	Yong Zhang (China)	Yangzhou, China	July 12, 1997
	Total	392.5	Pyrros Dimas (Greece)	Atlanta, GA	July 26, 1996
91 kg (200 lb.)	Snatch	187.5	Aleksei Petrov (Russia)	Atlanta, GA	July 27, 1996
	Clean and Jerk	228.5	Kakhi Kakhisahvili (Greece)	Warsaw, Poland	May 6, 1995
	Total	412.5	Aleksei Petrov (Russia)	Sokolov, Czech Republic	May 7, 1994
99 kg (218 lb.)	Snatch	192.5	Sergei Syrtsov (Russia)	Istanbul, Turkey	Nov. 25, 1994
	Clean and Jerk	235	Akakide Kakhiashvilis (Greece)	Atlanta, GA	July 28, 1996
	Total	420	Akakide Kakhiashvilis (Greece)	Atlanta, GA	July 28, 1996
108 kg (238 lb.)	Snatch	200	Timur Taimazov (Ukraine)	Istanbul, Turkey	Nov. 26, 1994
	Clean and Jerk	236	Timur Taimazov (Ukraine)	Atlanta, GA	July 29, 1996
	Total	435	Timur Taimazov (Ukraine)	Istanbul, Turkey	Nov. 26, 1994
Over 108 kg	Snatch	205	Alexander Kurlovich (Belarus)	Istanbul, Turkey	Nov. 27, 1994
	Clean and Jerk	260	Andrei Chemerkin (Russia)	Atlanta, GA	July 30, 1996
	Total	457.5	Alexander Kurlovich (Belarus)	Istanbul, Turkey	Nov. 27, 1994

Women

Bodyweight	Lift.	kg	Name and Country	Place	Date
46 kg (101 lb)	Snatch	81.5	Jiang Yinsu (China)	Pusan, South Korea	May 11, 1997
	Clean and Jerk	105.5	Xing Fen (China)	Yangzhou, China	July 8, 1997
	Total	185	Guan Hong (China)	Yachiyo, Japan	April 4, 1996
50 kg (110 lb)	Snatch	88	Jiang Baoyu (China)	Pusan, South Korea	July 3, 1995
	Clean and Jerk	110.5	Liu Xiuhua (China)	Hiroshima, Japan	Oct. 3, 1994
	Total	197.5	Liu Xiuhua (China)	Hiroshima, Japan	Oct. 3, 1994
54 kg (119 lb)	Snatch	93.5	Yang Xia (China)	Yangzhou, China	July 9, 1997
	Clean and Jerk	115.5	Liu Xiuhua (China)	Yangzhou, China	July 9, 1997
	Total	207.5	Yang Xia (China)	Yangzhou, China	July 9, 1997
59 kg (130 lb)	Snatch	100	Zou Feie (China)	Pusan, South Korea	May 13, 1997
	Clean and Jerk	124	Xiu Xiongying (China)	Warsaw, Poland	May 6, 1996
	Total	220	Chen Xiaomin (China)	Hiroshima, Japan	Oct. 4, 1994
64 kg (141 lb)	Snatch	107.5	Chen Xiaomin (China)	Yangzhou, China	July 10, 1997
	Clean and Jerk	130	Li Hongyun (China)	Istanbul, Turkey	Nov. 22, 1994
	Total	235	Li Hongyun (China)	Istanbul, Turkey	Nov. 22, 1994
70 kg (154 lb)	Snatch	103.5	Gao Shihong (China)	Yangzhou, China	July 13, 1997
	Clean and Jerk	130	Qu Lihua (China)	Yangzhou, China	July 13, 1997
	Total	230	Tang Weifang (China)	Hiroshima, Japan	Oct. 4, 1994
76 kg (167 lb)	Snatch	106.5	Gao Xiaoyan (China)	Seoul, South Korea	Nov. 24, 1996
	Clean and Jerk	140	Zhang Guimei (China)	Shilong, China	Dec. 18, 1993
	Total	235	Zhang Guimei (China)	Shilong, China	Dec. 18, 1993
83 kg (183 lb)	Snatch	115	Acikogöz Derya (Turkey)	Seville, Spain	June 29, 1997
	Clean and Jerk	142.5	Acikogöz Derya (Turkey)	Seville, Spain	June 29, 1997
	Total	257.5	Acikogöz Derya (Turkey)	Seville, Spain	June 29, 1997
Over 83 kg	Snatch	112.5	Wang Yanmei (China)	Yangzhou, China	July 14, 1997
	Clean and Jerk	155	Li Yajuan (China)	Melbourne, Australia	Nov. 20, 1993
	Total	260	Li Yajuan (China)	Melbourne, Australia	Nov. 20, 1993

Most titles (women)   The most gold medals is 12, by Peng Li Ping (China) with snatch, jerk and total in the 52-kg class each year, 1988–89 and 1991–92; and Milena Tendafilova (Bulgaria), 67.5-kg/70-kg classes, 1989–93.

BIG PLAYS

Youngest world record-holder   Naim Suleimanov set 56-kg world records for clean and jerk (160 kg) and total (285 kg), at 16 yr. 62 days, in Allentown, NJ on March 26, 1983.

Oldest world record-holder   The oldest is Norbert Schemansky (U.S.), who snatched 164.2 kg in the then unlimited Heavyweight class, aged 37 yr. 333 days, in Detroit, MI on April 28, 1962.

Most world records broken   Between January 24, 1970 and November 1, 1977, Vasily Alekseyev (USSR) broke 80 official world records in weightlifting.

Heaviest lift to body weight   Stefan Topurov (Bulgaria) managed to clean and jerk more than three times his body weight when he lifted 396$\frac{3}{4}$ pounds in Moscow, USSR on October 24, 1983.

Team deadlift (24 hours)   A team of 10 deadlifted 6,705,241 pounds in 24 hours at the Forum Health Club, Birmingham, England on March 30–31, 1996.

Individual deadlift (24 hours)   The 24-hour individual deadlift record is 818,121 pounds, by Anthony Wright at Her Majesty's Prison, Featherstone, England, August 31–September 1, 1990.

Individual bench press (12 hours)   An individual bench press record of 1,181,312 pounds was set by Chris Lawton at the Waterside Wine Bar, Solihull, England on June 3, 1994.

Team bench press (24 hours)   A bench press record of 8,873,860 pounds was set by a 9-man team from the Forum Health Club, Chelmsleywood, England, March 19–20, 1994.

Team squat (24 hours)   A squat record of 4,780,994 pounds was set by a 10-man team at St. Albans Weightlifting Club and Ware Boys Club, Hertfordshire, England, July 20–21, 1986.

Team arm curling (24 hours)   A record 133,380 arm-curling repetitions using three 48$\frac{1}{4}$-pound weightlifting bars and dumbbells was achieved by a team of nine from Intrim Health and Fitness Club in Gosport, England, August 4–5, 1989.

The next Winter Games are scheduled to take place in Nagano, Japan in 1998.

OLYMPICS

Records in this section include results from the Intercalated Games staged in 1906.

MEDALS (OVERALL)

Most gold medals Ray Ewry (U.S.) has won 10 gold medals in Olympic competition: standing high jump, 1900, 1904, 1906 and 1908; standing long jump, 1900, 1904, 1906 and 1908; standing triple jump, 1900 and 1904. The most gold medals won by a woman is nine, by gymnast Larissa Latynina (USSR): all-around, 1956 and 1960; vault, 1956; floor exercise, 1956, 1960 and 1964; team title, 1956, 1960 and 1964.

Most medals Gymnast Larissa Latynina (USSR) has won 18 medals (nine gold, five silver and four bronze), 1956–64. The most medals won by a man is 15 (seven gold, five silver and three bronze), by gymnast Nikolai Andrianov (USSR), 1972–80.

Most gold medals at one Olympics Swimmer Mark Spitz (U.S.) won a record seven gold medals at Munich in 1972. His victories came in the 100-meter freestyle, 200-meter freestyle, 100-meter butterfly, 200-meter butterfly, and three relay events. The most gold medals won at one Games by a woman athlete is six, by swimmer Kristin Otto (East Germany), who won six gold medals at the 1988 Games. Her victories came in the 50-meter freestyle, 100-meter freestyle, 100-meter backstroke, 100-meter butterfly, and two relay events. The most individual events won at one Games is five, by speed skater Eric Heiden (U.S.) in 1980. Heiden won the 500 meters, 1,000 meters, 1,500 meters, 5,000 meters, and 10,000 meters.

Double Champion

*M*ichael Johnson sprinted his way into the record books when he won the 200 meter sprint in a world record 19.32 seconds. Johnson's win was expected, but the margin of his victory and the toppling of the long-standing 200-meter mark by nearly half a second thrilled the crowd in the stadium and the millions watching on television around the world. But that was only half of his Olympian feat. He had already captured the 400 meters. Johnson was the first man to win these two sprint events.

"*I* was happy, of course, to have broken the world record. But at that moment, the important thing was to win the Olympic gold medal and to make Olympic history," says Johnson. "There were a lot of things going on in my mind as I crossed the finish line but I was very, very shocked to have broken the world record by that margin."

*J*ohnson's decision to attempt two sprint events in Atlanta stunned track and field experts. Some suggested that the world champion was jeopardizing his chances in the 400 meters by overextending himself. "It wasn't a matter of choosing events. The events chose me," says the Texan. "I was a 200-meter runner in high school, and started the 400 in college. I never put limits on myself. If I had I would still be a 200-meter runner."

Self-confidence is the key to Johnson's success. "You have to believe in yourself. That is most important. You have to learn as an athlete that there is a maturation process. I have learned from wins, losses, mistakes, and I try to carry it over to the next race." Should aspiring sprinters try to emulate Johnson's mastery of two events? "Go with where your talent lies," advises Johnson. "Try as many events as possible. If I had just stuck to the 200, I wouldn't have made Olympic history."

The Sydney Olympic Games in 2000 are definitely in Johnson's future. "I'd like to compete for another five or six years and break records and do things that haven't been done before," he says. Does Johnson think he can top his own 200 meter mark? "You never know," he muses. "I never put limits on myself. I think I'm capable of running faster."

200/400 METER DOUBLE

Only two athletes have won the 200-meter and the 400-meter events at the same Olympics. In 1996, Michael Johnson (U.S.) won both of the men's events and Marie-Jose Perec (France) won both of the women's events.

Most medals at one Olympics   Gymnast Aleksandr Dityatin (USSR) won eight medals (three gold, four silver and one bronze) at Moscow, USSR in 1980. The most medals won by a woman athlete is seven (two gold and five silver), by gymnast Maria Gorokhovskaya (USSR) in 1952.

Most consecutive gold medals (same event)   Two athletes have won four consecutive individual titles in the same event: Al Oerter (U.S.), who won the discus 1956–68; and Carl Lewis (U.S.), who won the long jump 1984–96. Yachtsman Paul Elvstrom (Denmark) won four successive golds at monotype events, 1948–60, but there was a class change: Firefly in 1948; Finn class, 1952–60.

Oldest gold medalist   Oscar Swahn (Sweden) was aged 64 yr. 258 days when he won an Olympic gold medal in 1912 as a member of the team that won the running deer shooting single-shot title. The oldest woman to win a gold medal was Queenie Newall (Great Britain), who won the 1908 national round archery event at age 53 yr. 275 days.

Youngest gold medalist   The youngest-ever winner was an unnamed French boy who coxed the Netherlands pair to victory in the 1900 rowing event. He was believed to be 7–10 years old. The youngest-ever woman champion was Kim Yoon-mi (South Korea), who at age 13 yr. 83 days won the 1994 women's short-track speed skating relay event.

Summer/Winter Games gold medalist   The only person to have won gold medals in both Summer and Winter Olympiads is Edward Eagan (U.S.), who won the 1920 light-heavyweight boxing title and was a member of the 1932 winning four-man bobsled team.

Summer/Winter Games medalist (same year)   The only athlete to have won medals at both the Winter and Summer Games held in the same year is Christa Rothenburger-Luding (East Germany). At the 1988 Winter Games in Calgary, Canada, Rothenburger-Luding won two speed skating medals: gold medal, 1,000 meters, and silver medal, 500 meters; and at the Seoul Games that summer she won a silver medal in the women's sprint cycling event.

MEDALS (WINTER GAMES)

Most gold medals   The most gold medals won in Winter Games competition is six, by two women: speed skater Lydia Skoblikova (USSR) won 500 meters, 1964; 1,000 meters, 1964; 1,500 meters, 1960–64; 3,000 meters, 1960–64; cross-country skier Lyubov Egorova (Unified Team/Russia) won 5 km classical, 1994, 10 km freestyle pursuit, 1992–94, 15 km freestyle, 1992, 4 × 5 km mixed relay, 1992–94. The most gold medals won by a man is five, by three athletes: speed skater Clas Thunberg (Finland), 500 meters, 1928; 1,500 meters, 1924–28; 5,000 meters, 1924; all-around title, 1924; speed skater Eric Heiden (U.S.), 500, 1,000, 1,500, 5,000 and 10,000 meters, all in 1980; and cross-country skier Bjorn Daehlie (Norway), 10 km classical, 1994, 15 km freestyle pursuit, 1992–94, 50 km classical, 1992, 4 × 10 km mixed relay, 1992.

Most medals Cross-country skier Raisa Smetanina (USSR/Unified Team) has won 10 medals (four gold, five silver and one bronze), 1976–92. The most medals won by a man is nine (four gold, three silver and two bronze), by cross-country skier Sixten Jernberg (Sweden), 1956–64.

Ski jumper Toni Neiminen is the youngest man to win a gold medal at the Winter Olympics.

Oldest gold medalist Jay O'Brien (U.S.) was aged 48 yr. 359 days when he won an Olympic gold medal in 1932 in the four-man bobsled event. The oldest woman to win a gold medal was Raisa Smetanina (Unified Team), who was a member of the 1992 4 × 5 km relay team at age 39 yr. 352 days.

Youngest gold medalist Maxi Herber (Germany) was aged 15 yr. 128 days when she won the 1936 figure skating title. The youngest-ever men's champion was Toni Neiminen (Finland), who at age 16 yr. 259 days was a member of the winning ski jumping team in 1992.

PARTICIPATION

Most participants The greatest number of competitors at a Summer Games celebration was 9,369 (6,659 men, 2,710 women), who represented a record 169 nations, in Barcelona, Spain in 1992. The greatest number at a Winter Games was 1,737 (1,216 men, 521 women) representing 64 countries, in Lillehammer, Norway in 1994.

Most Games The record for the most Olympic Games competed in by any one participant is nine, by yachtsman Hubert Raudaschl (Austria), 1964–96. The most appearances by a woman is seven, by fencer Kerstin Palm (Sweden), 1964–88.

Longest span The longest span of an Olympic competitor is 40 years, by Dr. Ivan Osiier (Denmark) in fencing, 1908–32 and 1948; Magnus Konow (Norway; 1887–1972) in yachting, 1908–20, 1928 and 1936–48; Paul Elvstrøm (Denmark) in yachting, 1948–1960, 1968–72 and 1984–88; and Durward Knowles (Great Britain 1948, then Bahamas) in yachting,

1948–72 and 1988. Raimondo d'Inzeo competed for Italy in equestrian events at a record eight celebrations from 1948–76, gaining one gold, two silver and three bronze medals. D'Inzeo's record was equaled by Paul Elvstrøm and Durward Knowles in 1988. The longest span by a woman is 28 years, by Anne Ransehousen (née Newberry; U.S.) in dressage, 1960, 1964 and 1988. Fencer Kerstin Palm (Sweden) competed in a women's record seven competitions, 1964–88.

The longest span of Olympic competition by a U.S. man is 32 years, by equestrian Michael J. Plumb, who competed in seven Olympics. Janice Lee York Romary competed in fencing in six Games.

Largest crowd   The largest crowd at any Olympic site was 104,102 in the 1952 ski-jumping competition at the Holmenkøllen, outside Oslo, Norway. Estimates of the number of spectators of the marathon race through Tokyo, Japan on October 21, 1964 ranged from 500,000 to 1.5 million. The total spectator attendance in Los Angeles in 1984 was given as 5,797,923.

Longest torch relay   The longest journey of the torch within one country was for the XV Olympic Winter Games in Canada in 1988. The torch arrived from Greece in St. John's, Newfoundland on November 17, 1987 and was transported 11,222 miles (5,088 miles on foot, 4,419 miles by aircraft/ferry, 1,712 miles by snowmobile and 3 miles by dogsled) until its arrival in Calgary on February 13, 1988.

RULES

The general requirements on this page apply to all Guinness record submissions. For specific rules for the "Top This" challenges, see pages 708–715.

PLANNING A GUINNESS RECORD ATTEMPT

- Choose to beat a record that is in the current edition of the book.
- Write to the following address, telling us exactly which record you want to break and requesting the guidelines for that record:

  The Guinness Book of World Records
  Six Landmark Square
  Stamford, CT 06901-2704

- Check with us again about 72 hours before you proceed with your attempt to make sure the record has not been broken since we sent you the guidelines.
- IF YOU WOULD LIKE TO ATTEMPT A POTENTIAL NEW RECORD CATEGORY, you *must* submit a written proposal outlining your idea to the address above.
- We are a very small editorial team, and we receive hundreds of letters every week. Please submit your request at least two months before your attempt so that we can give your inquiry the attention it deserves.
- Regrettably, it can take four to six weeks for us to get back to you, longer if your claim requires further research on our part.

DOCUMENTATION

Each published record category has its own customized rules and documentation requirements. You must ask us for these specific rules before your attempt.

All records require the following documentation:

• Two original signed statements of authentication from independent witnesses who are known and respected in your community. These statements must be typed or written by the witnesses on their own business stationery and must include their contact addresses and telephone numbers. The witnesses must confirm that they read the Guinness rules before the event, and that all of these rules were followed. Suitable witnesses include law enforcement officers; judges; elected officials; certified public accountants; surveyors; notaries public; clergypeople; legal, educational or medical professionals; postmasters; fire and rescue officers. Witnesses must not be related in any way to the participants, organizers or sponsors of the event.

• Independent corroboration in the form of local or national newspaper clippings.

• Good-quality color slides or reproducible color prints of the event.

REMEMBER: WRITE TO US IN ADVANCE FOR SPECIFIC RULES FOR YOUR ATTEMPT.

PUBLICATION CRITERIA

The criteria used to establish a record are as follows: the record must be measurable, must be independently corroborated, must be completely objective, and should preferably be the subject of worldwide interest and participation. Unique skills, one-of-a-kind occurrences and "firsts" do not qualify for entry into the book.

Even if the above criteria appear to have been met, the final decision on whether or not to include a record in the book rests with the Editorial Committee.

The Guinness Book of World Records reserves the right to determine in its sole discretion the records to be published.

Even if you do beat the existing record and we accept your claim, it does not necessarily mean that details will be included in the book, since your record may subsequently be beaten—we can only include the record that stands when we go to press.

LARGEST ONION (FRUIT, VEGETABLE, AND FLOWER RECORD GUIDELINES)

Rules

1. Only fruit and vegetables grown primarily for human consumption will be considered for publication. Documented claims for agricultural crops

and animal fodder produce such as sugar beets and mangolds are welcome, but these will be dealt with separately.

2. Priority will always be given to items entered and measured at officially recognized horticulture competitions, shows and events, where designated qualified judges are present. The competitions can be at local, national, or international level, but copies of the competition rules must be supplied with the record claim. In case of practical difficulties in getting to shows, it may be possible to arrange for judges to assess claims at the actual growing site.

3. Claims from the U.K. must be authenticated by National Vegetable Society or Horticulture Society judges as appropriate. Claims from overseas should be authenticated by suitably qualified national equivalents.

4. All entries must comply with the rules of the show/competition. Where the rules of the show/competition differ from our own, we will nominate an independent witness to see that the fruit/vegetable is eligible for inclusion in the book. In any case, we reserve the right to have the specimen examined by an expert nominated by us.

5. All claims should be made as soon as possible after judging. Generally speaking, retrospective claims will not be considered for publication unless the circumstances merit it or they are particularly interesting for historic or other reasons. To minimize delays and administrative problems, claims should be submitted by the actual grower(s) rather than by a third party.

Documentation

The following must be provided:

1. Signed and dated statements from the show judges and those responsible for weighing and measuring, with contact addresses and telephone numbers. Where applicable, completed and signed copies of any official entry forms should also be provided. The species and variety must be clearly stated. If possible, scientific names should also be given.

2. Two further signed statements of authentication by independent persons of some standing in the community or by representatives of a relevant organization (which could be the gardening press), including contact addresses and telephone numbers.

3. Independent corroboration in the form of local or national newspaper clippings, especially from the specialist gardening press. All clippings must be clearly marked with the date and source.

4. Good-quality color transparencies or prints of the object or event.

Preparing Vegetables for Record Claims

1. Foliage can only be included if it forms an integral part of the plant, for example on a leek, cabbage or celery.

2. Cauliflower leaves must be trimmed level with the curds.

3. Foliage must not be included in determining the weight/length of beets, broad beans, carrots, marrows, onions (which must be trimmed to the neck and showing no part of the green stem at all), parsnips, peas, potatoes, pumpkins, radishes, green beans, tomatoes and turnips. The definition of

beet does not include fodder beets, sugar beets or mangelwurzels (mangels, mangolds).

4. All roots must be cut cleanly from the main body of the specimen as near to it as possible, except where roots are an integral part of the specimen, for example in root crops. Therefore, roots can only be included with crops such as beets, carrots, radishes and parsnips.

5. Stalks must be trimmed as near to the main body of the specimen as possible.

6. All specimens must be in sound condition and should be available for examination by judges and any appointed representatives. Any specimen not judged at show that is also not made available for independent expert scrutiny is unlikely to be considered for publication in *The Guinness Book of World Records*.

7. No sticks, dirt, stones or any material not forming actual plant matter of the specimen may be included in weighing or measuring. Note that for very large specimens, the carrying tarp must be removed from beneath the vegetable before the weight is configured to ensure absolute accuracy.

8. Measurement of the weight must be carried out on professional weighing equipment, for example, Avery Scales. Weights registered on domestic kitchen or bathroom scales will not be accepted. The weight must be exact and absolutely no approximation or deduction may be used to produce the final figure.

9. Measurement of length must be carried out by placing the specimen on a plain surface (paper, if possible) and by marking the exact position of each end. Stalks or any part of the foliage must be excluded. A straight line should then be drawn between the two marks and this length measured exactly. Even with peas and beans, no part of the stalk should be included in the measurement, even though they are normally allowed on the showbench.

LARGEST EDIBLE FUNGUS

Rules

1. The record is for the circumference of the fungus, which must be measured with a steel tape.

2. The weight of the fungus must also be given. Measurement of weight must be carried out on professional weighing equipment.

3. No sticks, dirt, stones or any other material not forming part of the fungus itself may be included in the determination of either size or weight.

4. The fungus must be identified by a qualified mycologist, who must state the species of the fungus (and its common name, if it has one) and confirm that it is safe for human consumption.

5. The claimant must confirm that the fungus was found on public land or that permission was granted for the claimant to enter the area for the purpose of searching for fungi. Trespassing, disturbance of protected areas, or violation of any other law or ordinance will automatically invalidate the record claim.

In addition to the documentation listed on page 708, one of the witness statements must be from the mycologist (see Rule 4 above).

RAMP JUMPING (MOTORCYCLE)

Rules

1. This involves riding a motorcycle up a ramp, going through the air and landing either on the ground or on a ramp at the far end. The motorcycle must be a recognizable model, with no added "flying" aids.

2. If there is a ramp at the far end, and a successful landing is made on the ramp, the distance achieved would be the distance between the end of the takeoff ramp and a point directly below the point of contact on the landing ramp (which must be measured with a steel tape). If the motorcycle hits the front of the ramp at the far end, the attempt is invalidated. If the attempt is made without a ramp at the far end, the distance achieved would be the distance from the base of the takeoff ramp (i.e. directly below the point of take-off) to the point of landing. Again, a steel tape must be used to measure the distance.

3. The attempt must be made on level ground.

4. If the person attempting the record falls off the motorcycle in flight, the attempt is invalidated.

5. It is essential that stringent safety precautions are taken.

Documentation

See page 708.

CYCLING—ONE YEAR
(GENERAL SPORTS RECORD GUIDELINES)

Rules

1. These guidelines are for those sports events where the record concerned is either:
a) A performance for a specific time period OR
b) A singular performance

2. Officials are appointed by the organizer of the event. There must be at least two witnesses present at all times to act as officials and maintain a log book.

3. The log book must give a full description of the attempt, including:
a) Details of those attempting the record, with their names and ages.
b) The status and addresses of organizers, officials/umpires/referees and medical supervisors.
c) Complete details of scores, repetitions, time, etc.

4. The first entry is made by officials at the start of the event, and thereafter timekeepers, officials and observers sign as witnesses that the event is

under constant supervision and all rules are adhered to. The officials must therefore be fully aware of all the rules of the event. Help in obtaining suitably qualified people may be obtained from the association in charge of the sport (the governing body), who may be able to put the organizers in touch with an official, league or club in the area.

5. The chief official and referee/umpire/judge have complete jurisdiction over the event. Any problems that arise during the course of the attempt must be resolved by them, and their decision is final.

6. A regulation-size field, table, court, track, etc. and standard equipment must be used.

7. Participants may retire during the event as long as this does not mean a breach of the rules for the event in question. If it does, the event must be ended at that time. Once the event has begun, no participants may join the attempt as substitutes or replacements.

8. Rest breaks are at the participants' discretion. For example, if the event is one for 24 hours, the duration of it must be 24 hours only. Rest breaks taken during the time cannot be accumulated and added at the end to make the event one of 24 hours of activity. However, they must be noted in the log book, as they may be used in assessing the quality of the attempt.

9. We advise that medical attention should be available at all times.

Documentation

The following must be provided:

1. A signed and dated log book showing that the attempt has been the subject of unremitting surveillance.

2. Signed statements of authentication from two independent witnesses of some standing in the community or by a representative of a relevant organization of standing and by the qualified judges of the activity concerned.

3. Independent corroboration in the form of local or national newspaper clippings.

4. Good-quality color transparencies or prints of the event.

5. A signed and dated visitors' log book showing that attempt took place in a place open to the general public.

6. A surveyor's certificate confirming distance of course/performance (if applicable).

RUNNING A MARATHON WHILE
TOSSING A PANCAKE

Rules

1. The attempt must be made in a recognized marathon that is open to the public. Participants may not stage the event themselves for the sole purpose of making a record attempt.

2. The pancake must be tossed continuously throughout the run. On each toss, the pancake must flip over at least once before falling back into the pan.

The rules for Cycling—One Year (General Sports Record Guidelines) on page 711 must also be followed.

Documentation

See Cycling—One Year (General Sports Record Guidelines), page 711.

DARTS: A MILLION AND ONE

Rules

1. There are two categories for this event: Men's Team and Women's Team.

2. The team may consist of up to eight (8) players only and no substitutes are allowed.

3. The record is for the fewest darts to score.

4. The attempt must take place on only one dartboard, although it may be replaced if it becomes too worn.

5. The rules of darts must be observed regarding height of board, distance, throwing, retrieving and scoring.

6. The team starts with 1,000,001 points and subtracts in the normal manner.

7. The game must be started and finished by throwing a double. No dart counts toward the score until a double is thrown, but all darts must be included in the final figure of darts thrown.

8. To finish, a double must be thrown, reducing the score exactly to zero. However, if a greater score than is required is thrown, the whole throw of three darts does not count and the score remains as it was before the particular throw commenced. The darts thrown, however, do count toward the final total of darts thrown.

9. Darts only score when they remain in the board on completion of the three throws, but all darts thrown must be included in the total number, regardless of where they land.

10. The officials controlling the attempt should belong to the local darts league and the callers and scorers must be familiar with the rules of the game. If possible, a representative of the national association that controls the game should be present.

Documentation

See Cycling—One Year (General Sports Record Guidelines), page 711.

GOLF BALL BALANCING

Rules

1. The golf balls used must be new and not treated in any way. An independent witness must actually give the new balls to the person attempting the record, in full view of other witnesses.

2. No adhesive of any sort may be used.

3. The balls must be stacked one on top of the other, on a flat surface.

4. The stack must remain standing for at least 5 seconds, and must be photographed.

Documentation

See page 708.

PUSH-UPS

Rules

The body must remain straight throughout, i.e., no bending at knees or waist. The body must be lowered until at least a 90° angle is attained at the elbow. The body must then be raised until the arms are straight. This equals one push-up. This basic principle applies to all our push-up entries with minor modifications.

Finger tip: instead of the palm of both hands touching the floor, only the finger tips (including the tip of the thumb) may touch.

One arm: Only one arm may be used and the same arm must be used throughout the attempt. In this attempt the hand is placed flat on the floor.

correct body position for all push-up variations
left, correct position for fingertip push-ups;
right, correct position for one-finger push-ups

One finger: Only one finger of one hand may be used. The thumb may not be used. The record is for the number of repetitions; no rest breaks are permitted. The one-finger position must be maintained throughout. The side of the index finger must not be used as this means other parts of the hand will come into contact with the ground and therefore invalidate the attempt.

See also the diagrams below.

Documentation

See Cycling—One Year (General Sports Record Guidelines), page 711.

BASKETBALL DRIBBLING

Rules

1. The record attempt must be made under constant supervision by two independent witnesses not related to the participant. The officials can change throughout the attempt, but there must always be two judges present.

2. A log book of the attempt must be kept by the two officials. The log book must detail the name(s) and age(s) of the participants(s); the status and addresses of the organizers, officials and medical supervisors; the distances dribbled during each leg of the trip (noting starting and finishing points for both location and time); and any breaks taken during the attempt.

3. The record attempt must be measured either by a pedometer attached to the participant or by the odometer of the traveling vehicle(s) following the record attempt. Mileage for each leg of the journey must be noted in the log book.

4. The participant will dribble the basketball throughout the journey. (Note: the participant does not have to dribble the ball during breaks.)

5. The participant is allowed to take as many breaks as desired. The participant must mark the point where the journey breaks and restart the journey from that point.

Documentation

In addition to the documentation listed under Cycling—One Year (General Sports Record Guidelines) on page 711, a signed statement showing the method used to calculate the distance traveled must also be provided.

GOOD LUCK WITH YOUR ATTEMPT!

INDEX

r = On the Record

A

Aardman Animation, 447, *447*
abalone pearl, 299
abbreviations, 259
Abell (galaxy), 162
absorbent substance, 132
accidents, 217–21. see also disasters
  fireworks, 220
  helicopter, 220
  industrial, 217, *218,* 263
  mining, 217
  mountaineering, 220
  nuclear reactor, 221
  nuclear waste, 221
  offshore oil platform, 220
  road, 220
  ski lift, 221
  submarine, 220
  subway, 96
  tanker, 120
  yacht racing, 221
acid, strongest, 129
acquittals (trials), 265
acronyms, 259
Adler Planetarium, 176
administrative building, 287–88
advance sales, theater, 439
advertising, 283–85, *284*
  newspapers and magazines, 395
aerial acts (circus), 423
aerials, 638
aerobatics, 595
age span, movies, 444

agriculture, 300–304
Airbus Super Transporter A300-600 ST Beluga, 101, *102.*
aircraft, 101–5, *102.* see also airliners; flights; flying
  disasters, 217, 220, *219*
  land planes, 606
  model, 48–49, *49*
  speed record, 109
air force, 240–41
airliners, 103, *102*
  speed record, 109–10
airlines, 105
airports, 105–8, *106*
air racing, 595–96
airships, 104–5
airsickness bags, 44
Akers, Tom, 174
albatross, 338, *337*
Albright, Madeleine, 234–35, *234r*
albums (music), 418–19
alcoholic beverages, 37
alimony suit, 264
alloy, 129
alphabet, 258
alphabetic writing, 258
Alpha Centauri (star), 164
alphorn, 402
alpine skiing, 635–37
amateur championships (sports)
  squash, 565
  surfing, 630–31
amateur golf, 548
Amato, Joe, 586, *586*
amber, 299
American Bowling

Congress (ABC), 537–40
America Online, 157, *159*
America's Cup (sailing), 620
amphibians and reptiles, 333–36
amphibious circumnavigation, 73–74
amphitheater, 427
anagrams, 259
ancestor, distant, 136–37r
ancient structures, 135
animal-made structure, 321
animals. see also insects
  fossils, 311
  invertebrates, 319–23
  land animal, 311
  mammals, 342–343
  man-eating, 220
  movies, in, 446
  poisonous, most, 336
  prehistoric, 310–315
annual prize, 247
antiques and collectibles, 44, 381–88
antlers, moose, 343
APBA Gold Cup (powerboat racing), 628–30
Apollo 13 (spacecraft), 174
apology, belated, 395
applause, 406
apple, largest, 40
apple peeling, 10
apple picking, 10
aquariums, 57
aquatic sports,

620–35. see also
   sailing
aquatic weeds, 309
aqueducts, 99
arch, largest natural,
   179
archaeology, 135,
   138–40
archery, 679–81, *679*
archipelago, 184
aria (opera), 406
Arid Australia model
   railroad group,
   50–51
armed forces, 240–41
armies, 240
armor, antique, 381
arrest, mass, 268
artery, human, 365
artificial mound, 256
art nouveau, antique,
   381
arts and
   entertainment,
   376–448, 416–20
   antiques and
      collectibles,
      381–88
   circus, 423–26,
      424–25
   composers, 402–3
   dancing, 420–22
   literature, 388–94
   movies, 440–48
   music, 399–402
   newspapers and
      magazines,
      394–99
   performers, music,
      402–7
   radio, 415
   robbery of artwork,
      268
   television, 407–15,
      408–13
   theater, 427–40
   visual arts, 377–81
arts festival (theater),
   440
ascendants, 361
assassination
   attempts, 267
associate justice,
   Supreme Court, 267

asteroids, 166–67
astronauts, 171–74,
   173
AT-6 Class (air
   racing), 595–96
Atlantic Ocean,
   sailing, 622
atlas, antique, 381
atoll, largest, 184–85
atomic bomb, 217
attendance
   movie theaters, 448
   school, 243
   stockholder, 278
auctions, public, 280
audience
   circus, 423
   radio, 415
   television, 407
Australia
   floodlights, 291, *290*
Australia telescope,
   175–76
Australian Open
   championships
   (sports)
   tennis, 552–53,
      554–55r
authors, 393
automobiles, see
   automotive sports;
   cars
automotive sports,
   578–89
   championships,
      578–89
   Daytona 500, 579
   drag racing
      (NHRA), 586
   Formula One,
      583–84
   funny car, 586–87
   Indianapolis 500,
      583
   Indy car racing,
      579–83
   Le Mans, 584, *585*
   Monte Carlo Rally,
      585
   moto-cross, 589
   motorcycle racing,
      588–89
   NASCAR, 578–79,
      580–81r

pro stock, 587
   rallying, 585
avalanches, 205–6
aviation. see entries
   beginning air;
   flights; flying
awards, 247–48
   Cy Young awards,
      460
   Emmy awards, 414
   football, 501, 507
   Grammy Awards,
      417
   hockey, 518
   MVP awards, 460
   Oscar Awards,
      446–48, *447*
ax, largest, 2
Ayers Rock, 179, *179*

B

babies, human, *357,*
   358–59
baby teeth, 362
backgammon, 64
bacterium, 316–17
badminton, 562–63
bagel, 30
bags, collections, 44
Bailey, Donovan,
   658–59r
balance of payments,
   274
balance (scientific
   instrument), 140
balancing
   coin, 296
   on one foot, 10
baling, 301
ballet, 420–21
ballooning, 113,
   114–15r, 116–17,
   116
balloon release, 10
balloon sculpture, 2
ballroom dancing,
   421–22
banana split, 30
bands, 403
bank note forgery, 269
bankruptcy, 280
banks
   fraud, 269

largest, 280
robbery, 268
banner, 2
banquet, 37
barbecue, 37
Barbie dolls, 44
barefoot waterskiing, 632–34
barges, 120
barometer, 140
Barr, Dave, *84*
barrel rolling, 10, *11*
Barringer Crater, 168
Barrow, Alaska, *211*
barrow pushing, 10
barrow racing, 10
bars and restaurants, 55–56
barter deal, 280
baseball, 450–67
  awards, 460–62
  baserunning, 457–58, *458*
  college baseball, 465–66
  college World Series, 466
  consecutive games won, 457
  consecutive hits, 455
  Cy Young awards, 460
  games played, 461, 464–65
  generations, 460
  grand slams, 454
  hitting, *450,* 450–51, 454–55, 461
  home runs, 451, 452–53, *452r,* 461
  innings pitched, 456, 462
  League Championship Series, 461–62
  major leagues, 450–60
  managers, 460, 465
  MVP awards, 460
  no-hitters, 457
  pitching, *455,* 455–57, 461–62, 464–65

  runs batted in (RBIs), 451
  saves, 457
  shutouts, 456, 457
  stolen bases, 461
  strikeouts, 454, 455
  walks, 454, 456, 461
  wins (pitching), 455
  World Series, 463–65
baseball bat, 467
basket, 2
basketball, 467–91
  gold medals, 479
  Jordan, Michael, 477r
  National Basketball Association (NBA)
    assists, 475
    basket, valuable, 479
    coaches, 474, *474, 482,* 482–83r
    consecutive wins, 469
    dribbling, *478,* 479
    dunkheight, 479
    field goals, 472, 479
    finals, 474–75
    free throws, 469, 472, 479–80
    highest-scoring games, 468, 475
    individual records, 468–71, 474, *469*
    losses, 468
    lowest-scoring game, 468
    margin of victory, 475
    off-the-rim, 479
    players, 468
    playoff records, 472–73
    points, 469, 475, 480
    rebounds, 473
    spinning, 479
    tallest player, 468
    team records, 467–69, 474
    wins, 468, 474

    women, 479
  NCAA
    assists, 481, 487
    Championship, 486, 491
    coaches, 486, 491
    consecutive wins, 484
    Division I records, 481, 487–91
    field goals, 480, 487
    highest-scoring games, 490
    individual records, 480–84, 487–90
    losses, 484, 491
    lowest-scoring games, 490
    margin of victory, 484
    points, 484, 487, 490
    rebounds, 484, 488, 490
    team records, 484, 490–91
    undefeated seasons, 491
    wins, 486, 491
    women, 487, *488–89,* 490–91
  Olympic games, 479
  Smith, Dean, 482–83r
bass instruments, 401
bathtub racing, 11
baton twirling, 404
bats, 348
battery, 149
battery-powered car journey, 75
batting average (baseball), 450
battles, 237–38
bays, 187, *187*
beach volleyball, 534
beard, human, 361
Beatles, 416–17
  albums, 417
  clothing, 381, *381*
  song lyrics, 386
bed making, 11
bed pushing, 11

bed race, 11
beer, 37
beer cans, collections, 44
beer coaster flipping, 11
beer keg lifting, 11
beer labels, 44
beer stein carrying, 12
bees, mantle of, 18
beet, 40
Beetle (car), *71*
beetles, 324–25, *324*
Belmont stakes (horse racing), 248
bequests, 293
best man, 29
best-sellers
    books, 389, *390, 391r*
    music, recorded, 417–19
Betelgeuse (star), 163
beverage company, 281
Bhopal, India
    industrial accident, 217, 263
biathlon, 675–76
biceps, human, 364
bicycles, 82–83, *83*
big plays (sports)
    air racing, 596
    archery, 681
    automotive sports, 587–88
    badminton, 563
    barefoot waterskiing, 634
    boxing, 695
    canoeing, 625–27
    carriage driving, 574
    combat sports, 691–92, 695
    cycling, 591–93, 595
    diving, 619
    figure skating, 642
    horse racing, 571–72
    jai alai, 564
    judo, 689
    luge, 644–45

marathons, 664–66
martial arts, 689
polo, 575
powerboat racing, 630
rhythmic gymnastics, 651
rodeo, 577
rowing, 628
sailing, 624
shooting, 686
show jumping, 573
skateboarding, 603
skiing, 639–40
soccer, 529
speed skating, 642–43
swimming, 610
table tennis, 567
tennis, 560–62
track and field, 660–61, 664–70, 679
walking, 668–70
water polo, 635
weightlifting, 700
windsurfing, 624
wrestling, 691–92
billboards, advertising, 285
billionaire, 291
bills, birds, 341
bingo, 64
biotechnology, 133–37
birds, 336–41
    caged pets, *351*
    prehistoric, 311
bird-watching, 341
birth and life, 357–61
birthday party, 38
birthrates, 216
birth weight, pigs, 303
bites
    fish, 329
    snake, 335–36
bitterest substance, 129
bivouac, 185
blackout, 149
blanket, 2
    antique, 381
blast furnace, 142
blood, human, 365–66

blood alcohol level, 371
bloodsucking banded louse, *324,* 325
blood sugar level, 371
blown glass vessel, 2
board games, 64
boats. see ships and boats
bobsledding, 643–44
body, human, 361–66
body temperature, human, 371
boiling points, 128
bomber, speed record, 109
bombs
    atomic bomb, 217
    conventional bombing, 217
    nuclear weapons, 241
    terrorist bombings, 269
bones, human, 363
books
    antique, price of, 381–82
    best-sellers, 389, *390,* 391r
    collections, 44
    oldest, 388
bookstores, 56–57
boomerang juggling and throwing, 29
border crossings, 208
Boston Marathon, 661–64
bottle caps
    collections, 44
    pyramid, 2
bottle orchestra, 403–4
bottles, 2
    antique, 382
    collections, 44
boundaries, 208
bouquet of flowers, 6, *6*
bovine, 301
bowling, 536–41
    American Bowling Congress (ABC), 537–40

Ladies Professional
  Bowlers Tour
  (LPBT), 536–37
Professional
  Bowlers
  Association
  (PBA), 536
Women's
  International
  Bowling
  Congress
  (WIBC), 540–41
Bowman, Jean
  Lefcowitz, 243,
  244
box, antique, 382
boxing, 692–95
brains, human, 363
Branagh, Kenneth,
  434
brass musical
  instrument, 401
Brazil
  soccer, 524–25r
bread
  production of, from
  field, 301
breakwater, 196
breathing, human,
  364–65
breeders, mammals,
  342–43
Breeder's Cup series
  (horse racing), 569
breweries, 300
brick balancing, 12
brick carrying, 12
brick laying, 12
brick lifting, 12
brick throwing, 29
brickworks, 286
bride and bridegroom,
  oldest, 28, *28*
bridge (game), 67–68
bridges, 96–99, *97–98*
Britain
  ancestor, distant,
  136–37r
  pub, largest, *55*
British Open (golf),
  543
British Trans-Globe
  Expedition, 182
broadcast

radio, 415
television, 407
broadsheet, antique,
  382
broccoli, 40
bubble blowing, 12
bubble-gum blowing,
  12
Buddhist temple, 250
budget, largest, 274
Buffum, William, 436
buildings. see also
  structures
  commercial
    buildings, 286–87
  leisure, for, 51–57,
    55
  office, 287–88
  worship, 248–50
bungee jumping, 596
burrito, 30, *31*
Burton, Charles, 182
buses, 87
business, 278–83. see
  also corporations
Butler, Chris, *416*
butterflies, 325, 326

C

cabbage, 40
cable, telephone, 153
cable car, 144
cactus, *306*
caged pets, *351*
cake, 30, 32
calculator, 145, *146*
Calment, Jeanne
  Louise, 360, *360*
calm water, largest
  areas, 189
calves, 302
Cambodia
  mass killings, 269
camera, antique, 382
campers, 87
camping out, 12
Canada
  column of coins,
    295, 296
  cycling, 591
  edible fungus, *317,*
    318
  tower, *289,* 290

track and field,
  658–59r
Canadian Football
  League (CFL). see
  football
canals and locks,
  196–97
canal tunnel, 100
can construction, 2
candy, 32
cannon, 242
canoe, 117
canoeing, 625–27
can pyramid, 2
cantaloupe, 40
cantilever bridge, 98
canyons, 183
capital cities, 209,
  210
capital punishment,
  271
cardiac arrest, human,
  371–72
cards. see playing
  cards
career, longest, 277
cargo vessels, 120–21
Carnival Destiny
  (passenger liner),
  123, *125r*
carnivores, 342–43
carpets, 4
  antique, 383
carriage driving, 574
carriage pushing, 12
carrot, 40
cars, 71–73
  antique car
    collection, 44
  Beetle, 71
  driving, 73–75, 79
  gasoline, *76–78r*
  model, 48–51
  production, 71–72
  roads, 80–81
  services, 79–80
  speed record, 73
  washing, 12
cartoons (television),
  410r
cash, return of, 293
cash machines, 280
cassette, 416
castles, 222

catalytic cracker, 149–50

cathedrals, 248–49, *249*

cats
litter size, *355*
pets, 354

Cats (Broadway show), 427, *428–31*

cattle, 301–2

cattle ranch, 300

caves, 180

CD-ROM library, 160

celery, 40

cellos, 401–2

cells, human, 366

cemeteries, 254, 256

Centaurus (constellation), 164

ceramics, antique, 383

cereal treat, 32

Ceres (asteroid), 166

Cernan, Eugene Andrew, 171

CFL. see football

chainsaw, 4

chair, largest, 4

Challenger 5IL (space shuttle), 174

Challenger (space shuttle), 221

Challenger STS 61A (space shuttle), 171

champagne, 37

championships (sports)
aerials, 638
aerobatics, 595
alpine skiing, 636
archery, 680–81
automotive sports, 578–89
badminton, 562–63
barefoot waterskiing, 632–34
baseball, 461–62
basketball, 485, 491–92
biathlon, 676
bobsledding, 644
boxing, 692–94
canoeing, 625

carriage driving, 574

combat sports, 690, 691

curling, 645

cycling, 590

darts, 681

diving, 619

dressage, 574

fencing, 690

figure skating, 640

football, 495, 506, 510

golf, 541–44, 545–48

grass skiing, 639

gymnastics, 647–51

handball, team, 533–34

hockey, 518, 523

in-line skating (rollerblading), 598

jai alai, 564

judo, 686

karate, 689

lacrosse, 531

luge, 644

martial arts, 686, 689–90

moguls, 638

moto-cross, 589

motorcycle racing, 588–89

orienteering, 677–78

parachuting, 600–601

pentathlon, 676–77

polo, 574

racquetball, 564

rallying, 585

rhythmic gymnastics, 651

rodeo, 575–76

rowing, 627–28

sailing, 623

shooting, 684

short track speed skating, 643

show jumping, 573

snowboarding, 604

soaring, 605

speed skating, 642

squash, 565

surfing, 630, 631

swimming, 610, 617, 619

synchronized swimming, 617

table tennis, 566

taekwondo, 689–90

target sports, 679–86

tennis, 552–53

three-day event (equestrian sports), 573

track and field, 652–53, 661, 667–68, 676, 677–78

trampolining, 651

triathlon, 678

water polo, 634–35

waterskiing, 631–32

weightlifting, 695

windsurfing, 623

wrestling, 691, 700

chandelier, 4

charity
food bank, 280
fund-raising, 280

Charlie Elliott Wildlife Center, 25r

charts (music), 419–20

checkers, 65

checks (money), 294

"Cheddar Man," 136–37r

cheese, 32

chemistry and physics
elements, 128–29
extremes, chemical, 129–32
extremes, physical, 132–33

Chernobyl disaster, 221

cherry stem tying, 12

chess, *66*, 65–67

chest measurement, human, 364

chickens, 303

chimneys, 290

chip (computer), 157

Chiron, 169

chocolate model, 32

choir, 400
choral society, 400
chorister, 248
chorus lines, 422
Christmas cards, 394
Christmas cracker, 4
Christmas party, 38
Christmas tree, 5
chrysanthemum, 40
churches, 248–250
cigar box balancing, 13
cigarette lighters, 44
circulation (newspapers and periodicals), 394–96
circumnavigation amphibious, 73–74
cycling, 591
flying, 108, 111
helicopter, 104
sailing, 620–21
circus, 423–26, *424–25*
Cirque du Soleil, *424–25*
cities, 209–12
civil damages, 262–63
civil trial, 262–63
civil wars, 237
clam, 321
classical concert, 404
claws, dinosaurs, 315
Clemens, Roger, *455,* 456
click beetles, 325
clocks, 147–48, *147* antique, 383
cloning procedure, 133
clothesline, longest, *4,* 5
clothing, antique and collectible, 381, *381* 383
clovers, 308
CN Tower, *289,* 290
coaches basketball, 474, 482–83r, 486, 491
football, 493, 501, 507
hockey, 517–18, 522
coal shoveling, 13
coasters, 45

coastlines, 208–9
cockroaches, 326
cocktail, 37
codicils (wills), 264–65
Coffey, Paul, 517, *517*
coin collection, 295
coins, 294–96
collard, 40
collectibles, 381–87
collections, 44–48. see also specific collections (e.g., bags)
college baseball, 465–66
college presidents, 243
college World Series, 466–67
collegiate championships, rowing, 628
colonies bats, 348–49
rodents, 349
column of coins, *295,* 296
columns, 252
coma, 372
combat sports, 690–95
combine harvesting, 301
comets, 169
comic books, *397–98r,* 399
comic strips, 396, 399
commerce, 274–304 advertising, 283–85
agriculture, 300–304
business, 279–83
commercial buildings, 286–91
economics, 274–78
gems and precious metals, 296–300
money, 291–96
wealth, 291–93
commercial buildings, 286–91
commercials (television), 283
communications, 152–56

community garden, 300
composers, music, 402–3
computers, 157–60, *158, 159*
concerts, 404–5
concert series, 405
concert tour, 404
concrete dam, *194,* 195
conductors, 403
conga line (dance), 422
Congress United States, 233, 236–37
Connecticut income per capita, *275*
Conn Smyth trophies (hockey), 522
consonants, 258
constellation, *163,* 165. see also solar system
constitution, 228, *228*
construction housing, 221–22
project, 286
containership, 120
continent, largest and smallest, 178
contract bridge, 67–68
conveyor belt, 142
cookie, 32
cooling tower, 290
corals, 321
Corbillon Cup (table tennis), 566
corn, 40
corn cob, 42
corporations loss, 279
most valuable, 278
profit, 279
stock exchange, longest-listed company, 278
costs, litigation, 278
costumes, movies, 445–46, *445*
counties, 209
countries

geography, 208–9
population, 212
country line dance, 422
coup, 230
Covino, Charles P., *130*
cow, reproductive, 301
cow chip throwing, 29
cranes, 142–43
crawlers, 88
crawling, 13
crayfish, 322–23
credit cards, 45
crematorium, 256
crepe, 32
crepe tossing, 32
cribbage, 68
crime, 267–72
criminal trial, 263–64
crochet chain, 5
crocodilians, 333
croquet, 60
cross-country running, 667–68
cross-country skiing, 637–38
crossword puzzles, 68
crustaceans, 145, 321–23, *322*
Crux Australis (constellation), 165
cryonically preserved body, 133–34
crypts, 249
Cuba-Florida swimming, 617
cucumber
largest, 42
slicing, 13
cultured pearl, 299
curling, 645–46
currents (ocean), 189
curtain calls, 406
cut (diamond), 140
cycling, 589–95
Race Across AMerica, 590–91
records, 594
Tour de France, 589–90
Cy Young awards, 460

D

dahlia, 42
dairy farm, 300
daisy chain, 5
damages, litigation, 262
dams and reservoirs, 194–96
burst dams, 217
dancing, 420–22
dancing dragon, 422
Daniel, Marlene, 431
darts, 681–82, 684, *683*
Davis Cup (tennis), 559–60
Daytona 500, 579
death
leading cause of, 374
rates, 216
death row, 271
debate, longest, 257
deepest-living scorpion, 329
deer, 349–50
defamation, 264
degrees, honorary, 247
delta, 191
democracy
India, *229*
demolition project, 286
density, highest and lowest, 128
department stores, 281, *282*
deposit, gas, 150
descendants, 359–60
most distant ancestor, 136–37r
desert, 181
Detroit Lions, 498–99r
Devil Glitch, The (recorded music), *416*
diamond, 296–97
cut, finest, 140
diaries, 393
dictionary, 389
diesel car, 73

diesel engines, 143
dinosaurs, 314–15
directors, movies, 444
disasters, 217–21. see also accidents; hurricanes; tornadoes
aircraft, *219,* 220
avalanches, 205–6
dam burst, 217
earthquakes, 203–4
explosions, 204, 217
fire, 217
geysers, 206
landslides, 206
man-eating animals, 220
marine, 217, *218*
mass suicide, 217
natural disasters, 203–6
panic, 217
railroad, 220
riots, 217
shipwreck, 138
smog, 217
space, 221
spaceflight, 170–72
subway, *95,* 96
tsunamis, 189
volcanoes, 204–5
Discovery (space shuttle), 170
disease and medicine, 371–75
dish, 32
Disney fiber optics display, *154*
diving, 14
birds, 340
high diving (circus), 423
pinniped, 348
sport, 617–19
whales, 346
divorce
oldest divorcee, 28
rates, 216
settlement, 264
DNA, 310
doctorate, youngest, 243
doctors, 374
dogs, 352–54

litter size, *355*
doll, 5
dollhouse, 223–25r,
  223, 224
domestic animals,
  352–55
dominoes, 68
donors of blood, 366
doors, 288
double bass (musical
  instrument), 401
doughnut, 32
Douglas, William O.,
  265
dowry, 292
dragonflies, 326
drag racing (NHRA),
  586–87
drawing, price of, 380
dreaming, humans,
  363
dredgers (ships), 118
dress
  antique, 383, *383*
  jeweled, 299
dressage, 573–74
dress train, 5
Drew, J. D., *466*
dribbling, basketball,
  478, *478*
drilling, ocean, 186
drink, 37
drivers
  harness racing, 578
  worst and best, 79
driving, cars, 74–75,
  79
drugs (prescription),
  374, *374*
drug store chain, 283
drums, 402
ducks
  oldest, 303, *303*
  racing, *13,* 14
Duggan, Anne Marie,
  540
Du Maurier Classic
  (golf), 545–46
durable performers
  movies, 444
  theater, 439
durable programs
  radio, 415
  television, 407

Dutch words, 259

E

earrings, 45
ears, rabbits, *355*
earthmover, 143
Earth (planet)
  arch, largest
    natural, 179, *179*
  brightest star seen
    from, 164
  canals and locks,
    196–97
  caves, 180
  continent, largest
    and smallest, 178
  dams and
    reservoirs,
    194–96
  deserts, 181
  islands, 183–85
  lakes, 192–94
  land reclamation,
    197–98
  moon, longest
    distance, 167
  mountaineering,
    185–86
  mountains, 182–83
  natural disasters,
    203–6
  oceans, 186–88
  penetration into
    earth, deepest,
    178
  peninsula, largest,
    178
  polar exploration,
    181–82, *181*
  rivers, 190–92
  rock pinnacles, 180
  rocks, oldest and
    largest, 178–79,
    179
  sand dunes, 181
  solar system, place
    in, 166
  sun, longest
    distance, 165
  valleys, 183
  waterfalls, 192
  weather, 198–202,
    201, 203, 204

earthquakes, 203–4
earthworks, 254
earthworms, 319
Easter egg, 32
echo, longest, 133
eclipses, 169
economics, 274–78
edible fungus, *317,*
  318
Ednie, Mel, 41
education, awards
  and, 242–48
Edwin P. Hubble
  space telescope,
  176, *177*
egg farm, 300
eggplant, 42
eggs
  balancing, 14
  birds, 341
  chickens, 303
  dinosaurs, 315
  dropping, 303
  Easter egg, 32
  fish, 332
  hunt, 14
  insect, 325
  largest, 5
  racing, egg and
    spoon, 14
  shelling, 303
  spider, 328
  throwing, 29
elections
  government,
    227–32
  United States,
    232–33
electoral college
  majority (U.S.
    government), 233
electric current, 133
electric eel, 333
electricity, 148–49
elements (chemical),
  128–29
elephants, 342, 343,
  346–47
elevators
  fastest, 143
  incarceration in, 14
  lock elevator, 197
Eliason, Goran, *75,* 79
embroidery, 5

emeralds, 298
Emmy awards, 414
Emperor's Cup (sumo wrestling), 692
employer, largest, 279
employment, 276–77
single job, 277
employment agency, 277
Encke's Comet, 169
encore, opera, 407
encyclopedia, 389
Endeavor STS 49 (space shuttle), 174
endowment, educational, 246
energy
electricity, 148–49
gas, natural, 150–51
nuclear power, 151–52
oil, 149–50
steam and water power, 152
wind power, 152
Energya (spacecraft), 170
engagement, longest, 27
England, 318, *318*
Globe Theater, *437*
trains, 92, *92*
English Channel, swimming, 611, 616
English words, 258
entertainment. see arts and entertainment
equestrian sports. see also horse racing
carriage driving, 574
dressage, 573–74
harness racing, 577–78
polo, 574–75
rodeo, 575–77
show jumping, 572–73
three-day event, 573
escalators
longest, 143

riding, 14
shortest, 143
escapes from prison, 271–72
estuary, 191
Eta Carinae (star), 163, 164
Euler, Leonard, 147
evacuation, military, 239
executioners, 271
exercises, 649
exit (road), 81
explosions, 203, 217
extras, movies, 446
extraterrestrial search, largest, 176
extreme sports, 595–608

F

fabric, oldest, 138
fairs, 53–54
families, wealthiest, 291
family business, 279
family names, 260
fan, handpainted, 5
fangs, snake, 336
fantastic feats, 2–38
Farcus, Joe, *124–25r*
farms, 300–301
fax machines, 153
feasts and celebrations, 37–38
feathers, birds, 340
Federation Cup (tennis), 560
feet, human, 364
felines, 347, *347*
fences, 288
Fermat's Theorem, 146, *146*
ferret, litter size, *355*
ferry, 120–21
fiber optics transmission, 153–54, *154*
field hockey, 529–31
NCAA Division I, 531
Fiennes, Sir Ranulph, 181

FIFA World Cup (soccer), 523, 526
figure skating, 640–42
filibuster (United States Government), 237
filling station, 79
fines (crimes, for), 271
fingers, human, 361
fire, 217
fire bucket brigade, 14
fire engines, 88, *88,* 89
fireworks, 5
accidents, 220
first names, 260
fish, 329–33
fishing, recreational, 60, 62, *61*
fjord, 188
flag, 5–6
flagpole, 290
flame, hottest, 132
flamenco dancer, 422
fleas, 326
fleece (sheep), 304
flexible pole (circus), 423
flexible wing–multiplace distance records (hang gliding), 598
flexible wing–single place records (hang gliding), 596–98
flight attendant, 112
flights, 108–9. see also flying
space, 170–71, 174
float, 6, 32
floodlights, *290,* 291
floods, 200
flotation (stock exchange), 277
flower fossil, 310
flowers
bloom, largest, *307,* 308
largest bouquet, 6, *6*
leaves, 308
orchids, 308
plants, flowering, 308
rose tree, 308

sunflower, largest, 43

flying, 109–11
  birds, 338, 340
  personal aviation records, 112–13
flying birds, 338, 340
flying dinosaurs, 315
flying disc throwing, 30
flying return trapeze, 423
fog, 202
food, fantastic feats, 30–36
food and water, longest survival without, 372
food company, 281
footbag, 62
football, 493–513
  Arena football, 510–13
  Canadian Football League (CFL), 507–8, *508*
  The Grey Cup, 508, 510
  Moore, Herman, 498–99r
  National Football League (NFL)
    appearances, Super Bowl, 495
    awards, 501
    catches, 498–99r
    Championship, 495
    coaches, 493, 501
    consecutive wins, 493, 495
    highest scoring games, 493
    individual records, 496, 500–501
    margin of victory, 496
    NFL titles, 495
    pass completions, 500
    plays, longest, 493–94, 501
    points, 495, 496, 500
    receptions, 500–501
    records, 497
    scoring, 493
    streaks, 494–95
    Super Bowl, 495–96
    team records, 493, 495–96
    touchdowns, 494, 500
    wins, 493, 495
  NCAA, 224, 501–7, *502*
footprints, dinosaur, 315
foreign aid, 274
foreign language film, 440
forest, 310
forgery, 269
forging, 144
forklift, 144
Formula One, 583–84
Fossett, Steve, 114–15r
fossils, 310–11
fountain, 286
four-leaf clover, 45
Fouts, Dayton C., 21, *21*
France
  tourists, 213, *213*
fraud, computer, 160
free-living entity, 316
freestanding structure, oldest, 135, *139*
French Open (tennis), 553, 556
French words, 258
freshwater fish, 329
freshwater lake, 193
friction, 130–31r, 132–33
frisbee. see flying disc throwing
frogs, 336
fruits and vegetables, 40–43. see also specific types (e.g., apples)

fruit stickers, 45
fuel economy, 75, 76–78r
fumigation, hotel, 227
fungi, 318, *318*
funny car, 586–87
Furman, Ashrita, *82, 478*
furniture, antique, 384
fusion power, 151

G

galaxies, 162
gallbladder, human, 372
galleries, art, 377
gallstones, human, 372
games, 60–69. see also specific games (e.g., croquet)
gantry crane, 142–43
garage, service, 80
garbage can, 6
garbage collecting, 14
garbage dump, 287
garden, community, 300
garlic
  largest, 42
  string, 32
gas, natural, 150–51
gas fire, 151, *151*
gasoline, *76,* 76–78r
  lowest consumption, 74
gas tanks, 287
gastropods, 320
gender ratio imbalance, 216
General Motors, 279, *279*
generations of screen actors, 444
generator, 148
gentoo penguins, 338, *339*
geography, 208–12
Georgia Forestry Association, 24–25r, *24–25,* 26
gerbils
  caged pet, *351*

litter size, 355
German words, 259
Germany
  mass killings, 269
gestation periods,
  mammals, 343
geysers, 206
g force, 325, 372
Gielgud, Sir John, *435*
gingerbread house, 33
glass
  antique, 384
  balancing, 14, *15*
  sheets of, 288
  thinnest, 142
Gliese (star), 164
globe, 6
Globe Theater
  (London), *437*
gnomes, 45
goats, 302
Godwin, Thomas, 591
gold discs (records),
  417
Golden Gate Strait,
  swimming, 616–17
golden handshake,
  291
Golden Jubilee
  (diamond), 296–97,
  297
golden weddings, 28
goldfish, 332
gold medals
  (Olympics)
  alpine skiing,
    635–36
  basketball, 479
  biathlon, 675–76
  boxing, 694
  canoeing, 625
  cross-country
    skiing, 637–38
  cycling, 590
  diving, 617
  dressage, 573–74
  fencing, 690
  field hockey, 529
  figure skating, 640
  gymnastics, 646–47
  hockey, 523
  luge, 644
  pentathlon, 676
  rowing, 627

sailing, 620
shooting, 684
short track speed
  skating, 643
show jumping, 572
skateboarding, 608
ski jumping, 638
speed skating, 642
swimming, 609–10,
  617
synchronized
  swimming, 617
table tennis,
  565–66
target sports,
  679–86
three-day event
  (equestrian
  sports), 573
track and field,
  651–52, 661, 668,
  676
  walking, 668
water polo, 634
windsurfing, 623
gold (precious metal)
  largest mass, 299
  nugget, 299
  panning, 14
  price, stock
    exchange, 278
  reserves, 274
golf, 541–52
  amateur golf, 548
  balancing golf balls,
    550
  British Open, 543
  Du Maurier Classic,
    545–46
  LPGA
    Championship,
    545
  LPGA tour records,
    546
  majors
    men, 541–44
    women, 545–46
  Masters, 541
  Nabisco Dinah
    Shore, 545
  NCAA
    Championships,
    548
  PGA

    Championship,
    543
  PGA tour records,
    543–44
  Ryder Cup, 547
  Senior PGA tour,
    547
  U.S. Open, 541–42,
    545
golf balls, 45, *45*
goliath beetle, *323,*
  325
Gordon, Jeff, 579,
  580–81r
gorge, largest, 183
gorillas, 350
gourd, 42
gourd bushel, 42
government, 227–32
  constitution, 228,
    228
  coup, 230
  democracy, 232–33
  elections, 228–30
  heads of state, 231
  political party, 230
  royalty, 231–32
  United States,
    232–33
  women, U.S.
    government, *234,*
    234–35r
  world legislatures,
    227–28
governors, United
  States, 233
graduates, 242
Grammy Awards,
  417
Grandcamp (marine
  disaster), 218, *218*
Grande Dixence
  (dam), *194,* 195
grand piano, 401
grape catching, 15
grapefruit, 42
grapes, 42
grasses, 309
grasshopper, 326
grass skiing, 639–40
grave digging, 256
Great Britain
  cycling, 591
green bean, *40,* 42

Greenfarb, Louise J., 46–47r
Greenland, 183
greeting cards, 48
Grey Cup, 508
Griffey, Ken, Jr., *450*
grocery chain, 283
Groening, Matt, 410–11r
gross national product, 274
ground figures, *379*, 380
group, recording artists, 416
Grundig FIS World Cup (snowboarding), 604–5
guide dogs, 352
guinea pigs
    caged pet, *351*
    litter size, *355*
guitars, 401
gulf, 188
gum wrapper chain, 6
guns
    antique, 384
    military, 242
gymnastics, 646–51
    exercises, 649
    rhythmic gymnastics, 648, 651
    trampolining, 651

H

habituation, oldest, 138
hail, 202
hair, human, 361
hair cutting, 15
hair splitting, 16
Haise, Fred Wallace, Jr., 174
Hale-Bopp, *169*
Halley's Comet, 169
hamburger, 33
ham radio, 418
hamster, litter size, *355*
handball, team, 533–34

hands, human, 361
handshakes, 16
    U.S. presidents, 233
hangars, *107, 108*
hang gliding, 596–98, *597*
hanging basket, 6
hangings (capital punishment), 271
harness racing, 577–78
Harris, Julie, 438
Harrods (department store), *282*
Hartsfield, Hank, 171
Hart Trophy (hockey), 518
Hawaii Ironman, 678–79, *678*
heads of state, 231
hearing, bats, 348
heart transplants, 375
Heavyweight Division, boxing, 692–94
height, humans, 366–67, 370, 368–69r, *368*
helicopters, 103–4
    accidents, 220
    model, 49, *49*
Helios B (spacecraft), 170
helium ballooning, 114–15r
helmet, antique, 384
hemodialysis, 372
Henley, Suzanne, *292, 293*
herds, mammals, 343
hibernation, rodents, 349
hiccupping, 372
Hieb, Rick, 174
high diving (circus), 423
higher education institutions, 243
high school graduates, 243, 244–45r, *244*
high wire (circus), 423, 426
hijackings, 268, *270*
hill figures (sculpture), 380

Hindenberg, 219
Hingis, Martina, *554–55r*
hitting (baseball), *450,* 450–55, 461
hoard of coins, 296
hobbies and pastimes
    buildings for leisure, 51–57
    collections, 44–45
    fruit and vegetable growing, 40–43
    games, 60–69
    models, 48–51
hockey, 513–23
    awards, 518, 522
    field hockey, 529–31
    gold medals, 523
    National Hockey League (NHL), 513–18
    NCAA championships, 523
    Olympic games, 523
    Stanley Cup, 518–22
Hogenauer, Alan K., 58–59r, *58*
homelessness, 204
home runs (baseball), 451, 452–53r, 455, 461
hominid, 135
hominoid, 135
Homo, genus group, 135
Homo erectus, 135
Homo sapiens, 135
Hong Kong
    bridge, *98*
    cargo vessels, *126*
honorary degrees, 247
honors, 247
hopscotch, 16
horns, water buffalo, 343
horseback riding, circus, 426
horse racing, 567–72
    Belmont stakes, 568
    Breeder's Cup series, 568–69

horses, 570
jockeys, 569–70
Kentucky Derby, 567–68
Preakness Stakes, 568
trainers, 571
Triple Crown, 567
horses, 351–52
harness racing, 577–78
horse racing, 570
horseshoe pitching, 62–63
hospitals
number of, 213
stays in, 372
hot-air ballooning, 116–17, *116*
hotels, 226–27
house of cards, *3, 4*
houses, greatest number of, 212–13
housing, 221–22
hovercraft, 123
Hubble telescope, 176, *177*
Hudson Bay, 187, *187*
Hughes, Gryfudd, 303, *303*
hula dance, 422
human arrow (circus), 426
human beings, 357–75. see also human world
birth and life, 357–61
body, 361–66
disease and medicine, 371–75
height, 366–67, 368–69r, 370
weight, 370–71
human cannonball (circus), 426
human centipede, 16
human fly, 16
human origins, 135
human-powered submarine, 121
human-powered vehicles, 83–84

human pyramid (circus), 426
human structure, oldest, 135
human world, 208–72. see also human beings
accidents and disasters, 217–21
crime, 267–72
education and awards, 242–48
geography, 208–12
government, 227–37
housing, 221–22
languages, 256–62
law, 262–67
military and defense, 237–42
monuments, 252–56
population, 212–16
religion, 248–51
Hundley, Todd, 452–53r
hurricanes, 200–201
Hydra (constellation), 164
hydroelectric irrigation tunnel, 100
hymnists, 400
hymns, 400

I

ice, thickness, 199
icebergs, 190
ice breakers (ships), 118
ice-cream bar, 33
ice-cream sandwich, 33
ice-cream sundae, 33
ice palace, 226
identical twins, 359
height, 366–70, 368–69r
Iditarod Trail (sled dog racing), 646
illuminated advertising signs, 285

image wall, movie theaters, 448
immigrants, 213
imprisonment, 271–72
wrongful, 264
inaugural speeches, 232
income, highest, 291
income per capita, *275*
incubation, birds, 341
India
democracy, *229*
Indianapolis 500, 583
indoor theater, 427
indoor waterfall, 288
industries
accidents, 217, *218, 262–63*
building, largest, 286
oldest, 278
strikes, 276
Indy car racing, 579–83
infant mortality rates, 216
inflation, 276
infrared reflectors, 175
inhabited island, remotest, 212, 214–15r
injections (needle), 372
in-line skating (rollerblading), 598, *598,* 608
inpatient procedures, 375
insects, 323–26
fossil, 311
venomous insects, *324,* 327, 329
instruments, musical, 384, *384,* 400–402
instruments, scientific, 140–42
insurance companies, 281
insurance policies, 281
International Trans-Arctica Expedition, 181

Internet crash, 157
Internet service
    provider, 157, *159*
invasions, 239
invertebrates, 319–23
Iowa
    house of cards, 4
iron lung, 372
irrigation canal, 197
Irwin, James, 174
islands, 183–85
    artificial, 198
    remotest inhabited
        island, 212,
        214–15r
isotopes, 129
Italian Tethered
    Satellite, 170
Italy
    passenger liners,
        123, 124–25r, *124*

J

jack-o'-lantern, 7
jackpots, *292,* 293
Jacobs, Ted, 75, *76,*
    76–78r
jade, 299
Jahre Viking (tanker),
    119, *120*
jai alai, 564
jailbreaks, 272
James Clerk Maxwell
    telescope, 175
Japan
    Ocean Dome, 52,
        53
Japanese words, 258
jazz instrument,
    antique, 384, *384*
Jell-O, 33
jelly bean jar, 33
jellyfish, 321
jets, fastest, 109, *110*
jeweled objects,
    299–300
jewelry
    antique, 384–85
    robbery, 268
jigsaw puzzle, 7
    antique, 385
jockeys (horse racing),
    569–70

Johnson, Michael,
    702–3r
joints, artificial, 372
joke telling, 16
Jordan, Michael,
    476–77r
Joseph Papp Public
    Theater (New
    York), 435
judges, 262, 265,
    266–67
juggling, 16, 666,
    670–71
    boomerangs, 29
jukebox, 7
jumping
    bungee jumping,
        596
    dogs, 352–53, *353*
    kangaroos, *349,*
        350
    show jumping
        (sport), 572–73
    ski jumping, 638
    track and field, 660
jump rope, 63
Jupiter (planet), 165
justice, Supreme
    Court, 265–67

K

kaleidoscope, 142
kangaroos, *349,* 350
karate, 689
Karl Schwarzschild
    Observatory, 176
Kata championships
    (karate), 689
Keck telescopes, 174,
    175
Keh, Arceli and
    Cynthia, 357, *357*
Kentucky Derby
    (horse racing),
    567–68
keyboard, computer,
    159
kidnapping, ransom,
    269
kidney transplants,
    375
King, Stephen,
    390–91r, *390*

King Khalid
    International
    Airport (Saudi
    Arabia), 105, *106*
kissing, 17
kitchen, 287
kite flying, 17–18
knife, 7–8
knitting, 18
knot tying, 18
kohlrabi, 42
Krahenberg
    meteorite, 168
Kumite
    championships
    (karate), 689

L

Labatt Brier (curling),
    645
labor unions, 276
lacrosse, 531
    NCAA Division I,
    531
Lacy, Will, 181
ladder climbing, 18
Ladies Professional
    Bowlers Tour
    (LPBT), 536–37
lagoon, 193
lake in a lake, 194
lakes, 192–94
Lake Superior, 193
lambs, 304
land
    expensive, 281
    reclamation, 197
land planes, 606
land predator, 311
landslides, 206
land vehicles, 86
languages, 256–62
lasagna, 33
laser, 142
*Last Night of Ballyhoo,
    The,* 432
lathe, 144
lava (volcanoes), 205
Lavender, April, 24
law, 262–67
lawn mowers, 90
lawyers, 265
leaders, gathering

United States
  presidents, 233
world leaders, 232
leading roles, movies,
  444
League
  Championship
  Series (baseball),
  461–62
leapfrogging, 18
lease, longest, 264
leaves, flowers, *307,*
  308
lecture fees, 246
leek, pot, 42
legislation, 262–65
legislative bodies, 227
Le Mans, 584, *585*
lemon, 42
lemon, Ponderosa,
  43
lethal man-made
  chemical, 132
letter (alphabetic)
  most common, 259
  oldest, 258
letters, 394
  antique, 385
levees, 196, *196*
levy, tax, 291
Lexell's Comet, 169
libraries, 56–57
license plate, 72
life expectancy, 216
lifting with teeth, 23
light, brightest, 133
lightning, strikes of,
  202
lighthouse, 291
lima bean, 43
limbo dancer, 422
lineage, longest,
  359–60
line of coins, 296
liquid ranges, 129
liquor, 37
literature, 388–94
litigation, 262–65
litters
  pets, 355
  pigs, 302–3
  sheep, 304
  tenrecs, 343
lizards, 333–34

load, greatest raised,
  143
loaves, 33
  bread, production
  of, from field,
  301
lobby, hotel, 226
lobster roll, 33
lobsters, *322,* 323
Lockley, Martin G.,
  312–13, *312*
lock (water), 197
Loesser, Frank, 433r
log rolling, 18
lollipop, 33
longevity, 360–61, *360*
long-range attacks,
  239
Lost World, The, 440,
  441
lottery, jackpot, 293
louse (insect), *324,*
  325
Lovell, James Arthur,
  Jr., 174
Lowe, Jay, 76–78, *76,*
  78r
LPGA Championship
  (golf), 545
LPGA tour records
  (golf), 546–47
lubricant, 130–31, 133
Lucid, Shannon, 171
luge, 644–45

M

machines, scientific,
  142–45
Macy's (department
  store), *282*
Madonna, 445, *445*
magazines, 395
Magic the Gathering,
  68, *69*
magnetic field, 133
magnetic substance,
  133
magnets
  refrigerator magnet
  collections,
  46–47, *46, 47,*
  47r, 48
  scientific

instrument, 141,
  141
mail service, 156
major leagues
  (baseball), 450–55
Major League Soccer
  (MLS), 528
Mallard (train), 92, *92*
Malta temples, 135,
  139
mammals, 342–51
  pets and domestic
  animals, 351–55
  prehistoric, 311
man
  height, 366
  wealthiest, 291
managers, baseball,
  460, 465
man-eating animals,
  220
Manhattan Island
  swimming, 616
man-made chemical,
  132
mantle of bees, 18
manufacturing
  company, 279, *279*
manuscript, antique,
  385, *385*
maps, 212
marathons, 661–66
  Boston Marathon,
  661
  New York City
  Marathon, 664
  pancake tossing,
  663r, 666
marches
  military history, 239
  musical, 403
marching band, 403
marine disasters, 217,
  218
marriages, 27–29
married couples,
  height, 367
marsh, 192
Mars (planet), 166
*Mars
  Sojourner/Pathfinder*
  (Web site), *158*
Martinez, Tino, *450*
Massada, 217

mass arrest, 268
mass killings, 268
mass suicide, 217
mass tomb, 256
mast, 289
Masters (golf), 541
matchbook covers, 48
matchstick model, 8
mathematician, 147
mathematics
  computation, 18
  measures, 138,
    145–48
  problem, most
    difficult, 146
mayors (United
  States), 237
maypole, 290
McCandless, Bruce,
  II, 174
McCartney, Sir Paul,
  158, 386, 399
McCrary (McGuire),
  Billy Leon and
  Benny Loyd, 370,
  370
McEwan, Tom, 156,
  156
McMath solar
  telescope, 175
McNaught Russell
  Comet, 169
measures and
  calculations, 138,
  145–48
meat pie, 33
mechanically printed
  work, 388
medicine and disease,
  371–75
Meet the Press
  (television show),
  407
Megalosaurus, 312–13,
  313r, 408–9, 408,
  409r
Melbourne Cricket
  Ground, 290, 291
melting points, 128
membership
  (legislator), 228
memorization, 18–19,
  19
menhir, 252

Men's Professional
  Tour Records
  (ATP Tour), 558
merchant shipping,
  119
Mercury (planet), 166
message in a bottle,
  118
Messier 31 (galaxy),
  162
metals. see also gold
  (precious metal);
  silver (precious
  metal)
  pure metal,
    strongest, 129
meteorites, 168
meteor showers, 168
Mets (baseball), 453r
mice, litter size, 355
microbes, 315–18
microphone, 140
microscope, 141
migration
  butterfly, 326
  whales, 344–45
mileage
  cars, 74–78
  trains, 94
military and defense,
  237–42
milk bottle balancing,
  20
milk crate balancing,
  20
milking (agriculture),
  302
milk shake, 33
millionaire, 291
millipedes, 325
minaret, 250, 250
miniatures
  prices, 380
  White House,
    223–25, 225r
mining, accidents, 217
mints (money), 294
mirror, one-piece
  glass, 142, 142
Mississippi levees, 196
MMT (Multiple-
  Mirror Telescope),
  175
mobile crane, 143

mobile hotel, 227
mobile phones, 153
models, toy, 48–51
modem, 160
moguls, 638
mollusks, 320–21
monarch, 231–32
monkeys, 350–51
monolithic obelisk,
  254
Monte Carlo Rally,
  585
monuments, 252–56
moon, 167–68
Moore, Greg, 582, 582
Moore, Herman,
  498–99, 499r
moose, 343
Mormon temple, 250
mortality, human,
  373–74
mosaics, 377
mosque, 250
motherhood, 357–58,
  357
moths, 326
motionlessness, 20
moto-cross, 589
motorcycles, 84–86,
  84
  racing, 588–89
mound, artificial, 256
mountain bike racing,
  599–600
mountaineering,
  185–86
  accidents, 220
mountains, 182–83
  moon, 167
Mount Everest,
  climbing, 185
mouse, caged pet, 351
mousetrap, 7, 8
movie cameras, 48
movies, 440–48
  box office gross,
    440
  budget to box office
    ratio, 440
  characters, most
    portrayed, 445
  costumes, 445–46,
    445
  first run, 444

most seen by
individual, 445
Oscar Awards,
446–48, 447
prop, antique, 386
studios, 446
theaters, 448
moving sidewalks, 143
mules, 351
multievent sports,
675–79
multiplatinum discs
(records), 417
multiple births, 357,
358
multiple-mirror
telescope, 175
mummy, oldest, 138
Munchausen's
syndrome, 372–73
Munro, Minnie, 28, 28
murals, 138, 377
murders, 267–68
muscles, human,
363–64
museums, 57
Musgrave, Story,
172–73, 173, 173r
music, 399–407
composers, 402–3
Grammy Awards,
417
performers, 402–7
recorded music,
416–20
musical chairs, 404
musical instruments,
400–402
jazz instrument,
antique, 384, 384
musical manuscript,
antique, 386
music box, antique,
386
musicians, most
durable, 404, 405
mustache, human,
361, 362
MVP awards, 460

N

Nabisco Dinah Shore
(golf), 545

names, 259–62, 260
narcotics haul, 269
NASCAR, 578–79
national anthems,
399
National Basketball
Association (NBA).
see basketball
national boundaries,
208
National
Championship Air
Races (NCAR),
595
national debt, 274
National Football
League (NFL). see
football
National Hockey
League (NHL). see
hockey
National Science
Foundation, 176
natural disasters,
203–6
natural gas, 150–51
natural increase
(population), 216
naval battles, 238
navy, largest, 240
Nazca Desert, ground
figures, 379, 380
NBA. see basketball
NCAA. see
basketball; field
hockey; football;
golf; hockey;
lacrosse; NCAA
Championships;
soccer
NCAA
Championships
alpine skiing, 637
cross-country
running, 668
fencing, 690
gymnastics, 648
shooting, 684
track and field, 668
wrestling, 691
neck
dinosaurs, 315
human, 364
needle threading, 20

neon advertising sign,
285
nerve gas, 132
nest, birds, 341
Netherlands
clothesline, longest,
4, 5
tidal river barrier,
195, 195
Newman, Paul S.,
397–98, 398r, 399
newspapers and
magazines, 394–99
New York
Joseph Papp Public
Theater, 435
NFL. see football
NHL. see hockey
Nobel Prizes, 247–48
noodle making, 34
Norris Trophy
(hockey), 518
North Atlantic
lobster, 322, 323
northernmost
settlement and
capital city, 210
notes, musical, 402
nuclear power, 151–52
nuclear power station,
152
nuclear reactor, 152
accident, 221
nuclear waste
accident, 221
nuclear weapons, 241
atomic bomb, 217
nugget, gold, 299
numbers, 145
nuts (machine), 144

O

obelisk, 254
ocean descent,
greatest, 188
Ocean Dome (Japan),
52, 53
ocean drilling, 186
ocean liners, 123,
124–25, 125r
oceans, 186–90
O'Connor, Sandra
Day, 265, 266

office building, 288
offices, 287–88
  expensive, 281
offshore oil platform
  accident, 220
oil, 149–50
  offshore oil
    platform
    accident, 220
oil gusher, 150
oil spill, 150
okra, 43
Olympic games,
  701–6, *701, 705*
  alpine skiing,
    635–36
  archery, *679,* 680
  badminton, 562
  basketball, 479
  biathlon, 675, *675*
  bobsledding,
    643–44
  boxing, 694
  canoeing, 625
  combat sports, 690,
    694
  cross-country
    skiing, 637–38
  cycling, 590
  diving, 617
  double champion,
    702–3, 703r
  dressage, 573–74
  fencing, 690
  field hockey, 529
  figure skating, 640,
    641
  gold medals, 701,
    704
  gymnastics, 646–47,
    648
  handball, team, 533
  hockey, 523
  judo, 686
  luge, 644
  martial arts, 686
  medals
    overall, 701–4
    Winter games,
      704–5
  moguls, 638
  participation, 705–6
  pentathlon, 676
  rhythmic

gymnastics, 648,
    648
  rowing, 627
  sailing, 620, 623
  shooting, 684
  short track speed
    skating, 643
  show jumping, 572
  ski jumping, 638
  soccer, 528
  speed skating, 642
  swimming, 609–10,
    617
  synchronized
    swimming, 617
  table tennis,
    565–66, *566*
  target sports, 680
  tennis, 560
  three-day event
    (equestrian
    sports), 573
  track and field, 651,
    661, 668, 675
  volleyball, 534
  walking, 668
  weightlifting, 695
  windsurfing, 623
  Winter games,
    medals, 704–5
  wrestling, 690
omelet and omelet
  making, 34
one-man band, 403
one-man shows
  (theater), 439
one-piece glass
  mirror, 142, *142*
one-year drive, 74
onion, 41, *41,* 43
Oosterscheldedam
  tidal river barrier,
  195, *195*
opals, 298
opera, 405–7
opera company, 407
opera house, 405,
  406
opera singers, 406,
  407
operations (surgery),
  375
orchestra leaders, 403
orchestras, 403–4

orchids, 308
ordained priest, 248
organ, 400
origami, 8
Oscar Awards,
  446–48, *447*
ostrich, 336, *338,* 340,
  341
Owsley, Scott, *537,*
  540
oyster opening, 20
ozone levels, 198

P

paddle wheeler, 117
paintbrush, 377
painters, 377
  price of work, 380
paintings, 377
  prices, 380
palaces, 222–26, *226*
palindromic words,
  259
pancake tossing,
  marathons, 663r,
  666
panic, 217
paper chain, 8
paper clip chain, 20
paper money, 293–94
paperweight, antique,
  386
parachuting, 600–601,
  600, 601, 602–3
paragliding, 601–3
parasites, 315–16
parking lot, 80
parking tickets, 79
parks, 57, 58–59
Parreira, Carlos
  Alberto, 524–25
parsnip, 43
particle accelerator,
  141
party, largest, 38
par value (stock
  exchange), 278
passenger liners, 123,
  124–25, 125r
passengers
  aircraft, 103, 112,
    113
  airships, 105

aviation, oldest and youngest, 112
ballooning, 117
buses, 87
passports, collections, 48
pass the parcel, 20
pastry, 34
patent violation case, 264
patients, 375
Paturel, Georges, 162
pearls, 299
pedal-boating, 20
Pegasus (spacecraft), 256
pencil, 8
pendulum, 148
penetration into earth, deepest, 178
penguins, 338, *339,* 340
peninsula, largest, 178
pension, longest, 292–93
pens (writing)
  antique, 386
  collections, 48
  jeweled, 299
pentathlon, 676–77
pepper plant, 43
performers
  movies, 444
  music, 403–5
  television, 414
periodicals, 395–96
permafrost, 199
personal aviation records, 112–13
personal injury damages, 263
personal majority (elections), 230
personal names, 259–60
pesticide plant, industrial accident, 217, 263
petition (government), 227
pets and domestic animals, 351–55
petting, dogs, 354
petunia, 43

PGA Championship (golf), 543
philodendron, 43
Phoneutria, 327
photography, 378
physicians, 374
  number of, 213
pi, 147
  memorizing, 19
piano composition, 402
pianos, 401
  played at one time, 403
pie, 34
piggy banks, 8
  collections, 48
  largest, 280
pigs, 302–3
pile of coins, 296
pill-taking, 373
pilots, 112
  military, 241
piñata, 8
pineapple, 43
pinhole camera, 8
pinniped, 347
Pioneer 10 (spacecraft), 170
pipeline
  gas, 151
  oil, 150
piston-engined car, 73
pitching (baseball), 455–57, *455,* 461–62, 464
pizza, 34
pizza delivery, 34
place names, 262
plane pulling, 113
planetariums, 176
planets, 165–66
plants, 306–7
Plaskett, K., 163
plateau, 183
plate spinning (circus), 426
platforms (oil), 150
platinum, 299
platinum discs (records), 417
playing cards
  antique, 386
  games, 65

memorizing, 19, *19*
pliers, 48
plowing, 301
Pluto (planet), 166
poem, 393
pogo stick jumping, 20
poisonous animals, 336
polar exploration, 181–82
polder, 198
pole sitting, 20
political party, 230
polo, 574–75
Polyakov, Valeriy, 171
ponies, 352
pool (game), 63
popcorn, 34
popcorn ball, 34
popsicle, 34
popular majority (U.S. government), 233
population
  cities, most populous, 210
ports, 126
Portuguese words, 258
postal services, 156
posters, 171
  price of, 380
potato
  largest, 43
  peeling, 20–21
pottery, 8
poultry, 303
poverty, country, 274
powerboat racing, 628–30
power plant, 148, *148*
PRCA championship (rodeo), 575–76
Preakness Stakes (horse racing), 568
predators
  birds, 337
  fish, 329
  prehistoric, 311
prehistoric life, 310–15
premature babies, 358
presidential signatures, 394

presidents, United States, 232–33
Presley, Elvis, 416, 417
presses (machines), 144
pressure
  barometric, 202
  laboratory, highest, 132
prices
  antiques and collectibles, 381–87
  gold (precious metal), 278
  silver, 278
  visual arts, 380–81
priest, 248
primates, 350
  earliest, 135
print (artwork), price of, 380
printers, 389
prisoner, 271–72
prize, radio, 415
prize money, surfing, 631
producers
  gas, 150
  steel, 144
producers (arts and entertainment)
  movies, 444
  television, 414
Professional Bowlers Association (PBA), 536
professors, 243
projectile throwing, 29–30
proof, longest (mathematics), 146
propeller boats, 118
props, movies, 446
pro stock (automotive sport), 587
protozoan
  modern, 316
  prehistoric, 310–11
Proxima Centauri (star), 164
publication, largest, 389

publishers, 389–93
Pulitzer Prize winners, 395
pulling with teeth, 23
pulsars, 164
pumpkin, *42*, 43
pyramids, 252
  bottle caps, 2
  cans, 2
  human (circus), 426
  motorcycles, 86

Q

quadruplets, 358, 359
quasars, 162
quilt, 8
quintuplets, 358
quorum (government), 227

R

rabbits
  litter size, 354, 355
  pets, 351, 354–55
Race Across AMerica (cycling), 590–91
racquetball, 564
racquet sports, 562–67
  badminton, 562–63
  jai alai, 564
  racquetball, 564
  squash, 565
  table tennis, 565–67
  tennis. see tennis
radar, 156, *156*
radio, 415
Radio Astronomy Explorer (RAE), 170
radio stations, 415
radio telescope, 175
radish, 43
raffia palm, 308
raft, longest on, 188
railroads. see also trains
  disasters, 220
  tunnels, 100
  viaducts, 99
rainfall, 199–200
ramp jumping
  cars, 79

motorcycles, 85, 86
ransom, 269
rappelling, 21
rapper (music), 400
rat, caged pet, 351
Reader's Digest, 396, *396*
record, 416
recorded music, 416–20
recorder, 416
recording artists, 416–17
recording contract, 417
recordings (music), most, 417
record store, 416
reef, 185
refinery, oil, 149
reflectors, 174–75
refractor, 175
refractory substance, 132
refrigerator magnet collections, 46–47, *46, 47,* 47r, 48
refuse electrical generation plans, 287
registration, dogs, 353
Reid, Dudley, 28, *28*
reign, royalty, 231
religion, 248–51
representatives (U.S. Congress), 236
reptile fossil, 311
reptiles and amphibians, 333–36
resorts, 52
restaurants, 56
  most visited, 38
resting place, highest, 256
retailers, 281–83
reverse, cars driving in, 75
rhubarb, 43
rhythmic gymnastics, 648, *648*
Rice, John and Greg, 368–69, 369r
riding records, rodeo, 576

rigid wing—single place distance records (hang gliding), 598
rings, birds, 341
riots, 217
river basin, 190
river bore, 192
rivers, 190–92
riveting, 119
roads, 80–81
  accidents, 220
robbery, 268
robot, 160
rock concerts, 404
rockets, 170
rock pinnacles, 180
rock/pop festival, 404
rocks, 178–79. *179*
rodents, 349
rodeo, 575–77
rollerblading (in-line skating), 598, *598, 599,* 608
roller coasters, 54–55, *54*
roller hockey, 603
rolling pin throwing, 29
room, hotel, 226–27
roots (plant), 306–7
ropes, 8
  wire, 144
rope slide, 21
rose tree, 308
Ross Trophy (hockey), 518
rowing, 627
Royal Shakespeare Company, 435–36
royalty, 231–32
rubies, 298
rugby, 531–32
ruler, smallest, 142
ruling house, royalty, 231
rummage sale, 280
runner bean, 43
running backwards, 670
Russert, Tim, 408
Russia
  Chernobyl disaster, 221

explosions, 203
  nuclear waste accident, 221
Russian words, 259
rusty spotted cat, 347, *347*
rutabaga, 43
Ryder Cup (golf), 547

S

saguaro (cactus), 306, *306*
sailing, 620–24
  America's Cup, 620
  Atlantic Ocean, 622
  duration and distance, 623
  Olympic games, 620
  speed, 623
  windsurfing, 623
sailing ships, 117, 122–23
Sain, Kalyan Ramji, 361, *362*
salami, 34
salary, highest, 291
sales, business, 279
salvage, 118–19
sand castles, 222
sand dunes, 181
sand sculpture, 378–80
Santa Claus
  largest, 9
  portraying, 21, *21*
sapphires, 298
satellites, 167
Saturn (planet), 166
Saudi Arabia, airport in, 105, *106*
sausage, 34
savings and loan association, 280
scaffolding, 286
scarf, 9
Schmidt telescope, 176
school attendance, 243
schools, 243
Schumann, Robert, 182

science and technology, 127–60
  archaeology, 135–40
  biotechnology, 133–34
  chemistry and physics, 128–33
  communications, 152–56
  computers, 157–60
  energy, 148–52
  instruments, 140–42
  machines, 140–45
  measures and calculations, 145–48
Scott, David, 174
Scrabble, 68–69
scream, human, 365
screens, movie, 448
scriptwriter, television, 414
sculptures, 378–81
  oldest, 138
  price of, 380–81
sea cliffs, 183
sea lions, 347–48
seals, 347–48
seas, 186–90
seaway, artificial, 197
seeds (plants and trees), 308–9
Seinfeld, Jerry, 412–13
senators (United States), 236
Senior PGA tour (golf), 547
Serebrov, Aleksandr, 174
Servizio, Charles, 649, 650
SETI Program (Ohio State University), 176
settlements, 210
seven-generation family, 359
sewage works, 287
sewerage tunnel, 100
sexual harassment, damages, 263

Shakespeare, William, 434–38, 439
shaving, 21
shearing, sheep, 304
sheep, 300–301, 303–4, *304*
Shepard, Alan B., Jr., 171
Shepard, Oliver, 182
shipbuilding, 119
ship canal, 197
ships and boats, 117–26, *120, 125r*
  model boats, 50
shipwreck, oldest, 138
shoes, jeweled, 300
shoe shining, 22
shooting, 684–86
shopping centers, 56
shortcake, strawberry, 34
short track speed skating, 643
shout, human, 365
show dogs, 353
show jumping, 572–73
sidewalks, moving, 143
sieges, 239
signatures, presidential, 394
sign language, *257,* 258
signs, advertising, 283–85
silence (music), 402–3
silver (precious metal), 9
  antique, 386
  price, stock exchange, 278
Simpsons, The (cartoon), 410–11, 411r, 414
single birth, heaviest and lightest, 358
single recordings (music), 419
Sinope (satellite), 167
sire, dogs, 352
Sirius A (star), 164
skateboarding, 603, 608
skating

figure skating, 640–42, *641*
in-line skating (rollerblading), 598, *598,* 599, 608
short track speed skating, 643
speed skating, 642–43, *643*
skeleton, of distant ancestor, 136–37, 137r
skid marks, 74
skiing, 635–40
  acro-, 639
  aerials, 638
  alpine, 635–37
  cross-country, 637–38
  grass, 639
  moguls, 638
ski jumping, 638
ski lift accident, 221
ski orienteering, 678
skin, human, 361
skull, dinosaur, 315
sky surfing, 608
sled dog racing, 646
slingshot, 30
slot cars, 50
slot machine jackpot, 293
smell, sense of, 323
Smith, Dean, 482–83, 483r
Smith (name), 260, *260*
smog, 217
snails, 321
snakes, 335–36
  prehistoric, 311
snatching, coins, 296
sneezing, 373
snoring, 373
snowboarding, 604–5, *604*
snowfall, 202
snowman, 9
snow palace, 226
snow plows, 90
soaring, 605
soccer, 523–29
  big plays, 529

FIFA World Cup, 523–26
Major League Soccer (MLS), 528
  most world cup win, 525r
  NCAA Division I, 528
  Olympic games, 528
sofa, 9
softball, 532–33
solar power
  plant, 152
  vehicles, 90
solar system, 165–69
solar telescope, 175
soldiers, 240
solo performers, classical concerts, 404
solo recording artist, 416
Sondheim, Stephen, 433r
song lyrics, price, 386
songs, 399–400
songwriters, 399
Sonnenfeld, Jerry, 538–39, 539r
sounds
  animal, 346
  language, 257
southernmost settlement and capital city, 210, 212
Soyuz TM21 (spacecraft), 171
space. see also solar system; telescopes; universe
  disaster, 221
  exploration, 170–74
spacewalk, 174
spear throwing, 30
specialized vehicles, 86–91
speed records
  cars, 73
  flying, 109–11
  motorcycles, 84
speed skating, 642–43, *643*
  short track, 643

spice, 36
Spice Girls (recording artists), *419*
spiders, 327–28, *328*
spike driving, 94
spinoffs (television), 407
spiral staircase, 287
spires, 249
spitting, 22
sponges, 319–20
sports
 acro-skiing, 639
 aerials, 638
 aerobatics, 595
 air racing, 595
 alpine skiing, 635–37
 aquatic sports, 625–35
 archery, 679–81, *679*
 automotive, 578–89
 badminton, 562–63
 baseball, 450–67
 basketball, 467–92
 beach volleyball, 534
 biathlon, 675–76
 bobsledding, 643–44
 bowling, 536–41
 boxing, 692–95
 bungee jumping, 596
 canoeing, 625
 combat sports, 690–95
 cross-country running, 667–68
 cross-country skiing, 637–38
 curling, 645–46
 cycling, 589–95
 darts, 681–84
 diving, 617–19
 equestrian sports, 572–78
 extreme sports, 595–608
 fencing, 690
 field hockey, 529–31

 figure skating, 640–42, *641*
 football, 493–513
 golf, 541–52
 grass skiing, 639
 gymnastics, 646–51
 handball, team, 533–34
 hang gliding, 596–98, *597*
 Hawaii Ironman, 678–79
 hockey, 513–23
 horse racing, 567–72
 in-line skating (rollerblading), 598, *598*, 599, 608
 jai alai, 564
 judo, 686–89, *687*
 karate, *687*, 689
 lacrosse, 531
 luge, 644–45
 marathons, 661–66
 martial arts, 686–90
 moguls, 638
 mountain bike racing, 599–600
 orienteering, 677–78, *677*
 parachuting, 600–601, *600, 601*, 602–3
 paragliding, 601–3
 pentathlon, 676–77
 powerboat racing, 628–30
 racquetball, 564
 rhythmic gymnastics, 648, *648*
 rollerblading, 598, *598*, 599, 608
 roller hockey, 603
 rowing, 627
 rugby, 531–32
 sailing, 620–24
 shooting, 684–86
 short track speed skating, 643
 skateboarding, 603, 608
 skiing, 635–40
 ski jumping, 638

 ski orienteering, 678
 sky surfing, 608
 sled dog racing, 646
 snowboarding, 604–5, *604*
 soaring, 605
 soccer, 523–29
 softball, 532–33
 speed skating, 642–43, *643*
 squash, 565
 sumo wrestling, 692
 surfing, 630–31
 swimming, 609–19
 table tennis, 565–67
 taekwondo, *687*, 689–90
 target, 679–86
 tennis, 552–62
 track and field, 651–74
 trampolining, 651
 triathlon, 678–79
 ultralighting, 606
 volleyball, 534
 walking, 668–70
 water polo, 634–35
 waterskiing, 631–34, *633*
 weightlifting, 695–700, *695, 696, 697*
 windsurfing, 623–24
 winter sports, 640–46
 wrestling, 690–92
 X Games, 607–8
square dance caller, 422
squash (sport), 565
squash (vegetable), 43
stadiums, 51–52
Stafford, Thomas Patten, 171
stage set, movies, 446
stained glass windows, 250
stair climbing, 22
stairway, 287
stalagmites and stalactites, 180
stamp licking, 156

stamps, collectible,
388, *388*
standing, 22
Stanley Cup (hockey),
518–22
starfish, 321
stars, 163–65, *163*. see
also solar system
star sapphire, 298
Star Wars, 440, *442*
states, 209
station, train, 95
statues
monument, 252
prizes, 247
statute, 262
steam and water
power, 152
steam car, 73
steam engine, 152
steel producer, 144
step-ups, 22
Stevens, Harry, 28
Stevens, Thelma
(Lucas), 28
stilt-walking (circus),
426
stock exchanges,
277–78
stockholder
attendance, 278
stone-skipping, 22
store, largest, *282*
straits, 188–89
strawberry, 43
strawberry bowl, 36
streets, 80–81
stretcher bearing, 22
strike (labor), 276
string ball, 9
stringed musical
instruments, 400,
401
structures. see also
buildings
ancient, 135–38
animal-made, 321
students, 242, 243
studios, movie, 446
stuffed toy, 9
stupa, 250
submarine canyon,
183
submarine river, 191

submarines, 121
accidents, 220
submillimeter
telescope, 175
subways, 96
suicide
mass suicide, 217
rates, 216
sumo wrestling, 692
sun
closest approach to,
170
eclipses, 169
solar system,
relation to, 165
sundial, 148
sunflower, 43
Super Bowl, 496
supercomputing
speed record, 157
supernovas, 164
Supreme Court,
265–67
surfing, 630–31
surgical instrument,
antique, 386
survival at sea,
longest, 188
sushi roll, 36, *36*
suspended animation,
snail, 320–21
suspension bridge,
97–98
swallowing, 373
swallowtail butterfly,
325
swamp, 192
Swaythling Cup (table
tennis), 566
Swedish words, 258
sweetest substance,
129
sweet potato, 43
Swigert, John L., 174
swimming, 609–19
birds, 338
Cuba-Florida, 617
diving, 617–19
English Channel,
611–16
Golden Gate Strait,
616–17
long distance,
611–17

Manhattan Island,
616
Olympic games, 609
pinniped, 347
records, 612–13
short-course
records, 614–15
synchronized, 617
switchboard, 153
symphony, 402
synagogue, 248

T

table, 9
tablecloth, 9
table tennis, 565–67
taekwondo, *687,*
689–90
tailoring, 22
takeover bids, 279
talking, 365
backwards, 365
tankers, 119–20, *120*
tanks (military),
241–42
tap dancing, 420, *420*
tapestry, 9
antique, 386
target sports, 679–86
Targett, Adrian,
136–37, 137r
tattoos, 361
taxes
levy, 291
rate, 274
taxis, 90
teachers, 243, 246
technology. see
science and
technology
teddy bear, antique,
387
teeter board (circus),
426
teeth
dinosaurs, 315
human, 362–63
lifting and pulling
with, 23
whales, 346
telecommunications
exchange, 153
telephone calls, 153

telephones, 152–53
telescopes, 174–77, *175, 177*
television, 407–15
  advertising, 283, *284*
  cartoons, 410–11, 411r, 414
  Emmy awards, 414
  Seinfeld, 412–13, 413r
television sets, 414–15
temperatures
  equable, 198
  highest produced in laboratory, 132
  lowest produced in laboratory, 132
  moon, 168
  ranges, earth, 199
  seas, 188
  superconducting, highest, 132
temple (religious structure), 248
tennis, 552–62
  Australian Open championships, 552–53, 555r
  big plays, 560
  Davis Cup, 559
  Federation Cup, 560
  French Open, 553–56
  golden set, 562
  grand slam, 552
  Men's Professional Tour Records (ATP Tour), 558
  Olympic games, 560
  U.S. Open, 557–58
  Wimbledon, 556–57
  Women's Professional Tour Records (WTA), 559
tensile strength, 129
termite mounds, 326
terms of office, U.S. president, 232
territories, population, 212
terrorist bombing, 269

theater, 427–40
  advance sales, 439
  arts festival, 440
  · *Cats*, 428–31, *428, 429, 430*
  durable performer, 439
  one-man shows, 439
  runs, longest, 427, 428
  Shakespeare plays, 434–38, 439
  Tony Awards, 432, 433r, 439
theatergoer, 439
theorem, most-proved, 146
thermal expansion, 128
thermometer, 140
thermonuclear device, 241
Thomas, Clarence, 267, *267*
Thompson, Emma, *435*
Thornton, Kathryn, 174
three-day event (equestrian sports), 573
throwing, projectile, 29–30
Thuot, Pierre, 174
Thurmond, Strom, 236
tidal river barrier, 195, *195*
tides (ocean), 189–90
ties, 48
tightrope walking, 23
time, measure of, 147–48
titles, 247
Titov, Gherman Stepanovich, 171
toes, human, 361
tomato, 43
tomato, cherry, 43
tomato plant, 43
tombs, 254–56
Tony Awards, 432, 433r, 439
topaz, 298

top spinning, 23
tornadoes, 201–2, *201*
Torre, Joe, *465*
totem pole, 290
Tour de France (cycling), 589–90
tourists, greatest number of, 213, *213*
tower, 289–90, *289*
Tower of the Winds (observatory), 176
towns, 209–12
tow service, 80
toxic element, 129
toy brick tower, 10
toys, antique, 387
tracheostomy, 373
track and field, 651–74
  backwards, walking and running, 670
  biathlon, 675–76
  Boston marathon, 661–64
  cross-country running, 667
  gold medals, 652, 661, 668, 675
  Hawaii Ironman, 678
  indoor, records, 672–74
  long distance, 666–67
  marathons, 661–66
  marathon tossing a pancake, 663r, 666
  multievent sports, 675–79
  New York City marathon, 664
  Olympic games, 651–52, 661, 668
  orienteering, 677–78, *677*
  pentathlon, 676–77
  records, 654–55, 656–57, 659r, 662, 672–74
  ski orienteering, 678
  triathlon, 678–79

ultra long distance
records, 662
world
championships,
652, 661, 667
tracks
dinosaur, 313r
trains, 93–94
tractors, 90
traffic, 81
trainers, horse racing,
571
train pulling, 23
trains, 91–95
model, 50–51, *51*
stations, 95
tracks, 93–94
trampoline (circus),
426
trampolining (sport),
651
trans-Americas drive,
74
transformers, 148–49
transfusion of blood,
365–66
transistor, computer,
159–60
transmission lines,
149
transplantation of
organs, 375
transportation,
70–126
aircraft, 101–5, *102*
airlines, 105
airports, 105–8, *106,
107*
airships, 104–5
ballooning, 113–17,
115r, *116*
bicycles, 82–83
bridges, 96–99, *97,
98*
buses, 87
campers, 87
cars, 71–81
crawlers, 88
flights, 108–9
flying, 109–13
helicopters, 103–4
human-powered
vehicles, 83–84
land vehicles, 86–87

motorcycles, 84–86,
84
ships and boats,
117–26, *120,* 125r
solar-powered
vehicles, 90
specialized vehicles,
86–91
subways, 96
taxis, 90
trains, 91–95
tricycles, 83
trolleys, 91
trucks, 91
tunnels, 99–101
unicycles, 82, *82*
trapeze artists, 423
travel
most traveled, 23
train, 94
treaty, 228
tree fungus, 318, *318*
trees, 309–10
Christmas, 5
climbing, 23
planting, 24–25,
25r, 26
sitting, 26
trial, longest, 262–63
triathlon, 678–79
tricycles, 83
trilithons, 252
Triple Crown (horse
racing), 567
triplets, 358, 359
Tristan da Cunha,
212, 214–15, 215r
trolleys, 91
trucks, 91
Tsing Ma Bridge, 98,
98
tsunamis, 189
tugboat, 118
tug of war, 63–64
tumors, 375
tunnels, 99–101
accidents, 220
disasters, 217
turbines, 145
turtles, 334–35
tusks, mammals, 343
twins, 358, 359
height, 367, 368–69,
369r

weight, 370, *370*
Twister (game), 64
two-side-wheel
driving, 75–79, *75*
typewriting, 26
Tyrannosaurus rex,
314, 315

U

Uhry, Alfred, 433r
UKIRT (United
Kingdom Infrared
Telescope), 175
ultralighting, 606
ultrasound, 375, *375*
Ulysses (spacecraft),
170
underground lake,
194
underwater rescue,
118
underwater
submergence, 373
underwater tricycling,
83
unemployment,
276–77
unicycles, 82, *82*
Union Carbide
Corporation, 217,
263
United States
government,
232–37
inflation, 276
unemployment,
276–77
United States
championships
(sports)
badminton, 563
curling, 645–46
squash, amateur
championships,
565
table tennis, 566
United States
Constitution, 228,
228
universe, 162–65
university, 242
unsupported circle, 26
Uranus (planet), 166

U.S. Ballistic Early Warning System (BMEWS), 156
U.S. Open
golf, 541–42, 545
tennis, 557–58
U.S.A.F. Lockheed SR-71, 109

V

vacuum, 132
valleys, 183
vegetables. see fruits and vegetables
vein, human, 365
velocity, 133
venomous fish, 332
venomous snakes, 335
venomous spider, 327
Venus (planet), 166
verbs, irregular, 257
Versailles, 222, *226*
Vezina Trophy (hockey), 518
vice presidents, U.S., 233
videos, 415
vineyards, 300
vintners, 300
violins, 401
Virgo (constellation), 165
vision
birds, 340
human, 363
visual arts, 377–81
VLA (Very Large Array), 176
vocabulary, 257
voices, human, 365
singing, 400
volcanoes, 204–5
volleyball, 534
voltage, 133
vowels, 258

W

waist measurement, human, 364
walking, 26–27, 668–70
backwards, 670

dogs, 354
wallet, jeweled, 300
wall hanging, 377, *378*
wall of death, 86
walls, 288
wars, 237–39
warships, 121–22
watches, 147–48
antique, 387
water, bodies of
canals and locks, 196–97
dams and reservoirs, 194–96
lakes, 192–94
oceans, 186–90
rivers, 190–92
waterfalls, 192
water buffalo, 343
waterfalls, 192
indoor, 288
watermelon, 43
water mill, 152
water polo, 634–35
water power, 152
waterskiing, 631–34, *633*
water tower, 290
waterway, 191–92
waterwheel, 196
waves (ocean), 189
wealth
country, 274
personal, 291–93
weapons, oldest, 138
weather, 198–202
web, spider, 328, *328*
Webber, Andrew Lloyd, 387, *387*, 428, 429, 431
Web site, 158, *158*
wedding ceremonies, 28–29
weeds, 309
weight, human, 370–71
weightlifting, 695–700, *695, 696, 697*
weight loss, whales, 346
whales, 344–45, 346
wheelies, 83, 86
whip cracking, 27

Whipple Observatory, 175
whistle, human, 365
White House, miniature, 223–25, 225r
Wil Cwac Cwac (duck), 303, *303*
Wiles, Andrew, 146, *146*
wills, 264–65
Wimbledon (tennis), 556–57
wind generator, 152
windmill, 152
windows, 288
stained glass, 250
wind power, 152
winds, 200
windsurfing, 623–24
wind tunnel, 144
wine, 37
oldest, 140
wine cellar, 300
wine collection, 387, *387*
wine glass stacking, 27
wine tasting, 37
wings
birds, 338
insects, 325
wing walking (aircraft), 113
winter sports, 640–46. see also skiing
wired community, 158
women
basketball, 487–92
bowling, 536–37, 540–41
cross-country running, 667
cycling, 594
field hockey, 531
figure skating, 640–42
golf, 545–47
gymnastics, 646, 647, 648
hang gliding, 597
height, 366–67
in-line skating (rollerblading), 608

parachuting, 600
racquet sports, 564,
    565, 566
soccer, 526
speed skating, 642
swimming, 609, 610
tennis, 559, 562
track and field, 651,
    652
United States
    Government,
    235r
Women's
    International
    Bowling Congress
    (WIBC), 540–41
Women's Professional
    Tour Records
    (WTA), 559
wooden building, 287
wooden ships, 117
wooden structure,
    oldest, 135
Worden, Alfred M.,
    174
words, 258–59
world championships
    (sports)
    acro-skiing, 639
    aerials, 638
    aerobatics, 595
    alpine skiing, 636
    archery, 680–81
    automotive sports,
        585, 588
    badminton, 562
    barefoot
        waterskiing, 632
    biathlon, 676
    bobsledding, 644
    boxing, 694
    canoeing, 625
    carriage driving,
        574
    combat sports, 690,
        691, 694
    curling, 645
    cycling, 590
    darts, 681
    diving, 619
    dressage, 574
    fencing, 690
    figure skating,
        640–41

grass skiing, 639
gymnastics, 647
in-line skating
    (rollerblading),
    598
jai alai, 564
judo, 686
luge, 644
martial arts, 686,
    689–90
moguls, 638
moto-cross, 589
motorcycle racing,
    588
orienteering, 677
parachuting, 600
pentathlon, 676
polo, 574
racquetball, 564
rallying, 585
rhythmic
    gymnastics, 651
rodeo, 575–76
rowing, 627–28
sailing, 623
short track speed
    skating, 643
show jumping, 573
snowboarding, 604
speed skating, 642
squash, 565
surfing, 630–31
swimming, 610
synchronized
    swimming, 617
table tennis, 566
taekwondo, 689–90
target sports,
    680–81
three-day event
    (equestrian
    sports), 573
track and field,
    652–53, 661, 667,
    676, 677
trampolining, 651
triathlon, 678
water polo, 634–35
waterskiing, 631–32
weightlifting,
    695–700
windsurfing, 623
wrestling, 691
World Cup

alpine skiing,
    636–37
cross-country
    skiing, 638
field hockey, 530
rugby, 531
ski jumping, 638
world leaders,
    gathering, 232
World Series, 463–65
    college, 466–67
worms, 319
worship, buildings for,
    248–50
wreckers, 91
wrecking, car, 72
wrestling, 690–92
writing, 27

X

X Games, 607–8

Y

yacht racing accident,
    221
Yerkes Observatory,
    175
yodeling, 27
Young, John Watts,
    171
yo-yo, 10, 27

Z

Zantac (prescription
    drug), 374, *374*
Zehr, Nathan and
    Paula, *42*
ziggurat, 252
zipper, 10
zoos, 57
zucchini, 43
Zweifel, John, 223–25,
    225r

PHOTO CREDITS

4 W. Janssens; 11
Tecza Sports Club;
13 Ian Sumner/

Lubeck; 338 Wolfgang Kaehler/ Corbis; 339 Wolfgang Kaehler/ Corbis; 337 Animals Animals/ ©Johnny Johnson; 344 Animals Animals/©James D. Watt; 345t Animals Animals/©James D. Watt; 345b Animals Animals/©Dean Lee/OSF; 347 Animals Animals/ ©Zig Leszczynski; 349 Animals Animals/©Joe McDonald; 353 Linda Goldyn/ Monophoto; 355 Helen Smylye; 357 ©National Enquirer; 360 Sipa-Press/Rex Features; 362 Santosh Basak/Gamma/ Frank Spooner Pictures; 370 Bettmann/UPI/ Corbis; 374 Courtesy of Glaxo Wellcome; 375 Mehau Kulyk/ Science Photo Library; 379 Frantisek Brabec; 378 Takamatsu Winter Festival; 383bl Tim Graham; 383br Christie's Inc.; 381 Jan Olofsson/Redfern; 384 William Gottlieb/Library/ Redfern; 385 Christie's Images; 382 Christie's Images; 388 AP/Wide World Photos; 387 ©Sotheby's; 392 courtesy of Penguin Putnam, Inc.; 390

Mega Productions Inc./Rex Features; 396tl Readers Digest Association; 397 Jack French; 398 ©Golden Books Family Entertainment; 396b AP/Wide World Photos; 401 Mr. J. McNabb; 405 Martin's Studio; 406b © Diane Sobolewski; 406cr ©Diane Sobolewski; 408 NBC News; 410cr Anna Summa/Fox; 410cl The Simpsons™© 1997 20th Century Fox Film Corp.; 412 Jonas Public Relations/©Castle Rock Entertainment; 418b ©Warner Bros. Inc./Reprise Records; 418cl, 418cr ©Michelle Laurita/Maverick Recording Company; 419 Anthony Medley/ SIN; 416 Future Fossil Music; 420 David J.V. Meenan; 421 ©Michael Mew/Aloha Festivals; 424, 425 ©Al Seib; 440 Patrick Ward/ Corbis; 432t ©Carol Rosegg; 432b, 433 T. Charles Erickson; 434t Archive Photo/ PNI; 435t Mischal Daniel; 435b ©Tim O'Sullivan/Gamma Liaison; 434b ©Simon Grosset/ Gamma Liaison; 436 ©Michael

Halsband/Fox Searchlight; 438 AP/Wide World Photos; 437 ©Thompson/ Capital Pictures/ Gamma Liaison; 428 Nigel Teare; 430 Carol Rosegg; 429 Carol Rosegg; 441 © 1997 Universal City Studios, Inc. and Amblin Entertainment, Inc. Courtesy of MCA Publishing Rights; 442b Star Wars™ & ©Lucasfilm, Ltd. 1977; 443 Miramax Films; 441 Andrew Cooper/Columbia/ TriStar; 442cl The Return of the Jedi™ & ©Lucasfilm, Ltd., 1977; 442cr Star Wars™ & ©Lucasfilm, Ltd. 1977; 442t The Empire Strikes Back™ & ©Lucasfilm, Ltd. 1980; 445 Everett/ Corbis; 447 Wallace & Gromit/Aardman Animations Ltd. 1989; 450bl Jed Jacobson/Allsport; 450br Doug Pensinger/Allsport; 452 Bello/Allsport; 455 Doug Pensinger/Allsport; 458br Otto Greule/ Allsport; 458bl Jonathan Daniel/ Allsport; 462 Jonathan Daniel/ Allsport; 463 Doug Pensinger/Allsport; 465 Doug Pensinger/Allsport; 466 ©Ross Obley/ Florida State